Economic Geography and Public Policy

Economic Geography and Public Policy

RICHARD BALDWIN, RIKARD FORSLID,
PHILIPPE MARTIN, GIANMARCO OTTAVIANO
AND FREDERIC ROBERT-NICOUD

PRINCETON UNIVERSITY PRESS

PRINCETON AND OXFORD

Library of Congress Cataloging-in-Publication Data

Economic geography and public policy / Richard Baldwin ... [et al.].
p. cm.
Includes bibliographic references and index
ISBN 0-691-10275-9 (alk. paper)
1. Economic geography. 2. Policy sciences. I. Baldwin, Richard E.
HF1025 .E1917 2003
338.9–dc21

2002042722

This book has been composed in Times
Printed on acid-free paper ∞
www.pupress.princeton.edu

Printed in the United States of America

1 2 3 4 5 6 7 8 9 10

FOR TED, JULIA, NICKY and SOFIA

CONTENTS

Economic Geography and Public Policy

CHAPTER 1

Introduction

ECONOMISTS' interest in the location of economic activity has waxed and waned over the last two centuries, as Fujita and Thisse (2000) illustrate in their excellent monograph.

Policy makers' interest in the subject, by contrast, has never wavered. US President Alexander Hamilton advocated high tariffs as a means of shifting industrial production from Great Britain to the United States in the late 18th century. Throughout the 19th century, the captured-markets aspect of the global colonial system was viewed as essential to keeping and promoting industrial activity in Europe. In the mid-20th century, the European Union's founding treaty explicitly cited the reduction of economic inequality between regions and of the backwardness of less-favoured regions as a key goal of European integration. At the end of the 20th century, US presidential candidate Ross Perot argued against the US–Mexico free trade agreement, stating that it would result in a great 'sucking sound' of industrial jobs going south. The early 21st century sees Japanese policy makers wringing their hands over the 'hollowing out' of the Japanese economy, and the US Congress handing out billions of dollars to rural America. The amount and nature of the economic activity located within their districts is inevitably a prime concern for policy makers.

Given policy makers' intense and persistent interest, it strikes us as odd that the decade-old renaissance of location theory—what is usually called the 'new' economic geography—has been accompanied by so little policy analysis. The monograph, *The Spatial Economy*, by Fujita et al. (1999) all but ignores policy, and Peter Neary's excellent overview (Neary 2001) mentions not a single article that uses the new framework to analyse policy issues. This is also the case for Ottaviano and Puga (1998).

Our book's prime objective is to illustrate some of the new insights that economic geography models can provide for theoretical policy analysis. To limit the project to a manageable size, we focus on trade policy, tax policy, and regional policy. Much of this involves de novo analysis, but we also pull together insights from the existing literature. We wish to stress that our book only scratches the surface of what seems to be a very rich vein. Indeed, we had to abandon several promising lines of research in order to finish the book in a timely manner. The final chapter discusses these 'unfinished chapters' and provides our conjectures on the sort of policy insights that future researchers may uncover.

To keep this introduction brief, we limit it to four tasks. It explains the logic of our book's structure, provides a readers' guide, briefly surveys recent empirical evidence on economic geography models, and then acknowledges the help we have had in writing this book.

1.1 LOGIC OF THE BOOK'S STRUCTURE

The book is in five parts.

1.1.1 Part I: Analytically Tractable Model

Part I presents and thoroughly studies the positive aspects of the models we employ in our policy analysis.

Why devote so much space to the positive aspects of new economic geography models when this is the subject of the excellent Fujita–Krugman–Venables (FKV for short) monograph? The FKV book deals almost exclusively with the so-called core–periphery model. This model—introduced by Paul Krugman in a 1991 *Journal of Political Economy* article—has the unfortunate feature of being astoundingly difficult to work with analytically. None of the interesting endogenous variables can be expressed as explicit functions of the things that the model tells us are important—trade costs, scale economies, market size, etc. Particularly annoying is the fact that the core–periphery (CP) model does not afford a closed-form solution for the principal focus of the whole literature—the spatial distribution of industry. This has forced researchers to illustrate general points with a gallery of numerical examples. While the resulting gallery is beautiful and illuminating, it is less than fully satisfactory from a theorist's perspective; one simply cannot be certain that the gallery is complete.

Since the goal of our book is to illustrate new insights into public policy—and insights are best illustrated with logic—Part I presents a sequence of 'new economic geography' models that are analytically tractable. These models are not widely known, so we devote a good deal of space to presenting, motivating and studying their basic properties. The rest of the book uses these models to illustrate policy insights.

Before turning to the tractable models, however, the first substantive chapter, Chapter 2, presents the CP model in detail. Our particular aim here is to establish a definitive list of its key features: a list against which we benchmark the more analytically amenable models presented in subsequent chapters. Given the pivotal role of the CP model, appendices to Chapter 2 also provide analytic proofs of all the CP model's key features (these proofs emerged after FKV was published).

The next six chapters cover a range of models that display agglomeration forces but are, nonetheless, amenable to paper-and-pencil reasoning. The first is the most tractable, what we call the footloose capital model (FC model for short). The FC model, however, pays for its tractability by abandoning many of the CP model's most remarkable features, including, for example, catastrophic agglomeration. The next chapter presents the model that most closely mirrors the CP model's features. This model, the footloose entrepreneur model (FE model for short), turns out to be identical to the CP model at a very deep level, but despite this, it involves little of the CP model's obduracy.

While the models of Chapters 3 and 4 can be thought of as modifications of the CP model, Chapter 5 introduces a family of models that is based on an alternative framework, one that does not depend upon the many peculiar assumptions of the CP model (Dixit–Stiglitz, iceberg trade costs, etc.). These models, what we call the linear models, are entirely solvable, and they display most of the CP model's key features.

Chapter 6 continues expanding the CP family by introducing a model—the 'constructed capital' or CC model—that is almost as easy to work with as the FC model but which displays more of the CP model's features. We then go on, in Chapter 7, to present CP-like economic geography models that allow for endogenous growth, and, in Chapter 8, to introduce tractable models that include 'vertical linkages' (input–output relationships among firms).

1.1.2 Part II: Welfare

Part II of our book turns to general welfare and policy issues. The aim here is to extract some insights concerning policy that can be clearly demonstrated without reference to specific models.

1.1.3 Parts III, IV and V: Trade, Tax and Regional Policies

Parts III, IV and V form the 'meat' of our book. They deal with trade policy, tax policy, and regional policy, respectively.

1.2 READERS' GUIDE

Readers who are thoroughly familiar with the CP model may consider skipping most of Chapter 2 with the possible exception of the third section (which summarizes the key properties of the CP model). Readers who are less familiar with the CP model should find that Chapter 2 provides a complete and accessible presentation of this classic model.

All readers should find it profitable to work through Chapters 3 and 4 before turning to the policy analysis. These present the two models—what we call the footloose capital (FC) model and footloose entrepreneur (FE) model—with which the bulk of our policy analysis is conducted. Moreover, most of the other models presented in Part I are best thought of as extensions/modifications of the FC or FE models. Readers mainly interested in policy analysis may want to postpone reading the other Part I chapters until they are called upon in particular policy chapters.

Part II presents analysis that may be too abstract for those impatient to get to the new policy insights, but we suspect that it will prove useful for readers who wish to apply economic geography models to new policy issues.

The last three parts may be read in any order without loss of continuity. Moreover, these chapters provide nutshell summaries of the models employed as well as detailed references to the relevant Part I chapters.

1.3 EMPIRICAL EVIDENCE

In early 2002, we asked colleagues around the world to comment on the proposed outline for this book. By far the most frequent comment we received was: "Where are the empirics?"

Right at the start of this project in 2000, we quite intentionally left empirical work off the agenda. There are good reasons for this. First and foremost is the fact that this is not our comparative advantage. The world does need a monograph that provides a concise, insightful and penetrating presentation of empirical methods and results in the field, but it probably does not need one from us. Second, the empirical literature, which had barely begun to emerge in 2000, is now unfolding at a rapid pace. New data sets and empirical methodologies appear continually. It may, therefore, be premature for even the right set of authors to write a synthetic treatment.

Nevertheless, we do think it important to argue that the models we employ and the forces they emphasize are empirically relevant. We therefore turn to a brief synopsis of the most relevant empirical evidence.

To many, casual empiricism provides the most convincing evidence of agglomeration forces. Exhibit A is the concentration of economic activity in the face of congestion costs. Two-bedroom houses in Palo Alto, California, routinely change hands for hundreds of thousands of dollars while houses in northern Wisconsin can be had for a song. Despite the high cost of living and office space, Silicon Valley remains attractive to both firms and workers while economic activity in northern Wisconsin languishes. The fact that most of the world's economic activity is organized around cities of various sizes suggests that powerful agglomeration forces are ubiquitous.

A second line of informal evidence comes from the examination of the assumptions. Agglomeration forces will arise in almost any model that allows for economies of scale, imperfect competition and trade costs. Add in labour, capital and/or firm mobility and one gets circular causality. Given that real-world firms are not atomistic, many industrial firms are huge despite the obvious difficulties of communication and decision making in large organizations. This suggests that internal scale economies are important. Industrial firms also seem to be price setters, or so it seems given the frequency with which one observes anti-trust complaints and blocked mergers. The third and fourth elements, transport costs and factor or firm mobility, are equally evident to any observer. This sort of 'evidence' is completely unconvincing to one set of economists although it is the only sort of evidence that really matters to another. To address the former set, we now turn to econometric studies.

Davis and Weinstein (1998, 1999) find econometric evidence that one agglomeration force—the so-called home market effect—is in operation. Haaland et al. (1999) find evidence that circular causality plays a statistically significant role in explaining the location of European industry. Midelfart-Knarvik and Steen (1999) find direct econometric evidence that backward and forward linkages are operating in certain Norwegian industries. Redding and Venables (2000) estimate an economic geography model using cross-country data and find clear support for the presence of agglomeration forces. Midelfart-Knarvik et al. (2000) find that agglomeration forces are important in explaining the location and spatial evolution of European industry. Overman and Puga (2002) present evidence that agglomeration forces are responsible for the geographical clustering of unemployment in Europe. Finally, Hanson (1998) shows that factor rewards follow a spatial gradient that suggests the presence of pecuniary externalities of a type that is usually associated with agglomeration forces.

ACKNOWLEDGEMENTS

Many people have helped us with this work over its two-and-a-half years of gestation. We thank the dozen or so anonymous referees that read all or parts of this book in draft form. The least anonymous and most helpful of these was Jacques Thisse. We would like to single him out for special thanks. The many insightful comments that he provided in the course of his reading of two complete drafts of our manuscript immeasurably improved the final product. The European Commission and Swiss government have helped with financial support via a 'Research and Training Network' grant of which all the authors are members. Federica Sbergami and Matilde Bombardini spent countless hours proofing various versions of various chapters; without them this book would contain many more errors than it does. We would also like to thank Eric Reuben. Karen-Helene Midelfart-Knarvik directly and indirectly helped the authors meet in various combinations in Bergen, and on two occasions in Villars, Switzerland. The Graduate Institute of International Studies in Geneva provided office space for Gianmarco Ottaviano during the entire duration of this project. Finally, we would like to thank Richard Baggaley of Princeton University Press for his excellent input and energetic support.

   While we have checked the equations carefully for errors, some surely remain. We will post errors that we find to http://heiwww.unige.ch/~baldwin and we invite readers to alert us to any errors they find.

REFERENCES

Davis, Donald R. and David E. Weinstein. 1998. Market access, economic geography, and comparative advantage: an empirical assessment. Working Paper No. 6787, National Bureau of Economic Research.

_____. 1999. Economic geography and regional production structure: an empirical investigation. *European Economic Review* 43(2): 379–407.

Fujita, M. and J.-F. Thisse. 2002. *Economics of Agglomeration: Cities, Industrial Location and Regional Growth.* Cambridge: Cambridge University Press.

Fujita, M., P. R. Krugman and A. J. Venables. 1999. *The Spatial Economy: Cities, Regions, and International Trade.* Cambridge, MA: MIT Press.

Haaland, J., H. Kind, K. Midelfart-Knarvik, and J. Torstensson. 1998. What determines the economic geography of Europe? Discussion Paper No. 2072, Centre for Economic Policy Research.

Hanson, Gordon H. 1998. Market potential, increasing returns, and geographic concentration. Working Paper No. 6429, National Bureau of Economic Research.

Krugman, Paul. 1991. Increasing returns and economic geography. *Journal of Political Economy* 99: 483–499.

Midelfart-Knarvik, K. and F. Steen. 1999. Self-reinforcing agglomerations? An empirical industry study. *Scandinavian Journal of Economics* 101: 515–532.

Midelfart-Knarvik, Karen Helene, Henry G. Overman, Stephen J. Redding, and Anthony J. Venables. 2000. The location of European industry. Economic Papers 142, European Commission Directorate-General for Economic and Financial Affairs.

Neary, P. 2001. Of hype and hyperbolas: introducing the new economic geography. *Journal of Economic Literature* 49: 536–561.

Ottaviano, Gianmarco I. P. and Diego Puga. 1998. Agglomeration in the global economy: A survey of the 'new economic geography'. *World Economy* 21(6): 707–731.

Overman, Henry G. and Diego Puga. 2002. Unemployment clusters across European regions and countries. *Economic Policy* 34: 115–147.

Redding, S. and A. Venables. 2000. Economic geography and international inequality. Discussion Paper No. 2568, Centre for Economic Policy Research.

P A R T I

Preliminaries

The Core–Periphery Model

2.1 INTRODUCTION

This chapter studies the model that has been the backbone of the 'new economic geography' literature to date—the so-called core–periphery model (Krugman 1991a). Unfortunately, the core–periphery model (CP model for short) is astoundingly difficult to manipulate analytically and indeed most results in the literature are derived via numerical simulation. Since the goal of this book is to illustrate new insights into public policy—and insights are best illustrated with analytic reasoning—subsequent chapters work with more analytically tractable economic geography models. The particular aim of this chapter is, therefore, to establish a definitive list of the CP model's key features as a benchmark against which the more analytically amenable models will be gauged.

Before turning to the equations, we present the fundamental logic of the model informally. Section 2.2.2 and Appendix 2.B.1 examine the same fundamental logic more formally.

2.1.1 Logic of the CP Model

From a geographic point of view, the economy is a very lumpy place. Whether one partitions space into nations, provinces, cities, or neighbourhoods, the geographic distribution of economic activity is extremely unequal. Some of this clustering is trivial; it is not difficult to understand the concentration of oil extraction in Saudi Arabia, or logging in Canada. Yet much of the geographic grouping of production—especially that of industry—seems to be much more arbitrary and supported by 'agglomeration economies' where these are defined as the tendency of a spatial concentration of economic activity to create economic conditions that foster the spatial concentration of economic activity.

Explaining industrial clusters with agglomeration economies is both trivial and baffling. Trivial since its very definition shows that assuming agglomeration economies is tantamount to assuming the result. Baffling since it is hard to know how a clear-headed theorist should approach this seemingly self-referential problem. The chief concern of the CP model—and perhaps its principle contribution to economic theory—has been to "get inside this particular black box and derive the self-reinforcing character of spatial concentration from more fundamental considerations" (Fujita et al. 1999, p. 4).

While several forms of agglomeration economies have been discussed in the literature, the CP model highlights only one—self-reinforcing, linkage-based agglomeration. The basic notion is simple to describe. Firms will naturally want to locate their production in the largest market (to save on shipping and all the other costs involved in selling at a distance). The size of a market, however, depends upon the number of residents and their income levels, but these, in turn, depend upon how many jobs are available. Market size, in other words, is a chicken-and-egg problem. The size of a market depends on how many firms locate there, but this depends upon market size.

The CP model opens the black box using a highly parsimonious set-up. Indeed, just three effects drive the mechanics of the model. The first is the 'market-access effect' that describes the tendency of monopolistic firms to locate their production in the big market and export to small markets. The second is the 'cost-of-living effect' that concerns the impact of firms' location on the local cost of living. Goods tend to be cheaper in the region with more industrial firms since consumers in this region will import a narrower range of products and thus avoid more of the trade costs. The third is the 'market-crowding effect', which reflects the fact that imperfectly competitive firms have a tendency to locate in regions with relatively few competitors. As we shall see, the first two effects encourage spatial concentration while the third discourages it.

Combining the market-access effect and the cost-of-living effect with inter-regional migration creates the potential for 'circular causality'—also known as 'cumulative causality', or 'backward and forward linkages.' The idea is simple and can be illustrated by a thought experiment. Suppose there are just two regions—call them 'north' and 'south'—and suppose they are initially identical. Now consider a situation where this initial symmetry is broken by a single industrial worker migrating from the south to the north. Since workers spend their incomes locally, the southern market becomes somewhat smaller and the northern market becomes somewhat larger. Due to the market-access effect, the changing market size tends to encourage some industrial firms to relocate from the south to the north. However, this industrial relocation will, via the cost-of-living effect, make a given northern nominal wage look more attractive than the same wage in the south. For this reason, the initial migration shock may be self-reinforcing; migration may alter relative real wages in a way that stimulates further migration (this is circular causality).

However, this is not the only possibility. The south-to-north shifting of firms increases the competition for customers in the north and reduces it in the south. This 'market-crowding effect' means the northern firms will have to pay a lower nominal wage in order to break even, while the opposite happens in the south. For a given cost of living, this makes location in the north less attractive to workers/migrants. Plainly, there is a tension between the market-access/cost-of-living effects and the market-crowding effect.

If market-access/cost-of-living effects—what we call agglomeration forces—are stronger than the market-crowding effect—what we call the dispersion force—any migration shock will trigger a self-reinforcing cycle of migration that results in all industrial workers and thus all industry moving to one region. Yet if the dispersion force outweighs the agglomeration forces, the initial symmetric equilibrium is stable in the sense that a migration shock lowers the north's real wage relative to the south's and this reverses the initial shock. Migration shocks, in other words, are self-correcting when the dispersion force dominates but self-reinforcing when agglomeration forces dominate.

STRENGTH OF AGGLOMERATION AND DISPERSION FORCES

What determines the relative strength of these forces? Trade cost is the right answer, but explaining this requires a bit of background.

The strength of the dispersion force diminishes as trade gets freer. For example, if trade is almost completely free, competition from firms in the other region is approximately as important as competition from locally based firms. In other words, competition is not very localized, so shifting firms from south to north will have very little impact on firm's revenues and thus on the wages they can pay to industrial workers. At the other extreme, near-prohibitive levels of trade cost mean that a change in the number of locally based firms has a very large impact on competition for customers and thus a very big effect on wages.

The strength of agglomeration forces also diminishes as trade gets freer. This is most easily seen for the cost-of-living effect. If the regions are very open in the sense that trade costs are low, then there will be very little difference in prices between the two regions whatever the spatial allocation of production is. Thus, shifting industrial production has only a minor impact on the relative cost of living. However, if trade is very costly, the share of varieties produced locally will have a big impact on price indices. Similar reasoning shows that the market access advantage is strongest when trade costs are high.

As it turns out, the dispersion force is stronger than the agglomeration forces when trade costs are very high, but a reduction in trade costs weakens the dispersion force more rapidly than it weakens the agglomeration forces. Explaining this requires more formal methods, but taking it as given, it means that at some level of trade costs the agglomeration forces overpower the dispersion force and self-reinforcing migration ends up shifting all industry to one region. This level of trade costs is called the 'break point' for obvious reasons.

ENDOGENOUS ASYMMETRY AND CATASTROPHIC AGGLOMERATION

The existence of the break point underpins what is perhaps the most striking feature of the CP model—a symmetric reduction in trade costs between initially symmetric regions eventually produces asymmetric regions. Indeed, the progressive trade cost reduction initially has *no* impact on industrial location, yet once trade costs cross the break point, the agglomeration forces dominate and *all* industry moves to a single region. Moreover, the migration and industrial delocation that makes this possible does not happen gradually, it happens catastrophically.[1]

---

[1] The catastrophic nature of agglomeration can be reversed if migrants face different costs of relocation; see Appendix 9.B.5 and Tabuchi and Thisse (2002), and Murata (2003).

The result that a steady change in an underlying parameter leads to this sort of nothing-then-everything change is not very common in economics, but it is quite common in physical systems. Indeed, economic geography in the CP model acts in the same way plate tectonics shapes the earth's physical geography. The underlying forces are applied steadily but they manifest themselves as decades of quiescence punctuated by earthquakes and volcanic eruptions that suddenly and dramatically alter the landscape.

2.1.2 Organization of the Chapter

The next section, Section 2.2, presents the standard CP model more formally. After listing the basic assumptions, we work out the short-run equilibrium, that is, the equilibrium taking as fixed each region's supply of the mobile factor. Next, we introduce a series of normalizations that facilitate the analysis by making the expressions less cluttered, and then we turn our attention to the long-run equilibrium, that is, the equilibrium where the mobile factor has no incentive to change regions. After this, we consider the local stability properties of the various long-run equilibria and summarize both the equilibria and their stability properties in the so-called 'tomahawk diagram'.

Note that the presentation in Section 2.2 assumes familiarity with the basic properties of the Dixit–Stiglitz monopolistic competition model (Dixit and Stiglitz 1977). Appendix 2.A presents a complete and self-contained derivation of all the relevant properties of the Dixit–Stiglitz model.

Section 2.3 lists the key features of the CP model. The aim here is to establish a checklist against which we shall measure the other, more amenable economic geography models presented in subsequent chapters and used in all the policy chapters. The final section contains our concluding remarks and a brief review of the related literature.

THE APPENDICES

This chapter is intended to provide a complete and accessible treatment of the CP model while at the same time covering all the formal methods and results that are available, including those that have appeared after Fujita, Krugman and Venables (1999) (FKV for short) was published. To accomplish this without overburdening the text, we relegate most of the technicalities and formal demonstrations to Appendix 2.B. Moreover, while the literature has focused on the symmetric-region version of the CP model, many interesting policy questions turn on regional asymmetries. The CP model's acute intractability rules out its use in addressing such questions, but Appendix 2.C numerically explores the CP model's behaviour with various asymmetries. Again, this exercise is useful in providing a metre stick for the more analytically friendly models we use in the policy analysis.

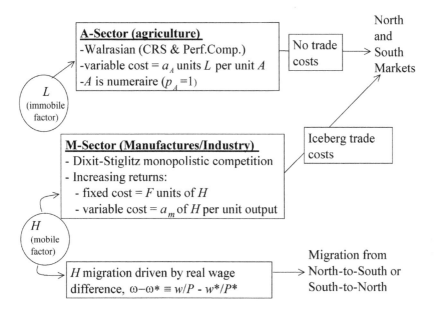

Figure 2.1 Schematic diagram of the CP model.

2.2 THE SYMMETRIC CP MODEL

The version of the CP model that we work with here is the one presented in FKV (Chapter 5). The vertical linkages version, which is critical in empirical work and some policy analysis, is dealt with in Chapter 8. Most of the assumptions of this model will be familiar to readers who are well acquainted with the new trade theory. Indeed, apart from migration, the CP model is very close to the model in Krugman (1980), especially as it is presented in Helpman and Krugman (1985, Chapter 10). See Fujita and Thisse (2002) for how CP model fits into the broader location literature and Section 2.4.1 for a brief description of related literature.

2.2.1 Assumptions

The basic structure of the CP model is shown schematically in Figure 2.1. There are two factors of production (industrial workers, H, and agricultural labourers, L), and two sectors (manufacturers, M, and agriculture, A).[2] There are two regions (north and south) that are symmetric in terms of tastes, technology, openness to trade, and, at least initially, in terms of their factors' supplies.

[2] As FKV argue, one does not have to think of the A sector literally as agriculture. Indeed, in practical terms, 'what the two sectors are' changes with the stage of development of the economy as well as with the epoch under consideration (Ottaviano and Thisse 2003). The key is that it uses the immobile factor intensively in its production. Readers who are familiar with FKV may find it useful to know that FKV's L^M and L^A correspond, respectively, to our mobile factor (H) and our immobile factor (L). Our notational choice is motivated by the fact that most of this book deals with issues where labour, or at least unskilled labour, is the immobile factor and physical, human and/or knowledge capital is the mobile factor.

The assumed technology is simple. The manufacturing sector (industry for short) is a standard Dixit–Stiglitz monopolistic competition sector, where manufacturing firms employ the labour of industrial workers to produce output subject to increasing returns. In particular, production of each variety requires a fixed input requirement involving 'F' units of industrial-worker labour (H), and a variable input requirement involving a_m units of H per unit of output produced. In symbols, the cost function is $w(F + a_m x)$, where x is a firm's output and w is an industrial worker's wage. By contrast, the A-sector produces a homogeneous good under perfect competition and constant returns; also, A-sector production uses only the labour of agricultural workers (L). More specifically, it takes a_A units of L to make one unit of the A-sector good regardless of the output level. The wage of A workers is denoted as w_A.

The goods of both sectors are traded, but trade in A-sector goods is frictionless while trade in M-sector trade is inhibited by iceberg trade costs.[3] Specifically, it is costless to ship industrial goods to local consumers but to sell one unit in the other region, an industrial firm must ship $\tau \geq 1$ units. The idea is that $\tau - 1$ units of the good 'melt' in transit (think of an iceberg melting as it is towed across an ocean).[4] As usual, τ captures all the costs of selling to distant markets, not just transport costs, and $\tau - 1$ is the tariff-equivalent of these costs.

The typical consumer in each region has a two-tier utility function. The upper tier determines the consumer's division of expenditure between the homogeneous good, on the one hand, and all differentiated industrial goods on the other hand. The second tier dictates the consumer's preferences over the various differentiated industrial varieties. The specific functional form of the upper tier is Cobb–Douglas (so the sectoral expenditure shares are constant) and the functional form of the lower tier is CES (constant elasticity of substitution). In symbols, preferences of a typical northern consumers are[5]

$$U = C_M^\mu C_A^{1-\mu}, \quad C_M \equiv \left(\int_{i=0}^{n+n^*} c_i^{1-(1/\sigma)} di \right)^{1/(1-1/\sigma)}; \quad 0 < \mu < 1 < \sigma \quad (2.1)$$

where C_M and C_A are, respectively, consumption of the composite of all differentiated varieties of industrial goods and consumption of the homogenous good A. Also, n and n^* are the 'mass' (roughly speaking, the number) of north and south varieties, μ is the expenditure share on industrial goods, and $\sigma > 1$ is the constant elasticity of substitution between industrial varieties. For a northern industrial worker, the indirect utility function for the preferences in (2.1) is

---

[3] The simplifying A-sector assumptions are very carefully matched, so relaxing any one of them individually can have seemingly outsized effects. For example, Davis (1998) showed that A-sector trade costs prevent agglomeration, but Krugman et al. (1999, Chapter 7) allowing trade costs and monopolistic competition in the second sector restores the main qualitative features of the CP model.

[4] In one of the earliest geography models, by von Thünen in 1826, the good was wheat and transportation was by horse-drawn wagon; $1 - \tau$ reflected the amount of wheat fed to the horse in transit. See Fujita and Thisse (2002) for a full account of the von Thünen model.

[5] Formally, we should also include the constant $\mu^\mu (1 - \mu)^{1-\mu}$, but this plays no role in the analysis.

$$\omega = \frac{w}{P}, \quad P \equiv p_A^{1-\mu}(\Delta n^w)^{-a}, \quad \Delta \equiv \frac{\int_{i=0}^{n^w} p_i^{1-\sigma} di}{n^w}; \quad a \equiv \frac{\mu}{\sigma - 1} \quad (2.2)$$

where ω is the indirect utility level, w is the wage paid to northern industrial workers, and P is the north's perfect price index that depends upon p_A, the northern price of A, and p_i, the consumer price of industrial variety i in the northern market (the variety subscript is dropped where clarity permits). Also, $n^w = n + n^*$ is the world number of firms and $n^w \Delta$ is the denominator of the CES demand function (see below). Observe that P is a 'perfect' price index in that real income defined with P is a measure of utility. Analogous definitions hold for southern variables, all of which are denoted by an asterisk.

Agricultural labourers are assumed to be immobile, and to keep things simple we suppose that each region has half the world's L. Thus taking L^w as the world endowment of unskilled labour, $L^w/2$ is the amount in each region (we consider asymmetric allocations of L in Appendix 2.C). The world supply of industrial workers—denoted as H^w—is also fixed but industrial workers can migrate between regions, so the inter-regional distribution of industrial workers is endogenously determined. As in FKV, migration is governed by the ad hoc migration equation:[6]

$$\dot{s}_H = (\omega - \omega^*)s_H(1 - s_H); \quad s_H \equiv \frac{H}{H^w}, \quad \omega \equiv \frac{w}{P}, \quad \omega^* \equiv \frac{w^*}{P^*} \quad (2.3)$$

where s_H is the share of the world's supply of industrial workers located in the north, H is the northern supply of industrial workers, w and w^* are the northern and southern wages paid to industrial workers, and ω and ω^* are the corresponding real wages. As (2.2) shows, real wages are also a utility index for industrial workers so the migration equation indicates that industrial workers migrate to the region that provides them with the highest level of utility. While this migration equation may seem rather arbitrary, and perhaps overly elaborate, there are good reasons for adopting it (see Box 2.1).

We note that many of these assumptions are made merely to simplify calculations or derivation of the equilibrium expressions. See Appendix 2.B.5 for a discussion of which assumptions are essential and which are merely for convenience.

Having covered the model's assumptions, we turn next to the equilibrium expressions.

2.2.2 Short-Run Equilibrium

Intuition is served by first working out the equilibrium taking as given the amount of the mobile factor located in each region. Focusing on this equilibrium—what we call the short-run equilibrium—allows us to study the dependence of key endogenous

---

[6] The FKV formulation, in our notation, has $(\omega - \omega')s_H$ on the right-hand side of the migration equation, where ω' is the weighted average of real wages in all regions, that is, $s_H\omega + (1 - s_H)\omega^*$. Our formulation is identical to that of FKV as simple manipulation reveals. Throughout the book, we use the standard 'dot' notation to indicate derivatives with respect to time.

BOX 2.1 HOW AD HOC IS THE MIGRATION EQUATION?

One amazing aspect of the early economic geography papers (Krugman 1991a; Krugman and Venables 1995; Venables 1996) is that they work with dynamic models where migration is the heart-and-soul of agglomeration without ever discussing dynamic equations or specifying a migration equation. The authors just assert that workers move to the region with the highest real wage. This omission was probably crucial in glossing over one of the model's key simplifications, namely that infinitely lived migrants are myopic rather than rational and forward-looking, but it may have been responsible for the error in Krugman (1991c) that was corrected by Fukao and Benabou (1993). Puga (1999) seems to be the first to deal explicitly with the CP model's dynamics, and FKV claim that although (2.3) is ad hoc, it might be justified on the grounds of 'replicator dynamics' used in evolutionary game theory.

Be that as it may, we note that (2.3) has one aspect that seems very natural—that the rate of migration is proportional the real wage gap—and one aspect that seems odd, namely the $s_H(1 - s_H)$ term. It is odd since although all migrants are assumed to be identical, this term means that they will not move all at once. That is a common result when there are adjustment costs that are proportional to the rate of change, but the CP model does not make such assumptions. Moreover, if it assumed the standard quadratic adjustment costs setup, the resulting law of motion would not be (2.3).

As with many of the model's assumptions, the $s_H(1 - s_H)$ term is best justified on the grounds of simplicity. This term makes it much simpler to deal with the dynamics formally since it makes it quite clear how the system behaves when the model is at a 'corner', $s_H = 0$ or $s_H = 1$. Moreover, if one does allow migrants to be forward-looking, this term is critical in avoiding the error pointed out by Fukao and Benabou. Finally as Appendix 2.B.4 shows, (2.3) can be justified as the outcome utility optimization by heterogeneous workers facing migration costs.

---

variables on the spatial allocation of the mobile factor. The subsequent section uses these results to characterize the long-run equilibrium, that is, the equilibrium that results when we allow industrial workers to migrate. (Formally, the short-run equilibrium requires optimization by consumers and firms as well as market clearing for a given distribution of H^w across regions.)

A-SECTOR RESULTS

The CP model, and indeed each model in this book, assumes that the A-sector is extremely simple (no imperfect competition, no increasing returns, no trade costs) and this makes it extremely simple to characterize the short-run equilibrium in this sector.

Perfect competition in the A sector forces marginal cost pricing, that is,

$$p_A = w_L a_A, \quad p_A^* = w_L^* a_A \tag{2.4}$$

Costless trade in A equalizes northern and southern prices, and this, in turn, indirectly equalizes wage rates for agricultural labours in both regions, viz. $w_L = w_L^*$. The short-run equilibrium additionally requires that the market for A clears. Consider first the demand for A. A well-known feature of the preferences in (2.1) is that utility maximization yields a constant division of expenditure between industrial goods and the agricultural good, with $(1 - \mu)E$ being the total spending by northern consumers on A-goods. Thus, the northern demand function for A is

$$C_A = \frac{(1 - \mu)E}{p_A} \tag{2.5}$$

where E is total expenditure in the north (this equals total northern income). The southern demand is isomorphic. Using the full employment of agricultural workers to write the global output of A as L^w/a_A, where L^w is the world endowment of agricultural labour, the market-clearing condition for the global A market is

$$(1 - \mu)(E + E^*) = p_A \left(\frac{L^w}{a_A} \right) \tag{2.6}$$

where E^* is southern expenditure (throughout the book we denote southern variables with an asterisk and northern variable with no superscript). Of course, Walras's law permits us to drop one of the market-clearing conditions; traditionally (2.6) is the omitted condition.

INDUSTRIAL SECTOR RESULTS

As just noted, northern consumers find it optimal to spend $(1 - \mu)E$ on A goods and μE on all industrial varieties. Utility optimization by northerners also yields a standard CES demand function for each industrial variety, namely

$$c_j \equiv \frac{p_j^{-\sigma} \mu E}{n^w \Delta}, \quad n^w \Delta \equiv \left(\int_{i=0}^{n+n^*} p_i^{1-\sigma} di \right), \quad E = wH + w_L L \tag{2.7}$$

The denominator of this demand function turns out to play an important role in the analysis, so it is convenient to denote it as Δ (a mnemonic for denominator). Observe that pure profits do not enter the definition of expenditure, E, since under monopolistic competition, free and instantaneous entry drives pure profits to zero.

An important aspect of Dixit–Stiglitz monopolistic competition is that each industrial firm is atomistic and thus rationally ignores the impact of its price on the denominator of the demand function in (2.7). Moreover, since varieties are differentiated, no direct strategic interaction among firms arises (Appendix 2.A.1 provides a more detailed exposition of these points). As a consequence, the typical firm acts as if it is a monopolist facing a demand curve with a constant elasticity equal to σ. Given the standard formula for marginal revenue, this implies that the profit-maximizing consumer price is a constant mark-up of marginal cost. More specifically, the first-order conditions for a typical industrial firm's sales to its local market and its export market are

$$p = \frac{wa_m}{1 - 1/\sigma}, \quad p^* = \frac{\tau wa_m}{1 - 1/\sigma} \tag{2.8}$$

where p and p^* are the local and export prices of a north-based industrial firm; the restriction $\sigma > 1$ ensures that p and p^* are positive and finite.

An important implication of (2.8) is that firms find it optimal to engage in so-called mill pricing. That is to say, a firm charges the same producer price for sales to both markets. To see that this is true, note that the producer and consumer prices are identical for local market sales (there is no trade cost), but for export sales the consumer price is p^*, while the producer price is p^*/τ. This, together with inspection of (2.8), reveals that $p = p^*/\tau$, and this confirms the assertion that mill pricing is optimal.

Mill pricing makes it very easy to calculate the equilibrium size of a typical industrial firm. With free entry, firms enter until the operating profit earned by a typical firm is just sufficient to cover its fixed cost. Because the producer price is a constant mark-up over marginal cost, regardless of where the good is sold, the operating profit earned on each unit produced is also constant regardless of where it is sold and this, in turn, means that breaking-even requires a firm to produce a number of units that is not sensitive to trade costs; mill-pricing, in other words, makes the division between local sales and export sales irrelevant for equilibrium firm scale. More specifically, a typical firm's operating profit is px/σ, where p is producer price and x is the firm's total production (see Appendix 2.A.2 for a fuller derivation). The zero-profit condition requires operating profit to equal the fixed cost wF, so using the mill-pricing rule in (2.8) and the fact that operating profit equals px/σ, the equilibrium firm size must satisfy

$$\bar{x} = \frac{F(\sigma - 1)}{a_m} \tag{2.9}$$

where $\bar{x}$ is the equilibrium size of a typical industrial firm. The break-even firm size in the south is identical.

To find the number of varieties produced in equilibrium, we calculate the amount of H employed by a typical industrial firm and then determine how many firms it would take to fully employ the economy's supply of H. In equilibrium, a typical firm employs $(F + a_m\bar{x})$ units of H, so the total demand for H is $n(F + a_m\bar{x})$. The supply and demand for H must match this in equilibrium, so using (2.9), the equilibrium number of firms is related to parameters and the north's supply of H according to

$$n = \frac{H}{\sigma F} \tag{2.10}$$

where H is the north's supply of H, which is fixed in the short run. An isomorphic expression defines the analogous southern variable n^*.

Two features of (2.9) and (2.10) are worth highlighting. First, the number of varieties produced in a region is proportional to the regional labour force. Migration of industrial workers is therefore tantamount to industrial relocation and vice versa. Second, the scale of firms is invariant to trade costs and everything else except the elasticity of substitution and the size of marginal and fixed costs. (The break-even firm size rises with the ratio of fixed to variable costs, F/a_m, and it falls as the operating profit margin, $1/\sigma$, rises.) Third, one measure of scale, namely the ratio of average cost to marginal cost, depends only on σ.[7]

The Mobile Factor's Reward: The Market Clearing Conditions. Since the location of industrial firms is tied to the location of skilled labour, and this, in turn, is determined by wage-driven migration, the relationship between the wage paid to H in the north and the north's supply of H is critical. Unfortunately, the CP model does not yield a closed-form expression for this relationship. Rather, the short-run equilibrium wages for H in the north and the south are implicitly defined by the so-called 'marketing-clearing conditions' for typical northern and southern varieties.[8]

These conditions are a combination of a supply-equals-demand condition and a zero-pure profit condition. They require prices to be such that each industrial firm can sell its break-even level of output $\bar{x}$. Since prices are directly linked to wages—via mill pricing—the market-clearing conditions indirectly define what northern and southern wages must be in equilibrium. It is traditional to define market-clearing in terms of quantities (i.e. quantity supplied equals quantity bought), but it turns out that the conditions are more intuitive when expressed in value terms (value of production equals value of consumption). We therefore write the market-clearing condition for a typical northern variety as

$$p\bar{x} = R \qquad (2.11)$$

The left-hand side is the value of the output of a firm making zero-pure profits; the right-hand side, R (a mnemonic for 'retail sales'), is the value of sales at consumer prices, namely $R = pc + p^* c^*$ where c and c^* are consumption of a typical northern variety in the north and south, respectively.[9]

This market-clearing condition and the isomorphic southern condition impose a pair of constraints on w and w^* because the consumption levels are linked—via the demand curves—to consumer prices and these prices are linked to north and south wages via mill pricing. Specifically, using the demand function, (2.7), the

---

[7] While commonly used, the scale elasticity (ratio of average to marginal cost) is a measure that has its limitations. For instance, if the cost function is not homothetic in factor prices, a given scale elasticity does not coincide one-to-one with firm size. If capital is used only in the fixed cost and labour only in the variable costs, then the scale elasticity is $rF/(wa_m x) + 1$. Even if this is constant in equilibrium, the corresponding firm size increases with the r/w ratio. Since trade costs can in general affect factor prices, this means that trade costs can also affect firm scale, even with monopolistic competition. See Flam and Helpman (1987) for details.

[8] FKV refer to the market-clearing conditions as the 'wage equations'.

[9] Due to mill pricing and iceberg trade costs, the value of a typical firm's retail sales at consumer prices always equals its revenue at producer prices, so R equally well stands for 'revenue'.

value of retail sales depends upon the prices of northern and southern varieties, but from mill pricing, (2.9), we know the prices depend upon trade cost and the wage paid to H in the north and the south, so R is[10]

$$R \equiv \frac{w^{1-\sigma}\mu E}{nw^{1-\sigma} + \phi n^*(w^*)^{1-\sigma}} + \frac{\phi w^{1-\sigma}\mu E^*}{\phi nw^{1-\sigma} + n^*(w^*)^{1-\sigma}}$$

where $\phi \equiv \tau^{1-\sigma}$. Note that $\phi \equiv \tau^{1-\sigma}$ measures the 'freeness' (phi-ness) of trade. That is, the freeness of trade rises from $\phi = 0$, with infinite trade costs, to $\phi = 1$, with zero trade costs. The market-clearing condition for a typical south-made variety is isomorphic.

In passing, we note that throughout the book we try to formulate the models such that the parameters and variables are defined on a compact space, typically $[0, ..., 1]$. This is handy for inspection of expressions, but it also makes numerical simulation more reliable. This is not standard practice in the literature. For example, typically the trade costs are left as τ and simulations are done for a finite range of τ's. This leaves the reader wondering whether the results that the simulations are supposed to illustrate also hold for near-infinite trade costs.

Of course the number of firms based in the north and south, n and n^*, respectively, are proportional to the amounts of H located in the two regions, as per (2.10). Thus, the market-clearing condition (2.11) provides an implicit relationship between the supply of H located in the north and wage paid to H. For example, if the northern wage, w, is too high given the southern wage w^* and the spatial allocation of firms, the value of sales of a typical north-based firm will not be large enough for it to break even. Thus, we know that the equilibrium northern wage must satisfy (2.11). The equilibrium w and w^* taking as given n and n^* (i.e. taking as given the allocation of the mobile factor between north and south) requires simultaneous solution of northern and southern market-clearing conditions.

Since our analysis focuses on the spatial allocation of industrial firms, and this in turn depends on the spatial allocation of expenditure (i.e. relative market size), it is convenient to re-write R in terms of shares—the share of world firms that are located in the north and the share of world expenditure that the north market represents. Thus, the retail sales of typical north-based and typical south-based firms are, respectively,

$$R \equiv \mu \frac{E^w}{n^w} B, \quad R^* \equiv \mu \frac{E^w}{n^w} B^* \tag{2.12}$$

where $E^w \equiv E + E^*$ is global expenditure, and the B's (mnemonics for bias in sales) are

---

[10] Using a bulky but explicit notation for prices, we denote the price of a good made in region i and sold in region j as p_{ij}, where $i \equiv N$ for north and S for south. With this, the CES demand functions imply that local sales of a northern variety are $(p_{NN})^{-\sigma}/D$ times μE, where $D \equiv n(p_{NN})^{1-\sigma} + n^*(p_{SN})^{1-\sigma}$. The expression for export sales is $(p_{NS})^{-\sigma}/D^*$ times μE^*, where $D^* \equiv n(p_{NS})^{1-\sigma} + n^*(p_{SS})^{1-\sigma}$. These volume terms are multiplied by their respective prices and then summed to get the value of revenue, R.

$$B \equiv \left(\frac{s_E}{\Delta} + \phi \frac{1 - s_E}{\Delta^*} \right) w^{1-\sigma}, \quad B^* \equiv \left(\phi \frac{s_E}{\Delta} + \frac{1 - s_E}{\Delta^*} \right) (w^*)^{1-\sigma}$$

where the symmetry of varieties produced within each region allows us to express the Δ's as[11]

$$\Delta \equiv s_n w^{1-\sigma} + \phi(1 - s_n)(w^*)^{1-\sigma}, \quad \Delta^* \equiv \phi s_n w^{1-\sigma} + (1 - s_n)(w^*)^{1-\sigma}$$

Here $s_n \equiv n/n^w$ and $s_E \equiv E/E^w$ are the north's share of world expenditure and industrial firms.

Market-Crowding Effect.   One reward for writing R in this form is that it clearly reveals the market-crowding effect. Starting from the symmetric outcome (where w obviously equals w^*), a small movement of firms from the south to the north raises s_n. This tends to raise Δ and lower Δ^* as long as trade is less than fully free ($\phi < 1$). Holding relative market size (s_E) and wage rates constant, this tends to lower a typical northern firm's sales and thus its operating profit. In order to break even, northern firms would have to pay their workers less, so the market-crowding effect is clearly a force that tends to discourage the concentration of workers/firms.[12] To be more precise, we note that starting from the symmetric outcome where wages and market sizes are equal and $s_n = 1/2$, a small shift in s_n leads to a change in B equal to $-2(1 - \phi)^2/w'(1 + \phi)^2$, where w' is the common wage. This shows that the market-crowding effect diminishes as trade gets freer (i.e. ϕ rises) and the relationship is roughly quadratic (See Appendix 2.B.1 for a fuller presentation).

Market-Access Effect.   The market-access effect can also be seen in the variable 'B', as the following thought experiment makes clear. Suppose for some reason that the northern market size increases, that is, that s_E rises. Again starting from symmetry (so the Δ's and everything else are equal), we see that a higher s_E raises B as long as $\phi < 1$. This means that the sales of a typical north-based firm rise and, by mill pricing, this raises northern operating profits. Since we start from zero-pure profits, re-establishing equilibrium will require an increase in the wage paid to northern industrial workers, and this, in turn, will tend to attract more workers to the north. To be more specific, note that the change in B with respect to a small change in s_E equals $1 - \phi$. Thus, the market-access effect diminishes as trade gets freer, but the relationship is linear.

For completeness, we use our expression for the equilibrium firm size, (2.9), and mill pricing, (2.8), to re-write the north and south market clearing conditions in terms of wages, w and w^*, the regional allocation of the world's supply of industrial workers, $s_H \equiv H/H^w$ and parameters. Expression (2.11) and its southern equivalent can be written as

$$w \sigma F = \mu \frac{E^w}{n^w} B, \quad w^* \sigma F = \mu \frac{E^w}{n^w} B^* \tag{2.13}$$

[11] The B's are biases in that $s_n B + (1 - s_n) B^* = 1$

[12] That is, full employment of industrial workers would require them to accept a lower wage.

Furthermore, (2.10) implies that the north's share of industrial firms (s_n) is identical to the north's share of the world's supply of H (s_H). Thus, we can substitute $s_H \equiv H/H^w$ into the definitions of the Δ's given in (2.12), and this gives us what FKV call the wage equations, that is, the w's in terms of the spatial allocation of H.

Unfortunately there is no way to solve the market-clearing conditions analytically. The w's in the B's are raised to the non-integer power $1 - \sigma$, so an analytic solution is impossible.[13] This inability to solve for the w's as explicit functions of the spatial allocation of the mobile factor is root of all the CP model's profound intractability. Without the w's, we cannot find real wages and since the real wage gap is the key to migration, and migration the key to agglomeration, it is difficult to say anything without resorting to numerical solutions. Numerical solutions for particular values of μ, σ and ϕ, however, are easily obtained (for a MAPLE spreadsheet that solves this model numerically, see http://heiwww.unige.ch/~baldwin/maple.htm).

The Market-Size Condition. The final short-run variable is the relative market size as measured by the north's share of world expenditure, s_E. The denominator of this is just total world expenditure/income, namely E^w, which equals $w_L L^w + wH + w^* H^*$. Due to the zero-profit condition, the total income earned by industrial workers just equals the total revenue of industrial firms and this, in turn, equals total spending on industrial goods. Thus, $wH + w^* H^*$ equals μE^w, so rearranging the definition of E^w, we get

$$E^w = \frac{w_L L^w}{1 - \mu} \qquad (2.14)$$

Using the definition of s_E and the definition of the north's income/expenditure, we have that s_E equals $(w_L L + wH)/[w_L L^w/(1 - \mu)]$. Using our share notation, this becomes

$$s_E = (1 - \mu)\left(s_L + \frac{wH^w}{w_L L^w} s_H\right) \qquad (2.15)$$

where $s_L = 1/2$ in the case we are considering (symmetric regions). The market size condition, (2.15), tells us that the north's share of expenditure is an average of its shares of the world's L and H endowments.

Observe that this expression shows how production shifting is related to expenditure shifting. Since industrial relocation (change in s_n) and migration (change in s_H) are perfectly tied in this model, anything that induces a relocation of firms from, say, south to north, will also increase the north's share of world expenditure.

2.2.3 Choice of Numeraire and Units

Both intuition and tidiness are served by appropriate normalization and choice of

---

[13] With Maple, one can solve for the special case of $\sigma = 2$, but the solution involves hundreds of terms.

numeraire. Such normalization, however, can be confusing at first, so we note that one could conduct all the analysis without these.

To start with we take A as numeraire and choose units of A such $a_A = 1$. This simplifies the expressions for the price index and expenditure since it implies $p_A = w_L = w_L^* = 1$. Turning to the industrial sector, we measure units of industrial goods such that $a_m = (1 - 1/\sigma)$. This implies that the equilibrium prices are $p = w$ and $p^* = \tau w$, and the equilibrium firm size is $\bar{x} = F\sigma$.[14]

The next normalization, which concerns F, has led to some confusion. Since we are working with the continuum-of-varieties version of the Dixit–Stiglitz model, we can normalize F to $1/\sigma$ (see Box 2.2 on this point). With this, $\bar{x} = 1$, and so from (2.10), we get a very simple relationship between regional supplies of industrial labourers and the number of varieties produced in each region, namely $n = H$ and $n^* = H^*$. These results simplify the market-clearing conditions and boost intuition by making the connection between migration and industrial relocation crystal clear.

We are also free to specify units for L and H. Choosing the world endowment of H such that $H^w = 1$ is useful since it implies that the total measure of varieties worldwide is fixed at unity (i.e. $n + n^* = n^w = 1$). The fact that $n + n^* = 1$ is useful in manipulating expressions. For instance, instead of writing s_H for the northern share of H^w, we could write s_n or simply n (notationally speaking, s_n is more explicit but n is easier to write). Finally, it proves convenient to have $w = w^* = 1$ in the symmetric outcome (i.e. where $s_n = n = H = 1/2$); manipulation of the market-clearing conditions with a few lines of algebra confirms that this can be accomplished by choosing units of L such that the world endowment of the immobile factor, that is, L^w, equals $(1 - \mu)/\mu$.[15] These normalizations also imply that at the full agglomeration outcome (i.e. $n = H = 1$ or 0), the industrial wage in the region that has all industry is also unity. For example, at the core-in-the-north outcome, $w = 1$ and $w^* < 1$.

In summary, the equilibrium values in the symmetric equilibrium are

$$p = w, \quad p^* = w\tau, \quad p_A = p_A^* = w_L = w_L^* = 1, \quad \bar{x} = 1,$$

$$n + n^* = H + H^* \equiv H^w = 1, \quad n = H = s_H = s_n, \quad n^* = H^*$$

$$L^w = \frac{1 - \mu}{\mu}, \quad E^w = \frac{1}{\mu} \tag{2.16}$$

and $w = w^* = 1$ in the symmetric outcome. In the core–periphery outcome, the nominal wage of industrial workers (i.e. their wage in terms of the numeraire) in the core is also unity. The nominal industrial wage in the periphery, which must be thought of as a 'virtual' wage since no H is working in the periphery in the CP outcome, is $[\phi(1 + \mu)/2) + (1 - \mu)/2\phi]^{1/\sigma}$ as manipulation of the market-clearing conditions reveals; this need not equal unity.

---

[14] To be more formal, we would add multiplicative constants in front of C_A and C_m in the utility function (2.1) to adjust to the change in units.

[15] KFV takes L^w as μ and A^w as $1 - \mu$, but wages are unity as long as L^w/A^w equals $\mu/(1 - \mu)$.

BOX 2.2 ONE TOO MANY NORMALIZATIONS?

Many authors who have worked with the original CP model (and its vertical-linkages variant) use two normalizations in the Dixit–Stiglitz sector in order to tidy the equations. In particular, they set the variable cost to $1 - 1/\sigma$ units of the sector-specific factor and they set the fixed labour requirement to $1/\sigma$ units of the same factor. Since units of the sector-specific factor are also normalized elsewhere, it may seem that there is one too many normalizations. Peter Neary makes the point elegantly in Neary (2001): "As Oscar Wilde's Lady Bracknell might have said, to normalise one cost parameter may be regarded as a misfortune, to normalise both looks like carelessness." In fact, dual normalization is not problematic in the continuum of varieties version of the model (i.e. it implies no loss of generality), but it is not OK in the discrete version (which is the version Neary (2001) works with). With a continuum of varieties, n is not, strictly speaking, the number of varieties produced in the north; indeed, as long as n is not zero, an uncountable infinity of varieties are produced in the north. Rather n corresponds to a mass of varieties that can be represented as the segment $[0...n]$ on a real line. But the units on this real line are arbitrary. Thus, the continuum gives us an extra degree of freedom that can be absorbed in an extra normalization. In the discrete varieties version, firms have a natural metric (defined by the size of the fixed labour requirement), so the second normalization does reduce generality.

2.2.4 Long-Run Equilibrium

The previous section works out the short-run equilibrium, that is, it ignores the migration equation, (2.3), and takes as given the spatial allocation of industrial workers. We now put migration explicitly back into the picture and study long-run equilibria defined as situations where no migration occurs. More formally, s_H is the state variable and the long-run equilibria are the steady states of the law of motion, (2.3), that is, the values of s_H where $\dot{s}_H$ equals zero (see Box 2.3 on the relationship between the mathematical concept of steady state and the concept of economic equilibrium).

THE LOCATION CONDITION

Inspection of the migration equation, (2.3), shows that there are two types of long-run equilibria: (1) interior outcomes ($0 < s_H < 1$) where industrial workers achieve the same level of utility (i.e. $\omega = \omega^*$) wherever they reside; (2) core–periphery outcomes ($s_H = 0$ or $s_H = 1$). Thus, the no-migration condition, which we call the 'location condition' is that either

$$\omega = \omega^*, \quad 0 < s_H < 1 \tag{2.17}$$

where

BOX 2.3 STEADY STATES AND ECONOMIC EQUILIBRIA

The ad hoc law of motion, (2.3), adopted by FKV raises problems of interpretation when it comes to the term 'long-run equilibrium'. In standard parlance, long-run equilibrium refers to a situation where no agent gains from unilateral deviation. According to the law of motion, if s_H starts out exactly at zero (all industrial workers in the south), then no worker would like to move north—even if the northern real wage is higher. This, of course, does not sound reasonable, but it is what the law of motion dictates. And, since the law of motion is not directly derived from optimizing behaviour, we cannot explain why workers would not want to move. This inconsistency is precisely the cost of ad hockery (Matsuyama 1991).

Be that as it may, to make our results readily comparable with FKV, we define 'long-run equilibria' as all the steady states of (2.3); thus, $s_H = 0, 1$ are always included. However, as we demonstrate below, such steady states are unstable unless trade is sufficiently free; in such cases, the corner outcomes would be observed with zero probability in a world that was subject to small random shocks. In other words, although we define all steady states as long-run equilibria, the only ones that are economically relevant are the *stable* long-run equilibria. Unstable steady states should be interpreted as landmarks for the mind rather than situations that are of interest in policy analysis.

$$\omega \equiv \frac{w}{P}, \quad \omega^* \equiv \frac{w^*}{P^*} \quad \text{and} \quad P \equiv \Delta^{-a}, \quad P^* \equiv (\Delta^*)^{-a}; \quad a \equiv \frac{\mu}{\sigma - 1}$$

and the Δ's are defined in (2.12), or $s_H = 0$ or $s_H = 1$.

To characterize the long-run equilibria, we must solve the location conditions for the geographical division of industrial workers between the north and the south, that is, s_H. As mentioned above, the w's are functions of the Δ's, but the Δ's are unsolvable functions of the w's, so we cannot in general solve the location conditions for the long-run equilibrium distribution of the mobile factor. Nevertheless, when the regions are intrinsically symmetric—as we have assumed them to be here—symmetry tells us that ω does equal ω^* when $s_H = 1/2$, so we know that $s_H = 1/2$ is always a long-run equilibrium. Moreover, the last two expressions in (2.17) show that the two core–periphery outcomes are also always long-run equilibrium, not because $\omega = \omega^*$, but because migration is zero when $s_H(1 - s_H) = 0$ according to (2.3).

To further our analysis and illustrate the agglomeration and dispersion forces, we turn to graphical methods.

DIAGRAMMATIC SOLUTION

The Wiggle Diagram. The earliest papers on the CP model evaluated local stability numerically using a 'wiggle diagram'. This approach is visually intuitive,

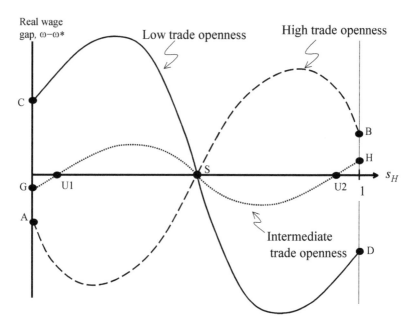

Figure 2.2 The wiggle diagram and local stability.

and the wiggle diagram comes in handy for more sophisticated analysis of the model (global stability analysis, etc.), so it is worth presenting here.

The wiggle diagram plots the real wage gap against the share of the mobile factor in the north, namely $\Omega[s_H]$, where $\Omega \equiv \omega - \omega^*$. As noted above, this function cannot be written explicitly since we cannot solve for w and w^* in terms of s_H and thus we cannot write w/P or w^*/P^* in terms of s_H. Instead, we must numerically solve for the w's and then substitute this into the price indices and form the real wages. Figure 2.2 plots the resulting real wage gap—which can be positive or negative—on the vertical axis against the share of industrial workers in the north.

When trade freeness (openness) is sufficiently low, the dispersion forces are stronger than the agglomeration forces. Thus, starting from symmetry, that is, point 'S' in the diagram where $s_H = 1/2$ and $\omega - \omega^* = 0$, a small increase in the north's share of H would make the wage gap negative and would therefore induce a self-correcting movement of workers back to the south. We see this in the diagram by noting the real-wage-gap curve (solid line) has a negative slope at the point 'S'. Given the migration equation, (2.3), we also know that the core–periphery outcomes are always steady states, but the 'low trade openness' curve shows that the real wage gap is positive at $s_H = 0$ (point C) and negative at $s_H = 1$ (point D). This means that these points are unstable; any shock starting from $s_H = 0$ would lead to south-to-north migration; any shock starting from $s_H = 1$ would produce north-to-south migration. In both cases, migration would proceed until the economy reached point S.

At the opposite extreme, when trade freeness is high, the symmetric outcome is unstable and the CP outcomes are stable. This is shown by the dashed line in Figure 2.2. This curve's slope is positive at S, while its level is positive at B and negative at A. What this means is that a slight increase in s_H starting at point S would make the real wage gap positive and thus lead to more south-to-north migration with the process continuing until all H was in the north, that is, the economy had reached point B. In other words, when trade is sufficiently free, the symmetric outcome is unstable since migration generates self-amplifying forces. We also know that point B (i.e. the core-in-the-north outcome) is stable since here the real wage gap is positive. Similarly, even the slightest north-to-south migration shock starting from S would bring the economy all the way to the stable core-in-the-south outcome shown as point A.

For a narrow range of intermediate levels of trade freeness, the real-wage-gap curve looks like the dotted curve. This crosses the zero line three times implying that there are three interior equilibria (the symmetric point S and the two points U1 and U2). The key features to note are that the line is negatively sloped at point S, while its endpoint G is below the line, and its endpoint at H is above the line. Applying the above reasoning, this indicates that for this range of trade costs, the symmetric and both CP outcomes are stable. Of course there is an unstable equilibrium between every two stable ones, and these are where the dotted line crosses the *x*-axis with a positive slope (namely U1 and U2). These outcomes are long-run equilibria (since the real wage gap is zero, there is zero migration), but the positive slope indicates that they are unstable.

What this diagram illustrates quite vividly is that although the CP model works with a highly parsimonious framework, it generates a range of results that are fascinatingly complex. The standard way of systematizing analysis of its behaviour is to realize that the model has three distinct types of behaviour according to the level of trade freeness (ϕ). Finding the two levels of trade freeness that partition the outcomes into the three distinctive behaviours is the classic means of characterizing the model's behaviour. This is the subject of the next section, but before turning to that we consider the forces that produce this captivatingly complex behaviour.

FORCES AT WORK

As discussed in the introduction, there are three distinct forces governing stability in this model. Two of them favour agglomeration, that is, they are de-stabilizing. These are the market-access and cost-of-living effects (also called 'demand-linked' and 'cost-linked' circular causalities, or 'backward' and 'forward' linkages). The third force favours dispersion; it is known as the market-crowding effect or 'local competition' effect.

Demand-Linked Circular Causality. The expression for s_E in (2.15) and the expression for firm-level sales in (2.12) help illustrate how the market-access agglomeration force is self-reinforcing. Starting from symmetry, a small migration from south to north increases s_E and decreases $1 - s_E$ since mobile workers spend their income locally. This makes the northern market larger and the southern market smaller. In the presence of trade costs, and all else being equal, firms will prefer to be located in the big market ('market-access effect'), so this migration-induced 'expenditure shifting' encourages 'production shifting'. More precisely, expenditure shifting raises sales of a typical northern firm, and lowers that of a typical southern firm. Since operating profit is proportional to sales with mill pricing, firms will tend to exit the south and enter in the north.

This mechanism becomes self-reinforcing since, as firms move northwards, the number of industrial jobs in the south shrinks and the number in the north expands, so the production shifting tends to encourage further expenditure shifting. The key point here is that if there were no change in industrial wages, the increase in northern industrial production would have to be *more than proportional* to the original expenditure shift in order to re-establish zero pure profits. (This, of course, is just the famous 'home-market effect' of Krugman 1980). Since the shifting in industrial jobs is more than proportional (holding wages constant), we see that production shifting tends to encourage further migration to the north.

We call this mechanism demand-linked circular causality; 'circular' since migration produces expenditure shifting that tends to encourage production shifting which in turn tends to encourage more migration; 'demand-linked' since changes in the spatial allocation of demand is the mechanism's fulcrum. This mechanism is also known by the somewhat cryptic moniker 'backward linkages'.

Cost-Linked Circular Causality.   The definition of the perfect price index in (2.2), the full employment condition for H, (2.10), and the migration equation, (2.3), help to illustrate how the second agglomeration force, the cost-of-living effect, is self-reinforcing.

Again starting from symmetry, a small migration from south to north would increase H and decrease H^* and thus, by the full employment condition, migration increases the share of varieties (s_n) produced in the north. Since selling locally produced varieties entails no trade cost, the shift in n's would, other things being equal, lower the cost of living in the north and raise living costs in the south ('cost-of-living effect'). The mechanism is self-reinforcing since the implied impact on the price indices tends to raise the northern real wage and lower the southern real wage. This, in turn, fosters additional migration that would result in a further increase in the north's share of industrial varieties.

We call this mechanism cost-linked circular causality; 'circular' since migration produces production shifting which changes the price indices in a way that tends to encourage more migration; 'cost-linked' since changes in the cost of living are the mechanism's fulcrum. This mechanism is also known by the somewhat cryptic moniker 'forward linkages'.

Market-Crowding Dispersion Force The lone stabilizing force in the model, the so-called 'market-crowding', or 'local-competition' effect, can be seen from the definition of retail sales, R, in (2.12), as we noted above. In particular, perturbing the symmetric equilibrium by moving a small mass of industrial workers northward, raises n and lowers n^*. From (2.12), we see that this tends to increase the degree of local competition for customers in the north and thus to lower R (as long as $\phi < 1$). To break even, northern firms would have to pay lower nominal wages to their workers and this, all else equal, would make the north less attractive than the south to industrial workers. In other words, the perturbation generates changes that tend to undo the initial perturbation. (See Appendix 2.B.1 for a more formal investigation of these three forces.)

CATASTROPHIC AGGLOMERATION

Figure 2.3 illustrates the dependence of agglomeration and dispersion forces on the level of trade costs by plotting the strength of the forces on the vertical axis and trade freeness on the horizontal axis (recall that trade freeness ranges from zero with infinite trade costs to unity with zero trade costs). As long as a regularity condition holds (more on this so-called no-black-hole condition below), the dispersion force is stronger than agglomeration forces when trade is very closed. As it turns out, however, the dispersion force is weakened more rapidly by rising openness than are the agglomeration forces, so at some point the agglomeration forces overpower the dispersion force and agglomeration occurs; this is called the break point, marked as ϕ^B in the diagram.

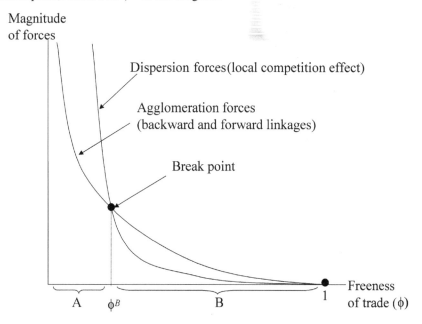

Figure 2.3 Agglomeration and dispersion forces erode with trade freeness.

What all this means is that a symmetric increase in openness between initially symmetric regions eventually produces asymmetric regions. Moreover, the migration that makes this possible does not happen gradually, it happens catastrophically. The reason why dispersion forces erode faster than agglomeration forces is somewhat involved and cannot really be illustrated fully without resort to equations (see Appendix 2.B.1).

2.2.5 Local Stability Analysis

As we illustrated with the 'wiggle diagram' (Figure 2.2), the CP model is marked by three distinctive types of dynamic behaviour. A major axis of investigation in the economic geography literature is to find two critical levels of trade openness that determine which of the three behaviours is relevant. One point marks the level of openness where the symmetric equilibrium becomes unstable. This is called the break point since it is where local stability of the symmetric outcome must break down. The other point is the level of openness where the core–periphery outcomes become stable. This is called the sustain point since it is the lowest level of openness where CP outcomes could be sustained.

Standard practice in the CP-model literature finds these points using the informal stability tests introduced by Krugman (1991a,b). For the symmetric equilibrium, one sees how a small northward migration *changes* the real wage gap $\omega - \omega^*$. If a migration shock leads to a negative change in the gap, the equilibrium is stable since migrants would regret their move and presumably return home. If the implied change in the real wage is positive, the symmetric equilibrium is taken to be unstable, since more migrants would be attracted by the higher real wage. This test is tantamount to checking slopes at the symmetric point in the wiggle diagram (Figure 2.2). For the CP outcomes, we look at the *level* of the real wage gap. The test is whether the *level* of the real wage in the periphery (i.e. the region with no industrial workers) exceeds the level of real wage in the core (the region with all the industrial workers); if the periphery real wage is higher, the CP equilibrium is unstable, otherwise, it is stable. This is equivalent to checking whether the end point of the Ω curve is above zero at $s_H = 1$, and below zero at $s_H = 0$. In symbols, the two informal stability tests are

$$\left. \frac{d(\omega - \omega^*)}{ds_H} \right|_{\text{sym}} < 0, \quad \omega_{\text{CP}} > \omega_{\text{CP}}^* \tag{2.18}$$

where sym and CP indicate that the variables are evaluated at $s_H = 1/2$ and $s_H = 1$, respectively. In passing, we note that these informal tests are equivalent to standard mathematical stability tests (see Appendix 2.B.2 for details).

BREAK POINT AND SUSTAIN POINT

To find the break point, we need to evaluate the slope of Ω at the symmetrical outcome. Totally differentiating the market-clearing condition, (2.11), and the price indices with respect to s_H, evaluating the results at $s_H = s_n = s_E = 1/2$, and using the definition of real wages, it is a straightforward, if tedious, matter to find the ϕ where the first expression in (2.18) holds with equality.[16] This is the break point ϕ^B since it is where the symmetric equilibrium switches from stable to unstable.

To find the sustain point ϕ^S, we again make use of the market clearing conditions and price indices, but this time without differentiation. Rather we use the second expression of (2.13) to find w^* by setting $s_H = 1$ and employing the fact that $w = 1$ at the core-in-the-north outcome (due to our normalizations). In particular, $s_H = 1$ and $w = 1$ imply that B^* equals $[\phi(1 + \mu)/2 + (1 - \mu)/2\phi]$ since s_E equals $(1 + \mu)/2$, Δ equals 1, and Δ^* equals ϕ. Solving, we find that w^* equals $[\phi(1 + \mu)/2 + (1 - \mu)/2\phi]^{1/\sigma}$. Noting the P^* equals ϕ^{-a} when all industry is in the north ($a \equiv \mu/(\sigma - 1)$ as usual), we find that the real wage in the south, ω^*, equals $\phi^a[\phi(1 + \mu)/2 + (1 - \mu)/2\phi]^{1/\sigma}$. At the sustain point, industrial workers are just indifferent to all staying in the north (where the real wage is unity), so the sustain point ϕ must satisfy the condition that $1 = \phi^a[\phi(1 + \mu)/2 + (1 - \mu)/2\phi]^{1/\sigma}$. To summarize, the break and sustain point levels of openness are

$$\phi^B = \left(\frac{1 - \sigma a}{1 + \sigma a}\right)\left(\frac{1 - \mu}{1 + \mu}\right), \quad 1 = (\phi^S)^{a\sigma}\left(\phi^S \frac{1 + \mu}{2} + \frac{1 - \mu}{2\phi^S}\right); \quad a \equiv \frac{\mu}{\sigma - 1}$$

$$(2.19)$$

with $\phi^B > \phi^S$ (more on this below). Observe that the break point is decreasing in the share of spending on industrial goods, μ. Intuitively this should be clear since a higher μ magnifies the strength of demand-linked circular causality by increasing the amount of expenditure shifting that accompanies migration. Thus, a higher μ results in agglomeration forces overcoming the dispersion forces at a lower level of openness. Likewise, the break point is decreasing in the combination of parameters that we define as 'a' since 'a' measures the strength of the cost-linked circular causality (i.e. it tells us how important cost-of-living differences are to workers). That is, as μ rises, workers care more about the price of industrial varieties, while as $\sigma - 1$ rises, workers care less about the cost of imported varieties since domestically produced varieties are a better substitute for imported ones.

The symmetric equilibrium is stable only for sufficiently low levels of trade freeness, specifically for $\phi < \phi^B$. CP outcomes (both of them) are stable only for sufficiently high levels of trade freeness, specifically for $\phi > \phi^S$. All this holds provided ϕ^B is positive, which requires

$$1 > \sigma a \qquad (2.20)$$

Were this not the case, CP outcomes would be the only stable equilibria for any level of openness; agglomeration forces would be so strong that even infinite trade costs would not counter them. For this reason, FKV call (2.20) the 'no-black-hole' condition. It is the regularity condition that we assume throughout the chapter.

---

[16] See the calculations in the Maple worksheet CPmodel.mws on http://heiwww.unige.ch/~baldwin/.

Agglomeration and Self-Fulfilling Expectations.   Before leaving this analysis we note that agglomeration may occur before trade openness reaches the break point. Fleshing out this observation fully requires a set of tools that is best relegated to the appendix (see Appendix 2.B.4). The point, however, is easily made heuristically. It turns on the fact that the break and sustain points characterize *local* stability of the system, but say nothing about *global* stability.

We know that if trade is less free than the break point, the symmetric outcome is locally stable, however, it is possible that such a point is *globally* unstable. Here is the argument. Suppose we start at a level of trade freeness that is between the break and sustain point, so we know that both symmetry and the CP outcomes would be locally stable. Moreover, suppose the economy is initially at the symmetric outcome. Now it is easy to understand that *all* industrial workers would prefer to be at either of the two CP outcomes than at the symmetric outcome. After all, if the entire mass of industrial workers clustered in one region, all industry would also be clustered in that region and so all industrial workers would enjoy a lower cost of living. In the terminology of game theory, the symmetric and CP outcomes represent multiple equilibria that can be Pareto ranked from the perspective of the mobile factor. Given this, it is not too difficult to imagine that a sufficiently large migration shock could push the system off of the symmetric outcome and to a CP outcome when ϕ is between ϕ^B and ϕ^S. For example, if a big group of southern workers decided to move north and everyone expected them to stay, then all remaining southern workers would also want to move north.

Pushing this even further, we can see that this opens the door to the very interesting possibility of self-fulfilling expectations. That is, to shift the economy from symmetry to a CP outcome, it might be sufficient that all the workers started to believe that everyone was moving to a CP outcome. See Appendix 2.B.4 for a more formal analysis of this possibility.

2.2.6 The Tomahawk Diagram

The nature and stability of the long-run equilibria can be conveniently summarized with the so-called 'tomahawk' diagram, Figure 2.4 (the 'tomahawk' name comes from viewing the stable part of the symmetric equilibrium as the handle of a double-edged axe).

The diagram plots s_H against the freeness of trade, ϕ, and shows locally stable long-run equilibria with heavy solid lines. Locally unstable long-run equilibria are shown with heavy dashed lines. As we know from the location condition, the three horizontal lines $s_H = 1$, $s_H = 1/2$ and $s_H = 0$ are long-run equilibria (i.e. steady states) for any level of ϕ, but the symmetric outcome is only locally stable between $\phi = 0$ and $\phi = \phi^B$. The CP outcomes are only stable between $\phi = \phi^S$ and $\phi = 1$. The bowed line also represents long-run equilibria but all of these are unstable. Note that for most levels of ϕ, there are three long-run equilibria, while for the levels of ϕ corresponding to the bowed curve, there are five equilibria—two CP outcomes, the symmetric outcome and two interior asymmetric equili-

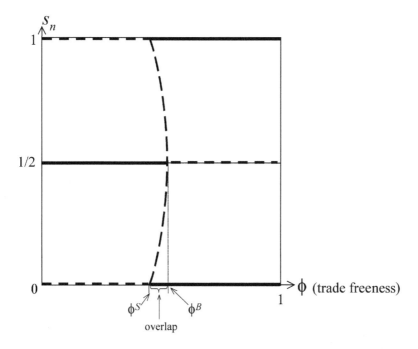

Figure 2.4 The tomahawk diagram for the CP model.

bria.[17] Importantly, in the range of ϕ with five equilibria, there are three over-lapping stable equilibria (symmetric and both CP outcomes).

PROVING THE TOMAHAWK DIAGRAM

Strange as it may seem, the CP model has enjoyed ten years of popularity without its crucial properties ever having been established formally (indeed, this is a good indication of the model's analytical obstinacy). For example, thousands of numerical simulations have shown that the sustain point comes before break point, and thousands of simulations have shown that there are at most three interior equilibria, but these properties have never been proved in published work. Fortunately, recent work (Robert-Nicoud 2002) established these properties and for completeness we include the demonstration in Appendix 2.B.2.

With all this in hand, we are ready to turn to the central purpose of this chapter, namely the establishment of a list of the CP model's main features.

2.3 KEY FEATURES

Here we summarize the key properties of the CP model. This creates a benchmark for the analytically solvable models we propose in subsequent chapters.

[17] The solid line in the wiggle diagram, Figure 2.2, corresponds to one particular value of $\phi \in (0, \phi^B)$. The dashed curve to a $\phi \in (\phi^S, 1)$, and the wiggly dotted curve to a $\phi \in (\phi^S, \phi^B)$.

2.3.1 Home Market Magnification

The 'home-market effect' is a key feature of the CP model. This effect reflects the fact that an exogenous change in the location of demand leads to a *more than proportional* relocation of industry to the enlarged region. Defining agglomeration as the tendency of a spatial concentration of economic activity to generate forces that encouraged further spatial concentration, it is clear that the home-market effect is an agglomeration force.

To see that the home-market effect is a feature of the CP model, we turn to the three expressions—the two market-clearing conditions (i.e. (2.11) and its southern equivalent) and the location condition for an interior location equilibrium, $\omega = \omega^*$. Totally differentiating these with respect to w, w^*, s_H, s_n and a parameter, ε, that allows us to increase the northern market size exogenously, we get a system of three equations.[18] These can be solved for the migration-induced change in the north's share of world labour that comes about in response to a small increase the north's market size, that is, $ds_H/d\varepsilon$. This derivative might be called the home-market derivative since it gauges that amount of industrial activity that is shifted by a small increase in the northern market size. As usual, the CP model is too complex to deal with generally, but if we evaluate the home-market derivative at the symmetric point ($\varepsilon = 0$ and $s_H = s_n = 1/2$), we get

$$\left.\frac{ds_H}{d\varepsilon}\right|_{1/2} = \mu \frac{1 + \sigma a + (1 - \sigma a)(\phi/\phi^B)}{(1 - \sigma^2 a^2)[1 - \phi/\phi^B]} \tag{2.21}$$

where ϕ^B is the breakpoint and $\sigma a > 1$, assuming that the 'no-black-hole' condition holds. As we know, the symmetric equilibrium is unstable if trade is free enough and in this case the home-market derivative does not exist. We therefore limit ourselves to a range of trade freeness where the symmetric equilibrium is stable, namely $\phi < \phi^B$. With this in mind, inspection of (2.21) shows two facts. First, the home market derivative exceeds unity since the numerator is greater than one and the denominator is less than one. This is what Krugman called the home-market effect. Second, $ds_H/d\varepsilon$ gets larger as trade gets freer. This is 'home-market magnification' (Baldwin 2000). The point is that freer trade magnifies the degree of relocation that comes from a given shift in economic activity. In other words, industry becomes more footloose, not less footloose, as trade gets freer. This is important for policy analysis since it means, for example, that regions/nations may be more tempted to engage in beggar-thy-neighbour production subsidies when trade is quite close to free. It also means that regional policies generally interact with trade openness in a very non-linear manner.

2.3.2 Circular Causality

Agglomeration forces in the CP model are self-reinforcing. This feature, so-called circular causality, is one of the hallmarks of the economic geography

---

[18] Specifically, ε increases north's L supply slightly.

literature. As described in Section 2.1.2, we can distinguish two such cycles of causality in the CP model. One linked to demand and one linked to costs. As we shall see in later chapters, not all economic geography models feature both forms of circular causality.

2.3.3 Endogenous Asymmetry

The next key feature might be called endogenous asymmetry. That is, a progressive lowering of trade costs between two initially symmetric regions eventually produces regional asymmetries.

Endogenous asymmetry is best highlighted by contrasting it with the results of lower trade barriers in a neoclassical model such as the standard $2 \times 2 \times 2$ neoclassical model. The Heckscher–Ohlin theorem tells us that gradual reduction of trade costs would lead a nation to specialize in the sector that is intensive in the use of the factor with which the nation is relatively well endowed. The Stolper–Samuelson theorem tells us that until trade costs are zero, the real wage of each factor is lowest in the nation that is relatively well endowed with the factor. Thus, in the Heckscher–Ohlin model, factors have an incentive to migrate in a pattern that tends to equalize relative factor supplies. For example, skilled workers would tend to migrate to the region that started with relatively few skilled workers. What this means is that migration in a model without agglomeration forces tends to reduce differences in production patterns.[19] To put it differently, a gradual opening of trade teamed with migration would make initially asymmetric regions more symmetric. In stark contrast, models with agglomeration forces suggest that factor mobility and opening eventually exaggerates initial differences with all industry ending up in one region before fully free trade is reached.

2.3.4 Catastrophic Agglomeration

The way in which endogenous asymmetry emerges in this model is spectacular, indeed catastrophic. This is perhaps the most celebrated feature of the CP model. As we have seen repeatedly, starting from a symmetric outcome and very high trade costs, marginal increases in the level of trade freeness ϕ has no impact on the location of industry until a critical level of ϕ, namely ϕ^B, is reached. Even a tiny increase in ϕ beyond this point causes a catastrophic agglomeration of industry in the sense that the only stable outcome is that of full agglomeration.[20]

2.3.5 Locational Hysteresis

The second famous feature of the CP model is locational hysteresis, but it arises only when the level of trade costs is such that the model has multiple stable equilibria, that is, for $\phi > \phi^S$. The importance of this lies in the fact that, in such situations, history matters. If the economy starts out near a CP outcome, it will

---

[19] This is the essence of the Mundell (1957) finding that factor mobility is a substitute for trade.

[20] In mathematical jargon, this catastrophe property is called 'sub-critical pitchfork bifurcation'; see Ottaviano (2000) or FKV (Chapter 3) for details.

move to it and stay there. Interestingly, if a temporary shock, say a temporary production subsidy in one region, moved the economy from one stable equilibrium to another, then the removal of the shock would not lead to a reversal of the effects of the shock. This hysteresis or path-dependency feature has important implications for policy analysis.

2.3.6 Hump-Shaped Agglomeration Rents

Another key feature of the CP model is that the mobile factor is not typically indifferent to location when the economy is at a core–periphery outcome. Another way to say this is that CP outcomes are marked by 'agglomeration rents', where these are measured as the loss that a worker would incur by relocating from the core to the periphery when full agglomeration is a stable equilibrium. Formally, such rents are given by (here we take the core-in-the-north case)

$$\omega - \omega^*|_{s_H=1} = 1 - \left[\frac{1}{\phi} \frac{1-\mu}{2} + \phi \frac{1+\mu}{2} \right]^{1/\sigma} \phi^a \qquad (2.22)$$

Importantly, the agglomeration rents are a concave function of trade freeness. Specifically, as inspection of (2.22) shows, the rents equal zero at $\phi = \phi^S$ and $\phi = 1$, while it is positive in between. Moreover, its maximum is at $\phi = \sqrt{\phi^B}$, where ϕ^B is the break point defined in (2.19). Accordingly, as trade gets freer (i.e. ϕ rises from ϕ^S towards 1), the agglomeration rents first rise and then fall ('hump shape').[21]

The concept of agglomeration rents will be crucial in many policy applications since it means that marginal policy changes may not produce marginal economic changes when the economy starts at a stable CP equilibrium.

2.3.7 The Overlap and Self-Fulfilling Expectations

The CP model has a range of ϕ where the symmetric and both CP outcomes are locally stable long-run equilibria (i.e. $\phi^S > \phi > \phi^B$); we call this range the 'overlap'.[22] The existence of this range provides the CP model with an interesting feature when workers are forward-looking. As it turns out (see Appendix 2.B for a rigorous exposition), a jump between the symmetric outcome and a CP outcome can be triggered by a shock to expectations. The logic behind this possibility was described in the discussion following (2.20).

2.4 CONCLUDING REMARKS AND RELATED LITERATURE

The chief aim in this chapter is to establish a definitive list of the CP model's key features and thus provide a benchmark for gauging the more analytically amenable models that we will use for our policy analysis.

---

[21] As subsequent chapters show ϕ^B is the apex of the hump even in other models; we have not been able to justify this result intuitively.

[22] Note that our 'overlap' is different from that of Krugman (1991c); he uses the term to refer to an interval of s_H rather than a range of ϕ.

2.4.1 Related Literature

The seminal CP model is found in Krugman (1991a,b), although the version we work with here is from Chapters 4 and 5 of FKV. Useful surveys of the theoretical work in the new economic geography literature can be found in Ottaviano and Puga (1998), Ottaviano (2000) and Neary (2001). The relationships between the CP model and the urban and regional literatures are discussed by Fujita and Thisse (1996), and in greater detail by Fujita and Thisse (2002). A critical assessment is provided by Martin (1999). For a non-mathematical presentation and empirical evidence, see Brakman et al. (2001).

The first formal treatment of the dynamic aspects of the CP model appeared in the PhD thesis of Diego Puga that was eventually published as Puga (1999). Puga (1999) also introduces an additional dispersion force (diminishing returns in agriculture) that implies that the symmetric outcome is stable for both very high and very low degrees of openness. Helpman (1997) shows that the presence of non-tradable goods can change the relation between trade freeness and agglomeration. In his setting, agglomeration takes place for high rather than low trade costs. We discuss this result in the linear version of the CP model presented in Chapter 5.

Additionally, a number of extensions and technical analyses of the CP model have appeared since FKV was published. Robert-Nicoud (2002) provides the first analytical proof of the CP model's main features, namely that the break point comes before the sustain point and that it has at most three locally stable equilibria for any given level of openness. The importance of the CP model's rather awkward assumption of myopic but infinitely lived migrants is explored in Baldwin (2001). That paper shows that allowing for forward-looking migrants and rational expectations has no effect on the break and sustain points, but it does change the model's global stability properties. The essence of these two papers is summarized in Appendix 2.B. Baldwin and Forslid (2000) solve the CP model allowing for endogenous growth.

An important variant of the CP model is the so-called vertical linkages version, due to Venables (1996) and Krugman and Venables (1995). In this alternative model, agglomeration is sustained by input–output relationships between firms and, importantly, it can arise even without inter-regional migration (so it may be easier to think of regions as nations rather than provinces). We call this the 'VL model' and postpone its consideration to Chapter 8. An elegant synthesis of the CP and VL models can be found in Puga (1999).

Basic elements of the CP model are found in the broader location literature. The struggle between dispersion and agglomeration forces is reminiscent of the spatial competition literature, which highlights a 'price competition effect' (the desire to relax competition by locating far from other firms) and a 'market area effect' (the desire to reduce trade costs by locating at the centre of the market). See, for example, d'Aspremont et al. (1979). The CP model also can be thought of as extending to a general equilibrium set-up the message of traditional models of firms location, that is, firms' locational behaviour is either sluggish or catastrophic (see Ottaviano and Thisse 2003). Likewise, the home-market effect bears some strong resemblance to the 'Principle of Minimum Differentiation' in spatial competition (Hotelling 1929). The fact that agglomeration takes place when trade costs are low concurs with what has been shown in spatial oligopoly theory; see Irmen and Thisse (1998) for a synthesis of the historical literature. More generally, the kind of complementarity that produces agglomeration in the CP model is the hallmark of models of monopolistic competition; see Matsuyama (1995) for a comprehensive analysis. Similar processes, however, have also been investigated in spatial competition theory when consumers are imperfectly informed about the characteristics of the products (Stahl 1987).

It is also worth noting that the dispersion force emphasized in the CP model is far from the only one that has been stressed in the literature. Some of these are unrelated to trade openness, like non-tradable goods as in Helpman (1997), for example, or comparative advantage as in Matsuyama and Takahashi (1998). Chapters 12 and 17 consider some of these.

APPENDIX 2.A: EVERYTHING YOU WANTED TO KNOW ABOUT DIXIT–STIGLITZ BUT WERE AFRAID TO ASK

CES preferences are at the heart of the Dixit–Stiglitz monopolistic competition model (Dixit and Stiglitz 1977). They can be expressed in terms of discrete varieties or a continuum of varieties:

$$U = C_M, \quad C_M \equiv \left(\int_{i=0}^{N} c_i^{1-(1/\sigma)} di \right)^{1/(1-1/\sigma)}$$

$$C_M \equiv \left(\sum_{i=1}^{N} c_i^{1-(1/\sigma)} \right)^{1/(1-1/\sigma)}, \quad \sigma > 1$$

where N is the mass of varieties in the former (continuum version) and the number of varieties in the latter (discrete version). The corresponding indirect utility functions of both versions can be written as E/P_M where the price indices are, respectively,

$$V = \frac{E}{P_M}, \quad P_M \equiv \left(\int_{i=0}^{N} p_i^{1-\sigma} di \right)^{1/(1-\sigma)}, \quad P_M \equiv \left(\sum_{i=1}^{N} p_i^{1-\sigma} \right)^{1/(1-\sigma)}, \quad \sigma > 1$$

P_M is called a 'perfect' price index since it translates expenditure, E, into utility; this is useful in many situations since it equates real income with utility.

The first-order condition of utility maximization is (with discrete varieties)

$$C_M \left(\sum_{i=0}^{N} c_i^{1-(1/\sigma)} \right)^{-1} c_j^{-1/\sigma} = \lambda p_j, \quad \forall j$$

Multiplying both sides by c_j, summing across varieties and using the budget constraint, $E = \Sigma_i p_i c_i$, yields one expression for the Lagrangian multiplier, namely $\lambda = C_M/E$. Alternatively, isolating c_j on the left-hand side, multiplying both sides by p_j, summing across varieties and using the budget constraint, λ can be show to be equal to $(\Sigma_i p_i^{1-\sigma})^{1/\sigma}(E^{-1/\sigma})C_M/(\Sigma_i c_i^{1-1/\sigma})$. Plugging the first or second expression for λ into the first-order condition yields the inverse or direct demand curves, respectively. These are

$$p_j = \frac{c_j^{-1/\sigma}}{\displaystyle\sum_{i=1}^{N} c_i^{1-(1/\sigma)}} E, \quad c_j = \frac{p_j^{-\sigma}}{\displaystyle\sum_{i=1}^{N} p_i^{1-\sigma}} E, \quad \forall j$$

It is convenient to use the indirect demand function when assuming quantity (Cournot) competition and to use the direct demand function when working with price (Bertrand) competition (as we shall see, these two forms of competition lead to the same behaviour when firms are atomistic). Derivation of demand functions for the continuum version is identical except, of course, the summations are replaced by integrals.

The CES utility function is often referred to as 'love of variety' preferences. To understand why, we show that the same level of expenditure spread over more varieties increases utility. If all varieties are priced at p, consumption of a typical variety is $E/(Np)$. Substituting this into the utility function implies that $U = N^{1/(\sigma-1)}(E/p)$ and we see that utility rises with N, so in this sense, consumers love variety for variety's sake. Moreover, even if each variety is priced differently, adding a new one increases utility if prices of the existing varieties are unchanged; this is very easily seen by using the expression for the perfect price index in the discrete case.

2.A.1 Dixit–Stiglitz Competition, Mill Pricing and Firms' First-Order Conditions

Dixit–Stiglitz monopolistic competition is highly tractable since a firm's optimal price is a constant mark-up over marginal cost. This is unusual since in most forms of imperfect competition, the optimal price–marginal cost mark-up depends upon the degree of competition, with the mark-up increasing as the degree of competition falls. For example, the optimal mark-up often depends upon the firm's market share, but since the market share depends upon prices, one needs to solve all firms' first-order conditions simultaneously. If, additionally, the number of firms is determined by free entry, finding equilibrium prices can require the simultaneous solution of many equations, some of which will be non-linear. Fixed mark-ups permit us to avoid all this.

To get started, consider Cournot competition among N firms in a single market, with each firm producing a symmetric variety subject to a homothetic cost function. The typical firm's objective function is revenue, $p_j c_j$, minus costs, $(a_m c_j + F)w$, where wF is the fixed cost, $wa_m c$ is the variable cost and w is the wage. Using the discrete-varieties version of the indirect demand function, the Cournot first-order condition is

$$p\left(1 - \frac{1}{\varepsilon}\right) = wa_m, \qquad \frac{1}{\varepsilon_{\text{Cournot}}} = \frac{1}{\sigma} + \left(1 - \frac{1}{\sigma}\right)s, \qquad \varepsilon_{\text{Bertrand}} = \sigma - (\sigma - 1)s$$

$$(2.A.1)$$

where s is the market share of the typical variety; with symmetry $s = 1/N$. Using the direct demand function and price competition yields the third expression. Note that under both conjectures, the perceived elasticity, ε, falls as s rises.

Note that as long as s is not zero, the degree of competition *does* affect the mark-up and thus pricing behaviour. For example, with symmetry and Cournot competition, the equilibrium mark-up is $(1 - 1/\sigma)(1 - 1/N)$, so the equilibrium mark-up falls as the number of competitors rises. This is called 'small-group' monopolistic competition. An interesting extreme case—which is at the root of the Dixit–Stiglitz monopolistic competition—is where N rises to infinity and the perceived elasticity ε equals σ (under both Cournot and Bertrand competition). Since the perceived elasticity is invariant to N, the mark-up is constant. This extreme case is what Chamberlain called the 'large-group' case and it is what Dixit–Stiglitz monopolistic competition assumes. Four comments are in order.

First, note that with an infinite number of atomistic competitors—that is, under Dixit–Stiglitz assumptions—equilibrium pricing does not depend upon the type of competition. Bertrand and Cournot competition produce the same result. While this is convenient, it is a strong assumption that rules out many interesting effects, such as the pro-competitive effect.

Second, in the discrete varieties version of Dixit–Stiglitz preferences (assumed in the original 1977 article), one must assume that N is large enough to approximate ε with σ. With the continuum of varieties case, there are an uncountable infinity of varieties, so s is automatically zero.

Third, the invariance of the Dixit–Stiglitz mark-up to changes in the number (mass) of firms is easily understood. One starts with the assumption that the number of competitors is infinite, so adding in more competitors has no effect. Infinity, after all, is a concept, not a number.

Fourth, the invariance of the mark-up implies that so-called mill pricing is optimal for firms. That is, with iceberg costs, if it costs T_1 to ship the goods to market 1, and T_2 to ship them to market 2, firms will fully pass the shipping costs on to consumer prices, so the ratio of consumer prices in market 1 to market 2 will be T_1/T_2. This is called mill pricing, or factory gate pricing, since it is as if the firm charged the same price 'at the mill' or at the factory gate, with all shipping charges being born by consumers. Another way of saying this is that with mill pricing, a firm's producer price is the same for sales to all markets.

2.A.2 Operating Profits, Free Entry and the Invariance of Firm Scale

One extremely handy, but not very realistic, aspect of Dixit–Stiglitz monopolistic competition is the invariance of equilibrium firm scale. This is a direct and inevitable implication of the constant mark-up, free entry and the homothetic cost function.

Plainly, a fixed mark-up of price over marginal cost implies a fixed operating profit margin. It is not surprising, therefore, that there is a unique level of sales that allows the typical firm to just break even, that is, to earn a level of operating profit sufficient to cover fixed costs. The first-order condition (the pricing equation) can be arranged as

$$p\left(1 - \frac{1}{\sigma}\right) = wa_m \quad \Rightarrow \quad (p - wa_m) = \frac{p}{\sigma} \quad \Rightarrow \quad (p - wa_m)c = \frac{pc}{\sigma}$$

$$\Rightarrow \quad (p - wa_m)c = \frac{wa_m}{\sigma - 1}c$$

The second to last expression shows that operating profit, $(p - wa_m)c$, equals an invariant profit margin (namely, $1/\sigma$) times the value of consumption at consumer prices. The last equation is derived using the formula for the equilibrium price. The constancy of equilibrium firm scale, that is, the volume of sales/production necessary for a typical firm to break even, is obvious when the scale economies take the familiar form of a linear cost function, namely $w(F + a_m c)$, where wF is the fixed cost and $wa_m c$ is the variable cost. The zero profit condition in this case is just

$$\frac{wa_m}{\sigma - 1}c = wF \quad \Rightarrow \quad c = \frac{F(\sigma - 1)}{a_m}$$

Observe that equilibrium firm scale depends on two cost parameters, F and a_m, and a demand parameter, σ.

As it turns out, the invariance of equilibrium scale economies demonstrated above is quite a general proposition, at least for one common measure of scale, viz. the scale elasticity. As long as the price–marginal cost mark-up is fixed and the zero profit condition holds, the scale elasticity, that is, $\chi \equiv (dC/dx)(x/C)$, where x is firm output/sales and C is the cost function, must be constant. To see this, note that with zero profit, price must equal average cost, so the first-order condition can be written as $AC/MC = (1 - 1/\sigma)$, where MC and AC are marginal and average cost, respectively. But, $(dC/dx)(x/C)$ is just MC/AC, so $1/\chi = (1 - 1/\sigma)$.

Note that the scale elasticity is a measure that has its limitations. For instance, if the cost function in not homothetic in factor prices, a given scale elasticity does not coincide one-to-one with firm size. For instance, if capital is used only in the fixed cost and labour only in the variable costs, then the scale elasticity is $(rF/(wa_M x) + 1)^{-1}$. Even if this is constant at, say, $1 - 1/\sigma$, the firm size that corresponds to this depends upon the r/w ratio. Since trade costs can, in general, affect factor prices, this means that trade costs can also affect firm scale, even in the Dixit–Stiglitz model.

2.A.3 Invariance of Firm Scale with Trade

The simplicity that comes with Dixit–Stiglitz monopolistic competition is especially apparent when dealing with multiple markets. In particular, when we assume that trade costs are 'iceberg' in nature (i.e. are proportional to marginal production costs since a fraction of shipped goods disappear in transit), solving the multi-market problem is no more difficult than solving the single market problem.

To understand the source of the simplifications, we start with a more general set of assumptions. Suppose there are two markets, local and export, and that it costs T^* to ship one unit of the good to the export market and T to ship it to the local market. These costs are *not* of the iceberg type.

A typical firm has $p(1 - 1/\sigma) = (wa_M + T)$ and $p^*(1 - 1/\sigma) = (wa_M + T^*)$ as its first-order conditions, where p^* is the consumer price in the distant market. Rearranging these conditions shows that operating profit—which we denote at π—is proportional to the value of retail sales, R. Specifically, $\pi = R/\sigma$, so the free entry condition requires that $R/\sigma = wF$ as in the single market case without trade costs. However, now $R = pc + p^*c^*$, where c and c^* are consumption in the local and export markets. Rearranging, we have that $c + c^* = wF\sigma/p - \psi c^*$, where $1 + \psi \equiv p^*/p$ and from the first-order conditions, p^*/p equals $(wa_m + T^*)/(wa_m + T)$. The left-hand side is clearly not constant because the right-hand side is not. Indeed, in general, both terms on the right-hand side may vary.

What is needed to make $c + c^*$ invariant to trade costs? If the cost function is homogenous, the fixed costs wF is proportional to the price (recall that price is proportional to marginal cost), so $wF\sigma/p$ will not vary with relative factor prices. Nevertheless, scale will vary since both ψ and c^* vary with trade costs. To make ψc^* constant, we assume that trade costs are 'iceberg' in the sense that a certain fraction of each shipment disappears in transit. This makes trade costs proportional to marginal cost. For example, if marginal costs are $wa_M(1 + t^*)$ for export sales and $wa_M(1 + t)$ for local sales, then ψ equals $(t^* - t)/(1 + t)$. In this case, we can without further loss of generality absorb $1 + t$ into the definition of a_m and define trade costs as zero for local sales and $t'' = t^* - t$ for distant sales (this is standard practice). Moreover, with iceberg costs we have that $(1 + t'')c^*$ equals the quantity produced for the distant market since the quantity produced and shipped is always $1 + t''$ times consumption.

In summary, the invariance of firm size (as measured by production) to trade costs is a result that is very sensitive to special assumptions and functional forms. Trade costs must be iceberg, the cost function must be homothetic and equilibrium prices must be proportional to marginal costs (this in turn requires mill pricing).

2.A.4 One Variety per Firm, and One Firm per Variety

So far we have *assumed* that there is one firm per variety. Here we show that this is a result rather than an assumption as it is well known in spatial competition theory. Working with the continuum version of preference, we can generate an expression for the perceived elasticity that is identical to (2.A.1) except that we must interpret s as the measure of a firm's range of products. Inspection of (2.A.1) shows that a firm that produces a range of varieties that has positive measure will perceive elasticity to be greater than σ. Since optimal pricing will always entail the expression $p(1 - 1/\varepsilon) = wa_M$, we know that a firm producing a positive range of varieties will 'over price' compared to a single-variety firm (here we rather loosely switch between the rough notion of a single-variety firm and the more formal notion of a firm that produces a range of varieties with measure zero). Moreover, since the multi-variety firm charges a higher mark-up, it will earn higher profits. While that would be advantageous for such a firm, competition will not let this situation stand. A single-variety firm can enter by producing the exact same variety and undercut the incumbent. In other words, while multi-variety firms might be more profitable, unless there is some entry barrier such as economies of scope (e.g. a fixed cost per firm regardless of the number of varieties produced) or a patent on the particular variety, competition will force the price down to the point where $p(1 - 1/\sigma)$ equals wa_M, regardless of how many varieties a firm produces. Given this, it makes no difference whether firms are single- or multi-variety producers; parsimony leads us to dictate one firm per variety.

We have also hereto assumed that there is only one firm per variety. It is easy to show that this is a result rather than an assumption. Suppose there is a firm already producing variety i, and another firm contemplating entering the market. If the entrant produces exactly variety i, then the mark-up and result profit will be that of a duopolist. In the case of Bertrand competition, this yields marginal cost pricing, but even in the case of Cournot competition, the profits earned by the entrant will be below those that he/she could earn by producing a unique variety. Since we assume that it costs the same to produce each variety, no entrant will ever find it profitable to encroach upon an existing variety.[23]

2.A.5 Quasi-Linear Dixit–Stiglitz Preferences

There are times when it is convenient to ignore income effects. An easy way to make this consistent with consumer optimization is to assume that preferences are quasi-linear. Specifically, consider the utility function of a typical consumer facing the choice of a homogenous good A, whose price is unity by choice of numeraire, and two types of differentiated goods where all varieties of each type enter preferences symmetrically. The specific utility function is

$$U = A + \mu\ln[(nc^{1-(1/\sigma)} + n^*c^{*1-(1/\sigma)})^{1/(1-1/\sigma)}]$$

where μ measures the intensity of preference for differentiated goods (as it turns out, μ is the expenditure on all differentiated goods), n and n^* are the number of the two types of differentiated good and c and c^* are the quantities consumed of a typical variety. Utility optimization (subject to the constraint that spending is E) is characterized by the necessary conditions

---

[23] This result agrees with what is called the principle of differentiation in industrial organization: "Firms want to differentiate to soften competition" (Tirole 1988, p. 286).

$$1 = \lambda p_A$$

$$\mu[nc^{1-(1/\sigma)} + n^* c^{*1-(1/\sigma)}]^{-1} c^{-1/\sigma} = \lambda p$$

$$\mu[nc^{1-(1/\sigma)} + n^* c^{*1-(1/\sigma)}]^{-1} c^{*-1/\sigma} = \lambda p^*$$

$$p_A A + npc + n^* p^* c^* = E$$

where $p_A = 1$, and p and p^* are the prices of the two types of varieties. Taking the ratio of the second and third expressions, we get

$$\frac{c}{c^*} = \left(\frac{p}{p^*}\right)^{-\sigma}$$

Using this and the fact that $\lambda = 1$, we have

$$\mu \left\{ n \left[\left(\frac{p}{p^*}\right)^{-\sigma} c^* \right]^{1-(1/\sigma)} + n^* c^{*1-(1/\sigma)} \right\}^{-1} c^{*-1/\sigma} = p^*$$

Rearranging, this yields the demand function for c^*,

$$c^* = \frac{\mu p^{*-\sigma}}{np^{1-\sigma} + n^* p^{*1-\sigma}}, \qquad c = \frac{\mu p^{-\sigma}}{np^{1-\sigma} + n^* p^{*1-\sigma}}$$

where we used symmetry to derive the demand function for typical c varieties. If we multiply both sides of the demand for c^* by p^* and the demand for c by p, and then sum across all n and n^* varieties (respectively), we see that total spending on these goods equals μ. Using these in the budget constraint, we get the demand function for A,

$$A = E - \mu$$

Note that we cannot use what might seem to be the most natural quasi-linear utility function $U = A + C_M$, where $C_M = [nc^{1-(1/\sigma)} + n^* c^{*1-(1/\sigma)}]^{1/(1-1/\sigma)}$ since the total expenditure on the differentiated good is either all or nothing. This is easily seen by noting that the CES sub-utility function is subject to constant returns. That is, doubling the spending on these goods will double the utility, so we can write the indirect utility function as $U = E_A/p_A + E_M/P_M$, where E_A and E_M are the spending on the two sectors. Either $dU/dE_M > dU/dE_A$ and all spending is on M goods, or the inequality is reversed and all spending is on the A good. If the two derivatives are just equal, the division of spending is indeterminate. Using the sub-utility function $\ln(C_M)$ remedies this problem by imposing diminishing marginal utility of expenditure on the M sector.

Appendix 2.B: Technicalities

This appendix covers various technical aspects of the CP model. It is organized in the order of topics addressed in the main text. Thus, the first section formally illustrates the three forces and the next proves the fundamental features of the CP model, as summarized by the tomahawk diagram. The next two sections explore the model's global stability properties and the model's behaviour when migrants are allowed to be rational. The final section considers which of the model's many assumptions are truly necessary.

2.B.1 The Three Forces in Detail

Focusing on each of the three forces separately boosts intuition and we accomplish this via a series of thought experiments. These focus on the symmetric equilibrium for a very pragmatic reason. In general, the CP model is astoundingly difficult to manipulate since the nominal wages are determined by equations that cannot be solved analytically. At the symmetric equilibrium, however, this difficulty is much attenuated. Due to the symmetry, all effects are equal and opposite. For instance, if a migration shock raises the northern wage, then it lowers the southern wage by the same amount. Moreover, at the symmetric outcome, $w = w^* = 1$, so much of the intractability—which stems largely from terms involving a nominal wage raised to a non-integer power—disappears.

THE MARKET-CROWDING OR LOCAL-COMPETITION EFFECT

To separate the production shifting and expenditure shifting aspects of migration, the first thought experiment supposes that industrial worker migration is driven by *nominal* wages differences (measured, of course, in terms of the numeraire) *and* that all industrial worker earnings are remitted to the country of origin.[24] Thus, migration changes n and n^* but not E and E^*.

We start with the market clearing condition for a typical northern industrial variety (M variety for short): $w\bar{x} = R$; see (2.11). What we are looking for is whether a slight increase in s_H, starting from $s_H = 1/2$, will increase or decrease the determinant of migration—which in this thought experiment is the nominal wage gap. Before starting, note that symmetry allows us to limit our investigation on the northern nominal wage since if the northern w rises, we know the southern w^* falls and vice versa. Consequently, a finding that w falls tells us that the wage gap falls and that the symmetric equilibrium is therefore stable when only the local competition effect is in operation. R can be written as

$$R \equiv \frac{w^{1-\sigma}\mu E}{\Delta n^w} + \frac{\phi w^{1-\sigma}\mu E^*}{\Delta^* n^w}$$

$$\Delta \equiv \frac{nw^{1-\sigma} + \phi n^*(w^*)^{1-\sigma}}{n^w}, \quad \Delta^* \equiv \frac{\phi nw^{1-\sigma} + n^*(w^*)^{1-\sigma}}{n^w}$$

---

[24] This may be thought of as corresponding to the case where H is physical capital whose owners are immobile. Note also that under these suppositions, the model closely resembles the pre-economic geography models with monopolistic competition and trade costs (e.g. Venables 1987; Helpman and Krugman 1989, Chapter 10).

so log differentiating $w\bar{x} = R$, recalling that firm size and the total number of firms n^w are fixed, we get

$$\hat{w} = (1 - \sigma)\hat{w} + s_R(\hat{s}_E - \hat{\Delta}) + (1 - s_R)(\hat{s}_E^* - \hat{\Delta}^*), \quad s_R \equiv \frac{nw^{1-\sigma}}{n^w \Delta}$$

$$\Rightarrow \quad \sigma\hat{w}|_{s_n=1/2} = 2\left(s_R - \frac{1}{2}\right)(\hat{s}_E - \hat{\Delta}) \qquad (2.A.2)$$

where we are using the standard trade-theory 'hat' notation (e.g. $\hat{x} = dx/x$); also, s_R is the share of a typical north firm's total revenue, R, that is earned in the north's market. We note that the second expression follows from the first due to the equal and opposite nature of all changes around symmetry. Observe that at the symmetric outcome (i.e. $s_n = s_H = 1/2$), s_R exceeds $1/2$ when trade is not perfectly free, that is, $\phi < 1$. Moreover, s_R falls toward $1/2$ as ϕ approaches unity; specifically, $s_R = 1/(1 + \phi)$ at $s_H = 1/2$.

Given the definition of Δ, we have

$$\hat{\Delta}|_{s_n=1/2} = 2\left(s_M - \frac{1}{2}\right)[\hat{n} - (\sigma - 1)\hat{w}] \qquad (2.A.3)$$

where s_M is the share of northern expenditure that falls on northern M varieties. With positive trade costs, s_M exceeds $1/2$ with the difference shrinking as ϕ increases; in fact using the demand functions and symmetry we can show that $2(s_M - 1/2) = (1 - \phi)/(1 + \phi)$.

By supposition, expenditure is repatriated so $\hat{s}_E = 0$; using (2.A.2) in (2.A.3) yields

$$\hat{w} = \frac{-4(s_R - 1/2)(s_M - 1/2)}{\sigma + (\sigma - 1)4(s_R - 1/2)(s_M - 1/2)}\hat{n} \qquad (2.A.4)$$

This is the 'market crowding' effect in isolation since it shows the change in w caused by a small increase in $n = H$ starting from symmetry. Note that s_R and s_M lie in the zero–one range.

There are four salient points.

1. Since the numerator is negative and the denominator positive (it is equal to $\sigma(1 - Z^2) + Z^2$, where $Z \equiv (1 - \phi)/(1 + \phi)$ is a convenient measure of closed-ness and $0 < Z < 1$), northward migration always lowers the northern nominal wage and, by symmetry, raises the southern wage. 'Nominal' wages are measured in terms of the numeraire, of course.

2. This shows directly that migration is not, per se, de-stabilizing. When the demand or cost linkages are cut, as in this thought experiment, the symmetric equilibrium is always stable despite migration.

3. The magnitude of this 'local competition', or more precisely 'competition for consumers' effect, diminishes roughly with the square of trade costs since as trade freeness rises, $(s_R - 1/2)$ and $(s_M - 1/2)$ fall. More specifically, $4(s_R - 1/2)(s_M - 1/2)$ equals Z^2 at the symmetric point. Note that in FKV terminology, $(s_R - 1/2)$ and $(s_M - 1/2)$ are both denoted as 'Z' since at the symmetric equilibrium both equal $(1 - \phi)/(1 + \phi)$.

In words, the dispersion force diminishes with the square of trade freeness. Roughly speaking, the strength of the market-crowding effect rises with the square of trade costs since two mechanisms operate in a way that compounds their joint strength. Freer trade lowers dependence of a north-based firm on the northern market (s_R is the share of northern sales in a typical north-based firm's total sales in value terms) *and* it shifts northern-market expenditure away from northern varieties and towards southern varieties (s_M is the share of northern expenditure that falls on northern *M* varieties).

4. The final point is that in this thought experiment the break and sustain points are identical; this can be seen by noting that s_H does not enter (2.A.4). Moreover, the break and sustain points both occur at $\phi = 1$ since, for positive trade costs, the dispersion force is operative. As usual, any locational outcome is an equilibrium when there are no trade costs.

DEMAND LINKAGES

In the next thought experiment, suppose that, for some reason, *H* workers base their migration decisions on nominal wages but spend all of their income in the region in which they are employed. While this would not make much sense to a rational *H* worker, the assumption serves intuition by allowing us to restore the connection between production shifting ($dH = dn$) and expenditure shifting dE without at the same time adding in the cost-linkage (i.e. cost-of-living effect).

By definition s_E equals E/E^w, and with our normalizations E equals $L + wn$ and E^w equals $1/\mu$. Thus, log differentiation with respect to w and n implies that the restored term from (2.A.2) is

$$\hat{s}_E = \frac{wn}{E}(\hat{w} + \hat{n}) = \mu(\hat{w} + \hat{n}) \qquad (2.A.5)$$

The second expression follows from the first since, with our normalization, $wn = 1/2$ and $E = \mu/2$ at the symmetric outcome. Using (2.A.5) and (2.A.3) in (2.A.2), we find

$$\hat{w}|_{1/2} = \frac{(\mu Z - Z^2)\hat{n}}{\sigma - Z^2(\sigma - 1) - Z\mu} \qquad (2.A.6)$$

where

$$Z \equiv \frac{1 - \phi}{1 + \phi} = 2\left(s_R - \frac{1}{2}\right)\Big|_{1/2} = 2\left(s_M - \frac{1}{2}\right)\Big|_{1/2}$$

Note that the denominator is always positive, since $0 \le Z \le 1$ and $\sigma > \mu$.

Seven aspects of (2.A.6) are worth highlighting.

1. The de-stabilizing aspects of expenditure shifting can be seen by the fact that the first term in the numerator is positive.

2. The size of the de-stabilizing expenditure shifting increases with industry's expenditure share, μ, because the impact of a given amount of expenditure shifting depends on the share that falls on industrial goods, namely μ.

3. The size of this de-stabilizing effect falls as trade gets freer since firms depend less on local sales as trade becomes more open. More specifically, s_R approaches 1/2 as ϕ approaches unity, so $2(s_M - 1/2) \rightarrow 0$.

4. The market-crowding effect shows up in the second term in the denominator, namely $-Z^2$; it is stabilizing since it is negative.

5. The symmetric outcome is stable when $dw/dn < 0$. This holds with very high trade costs, that is, when Z is close to unity.

6. At some point, namely when $\mu = Z$, dw/dn is zero; dw/dn is positive at higher levels of Z.

7. Finally, the level of trade freeness where $dw/dn = 0$ is $\phi^{bl} = (1 - \mu)/(1 + \mu)$. This critical value is useful in characterizing the strength of agglomeration forces since it defines the range of trade costs where agglomeration forces are stronger than the dispersion force. Thus, an expansion of this range (i.e. a fall in the critical value) indicates that agglomeration dominates over a wider range of trade costs.

COST-OF-LIVING LINKAGES

The above thought experiments isolate the importance of the local competition effect and demand-linked circular causality. The final force operating in the model works through the cost-of-living effect. Since the price of imported varieties bears the trade costs, consumers gain—other things being equal—from local production of a variety. This effect is a de-stabilizing force. A northward migration shock leads to production shifting that lowers the cost-of-living in the north and, thus, tends to makes northward migration more attractive. To see this more directly, we return to the full model with H basing its migration decisions on real wages and spending incomes locally.

Log differentiating the northern real wage, we have $\hat{\omega} = \hat{w} - a\hat{\Delta}$ where $a \equiv \mu/(\sigma - 1)$. Using our expression for $\hat{\Delta}$ evaluated at symmetry, we get

$$\hat{\omega}|_{s_n = 1/2} = \hat{w}\left[1 - \mu 2\left(s_R - \frac{1}{2}\right)\right] + \frac{\mu}{\sigma - 1} 2\left(s_R - \frac{1}{2}\right)\hat{n} \qquad (2.A.7)$$

The second term is the cost-of-living effect, also known as cost-linked circular causality, cost linkages or backward linkages. Since this is positive, the cost-of-living linkage is de-stabilizing in the sense that it tends to increase the real wage change stemming from a given migration shock. Moreover, consumers care more about local production as $\mu/(\sigma - 1)$ increases, so the magnitude of the cost-of-living effect increases as μ rises and σ falls. Higher trade costs also amplify the size of the effect since s_R rises towards 1 as ϕ approaches zero.

Two observations are in order. Observe first that the cost linkage can be separated entirely from the demand and local competition effects. The first term in (2.A.7) captures the demand linkage and the local competition effect, while the second term captures the cost linkage. Second, note that the coefficient on $\hat{w}$ is positive—since $2(s_R - 1/2) \leq 1$ and this means that the net impact of the demand linkage and local competition effects on ω depends only on the sign of $1 - \mu 2(s_R - 1/2)$.

2.B.2 'Proving' the Tomahawk Diagram

The key requirement for catastrophe is that full agglomeration is the only stable equilibrium for level of openness beyond the break point. The key requirement for locational hysteresis is the existence of a range of ϕ's where there are multiple, locally stable equilibria. We turn to the proof of each feature in turn, but first we establish that the informal local stability tests used in the literature are in fact identical to formal stability tests that are standard in the theory of differential equations.

EQUIVALENCE OF FORMAL AND INFORMAL LOCAL STABILITY TESTS

As Baldwin (2001) shows, formal tests for local stability are identical to the more intuitive informal tests in (2.18). The validity of the informal tests in (2.18) is easily understood. The CP model can be reduced to a single non-linear ordinary differential equation, namely

$$\dot{s}_H = s_H(1 - s_H)\Omega[s_H], \quad \Omega \equiv \omega - \omega^*$$

where $\Omega[s_H]$ is the implicit function relating s_H to the real wage gap. Local stability is formally evaluated by linearizing this around an equilibrium point s_H^o, and checking the coefficient on s_H. If it is negative, the system is locally stable; otherwise, it is locally unstable. The linear approximation is

$$\dot{s}_H = \left[s_H^o(1 - s_H^o)\frac{d\Omega[s_H^o]}{ds_H} + (1 - 2s_H^o)\Omega[s_H^o] \right](s_H - s_H^o)$$

Note that, at the symmetric equilibrium (i.e. $s_H^o = 1/2$), the necessary and sufficient condition for local stability is that $d(\omega - \omega^*)/ds_H < 0$. At the core–periphery outcome ($s_H^o = 1$ or $s_H^o = 0$), the necessary and sufficient condition is $(\omega - \omega^*) < 0$. These line up exactly with (2.18).

SUSTAIN POINT COMES BEFORE THE BREAK POINT

The fact that the sustain point occurs at a higher level of trade costs than the break point is well known and has been demonstrated in thousands of numerical simulations by dozens of authors. Yet a valid proof of this critical feature of the model was never undertaken until recently.[25]

The most satisfying approach to proving that $\phi^S < \phi^B$ would be direct algebraic manipulation of expressions for the two critical points. This is not possible since ϕ^S can only be defined implicitly as in (2.19). Instead, a two-step proof is necessary. First, we characterize the function

$$f(\phi) = \phi^{-1+\mu/(1-1/\sigma)}\frac{(1 + \mu)\phi^2 + (1 - \mu)}{2} - 1$$

---

[25] The first draft of the excellent paper by Peter Neary (2001) was seen by us before we wrote this section of the chapter. That draft contained a brief proof in a footnote that turned out to be incorrect. One of the authors showed the proof's error and provided a correct proof, which Peter Neary incorporated (with accreditation) in subsequent drafts of his paper. See also Robert-Nicoud (2002).

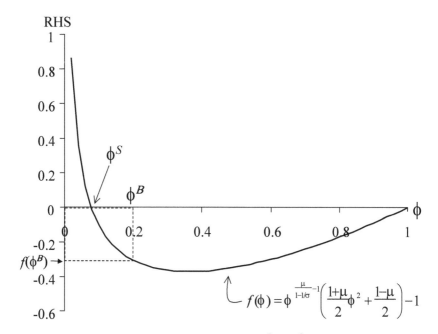

Figure 2.5 Proving that $\phi^B < \phi^S$.

which is just a transformation of the second expression in (2.19), changing with ϕ. This function is of interest since ϕ^S is one of its root. With some work, we can show three facts: (i) $f(1) = 0$ and $f'(1)$ is positive; (ii) $f(0)$ is positive and $f'(0)$ is negative; and (iii) f has a unique minimum. Taken together, these mean that f has a unique root between zero and unity. In short, it looks like the f drawn in Figure 2.5. Next, we show that $f(\phi^B) < 0$, so given the shape of f, it must be that $\phi^S < \phi^B$. In particular, observe that $f(\phi^B)$ is a function of μ and σ. Call this new function $g(\mu, \sigma)$ and note that the partial of g with respect to μ is negative and $g(0, \sigma)$ is zero regardless of σ. The point of all this is that the upper bound of g, and thus the upper bound of $f(\phi^B)$, is zero. We know, therefore, that for permissible values of μ and σ, $\phi^S < \phi^B$.

AT MOST FIVE DISTINCT STEADY STATES

Simulations also show that, for levels of the trade freeness parameter, ϕ, where asymmetric interior steady states exist, these steady states always feature three characteristics. First, they always come in symmetric pairs (this is hardly surprising given the symmetry of the model), namely, if some s_H other than 1/2 is a solution to $\Omega[s_H] = 0$, then $1 - s_H$ is also a solution. Second, these asymmetric steady states are always unstable (i.e. $d\Omega/ds_H$ is positive for all $s_H > 1/2$ such that $\Omega[s_H] = 0$). Finally, there are at most two of them (thus making five steady states for such values of ϕ when the CP outcomes are included).

To prove this, clearly it would be sufficient to invoke the result that $\phi^S > \phi^B$ (proved above) and then to show that the real wage gap is zero, namely $\Omega[\ ] = 0$, for at most three values of the state variable, s_H. The proof for this result is indirect. The first step is to rewrite the model in its 'natural' state space, namely the mobile nominal expenditure, $s_H w$, rather than the mass of mobile workers, s_H. To this end, it is useful to note that the Cobb–Douglas specification for tastes in (2.1) implies that $s_H w + (1 - s_H)w^* = 1$, hence $s_H w$ is the share of mobile expenditure spent in the north. The second step is to show that the 'footloose entrepreneur' (FE) model (Forslid and Ottaviano 2003)—described in detail in Chapter 4—is *identical* to the original CP model when both models are expressed in the natural state space. Finally, we note that Forslid and Ottaviano (2003) proved that there are at most three interior steady states in their model, so since the dynamic properties of a system are invariant to changes in state variables, we know there are at most three in the CP model. See Robert-Nicoud (2002) for details. As an aside, note that this indirect method extends to geography models in which agglomeration is driven by input–output linkages (e.g. see FKV Chapter 14).

The real work therefore is showing that the CP model and the FE model are identical in the natural state space. To this end, we first define M_R as the ratio of mobile expenditure in the north to its counterpart in the south, $M_R \equiv s_H w / [(1 - s_H)w^*]$. Since $s_H w + (1 - s_H)w^* \equiv 1$ by (2.16), this definition implies that $s_H w = M_R / (1 + M_R)$ and $(1 - s_H)w^* = 1/(1 + M_R)$. Next, we transform all the variables into similar ratios. For instance, we define P_R and E_R as P/P^* and E/E^*, respectively, where P and E are defined in (2.3) and (2.12). By the same token, ω_R is defined as $(\omega/\omega^*)^\sigma$. The reason why ω/ω^* has been raised at the power σ will become clear below.

Using the normalizations that yield (2.16), the instantaneous equilibrium of the model can entirely be described by the price indices from (2.1), the region-specific expenditures from (2.7), and the retail sales from (2.12). Using the ratio notation, this can be written as

$$M_R = P_R \frac{1 - \phi P_R^\theta}{P_R^\theta - \phi}, \quad E_R = \frac{M_R + \lambda}{1 + \lambda M_R}, \quad \omega = \frac{E_R P_R^\theta + \phi}{\phi E_R P_R^\theta + 1} \qquad (2.A.8)$$

where λ and θ are defined as $L/(1 + L)$ and $\sigma\mu/(\sigma - 1)$, respectively. These positive parameters are both less than unity. In particular, $\theta < 1$ holds as a consequence of the no-black-hole condition. It can be demonstrated that both the numerator and the denominator of the first equation in (2.A.8) are positive.

Importantly, the FE model can also be manipulated in a way such that (2.A.8) completely describes the model's long-run equilibrium conditions, with the parameter θ and the variable ω redefined judiciously. Since $s_H w$ is strictly increasing in s_H (this can be shown rather easily by contradiction) and the FE model can be shown to display at most three interior steady states ($\omega = 1$), this must also be true for the CP model. This is the essence of the proof developed in Robert-Nicoud (2002).

As it turns out, many new economic geography models (e.g., the FC model) can be rewritten as the system (2.A.8). In particular, the vertical-linkages version of the CP model (e.g. Chapter 14 of FKV) can be approximated by the three equations with judicious redefinition of θ and ω. This approximation is, however, exact at all steady states. As a consequence, the proof of at most three interior equilibria is also valid for the VL version of the CP model.

2.B.3 Global Stability Analysis

Local stability analysis is fine for most uses, but it is not sufficient for fully characterizing the model's behaviour when s_H is away from a long-run equilibrium (e.g. when the process of agglomeration is 'en route'). As with local stability, the literature has developed a heuristic approach to studying global stability properties. In this section, we show that the heuristic approach can be justified formally.

THE HEURISTIC AND FORMAL APPROACHES

The economic geography literature typically avoids discussing what happens between long-run equilibria, but where it does, it relies on a heuristic approach. Namely, it is asserted that the system approaches the nearest stable equilibrium that does not require crossing an unstable equilibrium. This reasoning does not constitute a rigorous analysis. For that, we turn to the mathematics of differential equations.

At a high level of abstraction, the CP model is just a non-linear differential equation with s_H or s_n (since $s_H = s_n$) as the state variable. One simple approach to global stability analysis of non-linear differential equations is called Liaponov's direct method. Instead of working with a potentially complicated function of the state variable (the solution to the non-linear equation for s_n, in this case), one works with a simple function—defined on a specific region—that attains its minimum at the long-run level of s_n. If the simple function (called the Liaponov function) and its domain are chosen judiciously, one can show that the value of the Liaponov function continuously approaches its minimum as time passes and that this implies that the state variable also approaches its long-run equilibrium as time passes. This is sufficient for showing that the system is globally stable in the region (see Beavis and Dobbs, 1990, p. 167 for details).

As shown above, the dynamics of the CP model depend upon the level of trade freeness and there are three qualitative cases. When ϕ is very low, only the symmetric equilibrium is stable; when ϕ is very high, only the CP equilibria are stable. The most interesting case, from a global stability point of view, is the case of intermediate trade costs. For an intermediate level of trade freeness, the model has five equilibria, three of which are stable (the symmetric and the two CP outcomes) and two of which are unstable. This case is shown in Figure 2.6, where the unstable equilibria are labelled U_1 and U_2.

What we wish to show is that, even in the five-steady-states case, the system is globally stable in the sense that the system always converges to one steady state

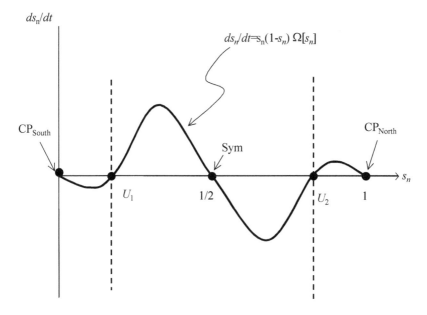

Figure 2.6 The wiggle diagram and global stability.

or another regardless of initial conditions. We also want to show that the system approaches the nearest stable steady state that does not require crossing of an unstable steady state.

Consider first stability in the open set $s_n \in (U_1, U_2)$. The Liaponov function we choose is $(s_n - 1/2)^2/2$. This satisfies the regularity conditions of Theorem 5.24 in Beavis and Dobbs (1990), namely the equilibrium point and initial point are in the set, the function is always positive on the set and the value of the function is zero at the equilibrium. Most importantly, $\dot{V} = (s_n - 1/2)\dot{s}_n < 0$ for all t and for all non-equilibrium values of s_n in the set. To see this, note that s_n is increasing when s_n is less than 1/2, but decreasing when s_n exceeds 1/2. Since V is always decreasing and attains its minimum at the symmetric steady state, we know that s_n converges to the symmetric steady state whenever the initial value is in the $s_n \in (U_1, U_2)$ range. This range is sometimes called the symmetric equilibrium's 'basin of attraction'.

Next consider stability in the $s_n \in (U_2, 1]$ interval with $(s_n - 1)^2/2$ as the Liaponov function. This function meets all the regularity conditions and time-derivative condition, so we know that $s_n \in (U_2, 1]$ is the basin of attraction for the core-in-the-north CP outcome. Similar reasoning implies that $s_n \in [0, U_1)$ is the basin of attraction for the core-in-the-south CP outcome.

Finally, analogous reasoning can show that the CP model is globally stable in the two simpler cases when only the symmetry outcome is stable and when only the CP outcome is stable. Moreover, in the latter case, it is straightforward to establish that (1/2, 1] and [0, 1/2) are, respectively, the basins of attractions for the core-in-the-north and core-in-the-south CP outcomes (see Baldwin 2001 for details).

2.B.4 Forward-Looking Expectations

Perhaps the least attractive of the CP-model assumptions concerns migrant beha-viour. Migrants are assumed to ignore the future, basing their migration choices on *current* real wage differences alone. This is awkward since migration is, after all, the key to agglomeration in this model. Moreover, workers are infinitely lived and migration alters wages in a predictable manner. While the shortcomings of myopia were abundantly clear to the model's progenitors, the assumption was thought necessary for tractability. This section shows that forward-looking expectations can be dealt with. Moreover, we show that allowing for forward-looking expectations does not overturn any of the main model results, but it does open to the door to a more rigorous thinking about issues like self-fulfilling prophecies concerning agglomeration.

THE MAIN DIFFICULTIES

CP-model dynamics with forward-looking agents are intractable for two distinct reasons: one is general, and the other is model specific. Forward-looking expec-tations demand consideration of the very difficult issues of global stability in non-linear dynamic systems with multiple equilibria. Although these are difficult, they are also important and interesting, as Matsuyama (1991)—the first to consider them formally—shows. For instance, such considerations open up a very impor-tant set of possibilities such as self-fulfilling expectations (i.e. spatial realloca-tions that are unrelated to changes in the economic environment but rather are triggered by shocks to expectations) and the idea that policies can work by deleting equilibria. The second source of intractability is model specific; the CP model cannot be reduced to a set of explicit differential equations since $\omega - \omega^*$ cannot be written as an explicit function of the state variable, s_n.[26] This, in turn, is because (2.13) cannot be solved analytically. This section considers a combination of analytical and numerical techniques that allow us to overcome both of these sources of intractability.

THE DYNAMIC PROBLEM AND OPTIMAL MIGRATION

The first task is to find a way of nesting the standard CP model within a closely related model that allows forward-looking expectations. To this end, none of the CP model assumptions, except the assumption concerning migrant myopia and the definition of households (i.e. the typical consumers), are altered. In particular, assume there are N households that are identical and endowed with H^w/N units of industrial labour and L/N units of agricultural labour. H_i units of the household's H are employed in the north and $1/N - H_i$ are employed in the south (recall that H^w is normalized to unity). A typical household's intertemporal preferences are defined by

[26] Since $H = n$ with our normalizations, either s_H or s_n can be taken as the state variable. Since other economic geography models can be written with s_n as the state variable, we prefer s_n to bolster comparability across models.

$$\int_{s=t}^{\infty} e^{-\rho(s-t)} U(s)\,ds$$

where ρ is the subjective discount rate, and U is as in (2.1). Migration is assumed to be costly; specifically the migration cost is quadratic in the flow of south-to-north migration, namely $m_i \equiv \dot{H}_i$ (this is a standard assumption intended to reflect congestion costs). Migration costs are also related to the existing inter-regional distribution of H. Thus, migration costs are $(\tilde{\gamma} m_i^2 / 2)$ times $(1/H_i)$ $(1/[1/N - H_i])$, where $\tilde{\gamma}$ measures overall migration costs. Given this, optimal migration behaviour is simple to derive.[27]

The typical household divides its labour between north and south to maximize its real earnings net of migration cost. Observing that the real wage is an index for worker's instantaneous utility (i.e. P is a perfect price index and w is the only source of income for the mobile factor), the typical household chooses migration to solve

$$\max_{m_i} \int_0^{\infty} e^{-\rho t} \left[\frac{1-\mu}{2\mu N} + H_i \omega + \left(\frac{1}{N} - H_i \right) \omega^* - \frac{\tilde{\gamma} m_i^2}{2 H_i [(1/N) - H_i]} \right] dt, \quad m_i \equiv \dot{H}_i$$

where the first term in the large brackets is the typical household's income from its immobile factor. This allows for almost any sort of migration behaviour, including the possibility that migrants will return and re-migrate.[28] Ignoring constants, the current valued Hamiltonian for the problem is $H_i \omega + (1/N - H_i)\omega^*$ minus $\tilde{\gamma} m_i^2 / [H_i (1/N - H_i)/2] + W m_i$ where W is the co-state variable that captures the asset value of migration. The solution to this is characterized by three necessary conditions $m_i = W H_i (1/N - H_i)$ and $\dot{W} = \rho W - (\omega - \omega^*)$, which must hold at all moments, and an endpoint condition $\lim_{t \to \infty} e^{\rho t} W m_i = 0$. Using our normalizations and household symmetry, we have $H = s_H = s_n = N H_i$ and $\dot{s}_n = \dot{s}_H = m$. Using these in the first necessary condition, and absorbing N terms into $\gamma = N\tilde{\gamma}$, the aggregate migration equation becomes

$$\dot{s}_n = W s_n \frac{1 - s_n}{\gamma} \tag{2.A.9}$$

As usual, W is governed by an asset-pricing-like expression,

$$\dot{W} = \rho W - (\omega - \omega^*) \tag{2.A.10}$$

MYOPIC AND FORWARD-LOOKING EXPECTATIONS

If migrants have rational and forward-looking expectations, (2.A.9) and (2.A.10) characterize their optimal behaviour. If migrants are myopic, that is, have static

---

[27] For justification of these assumptions, see Baldwin (2001).

[28] The main restriction is that we rule out an infinite number of migrations in a finite period. Moreover, since the co-state variable must be a continuous function of time, the migrants cannot expect to change their migration time path in the future.

expectations, they assume that the current real wage gap will persist forever, and (2.A.10) can be solved to yield $W = (\omega - \omega^*)/\rho$. Using this in (2.A.9) implies

$$\dot{s}_n = (\omega - \omega^*)s_n \frac{1 - s_n}{\gamma\rho}$$

The second expression—which is identical to (2.3) given our normalizations—follows from the first expression by choice of time units (such that $\rho\gamma = 1$). This result shows that the migration equation with myopic behaviour assumed in the CP model can be motivated by optimal migration behaviour with static expectations on the real wage gap. This is a special case of optimal migration with forward-looking behaviour that is characterized by the pair of differential equations, (2.A.9) and (2.A.10).

STABILITY ANALYSIS WITH FORWARD-LOOKING WORKERS

We turn next to the local and global stability properties of the CP model with forward-looking migrants.

Local Stability. Local stability is assessed by using a linear approximation to the non-linear system given by (2.A.9) and (2.A.10). The linearized system is $\dot{x} = J(x - x^{ss})$ where $x \equiv (s_n, W)^T$ and J is the Jacobian matrix (i.e. matrix of own and cross partials) evaluated at a particular steady state. Specifically, J is

$$J = \begin{bmatrix} W(1 - 2s_n)/\gamma & s_n(1 - s_n)/\gamma \\ -\dfrac{d\Omega}{ds_n} & \rho \end{bmatrix}, \quad \Omega \equiv \omega - \omega^*$$

Local stability is determined by checking J's eigenvalues at the symmetric and CP outcomes. As usual, saddle path stability requires one negative eigenvalue and one positive eigenvalue. If the eigenvalues are complex, then the test involves the signs of the real parts.[29] One useful fact reduces the work. A standard matrix algebra result is that the determinant of J equals the product of the eigenvalues (Beavis and Dobbs, 1990, p. 161). Thus, the system is saddle-path stable, if and only if $\det(J) < 0$. The determinant $\det(J)$ is equal to $(d\Omega/ds_n)s_L(1 - s_n)/\gamma + \rho W(1 - 2s_n)/\gamma$, so for the symmetric equilibrium—where $1 - 2s_n$ is zero—the stability test is $(d\Omega/ds_n)/4\gamma < 0$ and in the CP outcome—where $s_n(1 - s_n)$ is zero—the stability test is $\rho W/\gamma > 0$; in each case, the expressions and derivatives are evaluated at the appropriate steady state. Noting that W in the CP equilibrium equals $(\omega_{CP} - \omega_{CP}^*)/\rho$, this shows that the informal local stability test for the CP model with static expectations—viz. (2.18)—is exactly equivalent to the formal local stability test for the CP model with forward-looking expectations. An important and somewhat unexpected corollary of this result is that the break and sustain points are exactly the same with static and with forward-looking expectations.

[29]See the appendix to Barro and Sala-I-Martin (1995) for details and an excellent exposition of local stability and phase diagram analysis.

Global Stability. When trade costs are such that the CP model has a unique stable equilibrium, local stability analysis is sufficient. After any shock, W jumps to put the system on the saddle path leading to the unique stable equilibrium (if it did not, the system would diverge and thereby violate a necessary condition for intertemporal optimization, the transversality condition). For ϕ's where the model has multiple stable steady states, things are more complex. With multiple stable equilibria, there will be multiple saddle paths. In principle, multiple saddle paths may correspond to a given initial condition, thus creating what Matsuyama (1991) calls an indeterminacy of the equilibrium path. In other words, it is not clear which path the system will jump to, so the interesting possibility of self-fulfilling prophecies and sudden takeoffs may arise. These possibilities are explored next.

Recent advances in computing speed and simulation software have made it possible to numerically characterize non-linear systems with multiple steady states to a very high degree of accuracy. There are two key tricks to doing this: (1) it is much easier to find the unstable saddle path than the stable saddle path; and (2) the stable path becomes the unstable path in reverse time.[30] Numerical techniques are also used to solve the second source of intractability, namely the fact that $\omega - \omega^*$ cannot be written as an explicit function of the state variable. To get around this, the computer is used to solve the model for the exact values of $\Omega \equiv \omega - \omega^*$ corresponding to a grid of values of $s_n \in [0, ..., 1]$. A very high order polynomial of s_n is then fitted to these actual values. The result is an explicit polynomial function, $\Omega[s_n]$, in the simulations that follow, a 17th-order polynomial was fitted to 25 values of Ω.[31]

Numerical simulation (in reverse time) enables us to find the saddle paths for various parameter values; we always assume $\phi^S < \phi < \phi^B$ so that the system is marked by three stable steady states. Three qualitatively different cases are considered for the migration cost parameter, γ. In all simulations we take $\sigma = 5$, $\mu = 4/10$, $\rho = 1/10$ and $\phi = 1/10$. The first case is when γ, the migration cost parameter, is very large, so horizontal movement is very slow. This is shown in Figure 2.7. Importantly, there is no overlap of saddle paths in this case, so the global stability analysis with static expectations is exactly right. That is, the basins of attraction for the various equilibria are the same with static and forward-looking expectations. This is an important result. It says that if migration costs are sufficiently high, the global, as well as the local, stability properties of the CP model with forward-looking expectations are qualitatively identical to those of the model with myopic migrants.

The second case, shown in Figure 2.8, is for an intermediate value of migration costs. Here, the saddle paths overlap somewhat since the Jacobian evaluated at either unstable equilibrium has complex eigenvalues—this means that the system

---

[30]Dynamic systems marked by saddle path stability always have unstable saddle paths. In linear systems, the former correspond to the positive eigenvector, the latter to the negative eigenvector. See Baldwin (2001) for details.

[31]Algorithms showing how to find saddles paths and approximate $\Omega[s_n]$ are available from http://heiwww.unige.ch/~baldwin/.

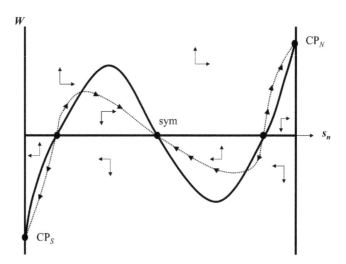

Figure 2.7 Global stability with forward-looking expectations and high migration costs.

spirals out from U_1 and U_2 in normal time. (The figure shows only the saddle paths in the right side of the diagram since the left side is the mirror image of the right).

The existence of overlapping saddle paths changes things dramatically, as Krugman (1991c) showed. If the economy finds itself with a level of s_n that lays in the overlap, namely the interval (A, B) shown in the figure, then a fundamental indeterminacy exists. Both saddle paths provide perfectly rational adjustment tracks. Forward-looking workers who are fully aware of how the economy works could adopt the path leading to the symmetric outcome. It would, however, be equally rational for them to jump on the track that will take them to the CP_N outcome.

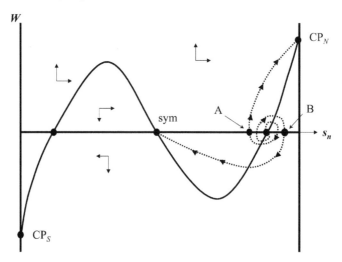

Figure 2.8 Global stability with intermediate migration costs.

Which track is taken cannot be decided in this model. Workers individually choose a migration strategy taking as given their beliefs about the aggregate path. Consistency requires that beliefs are rational on any equilibrium path. That is, the aggregate path that results from each worker's choice is the one that each of them believes to be the equilibrium path. Putting it more colloquially, workers choose the path that they think other workers will take. In other words, expectations, rather than history, can matter.

Because expectations can change suddenly, even with no change in environmental parameters, the system is subject to sudden and seemingly unpredictable takeoffs and/or reversals. Moreover, the government may influence the state of the economy by announcing a policy, say a tax, that deletes an equilibrium even when the current state of the economy is distant to the deleted equilibrium.

While it is difficult to fully characterize the constellation of parameters that corresponds to the overlap, it is easy to find a sufficient condition for there to be some overlap of saddle paths. If the eigenvalues of the Jacobian evaluated at the unstable equilibria are complex, then there must be some overlap. The eigenvalues at U_2 are

$$\frac{\rho \pm \sqrt{\rho^2 - 4(d\Omega/ds_n)s_n(1 - s_n)/\gamma}}{2}$$

so we get complex roots when migration costs are sufficiently low, namely when

$$\gamma < \frac{4(d\Omega/ds_n)s_n(1 - s_n)}{\rho^2}$$

To summarize, the possibility of history-versus-expectations dynamics, that is, that 'self-fulfilling prophecies' or self-fulfilling changes in expectations arise when the costs of migration (i.e. γ) are low relative to the patience of workers (i.e. $1/\rho^2$) and the impact that migration has on the real wage gap (i.e. $d\Omega/ds_n$) is large.

The final case, Figure 2.9, is the most spectacular. Here migration costs are very low, so horizontal movement is quite fast. As a result, the saddle path for CP_N originates from U_1 rather than U_2. Interestingly, the overlap of saddle paths includes the symmetric equilibrium. This raises the possibility that the economy could jump from the symmetric equilibrium onto a path that leads it to a CP outcome merely because all the workers expected that everyone else was going to migrate. Plainly, this raises the possibility of a big-push drive by a government, having some very dramatic effects.[32]

---

[32]Karp (2000) qualifies this insight by assuming that agents have 'almost common knowledge' in the sense of Rubinstein (1989) rather than common knowledge about history (economic fundamentals). In a setting akin to Matsuyama (1991) and Krugman (1991c), he shows that the equilibrium indeterminacy brought about by the possibility that expectations might prevail over history disappears. Common knowledge and rational expectations together give rise to the possibility that expectations might prevail over history in the first place, so it is not surprising that altering the information structure alters the equilibrium set considerably. We conjecture that the same holds true in the present CP model with forward-looking expectations. As Karp (2000) points out, the restoration of the determinacy implies that "the unique competitive equilibrium can be influenced by government policy, just as in the standard models."

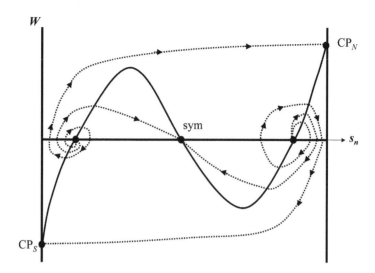

Figure 2.9 Global stability with low migration costs.

Finally, note that the region of overlapping saddle paths will never include a CP outcome. Thus, although one may 'talk the economy' out of a symmetric equilibrium, one can never do the same for an economy that is already agglomerated. To sum up, when migration costs are sufficiently low, and $\phi^B < \phi < \phi^S$, the symmetric equilibrium can be globally unstable while being locally stable and a coordinated change in expectations could produce migration that would shift the economy from the symmetric equilibrium to a CP outcome, even though there were no change in parameters or trade costs. In other words, a self-fulfilling prophecy could break the symmetric outcome even though it is locally stable.

2.B.5 Which Assumptions are for Convenience?

Solving a general equilibrium model is normally a difficult task. Usually, one has to simultaneously solve all the good-markets and factor-markets clearing conditions together with the free entry conditions. Many of the assumptions in the CP model simplify this task by making the model 'block recursive' in the sense that certain endogenous variables can be determined from a subset of the equilibrium conditions. With this in mind, we start by pointing out the truly important assumptions.

The assumption of increasing returns that are internal to industrial firms is absolutely essential. After all, if there is no loss to splitting up production there is really no location choice to be made.[33] Once we have scale economies, however, marginal cost pricing is out, so we must deal with imperfect competition. Dixit–Stiglitz

---

[33]In other words, as pointed out by Koopmans (1957), the location problem of a firm arises because some of its activities are indivisible.

monopolistic competition is assumed since this is by far the easiest form of imperfect competition to work with in a general equilibrium model, but other forms are also possible (see, e.g. Chapter 5). Likewise the locational choice is only interesting when trade in the increasing-return sector is subject to some sort of cost.

The assumption that workers share the same preferences makes it easy to characterize the point of catastrophic agglomeration. It is worth pointing out, however, that different assumptions concerning migration behaviour and/or the existence of some congestion in the core region can yield a smooth transition. For example, if workers display sufficiently different degrees of attachment to their original region, the economy can move from dispersion to agglomeration in a non-catastrophic way (Tabuchi and Thisse, 2002; Murata, 2003). These issues are explored to some extent in Chapter 9.

Most of the other assumptions are a matter of expediency. For example, the model assumes that there is only one non-industrial sector and to make this as trivial as possible, the model assumes that it is Walrasian and its output is traded costlessly (see FKV Chapter 7 for the CP model with transport costs and imperfect competition in the A sector). The only crucial assumption is that the non-industrial sector is intensive in its use of the immobile factor so that inter-regional factor mobility is associated with a concentration of industry. With more than one industrial sector, Krugman and Venables (1997) show that different sectors may agglomerate in different countries.

The assumption of two regions is not essential but it greatly simplifies the range of locational outcomes and thus greatly simplifies almost every calculation. The cost of this simplification is that the CP model cannot be used to study the many interesting issues that arise with multiple locations, for example, locational hierarchy. Likewise, the assumption of only two factors of production is not crucial, although we do need at least two, since one must be mobile to allow agglomeration and one must be immobile to keep the model interesting. (If all factors were mobile, then everyone would always have an incentive to avoid trade costs by agglomerating in one region or the other; in such a model, agglomeration would either happen immediately, with positive trade costs, or be irrelevant, with zero trade costs).

The CP model makes extreme assumptions about the factor intensity of the two sectors. Again this is for convenience, what really matters is that the mobile factor is used intensively in the increasing returns sector. The assumption is convenient in that it makes the two sectors quite independent of each other, allowing us to solve for many endogenous variables using only a subset of the equilibrium conditions.

The model also assumes a very particular form of trade costs, namely iceberg trade cost. This assumption is very convenient in a general equilibrium model because it allows us to avoid, for example, the issue of who gets the rents from trade barriers, how transport services are priced and which region's factors are used up in overcoming the trade costs.

Having trade cost only in one sector is also a simplifying assumption. The point is that agglomeration and dispersion forces do require trade cost in one sector. Moreover, if we allow trade costs in the other sector, we cannot maintain the simplifying assumption that that second sector is Walrasian. Davis (1998) showed that trade costs in the Walrasian sector shuts off all inter-industry trade and this, of course, means that each region cannot run a trade deficit in the M sector. Agglomeration is, therefore, impossible. Of course, Davis (1998) is not a critique of the basic logic of the CP model, it just shows how carefully simplifying assumptions must be fit together. Indeed one mark of an elegant model is that each assumption is critical; it should not be surprising that relaxing only one assumption produces different results. In particular, KFV (Chapter 7) show that one gets the same sort of results with trade costs in both sectors as long as one assumes differentiated varieties in both sectors (this permits intra-industry trade in both sectors).

The assumption of upper-tier Cobb–Douglas preferences greatly simplifies the algebra since it allows us to work out prices and demands separately in the A and M sector. For more general preferences, expenditure on M would depend upon relative prices, but relative prices would depend upon the level of M-sector expenditure (the expenditure level affects the number of varieties and this in turn affect the M-sector price index).

APPENDIX 2.C: EXOGENOUS ASYMMETRIES

The logic of demand-linked agglomeration depends crucially upon market size, so it is natural to wonder whether the crucial results—catastrophic agglomeration and locational hysteresis—would hold when regions are intrinsically asymmetric in terms of size. Another type of asymmetry to be considered is that of trade freeness. That is, if one nation's ϕ is larger but both ϕ's fall, do we still observe catastrophes?

2.C.1 Asymmetric Sizes

A nation's economic size depends on how much L and H it has. Since H is mobile and its international division is endogenous, intrinsic size asymmetries must come from different endowments of the immobile L. To this end, we assume that the two regions are endowed with different stocks of L and to be concrete, the south is 'bigger' in the sense that $L^* = L + \varepsilon$ with $\varepsilon > 0$.

Intuition on how size-asymmetry matters can be gained by considering a small change to a situation that starts out fully symmetric in terms of the division of both H and L. Formally, this involves consideration of a small perturbation, $d\varepsilon$, of the fully symmetric equilibrium where initially $\varepsilon = 0$ and $s_n = 1/2$. Mechanically, the ε enters into the equilibrium conditions via the definition of E's, namely $E = L + wH$ and $E^* = L^* + \varepsilon + w^* H^*$. Since the E's enter the market-clearing conditions (via the demand functions) and the market-clearing conditions determine nominal wages, a change in ε will generally affect w and w^*. To quantify this, we totally differentiate the two market-clearing conditions with respect to w, w^* and ε and evaluate the result at $s_n = 1/2$ and $\varepsilon = 0$. Solving these yields expressions for $dw/d\varepsilon$ and $dw^*/d\varepsilon$ and these tell us how equilibrium nominal wages are affected by a slight size asymmetry. Next, we totally differentiate the real wage gap, Ω, with respect to the nominal wages and plug in the expressions for $dw/d\varepsilon$ and $dw^*/d\varepsilon$. The result is an expression that tells us how the real wage gap, that is, $\Omega = \omega - \omega^*$, at full symmetry would be affected by a slight size asymmetry. The result is

$$\left.\frac{d\Omega}{d\varepsilon}\right|_{s_n=1/2} = -\frac{2^{1-a}\mu(1-\phi)(1+\phi)^a[(1+\mu)\phi+1-\mu]}{1-\mu+(1+\mu)\phi^2+2(2\sigma-1)\phi} < 0 \qquad (2.A.11)$$

where $a = \mu/(\sigma - 1)$ as usual.

Given the standard restrictions on the parameters (the no-black-hole condition and $\sigma > 1$ and $0 < \mu < 1$), (2.A.11) is negative by inspection. Since the real wage gap is zero at the initial point of full symmetry, and $\Omega = 0$ is a long-run equilibrium condition, we see that even a slight size asymmetry rules out the possibility of an even division of industry. In particular, if s_n were $1/2$, the southern real wage would be slightly higher so north-to-south migration would occur. What is the new equilibrium division on H? Unfortunately, the intense intractability of the CP model means that numerical simulation of the model for specific values of μ, σ and ε is the only way forward.

Figure 2.10 plots the real wage gap, Ω, against s_n (the share of mobile workers in the north) for various levels of trade freeness taking $\varepsilon = 0.01$, $\mu = 0.3$ and $\sigma = 5$. When ϕ is very low, say, 0.1, or very high, 0.9, we have three long-run

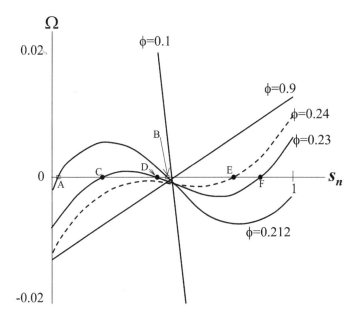

Figure 2.10 Wiggle diagram with size asymmetry.

equilibria. The two core–periphery outcomes, $s_H = 1$ and $s_H = 0$—which are always equilibria given the migration equation (2.3)—and an interior equilibrium at the point where the plot of Ω crosses the x-axis. As shown for $\phi = 0.1$ (this corresponds to trade costs of almost 80%), Ω is steeply declining in s_H over the whole range of s_H. This tells us that only the interior equilibrium is stable since Ω is positive at $s_H = 0$ and negative at $s_H = 1$ (see (2.18) for a formal statement of local stability criteria). When trade is very free, say $\phi = 0.9$ (i.e. 3% trade costs), we also have a unique interior equilibrium, but Ω is steeply rising, so only the two CP outcomes, $s_H = 1$ and $s_H = 0$, are stable and the interior equilibrium is unstable.

For intermediate values of ϕ, we have outcomes with one, two or three interior equilibria. For example, when $\phi = 0.212$ there are two interior equilibria marked A and B in the diagram; the first is unstable while the second is stable. For $\phi = 0.23$, we have three, C, D and F, of which only the middle one is stable. And for $\phi = 0.24$, the only one interior equilibrium, point E, is unstable. Plainly then, the asymmetric-size case presents a richer array of outcomes than does the symmetric case.

These simulation results can be parsimoniously illustrated in a diagram similar to the tomahawk diagram (Figure 2.11). This plots the long-run equilibrium division of industry on the vertical axis for all possible levels of trade freeness.

Interestingly, we see that size asymmetry 'breaks the handle' of the tomahawk from Figure 2.4 into two pieces and rotates the pieces in opposite directions. More precisely, from the above equation, we see that $d\Omega/d\varepsilon = 0$ at two values of trade freeness, $\phi = -(1 - \mu)/(1 + \mu)$ and $\phi = 1$. The first of these, while outside the range of economically meaningful ϕ, tells us that the fulcrum for the rotation of the right-hand part is $-(1 - \mu)/(1 + \mu)$; the left-hand part rotates around $\phi = 1$.

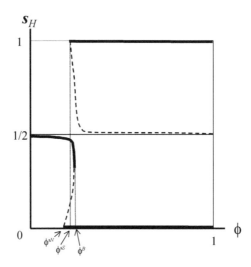

Figure 2.11   The broken tomahawk: size asymmetry in the CP model.

Notice that we now have two sustain points and a single break point and the stable interior equilibrium is no longer a straight line as in the symmetric-size case. These features significantly enrich the range of possibilities compared to the symmetric CP model. For instance, suppose we tell the usual story of how falling trade costs can affect the location of industry. Starting with very high trade costs and only slight size asymmetries, progressive reductions in trade costs have only a slight location impact, with some industry moving from the small region to the large region. However, as the level of trade freeness approaches the break point, ϕ^B, the location effect of a marginal increase in trade freeness is greatly magnified with a large share of northern industry relocating to the big region (the south). Once ϕ^B is surpassed, industry either all moves to the north or all to the south. Unlike in the symmetric case, the full agglomeration in the big region is much more likely. In short, this model displays the catastrophic features of the CP model, but also display a richer, pre-catastrophe behaviour.

The hysteresis features of this model are also richer. In the symmetric CP model, there is a single sustain point, so both regions become able to sustain full agglomeration at the same time. With size asymmetry, by contrast, the big region is able to sustain the core at a higher level of trade cost than is the small region. What this means is that at some intermediate level of trade costs, a sufficiently large location shock could switch the outcome from a fairly even division of industry to one dominated by the big region, but no shock could shift the outcome to having the core in the small region. At a somewhat higher level of trade freeness, however, a big location shock could—as in the symmetric CP model—shift industry to either extreme.

Further numerical simulation (not reported) shows that when the size asymmetry gets larger, the ordering of the break and sustain points can change. Specifically, the large region's sustain point always comes at a lower ϕ than the small region's but with very asymmetric regions the break point is between the two sustain points.

2.C.2 Asymmetric Trade Costs

A second type of asymmetry involves trade costs. As it turns out, the qualitative results for this type of asymmetry are quite similar to those described above, so we cover trade-cost-asymmetry rather quickly.

Assume the two regions differ in terms of their openness to imports (i.e. $\phi^* = \phi - \delta$, $\delta > 0$) with the north more open than the south. The first step to understanding what happens is again to consider a small perturbation, $d\delta$, of the symmetric equilibrium $s_n = 1/2$. Calculations similar to those described for the size-asymmetry case yield

$$\frac{d\Omega}{d\delta}\bigg|_{s_n=1/2} = -2^{-a}(1+\phi)^a \frac{\mu(1+\mu)(1-\phi) + 2[\sigma(1-\mu)-1]}{(\sigma-1)[1-\mu+(1+\mu)\phi^2+2(2\sigma-1)\phi]} < 0$$

where negativity is guaranteed by the no-black-hole condition.

This expression implies that a small decrease in southern openness makes the north–south real wage gap negative. Since at $s_n = 1/2$, Ω was zero, the perturbation triggers migration of industrial workers from north to south. As before, this asymmetry eliminates the $s_n = 1/2$ equilibrium and creates a situation with two sustain points and a break point.

REFERENCES

Baldwin, Richard E. 2000. Regulatory protectionism, developing nations and a two-tier world trading system. *Brookings Trade Forum*, The Brookings Institution, Washington, DC, 237–293.

_____. 2001. The core–periphery model with forward-looking expectations. *Regional Science and Urban Economics* 31: 21–49.

Baldwin, R. and R. Forslid. 2000. The core-periphery model and endogenous growth: stabilising and de-stabilising integration. *Economica* 67: 307–324.

Barro, R. and X. Sala-I-Martin. 1995. *Economic Growth*. New York: McGraw-Hill.

Beavis, B. and I. Dobbs. 1990. *Optimisation and Stability Theory for Economic Analysis*. Cambridge: Cambridge University Press.

Brakman, S., H. Garretsen, C. van Marrewijk. 2001. *An Introduction to Geographical Economics*. Cambridge: Cambridge University Press.

d'Aspremont, C., J., J. Gabszewicz and J.-F. Thisse. 1979. On Hotelling's "Stability in Competition". *Econometrica* 47: 1045–1050.

Davis, Donald. 1998. The home market, trade and industrial structure. *American Economic Review* 88(5): 1264–1276.

Dixit, A. K. and J. E. Stiglitz. 1977. Monopolistic competition and optimum product diversity. *American Economic Review* 67: 297–308.

Flam, Harry and E. Helpman. 1987. Industrial policy under monopolistic competition. *Journal of International Economics* 22: 79–102.

Forslid, Rikard and G. Ottaviano. 2003. An analytically solvable core-periphery model. *Journal of Economic Geography* in press.

Fujita, M. and J.-F. Thisse. 1996 Economics of agglomeration. *Journal of the Japanese and International Economies* 10: 339–378.

_____. 2002. *Economics of Agglomeration*. Cambridge: Cambridge University Press.

Fujita, M., P. Krugman and A. Venables. 1999. *The Spatial Economy: Cities, Regions and International Trade*. Cambridge, MA: MIT Press.

Fukao, K. and R. Benabou. 1993. History versus expectations: a comment. *Quarterly Journal of Economics* 108: 535–542.

Helpman, Elhanan. 1997. The size of regions. In *Topics in Public Economics. Theoretical and Applied Analysis*, ed. D. Pines, E. Sadka and I. Zilcha. Cambridge: Cambridge University Press.

Helpman, Elhanan and P. R. Krugman. 1985. *Market Structure and Foreign Trade*. Cambridge, MA: MIT Press.

_____. 1989. *Trade Policy and Market Structure*. Cambridge, MA: MIT Press.

Hotelling, H. 1929. Stability in competition. *Economic Journal* 39: 41–57.

Irmen, A. and J.-F. Thisse. 1998. Competition in multi-characteristics spaces: Hotelling was almost right. *Journal of Economic Theory* 78: 76–102.

Karp, Larry. 2000. Fundamentals versus beliefs under almost common knowledge. Mimeo, UC Berkeley.

Koopmans, T. C. 1957. *Three Essays on the State of Economic Science*. New York: McGraw-Hill.

Krugman, Paul. 1980. Scale economies, product differentiation, and the pattern of trade. *American Economic Review* 70: 950–959.

_____. 1991a. Increasing returns and economic geography. *Journal of Political Economy* 99: 483–499.

_____. *Geography and Trade*. Cambridge, MA: MIT Press.

_____. 1991c. History versus expectations. *Quarterly Journal of Economics* 106: 651–667.

Krugman, Paul and A. Venables. 1995. Globalization and the inequality of nations. *Quarterly Journal of Economics* 60: 857–880.

_____. 1997. Integration, specialization and adjustment. *European Economic Review* 40: 959–968.

Martin, R. 1999. The new 'geographical turn' in economics: some critical reflections. *Cambridge Journal of Economics* 23: 65–91.

Matsuyama, Kiminori. 1991. Increasing returns, industrialization and indeterminacy of equilibrium. *Quarterly Journal of Economics* 106: 617–650.

_____. 1995. Complementarities and cumulative processes in models of monopolistic competition. *Journal of Economic Literature* 33: 701–729.

Matsuyama, Kiminori and T. Takahashi. 1998. Self-defeating regional concentration. *Review of Economic Studies* 65: 211–234.

Mundell, Robert. 1957. International trade and factor mobility. *American Economic Review* 47: 321–335.

Murata, Y. 2003. Product diversity, taste heterogeneity, and geographic distribution of economic activities: market vs. non-market interactions. *Journal of Urban Economics*, in press.

Neary, Peter. 2001. Of hype and hyperbolas: introducing the new economic geography. *Journal of Economic Literature* 39: 536–561.

Ottaviano, G. I. P. 2000. *Ad usum delphini*: a primer in 'new economic geography'. *Giornale degli Economisti e Annali di Economia* 59: 89–116.

Ottaviano, G. I. P. and D. Puga. 1998. Agglomeration in the global economy: a survey of the 'new economic geography'. *The World Economy* 21: 707–731.

Ottaviano, G. I. P. and J.-F. Thisse. 2003. Agglomeration and economic geography. In *Handbook of Regional and Urban Economics*, Volume 3, ed. V. Henderson and J.-F. Thisse. Amsterdam: Elsevier, in press.

Puga Diego. 1999. The rise and fall of regional inequalities. *European Economic Review* 43: 303–334.

Robert-Nicoud, Frederic. 2002. The structure of simple 'New Economic Geography' models. Mimeo, London School of Economics.

Rubinstein, Ariel. 1989. The electronic email game: strategic behaviour under almost common knowledge. *American Economic Review* 79: 385–391.

Stahl, K. 1987. Theories of urban business location. In *Handbook of Regional and Urban Economics*, Volume 2, ed. E.S. Mills. Amsterdam: Elsevier, 759–820.

Tabuchi, T. and J.-F. Thisse. 2002. Taste heterogeneity, labor mobility and economic geography. *Journal of Development Economics*, in press.

Tirole, J. 1988. *The Theory of Industrial Organization*. Cambridge, MA: MIT Press.

Venables, Anthony. 1987. Trade and trade policy with differentiated products: a Chamberlinian-Ricardian model. *Economic Journal* 97: 700–717.

_____. 1996. Equilibrium locations of vertically linked industries. *International Economic Review* 37: 341–359.

The Footloose Capital Model

3.1 Introduction

While yielding valuable insights on the interactions between trade costs, factor mobility and agglomeration, the CP model is astoundingly difficult to work with, forcing numerical simulations for most results. In particular, the endogenous variables that are instrumental in determining the location of firms and workers (i.e. wages and prices) cannot be expressed as explicit functions of the spatial distribution of economic activities. As a consequence, numerical investigation can only provide a gallery of possible equilibrium outcomes; each obtained under a particular set of parameter values. From a theorist's perspective, this is less than fully satisfactory since, of course, one cannot be certain that the gallery is complete, and one wonders whether some unknown picture could change everything. Moreover, it is difficult to illustrate the new insights that geography models provide for policy making when the analysis consists of a handful of numerical examples.

This chapter (and the next one) considers modifications of the CP model's basic set-up that enhance tractability.

Following the principle of progressive complexity, this chapter focuses on the most tractable of all the economic geography models, that of Martin and Rogers (1995), which we refer to as the 'footloose capital' model. This model can be solved algebraically and it does display agglomeration forces, but it does not feature the circular causality that is the source of so much of the CP model's richness and intractability. In short, the price for this tractability is a model with a narrower range of effects and features.

3.1.1 Logic of the FC Model

The logic of the FC model is most easily seen by contrasting it with the logic of the CP model from the previous chapter. The CP model features demand-linked circular causality since migration leads to expenditure shifting (workers spend their incomes locally) and expenditure shifting leads to production shifting (via the market-access effect). The CP model also features cost-linked circular causality since production shifting leads to 'cost shifting' in the sense that it affects the cost of living (local production allows local residents to avoid trade costs) and cost shifting leads to production shifting (workers are attracted to regions with low costs-of-living). Both forms of circular causality turn on the fact that the mobile factor spends its income in the region where it works. That is, because workers spend their incomes locally, production shifting is tied to expenditure shifting *and* price indices are important in the migration decision.

The FC model cuts both demand-linked and cost-linked circular causality by assuming that the mobile factor repatriates all of its earnings to its country of origin. (It is for this reason that the mobile factor is most naturally viewed as a disembodied factor such as physical capital or knowledge capital.) To see how this single change cuts both demand- and cost-linked circular causality, note that inter-regional capital movements lead to production shifting without expenditure shifting and this cuts the demand linkage. This assumption also cuts the cost linkage since the cost-of-living is irrelevant to capital's location decision; capital's income gets spent in its owner's region regardless of where it is employed.

Nevertheless, the FC model features agglomeration, if we define agglomeration as the tendency of economic activity to generate forces that encourage further concentration of economic activity. In the FC model, agglomeration stems from the home-market effect, that is, a concentrate of economic activity—and thus income and spending—in one market creates forces that induce a more than proportionate share of industry to locate in the bigger market. Agglomeration in the FC model, however, is not self-reinforcing.

Cutting out self-reinforcing, agglomeration has two important ramifications. First, it means that the FC model is completely tractable. In fact, the main equilibrium expressions are linear in relative market size and the spatial allocation of industry, so we get closed-form solutions for all endogenous variables, including the variable that is the main focus of geography models—the spatial division of industry. The resulting model is tractable enough to allow for many asymmetries that will be of interest when we consider policy. The chapters on trade policy in particular draw heavily on this model. Second, it means that much of the CP model's richness is lost. As we shall see in the range of models considered in subsequent chapters, there is an inevitable trade-off between tractability and richness of features.

It is also worth noting that, since the FC model does not rely on labour migration, it is plausible to interpret the two regions as separate nations.

3.1.2 Organization of the Chapter

The chapter has three sections after the introduction. Section 3.2 presents the model in detail and works out the equilibrium. Section 3.3 compares the key features of the FC model to that of the CP model. Section 3.4 presents our concluding remarks as well as related literature.

The great merit of the FC model is its ability to deal with exogenous asymmetries such as region size and asymmetric trade costs. The appendix presents the model when we allow for such enriching factors.

3.2 THE SYMMETRIC FC MODEL

3.2.1 Assumptions

The basic structure of the FC model is quite similar to that of the CP model presented in Chapter 2, as Figure 3.1 shows schematically. There are two regions,

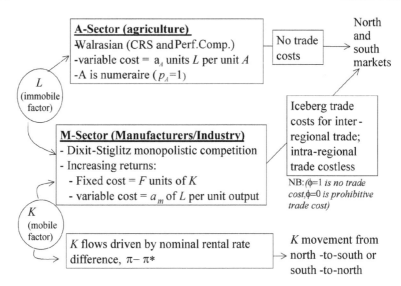

Figure 3.1 Schematic diagram of the FC model.

two sectors, and two productive factors. As in the CP model, the regions are referred to as the north and the south; they are symmetric in terms of tastes, technology, openness to trade, and factor endowments. The two sectors are referred to as industry and agriculture, and, just as in the CP model, industry is marked by increasing returns, monopolistic competition and iceberg trade costs. Since the main focus of all the models in this book, including the FC model, is the location of industry, we make assumptions that keep the second sector as simple as possible. Specifically, the agricultural sector is assumed to produce a homogeneous good under Walrasian conditions (constant returns and perfect competition) and its output is traded costlessly.

The first key difference between the FC and CP models lies in the productive factors. The product factors in the FC model are physical capital K and labour L, with K being the mobile factor and L being the immobile factor. The importance of this difference lies in the fact that physical capital can be employed in one region while its owner spends its reward in the other region—something that is clearly impossible when factors are associated with people as in the CP model. Moreover, capital is only employed in meeting the fixed costs of industrial firms; all variable costs involve labour.[1] Importantly, the FC model assumes that capital owners are completely immobile across regions. Thus, when pressures arise to concentrate production in one region, physical capital will move, but all of its reward will be repatriated to its country of origin. Worldwide supplies of capital and labour are fixed, with the world's endowment denoted as L^w and K^w.

Because physical capital can be separated from its owners, the region in which capital's income is spent may differ from the region in which it is employed. We

---

[1] Viewing K as physical capital, we can think of the fixed cost in the M sector as a factory. This resembles Flam and Helpman (1987) in which the source of increasing returns is also a firm specific input.

must therefore distinguish the share of world capital *owned* by northern residents (we denote this as $s_K \equiv K/K^w$) from the share of world capital *employed* in the north. Because we assume that each industrial variety requires one unit of capital (see below), the share of the world capital stock employed in a region exactly equals the region's share of world industry. Consequently, we can use north's industry share, that is, $s_n \equiv n/(n + n^*)$, to represent the share of capital employed in the north and the share of all varieties made in the north.

The second difference between the FC and CP models comes in the production technology of the increasing-returns sector. The cost function of a typical industrial firm in the FC model is non-homothetic; that is, the factor intensity of the fixed cost differs from the factor intensity of the variable cost. To keep things simple, we make the extreme assumption that the fixed cost involves *only* capital and the variable cost *only* involves labour. More specifically, each industrial firm requires one unit of K (so $F = 1$ in Figure 3.1) and a_m units of labour per unit of output. The implied cost function is

$$\pi + w_L a_m x \tag{3.1}$$

where π and w_L are the rewards to capital and labour, a_m is the variable unit input requirement, and x is firm-level output.

Technology in the A sector is kept as simple as possible. Producing A goods requires only labour, specifically, it takes a_A units of labour to make one unit of the A good. Note that this means that the increasing returns sector is intensive in the use of the mobile factor.

The tastes assumed here are identical to those assumed in the CP model. Thus, the representative consumer in each region has preferences given by

$$U = C, \quad C \equiv C_M^\mu C_A^{1-\mu}, \quad C_M \equiv \left(\int_{i=0}^{n^w} c_i^{1-1/\sigma} di \right)^{1/(1-1/\sigma)}; \quad 0 < \mu < 1 < \sigma \tag{3.2}$$

where C_M and C_A are, respectively, consumption of the composite of M-sector varieties and consumption of the A-sector good. Also, n^w is the mass (roughly speaking, the number) of industrial varieties available worldwide, μ is the expenditure share on industrial varieties, and σ is the constant elasticity of substitution between any two varieties. The indirect utility function for the preferences in (3.2) is

$$V = \frac{E}{P}, \quad P \equiv p_A^{1-\mu}(\Delta n^w)^{-a}, \quad \Delta \equiv \frac{\int_{i=0}^{n^w} p_i^{1-\sigma} di}{n^w}, \quad a \equiv \frac{\mu}{\sigma - 1} \tag{3.3}$$

where E is northern expenditure, P is 'perfect' price index, p_A is the price of A, p_i is the consumer price of industrial variety i (the variety subscript is dropped where clarity permits).[2] Analogous definitions hold for southern variables, all of which are denoted by an asterisk.

---

[2] Using standard terminology, P is 'perfect' since real income defined with P measures utility.

The last assumption concerns factor migration. Physical capital moves in search of the highest *nominal* reward rather than the higher real reward since its income is spent in the owner's region regardless of where the capital is employed (here nominal means the reward in terms of the numeraire; real means the reward in terms the consumption composite C). As in the CP model, inter-regional factor flows are governed by the ad hoc 'migration' equation,

$$\dot{s}_n = (\pi - \pi^*)(1 - s_n)s_n \tag{3.4}$$

Note that one of the great strengths of the FC model is its ability to deal with regional asymmetries, but to boost comparability among models, we focus on the symmetric-region case in the main text. That is, even though we keep the equilibrium expressions general as far as size asymmetry is concerned, we relegate discussion and analysis of size and openness asymmetries to the appendix.

3.2.2 Short-Run Equilibrium

As in the CP model, we distinguish between short- and long-run outcomes. That is, we first work out the equilibrium taking the spatial allocation of capital employment—that is, s_n—as exogenous, before working out what the equilibrium spatial allocation of capital will be once capital is allowed to seek out the highest rate of return.

A-SECTOR RESULTS

Derivation of A-sector short-run results is uncomplicated, and, indeed, identical to the derivation in the CP model. Specifically, utility optimization implies that the demand function for A is $C_A = (1 - \mu)E/p_A$ but we use Walras's Law to drop the A-sector market-clearing condition. Perfect competition in the A sector forces marginal cost pricing, that is, $p_A = a_A w_L$ and $p_A^* = a_A w_L^*$. In addition, costless trade in A equalizes northern and southern prices and thus indirectly equalizes wage rates internationally, viz. $w_L = w_L^*$, as long as some A good is made in both regions. This condition—the so-called non-full-specialization (NFS) condition—requires that no region has enough labour to satisfy world demand for A. The exact condition is that total world spending on A, namely $(1 - \mu)E^w$, is greater than the maximum value of A production that is possible by either region, namely $p_A(\max\{s_L, 1 - s_L\})L^w/a_A$ where s_L is the northern share of L^w. This is assumed to hold henceforth.

INDUSTRIAL SECTOR RESULTS

Utility optimization yields a constant division of expenditure between sectors and CES demand functions for industrial varieties:

$$c_j \equiv \frac{p_j^{-\sigma}\mu E}{\Delta n^w}, \quad n^w \Delta \equiv \left(\int_{i=0}^{n^w} p_i^{1-\sigma}di\right), \quad E = \pi K + w_L L \tag{3.5}$$

where E is region-specific expenditure (and income), π is the northern rental rate of K, n and n^* are the mass (number) of north and south varieties, w_L is the northern wage, and μ is the expenditure share on manufactured goods (μ is a mnemonic for manufactures). In the Dixit–Stiglitz monopolistic competition setting, free and instantaneous entry drives pure profits to zero, so E includes only factor income.

As usual, Dixit–Stiglitz monopolistic competition and (3.5) imply that 'mill pricing' is optimal for industrial firms, so the ratio of the price of a northern variety in its local and export markets is just τ (see Chapter 2 and its appendix for details). Thus,

$$p = \frac{w_L a_m}{1 - 1/\sigma}, \quad p^* = \frac{\tau w_L a_m}{1 - 1/\sigma} \tag{3.6}$$

Notice the way in which this differs from the corresponding pricing rules in the CP model. In the CP model, the marginal cost of industrial firms—and thus the price of industrial goods—depended on the wage earned by the mobile factor. Except in special cases, for example, perfectly symmetric regions, these factor prices were not equalized across regions, so the producer prices of industrial goods were not equalized internationally. In the FC model, the marginal cost of industrial firms involves only the immobile factor whose reward is equalized internationally by free trade in the A good. As a consequence, we have that producer prices are equalized in the industrial sector as well so consumer prices vary only with trade costs. Isomorphic mill-pricing rules hold for southern industrial firms.

The Mobile Factor's Reward. Since physical capital is used only in the fixed cost component of industrial production, the reward to capital is the Ricardian surplus of a typical variety, that is, the operating profit of a typical variety.[3] Under Dixit–Stiglitz competition, this operating profit is simply the value of sales divided by σ (see Chapter 2 and its appendix for details). In symbols, this means $\pi = px/\sigma$, where x is the scale of production, and an analogous expression holds for the southern operating profit, π^*. Using the demand function and mill pricing, we can write these equilibrium expressions for π and π^* as

$$\pi = bB\frac{E^w}{K^w}, \quad \pi^* = bB^*\frac{E^w}{K^w}; \quad b \equiv \frac{\mu}{\sigma} \tag{3.7}$$

where the B's (mnemonics for biases in sales) are

$$B \equiv \frac{s_E}{\Delta} + \phi\frac{s_E^*}{\Delta^*}, \quad B^* \equiv \phi\frac{s_E}{\Delta} + \frac{s_E^*}{\Delta^*}$$

$$\Delta \equiv s_n + \phi(1 - s_n), \quad \Delta^* \equiv \phi s_n + 1 - s_n$$

and E^w is world expenditure with s_E and $s_E^* \equiv 1 - s_E$ being the north's and the south's share of it; Δ is the denominator of the north's demand function, Δ^* is the southern equivalent, and s_n is the north's share of industry. Note that with one unit of

---

[3] Since each unit of capital can be used to produce one industrial variety, the reward to capital would be bid up to the point where it equalled operating profit.

capital per variety, s_n is both the north's share of industry and its share of world capital employed in the north while $n^w = K^w$.

As (3.7) shows, the mobile factor's reward depends upon the spatial distribution of industry s_n (which is taken as exogenous in the short run) and the spatial distribution of expenditure, namely s_E. Since capital reward is the key to capital flows and these in turn are the key to industrial agglomeration in the FC model, our next task is to characterize s_E.

We start with s_E's denominator, E^w. To find world expenditure, E^w, we note that with Cobb–Douglas preferences, total worldwide spending on industrial goods equals μE^w and since mill pricing with a constant mark-up implies that operating profit is simply the value of sales times $1/\sigma$, a straightforward manipulation of (3.7) reveals that the total payment to capital worldwide is bE^w, where E^w is the worldwide sum of factor income.[4] Employing this result in the definition of E^w, we get $E^w = w_L L^w + bE^w$, which solves to

$$E^w = \frac{w_L L^w}{1 - b} \qquad (3.8)$$

Since there is no savings in this model, expenditure and income are identical.

To finish our calculation of relative market size, we need north's income/expenditure, E. Labour is immobile so the labour-income part of E is easy; it equals $w_L L$. North's capital income is trickier. Since the distribution of firms is fixed in the short run, and may thus deviate from 1/2, the reward to capital will in general differ between regions (from (3.7) $\pi \neq \pi^*$ when $s_n \neq 1/2$ and $s_E \neq 1/2$). This, in turn, means that we have to know where north's capital is working to evaluate north's capital income. In the spirit of symmetry we make the straightforward assumption that half of the capital in each region belongs to northern capital owners regardless of s_n. That is, even if only a quarter of world capital is working in the south, we assume that half of that quarter comes from northern capital owners and half comes from southern capital owners. The ramification is that north's capital earns the world average reward. Now, an important simplifying feature of the FC model is that capital's average reward is constant regardless of the spatial allocation of industry and the degree of openness. The point is straightforward. Total payment to capital worldwide equals bE^w, where $b \equiv \mu/\sigma$, so the average operating profit per variety equals bE^w/K^w. Putting together the labour and capital earnings, $E = w_L s_L L^w + bs_K E^w$. Dividing by E^w and using (3.8), we get

$$s_E = (1 - b)s_L + bs_K, \quad s_L \equiv \frac{L}{L^w}, \quad s_K \equiv \frac{K}{K^w} \qquad (3.9)$$

where $s_L = s_K = s_E = 1/2$ in the symmetric-region case.

---

[4] For instance, using the pricing rule (3.6) for local sales, that is, $p(1 - 1/\sigma) = w_L a_m$, operating profit earned on local sales x_h—which is defined as $(p - w_L a_m)x_h$—equals px_h/σ. Doing the same for export sales and adding the two expressions yields px/σ as total operating profit.

A number of points concerning (3.9) are worth highlighting. First, the south's expenditure share, s_E^* is just $1 - s_E$. Second, north's expenditure share is a weighted average of its endowment shares of world labour and of world capital. The weighting factor, $b \equiv \mu/\sigma$, is increasing in the share of spending in industry and in the degree of market power in industry (as measured by the operating profit margin $1/\sigma$). Thus, when b is large, relative market size is determined mainly by the spatial distribution of capital owners, while labour owners are crucial for small values of b. This can be explained by the fact that, while in the former case capital reward is small, in the latter it is large due to sizeable expenditures on industrial goods. Finally, it is important to note that (3.9) implies that in the FC model, production shifting, namely changes in s_n, does not lead to expenditure shifting, namely changes in s_E. The reason, of course, is that capital's owners are immobile and earning the average reward, so the regional distribution of capital-income spending is unaffected by where capital is employed.

For completeness, we work out the equilibrium firm size even though this plays no explicit role in the analysis. Using (3.5) and the fact that $\pi = px/\sigma$, the equilibrium firm size is $(\sigma - 1)\pi/w_L a_m$. Note that as capital gets more expensive relative to labour, firms must sell more to cover the fixed cost. Thus, firm size increases with the ratio of K to L rewards. As we shall see below when we consider the long-run equilibrium, capital mobility ensures that π/w_L is equalized across regions and that neither π nor w_L change with trade costs or the spatial allocation of industry. As a consequence, firm size in the FC model is equalized across regions and invariant to policy changes.

3.2.3 Choice of Numeraire and Units

As in the CP model, appropriate normalization and choice of numeraire can 'clean' unenlightening complications from the equilibrium expressions. Indeed, most of the normalizations we choose for the FC model are identical to those we imposed on the CP model. However, again as in the CP model, we note that these are simply normalizations; interested readers can carry through all of the calculations below without them.

The A-sector good is chosen as numeraire, and we choose units of A such that $a_A = 1$, so $p_A = p_A^* = w_L = w_L^* = 1$. In the industrial sector, we measure output in units such that a_m equals $(1 - 1/\sigma)$, so the producer price for a typical industrial variety is $p = w_L = 1$ and its export-market consumer price is $p^* = \tau w_L = \tau$. We choose the world capital endowment, K^w, such that $K^w = 1$.[5] With one unit of capital per variety, this implies that the total measure (number) of varieties is unity (i.e. $n^w = 1$). The fact that $n + n^* = 1$ is useful in manipulating expressions. For instance, instead of writing s_n for the share of K^w employed in the north, we could write n.[6] Also, as (3.8) shows, E^w is proportional to L^w with $w_L = 1$. It

---

[5] See Chapter 2, Box 2.2, for a discussion of this kind of normalization.

[6] The notation s_n is more self-explanatory, but n is easier to write. In the policy chapters we often use n in preference to s_n in order to keep expressions tight.

proves convenient to have E^w equal to unity, so we choose units of labour such that L^w equals $1 - b$. Summarizing,

$$p = 1, \quad p^* = \tau, \quad p_A = p_A^* = w_L = w_L^* = 1, \quad n^w \equiv n + n^* = 1,$$

$$K^w \equiv K + K^* = 1, \quad n = s_n, \quad n^* = 1 - s_n, \quad L^w = 1 - b, \quad E^w = 1 \tag{3.10}$$

The only difference between these normalizations and those in the CP model is that here $E^w = 1$, so s_E is both the north's level of expenditure and its share of E^w.

We turn now to the long-run equilibrium location of firms.

3.2.4 Long-Run Equilibrium

In the long run, capital is mobile, so in addition to all the short-run equilibrium conditions mentioned above, the long-run equilibrium requires that capital migration stops. Formally, such equilibria are the steady states of the capital flow equation, (3.4).

THE LOCATION CONDITION

Inspection of the capital flow equation, (3.4), shows that there are two types of long-run equilibria: (1) interior outcomes where capital earns the same reward in both regions; and (2) core–periphery outcomes ($s_n = 0$ or $s_n = 1$). Thus, the no-capital-flow condition, which we call the 'location condition', is that either

$$\pi = \pi^*, \quad 0 < s_n < 1 \tag{3.11}$$

where π and π^* are given by (3.7), or $s_n = 0$ or $s_n = 1$.

To characterize the long-run equilibria, we must solve the location condition for the geographical division of the mobile factor between north and south, that is, s_n. While this was an impossible task in the CP model, it is trivial in the FC model. Using (3.7), the division of capital employment between the regions, namely s_n, that equates π and π^* is

$$s_n = \frac{1}{2} + \left(\frac{1 + \phi}{1 - \phi}\right)\left(s_E - \frac{1}{2}\right) \tag{3.12}$$

where this is valid as long as it implies an s_n that is economically relevant, that is, $1 \geq s_n \geq 0$. For values of ϕ and s_E that would imply a share below zero or above unity, all industry is clustered in one region; that is, $s_n = 0$ or 1 in the obvious manner. Specifically, (3.12) holds for combinations of ϕ and s_E that respect the condition $s_E \in [\phi/(1 + \phi), 1/(1 + \phi)]$; when $s_E < \phi/(1 + \phi)$, s_n is zero and when $s_E > 1/(1 + \phi)$, s_n is one.

In most economic geography models, we cannot obtain a closed-form solution for the endogenous variable that most interests us—the spatial division of industry as measured by s_n. Given the FC model's simplicity, however, such a closed-form expression for s_n is possible. Substituting (3.9) into (3.12), we get

$$s_n = \frac{1}{2} + \frac{1+\phi}{1-\phi}\left[(1-b)\left(s_L - \frac{1}{2}\right) + b\left(s_K - \frac{1}{2}\right)\right] \qquad (3.13)$$

Since this variable—the spatial division of industry—is at the heart of our concerns, the fact that it can be expressed as a simple, closed-form function of trade openness and factor endowments proves to be a great asset in policy analysis.

While (3.13) provides a full characterization of industrial location in this model, intuition for how the FC model works is bolstered by examining the key equilibrium expressions verbally and diagrammatically.

DIAGRAMMATIC SOLUTION

Analysis of the model is easily illustrated with the help of Figure 3.2. The figure plots the north's expenditure share s_E on the horizontal axis and the north's share of industry s_n on the vertical axis.

The Scissors Diagram. The two key equilibrium expressions are the location condition, which shows us how the spatial distribution of industry depends upon the spatial distribution of expenditure, and the relative market size condition, which shows us how the spatial distribution of expenditure depends on the spatial allocation of industry. The relative market size condition is given by (3.9), and, for interior equilibria, the location condition solves to (3.12).

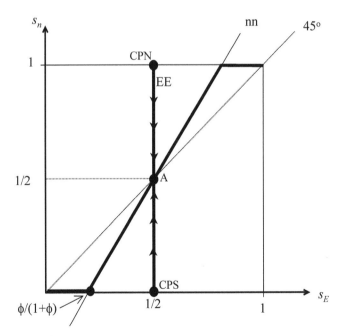

Figure 3.2 The scissor diagram for the FC model.

Expressions (3.12) and (3.9) are plotted as heavy solid lines, with (3.12) labelled nn, and (3.9) labelled as EE. The nn schedule shows how the north's share of industry changes with its share of expenditure. Notice that it is linear and its slope equals $(1 + \phi)/(1 - \phi)$, which means it gets steeper as trade gets freer, and it intersects the y-axis at $\phi/(1 + \phi)$. Moreover, it always passes through the point $(1/2, 1/2)$ regardless of the level of trade freeness, so changes in ϕ rotate nn around the midpoint. Importantly, the nn line is always steeper than the 45 degree ray, since $(1 + \phi)/(1 - \phi) > 1$. This is the 'home-market effect' diagrammatically, that is, a given change in market size leads to a more than proportional change in the share of industry in the big region. The shape of the EE curve is even simpler. In the symmetric-sized regions case that we focus on here, $s_E = 1/2$ regardless of s_n, so EE is a vertical line.

It is important to note that the EE line represents a *definition*, so the economy must *always* be on it—in both the short run and in the long run. The nn line, by contrast, represents the long-run equilibrium condition, so any long-run equilibrium must be on the nn line, but the economy may be off it in the short run.

Dynamics.   At all points to the right of the nn line, we have $\pi > \pi^*$ since for such points, the northern market is too large for rental rates to be equal and, following the logic of the market-access effect, this implies that capital's reward is higher in the north. Given this, capital and firms tend to flow northwards (thus raising s_n) if the economy finds itself at a point to the right of the nn line. For points to the left of the nn line, s_n is falling. Since we also know that the economy is always on the EE line, the facts that at the midpoint the nn line has a positive slope and the EE line has a negative slope (for any level of openness short of perfect openness, i.e. $\phi = 1$) imply that the symmetric outcome is always stable. This is illustrated by the arrows drawn on the EE line. This stability, of course, implies that the FC model never displays the spectacular catastrophes of the CP model.

FORCES AT WORK

Expressions (3.7) and (3.9) give the rental rates of capital in the two regions as functions of the spatial distribution of firms (s_n), workers (s_L), and capital owners (s_K). As Ottaviano (2001) shows, the resulting rental rate differential is zero/positive/negative when the right-hand side of the following expression is zero/positive/negative, that is,

$$\operatorname{sgn}(\pi - \pi^*) = (1 - \phi)\operatorname{sgn}\left\{(1 + \phi)\left(s_E - \frac{1}{2}\right) - (1 - \phi)\left(s_n - \frac{1}{2}\right)\right\} \quad (3.14)$$

where s_E is related to s_L and s_K by (3.9). When trade is perfectly free ($\phi = 1$), the right-hand side is always zero, which implies that rental rates are the same everywhere whatever the geographical distribution of firms. As intuition would have it, with no trade costs, the location of firms is immaterial.

More interestingly, when trade is not perfectly free ($\phi < 1$), expression (3.14) reveals that the pressure for firms to relocate is driven by the interaction of two opposing forces—the market-access effect and the market-crowding effect.

Market-Access Effect. The first term inside the curly brackets shows how the spatial distribution of expenditure affects the spatial distribution of firms. Since $(1 + \phi)$ is positive, this shows the market-access advantage of producing in the larger market in the presence of trade barriers. This is the sole agglomeration force in the model, that is, the sole effect that promotes agglomeration.

Market-Crowding Effect. The second term inside the curly brackets depends, instead, on the international distribution of firms s_n. Since $-(1 - \phi)$ is negative, this shows the market-crowding disadvantage of being in the region with the larger number of firms. This is the sole dispersion force in the model, that is, the only effect that counteracts agglomeration.

Recalling the definition of trade freeness $\phi = \tau^{1-\sigma}$, (3.14) shows that the weight of the access advantage with respect to the crowding disadvantage grows as the own- and cross-price elasticity of demand σ fall. In particular, the smaller the elasticity, the smaller is the relative weight of market crowding. The weight also rises as trade costs τ decrease. The reason is that, with lower trade costs, a larger fraction of a firm's operating profits is independent of the location of competitors. Thus, the lower the elasticity of demand and trade costs, the stronger is the pull of firms towards the region hosting the larger number of consumers. Notice, however, that when regional expenditures are the same, $s_E = 1/2$ and this force disappears.

3.2.5 Local Stability Analysis

The standard analysis of economic geography models requires us to find two critical levels of trade openness: (1) the level of openness where the symmetric equilibrium becomes unstable (break point); and (2) the openness where the core–periphery outcome becomes stable (sustain point). The FC model is simple enough to determine these two levels algebraically. Nevertheless, comparability across models and intuition are served by using the same methods we employed in studying the CP model.

To start with, we differentiate the mobile-factor reward-gap, $\pi - \pi^*$, to study the system's local stability at various long-run equilibria. Differentiating the gap and evaluating it at the symmetric equilibrium, we obtain

$$d(\pi - \pi^*)|_{s_E = s_n = 1/2} = 4b\left(\frac{1 - \phi}{1 + \phi}\right)ds_E - 4b\left(\frac{1 - \phi}{1 + \phi}\right)^2 dn \qquad (3.15)$$

where $ds_E = (\partial s_E / \partial s_n)dn$. Since capital owners are immobile and profits are repatriated, we have $\partial s_E / \partial s_n = 0$. Consequently, the destabilizing expenditure shifting effect does not operate. This leaves only the stabilizing market-crowding effect, so the symmetric outcome is always stable as long as trade is not perfectly free. If trade is fully free, $\phi = 1$, we see that industrial relocation (i.e. ds_n) has no effect on the reward gap. This means that when the movement of goods is entirely unrestricted, location is irrelevant, so any spatial allocation of industry is a long-run equilibrium. In other words, the break point in the symmetric-region FC model is $\phi = 1$.

This stability result is easy to understand from Figure 3.2. Given the relative slopes of the EE and nn lines, a small positive 'migration shock', that is, an increase in s_n, takes the economy to a point that is to the left of the nn line. At such points, $\pi < \pi^*$, so the initial shock would generate self-correcting capital flows. The opposite happens for negative migration shocks, so the symmetric outcome is stable as long as the nn line has a non-infinite slope.

Next we investigate the sustainability of the core–periphery outcome; take the core-in-the-north case to be concrete. Thus, we evaluate the reward gap at $s_n = 1$ and $s_E = 1/2$, to find

$$\pi - \pi^*|_{s_n=1} = -b \frac{(1 - \phi)^2}{2\phi} \tag{3.16}$$

What this says is that, when all industry is in the north, the southern reward to capital is always higher for any level of openness short of perfectly free trade. In other words, the sustain point in the symmetric-region FC model is $\phi = 1$.

This sustainability result is easy to understand from Figure 3.2. Again, given the relative slopes of the EE and nn lines, the core-in-the-north outcome, marked as CPN in the diagram, is always to the left of the nn line, so we know that $\pi < \pi^*$ at CPN for any level of openness short of perfect free trade. What this means is that there will always be a tendency for the system to move from CPN to the symmetric outcome, as long as $\phi < 1$.

The fact that the sustain point and break point are identical and coincide with free trade means that the symmetric-region FC model is rather uninteresting. Indeed, the FC model only comes into its own when we allow for regional asymmetries, including different degrees of openness, different sizes and different relative factor abundances. These issues are explored at length in the policy applications in later chapters; they are also explored more systematically in the appendix.

3.2.6 The Tomahawk Diagram

As we have seen, the model has one interior equilibrium—the symmetric outcome $s_n = 1/2$—and two core–periphery (CP) equilibria, $s_n = 0$ and $s_n = 1$. Thus, the symmetric FC model, unlike the symmetric CP model, never has more than one interior equilibrium. The Tomahawk diagram for the FC model is quite simple as Figure 3.3 shows. The symmetric outcome is locally stable for all ϕ up to $\phi = 1$, at which point any spatial distribution of industry becomes locally stable. Thus, the 'tomahawk' diagram for the FC model looks like a pickaxe.

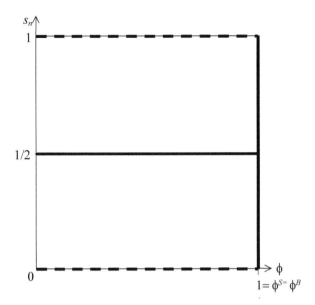

Figure 3.3   The tomahawk diagram for the FC model.

3.3 KEY FEATURES

Chapter 2 pointed out seven key features of the CP model: agglomeration via the home-market mechanism (with magnification by freer trade), demand and cost linkages, endogenous asymmetry, catastrophic agglomeration, locational hysteresis, hump-shaped agglomeration rents, and multiple long run equilibria in the 'overlap'. In comparing the FC model with the CP model, we discuss such features first and then we turn to new properties.

3.3.1 Comparison with the CP Model

To maintain comparability with the previous chapter on the CP model, and to present the model as simply as possible, we have so far only considered perfectly symmetric regions. As it turns out, the FC model is not very exciting in this knife-edge case. Indeed, with perfect symmetry, it displays few of the most interesting aspects of the CP model. Allowing for even small asymmetries, however, restores many CP-like features. In this section we mention these even though this anticipates the discussion in the appendix.

HOME-MARKET MAGNIFICATION

Agglomeration may be defined as the tendency of spatially concentrated economic activity to create forces that encourage further spatial concentration of economic activity. The FC model does display such a force in the form of the home-market effect. To stress this, we calculate the degree of relocation that is induced by a small, exogenous change in the location of expenditures. If the relocation of industry is *more than proportional* to the exogenous shift, spatial concentration of economic activity generates forces that encourage further concentration. Expression (3.15) shows the results of the total differentiation. Since firms move to equalize rental rates, we set $d(\pi - \pi^*) = 0$ and solve for dn/ds_E. The result is

$$d(\pi - \pi^*)|_{s_E=s_n=1/2} = 0 \quad \Rightarrow \quad \frac{dn}{ds_E} = \frac{(1 - \phi)/(1 - \phi)}{[(1 - \phi)/(1 + \phi)]^2} \qquad (3.17)$$

This exceeds unity for positive trade costs, so the home-market effect is indeed in operation. Moreover, the home-market effect gets more powerful as trade gets freer, so the FC model also displays home-market magnification.

Plainly, we could simplify the expression for dn/ds_E to $(1 + \phi)/(1 - \phi)$, however, intuition is served by showing that the home-market effect is the ratio of the market-access advantage and the market-crowding disadvantage. While freer trade reduces the strength of both, freer trade weakens the market-crowding effect much faster. As a consequence, when trade is quite free, a much larger relocation of firms is required to re-equalize rental rates after a given shock to the market-access advantage. This is the deep fundamentals of the home-market magnification effect.

CIRCULAR CAUSALITY

The FC model features neither demand-linked nor cost-linked circular caus-ality. The demand linkage is ruled out since all capital income is repatriated—expenditure shifting can lead to production shifting, but production shifting does not lead to expenditure shifting. The cost linkage is ruled out since physical capital is attracted by rewards defined in terms of the numeraire rather than rewards deflated by the local price index. Thus, while production shifting does have a cost-of-living effect, this does not in turn encourage further production shifting.

ENDOGENOUS ASYMMETRY

As we have seen, the symmetric-region FC model does not produce endogenous asymmetry. However, we would observe something akin to this for almost symmetric regions (see appendix for details).

CATASTROPHIC AGGLOMERATION

If one considers only the knife-edge case of perfectly symmetric regions, the FC model does not feature catastrophic agglomeration driven by lower trade costs. That is, a symmetric lowering of trade costs between perfectly symmetric regions never leads to a concentration of industry in one region. However, as soon as one allows for $s_E \neq 1/2$, trade-induced agglomeration does appear. And indeed, we get something akin to catastrophic agglomeration—what has been called 'near-catastrophic agglomeration' (Baldwin 1999). The reason is that, with low trade costs, capital is extremely footloose, so even small size asymmetries can trigger huge spatial reallocations.

LOCATIONAL HYSTERESIS

The FC model never features multiple locally stable equilibria, so hysteresis is not a possibility.

HUMP-SHAPED AGGLOMERATION RENTS

In the perfectly symmetric FC model, full agglomeration is only a long-run equilibrium when trade is costless (i.e. $\phi = 1$) and in this case, location has no ramifications. However, if factor endowments are even slightly asymmetric, then full agglomeration in the big region is a long-run equilibrium when trade is sufficiently free (see appendix for details). In this case, agglomeration rents in the FC model are a concave function of trade freeness just as they were in the CP model. This can be seen by considering a long-run equilibrium in which all capital is employed in the north ($s_E > 1/2$, $s_n = 1$ and $\phi^{CP} \leq \phi \leq 1$ where $\phi^{CP} = (1 - s_E)/s_E$, see Appendix 3.A). The agglomeration rents are then measured as the loss that a capital owner would incur by relocating its capital to the south. Formally, such rents are given by

$$\pi - \pi^*|_{s_n=1} = b\left\{1 - \left[\frac{1}{\phi}(1 - s_E) + \phi s_E\right]\right\} \qquad (3.18)$$

This is a function of ϕ. It equals zero at $\phi = \phi^{CP}$ and $\phi = 1$, while it is positive in between. Moreover, in the same interval, it is concave with a maximum at $\phi = \sqrt{\phi^{CP}}$, where ϕ^{CP} is the threshold freeness defined in the appendix. Accordingly, as trade gets freer (i.e. ϕ rises from ϕ^{CP} towards 1), the agglomeration rents first rise and then fall ('hump shape').

THE OVERLAP AND SELF-FULFILLING EXPECTATIONS

The absence of circular causality implies that the break and sustain points are both equal to 1 in the symmetric FC model. Thus, in the FC model there is no overlap.

3.3.2 New Features

The key new feature of the FC model is its tractability. There are also a number of features that depend upon asymmetric regions, but we relegate discussion of these to the appendix where such asymmetries are considered.

3.4 CONCLUDING REMARKS AND RELATED LITERATURE

3.4.1 Summary Results for Policy Modelling

The FC model has the great merit of displaying agglomeration forces while still being fully solvable in the sense that we get a closed-form solution for the location of industry (i.e. s_n). Indeed, the main expressions are linear, so we can solve the model while allowing for a wide range of regional asymmetries, including asymmetries in size, factor endowments and trade costs.

The FC model does not, however, display the threshold dynamics and locational hysteresis of the CP model. Analytically solvable models displaying such properties are the subject of the next chapters.

3.4.2 Related Literature

The FC model deals with the location of an industry when the spatial distribution of consumers is fixed, a topic investigated by Lösch (1940) and extensively studied in location theory since then. The central model featuring the home-market effect can be found in Krugman (1980). It differs from the FC model by Martin and Rogers (1995) only in that it assumes a unique immobile production factor and location is driven by firms creation/destruction rather than capital movements.

The central model has been amended under several ways. Krugman (1993) can be used to show that, in an economy with more than two countries, the home-market effect has no straightforward definition because there is no obvious benchmark against which to measure the 'more than proportionate' presence of imperfectly competitive firms.[7] Helpman (1990) specifies the demand conditions under which the home-market effect materializes: the cross-elasticity between varieties of the differentiated good must be larger than the overall price elasticity of demand for the differentiated good as a whole. Davis (1998) points out that, when transportation costs on perfectly competitive goods are considered, the home-market effect may disappear. Feenstra et al. (1998) show that there is nothing crucial in monopolistic competition per se in that the home-market effect can be expected even in homogenous-good sectors with restricted entry. Head et al. (2002) point out that, when goods are differentiated according to their place of production (Armington 1969), the home-market effect may again vanish. Finally, Ludema and Wooton (2000) present another tractable geography model based on homogenous product oligopoly.

APPENDIX 3.A: FC MODEL WITH EXOGENOUS ASYMMETRIES

The FC model's tractability permits us to analytically consider regional asymmetries. This is important in the policy chapters since much interest lies in

---

[7] As pointed out by Ottaviano and Thisse (2003), the home-market effect may be seen as extending the idea of a dominant place in Weber's (1909) transport cost minimization problem. Then, existing results in location theory (Beckmann and Thisse 1986) and traditional economic geography (Thomas 2002) suggest, in the multi-country case, the existence of a hierarchy of national markets, which depends on both the size of these markets and their relative position within the space economy.

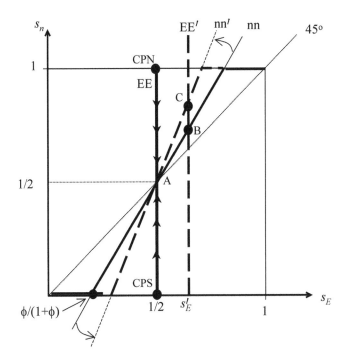

Figure 3.4   The scissors diagram for the asymmetric FC model.

situations where the two regions maintain different levels of taxes, trade barriers, infrastructure subsidies, etc.

3.A.1 Size asymmetry

When one region is larger, for example, when the north is bigger so $s_E' > 1/2$ as in Figure 3.4, the interior equilibrium is still unique and stable (unique since the nn and EE' are linear and stable since EE' is steeper). Since the nn line is always steeper than the 45 degree ray, the corresponding share of firms is $s_n' > s_E' > 1/2$. As already argued, this is the so-called 'home-market effect': a given change in expenditures leads to a more than proportional change in the share of industry in the big region.

For given expenditures, changing trade costs have an effect on industry location as (3.12) shows. That is, as trade gets freer, s_n rises and reaches the CP outcome, $s_n = 1$, before trade is fully free. Figure 3.4 shows this clearly. When north is larger, so EE' and nn are the relevant schedules, the long-run spatial division of industry is shown by the point B when the level of openness is ϕ. If openness increases (symmetrically) to, say, ϕ', the nn line rotates to nn'—see (3.12)—and the allocation of industry shifts towards the north, that is, to point C. Further liberalization continues to favour the large region until the core-in-the-north outcome is attained.

More carefully, we solve (3.12) for $s_n = 1$ to find the critical level of ϕ, beyond which all industry is in the north. This is

$$\phi^{CP} = \frac{1 - s_E}{s_E} \tag{3.A.1}$$

Also note that the magnification effect of lower trade costs on the relocation elasticity ('home-market magnification') can also be seen in (3.12). That is, a given increase in market size will result in a larger relocation when trade is freer.

3.A.2 Asymmetric Trade Costs

We consider asymmetries in trade cost by allowing the north's trade freeness parameter to differ from that of the south. We refer to the north's as ϕ and the south's as ϕ^*; when $\phi < \phi^*$, it is cheaper for northern firms to export to the southern market than for southern firms to export to the northern market. Carefully tracing through the impact of this change on the mill pricing of north and south firms and thus on operating profit, we can easily establish the more general version of the wage equations given by (3.7) for the symmetric ϕ case:

$$\pi = bB, \quad \pi^* = bB^*; \quad b \equiv \frac{\mu}{\sigma} \tag{3.A.2}$$

where we have used our normalizations of $E^W = K^W = 1$ to simplify the expressions and the B's are now

$$B \equiv \frac{s_E}{\Delta} + \phi^* \frac{s_E^*}{\Delta^*}, \quad B^* \equiv \phi \frac{s_E}{\Delta} + \frac{s_E^*}{\Delta^*}$$

$$\Delta \equiv s_n + \phi(1 - s_n), \quad \Delta^* \equiv \phi^* s_n + 1 - s_n$$

There is a unique solution to the location condition $\pi = \pi^*$, namely

$$s_n = \frac{1}{2} + \frac{(s_E - 1/2)(1 - \phi\phi^*) - 1/2(\phi - \phi^*)}{(1 - \phi)(1 - \phi^*)} \tag{3.A.3}$$

This is valid for ϕ's where s_n lies between zero and unity; for ϕ's outside this range, the left-hand side is either zero or unity as appropriate. The expression shows the role of both size asymmetries ($s_E \neq 1/2$) and trade costs asymmetric ($\phi \neq \phi^*$) for location.

Stability of the interior equilibrium is evaluated by differentiating $\pi - \pi^*$ with respect to s_n. Performing the differentiation and evaluating the result at the equilibrium s_n given by (3.A.3) yields $d(\pi - \pi^*)/ds_n = -b(1 - \phi^*)^2(1 - \phi)^2/[s_E(1 - s_E)(1 - \phi\phi^*)^2]$. Plainly this is negative or zero for all permissible values, so the interior equilibrium is always stable.

3.A.3 Asymmetric Factor Endowments and Capital Flows

The model can also easily handle regions that are asymmetric in terms of their K versus L endowments. Indeed, the case is already implicit in (3.13). One interesting question in such cases is the direction of capital flows, which boils down to the sign of $s_n - s_K$. If this difference is positive, north employs more of the world's capital than it owns, so it must be a capital importer. If the difference is negative, it is an exporter.

From the reasoning above, we know that if north is bigger but $s_L = s_K = s_E$, then north will be a capital importer (this is the home-market effect). An interesting case is when north is both larger and relatively well endowed with capital, that is, $s_K > s_E > 1/2$. In this case, the north's relative abundance of capital tends to offset the home-market effect (Baldwin and Robert-Nicoud 2000). In particular, manipulating (3.9) and (3.12) yields

$$s_n - s_K = \frac{2\phi}{1 - \phi}\left(s_E - \frac{1}{2}\right) + (s_E - s_K) \qquad (3.A.4)$$

This shows that if north's factor endowment is sufficiently skewed towards capital, then the north may be a capital exporter despite the home-market effect. However, the home-market effect will eventually dominate for sufficiently low trade costs.

3.A.4 New Features

While the FC model displays only a few of the CP model's key features, it does allow consideration of a novel phenomenon. This stems from the fact that, in the FC model, the mobile factor can be spatially separated from its owner. In particular, when capital is mobile and one region starts out richer than the other, then changing trade costs can alter the size and even the direction of capital flows.

TRADE DEPENDENT FACTOR FLOWS

To study this, suppose the two regions are equal in their fundamental size, that is, s_L equals 1/2 but the north just happens to start with a higher capital/labour ratio, that is, $s_K > 1/2$. This is the same as saying that the north is richer than the south since the higher capital/labour ratio implies a higher per capita income. Rearranging (3.13), we get a relation between the share of firms located in the north and the share of firms owned by northerners:

$$\frac{s_n - 1/2}{s_K - 1/2} = b\frac{1 + \phi}{1 - \phi} \qquad (3.A.5)$$

This allows us to answer the following question: 'What is the difference between the geography of capital ownership and the geography of production?' Or more formally, 'What is the difference between the share of firms owned by the North s_K and the share of firms producing in the north s_n and how does freeing trade change this?'

In the symmetric equilibrium, where both regions are endowed originally with the same amount of capital, there is no relocation, of course. If the initial distribution of capital is such that $s_K > 1/2$, so that the north is richer than the south, then the direction of the capital flows is ambiguous and depends on trade costs. When trade costs are very high, namely ϕ is near zero, the rich region's share of industry is less than its share of capital. In other words, when goods markets are not very integrated, but capital markets are, capital will flow from the rich region to the poor region. But when trade gets freer than a certain critical value, the direction of capital flows is reversed; s_n will exceed s_K, so the poor region will be a net exporter of capital. The threshold value of trade freeness is

$$\phi^K = \frac{1-b}{1+b}, \quad b \equiv \frac{\mu}{\sigma} \tag{3.A.6}$$

Thus, the level of trade freeness where capital flows are reversed decreases with the strength of the agglomeration forces, as measured by b.

The ambiguity of the direction of relocation is due to the opposite effects of market crowding and market access. The former makes the poor capital region attractive because firms installed there face less competition. The latter, which in this context can be thought of also as a capital-income effect, makes the capital rich region attractive because it represents a larger market given its high level of income and expenditure. The market-crowding effect dominates when trade is quite restricted (ϕ is low) because the southern market is well protected from northern competition. The market-crowding effect also dominates when capital's share of income is low relative to labour income so that the capital-income effect is small.[8]

NEAR-CATASTROPHIC AGGLOMERATION

The symmetric opening of trade produces a gradual relocation of firms to the north when $s_E > 1/2$, as inspection of (3.12) reveals. An important feature of the model is the so-called near-catastrophic agglomeration. Observe that the rate of relocation gets very large when the regions are only slightly different in size and ϕ approaches ϕ^{CP} (the level of trade costs at which full agglomeration of industry first occurs). To see this, we note that the fundamental metric for catastrophic agglomeration is the percent change in s_n with respect to a percent change in the freeness of trade, or $(ds_n/d\phi)(\phi/s_n)$ in symbols. In the CP model in which agglomeration is catastrophic, this 'delocation elasticity' switches from zero to infinite at the break point. From (3.12), we can calculate such elasticity for the FC model. This yields

$$\frac{ds_n/s_n}{d\phi/\phi} = \frac{2\phi(s_E - 1/2)}{(1-\phi)[s_E(1+\phi) - \phi]}, \quad \frac{ds_n/s_n}{d\phi/\phi}\bigg|_{\phi=\phi^{CP}} = \frac{s_E(1-s_E)}{2(s_E - 1/2)} \tag{3.A.7}$$

The first expression shows that with $s_E = 1/2$, the delocation elasticity is always zero. It also shows that, if $s_E > 1/2$, the elasticity is positive. The second expres-

---

[8] Thus, the asymmetric FC model provides an answer to the question raised by Lucas (1990): "Why doesn't capital flow from rich to poor countries?" The answer is the same as Lucas's and stresses the importance of 'local enough' (p. 94) external economies that make capital more profitable in rich countries. The difference is that, while the FC model focuses on pecuniary externalities (market-access effect), Lucas's approach highlights technological externalities (knowledge spillovers).

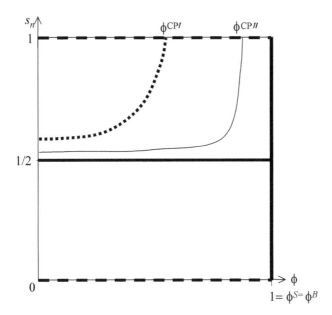

Figure 3.5   The tomahawk diagram for the asymmetric FC model.

sion is the elasticity evaluated at ϕ^{CP}, where this is defined by (3.A.1). In the tomahawk diagram for the asymmetric region case (Figure 3.5), this is the slope of the dotted line at the point where it meets the $s_n = 1$ line at $\phi^{CP\prime}$. The full line which crosses the $s_n = 1$ one at $\phi^{CP\prime\prime}$ represents a case where s_E is closer to 1/2. This shows that the elasticity evaluated at the point where full agglomeration first occurs approaches infinity as the two regions become nearly equal in size.

REFERENCES

Armington, P. 1969. A theory of demand for products distinguished by place of production. *IMF Staff Papers* 16: 159–176.

Baldwin, Richard E. 1999. Agglomeration and endogenous capital. *European Economic Review* 43: 253–280.

Baldwin, Richard E. and F. Robert-Nicoud. 2000. Free trade agreements without delocation. *Canadian Journal of Economics* 33(3).

Beckmann, M. J. and J.-F. Thisse. 1986. The location of production activities. In *Handbook of Regional and Urban Economics*, Volume 1, ed. P. Nijkamp. Amsterdam: North-Holland, 21–95.

Davis, D. R. 1998. The home market effect, trade, and industrial structure. *American Economic Review* 88: 1264–1276.

Feenstra, R. C., J. R. Markusen and A. K. Rose. 1998. Understanding the home market effect and the gravity equation: the role of differentiated goods. Discussion Paper No.2035, Centre for Economic Policy Research.

Flam, H. and E. Helpman. 1987. Industrial policy under monopolistic competition. *Journal of International Economics* 22: 79–102.

Head, K., T. Mayer and J. Ries. 2002. On the pervasiveness of the home market effect. *Economica* 69: 371–390.

Helpman, E. 1990. Monopolistic competition in trade theory. Special Paper in International Economics 16, Princeton University, International Finance Section.

Krugman, P. R. 1980. Scale economies, product differentiation, and the pattern of trade. *American Economic Review* 70: 950–959.

_____. 1993. The hub effect: or, threeness in international trade. In *Theory, Policy and Dynamics in International Trade*, ed. W. J. Ethier, E. Helpman and J. P. Neary. Cambridge: Cambridge University Press.

Lösch, A. 1940. *Die Räumliche Ordnung der Wirtschaft*. Jena: Gustav Fischer. English translation: 1954. The Economics of Location. New Haven, CT: Yale University Press.

Lucas, R. E. 1990. Why doesn't capital flow from rich to poor countries? *American Economic Review* 80(Papers and Proceedings): 92–96.

Ludema, R. and I. Wooton. 2000. Economic geography and the fiscal effects of regional integration. *Journal of International Economics* 52: 331–357.

Martin, P. and C. A. Rogers. 1995. Industrial location and public infrastructure. *Journal of International Economics* 39: 335–351.

Ottaviano, G. I. P. 2001. Home market effects and the (in)efficiency of international specialization. Mimeo, Graduate Institute of International Studies.

Ottaviano, G. I. P. and J.-F. Thisse. 2003. Agglomeration and economic geography. In *Handbook of Regional and Urban Economics*, Volume 3, ed. V. Henderson and J.-F. Thisse. Amsterdam: North-Holland, in press.

Thomas, I. 2002. *Transportation Networks and the Optimal Location of Human Activities. A Numerical Geography Approach*. Cheltenham: Edward Elgar.

Weber, A. 1909. *Über den Standort der Industrien*. Tübingen: J. C. B. Mohr. English translation: 1929. The Theory of the Location of Industries. Chicago, IL: Chicago University Press.

The Footloose Entrepreneur Model

4.1 INTRODUCTION

The FC model presented in Chapter 3 redresses the CP model's obdurate intractability by eliminating circular causality. While this permits closed-form solutions for all variables, the natural cost for this tractability is that the FC model displays only some of the key features of the CP model. In particular, the FC model does not allow for catastrophic agglomeration or locational hysteresis.

This chapter presents a model that relies on a much less radical approach to redressing the CP model's intractability. Indeed, the model displays *all* the key features of the CP model while still remaining amenable to analytic reasoning. The model, which we call the 'footloose entrepreneurs' model (FE model for short), was put forth independently by Ottaviano (1996) and Forslid (1999). The version of the model used here is based on Forslid and Ottaviano (2002).

4.1.1 Logic of the FE Model

The FE model may be thought of as the progeny of a marriage between the CP model and the FC model. It resembles the CP model in that the spatial concentration of activity requires labour migration and this migration is driven by real wage differences. As we saw in Chapter 2, such migration is the key to both demand-linked and cost-linked circular causality. When the mobile factor and its owners move together, the model displays demand-linked circular causality (production shifting leads to expenditure shifting which in turn fosters further production shifting). And since the mobile factor judges the attractiveness of locations based on real wages, we get cost-linked circular causality (migration leads to production shifting that changes the relative cost-of-living in the two regions in a way that fosters further migration). Because these two forms of circular causality were responsible for the main features of the CP model, their presence guarantees the existence of these same features in the FE model.

The FE model resembles the FC model in the way the mobile factor is used. A large measure of the FC model's tractability stems from the fact that we can get a closed-form solution for the reward to the mobile factor, and this in turn is due to the assumption that it is used only in meeting the fixed cost of producing a manufactured variety. To profit from this tractability, the FE model makes the same assumption. Indeed, this motivates the moniker 'footloose entrepreneur' model; producing a variety of the industrial good requires one unit of human capital—that is, one entrepreneur—regardless of the firm's output, and thus firms move with their entrepreneur. The consequence is that the FE model shares most of the FC model's tractability. In particular, the FE model allows for closed-form solutions for most endogenous variables and an analytical assessment of the number of equilibria as well as their global stability. We note that the coupling of a higher level of skills with higher interregional mobility is also in line with empirical evidence (Shields and Shields 1989).

4.1.2 Organization of the Chapter

The chapter has three sections after the introduction. Section 4.2 presents the model formally and derives the short-run and long-run equilibrium conditions. Section 4.3 compares the FE and CP models in terms of their key features. Section 4.4 contains our concluding remarks and a brief survey of related literature.

As in the previous chapter, the asymmetric version of the FE model—which is frequently the version we use in the policy chapters—is dealt with in the appendix.

4.2 THE SYMMETRIC FE MODEL

The FE model is almost identical to the CP model presented in Chapter 2, as a comparison between Figure 4.1 and the corresponding figure in Chapter 2 reveals. The only substantial difference lies in the manufacturing sector's production technology. While the CP model assumes a homothetic production function (i.e., fixed and variable costs involve the same factor intensity), the FE model

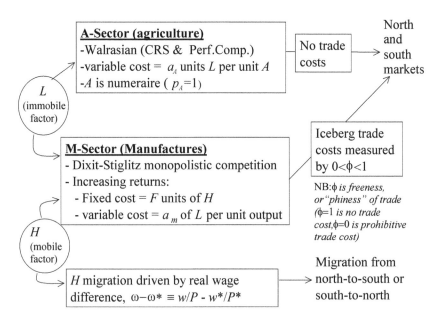

Figure 4.1   Schematic diagram of the FE model.

assumes that the fixed cost and the variable cost are associated with different factors. Specifically, the fixed cost involves only human capital and the variable cost only unskilled labour. We view the fixed cost as R&D activities or head-quarter services, which naturally make it relatively skill intensive.

4.2.1 Assumptions

Most of the formal assumptions of the FE model are the same as those of the CP model, but we repeat them here for completeness. The FE model works with two regions, two sectors and two factors. The two regions, called north and south, are symmetric in terms of tastes, technology, trade costs and endowments. The two sectors are agriculture (A for short) and manufacturing (M or industry for short). The two factors of production are entrepreneurs (H) and workers (L).

The representative consumer in each region has the usual two-tier preferences, with the upper tier consisting of a Cobb–Douglas 'nest' of consumption of the agricultural good and a composite of all industrial goods; this composition is a CES sub-utility function defined over all varieties of industrial goods. In symbols,

$$U = C_M^\mu C_A^{1-\mu}, \quad C_M \equiv \left(\int_{i=0}^{n+n^*} c_i^{1-1/\sigma} di \right)^{1/(1-1/\sigma)} ; \quad 0 < \mu < 1 < \sigma \quad (4.1)$$

where C_M and C_A are, respectively, consumption of the CES composite of industrial varieties and consumption of A. Also, n and n^* are the mass (number) of north and south varieties, μ (a mnemonic for manufacturers' share) is the expenditure share on industrial varieties, and σ is the constant elasticity of substitution between varieties. The corresponding indirect utility functions for typical northern entrepreneurs and workers are ω and ω_L, where

$$\omega \equiv \frac{w}{P}, \quad \omega_L \equiv \frac{w_L}{P}, \quad P \equiv p_A^{1-\mu}(\Delta n^w)^{-a}, \quad \Delta \equiv \frac{\int_{i=0}^{n^w} p_i^{1-\sigma} di}{n^w}, \quad a \equiv \frac{\mu}{\sigma - 1}$$
$$(4.2)$$

Here, w is the northern wages for entrepreneurs (the mobile factor H) and w_L is the northern wage for workers. Expressions for the corresponding southern values are isomorphic.

The manufacturing sector (industry) is monopolistically competitive and faces increasing returns. Specifically, production of a typical variety of the manufactured good involves the services of one entrepreneur—this is the fixed cost $F = 1$—and a_m units of worker's labour for each unit of output produced. Thus, the total cost of producing x units of a variety is $w + w_L a_m x$. Trade in industrial goods is subject to iceberg trade costs; a firm wishing to sell one unit of its good in the other region must ship $\tau \geq 1$ units since $\tau - 1$ units 'melt' in transit.[1]

---

[1] Alternatively, we can think of these trade costs as involving real resources. Specifically, for each unit exported, the industrial firm must hire $(\tau - 1)a_M$ units of local L in order to overcome the natural and man-made trade barriers.

   The agricultural good is homogeneous, is produced using workers only, and is subject to constant returns to scale and perfect competition. The specific cost function is $w_L a_A$, where a_A is the unit input coefficient. Trade in the homogeneous A good is costless.

   Workers are *not* inter-regionally mobile, and regions are endowed with equal supplies of the immobile factor, L, thus $L = L^* = L^w/2$ (see the appendix for a treatment of the model with asymmetric regions). Entrepreneurs, by contrast, are mobile inter-regionally, so the spatial allocation of the mobile factor, H, across the two regions is endogenous in the model. Entrepreneurs' migration decisions are based on the indirect utility difference, that is, the real wage difference. To formalize this, we assume the by now familiar ad hoc 'migration equation':

$$\dot{s}_H = (\omega - \omega^*)s_H(1 - s_H), \quad s_H \equiv \frac{H}{H^w} \tag{4.3}$$

where s_H is the share of entrepreneurs in the north, H is the north's stock of entrepreneurs, H^w is world's supply, ω and ω^* are the northern and southern real wages for H.

4.2.2 Short-Run Equilibrium

To build intuition, we first work out the 'short-run' equilibrium, that is, the equilibrium taking as given the spatial distribution of entrepreneurs (s_H); this becomes endogenous in the long run.

A-SECTOR RESULTS

Most of the equilibrium expressions for the FE model are identical to those of the CP model, or to those of the FC model. We repeat them here very briefly for the sake of completeness; see Chapters 2 and 3 for a thorough exposition. On the supply side, perfect competition forces marginal cost pricing in the sector A, so $p_A = a_A w_L$ and $p_A^* = a_A w_L^*$. Trade in A goods is costless so the price of A in both regions is equalized. Assuming the non-full-specialization (NFS) condition holds, both regions produce some A, so the equalization of the price of A indirectly equalizes the wage paid to workers in the two regions, that is, $w_L = w_L^*$. In the symmetric case that we consider here, the NFS condition is $(1 - \mu)E^w > 1/2L^w/a_A$, where $(1 - \mu)E^w$ is world expenditure on good A (see Chapter 3 for details). As usual, worldwide demand for A is $C_A = (1 - \mu)(E + E^*)/p_A$, where E and E^* are northern and southern consumption expenditure, respectively. Supply and demand for A must match, but we use Walras's law to drop this market clearing condition.

INDUSTRIAL SECTOR RESULTS

Utility optimization implies that a constant expenditure share, μ, is spent on industrial goods. Northern consumption of a typical variety j is

$c_j = p_j^{-\sigma}(\mu E/\Delta n^w)$, where $E = wH + w_L L$ is northern expenditure, and Δ is defined in (4.2). The south has isomorphic expressions. Given monopolistic competition and the demand functions, mill pricing is optimal for all firms in the industrial sector (see Chapter 2 for details). Thus,

$$p = \frac{w_L a_M}{1 - (1/\sigma)}, \quad p^* = \frac{\tau w_L a_M}{1 - (1/\sigma)} \tag{4.4}$$

where p and p^* are the consumer prices for a typical north-made variety in the northern market and the southern market, respectively. These pricing equations have important differences from those of the CP model. In the CP model, industrial good prices depended on the wage of the mobile factor. In the FE model, as in the FC model, they depend on the wage of the *immobile* factor. Since these are equalized across regions via costless trade in the A good, the prices involve significantly less complexity. As in the FC model, this is one of the keys to the FE model's analytical friendliness.

The Mobile Factor's Reward. As in the FC model, the reward to entrepreneurs is the operating profit of a typical variety, that is, $w = \pi$, where π is the operating profit of a typical north-based industrial firm. With mill pricing and constant mark-ups, π equals the value of sales times the profit margin $1/\sigma$ (see Chapter 2 for details). Using the demand function and mill pricing, we have that the reward to H satisfies

$$w = bB\frac{E^w}{n^w}, \quad w^* = bB^*\frac{E^w}{n^w} \tag{4.5}$$

where $b \equiv \mu/\sigma$ and

$$B \equiv \frac{s_E}{\Delta} + \phi\frac{1 - s_E}{\Delta^*}, \quad B^* \equiv \frac{\phi s_E}{\Delta} + \frac{1 - s_E}{\Delta^*}$$

$$\Delta \equiv s_n + \phi(1 - s_n), \quad \Delta^* \equiv \phi s_n + 1 - s_n$$

The notation here is standard; E^w is world expenditure, n^w is world mass (number) of varieties, and s_E and s_n are the north's share of E^w and n^w, respectively. The Δ's are the denominators of the demand functions for a typical variety. Variables marked with an asterisk denote the corresponding southern values.

Observe that in contrast to the CP model, we easily obtain a closed-form solution for how the nominal reward to the mobile factor varies with market size and the spatial distribution of industry (in the CP model, the 'wage equations' could not be solved analytically). This is crucial to the FE model's tractability.

THE MARKET SIZE CONDITION

To characterize the dependence of the spatial allocation of expenditure (s_E) on the spatial distribution of industry (s_n) and parameters, we first calculate the denominator of s_E, namely world expenditure. World expenditure (E^w) is the sum of $w_L L^w$ and total payments to entrepreneurs, where the latter equals the worldwide sum of operating profits. Since mill pricing implies that operating profit is the value of sales times $1/\sigma$, and worldwide spending on industrial goods is μE^w, total payments to entrepreneurs is bE^w. Thus, $E^w = w_L L^w/(1 - b)$ and full employment of entrepreneurs implies $n^w = H^w$.

The numerator of s_E is the north's income/expenditure, that is, $(w_L L + wH)$, so using the expression for E^w that we just derived and (4.5), simple manipulations using the fact that n^w equals H^w yield

$$s_E = (1 - b)s_L + bBs_H, \quad s_L \equiv \frac{L}{L^w}, \quad s_H \equiv \frac{H}{H^w} \qquad (4.6)$$

where $s_L = 1/2$ in the symmetric-region case we are considering.[2] This is very similar to the corresponding expression in the FC model, but here relative market size depends upon where the mobile factor is working (s_H) as well as on its profitability (B). In particular, s_E is increasing in the number of firms in the north (s_H) and their profitability (B). As a consequence, production shifting (i.e. changes in s_H) will lead to expenditure shifting (i.e. changes in s_E). This is one of the key differences between the FC and FE models.

Although equilibrium firm size plays no explicit role in our analysis, we calculate it for completeness's sake. As in the FC model, the typical industrial firm's cost function is non-homothetic, so the equilibrium firm size depends on relative factor prices. Specifically, firm size x equals $\pi\sigma/p$ (see Chapter 3 for details).

4.2.3 Choice of Numeraire and Units

The normalizations we adopt for the FE model are quite close to those of the FC model and they provide the same sort of simplifications. We take A as numeraire and choose units such that $a_A = 1$ so $w_L = w_L^* = 1$. We also choose units such that a_m equals $1 - (1/\sigma)$, so the consumer price of a typical northern variety in the north and south markets are $p = 1$ and $p = \tau$. Similar pricing rules hold for southern firms. We choose units of H such that the world's endowment equals unity, so, as in the FC model, a region's supply of the mobile factor equals the number of industrial varieties produced locally, that is, $n = H$ and $n^* = H^*$. Moreover, with $n^w = H^w = 1$, n and n^* are both the level and share of firms in the north and south, respectively, so instead of writing s_H for the northern share of H^w, we could write s_n or simply n. These results simplify several expressions and the results that $n = H$ and $n^* = H^*$ boost intuition by highlighting the connection between migration and industrial relocation. Finally, we choose units of L such that the world endowment, L^w, equals $1 - b$; this implies that $E^w = 1$. To summarize, with these normalizations,

---

[2] Note that using (4.5) in (4.6) and collecting all s_E terms on the right-hand side yields

$$s_E = \frac{(1 - b)s_L + b(\phi/\Delta^*)s_H}{1 - bs_H/\Delta + bs_H\phi/\Delta^*}$$

This shows the explicit dependence of s_E on s_L and s_H, that is, it is a closed-form solution, but the formulation in the text stresses the similarity between models.

$$p = 1, \quad p^* = \tau, \quad p_A = p_A^* = w_L = w_L^* = 1, \quad n^w \equiv n + n^* = 1,$$

$$H^w \equiv H + H^* = 1, \quad n = H = s_n = s_H, \quad n^* = H^* = s_H^* = 1 - s_n, \quad (4.7)$$

$$L^w = 1 - b, \quad E^w = 1$$

The next task is to find the long-run equilibrium location of firms and to characterize their local stability properties.

4.2.4 Long-Run Location

The long-run equilibrium is characterized by the same properties as a short-run equilibrium with the additional condition that all migration stops. This happens in two cases. For interior outcomes ($0 < s_H < 1$), migration stops whenever entrepreneurs achieve the same level of utility in the two regions ($\omega = \omega^*$). For core–periphery outcomes ($s_H = 0$ or $s_H = 1$) migration is always zero given the migration equation, (4.3).

THE LOCATION CONDITION

To summarize, the 'location condition' is that either

$$\omega = \omega^*, \quad 0 < s_n < 1 \tag{4.8}$$

where ω and ω^* are defined in (4.2), or $s_n = 0$ or $s_n = 1$. Note that we have used our normalizations to write the location condition in terms of the spatial allocation of industry (s_n) instead of the spatial allocation of entrepreneurs (s_H).

To obtain a closed-form solution for the equilibrium, spatial allocation of industry would require us to solve the location conditions for the geographical division of industry between north and south, that is, s_n. Since the location condition involves the real wages and thus the CES price indices that involve a non-integer power, we cannot solve the location condition except in special cases. This is a key difference between the FC and FE models. We can, nevertheless, characterize the long-run equilibria using graphical methods.

DIAGRAMMATIC SOLUTION AND FORCES

As in the FC model, we can find the long-run equilibria and characterize their stability properties with the scissors diagram shown in Figure 4.2. The scissors diagram, which was introduced in Chapter 3, shows two schedules. The nn curve, which defines the spatial allocation of industry, s_n, implied by any given relative market size, s_E, and the EE curve which shows how the relative market size depends upon the spatial allocation of industry.

The Scissor Diagram. Given the powers involved in the price indices, analysis is simplified by working with the log's of the real wages, namely $\ln(\omega)$ and $\ln(\omega^*)$, instead of the levels. The location condition, (4.8), of course, applies

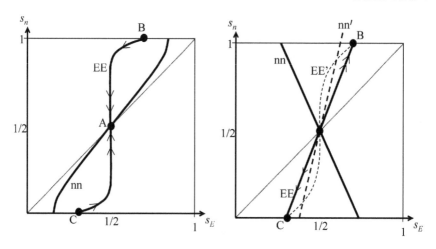

Figure 4.2 The scissors diagram for the FE model.

equally to the log and the level of real wages. Turning to Figure 4.2, we note that the nn curve plots the combinations of s_n and s_E for which the log real wage gap is zero, that is, $\Omega \equiv \ln(\omega/\omega^*) = 0$. Equation (4.5) gives w and w^* in terms of s_n and s_E, and using this in the definition of the price indices in (4.3), together with $w_L = w_L^* = 1$, the nn curve can be written in implicit form as

$$\Omega = \ln\left[\frac{s_E \Delta^* + \phi(1-s_E)\Delta}{\phi s_E \Delta^* + (1-s_E)\Delta}\right] + a\ln\left(\frac{\Delta}{\Delta^*}\right) = 0 \qquad (4.9)$$

where the Δ's, which are defined in (4.5), depend upon s_n.

Three features of the nn curve facilitate analysis with the diagram. First, given the symmetry of the model, the nn curve passes through the midpoint, $(1/2, 1/2)$. Second, the slope of the nn curve depends on trade freeness, ϕ. Specifically, differentiation of (4.9) shows that ds_n/ds_E equals $(1 + \phi)/[(1 - a) - (1 + a)\phi]$ at the midpoint. Importantly, the slope is negative when trade is very free and positive when trade is highly restricted. Third, as in the FC model, s_n has a tendency to increase for combinations of s_n and s_E to the right of the nn curve because $\omega/\omega^* > 1$ in this region. To understand this, take the left panel of the diagram and consider a point on the nn curve and another point that is a horizontal shift to the right of it. At the point on the nn curve, real wages are equal, but for the point to the right, the northern market is larger and this makes the northern real wage higher by the usual logic of the market-access effect (more formally this can be shown by differentiating (4.5) with respect to s_E). Correspondingly, s_n tends to fall at all points to the left of nn.

The EE line plots the definition of s_E as a function of s_n, namely (4.6). Three facts concerning the EE curve assist the diagrammatic analysis. First, the curve passes through the midpoint. Second, the slope of EE (i.e. ds_n/ds_E) at the midpoint is infinite when $\phi = 0$ and falls to $1/b \equiv \sigma/\mu$ when $\phi = 1$; specifically, the slope is $\{(1 + \phi)[(1 + \phi) - b(1 - \phi)]\}/(4b\phi)$. Third, the endpoints of EE are unaffected by trade costs; specifically s_E equals $(1 - b)/2$ and $(1 + b)/2$ for $s_n = 0$ and 1, respectively.

Finally, we note that the economy is always on the EE curve since EE holds at any short-run equilibrium. By contrast, the nn line shows all the combinations of s_n and s_E that satisfy one of the conditions for an interior long-run equilibrium, namely real wage equalization.

Catastrophic Agglomeration. The two panels in Figure 4.2 depict two alternative scenarios. The left panel shows the case when the regions are rather closed to trade (i.e. ϕ is low), so EE is very steep and nn is close to the 45-degree line. For this level of trade costs, the economy has three long-run equilibria, the symmetric outcome, shown as point A, and the two CP outcomes, shown as points B and C.[3]

The symmetric outcome, point A, is stable since a small increase in s_n (moving along the EE curve as usual) would bring the economy to the left of the nn curve, and this, in turn, would result in a falling s_n. In this way, the migration shock generates self-correcting forces. The CP outcomes, shown as points B and C, are unstable. B, where $s_n = 1$, is to the left of the nn curve so s_n would fall, following the EE curve to point A. C is unstable for isomorphic reasons.

The right panel shows the situation for a more open economy. As trade freeness rises, the EE line straightens out even though its endpoints do not move. The nn curve also rotates around the centre point, but its endpoints move since trade cost changes continue to move the ratio of price indices even with $s_n = 0$ or $s_n = 1$. Indeed, the nn curve switches from a positive slope to a negative slope at a sufficiently high ϕ.

The heavy solid EE and nn curves in the right panel show the situation where ϕ has risen to the point where the nn curve has a negative slope. Here, the symmetric outcome is unstable (a shock along the EE curve would take the economy to the right of nn, so the shock generates self-reinforcing forces). The core-in-the-north outcome, point B, is stable since it is to the right of the nn line. The core-in-the-south outcome is stable for symmetric reasons.

The dashed EE and nn curves in the right panel show the situation when the level of openness falls in an intermediate range. Here, there are five long-run equilibria, but only three are stable. The symmetric outcome is stable since a small movement along EE takes the economy to the left of the nn curve (so s_n tends to fall back toward 1/2). The CP outcomes, points B and C, are stable since they are, respectively, to the right and left of nn. The dashed lines also intersect between the symmetric and CP outcomes. These are the unstable interior outcomes. Proving that there is a range of ϕ where there are three interior equilibria (and that they are at most three) requires more formal methods, which we relegate to the appendix.

To more fully characterize the local stability properties of the symmetric and core–periphery outcomes, we turn to standard stability analysis.

---

[3] Given the ad hoc migration equation (4.3), the core–periphery outcomes are always steady states. They are not, however, always stable, as we shall see.

4.2.5 Local Stability Analysis

By differentiating (4.8) with respect to s_n and evaluating the derivative at $s_n = 1/2$, it is readily established that the symmetric equilibrium becomes unstable for trade costs such that the corresponding values of ϕ are lower than the 'break' point[4]

$$\phi^B = \left(\frac{1-b}{1+b}\right)\left(\frac{1-a}{1+a}\right) \tag{4.10}$$

Given that $b \equiv \mu/\sigma$ and $a \equiv \mu/(\sigma - 1)$, the break point is decreasing in μ and increasing in σ, which means that the range of trade freeness for which the symmetric outcome is unstable expands as the expenditure share on manufacturing increases. A larger σ works in the opposite direction since it implies a lower mark-up in manufacturing and therefore weaker agglomeration forces.

A value of $a \equiv \mu/(\sigma - 1)$ larger than unity makes ϕ^B negative. In this case, ϕ cannot be smaller than ϕ^B and the symmetric equilibrium is always unstable whatever the parameter values. This situation is ruled out by imposing the no-black-hole condition, which, in the FE model, is just $a < 1$.

The core–periphery equilibrium in turn cannot be sustained for trade costs above the sustain point, where this is defined, as usual, as the level of trade openness for which $\Omega = 0$ when evaluated at $s_n = 0$ or $s_n = 1$. The sustain point level of trade costs, which we denote as ϕ^S, is implicitly defined as the lowest root of

$$1 = (\phi^S)^a \left(\frac{1+b}{2}\phi^S + \frac{1-b}{2\phi^S}\right) \tag{4.11}$$

In the appendix, we show that, as in the CP model, ϕ^S cannot be larger than ϕ^B.

To summarize our findings, the symmetric equilibrium is stable only for sufficiently low levels of trade freeness, specifically for $\phi < \phi^B$, and core–periphery outcomes are stable only for sufficiently high levels of trade freeness, specifically for $\phi > \phi^S$.

4.2.6 The Tomahawk Diagram

The foregoing results can be summarized by Figure 4.3, which plots $s_n = s_H$ against the freeness of trade ϕ.[5] The stable long-run equilibria are illustrated with solid lines, while the unstable long-run equilibria are marked by dashed lines. For $\phi < \phi^S$, $s_n = 1/2$ is the only steady state of (4.3) that is stable. For $\phi > \phi^B$, $s_n = 1/2$, $s_n = 0$ and $s_n = 1$ are all steady states but only the CP ones are stable. Finally, for $\phi^S < \phi < \phi^B$, there are five steady states. Two are CP outcomes and are stable, two are interior asymmetric equilibria and are unstable, and the last one is the symmetric outcome and it is also stable.[6]

---

[4] See Chapter 2 for formal justification of this informal stability evaluation procedure.

[5] Recall that our normalizations imply that $s_n = s_H = n$.

[6] Of course, when distance has no meaning, that is, $\phi = 1$, the location of production is not determined, so any division of H^w is a steady state.

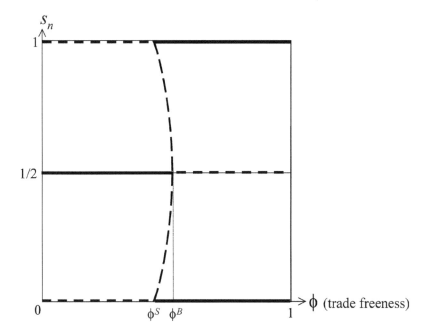

Figure 4.3   The tomahawk diagram for the FE model.

We can therefore conclude that the equilibrium and local stability properties of the FE and CP models are qualitatively identical. The global stability properties and the implications of forward-looking behaviour are also qualitatively identical in the two models. The formal demonstration of this is somewhat involved (see Ottaviano 2001). But, more heuristically, this result should not be hard to believe. The analysis in Chapter 2 worked with a numerical approximation to the Ω function that had properties qualitatively identical to those of (4.8). Since the behaviour of the dynamic system depends only on Ω, it should be easy to believe that the FE and CP models display similar behaviour even with forward-looking migrants (see the appendix to Chapter 2 for an analysis of forward-looking behaviour in the CP model).

4.3 KEY FEATURES

Chapter 2 pointed out seven key features of the CP model: agglomeration via the home-market mechanism (with magnification by freer trade), demand and cost linkages, endogenous asymmetry, catastrophic agglomeration, locational hysteresis, hump-shaped agglomeration rents, and multiple long-run equilibria in the 'overlap'. In comparing the FE model with the CP model, we discuss such features first and then we turn to new properties.

Before proceeding, however, a general comment is in order. The FE model displays all the key features of the CP model even though it is analytically more tractable. This is not surprising since in essence the two models are qualitatively identical. In both models migration is the key to agglomeration and in both the migrating factor and its owners move together, basing their decisions on real wages. The big difference is that the migrating factor in the FE model is used for only a fraction of the total cost of producing an industrial variety. This weakens the link between production and expenditure shifting, so agglomeration forces are weaker in the FE model. Specifically, the expenditure of a unit of H in the CP model equals the total revenue of a typical industrial firm; in the FE model it equals only a fraction of this, namely the operating profit that is $1/\sigma$ times revenue. For this reason, most of the key expressions of the FE model are those of the CP model with μ divided by σ.

Since agglomeration forces are weaker in the FE model, the sustain point occurs at a higher level of freeness than it does in the CP model. Similarly, the break point is larger while the no-black-hole condition is less stringent in the FE model. Indeed, the FE expressions for these are just those of the CP model with μ everywhere divided by σ.[7]

4.3.1 Comparison with the CP Model

HOME-MARKET MAGNIFICATION

As in the CP model, the FE model features the home-market effect, as can be seen from Figure 4.2. A slight increase in the northern market size leads to a shift of the EE curve to the right. Presuming that trade costs are high enough for the interior equilibrium to be stable, the shock will lead to a more than proportional increase in the north's share of industry since, in this case, the nn line is steeper than the 45-degree line. Moreover, we see that home-market magnification also occurs (i.e. the home-market effect gets stronger as trade gets freer) since freeing up trade makes the nn line steeper. Thus, the same rightward shift in the EE curve would result in a higher degree of relocation.

CIRCULAR CAUSALITY

In the FE model, as in the CP model, agglomeration is driven by and drives inter-regional factor movement involving people. Because people spend their incomes locally, they care about the local cost of living. This, in turn, means that migration decisions will be based on the real reward to human capital so cost-linked circular causality comes into play via the cost-of-living effect. The fact that migrants spend their incomes locally ties production shifting to expenditure shifting, so that demand-linked circular causality operates in both models.

[7] More generally, Robert-Nicoud (2001) shows that the collection of parameters that captures the forward linkages in the FE model is $1/\sigma$ times the equivalent in the CP model.

ENDOGENOUS ASYMMETRY

As in the symmetric CP model, a gradual opening of trade in the symmetric FE model eventually leads to full agglomeration. Moreover, just as in the CP model, partial agglomeration is never a stable outcome—the location of industry is either symmetric or involves all industry in one region or the other. Thus, the steady lowering of trade costs results in a perfectly symmetric model becoming asymmetric.

CATASTROPHIC AGGLOMERATION

As the tomahawk diagram shows, the FE model is subject to sudden and massive agglomerations in reaction to minor changes in trade costs. For example, when trade gets just a bit freer than ϕ^B. The same occurs in the CP model.

LOCATIONAL HYSTERESIS

Whenever $\phi > \phi^S$, the FE model features multiple, stable, long-run equilibria. As in the CP model, this means that temporary shocks, including temporary policy changes, may have hysteretic effects on the location of industry.

HUMP-SHAPED AGGLOMERATION RENTS

As in the CP model, agglomeration rents in the FE model are a concave function of trade freeness. This can be established by considering a long-run equilibrium in which all entrepreneurs are located in the north ($s_n = 1$ and $\phi^S \leq \phi \leq 1$). In this case, agglomeration rents are measured as the loss that an entrepreneur would incur by relocating to the south. Formally, such rents are given by

$$\Omega|_{s_n=1} = \ln\left[\left(\frac{1-b}{2\phi} + \phi\frac{1+b}{2}\right)\phi^a\right] \qquad (4.12)$$

This is a function of ϕ. It equals zero at $\phi = \phi^S$ and $\phi = 1$ while it is positive in between. Moreover, in the same interval, it is concave with a maximum at $\phi = \sqrt{\phi^B}$, where ϕ^B is the break point defined in (4.10). Accordingly, as trade gets freer (i.e. ϕ rises from ϕ^S towards 1), the agglomeration rents first rise and then fall ('hump shape').

THE OVERLAP AND SELF-FULFILLING EXPECTATIONS

Since $0 < \phi^S < \phi^B < 1$, the FE model features an overlap. Thus, as in the CP model, shocks to expectations may result in large spatial reallocations when migrants are forward looking.

4.3.2 New Features

The main new feature of the FE model is its tractability. While it is somewhat less tractable that the FC model (we cannot in general solve the location condition for the spatial allocation of industry), it is far more amenable to paper-and-pencil analysis than the CP model while still displaying all of the CP model's richness. Given its tractability, the FE model is able to analytically deal with asymmetric regions. This in turn allows us to highlight some features that we could not establish in the CP model, but illustration of such points is relegated to the appendix where asymmetries are explicitly treated.

4.4 CONCLUDING REMARKS AND RELATED LITERATURE

4.4.1 Summary Results for Policy Modelling

While yielding valuable insights on the interactions between trade costs, factor mobility, and agglomeration, the CP model is astoundingly difficult to work with, forcing numerical simulations for most results. This chapter has presented the footloose entrepreneurs model, which can be thought of as a modified version of the CP model that exhibits all qualitative properties of the original model while still yielding closed-form solutions for most endogenous variables. Indeed, most of the key expressions of the FE model are those of the CP model with μ divided by σ.

Since an explanation of agglomeration based on migration might be unappealing when we view north and south as nations rather than regions within a nation, it is worth noting that the FE model can be extended to include 'vertical linkages' (Krugman and Venables 1995). In this model, the gradual opening of trade eventually produces full agglomeration without international labour migration. Consideration of this model is postponed to Chapter 8.

4.4.2 Related Literature

The FE model was independently proposed by Forslid (1999) and Ottaviano (1996, 1998). Its detailed presentation appears in Forslid and Ottaviano (2002). The implications of forward-looking behaviour are studied by Ottaviano (1996, 1999, 2001). He shows that, as in the CP model, self-fulfilling expectations are possible when entrepreneurs are patient and mobility costs as well as trade barriers are low. Robert-Nicoud (2002) points out the fundamental similarities of the CP model (both the original version and the vertical linkages model in Krugman and Venables 1995) and the FE model. In so doing, he extends the results by Puga (1999), who considers CP and VL models only. A model that has elements similar to that of the FE model is explored by Mori and Turrini (2000). The distinctive feature of their model is that it allows for skill (productivity) heterogeneity of the mobile labour and they find that symmetry is never an outcome since higher skilled workers tend to congregate in the wealthier region, thus making it even wealthier.

APPENDIX 4.A: TECHNICALITIES AND EXOGENOUS ASYMMETRIES

4.A.1 Formal Characterization of Long-Run Equilibria

The existence of the core–periphery equilibria is not in question (we see this from inspection of the migration equation), but the interior equilibria pose greater difficulties. Their number is of particular interest because Appendix 2.B appealed to the FE model in establishing the number of such equilibria in the CP model.

The study of interior equilibria requires us to characterize the real wage gaps as a function of the spatial division of industry/entrepreneurs.[8] To find the real wages, we first solve for w and w^* in terms of the spatial distribution of industry, n, and parameters (given our normalization, n and s_n are interchangeable, but we use n in this appendix in an effort to keep the expressions tidy). Using (4.6) in (4.9), the north and south wages, w and w^*, are related to the distribution of industry/entrepreneurs, n, and parameters by

$$w = b\frac{\phi n + \psi m^*}{D}, \quad w^* = b\frac{\phi n^* + \psi m}{D}$$

$$\psi \equiv \frac{(1 + b)\phi^2 + 1 - b}{2} \qquad (4.A.1)$$

$$D \equiv (n + \phi n^*)(n^* + \phi n) - b(1 - \phi^2)nn^*$$

Next, we use the definition of the price indices to show that the log difference of real wages is

$$\Omega = \ln\left(\frac{\phi n + \psi[\phi]n^*}{\psi[\phi]n + \phi n^*}\right) + a\ln\left(\frac{n + \phi n^*}{n^* + \phi n}\right) \qquad (4.A.2)$$

where we write $\psi[\phi]$ to emphasize the dependence of ψ, which is defined in (4.A.1), on trade freeness. Noting that $n^* = 1 - n$, (4.A.1) gives the real wage gap as an explicit function of the spatial distribution of industry and parameters. Given symmetry, it is plain that real wages are equal at the symmetric outcome, $n = 1/2$, so this is always a long-run interior equilibrium. Are there other interior long-run equilibria?

Here we show analytically that the FE model has one or three interior long-run equilibria depending upon trade openness. An interior equilibrium requires Ω to equal zero, so finding the number of interior equilibria is tantamount to finding the number of roots of Ω. We know Ω crosses the zero line at $n = 1/2$, so the question of whether and how often it re-crosses the zero line depends upon Ω's concavity. The key to our demonstration is to show that Ω changes concavity at most once. Indeed, it is readily established that the sign of its first derivative $d\Omega/dn$ depends on the sign of its quadratic numerator and therefore changes sign

---

[8] Recall that our normalizations imply that $s_n = s_H$.

at most twice. Together with the fact that Ω always equals zero at $n = 1/2$, this implies that it crosses the horizontal axis either once or (no less and no more than) three times. That is, either $n = 1/2$ is the only root of Ω or there are exactly two other roots. Symmetry implies that when the asymmetric interior equilibria exist, they are symmetric around $n = 1/2$. Thus, as claimed, the model exhibits either one or three interior long-run equilibria.

The ease of this demonstration illustrates how much more tractable the FE model is compared to the CP model. Nonetheless, the above discussion makes it clear that the wiggle diagram—that is, the plot of Ω against n—is qualitatively identical to that of the CP model discussed in Chapter 2.

Next we show, that, as in the CP model, ϕ^S cannot be larger than ϕ^B in the FE model. This can be achieved by using the same procedure we followed in the CP model. The argument is two-stepped. First, we study the function

$$f_{\text{FE}}(\phi) = \phi^{a-1}\psi[\phi] - 1 \qquad (4.A.3)$$

which is a transformation of (4.11). This function exhibits the same properties as $f[\phi]$ in the CP model (see Chapter 2). Indeed, $\psi[\phi]$ and $f[\phi]$ are the same function except for the fact that to pass from the former to the latter, one has to multiply μ by σ wherever it appears. Given this and the results in Appendix 2.B, we know that $\psi[\phi]$ has a unique root, that is, ϕ^S, between zero and one. In addition $\psi[\phi^B] < 0$, which is possible only if $\phi^S < \phi^B$.

4.A.2 Asymmetries

The analytical convenience of the FE model is readily gauged by considering situations in which regions differ in terms of market size or market access. (Recall that characterizing the behaviour of the CP model with size asymmetry required numerical simulation).

ASYMMETRIC SIZES

The focus is on the exogenous components of market sizes, that is, the regional endowments of immobile unskilled workers L. To fix ideas, we abandon the normalization of L^w and assume that $L^* = \varepsilon L$ with $\varepsilon > 1$ so that the south is larger. Then, in equilibrium

$$w = \left(\frac{bL}{1-b}\right)\frac{(1+\varepsilon)\phi n + [(\varepsilon+b)\phi^2 + (1-b)]n^*}{(1+\varepsilon)D} \qquad (4.A.4)$$

$$w^* = \left(\frac{bL}{1-b}\right)\frac{(1+\varepsilon)\phi n^* + [(1+\varepsilon b)\phi^2 + \varepsilon(1-b)]n}{(1+\varepsilon)D}$$

with a corresponding log real-wage difference,

$$\Omega = \ln\left(\frac{\phi n + \psi(\phi,\varepsilon)n^*}{\psi^*(\phi,\varepsilon)n + \phi n^*}\right) + a\ln\left(\frac{n + \phi n^*}{n^* + \phi n}\right) \qquad (4.A.5)$$

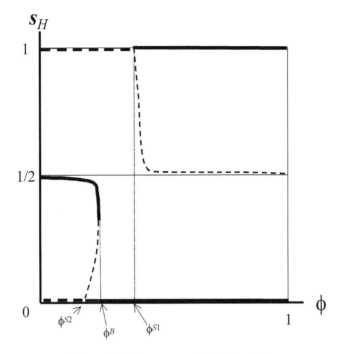

Figure 4.4 Asymmetry in the FE model.

$$\psi(\phi, \varepsilon) \equiv \frac{(\varepsilon + b)\phi^2 + (1 - b)}{1 + \varepsilon}, \quad \psi^*(\phi, \varepsilon) \equiv \frac{(1 + b\varepsilon)\phi^2 + \varepsilon(1 - b)}{1 + \varepsilon}$$

Given $n^* = 1 - n$, expression (4.A.5) has the real wage gap Ω as an explicit function of the share of skilled workers in the north.

Since ε appears only in the first logarithmic term in (4.A.5), it is readily verified that $d\Omega/d\varepsilon > 0$ for any n, which points out that the analytic properties of the asymmetric-regions FE model are qualitatively the same as the numerical properties of the asymmetric-sized CP model (see Chapter 2). These properties are summarized in Figure 4.4, which shows that there are two sustain points and the stable equilibrium is no longer a straight line as in the symmetric case.

Talking through this 'broken tomahawk' diagram in the usual fashion, we note that when trade is completely closed, there is more industry in the large south but the difference is only ε. As trade gets free (i.e. ϕ rises), industry and entrepreneurs migrate to the south in a gradual fashion up until ϕ reaches the break point. Just beyond this point, full agglomeration in the south is the only stable long-run equilibrium. However, when trade costs fall enough to push ϕ beyond ϕ^{S1}, full agglomeration in the small region is also possible. A key contrast between Figures 4.3 and 4.4 is the existence of a unique, unstable, asymmetric equilibrium for values of ϕ beyond ϕ^{S1}.

ASYMMETRIC TRADE COSTS

Regions can also differ in terms of market access. For identical exogenous market sizes $(L = L^*)$, this happens when trade costs are asymmetric. To analyse this situation, call ϕ the freeness of trade from south to north, ϕ^* trade freeness from north to south, and posit $\phi^* = \varepsilon\phi$ with $\varepsilon > 1$. Then, in equilibrium, skilled wages become

$$w = \frac{bL}{1-b} \frac{2\varepsilon\phi n + [(1+b)\varepsilon\phi^2 + (1-b)]n^*}{(n + \phi n^*)(\varepsilon\phi n + n^*) - b(1 - \varepsilon\phi^2)nn^*}$$

$$w^* = \frac{bL}{1-b} \frac{2\phi n^* + [(1+b)\varepsilon\phi^2 + (1-b)]n}{(n + \phi n^*)(\varepsilon\phi n + n^*) - b(1 - \varepsilon\phi^2)nn^*} \qquad (4.A.6)$$

with a corresponding real wage gap

$$\Omega = \ln\left(\frac{\phi n + \psi_\tau(\phi)n^*}{\varepsilon\psi_\tau(\phi)n + \phi n^*}\right) + a\ln\left(\frac{n + \phi n^*}{n^* + \varepsilon\phi n}\right) \qquad (4.A.7)$$

where $\psi_\tau(\phi) \equiv [(\sigma + \mu)\varepsilon\phi^2 + (\sigma - \mu)]/(2\varepsilon\sigma)$. Given $n^* = 1 - n$, expression (4.A.7) has the real wage gap Ω as an explicit function of the share of skilled workers in the north.

Since both logarithmic terms in (4.A.7) are increasing in ε, we have $d\Omega/d\varepsilon > 0$ for any n, which points out that the analytic properties of the asymmetric-sized FE model are qualitatively the same as the numerical properties of the asymmetric-sized CP model. In particular, such properties are qualitatively similar to those described above in the case of size asymmetries (see Figure 4.4). The reason is that relatively protected and large regions both provide better access to world markets than relatively open and small regions.

REFERENCES

Forslid, R. 1999. Agglomeration with human and physical capital: an analytically solvable case. Discussion Paper No. 2102, Centre for Economic Policy Research.

Forslid, Rikard and G. Ottaviano. 2002. An analytically solvable core-periphery model. *Journal of Economic Geography*, in press.

Krugman, P. R. and A. Venables. 1995. Globalization and the inequality of nations. *Quarterly Journal of Economics* 60: 857–880.

Mori, T. and A. Turrini. 2000. Skills, agglomeration and segmentation. Discussion Paper No. 2645, Centre for Economic Policy Research.

Ottaviano, G. I. P. 1996. Monopolistic competition, trade, and endogenous spatial fluctuations. Discussion Paper No. 1327, Centre for Economic Policy Research.

———. 1998. Dynamic and strategic considerations in international and interregional trade. PhD Thesis, Université Catholique de Louvain (Louvain-la-Neuve: CIACO).

———. 1999. Integration, geography and the burden of history. *Regional Science and Urban Economics* 29: 245–256.

———. 2001. Monopolistic competition, trade, and endogenous spatial fluctuations. *Regional Science and Urban Economics* 31: 51–77.

Puga, D. 1999. The rise and fall of regional inequalities. *European Economic Review* 43: 303–334.

Robert-Nicoud, F. 2001. A simple geography model with vertical linkages and capital mobility. Mimeo, London School of Economics.

_____. 2002. The structure of simple 'New Economic Geography' models. Mimeo, London School of Economics.

Shields, G. M. and M. P. Shields. 1989. The emergence of migration theory and a suggested new direction. *Journal of Economic Surveys* 3: 277–304.

Linear Models

5.1 INTRODUCTION

Since the publication of the core–periphery (CP) model by Krugman (1991), the new economic geography has suffered from tension between the broadness of the issues addressed and the relative narrowness of the modelling strategy adopted. This narrowness is summarized by Krugman (1998, p. 164): ''To date, the new economic geography has depended heavily on the tricks summarized in Fujita et al. (1999) with the slogan 'Dixit–Stiglitz, icebergs, evolution, and the computer'.''

This chapter considers a family of models that are based on an alternative framework due to Ottaviano et al. (2002)—a framework that does not rely on Dixit–Stiglitz, icebergs, evolution or the computer. The models are fully tractable since the main expressions are linear, yet they display many of the main features of the CP model, including elements that were not present in the footloose capital (FC) model of Chapter 3, such as circular causality and catastrophic agglomeration. Before turning the logic of this alternative framework—what we call linear models—we consider the problems that come with Dixit–Stiglitz monopolistic competition, CES utility, and iceberg trade costs (henceforth, 'DCI').

5.1.1 Problems with the DCI Framework

One issue is that the stability analysis normally used to select spatial equilibria in the CP and related models rests on *myopic adjustment processes*, in which the location of mobile factors is driven by differences in current returns. Despite some analogy with evolutionary game theory (hence, 'evolution'), this approach neglects the role of expectations, which may be crucial for location decisions since they are often made once and for all. Chapter 2 used numerical simulation to show that neglecting expectations is wrong when barriers to goods and factors mobility are low (provided agents care enough about the future). In the linear model framework we can deal with such issues analytically.

Another issue is that, notwithstanding their simplifying assumptions, many new economic geography models are beyond the reach of analytical resolution so that authors have to appeal to *numerical investigations* (hence, 'the computer'). In Chapter 3 and 4, we presented models that, while retaining all the key features of the CP and related models, turn out to be analytically much more amenable to analytic reasoning, yet the only model that was 100% tractable (the FC model) also lacked many of the key features of the CP model. As we shall see, the linear models retain 100% tractability while retaining most of the main features of the CP model.

A third problem arises from the combination of Dixit–Stiglitz monopolistic competition and iceberg trade costs (hence, 'Dixit–Stiglitz' and 'icebergs'). It is a *lack of identification*. In equilibrium, the number of independent parameters is smaller than the number of exogenous variables. This implies that comparative static analysis is not able to disentangle the logically distinct impacts on endogenous outcomes of different exogenous events. More specifically, the DCI framework yields a demand system in which the own-price elasticities of demands are constant and identical to the elasticities of substitutions. Accordingly, comparative statics is unable to investigate the impact of different own and cross elasticities on firms' location. This is a major shortcoming in that such elasticities can be expected to be key determinants of the relative strength of market access, market crowding, and cost-of-living effects. Furthermore, when coupled with constant fixed and marginal costs of production, DCI implies that the own and cross elasticities of demand are also an inverse measure of the returns to scale that remain unexploited in equilibrium. Thus, the impacts of demand and supply parameters cannot be told from one another. When further associated with iceberg costs, the constant elasticity of demand implies equilibrium prices that are independent of the spatial distribution of firms and consumers. Although convenient from an analytical viewpoint, such a result conflicts with research in spatial competition, which shows that demand elasticity varies with distance while prices change with the level of demand and the intensity of competition (see, e.g. Anderson et al. 1992). Finally, the iceberg assumption also implies that any increase in the price of the transported good is accompanied by a proportional increase in its trade cost, which is unrealistic.

To address these weaknesses, this chapter describes an alternative framework put forth by Ottaviano et al. (2002). With respect to previous chapters, the crucial difference is that utility is quasi-linear quadratic rather than Cobb–Douglas nested-CES and trade costs are not of the frictional kind. The framework is applied to set-ups that mimic the factor mobility assumptions of the FC model and the FE models. Since the resulting models are easier to handle, we can also introduce congestion costs that act as an additional dispersion force.

5.1.2 Logic of Linear Models

The linear models display all the agglomeration and dispersion forces that are present in the DCI model, so it is not surprising that the fundamental logic of agglomeration and the role of trade costs is quite similar for both families of models. This logic was explained in all three preceding chapters so we will not repeat it here. We do note, however, that the economic logic of models in the linear framework differs from that of the DCI models in two respects.

First, since industrial firms face linear demand curves, the optimal price–cost mark-up depends upon a whole host of factors including the number of competitors in the local market. This opens the door to a pro-competitive effect that acts as a distinct dispersion force. That is, since both per firm sales and mark-ups are lower in the 'crowded' market, firms are more interested in locating in the market with the fewest firms in the linear models than they are in the DCI models. (Recall that firms in the DCI framework perceive the demand elasticity to be constant and so charge the same mark-up regardless of the degree of competition.)

Second, the quasi-linear structure of preferences implies—as always—that per consumer spending on industrial varieties is independent of income. As a consequence, relative market size depends only upon the number of consumers residing in each region. Their income levels are irrelevant. The lack of such income effects in the linear models has little impact on the fundamental logic of agglomeration. In linear models where factors move with their owner (the linear FE model of Section 5.3, for example), production shifting is associated with population changes that imply changes in relative market size, and these changes in turn promote production shifting. In short, demand-linked circular causality operates in the linear FE model very much as it does in the DCI version. The main impact of the lack of income effects shows up in the lack of an overlap. That is, the break and sustain points of the symmetric linear models always coincide. The reason for this is straightforward. In all the models considered up to this point, the mobile factor earns a higher reward when it is fully agglomerated in one region (this is the so-called hump-shaped feature). When income effects are present, as they are in the DCI framework, this higher level of income exaggerates the market size difference and this, in turn, means that full agglomeration can be sustained at levels of trade costs where the symmetric outcome is still stable. In the linear model, income levels are irrelevant so the symmetric outcome becomes unstable at the same level of trade cost that makes full agglomeration stable.

5.1.3 Organization of the Chapter

The chapter is organized in four further sections. Section 5.2 presents the quasi-linear quadratic set-up and applies it to a set-up that resembles the FC model. Section 5.3 does the same for an FE-like framework. Section 5.4 exploits the superior analytical tractability that derives from linearity to deal with the important issue of spatial congestion. Section 5.5 concludes and presents the related literature.

5.2 THE LINEAR FC MODEL

The basic structure of the linear FC model closely follows the outlines of the FC model presented at length in Chapter 3. This section is based on Ottaviano et al. (2002) and Ottaviano (2001) and modify this setting in two respects.

5.2.1 Assumptions

There are two regions, north and south. Each region has two factors of production (capital K and labour L) and two sectors (industry M and agriculture A). Both L- and K-factor owners are geographically immobile. The two groups, however, differ in that, while the services of L are embodied in its owners, the services of K can be provided wherever convenient, so capital can be employed in one region while its owner resides in the other. We call $s_L \equiv L/L^w$ the share of the world endowment of L that is owned and employed in the north, $s_K \equiv K/K^w$ the share of the world endowment of K owned by northern residents, and s_n the share of the world K employed in the north.

Physical capital moves freely across regions, seeking the highest nominal reward π; capital flows are driven by nominal rather than real rewards since the income is sent to the owner's region regardless of where the capital is employed.[1] Specifically, inter-regional capital flows are governed by the ad hoc equation:

$$\dot{s}_n = (\pi - \pi^*)(1 - s_n)s_n \qquad (5.1)$$

where π is the northern rental rate of capital (an asterisk indicates southern variables).

The A sector is perfectly competitive. It supplies a homogeneous good under constant returns to scale using labour L as its only input. In particular, A-sector unit cost is $a_A w_L$ where w_L is the wage. The industry sector is monopolistically competitive. It produces a horizontally differentiated good under increasing returns to scale using both L and K as its inputs. Increasing returns are captured through a linear cost function with fixed and variable costs. Specifically, fixed and variable costs are undertaken in terms of K and L, respectively. The total cost of producing x units of a variety of the M good is $\pi F + w_L a_m x$.

As in the standard FC model, we assume that the A good is freely traded, however, instead of assuming iceberg trade costs in the M sector, we assume that it costs τ units of the A good to ship a unit of the industrial good between regions. The resources of the sending region are used to pay the trade cost.

Preferences over goods are described by the quasi-linear quadratic utility function

$$U = \alpha \int_{i=0}^{n+n^*} c_i di - \frac{\beta - \delta}{2} \int_{i=0}^{n+n^*} c_i^2 di - \frac{\delta}{2} \left(\int_{i=0}^{n+n^*} c_i di \right)^2 + C_A \qquad (5.2)$$

$$0 < \alpha, \quad 0 < \delta < \beta$$

where c_i is consumption of variety i of the M good, C_A is consumption of the A good, and n is the number (mass) of northern varieties. Analogous definitions hold for southern variables, which are denoted by an asterisk. As to parameters, α expresses the intensity of preferences for the differentiated product, whereas $\beta > \delta$ means that consumers are biased toward a dispersed consumption of varieties. In particular, the quadratic utility function exhibits love of variety as long as $\beta > \delta$. Finally, for a given value of β, the parameter δ expresses the substitutability between varieties: the higher δ, the closer substitutes the varieties.

---

[1] The rewards are nominal in the sense that they are measured in terms of the numeraire good rather than the price index.

5.2.2 Short-Run Equilibrium

As usual, we first work out the 'short-run' equilibrium defined as the equilibrium taking as given the allocation of capital across the regions. Utility optimization yields a linear demand for the typical M variety, which may be written as

$$c_j = a - (b + cn^w)p_j + cP$$

$$a \equiv \frac{\alpha}{\beta + \delta(n^w - 1)}, \quad b \equiv \frac{a}{\alpha}, \quad c \equiv \frac{\delta b}{\beta - \delta}, \quad P \equiv \int_{i=0}^{n+n^*} p_i di \quad (5.3)$$

where we use the usual notation $n^w = n + n^*$. In this demand function, p_i is the price of variety i and P/n^w is the average price prevailing in the north. Thus, the demand function encapsulates the idea that the demand of a certain variety falls when its own price rises, not only in absolute terms (*own price effect*) but also relatively to the average price (*differential price effect*), which is the essence of monopolistic competition. Finally, it shows that the demand for an M variety is independent of income, so all income effects are absent. Consequently, the demand for A is determined as a residual. Accordingly, aggregate demand is simply (5.3) times the number of consumers. Note that the parameters a and b here are unrelated to those in other chapters.

On the supply side, perfect competition in sector A forces marginal cost pricing, that is, $p_A = a_A w_L$ and $p_A^* = a_A w_L^*$. In addition, costless trade in A equalizes northern and southern prices and thus indirectly equalizes L wage rates internationally, viz. $w_L = w_L^*$. Setting units such that $a_A = 1$ and choosing the A good as numeraire gives $p_A = p_A^* = w_L = w_L^* = 1$.

In the M sector, assuming market segmentation, a typical northern firm maximizes operating profit

$$(p - a_M)[a - (b + cn^w)p + cP]M + (\bar{p} - a_M - \tau)[a - (b + cn^w)\bar{p} + cP^*]M^*$$

$$M \equiv s_L L^w + s_K K^w, \quad M^* \equiv (1 - s_L)L^w + (1 - s_K)K^w \quad (5.4)$$

where p and $\bar{p}$ are the consumer prices set by a typical northern firm in the northern and southern markets, respectively, while $M = s_L L^w + s_K K^w$ and $M^* = (1 - s_L)L^w + (1 - s_K)K^w$ are the number of consumers in the north and south. Assuming that firms compete in prices in segmented markets equilibrium, consumer prices in the north are[2]

$$p = \frac{1}{2} \frac{2[a + a_M(b + cn^w)] + \tau cn^*}{2b + cn^w}, \quad \bar{p}^* = p + \frac{\tau}{2} \quad (5.5)$$

with a symmetric expression holding for the south.

Importantly, these pricing rules do not imply mill pricing, so equilibrium prices depend on the geographic distribution of firms. In particular, the price firms charge in their local market is positively affected by trade costs, but the

---

[2] As in the DCI framework, since there is a continuum of firms, nothing would change if firms competed in quantities rather than prices.

effect is larger when more of their competitors are located in the other market. The reason is that high trade barriers shelter domestic producers against distant competitors. Finally, there will be two-way trade as long as $\bar{p} - a_M - \tau > 0$ and $\bar{p}^* - a_M - \tau > 0$, that is, as long as trade costs are not too high. The critical level of trade costs is

$$\tau < \tau_{\text{trade}} \equiv \frac{2(a - ba_M)}{2b + cn^w} \tag{5.6}$$

We assume this inequality holds.

As in the FC model, the reward to a firm's F units of capital is the firm's operating profit, so evaluating (5.4) at equilibrium prices gives the rental rate of capital as

$$\pi = (b + cn^w)\frac{(p - a_M)^2 M + (\bar{p} - a_M - \tau)^2 M^*}{F} \tag{5.7}$$

where the prices are defined by (5.5). The expression for the southern rental rate is isomorphic.

As to firms' location, recall that any active firm requires F units of K, regardless of output. Thus, by the K-factor market-clearing condition, we have that the equilibrium number of firms in the north is

$$n = \frac{s_n K^W}{F} \tag{5.8}$$

Appropriate normalization can be used to clean the equations from unenlightening complications. Specifically, we can choose units such that $K^W = F$. With this, $n^w = 1$, $n = s_n$ and $n^* = 1 - s_n$.

5.2.3 Long-Run Location

In the long run, capital becomes mobile and, as in the FC model, it flows freely between the regions seeking the highest reward. Since each firm requires a fixed amount of capital, these capital flows also determine the spatial distribution of firms.

CHARACTERIZATION OF EQUILIBRIA

A long-run equilibrium is characterized by the same properties as a short-run equilibrium, plus the fact that capital has no incentive to move. More precisely, from the migration equation (5.1), equilibrium arises when no capital owner can earn a strictly higher rental rate by changing the country serviced by his/her capital endowment. This happens when

$$\begin{aligned} \pi = \pi^*, \quad 0 < n < 1 \\ \pi > \pi^*, \quad n = 1 \end{aligned} \tag{5.9}$$

where the first expression holds for interior equilibrium and the second for the core-in-the-north equilibrium; the condition for the other CP equilibrium is isomorphic.

Plugging (5.7) into (5.9) and using (5.5), the resulting rental rate differential is zero/positive/negative when the following expression is zero/positive/negative:

$$\tau \left\{ 2(2a - 2ba_M - b\tau) \left[\left(s_L - \frac{1}{2} \right) L^w + \left(s_K - \frac{1}{2} \right) K^w \right] - c\tau (L^w + K^w) \left(n - \frac{1}{2} \right) \right\}$$

(5.10)

In the absence of trade costs ($\tau = 0$), the expression is always zero, which implies rental rate equalization whatever the geographical distribution of firms. As intuition would have it, with no trade costs, the location of firms is immaterial.

When trade costs are positive ($\tau > 0$), expression (5.10) reveals that the location of firms is driven by the interaction of two opposing forces. One force, which corresponds to the first term inside the curly brackets, depends on the spatial distribution of customers, that is, workers s_L and capital owners s_K. Since $(2a - 2ba_M - b\tau)$ is positive under the trade condition (5.6), the first term shows the market-access advantage of producing in the larger country in the presence of trade barriers. The second term inside the curly brackets depends, by contrast, on the international distribution of firms, n. Since $c\tau$ is positive, that term is negative and so it reflects the market-crowding disadvantage of the country that hosts a larger number of firms.

Plainly the relative weight of the market-access advantage to the market-crowding disadvantage grows as the substitutability between varieties, that is, c, falls. For example, in the limiting case of monopoly, where $c = 0$, the market-crowding disadvantage disappears altogether. Since a firm does not have any competitor, all that matters for its location decision is the better market access offered by the larger region. The relative weight of market access also rises as trade costs τ fall. The reason is that, with lower trade costs, a larger fraction of a firm's operating profits is independent of the location of competitors. Thus, the lower the substitutability between varieties and the smaller the trade costs, the stronger the attraction of firms towards the region hosting the larger number of consumers.

This is highlighted by finding the value of n for which (5.10) is zero, namely

$$n = \frac{1}{2} + \frac{2(2a - 2ba_M - b\tau)}{c\tau} \left(s_E - \frac{1}{2} \right), \quad s_E \equiv \frac{M}{L^w + K^w}$$

(5.11)

where s_E is the northern share of expenditures on the M good (i.e. the northern share of consumers). When $s_E \neq 1/2$, this expression holds only if trade costs are not too small. Otherwise, a core–periphery outcome emerges. In particular, if $s_E > 1/2$, all firms end up in the north when trade costs fall short of the threshold value

$$\tau^{CP} = \frac{8(a - ba_M)(s_E - 1/2)}{4b(s_E - 1/2) + c}$$

(5.12)

Finally, location depends on the spatial distribution of both factor owners. Obviously, the more abundant factor is more important. For example, if $L^w >$

K^w, the distribution of workers is more important. Notice, however, that, in contrast to the standard FC model from Chapter 3, what matters in the linear FC model is the number of residents rather than income levels since M-sector expenditure per person is fixed by the quasi-linear aspects of the assumed preferences.

DIAGRAMMATIC SOLUTION AND FORCES

The Scissors Diagram.   The analysis of the model is easily illustrated with the help of Figure 5.1. The figure plots the north's expenditure share s_E on the horizontal axis and the north's share of industry s_n on the vertical axis.

The two key equilibrium expressions in (5.11) are plotted as heavy solid lines, with the first expression for s_n labelled nn, and the second expression for s_E labelled EE. The nn schedule shows how the north's share of industry changes with its share of expenditure. Notice that its slope is equal to $2(2a - 2ba_M - b\tau)/(c\tau)$, which means it gets steeper as trade gets freer, and it intersects the y-axis at $-(1/2)[2(2a - 2ba_M - b\tau)/(c\tau) - 1]$. Moreover, it always passes through the point $(1/2, 1/2)$ regardless of the level of trade freeness, so changes in τ rotate nn around the midpoint. It is also worth noting that the nn line is always steeper than the 45-degree ray as long as the trade condition (5.6) is

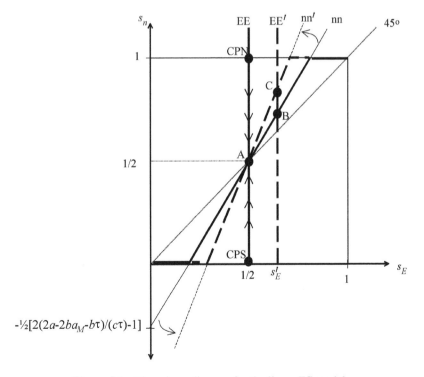

Figure 5.1   The scissor diagram for the linear FC model.

satisfied. This is the 'home-market effect' diagrammatically, that is, a given change in market size leads to a more than proportional change in the share of industry in the big region.

In (5.11) the expression for s_E does not depend upon s_n so the EE schedule is a vertical line. In particular, the figure depicts the two cases, that of symmetric expenditure, $s_E = 1/2$, and that of larger northern expenditure, $s_E > 1/2$. These correspond to EE and EE′, respectively.

By construction, the nn line shows the combinations of s_E and s_n where rental rates are equalized. It is clear therefore that $\pi > \pi^*$ at all points to the right of the nn line, because the northern market is too large for rental rates to be equal and, following the logic of the market access advantage, this corresponds to $\pi > \pi^*$. What this means is that, if the economy finds itself at a point to the right of the nn line, capital and firms will flow northwards, thus raising s_n. For points to the left of the nn line, s_n is falling. Therefore, the long-run equilibrium of the model is both unique since nn and EE are linear and stable since EE is steeper. Moreover, the CP outcomes are always unstable in the symmetric region case. The CP outcomes are marked as points CPN and CPS in the diagram. These points must be on the EE line, since the EE line is the plot of a definition, rather than a relationship that must hold only in equilibrium. The instability can be seen by noting that CPN is to the left of the nn line for any level of trade freeness. This means a small shock to CPN would take the economy into a region where capital would flow southwards and indeed this would continue until the symmetric point was reached. Analogous reasoning establishes the instability of the core-in-the-south, CPS, equilibrium.

For a given distribution of expenditure, changing trade costs have an effect on industry location. When the level of trade costs is τ, then the equilibrium s_n will be at the level of point B. If trade gets freer, s_n will shift up to the level of point C.

The Tomahawk Diagram. The foregoing results can be summarized by the tomahawk diagram in Figure 5.2. When regions are symmetric, $s_E = 1/2$, the symmetric outcome is always stable, as shown by the heavy, horizontal line at $s_n = 1/2$. The CP outcomes—which are steady states of the capital flow equation (5.1)—are always unstable as shown by the dashed horizontal lines at $s_n = 1$ and $s_n = 0$. In other words, the blade of the tomahawk is very thin and located at $\tau = 0$. We should also note that the break and sustain points coincide with both occurring at $\tau = 0$. Thus, in the symmetric-region case, symmetry does not break until all trade costs vanish, but, of course, at this point, location is irrelevant. For this reason, catastrophic agglomeration does not occur.

In the asymmetric case, $s_E > 1/2$, the home-market effect gives $s_n > s_E > 1/2$. In this case, the progressive freeing of trade leads to negligible relocation for high levels of trade costs, but as τ approaches τ^{CP}, the rate of relocation becomes extremely rapid—the more so the more similar countries are. To illustrate this, we draw two thin lines in Figure 5.2 that correspond to $s_E′$ and $s_E″$ with $s_E′ > s_E″ > 1/2$. The latter shows the agglomeration path when the regions are almost equal in size.

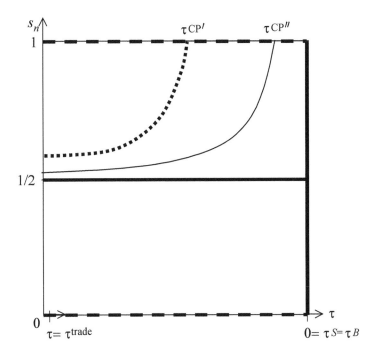

Figure 5.2   The tomahawk diagram for the linear FC model.

5.2.4 Key Features

Chapter 2 pointed out seven key features of the CP model: agglomeration via the home-market mechanism (with magnification by freer trade), circular causality via demand and cost linkages, endogenous asymmetry, catastrophic agglomeration, locational hysteresis, hump-shaped agglomeration rents and multiple long-run equilibria in the 'overlap'. Chapter 3 argued that circular causality, endogenous asymmetry, locational hysteresis and the multiple equilibria do not appear in the FC model. Since this is also the case in the linear version, we focus on the remaining features before highlighting some new properties.

COMPARISON WITH THE FC MODEL

Home-Market Magnification.   The linear FC model, in line with the Chapter 3 version, displays agglomeration forces in the form of the home-market effect. A small, exogenous change in the location of expenditures causes a more than proportional relocation of firms. This can be ascertained by differentiating (5.11) with respect to s_E to get

$$\frac{dn}{ds_E} = \frac{2(2a - 2ba_M - b\tau)}{c\tau} \tag{5.13}$$

This exceeds unity if the trade condition (5.6) holds, so the home-market effect is indeed in operation. Moreover, the home-market effect gets more powerful as trade gets freer, so the FC model also displays home-market magnification.

Catastrophic Agglomeration. If one considers only the knife-edge case of perfectly symmetric regions, the linear FC model, like its Chapter 3 relative, does not feature catastrophic agglomeration driven by lower trade costs. That is, a symmetric lowering of trade costs between perfectly symmetric regions need not lead to a concentration of industry in one region. However, when $s_E \neq 1/2$, trade-induced agglomeration does appear, but it never occurs catastrophically. Specifically, in the linear FC model, (5.11) implies that the 'delocation elasticity' $(ds_n/d\tau)(\tau/s_n)$ is

$$\frac{dn}{d\tau}\frac{\tau}{n} = -\frac{8(a - ba_M)(s_E - 1/2)}{4(2a - 2ba_M - b\tau)(s_E - 1/2) + c\tau} \tag{5.14}$$

While the delocation elasticity in the standard FC model approaches infinity as trade costs approach the level that results in full agglomeration, this is not true in the linear version. To see this, we evaluate (5.14) at τ^{CP} and find

$$\frac{dn}{d\tau}\frac{\tau}{n}\bigg|_{\tau=\tau^{CP}} = -\frac{1}{2} - \frac{2b(s_E - 1/2)}{c} \tag{5.15}$$

This shows that the linear FC model does not exhibit 'near-catastrophic agglomeration' in the sense of Baldwin (2000).

Hump-Shaped Agglomeration Rents. Agglomeration rents are a concave function of trade freeness in both versions of the FC model. For the linear version, we illustrate this by considering a long-run equilibrium in which all capital is employed in the north $(s_E > 1/2, \; n = 1 \; \text{and} \; \tau \leq \tau^{CP})$. The agglomeration rents are measured as the loss that a capital owner would incur by relocating its capital to the south. Formally, such rents are given by

$$\pi - \pi^*\big|_{n=1} = \frac{L^W + K^W}{K^W}\frac{b + c}{4(2b + c)}\tau\{8(a - ba_M)(s_E - 1/2) - \tau[4b(s_E - 1/2) + c]\} \tag{5.16}$$

This is a function of τ. It equals zero at $\tau = 0$ and $\tau = \tau^{CP}$, while it is positive in between. Moreover, in the same interval, it is concave with a maximum at $\tau = \tau^{CP}/2$, where τ^{CP} is defined in (5.12). Accordingly, as trade gets freer (i.e. τ falls from τ^{CP} towards 0), the agglomeration rents first rise and then fall ('hump shape').

Trade Dependent Factor Flows. In the standard FC model with asymmetric regions, changes in trade costs can alter the size and even the direction of capital flows. To show that this is also the case in the linear FC model, suppose the two regions have equal L endowments but the north just happens to start with a higher capital/labour ratio, that is, $s_L = 1/2$ and $s_K > 1/2$. This is equivalent to saying that the north has more consumers since we identify each unit of capital with a capital owner. Rearranging (5.11), we get a relation between the share of firms located in the north and the share of firms owned by northerners:

$$\frac{s_n - 1/2}{s_K - 1/2} = \frac{K^w}{L^w + K^w} \frac{2(2a - 2ba_M - b\tau)}{c\tau} \tag{5.17}$$

This allows us to compare the geography of capital ownership (i.e. s_K) and the geography of production (i.e. $n = s_n$). In the symmetric equilibrium, where both regions are endowed originally with the same amount of capital, there is no relocation. If the initial distribution of capital is such that $s_K > 1/2$, so that the north is richer than the south, then the direction of the capital flows is ambiguous and depends on trade costs. When trade cost are very high, namely τ is near τ_{trade}, the rich region's share of industry is less than its share of capital. In other words, when goods markets are not very integrated, but capital markets are, capital will flow from the big region to the small region. But when trade gets freer than a certain critical value, the direction of capital flows is reversed; s_n will exceed s_K, so the small region will be a net exporter of capital. The threshold value of trade freeness is

$$\tau^K = \frac{2(a - ba_M)}{b + c(L^w + K^w)/K^w} \tag{5.18}$$

Thus, the level of trade costs where capital flows are reversed increases with the share of the mobile factor, $K^w/(L^w + K^w)$.

The ambiguity of the direction of relocation is due to the opposite effects of market crowding and market access. The former makes the poor capital region attractive because firms installed there face less competition. The latter, which in this context can also be thought of as a capital owners' demand effect, makes the capital-rich region attractive because it represents a larger market given its high population. The market-crowding effect dominates when trade is quite restricted (τ is high) because the southern market is well protected from northern competition. The market-crowding effect also dominates when the capital owners' share of the population is low relative to workers so that the capital owners' demand effect is small.

NEW FEATURES: SUBSTITUTABILITY AND VARIABLE MARK-UPS

As we have seen, the linear FC model shares almost all the properties of the FC model presented in Chapter 3. We turn now to its distinct features.

Role of Product Substitutability.   As mentioned above, a major limitation of the DCI framework is that it makes it impossible to distinguish the own and cross elasticities of demand from one another since both are constant and equal to σ. With linear demands, such elasticities are not constant and are related to different parameters. Thus, we can distinguish between own and differential price effects, filtered by parameters, b and c, respectively. The substitutability parameter, c, turns out to be crucial for most results. In particular, lower substitutability (smaller c) facilitates trade (see (5.6), weakens the market-crowding effect (see (5.10)), thus fostering agglomeration (see (5.11)), strengthens the home-market effect and home-market magnification (see (5.13)), increases the delocation elasticity (see (5.15)) as well as the agglomeration rents (see (5.16)).

Location Dependent Mark-Ups. Combined with non-iceberg trade costs, variable elasticity of demand gives rise to producer prices that vary according to the location of sales. In particular, (5.5) shows that a firm sets its prices considering the geographical distribution of both customers and competitors. It absorbs part of the trade costs on distant sales (which generates 'reciprocal dumping'; see Brander and Krugman 1983) and keeps its price low where it faces many local competitors (we will come back to this when discussing the linear FE model), the more so the greater is the substitutability among varieties (i.e. the larger is the parameter c).

   This feature introduces an additional dispersion force with respect to the DCI framework. Specifically, all the rest being equal, an increase in the local number of firms not only makes the whole array of M varieties cheaper because of trade cost-saving for given producer prices; it also makes each M variety cheaper because its producer price falls ('procompetetive effect'). This reinforces the market crowding disadvantage.

5.3 THE LINEAR FE MODEL

5.3.1 Assumptions

As discussed in Chapter 4, the FE framework departs from the FC setting in one major respect. K is not physical capital but rather human capital that is embodied in K-factor owners. The crucial implication is that a K owner can offer his/her services only in the region where he/she resides, that is, $n = s_K$ and $n^* = 1 - s_K$. Accordingly, K can be interpreted as 'entrepreneurs', who are mobile between regions. To emphasize this difference, we use H (a mnemonic for human capital) to symbolize the mobile factor rather than K, and we call its reward w rather than π. By contrast, workers L are immobile across regions, and, in the symmetric-region version, they are equally distributed between regions ($s_L = 1/2$).

   As usual, the migration of entrepreneurs is governed by

$$\dot{s}_H = (\omega - \omega^*)(1 - s_H)s_H \tag{5.19}$$

where ω and ω^* are the northern and southern entrepreneurs' indirect utilities associated with (5.2). As to the former, we have

$$\omega = \frac{a^2 n^w}{2b} - a \int_{i=0}^{n+n^*} p_i di + \frac{b + c(n^w)}{2} \int_{i=0}^{n+n^*} p_i^2 di - \frac{c}{2} \left(\int_{i=0}^{n+n^*} p_i di \right)^2 + w \tag{5.20}$$

where (5.7) gives the equilibrium rental rate w (keeping in mind the change in notation), and the equilibrium prices p_i are given by (5.5). A symmetric expression holds for southern entrepreneurs.

5.3.2 Short-Run Equilibrium

In the short run, workers and entrepreneurs are immobile. Therefore, in a short-run equilibrium, consumers maximize utility, firms maximize profits, and markets clear for any given distribution of H across regions. All short-run equilibrium expressions for the linear FE model are identical to those of the linear FE model reported above but for the fact that $n = s_K$ and $n^* = 1 - s_K$.

5.3.3 Long-Run Location

In the long run, entrepreneurs are mobile. Therefore, a long-run equilibrium is characterized by the same properties as a short-run equilibrium plus the fact that entrepreneurs have no incentive to move.

CHARACTERIZATION OF EQUILIBRIA

From (5.19) entrepreneurs are unwilling to relocate in two cases: (1) for interior outcomes ($0 < s_H < 1$), whenever they achieve the same level of indirect utility wherever they reside ($\omega = \omega^*$); (2) for core–periphery (CP) outcomes ($s_H = 0$ or $s_H = 1$).

By using short-run equilibrium prices and rewards, the instantaneous indirect utility differential can be evaluated as

$$\omega - \omega^* = \Theta(\tau^T - \tau)\tau\left(n - \frac{1}{2}\right) \tag{5.21}$$

where $\Theta > 0$ is a bundle of parameters that do not involve τ. Adopting the normalization of units that implies $F = H^w$, we have

$$\tau^T \equiv \frac{4(a - ba_M)(3b + 2c)H^w}{2b[3(b + c)H^w + cL^w] + c^2(L^w + H^w)} \tag{5.22}$$

It follows immediately that $n = 1/2$ is always an equilibrium. Moreover, if $\tau < \tau^T$, the differential $\omega - \omega^*$ has the same sign as $n - 1/2$, while it has the opposite sign for $\tau > \tau^T$. Thus, when $\tau < \tau^T$, the symmetric equilibrium is unstable and entrepreneurs agglomerate in the region that initially hosts the larger fraction of them. In other words, as usual, agglomeration arises when trade costs are small enough. In contrast, for large trade costs, that is, when $\tau > \tau^T$, it is straightforward to see that the symmetric configuration is the only stable equilibrium. Hence, the threshold τ^T corresponds to both the critical value of τ at which symmetry ceases to be stable (the 'break point') and the value below which agglomeration is stable (the 'sustain point'). This follows from the fact that (5.21) is linear in n.

We must also characterize situations where τ^T is lower than τ_{trade} as defined in (5.6). This is so if and only if

$$\frac{L^w}{H^w} > \frac{6b^2 + 8bc + 3c^2}{c(2b + c)} > 3 \tag{5.23}$$

which requires the number of L owners to be large relative to the population of skilled workers. When (5.23) does not hold, the coefficient on $(n - 1/2)$ is always positive implying that agglomeration is the only stable equilibrium whatever the trade costs. Therefore, (5.23) plays a role similar to the 'no-black-hole' condition in the CP and FE models. When it is violated, the region with the larger initial share of M firms ends up attracting all of them regardless of the value of the trade costs. As in those models, more product differentiation (lower c) makes the no-black-hole condition less likely. Moreover, although the size of the industrial sector is captured here through the relative population size L^w/H^w and not through its share in consumption, the intuition is similar. The ratio L^w/H^w must be sufficiently large for the economy to display different types of equilibria according to the value of τ.[3] This result, however, does not depend on the expenditure share of the manufacturing sector because of the absence of general equilibrium income effects. Small or large sectors in terms of expenditure share may be agglomerated when τ is small enough.

Low substitutability between M varieties and low trade costs tend to favour agglomeration over dispersion. The intuition is similar to the FC model. The smaller c and τ are, the stronger the market access advantage against the market-crowding disadvantage. However, in contrast to the linear FC model, because market size is now endogenous, once a region is even slightly larger than the other, the market-access advantage snowballs and triggers complete agglomeration.

DIAGRAMMATIC SOLUTION AND FORCES

The Scissors Diagram. As in the FC model, we can find the long-run equilibria and characterize their stability properties with the scissors diagram shown in Figure 5.3.

The nn curve plots the combinations of s_n and s_E for which the indirect utility differential is zero, that is, $\omega = \omega^*$. Equation (5.7) gives $w \, (= \pi)$ and $w^* \, (= \pi^*)$ in terms of s_n and $s_E = M/(M + M^*)$. Using the equilibrium prices (5.5), the nn curve can be written in explicit form as

$$s_n = \frac{1}{2} - \frac{2(2(a - ba_m) - \tau b)(2b + c)(L^w + H^w)}{4(a - ba_m)(b + c)H^w - \tau[2b(b + c)H^w + c(2b + c)(L^w + H^w)]}\left(s_E - \frac{1}{2}\right) \tag{5.24}$$

Diagrammatic analysis is facilitated by three features of the nn curve. First, given the symmetry of the model, the nn curve passes through the midpoint, $(1/2, 1/2)$.

---

[3] Recall that, by choice of units, $(1 - \mu)/\mu$ is proportional to L^w/H^w in the CP model (see Chapter 2).

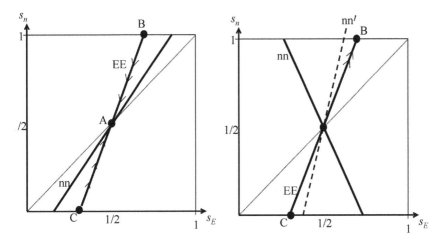

Figure 5.3 The scissors diagram for the linear FE model.

Second, the slope of the nn curve is a function of trade costs τ, and is positive for large τ's and negative for low τ's. Third, as in the FC model, n has a tendency to increase for combinations of n and s_E to the right of the nn curve because $\omega - \omega^* > 0$ in this region. To see this, take the left panel of the diagram and consider a point on the nn curve and another point that is a horizontal shift to the right of it. At the point on the nn curve, real wages are equal but for the point to the right the northern market is larger and this makes the northern real wage higher by the usual logic of the market-access advantage. Correspondingly, n is falling at all points to the left of nn.

The EE line plots the definition of E as a function of n, viz. $s_E = M/(M + M^*)$ which also equals $(L^w/2 + s_n H^w)/(L^w + H^w)$. Thus, due to the absence of income effects, the EE curve is

$$s_n = \frac{1}{2} + \frac{L^w + H^w}{H^w}\left(s_E - \frac{1}{2}\right) \tag{5.25}$$

The diagrammatic analysis is assisted by noting three facts concerning the EE curve. First, (5.25) passes through the midpoint, given symmetry. Second, it is independent of trade costs.[4] In particular, its slope is always positive. Importantly, the economy is always on the EE curve since EE is a definition. By contrast, the nn line shows all the combinations of n and s_E that satisfy the condition for an interior long-run equilibrium, namely indirect utility equalization.

The two panels in Figure 5.3 depict two alternative scenarios. The left panel of the diagram shows the case when the regions are rather closed to trade (i.e. τ is large), so nn is positively sloped. The symmetric outcome, point A, is stable since a small increase in n (moving along the EE curve as

[4] In the FE model of Chapter 4, only the endpoints of EE are unaffected by trade costs.

usual) would bring the economy to the left of the nn curve, and this, in turn, would result in a falling n. In this way, the migration shock generates self-correcting forces. The CP outcomes—shown as points B and C—which are always steady states given (5.19), are unstable. B, where $s_n = 1$, is to the left of the nn curve so n would fall, following the EE curve to point A. C is unstable for isomorphic reasons.

The right panel shows the situation for a more open economy. As trade barriers fall, the nn curve rotates around the centre point. Indeed, the nn curve switches from a positive slope to a negative slope at a sufficiently low τ. The heavy solid EE and nn curves in the right panel show the situation where τ has risen to the point where the nn curve has a negative slope. Here, the symmetric outcome is unstable (a shock along the EE curve would take the economy to the right of nn, so the shock generates self-reinforcing forces). The core-in-the-north outcome, point B, is stable since it is to the right of the nn line.

It is important to note that, in contrast to the standard FE model of Chapter 4, both the nn and EE curves, (5.24) and (5.25), are linear. As a consequence the break and sustain points coincide.

The Tomahawk Diagram. The foregoing results can be summarized by Figure 5.4, which plots $n = s_n = s_H$ against the trade cost τ and shows stable long-run equilibria with solid lines. For $\tau > \tau^T$, $n = 1/2$ is the only stable steady state of (5.19). For $\tau < \tau^T$, $n = 1/2$, $n = 0$ and $n = 1$ are all steady states but only the CP ones are stable. Given the coincidence between the break and sustain points, no overlap exists in the linear FE model.

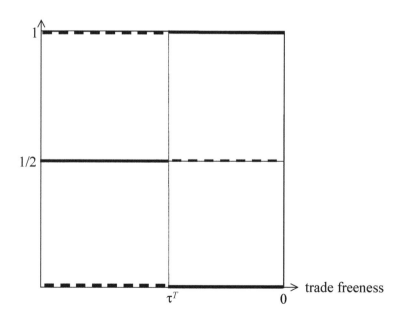

Figure 5.4 The tomahawk diagram for the linear FE model.

5.3.4 Key Features

COMPARISON WITH THE FE MODEL

Home-Market Magnification. As is true for the standard version, the linear FE model displays the home-market effect. This can be seen from inspection of Figure 5.3. A slight increase in the northern market size leads to a shift of the EE curve to the right. Presuming that trade costs are high enough for the interior equilibrium to be stable, the shock will lead to a more than proportional increase in the north's share of industry since, in this case, the nn line is steeper than the 45-degree line. Moreover, home-market magnification also occurs (i.e. the home-market effect gets stronger as trade gets freer) since freeing up trade makes the nn line steeper. Thus, the same rightward shift in the EE curve would result in a higher degree of relocation.

Circular Causality. The home-market effect is amplified by demand-linked and cost-linked circular causality. As in the FE model, agglomeration is driven by and drives inter-regional factor movement that involves people. Because people spend their incomes locally, they care about the local cost of living. This, in turn, means that migration decisions will be based on the real reward to human capital so cost-linked circular causality comes into play via the cost-of-living effect. The fact that migrants spend their incomes locally ties production shifting to expenditure shifting, so that demand-linked circular causality also operates.

Endogenous Asymmetry. Steadily falling trade costs result in an initially symmetric model becoming asymmetric. As in the symmetric FE model, the gradual reduction of trade costs starting from a high level eventually leads to full agglomeration and results in a perfectly symmetric model becoming asymmetric. However, differently from the FE model of Chapter 4, its linear version never displays (unstable) outcomes with partial agglomeration.

Catastrophic Agglomeration. As in the FE model of Chapter 4, the tomahawk diagram of its linear version shows that the endogenous asymmetry is both extreme (all industry ends up in one region) and catastrophic in the sense that, once symmetric becomes unstable, the only stable outcome is full agglomeration. Thus, the linear FE model may be subject to sudden and massive agglomeration in reaction to minor changes in trade costs, namely, when trade gets just a bit freer than τ^T.

Locational Hysteresis. Since the core can end up in either region, the linear FE model is subject to locational hysteresis. For $\tau < \tau^T$, the model features multiple stable CP equilibria. As in Chapter 4, this implies that temporary shocks, including temporary policy changes, may have hysteretic effects on the location of industry.

Hump-Shaped Agglomeration Rents.   As in the FE model, its linear version features agglomeration rents that are concave function of trade freeness. This can be established by considering a long-run equilibrium in which all entrepreneurs are located in the north ($n = 1$ and $\tau < \tau^T$). In this case, agglomeration rents are measured as the loss that an entrepreneur would incur by relocating to the south. Formally, such rents are given by

$$\Omega|_{n=1} = \frac{\Theta}{2}(\tau^T - \tau)\tau \qquad\qquad (5.26)$$

where τ^T is the threshold defined in (5.22). Agglomeration rents are thus a function of τ, which equals zero at $\tau = \tau^T$ and $\tau = 0$, while it is positive in between. Moreover, in the same interval, (5.26) is concave in τ with a maximum at $\tau = \tau^T/2$. Accordingly, as trade gets freer (i.e. τ falls from τ^T towards 0), the agglomeration rents first rise and then fall ('hump shape').

The Overlap and Self-fulfilling Expectations.   Since the break and sustain points coincide, the linear FE model does not feature any overlap. Thus, shocks to expectations cannot result in large spatial re-allocations between stable long-run equilibria.

NEW FEATURES: SUBSTITUTABILITY AND VARIABLE MARK-UPS

The linear FE model shares almost all the properties of the FE model presented in Chapter 4 except one, namely, the overlap. At the same time, it exhibits additional features that stem from the adoption of a more flexible utility function.

Role of Product Substitutability.   As in the FC model, linear demand has allowed us to distinguish between own and differential price effects captured by the parameters b and c, respectively. This has pointed out the centrality of parameter c (viz. the substitutability between varieties of the M sector) for most results. In particular, lower substitutability (smaller c) facilitates trade, weakens the market-crowding effect, thus fostering agglomeration, strengthens the home-market effect and home-market magnification. Consequently, it increases the threshold level of trade cost below which agglomeration takes place (see (5.22)) and the associated agglomeration rents (see (5.26)).

Location Dependent Mark-Up.   As in the linear FC model, the combination of non-iceberg trade costs and variable elasticities of demand gives rise to producer prices that vary according to the location of sales. Firms absorb part of the trade costs on distant sales ('dumping') and keep prices low in those markets where they face many local competitors—the more so the easier the substitutability between M sector varieties (viz. the larger c). However, differently from the linear FC model, this procompetitive effect reinforces both the market-crowding and the cost-of-living effects.

5.4 Congestion in the Linear FE Model

In previous chapters and in the present chapter so far, we have assumed that the agglomeration of workers into a single region does not involve any agglomeration costs. Yet, it is reasonable to believe that a growing settlement in a given region congests the use of local non-tradable resources. As pointed out by Helpman (1998), and Puga (1999), allowing for such phenomenon generates an additional dispersion force.

The simplest way to investigate the implications of this line of argument is to follow Ottaviano et al. (2002) in considering the natural example of land use. In particular, think of regional settlements that take the form of cities, which allows us to introduce the central variables of urban economics in the analysis (see Fujita 1989).

5.4.1 Assumptions

Assume that space is continuous and one-dimensional. Each region has a spatial extension and involves a linear city whose centre is given but has a variable size. The city centre stands for a central business district (CBD) in which all firms locate once they have chosen to set up in the corresponding region.[5] To avoid any overlap between cities, the two CBDs are assumed to be two remote points of the location space. Inter-regional trade flows go from one CBD to the other.

Housing is a new good in our economy and is described by the amount of land used by entrepreneurs. While firms and workers are assumed not to consume land, entrepreneurs, when they live in a certain region, are urban residents who consume land and commute to the regional CBD where manufacturing firms are located. Hence, each agglomeration has a spatial extension that imposes commuting and land costs on the corresponding entrepreneurs. The migration equation is modified accordingly:

$$\dot{s}_H = [(\omega - R) - (\omega^* - R^*)](1 - s_H)s_H \qquad (5.27)$$

where $(\omega - R)$ and $(\omega^* - R^*)$ are the northern and southern indirect utility levels net of commuting and land costs.

For simplicity, entrepreneurs consume a fixed lot size normalized to unity, while commuting costs are linear in distance, the commuting cost per unit of distance being given by $\theta > 0$ units of the numeraire A good. Without loss of generality, the opportunity cost of land is normalized to zero. Entrepreneurs are equally distributed around its CBD. Thus, the northern and southern cities cover n and $1 - n$ units of land, respectively, which are symmetrically located around the corresponding CBDs. This implies that the borders of the two cities are at distances $n/2$ and $(1 - n)/2$ from the CBDs, respectively.

---

[5] All these assumptions are standard in urban economics (Fujita 1989). See Fujita and Thisse (1996) as well as Lucas and Rossi-Hansberg (2002) for various explanations of why firms want to cluster in a CBD.

5.4.2 Short-Run Equilibrium

In the short run, entrepreneurs are immobile. Therefore, in a short-run equilibrium, consumers maximize utility, firms maximize profits, and markets clear for any given distribution of H across regions. All the equilibrium conditions of the linear FE model apply. In addition, however, we have to characterize the equilibrium of the land market.

In equilibrium, since all entrepreneurs residing in a certain region earn the same wage, they all reach the same utility level. For example, all northern entrepreneurs achieve the indirect utility level ω. Furthermore, since they all consume one unit of land, the equilibrium land rent at distance $\chi < n/2$ from the northern CBD is given by

$$R(\chi) = \theta\left(\frac{n}{2} - \chi\right) \tag{5.28}$$

Hence, an entrepreneur located at the average distance $n/4$ from the CBD bears a commuting cost equal to $\theta n/4$ and pays the average land rent $\theta n/4$. For simplicity, we assume that all the land rents are collected and equally redistributed among the northern entrepreneurs. Consequently, the individual urban costs after redistribution are equal to $\theta n/4$. This shows that commuting and land costs rise as city size increases, thus acting as an additional dispersion force that does not depend on trade costs.

5.4.3 Long-Run Location

In the long run, entrepreneurs are mobile. Therefore, a long-run equilibrium is characterized by the same properties as a short-run equilibrium plus the fact that entrepreneurs have no incentive to move.

CHARACTERIZATION OF EQUILIBRIA

From (5.27), entrepreneurs are unwilling to relocate in two cases. For interior outcomes ($0 < s_H < 1$) whenever they achieve the same level of net indirect utility wherever they reside ($\omega - R = \omega^* - R^*$). For core–periphery (CP) outcomes ($s_H = 0$ or $s_H = 1$) whenever their utility is higher in the region where they are clustered ($\omega - R < \omega^* - R^*$ or $\omega - R > \omega^* - R^*$, respectively). Using (5.28), the incentive to move from north to south is given by

$$\Omega^C = (\omega - R) - (\omega^* - R^*) = \left[\Theta(\tau^T - \tau)\tau - \frac{\theta}{2}\right]\left(n - \frac{1}{2}\right) \tag{5.29}$$

where the term $-(\theta/2)$ within the square brackets accounts for the difference in urban costs. The threshold values of trade costs in this expression are

$$\tau_1^C \equiv \frac{\tau^T - \sqrt{(\tau^T)^2 - 2\theta/\Theta}}{2}, \qquad \tau_2^C \equiv \frac{\tau^T + \sqrt{(\tau^T)^2 - 2\theta/\Theta}}{2} \tag{5.30}$$

Intuitively, these thresholds reach 0 and τ (defined in (5.22)) when commuting costs θ go to zero; without commuting costs, city dimension is immaterial.

Inspecting (5.27) together with (5.28) shows that the symmetric outcome $n = 1/2$ is always an equilibrium. Moreover, if $\tau_1^C < \tau < \tau_2^C$, the differential Ω^C has the same sign as $n - 1/2$, while it has the opposite sign for $0 < \tau < \tau_1^C$ and $\tau_2^C < \tau < \tau_{\text{trade}}$. Thus, when $\tau_1^C < \tau < \tau_2^C$, the symmetric equilibrium is unstable and entrepreneurs agglomerate in a single region. In other words, agglomeration arises for intermediate values of trade costs. In contrast, for small and large trade costs, the symmetric configuration is the only stable equilibrium. Moreover, the thresholds τ_1^C and τ_2^C correspond to both the critical values of τ at which symmetry ceases to be stable ('break points') and the values at which agglomeration becomes stable ('sustain points'). This follows from the fact that (5.29) is linear in n.

These results show that the existence of positive commuting costs within the regional centres is sufficient to yield dispersion when trade costs are sufficiently low. In particular, an increase in the commuting costs fosters dispersion by widening the range of values of τ for which symmetry is the only stable equilibrium. Indeed, sufficiently high commuting costs always yield dispersion.

It is interesting to point out that, while dispersion arises for both high and low trade costs, this happens for very different reasons. In the former case, firms are dispersed as a response to product market crowding. In the latter, firms are dispersed as a response to land market crowding.

DIAGRAMMATIC SOLUTION AND FORCES

The Scissors Diagram As in the plain FE model, we can draw a scissors diagram that is qualitatively identical to Figure 5.3. Indeed, the EE curve is exactly the same as (5.25), while the nn curve is still linear in s_E and coincides with (5.24) for $\theta = 0$:

$$s_n = \frac{1}{2} - \frac{2\tau(2a - \tau b)(b+c)(2b+c)(L^w + H^w)(s_E - (1/2))}{-\theta(2b+c)^2 H^w + \tau(b+c)\{4a(b+c)H^w - \tau[2b(b+c)H^w + c(2b+c)(L^w + H^w)]\}} \quad (5.31)$$

The presence of θ implies that the slope of nn is positive for large and small τ's. Accordingly, the two panels in Figure 5.3 cover three possible scenarios.

The left panel of the diagram shows the case when the regions are either rather closed or rather open to trade (i.e. τ is either large or small), so nn is positively sloped. For these levels of trade costs, the economy has three long-run equilibria, the symmetric outcome, shown as point A, and the two CP outcomes, shown as points B and C. While the former outcome is stable, the latter ones are not.

The right panel shows the situation for intermediate openness. As trade barriers fall from some high level, the nn line rotates around the centre point and its slope switches from positive to negative. Here, the symmetric outcome A is unstable, while the CP outcomes, B and C, are stable. However, as barriers continue to fall, the nn line reverses its rotation and eventually its slope switches back from negative to positive as in the left panel. The reason for this reversal is as follows. Lower trade costs end up eroding both the market-access and the market-crowd-

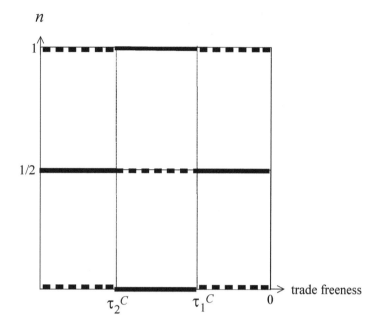

Figure 5.5 The tomahawk diagram for the linear FE model with congestion.

ing effects. They do not erode, however, the congestion effect in the land market, which thus becomes the driving force of location.

The Tomahawk Diagram. The foregoing results can be summarized by the tomahawk diagram. This is reported in Figure 5.5, which plots $n = s_n = s_H$ against the trade cost τ and shows long-run equilibria with solid lines. For $\tau < \tau_1^C$ and $\tau > \tau_2^C$, $n = 1/2$ is the only stable steady state of (5.27). For $\tau_1^C < \tau < \tau_2^C$ only the CP outcomes are stable steady states. Given the coincidence between the break and sustain points, no overlap exists as in the plain linear FE model.

5.4.4 Key Features

COMPARISON WITH THE LINEAR FE MODEL

The introduction of an inner spatial dimension of regions alters some of the fundamental properties of the linear FE model.

Home-Market Magnification. In the linear FE model with congestion, the home-market effect is not a robust feature. This can be seen from inspection of Figure 5.3. A slight increase in the northern market size leads to a shift of the EE curve to the right. Even when trade costs are high or low enough for the interior equilibrium to be stable, the shock does not lead necessarily to a more than proportional increase in the north's share of industry since, due to congestion costs, the nn line may not be steeper than the 45-degree line. Accordingly, also home-market magnification does not always occur, that is, freeing up trade makes the nn line flatter when trade costs are low enough. Thus, the same rightward shift in the EE curve does not necessarily result in a higher degree of relocation.

Circular Causality. The home-market effect is amplified by demand-linked and cost-linked circular causality and dampened by congestion. Since agglomeration is still driven by and drives inter-regional factor movement involving people, there is both cost- and demand-linked circular causality.

Endogenous Asymmetry. For a while the gradual reduction of trade costs starting from a high level leads to full agglomeration and causes a perfectly symmetric model to become asymmetric. Moreover, as in the plain linear FE model, its congested version never displays (unstable) outcomes with partial agglomeration.

Catastrophic Agglomeration. As in the plain linear FE model, the tomahawk diagram of its congested version shows that the endogenous asymmetry is both extreme (all industry ends up in one region) and catastrophic in the sense that, once symmetry becomes unstable, the only stable outcome is full agglomeration. Thus, sudden and massive agglomerations in reaction to minor changes in trade costs are possible.

Locational Hysteresis. Since for $\tau_1^C < \tau < \tau_2^C$, it features multiple stable CP equilibria, the linear FE model with congestion is subject to locational hysteresis. Accordingly, temporary shocks, including temporary policy changes may have hysteretic effects on the location of industry.

Hump-Shaped Agglomeration Rents. Also the congested FE model features agglomeration rents that are a concave function of trade freeness. This can be established by considering a long-run equilibrium in which all entrepreneurs are located in the north ($n = 1$ and $\tau_1^C < \tau < \tau_2^C$). In this case, agglomeration rents are measured as the loss that an entrepreneur would incur by relocating to the south. Formally, such rents are given by

$$\Omega^C\big|_{n=1} = \frac{1}{2}\left[\Theta(\tau^T - \tau)\tau - \frac{\theta}{2}\right] \tag{5.32}$$

where τ^T is the threshold defined in (5.22). Therefore, agglomeration rents are a concave function of τ with a maximum at $\tau = \tau^T/2$ ('hump shape'). However, with respect to (5.26), the agglomeration rents (5.32) are smaller than in the plain linear FE model for any τ. The extent of this downward shift is an increasing function of the commuting cost θ. Thus, intuitively, congestion reduces the gains from agglomeration.

The Overlap and Self-fulfilling Expectations. Since the break and sustain points coincide, also the congested version of the linear FE model does not feature any overlap. Shocks to expectations cannot trigger large spatial re-allocations between stable long-run equilibria.

Product Substitutability and Variable Mark-Ups. The introduction of commuting and land costs in the linear FE model does not affect previous results. Lower substitutability between varieties fosters agglomeration. Moreover, variable elasticity of demand generates equilibrium prices that vary in space, being lower where many firms are located.

Re-Dispersion. In the linear FE model with congestion, falling trade costs drive the economy through dispersion, agglomeration, and re-dispersion. Thus, the presence of non-tradable resources in limited supply gives rise to a 'bell-shaped curve' in spatial development (Alonso 1980).[6]

Reverse Tomahawk. In contrast to the plain FE model, in the present setting the absence of immobile L would not remove all the dispersion forces. To see this, notice that if $L^w = 0$, it is readily verified that $\tau_{\text{trade}} < \tau^T/2 < \tau_2^C$ so that dispersion does not arise when trade costs are high. Consequently, the economy moves from agglomeration to dispersion when trade costs fall as in Helpman (1998). This can be summarized by a tomahawk diagram that is the mirror image of Figure 5.4.

5.5 CONCLUDING REMARKS AND RELATED LITERATURE

5.5.1 Summary Results for Policy Modelling

The models of the new economic geography have been questioned for their heavy dependence on Dixit–Stiglitz monopolistic competition, CES utility and iceberg trade costs—what we called the DCI framework. This chapter has shown that their insights hold true in an alternative set-up based on quasi-linear quadratic utility and linear trade costs. The alternative set-up is also more flexible. This has allowed us to enrich previous results. First, lower substitutability between M varieties reinforces agglomeration against dispersion. Second, firms apply lower mark-ups to sales in markets where they face more competitors. This procompetitive effect affects both the cost-of-living and the home-market effects and thus agglomeration and dispersion forces.

The linear set-up is also easier to handle, yielding closed-form answers to all questions. This has allowed us to introduce congestion costs that act as an additional dispersion force. The result is the emergence of a 'bell-shaped curve' of

---

[6] The connection between the evolution of the spatial distribution of economic activities and the various stages of development is investigated, among others, by Williamson (1965) and Wheaton and Shishido (1981).

spatial development: as trade costs fall, the economy goes through dispersion, agglomeration, and re-dispersion.

Nonetheless, all these additional insights are gained at some cost. In particular, due to linearity the break and sustain points coincide so that shocks to expectations cannot trigger large spatial re-allocations.

5.5.2 Related Literature

The origin of the linear models proposed is to be found in Ottaviano et al. (2002), who adopt a quasi-linear utility function in the FE model. Ottaviano (2001) applies the same demand system to the FC model.

The role of non-traded goods and factors in models of the new economic geography is studied by Helpman (1998) and Puga (1999). Krugman and Livas Elisondo (1996) as well as Tabuchi (1998) deal with commuting costs and land rents in linear cities. Richer models involving these costs can be found in Alonso (1964), Fujita (1989), as well as Papageorgiou and Pines (1999).

REFERENCES

Alonso, W. 1964. *Location and Land Use*. Cambridge, MA: Harvard University Press.
_____. 1980. Five bell shapes in development. *Papers of the Regional Science Association* 45: 5–16.
Anderson, S. P., A. de Palma and J.-F. Thisse. 1992. *Discrete Choice Theory of Product Differentiation*. Cambridge, MA: MIT Press.
Baldwin, R. 2000. In *Regulatory Protectionism, Developing Nations and a Two-Tier World Trading System*, Brookings Trade Forum, ed. Susan Collins and Dani Rodrik. Washington DC: The Brookings Institution, 237–293.
Brander, J. and P. Krugman. 1983. A 'reciprocal dumping' model of international trade. *Journal of International Economics* 15: 313–323.
Fujita, M. 1989. *Urban Economic Theory. Land Use and City Size*. Cambridge: Cambridge University Press.
Fujita, M. and J.-F. Thisse. 1996, Economics of agglomeration. *Journal of the Japanese and International Economies* 10: 339–378.
Fujita, M., P. Krugman and A. J. Venables. 1999. *The Spatial Economy. Cities, Regions and International Trade*. Cambridge, MA: MIT Press.
Helpman, E. 1998. The size of regions. In *Topics in Public Economics. Theoretical and Applied Analysis*, ed. D. Pines, E. Sadka and I. Zilcha. Cambridge: Cambridge University Press, 33–54.
Krugman, P. 1991. Increasing returns and economic geography. *Journal of Political Economy* 99: 483–499.
_____. 1998. Space: the final frontier. *Journal of Economic Perspectives* 12: 161–174.
Krugman, P. and R. Livas Elisondo. 1996. Trade policy and the third world metropolis. *Journal of Development Economics* 49: 137–150.
Lucas, R. E. and E. Rossi-Hansberg. 2002. On the internal structure of cities. *Econometrica* 70: 1445–1476.
Ottaviano, G. I. P. 2001. Home market effects and the (in)efficiency of international specialization. Mimeo, Graduate Institute of International Studies.

Ottaviano, G. I. P., T. Tabuchi and J.-F. Thisse. 2002. Agglomeration and trade revisited, *International Economic Review* 43: 409–436.

Papageorgiou, Y. Y. and D. Pines. 1999. *An Essay in Urban Economic Theory.* Dordrecht: Kluwer.

Puga, D. 1999. The rise and fall of regional inequalities. *European Economic Review* 43: 303–334.

Tabuchi, T. 1998 Agglomeration and dispersion: a synthesis of Alonso and Krugman. *Journal of Urban Economics* 44: 333–351.

Wheaton, W. and H. Shishido. 1981. Urban concentration, agglomeration economies, and the level of economic development. *Economic Development and Cultural Change* 30: 17–30.

Williamson, J. 1965. Regional inequality and the process of national development. *Economic Development and Cultural Change* 14: 3–45.

The Constructed Capital Model

6.1 INTRODUCTION

At a very abstract level, the models presented in the previous chapters can be thought of as representing points on the trade-off between richness of features and tractability. The FC model of Chapter 3 is entirely tractable in the sense that closed-form solutions could be had for all endogenous variables including the spatial distribution of industry. Unfortunately, this tractability comes at the cost of losing many of the most exciting features of the CP model of Chapter 2, including circular causality, catastrophic agglomeration, locational hysteresis and the overlap.

The FE model of Chapter 4 restores all of these features, but even though it is far more tractable than the CP model, one cannot find a general closed-form solution for the endogenous variable that is usual the focus of policy analysis, namely the spatial location of industry. As we explained at length in Chapters 2 and 4, the source of this intractability is the non-integer power that enters the price index.

The linear FE model of Chapter 5 provides a different point on the tractability-richness trade-off. It displays more of the CP model's features than the FC model while remaining perfectly tractable in the sense that we get closed-form solutions for all variables, including the critical spatial allocation of industry. It also exhibits some additional features such as variable mark-ups.

Here we enrich this gallery by adding a model in the CP family (Dixit–Stiglitz, icebergs, etc.) that is as tractable as the FC model while displaying more CP features. In particular, the model features catastrophic agglomeration and circular causality even though we get closed-form solutions for all endogenous variables and agents are forward looking. The model, which we refer to as the constructed capital model (CC model for short), is due to Baldwin (1999).

6.1.1 Logic of the CC Model

The key to industrial relocation in the CC model is the construction and depreciation of capital. In the CP model, various changes (trade costs, region size, etc.) produced inter-regional factor flows. In the CC model, the same pressures lead to the construction of capital in the attractive region and depreciation of capital in the other region (inter-regional capital flows are assumed away). As the capital stock rises in the attractive region and depreciates in the other, total expenditure rises in the attractive region and declines in the other. This generates demand-linked circular causality that can support further accumulation of capital in the attractive region and depreciation in the other. As in the CP and FE models, the strength of this pro-agglomeration circular causality dominates the anti-agglomeration market-crowding effect when trade is sufficiently free. Initially symmetric regions will, therefore, experience a catastrophic agglomeration of industry when the degree of openness surpasses a critical level (the break point).

6.1.2 Organization of the Chapter

We begin with a formal presentation of the CC model assuming regions are symmetric. The CC model shares almost all the basic assumptions of the FC model, so this presentation is kept brief. We then go on to examine the locational equilibria, working first with the short-run equilibrium (where capital stocks are taken as exogenous) before carrying on to the long-run equilibrium where regional capital stocks are endogenous. As part of this, we study the local stability properties of long-run equilibrium and provide an analysis of forces. The following section extends the model to study the implications of capital mobility/immobility. The resulting model with capital mobility has properties that are qualitatively identical to those of the FC model; in particular, all the long-run equilibria are locally stable so catastrophes are impossible. This highlights the fact that capital mobility—at least capital mobility without its owner—is actually a force for spatial stability. As usual, we close the chapter with a comparison of CC and CP model features as well as some concluding remarks that include bibliographic notes.

6.2 THE SYMMETRIC CC MODEL

The CC model is best thought of as a slight modification of the FC model (Chapter 3). The crucial difference between the two models lies in the mechanics of regional imbalances. In the FC model, divergence in the regional stocks of firms is fuelled by capital mobility. In the CC model, it is fostered by the local accumulation of capital.

6.2.1 Assumptions

The CC model works with a global economy consisting of two nations/regions (north and south), two sectors (agriculture and industry), and two factors (physical capital K and labour L). The distribution of factor ownership is such that s_K units of the world capital supply and s_L units of world labour are owned by northern residents; southerners own the balance.

From the modelling perspective, the agriculture sector serves the very modest role of allowing trade imbalances in the industrial goods sector (as is true in all the models in this book). The principle of parsimony thus leads us to keep it as simple as possible. Specifically, the A sector is Walrasian, uses only labour to produce its homogenous output (one unit of L per unit of output) and its output is sold costlessly both inter- and intra-regionally. The A sector good is our numeraire.

The industrial sector's technology and market structure are identical to that of the FC model. Namely, industry supplies a set of differentiated varieties subject to increasing returns and Dixit–Stiglitz monopolistic competition. Industrial production uses only capital in its fixed cost (one unit of K per variety) and only labour in the variable cost (a_M units of L per unit of variety). Intra-regional sales are costless, but inter-regional trade in industrial goods is subject to iceberg trade costs with only one unit arriving at its destination for every $\tau > 1$ units of shipped. Each region's supply of labour is fixed and inter-regionally immobile.

One critical difference between CC and FC models is that the CC model assumes that capital, as well as labour, is immobile across regions.

There are two further differences between the CC and FC models. First, the FC model assumed that physical capital never depreciates. Here, we allow depreciation, and—because capital is used in the fixed cost—it is convenient to assume a particular form of depreciation.[1] Specifically, a unit of capital is either in perfect working order, or it 'dies', that is, it becomes completely useless. We assume that each unit of capital faces a constant probability of 'dying' at every instant, with the probability equal to δ. Given the continuum of varieties, the law of large numbers implies that the proportion of the capital stock—and thus a proportion of the industrial varieties—that disappears each period is exactly equal to δ.[2]

Second, we assume that a new unit of physical capital can be constructed from primary resources (labour). Formally, this means introducing a perfectly competitive capital-construction sector, which we refer to as the I sector (a mnemonic of investment goods sector). Specially, we assume that a new unit of capital can be made with a_I units of L, so the cost of a new unit of capital, what we call F, is equal to $w_L a_I$, where w_L is the wage. Also, the amount of new capital constructed equals L_I/a_I where L_I is the amount of L employed in the I sector. To summarize, the I sector technology,[3]

$$F = w_L a_I, \quad Q_K = \frac{L_I}{a_I} \tag{6.1}$$

where Q_K is the I sector's output, that is, the flow of newly constructed capital, and F is the cost of a new unit of capital.

As to demand, the CC and FC models are identical. Preferences over agricultural and industrial goods consist of CES preferences for a continuum of industrial varieties nested in an upper-tier Cobb–Douglas function that ensures a constant fraction of expenditure, namely μ, is spent on industrial goods.

To summarize, apart from three assumptions—that capital can depreciate, can be constructed, and is immobile across regions—the CC model is identical to the FC model. We also note that one can interpret the CC model as a neoclassical growth model (see Baldwin 1999 for a development of this theme).

[1] Since capital is immobile in this model, we could never reach the CP outcome without depreciation.

[2] More technically, the probability at time t that a unit of K will still be working at time s is $e^{-\delta(s-t)}$, where δ is the instantaneous failure rate. See Baldwin (1999) for details.

[3] Given our assumptions on depreciation and construction of capital, the north's capital stock evolves according to $dK/dt = Q_K - \delta K$. The south has an isomorphic expression.

Since capital must work in the same region as its owner, there can be no distinction between the ownership and employment distribution of world capital. In symbols, this means that s_n and s_K are identically equal. Plainly we could use either symbol but since s_n is endogenous in the FC model while s_K is exogenous, we use s_n to represent the spatial division of firms/capital. In symbols, this can be expressed as $n = s_n K^w$ and $n^* = (1 - s_n) K^w$.

6.2.2 Short-Run Equilibrium

As usual, we distinguish between short- and long-run equilibria. The key to this distinction in the CC model is capital. Specifically, the world capital stock K^w and its inter-regional division s_n are fixed in the short run but endogenous in the long run. As usual, taking the long-run variables as given in the short run allows us to work out prices, quantities and relative market size, s_E, in a conceptually uncluttered setting.

Since the regional capital stocks are fixed in the short run, the distinction between the FC and CC models—that is, relocation versus construction/destruction of capital—is immaterial. For this reason, most of the CC model's short-run equilibrium expressions are identical to those of the FC model. In particular, using the same normalizations and choice of units as in the FC model, mill pricing by industrial firms (together with iceberg trade costs), and marginal cost pricing by agriculture firms (together with costless trade), we get

$$p = 1, \quad p^* = \tau, \quad p_A = p_A^* = w_L = w_L^* = 1 \qquad (6.2)$$

using the standard notation (w_L is wages, π is operating profits, p is the producer price of a typical industrial variety, and p_A the price of the A good). See Chapter 3 for derivations.

It is important that we do not normalize the world stock of capital to unity as we did in the FC model, the reason being that the world capital stock is endogenous in the CC model.

In the CC model, as in the FC model, physical capital's reward is the operating profit earned by a typical unit of variety. Given (6.2) and the standard demand functions, operating profits are (see Chapter 3 for details)

$$\pi = bB \frac{E^w}{K^w}, \quad \pi^* = bB^* \frac{E^w}{K^w}; \quad b \equiv \frac{\mu}{\sigma} \qquad (6.3)$$

where as in the FC model

$$B \equiv \frac{s_E}{\Delta} + \phi \frac{s_E^*}{\Delta^*}, \quad B^* \equiv \phi \frac{s_E}{\Delta} + \frac{s_E^*}{\Delta^*}; \quad \Delta \equiv s_n + \phi s_n^*, \quad \Delta^* \equiv \phi s_n + s_n^*$$

Here, we use the standard notation (s_E is the northern share of world expenditures E^w, $\phi \equiv \tau^{1-\sigma}$ is our measure of trade freeness, $s_E^* \equiv 1 - s_E$, and $s_n^* \equiv 1 - s_n$).

As (6.3) shows, the mobile factor's reward depends upon the spatial distribution of industry, namely s_n, and the spatial distribution of expenditure, namely s_E. Since capital's reward is the fulcrum of our analysis and we are taking s_n as given here, our next task is to characterize s_E. We begin with s_E's denominator, E^w.

A crucial difference between the CC and FC models is that the construction of capital uses up some resources, so consumption expenditure does not equal income. At the world level, consumption expenditure equals world income minus world spending on new capital. World income is the wage bill plus operating profits, that is, $L^w + bE^w$.[4] Spending on capital construction is just equal to the value of resources employed by I sectors worldwide; this quantity is denoted as L_I^w.[5] With $w_L = w_L^* = 1$, E^w equals $L^w + bE^w$ minus L_I^w. To express this in term of parameters and long-run variables, we note from (6.1) that the amount of labour necessary to maintain the world capital stock, that is, L_I^w, equals $\delta K^w a_I$. Using this together with the fact that $E^w = L^w + bE^w - L_I^w$, we get

$$E^w = \frac{L^w - \delta K^w a_I}{1 - b} \tag{6.4}$$

where K^w is the worldwide capital stock (to be determined below).

To finish our characterization of s_E, we calculate northern expenditure E. The north's labour income is $s_L L^w$, its capital income is $s_n b B E^w$ given (6.3) and its share of depreciation is $s_n \delta K^w$. Using these facts in the north's expenditure definition yields $E = s_L L^w + s_n b B E^w - s_n \delta K^w a_I$. Taking the ratio of this to our expression for world expenditure, (6.4), we get

$$s_E = \frac{(b\phi s_n/\Delta^*) + (1 - b)(s_L L^w - s_n \delta K^w a_I)/[L^w - \delta K^w a_I]}{1 - (b s_n/\Delta) + (\phi b s_n/\Delta^*)} \tag{6.5}$$

after gathering terms and simplifying. What this shows is that relative market size s_E depends upon the long-run variables, namely the spatial distribution of firms/capital, that is, s_n, and the global capital stock K^w.[6]

6.2.3 Long-Run Equilibrium

In the long run, regional capital stocks are endogenous and rise or fall until the cost of constructing/replacing a new unit of capital just equals the present value of the income stream it would generate.[7] Finding the long-run equilibrium capital stock therefore requires evaluation of the costs and benefits of having an extra unit of capital. The condition yields what may be thought of as the location condition for the CC model.

---

[4] With mill pricing, operating profit is $1/\sigma$ times sales and worldwide industry sales equal μE^w

[5] Spending on capital accumulation equals the I sector total cost since, by perfect competition, its revenue always equals its total costs.

[6] Although we do not use them in the analysis, we note that the equilibrium firm size equals $\pi\sigma$ in the north and $\pi^*\sigma$ in the south; the long-run equilibrium values of these turn out to be identical across regions and invariant to industrial delocation and changes in openness (as in the FC model).

[7] To put this differently, national capital stocks rise or fall until the typical variety earns an operating profit that provides a normal rate of return on the construction investment.

In any interior long-run equilibrium (i.e. where $0 < s_n < 1$), both regions must be actively constructing enough capital to replace depreciation. Thus, in both regions, the capital stock (i.e. number of industrial firms) adjusts to the point where the value of extra capital v equals its construction cost F. If a core–periphery outcome emerges, it must be that the value of a unit of capital is below its construction/replacement cost in the 'periphery', while capital's value exceeds its construction costs in the 'core'. To summarize, the 'location conditions' of the CC model are

$$v = F, \quad v^* = F^*; \quad 0 < s_n < 1$$
$$v = F, \quad v^* < F^*; \quad s_n = 1 \tag{6.6}$$

where F is the construction/replacement costs and from (6.1), $F = a_I$. The condition for the core-in-the-south CP equilibrium (not shown) is isomorphic to the second-row condition in (6.6). Note that this expression implies that $q \equiv v/F = 1$ and $q^* \equiv v^*/F^* = 1$ at interior equilibria, where q (",4>Tobin's q from Tobin 1969) is the ratio of the value of K to its replacement cost.

To finish our characterization of the long run, we need to find v. If we could ignore depreciation, calculating the value of a unit of capital in equilibrium would be trivial. Once operating profit reaches its equilibrium level, say π', the value of having a unit of capital would be the present value of a permanent income stream equal to π'; with a discount rate of ρ, the present value would be π'/ρ. Recognizing that the unit of capital may depreciate lowers its present value. Given the particular form of the depreciation assumed, the probability that the unit is still alive declines at the rate δ, so the present value of a unit of capital is $\pi/(\rho + \delta)$.[8] A similar condition holds for southern varieties, so

$$v = \frac{\pi}{\rho + \delta}, \quad v^* = \frac{\pi^*}{\rho + \delta} \tag{6.7}$$

where v and v^* are our symbols for the value of a unit of capital in the north and the south, respectively.

It immediately follows from (6.6) and (6.7) that $\pi = \pi^*$ at all interior equilibria in the CC model. This in turn means that CC model interior equilibria are characterized by exactly the same relationship between relative market size and trade freeness as in the FC model; namely

$$s_n = \frac{1}{2} + \left(\frac{1 + \phi}{1 - \phi}\right)\left(s_E - \frac{1}{2}\right) \tag{6.8}$$

---

[8] More formally, the value v is $v = \int e^{-(\rho + \delta)} \pi_t dt$ integrated from $t = 0$ to $t = \infty$; note that the long-run equilibrium π is constant and the probability of the unit of capital being alive at time s is $e^{-s\delta}$.

where, as usual, this only holds when it implies economically relevant values for the spatial division of industry.[9]

We turn next to finding K^w. We saw that at any interior equilibrium $\pi = \pi^*$ but it is also true that, at any core–periphery outcome, all capital earns the same. This equality of earnings in any long-run equilibrium means that each unit must earn the world average reward, which, given (6.3), is just total payments to capital bE^w divided by K^w. From (6.6), this reward (bE^w/K^w) must equal $a_I(\rho + \delta)$; rearranging implies that $K^w = bE^w/[(\rho + \delta)a_I]$. Solving this together with (6.4), we find

$$K^w = \frac{\beta L^w}{(1 - \beta)\rho a_I}, \quad E^w = \frac{L^w}{1 - \beta}; \quad \beta \equiv \frac{b\rho}{\rho + \delta} \tag{6.9}$$

where β is a group of parameters that frequently appears, and $b \equiv \mu/\sigma$ as usual.[10]

A second useful implication of the equality of capital earnings in long-run equilibria is that the north's share of global expenditure can be written in a highly intuitive form. In particular, earnings equalization implies that B from (6.3) is always unity in long-run equilibria, so $E = s_L L^w + s_n bE^w - s_n \delta K^w a_I$. Using (6.9), this simplifies to

$$s_E = \frac{1}{2} + \beta\left(s_n - \frac{1}{2}\right) + (1 - \beta)\left(s_L - \frac{1}{2}\right) \tag{6.10}$$

Alternatively, (6.10) can be written as $s_E = \beta s_n + (1 - \beta)s_L$, so the north's share of world expenditure takes the very intuitive form of being a weighted average of the north's share of world L and world K. This expression shows the key difference between the CC model and the FC model. In the FC model, s_E is fixed by initial endowments of L and K. Here, s_E is endogenous, because it depends upon s_n. What this means is that the production shifting leads to expenditure shifting in the CC model.

To complete the analysis, we note that the long-run equilibria, s_E and s_K, are given by using (6.10) in (6.8), to get

$$s_n = \frac{Z/2 + [(1 - \beta)(s_L - 1/2) - \beta/2]Z}{Z - \beta}; \quad Z \equiv \frac{1 - \phi}{1 + \phi} \tag{6.11}$$

In the symmetric region case where $s_L = 1/2$, the even division of industry is always a long-run equilibria. It is not, however, always stable. This is the next topic.

6.2.4 Diagrammatic Solution

THE SCISSORS DIAGRAM

Analysis of the model is easily illustrated with the help of Figure 6.1. The figure plots the north's expenditure share, s_E, on the horizontal axis and the north's share

---

[9] More specifically, it holds for $s_E \in [\phi/(1 + \phi), 1/(1 + \phi)]$; outside these bounds, s_n is zero or unity, that is, $s_n = 1$ for $s_E < \phi/(1 + \phi)$ and $s_n = 0$ for $s_E > 1/(1 + \phi)$.

[10] More specifically, β is the ratio of capital's net income, that is, $(\pi - \delta F)K$, to total income in equilibrium. It thus measures how much expenditure shifting occurs for a given amount of production shifting and therefore can be viewed as a gauge of the strength of the demand-linked circular causality in this model.

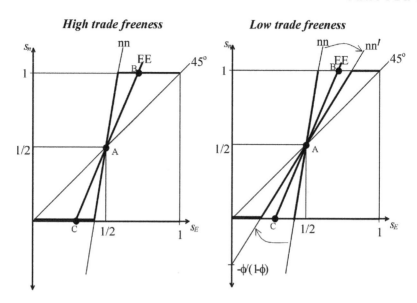

Figure 6.1 The scissor diagram for the CC model with symmetric nations.

of industry, s_n, on the vertical axis. For simplicity, we consider symmetric nations, that is, $s_L = 1/2$.

The two key equilibrium expressions, (6.8) and (6.10), are plotted as heavy solid lines, with the expression for $s_K \equiv s_n$, namely (6.8), labelled nn, and the expression for s_E, (6.10), labelled EE. The diagram is quite similar to that of the FC model. Indeed, as in the FC model, the slope of the nn curve is $(1 + \phi)/(1 - \phi)$. This slope always exceed unity so we know the home-market effect is in operation. The nn curve also becomes steeper as trade gets freer, so the home-market magnification effect is also in evidence. The big difference with the FC model is that the EE curve is no longer vertical; the EE curve slopes upward with a slope equal to $1/\beta$. In other words, expenditure shifting leads to production shifting (nn slopes upward) as in the FC model, but additionally, production shifting leads to expenditure shifting (EE slopes upward). This, of course, is exactly why circular causality can operate in the CC model, but not in the FC model.

Since the regions have equal endowments of labour in the symmetric case that we are considering, both nn and EE pass through the midpoint (1/2, 1/2). The symmetric outcome ($s_E = 1/2$ and $s_n = 1/2$) is therefore a long-run equilibrium. The core–periphery outcomes are shown as points B and C in the diagram. At point B, for example, the expression of the north's expenditure share continues to hold, but capital rates of return are not equalized so the point is off the nn line.

As in the FC model, all points to the right of the nn line imply $\pi > \pi^*$ since the north market is too large to allow for the equalization of rates of return (by the usual market size logic). In the FC model, this price pressure induced inter-regional capital flows. Here, capital is immobile, but the same pressure results in above-normal rates of capital construction in the north and zero construction in the south. More precisely, since $\pi = \pi^* = a_I(\rho + \delta)$ on the nn line, it must be that, $\pi > a_I(\rho + \delta)$ and $\pi^* < a_I(\rho + \delta)$ to the right of the nn line. In other words, for points to the right of nn, the north's capital stock will be rising and the south's will be depreciating. What this means is that s_n will be increasing for all points to the right of the nn line and it will be decreasing for all points to the left.[11]

SOLVABLE CATASTROPHES

The two panels in Figure 6.1 depict two alternative scenarios. The left panel of the figure shows the case where trade is very free, so nn is steeper than EE. To investigate local stability, consider what would happen if there were a small increase in s_n starting from $s_n = 1/2$ and we allowed this production shock to alter market sizes according to EE. Such a shock would take the economy to a point that is to the right of nn, so the shocked s_n would tend to increase. This equilibrium is clearly unstable; any positive shock to s_n would drive the system to the core-in-the-north outcome, namely point B. Any negative shock would lead it to the core-in-the-south equilibrium at point C.

The right panel shows the case where trade is sufficiently restricted for the nn line, marked as nn′, to be flatter than the EE line (falling openness pivots the nn around point A as shown). The symmetric equilibrium A is stable since a slight increase in s_n would take us to a point to the left of nn, where s_n tends to decrease back to its initial value.

The diagram also allows us to evaluate the stability of the CP outcomes. When ϕ is low, point B is to the left of nn, and point C is to right. Thus, perturbations from B will result in a falling s_n, so the core-in-the-north outcome is unstable. Likewise, the core-in-the-south outcome is also unstable. When ϕ is high enough, B is to the right of the nn line and C is to the left, so both CP outcomes are stable.[12]

The break and sustain points occur when the slopes of the nn and EE curves coincide. At this point a catastrophic agglomeration would occur since the symmetric outcome becomes unstable and the core–periphery outcome becomes stable.

6.2.5 Stability Analysis

As the scissors diagram makes clear, the linearity of the model implies that the break and sustain points are identical. Comparing the slopes of nn and EE, we see

[11] Another way to say this is that for combination of s_K and s_E to the right of nn, northern capital earns an above-normal rate of return, and southern capital earns a below-normal rate of return.

[12] The CC model can be easily extended to the case of asymmetric regions. In particular, if regions are different in their fundamental sizes, then the EE line does not pass through the midpoint in the scissor diagram. If, for example, the south is bigger ($s_L < 1/2$), the EE line moves left. In this case, when the interior equilibrium is stable, a smooth decrease in trade barriers produces a gradual increase in the share of capital in the south (home-market effect). In contrast, when the interior equilibrium is unstable, lower trade costs drive this equilibrium closer to the core-in-the-north outcome, thus enlarging the set of initial s_K's that lead to agglomeration in the south. This is reminiscent of what happens in the CP and FE models of Chapters 2 and 4, respectively.

that the break point is when the denominator of (6.11) becomes zero, namely when $Z = \beta$. Using our definition of Z, we find that the break and sustain levels of trade freeness are

$$\phi^B \equiv \phi^S = (1 - \beta)/(1 + \beta) \qquad (6.12)$$

From the definition of β in (6.9), we see that the set of unstable ϕ's expands as μ and ρ rise and σ and δ fall. The impact of σ and μ on the instability set is familiar from the FC and FE models. The novel elements here are ρ and δ. As δ falls, the expenditure shifting that comes with production shifting gets stronger, expanding the instability set. To see this, note that δ dampens the expenditure rise that comes with a higher K stock, since depreciation means that some additional resources must be devoted to maintenance instead of consumption. The lower δ is, the lower will be this dampening effect. Turning to ρ's impact, note that ρ raises the equilibrium profit rate, $a_l(\rho + \delta)$. Thus, a higher ρ amplifies the expenditure shifting that accompanies a given amount of production shifting, thereby strengthening the agglomeration forces.

To gain insight on the stability properties of the model, we can study the agglomeration and dispersion forces at work by considering a perturbation of the symmetric equilibrium. As usual, the equilibrium is stable only if $\partial(\pi - \pi^*)/\partial s_n$ is negative because in this case, a positive shock to s_n lowers π, raises π^* and thus generates capital construction/destruction that 'corrects' the initial perturbation. Since we work with the symmetric equilibrium, $\partial\pi/\partial s_n$ and $\partial\pi^*/\partial s_n$ are equal in absolute value but have opposite signs. Therefore, we only need to calculate $\partial\pi/\partial s_n$ to determine the sign of $\partial(\pi - \pi^*)/\partial s_n$. Using (6.3) to form $\pi - \pi^*$, differentiating with respect to s_n and evaluating it at the symmetric equilibrium, we have

$$\frac{d(\pi - \pi^*)|_{\text{sym}}}{a_l(\rho + \delta)} = 4\frac{1 - \phi}{1 + \phi}ds_E - 4\left(\frac{1 - \phi}{1 + \phi}\right)^2 ds_n; \quad ds_E = \beta, \quad ds_n > 0 \quad (6.13)$$

Notice that unlike the FC model, a change in the distribution of industry, ds_n, does alter the size of the two markets as production shifting does lead to expenditure shifting. Consequently, the destabilizing market-access advantage does come into play. The impact of ds_n on s_E depends upon the share of capital's net income in expenditure spending, namely β. For this reason, β can be viewed as a summary statistic for the fundamental strength of agglomeration forces in this model. As the first right-hand term shows, increasing openness weakens the agglomeration force, as usual, but openness weakens the dispersion force—that is, the second right-hand term—even more. The break point comes when the positive first right-hand term overpowers the negative second right-hand term. By inspection, this is where $(1 - \phi)/(1 + \phi) = \beta$.

6.2.6 The Tomahawk Diagram

To summarize the analysis, Figure 6.2 shows the equivalent to the tomahawk diagram for the CC model. Its crucial feature is that the break and sustain points

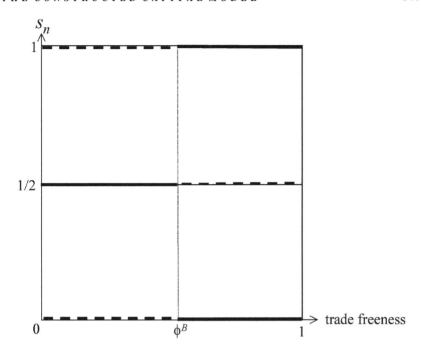

Figure 6.2   The tomahauk diagram for the CC model.

are equal and occur at an intermediate level of ϕ. This makes the diagram look more like a sledgehammer than a tomahawk.

6.3 THE CC MODEL WITH CAPITAL MOBILITY

6.3.1 Perfect Capital Mobility

It is easy and fruitful to extend the CC model to the case of perfect capital mobility—continuing to assume that capital owners are immobile. Given the analysis of the FC model in Chapter 3, the features of this variant are easily understood.[13]

When capital is freely mobile across regions, the north's share of industry can differ from its share of capital, that is, $s_n \neq s_K$. Capital flows quickly to equalize K's nominal reward in the two regions, so $\pi = \pi^*$ at all moments as long as not all the K is in one region, otherwise $\pi < \pi^*$ and $s_n = 0$, or $\pi > \pi^*$ and $s_n = 1$. Solving $\pi = \pi^*$ for the spatial pattern of capital's employment, we get (6.8) with s_n substituted for s_K and now s_E is parametrically fixed at its initial level for the same reasons it was fixed in the FC model. Moreover, with all capital income repatriated and capital's reward equalized, workers/investors in both regions always have identical incentives to invest in new capital.

[13] See Baldwin (1999, p. 266) for a detailed analysis.

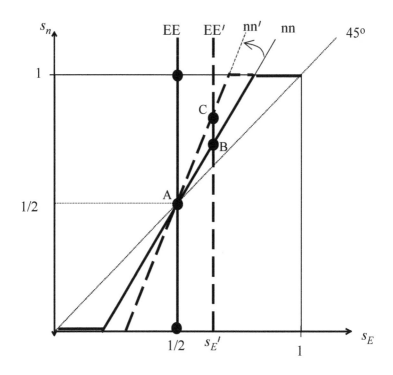

Figure 6.3 Capital mobility as a stabilizing force.

6.3.2 Circular Causality Broken

When capital is mobile, but capital owners are not, capital income gets repatriated to its region of origin regardless of where it works. Consequently, all circular causality is broken and the outcome is stable for all levels of trade costs.[14] This can be seen in Figure 6.3, which depicts the scissors diagram with perfect capital mobility.

If regions are perfectly symmetric to start with, the symmetric outcome, point A in the diagram, remains stable until trade becomes costless. The reason is that lower trade costs simply pivot the nn curve around A. If the regions are asymmetric to begin with, say the north's expenditure share is somewhat above 1/2 at s_E', then the rotation of nn driven by the freeing of trade will lead to industrial delocation from south to north. In the diagram, this is shown as a move from point B to point C. The interior equilibrium does not, however, ever become unstable since nn is flatter than EE as long as trade costs are positive.

The main import of this extension is that capital market barriers can also have important effects on the spatial distribution of industry. In particular, removing

---

[14] Observe that the stability properties of the CC model with capital mobility are identical to those of the FC model.

barriers to the movements of goods and capital can produce effects on economic geography that are substantially different from the impact of lowering trade costs while capital is immobile. In short, capital mobility per se is not destabilizing, rather it actually helps to stabilize the spatial distribution of industry.

6.4 KEY FEATURES

Chapter 2 pointed out seven key features of the CP model: agglomeration via the home-market mechanism (with magnification by freer trade), demand and cost linkages, endogenous asymmetry, catastrophic agglomeration, locational hysteresis, hump-shaped agglomeration rents and multiple long-run equilibria in the overlap. This section starts by studying which of these are shared by the CC model.

6.4.1 Comparison with CP Model

HOME-MARKET MAGNIFICATION

As the analysis in Figure 6.1 showed, the home-market effect operates in the CC model, so the spatial concentration of economic activity does generate forces that encourage further spatial concentration. Moreover, the effect is stronger when trade is freer (magnification effect), since the nn line gets steeper as ϕ rises. Thus, as in the CP, FC and FE models, industry becomes more footloose, not less footloose, as trade gets freer.

CIRCULAR CAUSALITY

In the CC model, the home-market effect is amplified into demand-linked circular causality by the fact that production shifting leads to capital construction and destruction that in turn produces expenditure shifting. Unlike the CP model, this occurs without factor mobility. The CC model does not, however, feature cost linkages since there is no factor migration to be concerned with price indices. The point is that the incentive to produce physical capital does not depend upon the local price index. This, of course, is exactly why the CC model remains perfectly tractable.

ENDOGENOUS ASYMMETRY

As we showed above, the symmetric CC model does produce endogenous asymmetry. As in the CP model, the gradual reduction of trade costs starting from a high level eventually leads to full agglomeration. Thus, the steady lowering of trade costs results in a perfectly symmetric model becoming asymmetric.

CATASTROPHIC AGGLOMERATION

The CC model does feature catastrophic agglomeration at the break point, as the tomahawk diagram in Figure 6.2 makes clear. Indeed, the model may be subject to sudden and massive agglomerations in reaction to minor changes in trade costs. This happens, for example, when trade gets just a bit freer than ϕ^B. The same occurs in the CP model.

LOCATIONAL HYSTERESIS

Whenever $\phi > \phi^B$, the CC model features multiple stable equilibria. As in the CP model, this means that temporary shocks, including temporary policy changes, may have hysteretic effects on the location of industry.

HUMP-SHAPED AGGLOMERATION RENTS

As in the CP model, the agglomeration rents in the CC model are concave function of trade freeness. To see this, consider a long-run equilibrium in which no capital is left in the south ($s_n = 1$ and $\phi \geq \phi^B$). The agglomeration rents are then measured as the difference between northern and southern ratios of the value of K to its cost ('Tobin's q'). Such difference can be evaluated by substituting $s_n = 1$, (6.1), (6.3) and (6.7) in the definitions of q and q^* (taking $s_L = 1/2$ for comparability). This yields

$$q - q^*|_{s_n=1} = 1 - \frac{1}{2}\left[\frac{1}{\phi}(1 - \beta) + \phi(1 + \beta)\right] \qquad (6.14)$$

This is a function of ϕ. It equals zero at $\phi = \phi^B$ and $\phi = 1$, while it is positive in between. Moreover, in the same interval, it is concave with a maximum at $\phi = \sqrt{\phi^B}$, where ϕ^B is the break-and-sustain point defined in (6.12). Accordingly, as trade gets freer (i.e. ϕ rises from ϕ^B towards 1), the agglomeration rents first rise and then fall ('hump shape').

THE OVERLAP AND SELF-FULFILLING EXPECTATIONS

Since the break and sustain points coincide, the CC model does not feature any overlap. Thus, shocks to expectations cannot result in large spatial reallocations between stable long-run equilibria.

6.4.2 New Features

The CC model shares all the properties of the CP model presented in Chapter 2 except two, namely, cost linkages and the overlap, while remaining entirely tractable. At the same time, it displays a number of useful features that go beyond those present in the CP model.

GROWTH AFFECTS GEOGRAPHY

The first novel element that arises is that growth can affect geography. To see this, note that the source of per capita growth is the accumulation of capital. In the FC model, where capital was not accumulated, the symmetric equilibrium was always stable. However, once we allow capital to be accumulated, as in the CC model, we find that symmetry breaks down when trade becomes sufficiently free. The key to this is the fact that forces that encourage production in one region also tend to encourage capital accumulation in that region. To put it differently, capital accumulation is another way in which expenditure shifting can be tied to production shifting.

GROWTH POLES AND GROWTH SINKS

When capital is immobile, the model displays a second novel feature—geography can affect regional growth, at least in the medium run. In particular, Perroux's (1955) notion of 'growth poles and growth sinks' appears very clear.

Consider, for instance, initially symmetric regions facing trade costs that are high enough to ensure that the symmetric outcome is stable. When trade becomes sufficiently free, symmetry becomes unstable. To be concrete, assume that a small shock puts the north a bit ahead so the core will eventually end up in the north. The instability arises since the reward to capital rises in the north and falls in the south. This, in turn, would induce northern residents to raise their investment rate above the rate necessary to sustain the initial capital stock. The consequence might be called agglomeration-induced, investment-led growth. The north's investment rate rises, boosting its capital/labour ratio, and thus its per capita income and output. This expansion of market size further favours investment in the region. In short, the north has become a growth pole.

Circular causality has an interesting interpretation in this context. Investment in the growing region is favoured precisely because expenditure in the region is growing. And expenditure is growing due to the high investment rate. The reverse process operates in the south. The lower rate of return induces southern consumers/savers to stop investing, so depreciation erodes the southern capital stock so that southern per capita income and output begin to drop. Given the particular depreciation process assumed, southern firms shut down one by one. In the simple model we work with, workers displaced by the downsizing of the south's M sector immediately find new jobs in the A sector. However, if finding a new job or expanding the A sector took time, the periphery's downward spiral would be associated with above-normal unemployment; the same labour market features would imply 'labour shortages' in the growing region. More colloquially, the declining region would resemble a 'rust belt' and the ascending region would resemble a 'boom belt'.

PERMANENT INCOME DIFFERENCES

In the CP model, falling trade costs can produce asymmetries in initially symmetric regions. At intermediate trade costs, the two regions also experience divergence of their real per capita incomes, but eventually, free trade re-equalizes incomes. This is illustrated in the left panel of Figure 6.4 with the heavy solid lines.

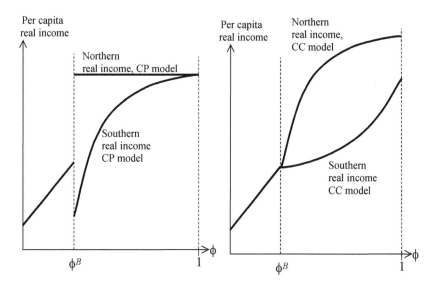

Figure 6.4   Real per capita income changes, CP versus CC models.

At the break point, all industry moves north (for convenience, the diagram assumes it moves immediately) and this raises northern per capita income (recall that, in the CP model, normalization renders $w = w_L = 1$ at all long-run equilibria, so the changes and the north–south income gap is driven entirely by cost-of-living effects).

In the CC model, which assumes that capital is immobile, the core–periphery outcome comes about as a result of a change in the two region's capital/labour ratios, with the north's rising and the south's falling. Thus, even at free trade, the per capita income of the north is permanently higher than that of the south. This is shown in the right panel of the diagram.

Thus, the CC model adds a new element to the growth literature, which presumes that neoclassical growth models (such as the CC model) predict convergence of regional income levels (see, e.g. Barro and Sala-i-Martin 1995). In this CC model, however, progressive trade liberalization between symmetric nations eventually produces the core–periphery outcome. Thus, contrary to the standard assertion in the growth literature, in this neoclassical growth model, economic integration produces divergence in real per capita income levels.

A RICHER DEFINITION OF ECONOMIC INTEGRATION

Closer economic integration in the CP model has only one substantive meaning—lower trade costs. It is possible to lower migration costs, but this has little impact on the main operation of the model.[15]

[15] The exception concerns the CP model extended to allow for forward-looking expectations; here, lower migration costs can produce situations where expectations may be self-fulfilling. See Chapter 2 for details.

Once we allow for growth, however, economic integration of the regions can vary in two dimensions—trade costs and capital mobility. In particular, the CC model shows what happens when trade gets freer, but capital remains immobile between the regions. Eventually, a CP outcome emerges and regional incomes diverge.

What happens if we allow for the joint mobility of goods, capital and capital owners? The result is something like the FE model, but agglomeration occurs at any level of trade costs. The reason is that everyone is always better off avoiding trade costs by all co-locating in the same region.

6.5 CONCLUDING REMARKS AND RELATED LITERATURE

6.5.1 Summary Results for Policy Modelling

This chapter has presented a model that is completely solvable and yet it displays all the key feature of the CP model except two, namely, cost linkages and the overlap. Moreover, it features three new characteristics. First, when capital is immobile, geography can affect regional growth, which formalizes Perroux's notion of 'growth poles'. Second, with immobile capital, even at free trade, per capita incomes can differ permanently across regions when core–periphery outcomes emerge. Third, the model allows for the analysis of two different dimensions of economic integration: trade freeness and capital mobility. In particular, the CC model points out that capital mobility can act as an additional dispersion force.

The first feature is clearly central for policy design. However, in the CC model, geography affects growth only in the medium run. Indeed, being a neoclassical growth model, the long-run growth rate is completely exogenous (here we set it to zero for the sake of simplicity): in the long run, location has no effect on the rate of growth. This limitation is overcome in Chapter 7, which deals with 'new' growth models, that is, models where the long-run growth rate is endogenously determined (Grossman and Helpman 1991).

6.5.2 Related Literature

The role of cumulative growth processes in regional development has a long tradition in spatial economics. Among others, it plays a central role in the works of Myrdal (1957) and Perroux (1955). For a wider survey, see Fujita and Thisse (2002).

REFERENCES

Baldwin, R. E. 1999. Agglomeration and endogenous capital. *European Economic Review* 43: 253–280.

Barro, R. and X. Sala-i-Martin. 1995. *Economic Growth*. New York: McGraw-Hill.

Fujita, M. and J.-F. Thisse. 2002. *Economics of Agglomeration*. Cambridge: Cambridge University Press.

Grossman, G. and E. Helpman. 1991. *Innovation and Growth in the Global Economy*. Cambridge: MIT Press.

Myrdal, G. 1957. *Economic Theory and Under-Developed Regions*. London: Duckworth.

Perroux, F. 1955. Note sur la notion de 'pole de croissance'. *Economie Appliquée* 8. English translation in McKee, D., R. Dean and W. Leahy, ed. 1970. *Regional Economics*. New York: Free Press, 93–103.

Tobin, J. 1969. A general equilibrium approach to monetary theory. *Journal of Money, Credit and Banking* 1: 15–29.

Global and Local Spillovers Models

7.1 INTRODUCTION

The models we have examined in the previous chapters focus on the long-run spatial distribution of industry. While this is a concern of policy makers, it is certainly not all they care about and indeed it may not be the main thing they care about. When policy makers argue that something should be done to help encourage economic activity in poor regions, the goal is to promote growth, not just a one-off shift of industry. Likewise, the main goal of national policies aimed at influencing the international distribution of industry—that is, pro-industrialization policies—is growth; promoting industrialization is merely a means of promoting growth. Indeed, emergence and dominance of spatial concentration of economic activities is one of the facts traditionally associated with modern economic growth.

To provide a framework in which we can evaluate such policies, the present chapter considers two models in which the long-run growth rate is endogenous. The mechanism of endogenous growth is quite simple and we introduce it in a framework that can be thought of as an extension of the CC model.[1] Due to technological spillovers in the capital-creation section, firms find it optimal to continually invest in new capital. As in the FC and CC models, each unit of capital is associated with a new variety of the industrial good, so the continual investment produces an ever-expanding range of varieties. This, in turn, yields an ever-falling price index so real output and real wages rise at a steady pace.

The first model assumes that spillovers are perfectly transmitted between firms in different regions. Accordingly, we call it the 'global spillovers' (GS) model. Despite the endogenization of the long-run growth rate, the GS model is fundamentally no more difficult to work with than the CC model. It shows that growth could dramatically alter economic geography in the sense that the process of accumulation of capital could lead to catastrophic agglomeration. However, as in the CC model, geography has no impact on the long-run growth rate of the GS model. This is not the case in the second model, which assumes that spillovers are harder to transmit between rather than within regions. For this reason, we call it the 'localized spillovers' (LS) model and show that, in this model, long-run location does affect the long-run rate of growth. The GS and LS models were introduced by Martin and Ottaviano (1999) and Baldwin et al. (2001). They are reviewed in detail in Baldwin and Martin (2003).

[1] Note, however, the first endogenous growth and economic geography model, Martin and Ottaviano (1999), came before the CC model.

7.1.1 Logic of Endogenous Growth Models

At one level, all per capita growth is driven by the accumulation of capital, where capital is broadly defined to include physical capital (machines), human capital (skills) and/or knowledge capital (technology). In neoclassical growth models (otherwise known as exogenous growth models), the focus is on the endogenous accumulation of physical capital. Since physical capital is assumed to experience diminishing returns, the steady state is marked by a given level of the capital/labour ratio and from then on any growth must be driven by exogenous factors such as exogenous technological progress. In the endogenous growth literature, such diminishing returns are overcome by various mechanisms, most of which focus on knowledge capital since it is much easier to believe that knowledge creation does not face diminishing returns.

The CC model can be viewed as an exogenous growth model. One-time changes can alter the long-run equilibrium capital stock and the regional economies will experience medium-run growth (positive or negative) as their capital stocks approach their new long-run levels. The long-run growth rate, however, is always zero. The deep reason for this is diminishing returns to capital accumulation. Since firms' fixed costs are paid in units of capital, new capital allows for the entry of new firms. However, as new firms enter, the market becomes more crowded, operating profits drop, and eventually their discounted flow is not enough to cover the constant cost of new capital. When this happens, capital accumulation comes to a halt. Thus, in the long run growth ceases because the rising capital stock depresses the return to new capital, while leaving its cost unaffected.

Endogenizing the long-run growth rate requires us to get around the diminishing returns to capital accumulation. To achieve this, two options are available in principle. First, we could prevent capital's reward from falling with the rising capital stock. Second, we could have the cost of making new capital fall. For consistency with previous models, we favour this latter option. In particular, we assume that capital construction follows a learning curve.[2] The idea is that we view capital as knowledge capital or ideas for short, and assume that the marginal cost of producing an idea declines as the cumulative production of ideas rises. In other words, the experience gained on past innovation improves the efficiency of current innovation. This is modelled as a technological externality; all current innovators benefit from past innovation no matter whether they contributed to it or not ('spillover'). However, the intensity of the spillovers could fade away with distance. When this is the case, the localized externality creates an additional agglomeration force.[3]

---

[2] Many justifications of this learning curve are possible. Romer (1990), for instance, rationalizes it by referring to the non-rival nature of knowledge.

[3] Empirical evidence in favour of localized spillovers is provided by Jacobs (1969), Ciccone and Hall (1996), Coe and Helpman (1995), Coe et al. (1997), Jaffe et al. (1993) and Keller (2002).

7.1.2 Organization of the Chapter

The chapter has four sections after the introduction. Section 7.2 presents the GS model and derives its key features. Section 7.3 introduces the LS model and its key properties. In both sections, the new models are extensively compared with those seen in previous chapters. Section 7.4 contains our concluding remarks and presents some related literature.

7.2 THE SYMMETRIC GS MODEL

7.2.1 Assumptions

The basic structure of the GS model closely parallels that of the CC model of Chapter 6 (which itself is based on the FC model of chapter 3). The various assumptions underlying this structure are explained and motivated at length in Chapter 6, so here we cover them rather quickly. The world economy consists of two regions (north and south), two consumption-good sectors (a traditional sector, the A sector, and industry, the M sector), and two factors of production (capital, K, and labour, L). The A sector is Walrasian and uses only L to produce its homo-genous output. Units are chosen such that one unit of labour is required to produce one unit of A. Inter-regional and intra-regional trade in A is costless. The M sector (industry) is subject to Dixit–Stiglitz monopolistic competition and increasing returns. This sector uses only K in its fixed cost (one unit of K per variety) and only L in the variable cost (a_M units of L per unit of variety). Inter-regional trade in M goods is subject to iceberg trade costs; intra-regional sales are costless.

Each region is endowed with half the world's supply of labour, and labour is assumed to be inter-regionally immobile. As in the CC model, labour is a primary factor—its endowment is immutably fixed—but capital is 'constructed' by a sector that we call the I sector. Capital depreciates as in the CC model (a proportion, equal to δ, disappears each period) and it is assumed to be inter-regionally immobile.

While unimportant for the mechanics of the model, it proves helpful to think of capital in the GS model as knowledge capital rather than physical capital, so the one unit of K that is necessary per variety represents one idea or one technique.

THE I SECTOR LEARNING CURVE

The GS model departs from the CC set-up when it comes to the I sector's technology. Before laying out the new assumption, we motivate it by explaining why it is necessary.

Continuous growth in the GS model is driven by the continuous expansion of the world's knowledge stock. Since each unit of knowledge capital is associated with a variety, this means that the range of varieties will be continually expanding. In a Dixit–Stiglitz setting, such an expansion is inevitably associated with a falling rate of operating profit per variety. Now, if—as in the CC model—the cost of 'constructing' a new unit of knowledge capital were constant in terms of the numeraire, then the capital stock would eventually rise to the point where the present value of operating profits from a new variety would be insufficient to cover the marginal capital construction costs. At this point, no one would pay for net additions to the capital stock. The expansion of varieties and thus growth would stop.

To get around this while remaining in the Dixit–Stiglitz setting, we need the cost of new units of capital to fall over time. What sort of economic logic implies falling costs? A learning curve is one possibility, and indeed this is the tactic adopted by the GS model (and much of the endogenous growth literature[4]).

The specific assumption is that the marginal cost of producing a unit of knowledge capital—think of it as an idea—declines as the cumulative production of ideas rises. As usual, we justify this learning curve by asserting that the experience gained on past innovation improves the efficiency of current innovation. We continue to assume that the I sector (a mnemonic for the innovation sector in this case) employs only labour and produces one unit of K with a_I units of L, so the marginal cost, what we call F, is equal to $w_L a_I$. The sector-wide learning curve assumed implies that a_I decreases as the sector's cumulative output rises, due to a learning-effect, that is, an inter-temporal technological externality or technological spillovers.

One entirely novel element that arises in this class of models concerns the extent to which learning effects in the innovation sector are transmitted over distance. We discuss this at length below, but for now we start with the simplest assumption, that learning effects are global. That is, the north's marginal cost of producing ideas depends as much on experience gained in the south as it does on the north's own past production of ideas, and the same is true in the south.[5] The precise learning curve in this global spillovers case is[6]

$$F = w_L a_I, \quad F^* = w_L^* a_I^*; \quad a_I = a_I^* = 1/K^w, \quad K^w = K + K^* \quad (7.1)$$

Finally, we maintain perfect competition despite the dynamic scale economies by assuming that each firm in the I sector is too small to internalize the spillovers. Thus, each I firm considers a_I as a parameter when it sets its price for new capital.

It may boost intuition to think of the innovation sector as producing two distinct outputs every time it invents a new idea. The first output is a unit of private knowledge, which can be patented and therefore sold to someone wishing to

---

[4] See, for instance, Romer (1990) and Lucas (1988). See Grossman and Helpman (1991) for its application to trade.

[5] Another way to think of this is to view the experience gained on past innovations as a public good. Specifically, in the case at hand, it is a global public good. The local public good case is addressed by the LS model below.

[6] Since we allow depreciation here as in the CC model, we note that learning spillovers for new ideas is based only on ideas that have not yet become obsolete, that is, have not yet depreciated.

start supplying a new M variety. The second output is a unit of public knowledge, which cannot be patented but helps every I sector firm produce additional units of K with less effort. Private knowledge capital is immobile, that is, patents must be used in the nation in which they are developed (the idea here is that at least some of the private knowledge is tacit, so industrialists must be near innovators). Public knowledge, on the other hand, is instantly and freely disseminated worldwide.

INTER-TEMPORAL ISSUES

Our presentation of the models in Chapters 2–6 followed mainstream, economic geography tradition by leaving all inter-temporal aspects of the model in the background.[7] Here, we switch to the more explicit treatment that is standard in growth theory. In particular, the instantaneous utility we assume is identical to the one in previous chapters, namely a CES sub-utility for M varieties nested in an upper-tier Cobb–Douglas function. The inter-temporal utility is also CES with the elasticity of inter-temporal substitution set to one for simplicity (log utility). Thus, we have

$$U = \int_{t=0}^{\infty} e^{-\rho t}\ln C dt, \quad C = C_A^{1-\mu}C_M^{\mu}, \quad C_M = \left(\int_{i=0}^{n^w} c_i^{1-1/\sigma}di\right)^{1/(1-1/\sigma)} \tag{7.2}$$

where ρ is the rate of time preference.

Our treatment of uncertainty in Chapter 6 was also pushed into the background. The owner of a particular unit of capital faces depreciation uncertainty, but given the continuum of varieties, there is no aggregate uncertainty. To deal with this explicitly, we assume a perfect financial market that allows perfect diversification and the existence of a safe bond that bears an interest rate r in units of the A good. This market is where investment in innovation is financed and it is local in the sense that there is no trade in financial assets among regions. We define r^* as the southern interest rate.

7.2.2 Short-Run Equilibrium

As usual, we distinguish between short- and long-run equilibria. Just as in the CC model, capital is the crucial variable; however, in the GS model, the world capital stock never stops growing, so instead of taking the level of K^w as the long-run variable, we take the growth rate of K^w as the long-run variable. This growth rate, which is denoted as g, together with the spatial allocation of capital, s_n, are our long-run variables. They are taken as given in the short run.

A SECTOR RESULTS, M SECTOR RESULTS AND CAPITAL'S REWARD

Most of the short-run expressions in the GS model are identical to those of the CC model provided we keep in mind that now $a_I = 1/K^w$. Accordingly, we can write

[7] Throughout the entire FKV book, for example, consumers are implicitly assumed to be infinitely lived, but their intertemporal preferences are never specified.

$$p = 1, \quad p^* = \tau, \quad p_A = p_A^* = w_L = w_L^* = 1, \quad s_n = s_K \qquad (7.3)$$

where w_L is the wage of labour, p and p^* are the consumer prices of a typical M variety in its local and export markets, respectively, and p_A is the price of the A good, which is chosen as numeraire. (As in the CC model, we use s_n to indicate the spatial division of capital instead of s_K since the GS and CC models should be thought of as extensions of the FC model and s_n is endogenous in the FC model while s_K is exogenous.) Operating profits are

$$\pi = bB\frac{E^w}{K^w}, \quad \pi^* = bB^*\frac{E^w}{K^w}; \quad b \equiv \frac{\mu}{\sigma} \qquad (7.4)$$

where

$$B \equiv \frac{s_E}{\Delta} + \phi\frac{s_E^*}{\Delta^*}, \quad B^* \equiv \phi\frac{s_E}{\Delta} + \frac{s_E^*}{\Delta^*}; \quad \Delta \equiv s_n + \phi(1 - s_n),$$

$$\Delta^* \equiv \phi s_n + 1 - s_n$$

Here, we employ the standard notation: s_E and s_n are the north's share of world expenditures and capital, respectively, and $\phi \equiv \tau^{1-\sigma}$ is our measure of trade freeness (see Chapter 3 for derivations).

THE MARKET SIZE CONDITION

As in the FC and CC models, the mobile factor's reward in the GS model depends upon the spatial distribution of industry, s_n, and relative market size, namely s_E. Capital's reward is pivotal to our analysis and we are taking s_n as given here, so our next task is to characterize s_E. We commence with s_E's denominator.

At the world level, expenditure equals world factor income minus world spending on new capital. World factor income is the wage bill plus operating profits, and using (7.4), this is just $L^w + bE^w$ (see Chapter 3 for details). Spending on innovation, that is, capital construction and replacement, is just equal to the value of resources employed by I sectors worldwide and this is L_I^w.[8] Thus, E^w equals $L^w + bE^w$ minus L_I^w, and this solves to $E^w = (L^w - L_I^w)/(1 - b)$ as in the CC model. A difference arises, however, in that now L_I^w involves the creation of net new capital as well as the replacement of depreciation. The amount of new capital required to replace depreciation and keep the world capital stock growing at g is $(g + \delta)K^w$.[9] Given the I sector technology in (7.1), viz. $a_I = 1/K^w$, the amount of labour required to produce this is $L_I^w = g + \delta$. Using this, we have

$$E^w = \frac{L^w - g - \delta}{1 - b} \qquad (7.5)$$

[8] Spending on capital accumulation equals the I-sector total cost since, by perfect competition, its revenue always equals its total costs.

[9] The amount of capital needed to replace depreciation is just δK^w. To keep K^w growing at the rate of $g = \dot{K}^w/K^w$ requires a flow of new capital equal to gK^w. Thus, overall, the production flow of new capital must be $(\delta + g)K^w$.

To find the north's share of E^w, we note that northern expenditure E equals northern income, which is just $L + \pi K$, minus northern spending on new units of capital.

To finish our characterization of s_E, we must calculate northern expenditure E. The north's labour income is $s_L L^w$ plus its capital income $s_n b B E^w$ while its share of depreciation is $s_n \delta K^w$. Using these facts in the definition of the north's expenditure, we find that E equals $s_L L^w + s_n b B E^w - s_n (\delta + g) K^w a_I$. Taking the ratio of this to our expression for world expenditure and using the fact that $a_I = 1/K^w$ yields

$$s_E = \frac{(b\phi s_n/\Delta^*) + (1 - b)[s_L L^w - s_n(\delta + g)]/[L^w - \delta - g]}{1 - (b s_n/\Delta) + (\phi b s_n/\Delta^*)} \qquad (7.6)$$

after gathering terms and simplifying. What this shows is that relative market size s_E depends upon the long-run variables, s_n and g. As in the CC model, the expression for s_E in the long run is significantly simpler.

To deal explicitly with inter-temporal issues, we turn next to characterizing the optimal inter-temporal division of expenditure. The classic way of expressing optimal inter-temporal consumption behaviour is the so-called Euler equation:

$$\frac{\dot{E}}{E} = r - \rho \qquad (7.7)$$

This can be easily derived using the Hamiltonian approach (see Barro and Sala-I-Martin 1995), but intuition is served by justifying it with classic arguments. The marginal cost of postponing consumption for an instant is ρ plus the rate of decline of marginal utility, which, given the log preferences is just $\dot{E}/E$. The marginal benefit of postponing consumption for an instant is r since this is what is earned by holding bonds. Noting that agents can lend and borrow freely across periods, the optimal consumption path must be such that any small re-allocation would leave consumers indifferent, that is, the marginal benefit and marginal cost of postponing consumption must be equal at all points in time so $\dot{E}/E + \rho = r$; rearranging this yields the Euler equation.

7.2.3 Long-Run Location

Long-run equilibrium in the GS model is defined by the growth rate of the global capital stock (i.e. g) and its regional division s_n as well as all the usual prices and quantities calculated in the short-run equilibrium. To find g, we look for the rate of capital accumulation where the value of employing a new unit of capital just equals its cost. The condition that characterizes this can be thought of as a location condition.

THE LOCATION CONDITION

As usual, the model will have one or more interior equilibria, where both regions are producing capital, and the two CP outcomes where only one is doing so. For interior solutions, both regions must find it just worthwhile to continually invest in raising the capital stock at rate g. For a core-in-the-north outcome, only the north must find it just worthwhile to invest. So, as in the CC model it must be that

$$q \equiv \frac{v}{F} = 1, \quad q^* \equiv \frac{v^*}{F^*} = 1; \quad 0 < s_K < 1$$

$$q = 1, \quad q^* < 1; \quad s_K = 1 \tag{7.8}$$

where q is the ratio of the value of K to its cost (called Tobin's q ratio), and the condition for the core-in-the-south is isomorphic to that of the second line in (7.8).

The first task is to relate the value of employing a new unit of capital (i.e. introducing a new industrial variety) to the growth rate of capital. The calculation is quite similar to those of the CC model, but there is an important difference. In the CC model, the long-run operating profit was constant and we found the value of a unit of K by taking the present value of its constant income stream. With a discount rate of ρ, and a depreciation rate of δ, the present value was $\pi/(\rho + \delta)$. With long-run growth, however, the operating profit earned per variety is not constant—it is decreasing since the continuous introduction of new varieties crowds the market for industrial goods thus depressing operating profit per variety.

To find the constant rate at which the operating profit falls, we recall that, by the above definition of long-run equilibrium—that is, that both g and s_n settle down to their long-run levels—both the level E^w and the spatial distribution s_E of world expenditures are constant; see (7.5) and (7.6). By (7.4), it implies that the sum of operating profits worldwide is also constant, since a constant fraction of expenditures falls on M varieties and the operating profit margin is constant. What this means is that the average π is just the constant total expenditures on industrial goods divided by the number of firms, $\pi = \mu E^w/(\sigma K^w)$, so the average π must fall at the same rate as the number of firms rises (recall that $n^w = K^w$). In the symmetric outcome, firms in both regions clearly earn the average π (hence, $B = B^* = 1$) and the same is obviously true when all firms are concentrated in a single region (hence, $B = 1$ or $B^* = 1$). Thus, for the symmetric and CP outcomes, we know how fast the individual firm's profit stream falls. It falls at the long-run rate at which the world capital stock K^w grows in equilibrium, namely g. This changes our discounting procedure.

The present value of the profit flow is simply $\pi/(\rho + \delta + g)$, where π is the initial level of operating profit.[10] Hence, we can write the value of an extra unit of capital in the north and south, respectively, as

$$v = \frac{\pi}{\rho + \delta + g}, \quad v^* = \frac{\pi^*}{\rho + \delta + g} \tag{7.9}$$

where g is the long-run equilibrium growth rate of K^w. See Box 7.1 for why we can use ρ in this discounting procedure.

---

[10] π's time path is $\pi^o e^{-gt}$, the probability that the unit is un-depreciated is $e^{-\delta t}$, and the discount factor is e^{-rt}, so v equals the integral of $\pi^o e^{-gt} e^{-rt} e^{-\delta t}$ over $t = 0$ to infinity.

BOX 7.1. EULER EQUATION AND FIRM VALUE.

The Euler equation, (7.7), is useful for two purposes in the GS model. First it allows us to define the behaviour of the model when it is away from long-run equilibria, that is, out of steady state. Following standard practice in the economic geography literature, this chapter focuses on long-run equilibria and their stability properties, so we do not use this aspect here; see Martin and Ottaviano (1999) for how it is done. The second purpose is to pin down the discount rate. The logic of discounting an income stream is based on arbitrage. That is, instead of holding the asset which provides the income stream under consideration, the owner could have sold the asset and placed his/her money in safe bonds yielding an interest rate of r. But what is r, and does it vary over time?

Having taken g and s_n as the state variables in the GS model (i.e. long-run variables), we know from (7.5) that E^w is time-invariant and from (7.6) that s_E is time-invariant. As a consequence both E and E^* are time-invariant so the Euler equation tells us that $r = \rho$. This is the formal justification for discounting with ρ.

CHARACTERIZING THE LONG-RUN EQUILIBRIA

Next we find the long-run rate of capital accumulation, g. Given (7.9), (7.5), (7.4), $B = 1$ and $F = 1/K^w$, the $q = 1$ condition reduces to

$$q \equiv \frac{v}{F} = \frac{b(L^w - g - \delta)/(1 - b)}{\rho + \delta + g} = 1 \qquad (7.10)$$

Thus, solving Tobin's $q = 1$, we get the long-run rate of growth of capital; using the result in (7.5) provides us with the long-run E^w. These are[11]

$$g = bL^w - (1 - b)\rho - \delta, \qquad E^w = L^w + \rho \qquad (7.11)$$

Capital's earning is always equalized across regions in the GS model (just as in the FC and CC models). To see this note that at interior long-run equilibria, (7.9) and (7.8) tell us that $\pi = \pi^*$, and at any core–periphery long-run outcome, all capital units obviously earn equal rewards (by symmetry of varieties). There are two useful implications of this spatial equalization of capital's long-run reward. At any interior equilibrium, just as in the FC and CC models,

$$s_n = \frac{1}{2} + \left(\frac{1 + \phi}{1 - \phi}\right)\left(s_E - \frac{1}{2}\right) \qquad (7.12)$$

where we derived this from (7.4), (7.8), (7.9) and (7.11); see Chapter 3 for details. The second implication is that it simplifies the expressions for the long-run spatial division of expenditure, as we shall see.

---

[11] Note that E^w is the 'permanent income' level; L^w is the constant flow of labour income and the net permanent income from capital is $\rho v K^w$ but from $q = 1$, $v = F = a_I = 1/K^w$.

Northern expenditure is northern income minus northern gross investment, where northern gross investment in equilibrium is just the north's share of world investment, namely $s_n(g + \delta)$. Northern income is L plus s_n times the world capital income, namely $\mu E^w / \sigma$. Putting these elements together, $E = L + s_n b E^w - s_n(g + \delta)$, gathering terms and using the equilibrium expressions for g and E^w from (7.11), we have

$$s_E = \eta s_n + (1 - \eta)s_L, \quad \eta \equiv \frac{\rho}{L^w + \rho} \tag{7.13}$$

That is, the north's expenditure share is a weighted average of its share of world K and L; the weights are such that as the equilibrium rate of return to K rises, via ρ, the importance of s_K rises.

In the symmetric equilibrium, capital grows at the same rate in both regions, that is, $g = g^*$. In core–periphery outcomes, only one region builds capital. As it turns out, however, the growth rate is identical in the symmetric and core–periphery equilibria. Intuitively, this is due to the fact that the equilibrium rate of return to capital is independent of its spatial distribution for one simple reason. Capital continues to exist only in regions where it earns enough to repay its owner for investing in it, and due to the global spillovers assumption, the investment cost (i.e. the cost of a unit of capital, F or F^*) is the same regardless of where it is made. Consequently, the growth rate that pushes capital's return down to its equilibrium level is independent of K's spatial distribution. More mechanically, note that g was solved from $q = 1$, where q was given in (7.10). Finding g required us only to find world variables, for example, E^w and L_l^w. Given this, it is clear that the procedure for finding the equilibrium g at a core–periphery outcome will be identical and will thus yield the same answer.

LONG-RUN REAL INCOME GROWTH

The growth rate of capital is directly linked to real income growth. World income in terms of the numeraire is $Y^w = L^w + b E^w$, so with $E^w = L^w + \rho$ in equilibrium, the equilibrium world income is $L^w(1 + b) + b\rho$. This does not grow over time (it is, after all, essentially measured in units of the primary factor L since $p_A = w_L = 1$), but the price index in both nations falls as the number of varieties rises and this implies continual real income growth. Specifically, in the symmetric equilibrium $P = P^* = [(1 + \phi)n^w/2]^{-a}$, where as usual $a \equiv \mu/(\sigma - 1)$, so the fact that n^w is rising at a rate of g means that the price index is falling at a rate of a times g. In symbols,

$$g_{GDP} = ag, \quad a \equiv \frac{\mu}{\sigma - 1} \tag{7.14}$$

Importantly, the GDP growth rates in the two regions are identical in both the interior equilibrium where both are innovating, and in the CP equilibria where only one is doing so. This is due to the fact that real growth stems from the constant fall in the price index that is driven by a continuously widening range of varieties. In short, the level of real incomes can differ across regions, but the growth rates can only differ in the medium run, that is, as the economy approaches its long-run equilibrium. In the long run, regional real income growth rates are identical.

DIAGRAMMATIC SOLUTIONS AND FORCES

Investment and Growth. Economic intuition can be boosted by a graphical representation. In the CC model, the level of the world capital stock was the equilibrating variable. More specifically, the q ratio fell as K^w rose—and this for two reasons. First, a higher K^w meant more competing varieties and this reduced π and thus v directly, that is, for a given level of expenditures on M goods. Second, as K^w rose, more resources were diverted away from expenditures and towards the I sector in order to replace the depreciation. This reduced total spending on industry and thus lowered π and v for any given number of competing varieties. The same logic applies to the GS model.

In the GS model, the equilibrating variable is the growth rate. In particular, q falls as g rises since a higher g lowers v directly (i.e. even holding world expenditure constant, the higher g means competitors are being introduced faster so owning a unit of capital today is worth less), and via the expenditure channel (see (7.5) which says that as g increases, more labour resources are diverted from the M and A sectors to the I sector so that expenditures must decrease). Given I-sector technology, the equilibrium capital stock in the CC model and the equilibrium growth rate in the GS model are both proportional to L_I^w. Moreover, in both models q declines with L_I^w, so the equilibrium for both models can be illustrated with the help of Figure 7.1, noting that from (7.1), $g = L_I^w - \delta$ in the GS model and $K^w = L_I^w / \delta a_I$ in the CC model.

The Scissors Diagram. As usual, we can characterize the location equilibria of the GS model and their local stability properties with the scissors diagram in Figure 7.2.

The left panel of Figure 7.2 depicts (7.12) as the nn curve and (7.13) as the EE curve for equal-sized regions ($s_L = 1/2$). As in the FC and CC models, s_n tends to increase for points to the right of the nn curve and tends to decrease for points to the left. For points to the right of nn, $B > B^*$, so for such points we know that $q = 1$ and $q^* < 1$. Since, in south, the value of K is lower than its cost (viz. $q^* < 1$), s_n tends to rise for points to the right of nn. Moreover, ϕ has no impact on EE, but it rotates the nn curve around the symmetric point. As in the CC model, the symmetric point is stable for low levels of openness, but at some point nn becomes steeper than EE and at this level of ϕ the symmetric equilibrium becomes unstable.

By now it should be clear that the GS model functions in a manner that is quite similar to that of the CC model with the important additional feature of continual real income growth. As such, the GS model can be easily analysed assuming asymmetric regions. In particular, if regions are fundamentally different in size,

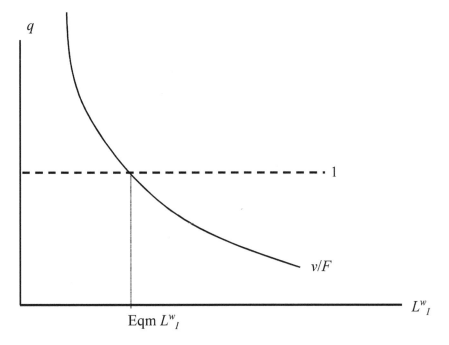

Figure 7.1 Finding the growth equilibrium.

that is, $s_L \neq 1/2$, then the EE line does not pass through the midpoint in the scissor diagram, as shown in the right panel of Figure 7.2. In this case, the interior equilibrium D is always stable, but freeing trade will produce a gradual increase in the share of capital in the initially big region until the core–periphery outcome is reached (just as in the asymmetric FC model).

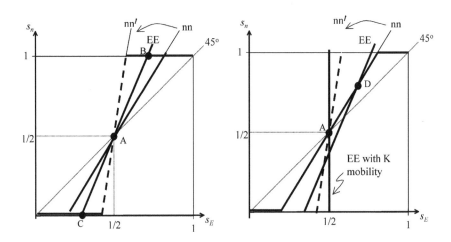

Figure 7.2 The scissor diagram for the GS model.

STABILITY ANALYSIS

The stability properties of the GS model are easily characterized by inspecting the scissors diagram. Since the nn and EE curves are linear (as they are also in the CC model), the two core–periphery outcomes in the GS model become stable long-run equilibria at the same level of trade freeness that renders the symmetric outcome unstable. More formally, the break-and-sustain points are both where the slopes are equal. Thus, using (7.12) and (7.13), their slopes coincide when

$$\phi^S = \phi^B = \frac{1 - \eta}{1 + \eta} \tag{7.15}$$

where η is defined as in (7.13).

When trade costs are high, the symmetric equilibrium is stable and for a while gradually reducing trade costs have no impact on industrial location. As trade freeness moves beyond ϕ^B, however, the equilibrium enters a qualitatively distinct phase. The symmetric distribution of industry becomes unstable, and northern and southern industrial structures begin to diverge; to be concrete, assume industry agglomerates in the north. Thus, crossing ϕ^B triggers transitional dynamics in which northern industrial output and investment rise and southern industrial output, investment and capital stock fall. Moreover, in a very well-defined sense, the south appears to be in the midst of a 'vicious cycle'. The demand linkages have southern firms lowering employment and abstaining from investment, because southern wealth is falling, and southern wealth is falling since southern firms are failing to invest. By the same logic, the north would appear to be in the midst of a 'virtuous cycle'. In the words used by Perroux (1955), the north acts as a growth pole while the south behaves as a growth sink.

To gain more intuition on this result, we can also study the stability in a different and more rigorous way. Specifically, we can analyse the effect of an exogenous increase in s_K by a small amount and check the impact of this perturbation on Tobin's q, while allowing expenditure shares to adjust according to the optimal saving relation.

The symmetric equilibrium is stable, if and only if $\partial q / \partial s_n$ is negative: in this case, an increase in the share of northern capital lowers Tobin's q in the north (and therefore the incentive to innovate) and raises it in the south (by symmetry $\partial q / \partial s_n$ and $\partial q^* / \partial s_n$ have opposite signs). Thus, when $\partial q / \partial s_n < 0$, the perturbation generates self-correcting forces in the sense that the incentive to accumulate more capital in the north falls while it increases in the south. If the derivative is positive, the increase in the northern share of capital reinforces the incentive to accumulate even more capital in the north; the symmetric equilibrium is unstable in this case. Differentiating the definition of q with respect to s_n, and estimating it at the symmetric equilibrium, we have[12]

$$\left. \frac{dq}{q} \right|_{s_K = 1/2} = 2 \left(\frac{1 - \phi}{1 + \phi} \right) \left. \frac{\partial s_E}{\partial s_K} \right|_{s_K = 1/2} ds_K - 2 \frac{(1 - \phi)^2}{(1 + \phi^2)} ds_K \tag{7.16}$$

[12] The following equation is valid both in the neo-classical case of Chapter 6 and the present endogenous growth case. The reason is that $K^w / F(g + \rho)$ is a constant in both cases.

This expression illustrates the two forces affecting stability. The first term is positive, so it represents the destabilizing force, namely the demand-linked effect that shifts expenditure; an increase in the capital share of the north increases its capital income and its expenditure share. In turn, it raises profits and the value of capital (the numerator of Tobin's q) in the north. The negative second term reflects the stabilizing market-crowding effect. Clearly, reducing trade costs (an increase in ϕ) erodes the stabilizing force more quickly than it erodes the destabilizing demand linkage.

In the core-in-the-north outcome, $q = 1$, means continuous accumulation is profitable. In the south $v^* < F^*$, so no agent would choose to set up a new firm. Defining the core–periphery equilibrium this way implies that it is stable whenever it exists. Using the definition of q^* with $s_n = 1$, $E^w = L^w + \rho$, (7.4) and (7.9), we get

$$q^*|_{s_K=1} = \frac{(1 - \eta) + \phi^2(1 + \eta)}{2\phi} \qquad (7.17)$$

If q^* is less than 1 when $s_n = 1$, then the CP equilibrium exists and is stable as there is no incentive for the south to replace depreciated capital or innovate in this case. The threshold ϕ that solves $q^* = 1$ defines the threshold freeness above which the core-in-the-north outcome is a stable long-run equilibrium. Again, the solution to this quadratic equation in ϕ is the ϕ^B given in (7.15). Therefore, at the level of the transaction costs for which the symmetric equilibrium becomes unstable, the CP outcome becomes stable.

The intuition is simple. When trade costs are high enough, the CP equilibrium is not stable since the south has an incentive to replace its depreciated capital and innovate. This is because, even though the southern market is small in this case (it has no capital income in the core-in-the-north outcome), it is protected from northern competition thanks to high trade costs. When these costs are low, this protection diminishes and the fact that the market in the south is smaller becomes more important.

THE TOMAHAWK DIAGRAM

To summarize the foregoing analysis, Figure 7.3 shows the tomahawk diagram for the GS model. As in the CC model, its crucial feature is that the break-and-sustain points are equal and occur at an intermediate level of ϕ. This makes the diagram look more like a sledgehammer than a tomahawk.

7.2.4 The GS Model with Capital Mobility

The natures of the I sector's two outputs—private knowledge capital and public knowledge capital—are quite different. Private knowledge is only useful in the M sector and public knowledge is only useful in the I sector. Accordingly, it seems entirely plausible that their spatial diffusion could also differ. Indeed, the GS model assumes that public knowledge is perfectly mobile while private knowl-

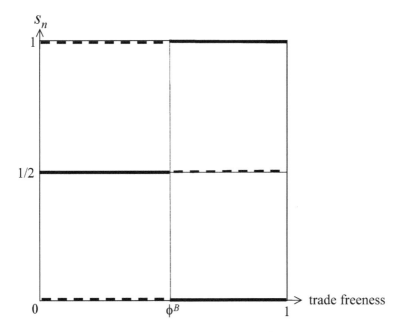

Figure 7.3   The tomahawk diagram for the GS model.

edge capital is perfectly immobile, but we can easily study the consequences of
the alternative polar assumption. The subject of this section is to consider the
consequences of allowing perfectly mobile capital in the sense of allowing inter-
regional trade in private knowledge (think of them as patents or blueprints).

In particular, we stick to the assumption that capital owners are immobile, so
once again the ownership and employment patterns of capital may differ and, as
in the FC model, we use s_K to indicate owner and use s_n to continue to denote
employment. Moreover, since all capital income is repatriated, the EE curve is
vertical as shown in the right panel of Figure 7.2. Thus, the symmetric equilibrium ($s_K = 1/2$) remains stable as long as trade is not perfectly free (and then
location becomes irrelevant).

The share of firms located in the north, s_n, can now differ from s_K. Hence, as in
the CC model, (7.12) now describes the location of firms. Using (7.13), which is
still valid, with s_n replaced by s_K we can analyse the difference between the
geography of capital ownership and the geography of production in the case of
equal-sized regions ($s_L = 1/2$). This is simply given by the difference between s_n
and s_K (this uses the expression for the EE curve in the expression for the nn
curve):

$$s_n - s_K = \left(s_K - \frac{1}{2} \right) \frac{\eta(1 + \phi) - 1 + \phi}{1 - \phi} \tag{7.18}$$

Contrary to the CC model, because new firms are constantly created, some of
those firms constantly relocate either to the north or the south depending on the

sign of the expression (7.18). If the initial distribution of capital is such that $s_K > 1/2$, so that the north is richer than the south, then the direction of the capital flows is ambiguous. The sign of (7.18) depends on whether ϕ is above or below the level defined in (7.15), the break-and-sustain points when capital is immobile. If $\phi < \phi^B$, then $s_K > s_n$ so that some of the capital owned by the north relocates to the south. The reason is that the market-crowding effect is strong when capital income is low relative to labour income.

When trade costs are sufficiently low, relocation takes place towards the north and vice versa. An interesting feature of the GS model compared to the CC model is that concentration in the north (if $s_K > 1/2$ then $s_n > 1/2$), is compatible with constant relocation over time of firms from north to south ($s_K > s_n$).

A related interesting question we can ask is the following. If all capital is owned by the north, under which conditions will all firms be located in the north with no relocation towards the south? That is, under which conditions is $s_n = 1$ when $s_K = 1$? (Recall that s_K is exogenous while s_n is endogenous.) We can think of this situation as the mobile capital version of the core–periphery equilibrium. It is easy to see that this is the case when freeness is larger than ϕ^B as defined in (7.15).

As is the case for the FC and CC models with capital mobility, the GS model with capital mobility does not feature catastrophic agglomeration. The absence of labour mobility eliminates the cost-of-living effect and, thus, cost-linked circular causality. The mobility of capital together with the repatriation of profits eliminates the demand-linked circular causality. The reason is that income from capital is not linked to the spatial location of production. Even when all firms produce in the north, capital owners in the south are not poorer.

7.2.5 Key Features

Chapter 2 pointed out seven key features of the CP model: agglomeration via the home-market mechanism (with magnification by freer trade), demand and cost linkages, endogenous asymmetry, catastrophic agglomeration, locational hysteresis, hump-shaped agglomeration rents and multiple long-run equilibria in the overlap. This section starts by studying which of these features appear in the GS model. Then, it turns to the additional features that the GS model shares with the CC model. Finally, it discusses new features that are peculiar to the GS model.

COMPARISON WITH CP MODEL

The GS model displays most of the features of the CP model.

Home-Market Magnification.   The nn curve shows that the home-market effect operates in the GS model as in the CP model. Indeed, when regions differ in terms of initial income and the interior equilibrium is stable, the initially richer region eventually hosts a more than proportionate share of accumulated capital (home-market effect). Freeing trade magnifies this effect by inducing a gradual increase of the share of capital in the initially richer region until the core–periphery outcome is reached (home-market magnification).

Circular Causality. As the CP model, the GS model also exhibits demand-linked circular causality. Specifically, as in the CC model, the home-market effect is amplified by the connection between production shifting and expenditure shifting that stems from the construction and destruction of capital. However, the GS model does not feature cost-linked circular causality since factor 'migration' (more precisely, differential capital accumulation) is unrelated to the regional price indices.

Endogenous Asymmetry. In the GS model, steadily increasing openness eventually leads to initially symmetric regions becoming asymmetric in terms of their production structures. In particular, all industry concentrates in one region. Thus, the steady lowering of trade costs results in a perfectly symmetric economy becoming asymmetric. This also happens in the CP model.

Catastrophic Agglomeration. The tomahawk diagram in Figure 7.3 makes it clear that the GS model also features catastrophic agglomeration at the break point. Therefore, as in the CP model, the GS model may be subject to sudden and massive agglomerations in reaction to minor changes in trade costs when trade gets just a bit freer than ϕ^B.

Locational Hysteresis. As in the CP model, the ultimate region of concentration is indeterminate so the economy can be subject to locational hysteresis. In particular, whenever $\phi > \phi^B$, the GS model features multiple stable core–periphery equilibria. This implies that temporary shocks, such as temporary policy changes, may have hysteretic effects on the location of industry.

Hump-Shaped Agglomeration Rents. As in the CP model, agglomeration rents in the GS model are a concave function of trade freeness. To see this, consider a long-run equilibrium in which countries have equal populations ($s_L = 1/2$) and no capital is left in the south ($s_K = 1$ and $\phi \geq \phi^B$). The agglomeration rents are then measured as the difference between northern and southern ratios of the value of K to its cost (Tobin's q). Such difference can be evaluated by substituting $s_K = 1$ in the definitions of q and q^* (using all the equilibrium expression to get q's in terms of parameters). This gives

$$q - q^*|_{s_n=1} = 1 - \frac{1}{2}\left[\frac{1}{\phi}(1 - \eta) + \phi(1 + \eta)\right] \tag{7.19}$$

This is a function of ϕ. It equals zero at $\phi = \phi^B$ and $\phi = 1$, while it is positive in between. In the same interval, it is concave with a maximum at $\phi = \sqrt{\phi^B}$, where ϕ^B is the break-and-sustain point defined in (7.15). Accordingly, as trade gets freer (i.e. ϕ rises from ϕ^B towards 1), the agglomeration rents first rise and then fall ('hump shape').

The Overlap and Self-Fulfilling Expectations.   In the GS model, the lack of cost-linked circular causality makes the break-and-sustain points coincide so that the GS model does not feature any overlap. Therefore, shocks to expectations cannot result in large spatial re-allocations between stable long-run equilibria. Expectations cannot overrule history.

COMPARISON WITH CC MODEL

The GS model, like the CC model, displays a number of interesting features that do not arise in the CP model. Specifically, the GS model has all the new features of the CC model: growth affects geography; agglomeration is driven by the appearance of growth poles and sinks; regional income differentials do not disappear as trade gets perfectly free; and economic integration has a twofold meaning.

Growth Affects Geography.   Since capital accumulates in the GS model and capital's income is spent locally, growth can affect geography.

Growth Poles and Growth Sinks.   Although we have not stressed transitional dynamics, the GS model is also marked by behaviour that could be called 'growth poles and growth sinks'. Specifically, the move from the symmetric equilibrium to a core–periphery equilibrium involves faster-than-normal investment, capital accumulation and growth in the region gaining industry and below-normal investment, capital accumulation and growth in the region losing it.

Permanent Income Differences.   As in the CC model, the connection between the spatial distribution of income and the spatial distribution of capital ownership implies that regional asymmetries in industrial structure cause and are caused by regional asymmetries in factor endowments. In the end, the core region has a higher capital/labour ratio, so income per worker (workers own all capital) is higher in the core. Importantly, this difference does not disappear as trade becomes perfectly free as it did in the CP model (see Chapter 6 for a more thorough discussion of this feature).

A Richer Definition of Economic Integration.   Closer economic integration means capital mobility or freer trade in the GS model. In the CP model, only the latter interpretation was possible.

NEW FEATURES: ENDOGENOUS GROWTH

The GS model exhibits an important novel feature. This is, of course, endogenous long-run growth, something that does not appear in the CC model. From a positive perspective, endogenous growth also makes the flow of relocating capital permanent rather than transitional as it is in the CC model. When regions are asymmetric in terms of capital stocks and private knowledge capital is mobile, capital relocates continually either from the rich region to the poor region, or vice versa, with the direction being determined by the level of trade openness. Capital flows out of the capital abundant region when trade is relatively restricted, but flows into the capital abundant region when trade is sufficiently free.

7.3 THE SYMMETRIC LS MODEL

The previous section has shown that growth can dramatically alter economic geography in the sense that the process of accumulation of capital can lead to catastrophic agglomeration. However, geography has no impact on growth in the GS model. The long-run growth rate is independent of the spatial distribution of industry and innovation. This 'neutrality' of geography is due to the fact that the GS model assumes global spillovers in the innovating sector. The corresponding learning curve, which is at the origin of sustained growth, is global in the sense that the north and the south learn equally from an innovation made in either region. In other words, the transmission of knowledge in innovation is unaffected by distance. This downsizes the importance of proximity and face-to-face inter-actions for the transmission of knowledge.

In this section, we investigate the implications of letting distance affect knowl-edge diffusion. In so doing, we assume that some frictional barrier reduces the diffusion of public knowledge to distant innovators—hence the name 'localized spillovers' model, or LS model for short.

7.3.1 Assumptions

The introduction of localized spillovers requires only a minor modification of the I sector learning curve. The innovating sector in the GS model assumed that the marginal cost of an innovation was identical in both regions, that is, $F = F^* = a_I = 1/K^w$. By contrast, the LS model assumes that the cost of R&D in one region also depends on the location of capital. Specifically,

$$F = w_L a_I, \quad a_I \equiv \frac{1}{K^W A}, \quad A \equiv s_K + \lambda (1 - s_K) \qquad (7.20)$$

where λ (a mnemonic for learning spillover) measures the degree of globalization of learning spillovers. The south's cost function is isomorphic, that is, $F^* = w_L/K^w A^*$, where A^* equals $\lambda s_K + 1 - s_K$.

In a sense, λ measures the freeness with which public knowledge capital traverses distance, much in the same way as ϕ measures the freeness with which goods traverse distance. Consequently, $\lambda = 1$ means that ideas move at no cost, so learning spillovers are global; $\lambda = 0$ means ideas cannot move, so learning spillovers are purely local. For $0 < \lambda < 1$, we could view $1 - \lambda$ as the fraction of public knowledge that 'melts' in transit to the other region.

As to private knowledge capital—that is, the appropriable output of the I sector—we continue to suppose that it is inter-regionally immobile, so firms must be set up in the region where their knowledge capital has been invented. Due to this assumption $s_n \equiv s_K$; here we use s_K to represent the two.

7.3.2 Short-Run Equilibrium

Once more we distinguish between short- and long-run equilibria. In a short-run equilibrium, consumers maximize utility, firms maximize profits, and markets clear for given s_K and g. Thus, all the equilibrium expressions are the same as those of the GS model, except for the fact that, by (7.20), now we have $a_I = 1/\{K^w[s_K + \lambda(1 - s_K)]\}$. Accordingly, the short-run equilibrium of the LS model is also characterized by conditions (7.3), (7.4), (7.6) and (7.7).

7.3.3 Long-Run Location

>In the long run, the capital stocks of the two regions change due to capital construction and destruction. As in the GS model, in each region the capital stock rises or falls until the operating profit of the typical M variety provides a rate of return for its unit of capital that exactly matches the cost of new capital (i.e. conditions (7.8) hold). When this happens, the economy reaches its long-run equilibrium: the growth rate of the world capital stock, K^w, the level of world expenditures, E^w, as well as their spatial distributions, s_K and s_E, are all constant.

Moreover, the LS model has only two categories of long-run equilibria. Interior equilibria, where both regions are innovating at the same rate, that is, $g = g^*$ and $0 < s_K < 1$, and core–periphery equilibria where one region has all the world's capital and is the only region creating new capital. The point is easily made. The division of the world capital and industry is given by s_K. Plainly, the rate of growth of the north's capital stock, g, and the rate of growth the south's capital stock, g^*, will influence the level of s_K over time. In particular, differentiating the definition of s_K with respect to time and gathering terms, we have the identity

$$\dot{s}_K \equiv (g - g^*)s_K(1 - s_K) \qquad (7.21)$$

As part of the definition of a long-run equilibrium, the spatial division of industry must reach a steady level and, given (7.21), this can only happen when $g = g^*$, or $s_K(1 - s_K) = 0$.

CHARACTERIZATION OF EQUILIBRIA

Growth. We start by finding the common, long-run rate of capital accumulation, $g = g^*$ for the symmetric interior equilibria, that is, where $q = 1$ and $q^* = 1$. Given symmetry, that is, $s_K = 1/2$, we know from (7.4) that $B = B^*$, so (7.9), (7.3), (7.4) and (7.20) imply that the $q = 1$ condition reduces to

$$q \equiv \frac{v}{F} = \frac{b}{1 - b} \frac{[(1 + \lambda)L^w - 2(g + \delta)]}{2(g + \delta + \rho)} = 1 \qquad (7.22)$$

Thus, solving Tobin's $q = 1$, we get the long-run rate of growth of capital; using the result in (7.5) provides us with the long-run E^w. These are

$$E^w = L^w + \rho \frac{2}{1 + \lambda}$$

$$g = bL^w \frac{1 + \lambda}{2} - (1 - b)\rho - \delta \tag{7.23}$$

The growth rate, of course, increases with λ because easier spillovers between regions help to decrease the cost of innovation. As the intensity of learning spillovers rises to the limiting case of global spillovers, $\lambda = 1$, the growth rate of the LS model approaches that of the GS model. By construction $g = g^*$, so g is also the growth rate of the world's capital stock. As before, the implied real income growth rate is just g times $\mu/(\sigma - 1)$.

In the core-in-the-north outcome ($s_K = 1$), the λ parameter is irrelevant since all knowledge creation and all industry is located in the north. As mentioned above, we may view λ as the fraction of public knowledge capital (i.e. the unappropriable learning effect generated by the I sector) that melts as it flows between innovators who are geographically separated. In the CP outcome, all innovation occurs in the same region, so none of the learning melts—just as in the case when $\lambda = 1$. Accordingly, $A = 1$ and $B = 1$. This implies that the long-run outcome (7.11) holds here, that is, the fully agglomerated LS model has the same long-run growth rate and expenditure as the GS model. This is also true for the core-in-the-south equilibrium.

The difference between the real income growth rate in core–periphery and symmetric outcomes is then

$$abL^w \left(\frac{1 - \lambda}{2} \right), \quad a \equiv \frac{\mu}{\sigma - 1} \tag{7.24}$$

As intuition would have it, this gap decreases with the intensity of learning spillovers and is magnified by the underlying growth rate, which is proportional to L^w. Note that this expression shows how geography affects growth.

Location. As for the GS model, a simple way to characterize the locational equilibria of the LS model is by means of the EE and nn curves. To calculate the EE relationship, we need E and E^*. Expenditure on consumption is just income less spending on new and replacement capital. From $q = 1$, we know πK equals $(\rho + \delta + g)FK$, and from the I sector production function, we know $L_I = (g + \delta)FK$, so E equals $L + \rho FK$. Likewise, $E^* = L + \rho F^* K^*$. Taking the ratio of $E/(E + E^*)$, imposing $s_n = s_K$, and using (7.20), we get

$$s_E = \frac{1}{2} + \frac{\rho \lambda (s_K - 1/2)}{AA^* L^w + \rho(A(1 - s_K) + A^* s_K)} \tag{7.25}$$

Note that for global spillovers, that is, $\lambda = 1$, $A = A^* = 1$, so (7.25) reduces to corresponding expression for the GS model, (7.13) with $s_L = 1/2$.

Since both nations are investing at interior equilibria, $q = q^* = 1$. Using the expressions for the v's and F's in (7.9) and (7.20), $q = q^*$ is true if and only if $A\pi = A^*\pi^*$. Intuitively, this equality means that, for both regions to invest, larger

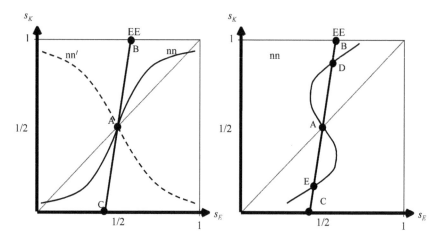

Figure 7.4 The scissor diagram for the LS model.

profits in one region must be compensated by a higher cost of capital (i.e. lower A) in that same region. Imposing $s_K = s_n$ again, and using the definitions of the π's and A's in (7.4) and (7.20), the nn curve for interior equilibria becomes

$$s_E = \frac{1}{2} + \frac{(s_K - 1/2)(\lambda(1 + \phi^2) - 2\phi)}{(1 - \phi^2)(A(1 - s_K) + A^* s_K)} \qquad (7.26)$$

As in the GS model, perfect symmetry, $s_E = s_K = 1/2$, is an obvious solution. However, here two other interior solutions exist in addition to the symmetric equilibrium. To find them, we use (7.20), (7.25), and (7.26) and obtain

$$s_K = \frac{1}{2} \pm \frac{1}{2}\sqrt{\left(\frac{1 + \lambda}{1 - \lambda}\right)\left(\frac{1 + \lambda\Lambda}{1 - \lambda\Lambda}\right)}, \quad \Lambda \equiv \left[1 - \frac{4\rho\phi(1 - \lambda\phi)}{L^w[\lambda(1 + \phi^2) - 2\phi]}\right]^{-1}$$
$$(7.27)$$

These additional interior solutions only exist for an intermediate range of ϕ.[13]

DIAGRAMMATIC SOLUTIONS AND FORCES

Figure 7.4 plots the EE and nn curves, (7.25) and (7.26), respectively. Note that the EE curve does not depend upon trade costs and it has a positive slope since a higher share of world capital implies a higher share of world expenditures. As usual, the two intersect at the mid-point (shown as point A), and changing the level of trade freeness rotates the nn curve around point A. For points to the right of nn, the northern market is too large for both q and q^* to equal unity. In particular, since $q = q^* = 1$ on the nn curve, to the right of it, $q = 1$ and

[13] Since we have an analytic solution for the stable interior equilibria, we could find the corresponding rate of growth. The result, however, is too unwieldy to be revealing, beyond showing that the growth rate thus derived increases smoothly from the symmetric to the CP values. See Baldwin et al. (2001) for details.

$q^* < 1$, so only the north innovates and, as a consequence, s_K tends to rise for points to the right of nn. Similarly, s_K tends to fall for points to the left of nn.

The left panel shows nn for two levels of trade freeness. When the level of freeness is quite low, as shown by the solid nn curve, the nn curve is flatter than EE. As usual, this implies that the symmetric equilibrium is stable. Since a shock to s_K from point A takes the economy slightly up the EE curve and since the EE curve is steeper than the nn curve, the perturbed economy finds itself to the left of nn. Since s_K tends to fall for such points, we can say that the shock generates self-correcting pressures when the regions are not very open to trade. The CP equilibria are marked as B and C. They are on EE but off nn since the EE relationship must hold at any equilibrium (it is based on a definition and utility maximization), but the nn curve only holds for interior equilibria. Plainly both CP outcomes are unstable since the core-in-the-north outcome is to the left of nn and the core-in-the-south point is to the right of nn. The intuition for why the symmetric outcome is stable when the regions are very closed to trade is the same as we saw in the FC, CC and GS models—the dispersion force (market crowding effect) gets very strong as trade gets closed, and so dominates the agglomeration forces.

The second nn curve in the left panel, marked as nn′, shows the curve when the economy is quite open to trade. In this case, the nn curve is negatively sloped, so the symmetric equilibrium is unstable. A shock to s_K from point A takes the economy slightly up the EE curve and since EE is positively sloped, the perturbed economy finds itself to the right of nn. Since s_K tends to rise for such points, we can say that the shock generates self-reinforcing pressures that amplify the original shock. Similarly, both CP equilibria are stable since the core-in-the-north outcome is to the right of nn and the core-in-the-south point is to the left.

The right panel of Figure 7.4 shows the case for a range of intermediate levels of trade freeness. Two other intersections, points D and E, between the EE and nn curves exist in addition to the symmetric equilibrium. The same logic used above allows us to conclude that they are stable.

STABILITY ANALYSIS

The foregoing graphical analysis shows that the symmetric outcome is the only stable long-run equilibrium when trade freeness is small. The CP outcomes are the only stable long-run equilibria when trade freeness is large. For intermediate freeness, both symmetry and core–periphery are unstable long-run equilibria. In this case, two extra interior equilibria exist and they are stable.

These additional interior solutions only exist for the range of ϕ between the break-and-sustain points. The break point can be found by noting that the two values of s_K given by (7.27) converge to 1/2 as ϕ approaches the value

$$\phi^B = \frac{L^w(1 + \lambda)/2 + \rho - \sqrt{(1 - \lambda^2)[L^w(1 + \lambda)/2 + \rho]^2 + \lambda^2\rho^2}}{\lambda[L^w(1 + \lambda)/2 + 2\rho]} \quad (7.28)$$

from above. For levels of ϕ below ϕ^B, the symmetric point is the only solution to the nn and EE curves since the other two interior solutions are imaginary. In addition, for levels of ϕ above the sustain point,

$$\phi^s = \frac{L^w + \rho - \sqrt{(L^w + \rho)^2 - 2\lambda\,^2L^w(L^w/2 + \rho)}}{2\lambda(L^w/2 + \rho)} \tag{7.29}$$

the solutions in (7.27) are out of the economically relevant range (one is negative and the other exceeds one). Note that for $\lambda = 1$, (7.28) and (7.29) coincide and attain the same value as (7.15) in the GS model.

The stability of the symmetric equilibrium can also be studied with the method we used in the GS model. That is, we ask what a slight change in s_K would do to Tobin's q or the incentive to innovate in the north, holding constant the common growth rate and world expenditure. If it turns out that dq/ds_K evaluated at the symmetric equilibrium is positive, we know that a small positive shock to s_K would generate forces that would be self-reinforcing in the sense that the shock would hasten innovation in the north and hinder it in the south. If the derivative is negative at the symmetric point, the shock generates self-correcting forces. Using our expression for π in our expression for v and taking the ratio of this to our expression for F yields

$$q = \frac{bE^w}{\rho + \delta + g}AB \tag{7.30}$$

where A is defined in (7.20) and B in (7.4). Differentiating this with respect to s_K, we get

$$\left.\frac{dq}{q}\right|_{s_K=1/2} = 2\left(\frac{1 - \phi}{1 + \phi}\right)\frac{\partial s_E}{\partial s_K}ds_K - 2\frac{(1 - \phi)^2}{(1 + \phi)^2}ds_K + 2\left(\frac{1 - \lambda}{1 + \lambda}\right)ds_K$$

$$\left.\frac{\partial s_E}{\partial s_K}\right|_{s_K=1/2} = \frac{2\lambda\rho/(1 + \lambda)}{(L^w/2)(1 + \lambda) + \rho} \tag{7.31}$$

where the derivatives are evaluated at the symmetric outcome, and the expression for $\partial s_E/\partial s_K$ is derived from (7.25).

This shows that, in addition to the two effects that were in operation in the GS model—that is, the destabilizing demand-linked effect shown in the first term, and the stabilizing market-crowding effect shown in the second term—a third force operates in the LS model. Since learning spillovers are localized, a small increase in s_K raises the relative productivity of the north's innovating sector and thus makes the north more attractive for innovation. This is what we call the 'localized spillover effect' and we note that it is destabilizing. It is also worth remarking that the strength of the localized spillover effect is independent of trade costs since it reflects the cost of trading ideas rather than goods, and its strength diminishes as learning gets less localized, that is, as λ approaches 1. Finally, one may think of the localized spillover effect as being akin to the cost-linked circular causality in the vertical linkage version of the CP model. As the share of capital in the north rises, the north's capital producing sector gets more productive because of the proximity of capital. Since this higher I sector productivity encourages further increases in s_K, circular causality is in operation.

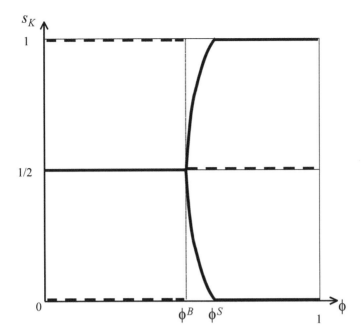

Figure 7.5   The tomahawk diagram for the LS model.

Equation (7.31) shows that the system is unstable for sufficiently low trade costs. As ϕ approaches unity, the first two right-hand terms go to zero, leaving the positive third term. It can be checked that the critical level at which the expression in (7.31) becomes positive is ϕ^B. It is also possible to show that the break point in the LS model comes at a lower level of openness than does the break point in the GS model. This is quite intuitive as the introduction of localized spillovers adds a destabilizing effect.

THE TOMAHAWK DIAGRAM

The foregoing results can be gainfully summarized by the usual tomahawk diagram. This is reported in Figure 7.5. As manipulation of (7.28) and (7.29) would show, the break point ϕ^B is smaller than the sustain point ϕ^S. Thus, as trade freeness increases from autarky, the symmetric equilibrium turns from stable to unstable before the CP outcomes become stable. In between there exist two other stable interior equilibria. As revealed by (7.27), these are located at equal distance from $s_K = 1/2$. This implies that Figure 7.5 looks more like a pitchfork than a tomahawk.

7.3.4 Key Features

The LS model exhibits most of the CP model's seven key features. While it also shares all of the new properties of the CC and GS models, it is even richer.

COMPARISON WITH THE CP MODEL

Home-Market Magnification.   As is true for all the models in this book, the LS model displays agglomeration forces in the form of the home-market effect. This is magnified when the economies are more open to trade. Thus, small differences among regions/nations become more important, not less important, as trade gets freer (home-market magnification).

Circular Causality.   In the LS model, as in the GS and CC models, the home-market effect is amplified by the connection between production shifting and expenditures. In contrast to the CP model, the expenditures–production connection is not based on the physical mobility of the factor used intensively in the industrial sector. Rather, as in the GS and CC models, pressures that were relieved by migration in the CP and other models find vent here in capital construction and destruction. This alters relative market size because capital's income is spent locally.

  Like the CP model but differently from the GS and CC models, the LS model also features cost-link circular causality. This, however, is based on a different mechanism than the one in the CP model. Knowledge spillovers in both the GS and LS models imply that the current productivity of I sector workers depends upon cumulative past production. In the GS model, the location of past production is irrelevant since learning spillovers are global. In the LS model, however, I workers learn more from past production that took place in their own region. This gives rise to what might be called an 'intertemporal vertical linkage'. The north's share of capital and industry depends upon its past production relative to that of the south, but as the north's share rises, its innovators get more productive. This makes innovation relatively more attractive in the north and thus tends to raise the north's share of industry even further.

Endogenous Asymmetry.   As shown in Figure 7.5, regional asymmetries arise endogenously in response to falling trade costs in the LS model. This also happens in the CP, FE, CC and GS models.

Catastrophic Agglomeration.   As the tomahawk diagram shows in Figure 7.5, the symmetric equilibrium in the LS model does not break in a catastrophic manner. Increasing trade freeness destabilizes the symmetric equilibrium, before stabilizing the CP ones. This happens because the break point is smaller than the sustain point. When freeness lies between these two points, the only stable equilibria are two interior equilibria with asymmetric location. As trade freeness moves towards the sustain point, the asymmetric interior equilibria approach the two CP outcomes. Beyond the sustain point, only the CP equilibria are stable.

Locational Hysteresis.   Once the regions are sufficiently open to trade ($\phi > \phi^B$), there are two locally stable equilibria, so temporary policies could have permanent effects by selecting one of the two equilibria, or shifting the economy from one to the other.

Hump-Shaped Agglomeration Rents.   As in the CP model, in the LS model the agglomeration rents are also a concave function of trade freeness. To see this, consider a long-run equilibrium in which no capital is left in the south ($s_K = 1$ and $\phi \geq \phi^S$). In this scenario, the agglomeration rents are measured as the difference between q and q^*. Such difference can be evaluated by substituting $s_K = 1$, into the equilibrium expression to get

$$q - q^*|_{s_n=1} = 1 - \frac{\lambda}{2}\left[\frac{1}{\phi}(1 - \eta) + \phi(1 + \eta)\right] \qquad (7.32)$$

where $\eta \equiv \rho/(L^w + \rho)$ as in (7.19). Indeed, (7.32) differs from (7.19) only for the presence of λ before the square bracket. In particular, (7.32) is a function of ϕ, which equals zero at $\phi = \phi^S$ and $\phi = 1$ while being positive in between. Moreover, in the same interval, it is concave with a maximum at $\phi = \sqrt{\phi^B}$. Therefore, as trade gets freer (i.e. ϕ rises from ϕ^S towards 1), the agglomeration rents first rise and then fall ('hump shape'). Notice, however, that here, while ϕ^S is the sustain point of the LS model as defined in (7.29), ϕ^B is the break-and-sustain point of the GS model as defined in (7.15).

The Overlap and Self-Fulfilling Expectations.   In the LS model, the sustain point occurs at a higher level of freeness than does the break point, so there is no overlap where symmetry and both CP outcomes are stable. Shocks to expectations cannot therefore result in reallocations between symmetric and CP outcomes.

COMPARISON WITH CC AND GS MODELS

The LS model, like the CC and GS models, also displays a number of interesting features that do not appear in the CP model. Specifically, the LS model shares all the additional features of the CC model: growth affects geography; agglomeration is driven by the appearance of growth poles and sinks; regional income differentials do not disappear as trade gets perfectly free; and economic integration has a twofold meaning. In addition, the LS model shares the crucial new feature of the GS model: endogenous growth.

Growth Affects Geography.   As in the CC and GS models, since capital accumulates in the LS model and capital's income is spent locally, growth can affect geography.

Growth Poles and Growth Sinks.   The transitional dynamics of the LS model are characterized by the emergence of 'growth poles and growth sinks'. The shift from symmetric to asymmetric location is driven by faster growth in the region gaining industry and slower growth in the region losing it. This also happens in the CC and GS models.

Permanent Income Differences.   Since the spatial distributions of income and capital ownership are intertwined, as in the CC and GS models, in the LS model, regional asymmetries in location also cause and are caused by regional asymmetries in factor endowments. In the end, the core region has a higher capital/labour ratio and therefore higher income per worker (workers own all capital). This difference does not disappear as trade becomes perfectly free.

A Richer Definition of Economic Integration. Even if, for the sake of parsimony, we have not presented the case of perfect capital mobility, in the LS model, closer economic integration can also be studied as freer capital movement or freer trade. (We have not worked out the perfect capital mobility case in the LS model since it functions in a qualitatively identical fashion as in the GS model. See Martin and Ottaviano (1999) for a detailed analysis of perfect capital mobility in the extreme case of $\lambda = 0$).

NEW FEATURES: GEOGRAPHY AFFECTS GROWTH

While sharing most of the features of the CP, CC and GS models, the LS framework also exhibits a number of new properties.

An Even Richer Definition of Economic Integration. Economic integration is a multi-faceted phenomenon. In all the models presented, the cost of selling goods at a distance plays centre stage. In the CP and FE models, the costs of human capital migration are also important. In the FC, CC and GS models, barriers to physical capital mobility are relevant too. Lowering the cost of trade in goods and private capital mobility, however, is only one aspect of integration. Indeed, lowering the barriers to the spatial diffusion of public knowledge can also be crucial. This comes out nicely from the LS model, in which the parameter λ measures the freeness of the learning spillover.

To investigate a scenario in which the cost of sharing ideas, λ, changes together with the cost of trading goods, ϕ, Figure 7.6 depicts what Baldwin and Forslid (2000) call a 'stability map'. This shows how the LS model's stability properties vary with λ and ϕ. The diagram plots the break-and-sustain points, (7.28) and (7.29), against the various possible values of λ. The dashed curve is the break point and the solid curve is the sustain point. The curves partition the map into three regions. When trade is not very free, and/or knowledge spillovers are very free, then the symmetric outcome is stable and the CP outcomes are unstable. This is the northwest region in the diagram. When trade is quite free and/or knowledge flows are very restricted, only the CP outcomes are stable. This is the southeast region of the map. For a narrow range of ϕ's, two asymmetric interior equilibria are the only stable equilibria and this is shown as the area between the two curves.

Endogenous Growth as Agglomeration Force. In the LS model, endogenous growth is an agglomeration force per se. When $\lambda = 0$ (no learning spillovers between regions), the system is always unstable, regardless of the level of trade freeness. This can be seen in the diagram by noting that the break-and-sustain points are both zero when λ is zero.

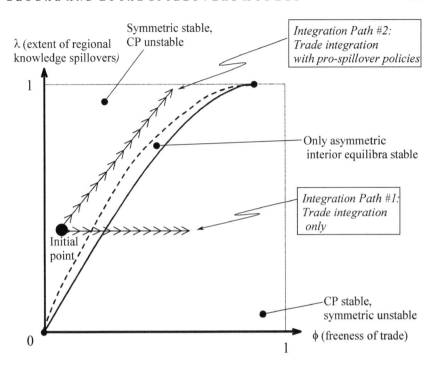

Figure 7.6 Stability map for the LS model: stabilizing and destabilizing integration.

Intuition for this result is simple. Any perturbation will cause the relative capital stocks (of initially symmetric nations) to diverge forever. The reason is that the nation with the slight head start finds that it accumulates *I*-sector experience faster than the other nation. This lowers the replacement cost of capital—the denominator of its Tobin's *q*—faster and this in turn attracts more resources to the *I* sector of the fast-accumulating nation. If trade is prohibited between the nations, the peripheral region will continue to innovate, but at a slower rate, so that s_K will approach unity.

Knowledge Spillovers as Dispersion Force.   While endogenous growth fosters agglomeration, in the LS model, knowledge spillovers favour dispersion. There are two ways to see this. First, with $\lambda = 1$ (perfect knowledge spillovers between regions), the symmetric equilibrium is stable for sufficient low levels of trade freeness (i.e. for high levels of trade costs). Second, as is clear from Figure 7.6, the range of ϕ's for which symmetry is stable expands as λ rises. In this sense, knowledge spillover is a dispersion force that goes a long way to countering the agglomerating effects of growth.

The intuition for this result is also straightforward. The spillovers in the *I* sector (which are necessary for growth) create their own circular causality encouraging agglomeration. The strength of this force, however, depends upon the extent to which such spillovers are localized. As λ rises to unity, the growth-linked agglomeration force disappears.

Integration as Agglomeration and Dispersion Force. Given the above results, it is clear that integration may be stabilizing or destabilizing in the LS model. This is an important feature since one of the shortcomings of the CP model is that it predicts that economic integration eventually ends up creating extreme divergence between initially symmetric regions, that is, that integration always fosters agglomeration.

As shown by the path marked as 'integration path #1' in Figure 7.6, a purely trade-cost reducing integration policy encourages agglomeration and eventually results in extreme agglomeration. By contrast, a policy that lowers the cost of transporting both goods and public knowledge may avoid extreme agglomeration. This is shown by the path marked 'integration path #2' in the diagram. Indeed, an integration policy that sufficiently raises learning spillovers can lead to the dispersion of economic activity. For example, if the economy started off with moderate ϕ and λ, an increase in λ with no increase in ϕ could move the system from a point where only CP outcomes are stable to another point where only the symmetric outcome is stable.

Growth Take-Offs. Perhaps the most important new feature of the LS model is that economic geography can affect the growth rate.

One way to highlight this is to consider the impact of lowering trade costs, while leaving the intensity of learning spillovers unchanged. When trade freeness is below the break point ϕ^B, the equilibrium location is such that both industry and innovation are dispersed. In this situation, learning spillovers are as weak as possible and the cost of innovation as large as possible. The corresponding growth rate of capital is given by (7.23). As trade freeness increases above the sustain point ϕ^S, CP outcomes become the only stable equilibria. Once all industry is agglomerated in one region, learning spillovers are as strong as possible and the cost of innovation as small as possible. The resulting growth rate of capital is thus higher, as (7.11) shows. Therefore, by triggering agglomeration, trade integration raises the economy to a higher growth path ('growth take-off') (see Baldwin et al. 2001 for details).

Growth Compensation for the Periphery. In all previous models, the loss of industry is unambiguously harmful to the residents of the periphery, as long as trade is not perfectly costless. In the LS model, the result is not so stark.

The continual lowering of trade costs in the LS model does produce uneven spatial development—real per-capita income rises in the core region (since it saves the trade costs on all M varieties) and falls in the peripheral one (since it pays the trade costs on all M varieties). However, the emergence of regional imbalances is accompanied by faster growth in all regions (growth take-off). Of course, this is good also for the periphery and creates a tension between the static loss due to relocation and the dynamic gain due to faster growth. Thus,

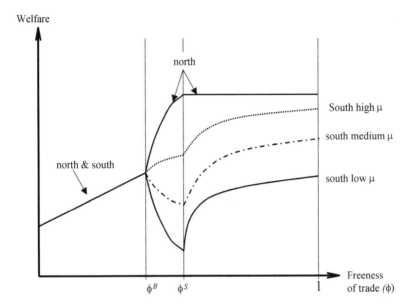

Figure 7.7   Can the periphery gain from agglomeration?

while the core is unambiguously better off, the take-off has ambiguous effects on peripheral welfare.

Intuition is served by Figure 7.7, which plots the long-run levels of welfare in the two regions as functions of trade freeness. In particular, it depicts a scenario in which lower trade costs drive all industry towards the north.

When trade is sufficiently closed, freer trade raises welfare in both regions because it lowers the price of imported manufactured goods. As trade freeness rises above the break point, north and south welfare levels diverge. The north benefits from agglomeration and faster growth. The south benefits only from the latter, while it is harmed by the former. This explains why the south's post-take-off welfare is always below the north's. Once full agglomeration has been reached (i.e. freeness has raised above the sustain point), the north's welfare is constant.

The behaviour of south's welfare is more complex. If the expenditures share of manufacturing goods, μ, is low enough, the increase in the growth rate has only a mild impact on welfare and the static loss dominates. In this case, the south loses from the take-off. This case is shown by the solid line (the lowest one in the diagram). On the contrary, if the share μ is sufficiently large, the dynamic gain dominates and the take-off benefits both regions, as shown by the dotted line. Finally, for intermediate values of μ, the south initially loses but eventually attains a welfare level that exceeds its pre-take-off situation. This is illustrated by the dashed curve.

Importantly, after the take-off, lowering transaction costs always improves welfare in the south because it decreases the price of goods imported from the north. Thus, even though the south may have been made worse off by agglomeration in the north, resisting further reductions in transaction costs is not welfare improving.

7.4 CONCLUDING REMARKS AND RELATED LITERATURE

7.4.1 Summary Results for Policy Modelling

This chapter has presented two models of endogenous growth, the GS and LS models, in which economic geography is important. It has shown that adding endogenous growth to economic geography models expands the range of features well beyond those of the CP model—and of the CC model as well. At the same time, endogenous growth models are also much easier to work with than the CP model.

In both models, the long-run accumulation of knowledge capital is supported by learning effects in an innovating sector. Innovation has a public good component that makes it possible for current innovators to benefit from the experience of past innovators (learning spillover). In the GS model, such spillover is global in that its positive effects are equally available to all innovators wherever they operate. In the LS model, the spillover is local: its positive effects fade away with distance.

The GS model enriches the CC model by adding endogenous long-run growth. This makes trade-freeness-dependent capital flows a permanent rather than a transitional feature of the model. When regions are asymmetric in terms of capital stocks and we assume that private knowledge capital is mobile, the GS model predicts a continual relocation of capital either from the rich region to the poor region, or vice versa, depending on whether trade is more or less restricted, respectively.

The LS model moves one step further by showing that endogenous growth per se provides an additional agglomeration force while the strength of spatial spillovers acts as an additional dispersion force. This latter result suggests a third dimension of trade integration in addition to trade freeness and private capital mobility: public knowledge diffusion.

The LS model also shows that trade integration can help an economy to take off at the price of regional imbalances. This creates a trade-off for peripheral regions between the static loss due to lower real income and the dynamic gain due to faster growth.

7.4.2 Related Literature

The GS and LS models have their antecedents in the FC model of Chapter 3 and the endogenous growth model with expanding product variety by Grossman and Helpman (1991).

The first paper to introduce endogenously expanding product variety in a CP-like model was Martin and Ottaviano (1999), who presented versions of both GS and LS models with perfect capital mobility. They considered, however, only the cases of purely global and purely local learning spillovers. The intermediate case is studied by Baldwin et al. (2001) in a setting that rules out capital mobility. The solution of endogenous growth models in terms of Tobin's q is put forth by Baldwin and Forslid (1997).

This set of basic results is enriched by other contributions. Baldwin and Forslid (2000) introduce endogenous growth in the CP model of Chapter 2. This allows them to consider human capital migration together with human capital. They also point out that integration fosters agglomeration if pursued along the line of freer trade, while it favours dispersion if fostered along the line of better knowledge transmission. Basevi and Ottaviano (2002) modify the LS model to investigate the intermediate situation in which capital mobility is neither absent nor perfectly free. Ottaviano (1996) as well as Manzocchi and Ottaviano (2001) extend the model of Martin and Ottaviano (1999) to a three-region economy. Martin and Ottaviano (2001) generate a feedback between growth and agglomeration by assuming vertical linkages rather than local spillovers in innovation. Yamamoto (2002) presents a similar model but with the circular causation between growth and agglomeration coming from the vertical linkages between the intermediate goods sector and the innovation sector. Urban (2002) integrates a neo-classical growth model into a static geography model without capital mobility. Contrary to the models presented here, he shows that lower transaction costs lead to convergence between the poor and the rich country. The reason is that the classic, local, decreasing-returns effect implies that there is more incentive to accumulate capital in the poor country and this effect does not depend on transaction costs. On the contrary, the home-market effect, the divergence force, decreases as transaction costs diminish. Bottazzi (2001) presents related analysis.

An early attempt to link growth and geography models was Walz (1996) who introduces endogenously expanding product variety in a model with vertical linkages and migration. His assumption of costless migration leads to a bang-bang migration behaviour. Walz (1997) extends the model to a three-region setting.

Fujita and Thisse (2002a,b, Chapter 11) propose a combination of a Krugman type core–periphery model and a Grossman–Helpman type model with horizontally differentiated products. As in this chapter and the earlier literature on growth and agglomeration, they use a set-up where the fixed cost of firms is a patent which they assume to be tradable with no cost. This means they work with a perfect capital mobility assumption which we know is a stabilizing factor. The skilled workers who produce these patents are themselves mobile, an assumption which we know from the FE model (Chapter 4) is destabilizing. Finally, they work with localized spillovers so that agglomeration enhances growth.

Black and Henderson (1999) model the relation between urbanization and growth: there are localized knowledge spillovers so that urbanization affects the endogenous growth of the economy. Growth itself affects the size of cities. However, the assumption of a migration process that is determined by a city developer seems rather restrictive. Duranton and Puga (2001) provide micro-foundations for the link between local diversity and innovation in a model with localized spillovers. Firms that innovate locate in diversified cities and then relocate in specialized cities to commence mass production.

A different type of geography and growth model where trade is absent is proposed by Quah (2002). The knowledge spillovers are imperfect both across space and time so that quite intuitively spatial clusters can appear. The reasoning is not very different from Grossman and Helpman (1991) who show that when knowledge spillovers are localized, the increasing returns activity concentrates in one location.

REFERENCES

Baldwin, R. and R. Forslid. 1997. Trade liberalization and endogenous growth: a q-theory approach. *Journal of International Economics* 50: 497–517.

_____. 2000. The core-periphery model and endogenous growth: stabilising and de-stabilising integration. *Economica* 67: 307–324.

Baldwin, R. and P. Martin. 2003. Agglomeration and regional growth. In *Handbook of Regional and Urban Economics: Cities and Geography*. ed. V. Henderson and J.-F. Thisse. Amsterdam: North-Holland, forthcoming.

Baldwin, R., P. Martin and G. Ottaviano. 2001. Global income divergence, trade and industrialization: the geography of growth take-off. *Journal of Economic Growth* 6: 5–37.

Barro, R. and X. Sala-i-Martin. 1995. *Economic Growth*. New York: McGraw-Hill.

Basevi, G. and G. Ottaviano. 2002. The district goes global: export vs FDI. *Journal of Regional Science* 42: 107–126.

Black, D. and V. Henderson. 1999. A theory of urban growth. *Journal of Political Economy* 107: 252–284.

Bottazzi, L. 2001. Globalization and local proximity in innovation: a dynamic process. *European Economic Review* 45: 731–741.

Ciccone, A. and R. Hall. 1996. Productivity and the density of economic activity. *American Economic Review* 87: 54–70.

Coe, D. and E. Helpman. 1995. International R&D Spillovers. *European Economic Review* 39: 859–887.

Coe, D., E. Helpman and A. Hoffmaister. 1997. North-south R&D spillovers. *The Economic Journal* 107: 134–149.

Duranton G. and D. Puga. 2001. Nursery cities: urban diversity, process innovation and the life cycle of products. *American Economic Review* 5: 1454–1477.

Fujita, M. and J. Thisse. 2002a. Does geographical agglomeration foster economic growth? and who gains and loses from it? Discussion Paper No. 3135, Centre for Economic and Policy Research.

_____. 2002b. *Economics of Agglomeration*. Oxford: Oxford University Press.

Grossman, G. and E. Helpman. 1991. Innovation and Growth in the World Economy. Cambridge, MA: MIT Press.

Jacobs, J. 1969. The Economy of Cities. New York: Vintage.

Jaffe, A., M. Trajtenberg and R. Henderson. 1993. Geographic Localization of Knowledge Spillovers as Evidenced by Patent Citations. *Quarterly Journal of Economics* 108: 577–598.

Keller, W. 2002. Geographic localization of international technology diffusion. *American Economic Review* 92: 120–142.

Lucas, R.E. 1988. On the mechanics of economic development. *Journal of Monetary Economics* 22: 3–42.

Manzocchi, S. and G. Ottaviano. 2001. Outsiders in economic integration: the case of a transition economy. *Economics of Transition* 9: 229–249.

Martin, P. and G. Ottaviano. 1999. Growing locations: industry location in a model of endogenous growth. *European Economic Review* 43: 281–302.

Martin, P. and G. Ottaviano. 2001. Growth and agglomeration. *International Economic Review* 42: 947–968.

Ottaviano, G. I. P. 1996. The location effects of isolation. *Swiss Journal of Statistics and Economics* 132: 427–440.

Perroux, F. 1995. Note sur la croissance. *Economie Appliquée* 1–2: 307–320.

Quah, D. 2002. Spatial agglomeration dynamics. Discussion Paper No. 3208, Centre for Economic and Policy Research.

Romer, P. 1990. Endogenous technological change. *Journal of Political Economy* 98.5(part II): S71–S102.

Urban, D. 2002. Neoclassical growth, manufacturing agglomeration and terms of trade. Mimeo, London School of Economics.

Walz, U. 1996. Transport costs, intermediate goods and localized growth. *Regional Science and Urban Economics* 26: 671–795.

Walz, U. 1997. Growth and deeper regional integration in a three-country model. *Review of International Economics* 5: 492–507.

Yamamoto, K. 2001. Agglomeration and growth with innovation in the intermediate goods sector. Mimeo, Graduate School of Economics, Kyoto University (*Regional Science and Urban Economics* in press).

CHAPTER 8

Vertical Linkages Models

8.1 INTRODUCTION

Migration drives agglomeration in both the CP and the FE models. Inter-regional migration, however, is not always a reasonable assumption. While labour is quite mobile among US states, labour mobility across and even within EU countries is rather limited. This observation encouraged the development of an alternative agglomeration mechanism. Perhaps the most important is that of the so-called 'vertical linkage' models (VL models for short). In these models, input–output linkages in the presence of inter-sectoral, rather than inter-regional labour mobility, support agglomeration.[1]

The seminal paper, Venables (1996a), introduces cost linkages between an upstream sector and a downstream sector. For the sake of simplicity, Krugman and Venables (1995) and Fujita et al. (1999, Chapter 14) collapse the two sectors into one, so input–output relationships switch from 'vertical' linkages to 'horizontal' linkages (nevertheless the VL label is retained). In this modified model, the functional forms are very similar to those that Krugman (1991) used in the CP model. For this reason, we refer to this model as the 'core–periphery vertical-linkage' model (CPVL model for short).

The CPVL is at least as analytically impenetrable as the CP model and is thus equally inapt for policy analysis. For this reason, we cover two alternative models in which agglomeration stems from vertical linkages that are more tractable.

One such alternative is the FEVL model. As its name suggests, it is the vertical-linkage parallel of the FE model of Chapter 4. The CPVL model differs from the CP model in that it replaces inter-regional migration of a primary factor with input–output linkages among firms. Likewise, the FEVL uses similar functional forms as the FE model but differs from it in exactly the same way that the CPVL models differs from the CP model. In both the CPVL and FEVL models, labour is the unique primary factor and both sectors draw from a common, local pool of workers. Also, all firms in the manufacturing sector use each other's output as intermediate input. Despite these similarities, the FEVL model is much simpler to work with. Like the FE model, for instance, the FEVL model is analytically solvable. This implies that we can entirely characterize its dynamic properties.

The other alternative VL model we propose is the 'footloose-capital vertical-linkage' model (FCVL model). Like the FC model, the FCVL model has two

---

[1] This approach also captures what seems to be an essential ingredient of an urban agglomeration, namely the existence of a diversified intermediate sector (Fujita and Thisse 2002, Chapter 4).

primary factors, labour and capital, the latter being inter-regionally mobile. As we saw in Chapter 3, inter-regional mobility of some factor alone is not sufficient to trigger agglomeration. In the FC model, agglomeration forces of the cumulative sort are inexistent because capital is disembodied and as a result capital owners allocate their factor so as to maximize nominal returns (this cuts the cost-linked agglomeration force) and spend their income locally (which cuts the demand-linked agglomeration force). As it turns out, if we add vertical linkages to the story, the resulting model displays self-enforcing agglomeration forces. The resulting model is useful because it encompasses the FC model, which is the simplest of all geography models. Hence, in many applications we can work with the handy FC model and see the associated results as a limiting case of a richer set-up. We can then use the FCVL framework to see how agglomeration forces change the picture that emerges from the previous analysis. We shall pursue this strategy in the trade chapters of Part III.

8.1.1 Logic of VL Models

Like all the models in this book, the main concern of the three VL models we cover is the geographic location of industry. They assume a world of two regions, two sectors, and either two primary factors (FCVL model) or—in contrast to the CP and FE models—only one such factor (CPVL and FEVL models). One of the sectors—call it 'industry'—is marked by increasing returns and monopolistic competition in differentiated varieties. To make the location choice of industrial firms interesting, the model assumes that it is costly to sell industrial goods across regional borders. The other sector is kept as simple as possible by assuming perfect competition, constant returns and costless trade. The factor that is intensively used in such a Walrasian sector is assumed to be inter-sectorally mobile, while being inter-regionally immobile. The final main assumption concerns input–output linkages. All firms in the industrial sector buy each other's output as intermediate input (as in Ethier 1982).

As in the migration-based CP and the FE models, the mechanics of the FCVL and FEVL models are driven by two well-known results in the theory of international trade. The first is the 'market-access effect' that describes the tendency of imperfectly competitive firms to concentrate production in the big market and export to the small markets. The second result concerns the impact of firms' location on the production cost of other firms ('cost-of-production effect').[2] Each industrial firm produces a differentiated variety, and, because of trade coststrade costs, a variety is cheaper in the region in which it is produced. Thus, consumers and firms in the region with more firms import a narrower range of varieties and so avoid the trade costs more.

In the Walrasian sector the workers are paid their marginal product. By contrast, industry is imperfectly competitive and its workers generate a product that is priced above its cost of labour. This is a pecuniary externality for the worker

---

[2] In the CP and FE models, this is a cost-of-living effect (see Chapters 2 and 4).

does not take it into account when he/she decides to join the manufacturing force as, in so doing, he/she simply compares the nominal wages between sectors.

Combining the market-access effect, the cost-of-production effect and inter-sectoral mobility creates the potential for 'circular causality'—also known as 'cumulative causality', or 'backward and forward linkages.' The idea is simple and can be illustrated by a thought experiment. Suppose the two regions, north and south, are initially identical, but this symmetry is broken by a single worker in the north leaving the Walrasian sector to join the local industrial workforce. Assume also that simultaneously an industrial worker in the south leaves the industrial sector to join the Walrasian one. Clearly, this expands industrial output in the north and decreases it in the south. In turn, the northern expansion of industrial output must be accompanied by an increase in demand for intermediates. The existence of trade costs implies that supplementary demand in the north is biased towards northern inputs, which in turn raises the profitability of local firms relative to southern ones (by mark-up pricing). This increase in profitability is matched by the entry of new firms in the north. These firms in turn hire workers from the northern Walrasian sector, so the cycle repeats. For symmetric reasons, the opposite happens in the south. This is the essence of the demand (or backward) linkage.

The foregoing discussion points out that in the VL models the market-access and the cost-of-living (here, the cost-of-production) effects act as agglomeration forces as in the CP and the FE models. These forces are opposed by the market-crowding effect, which acts as a dispersion force. When the agglomeration forces are stronger than the dispersion forces, any inter-sectoral employment shock will trigger a self-reinforcing cycle of inter-sectoral labour reallocation that results in one region specializing in the Walrasian sector while the whole industry clusters in the other region. On the contrary, when the dispersion force outweighs the agglomeration forces, then any inter-sectoral employment shock lowers the northern firms' profitability relative to the southern firms' and this reverses the initial shock. In other words, employment shocks are self-correcting when the dispersion force dominates but self-reinforcing when the agglomeration forces dominate.

What determines the relative strength of agglomeration and dispersion forces? Trade cost is the usual suspect. As we will see, the strength of the dispersion force diminishes as trade gets freer. For example, if trade is almost completely free, competition from firms in the other region is approximately as important as competition from locally based firms. In other words, competition is not very localized, so shifting firms from south to north will have very little impact on firm's revenues and thus on their profits and entry.[3] At the other extreme, near-prohibitive levels of trade costs mean that a change in the number of locally based firms has a very large impact on competition for customers and thus a very big effect on profits and entry.

The strength of agglomeration forces also diminishes as trade gets freer. This is most easily seen for the cost-of-production effect. If the regions are very open,

---

[3] As usual, pure profits are eliminated by free entry and exit in the 'long run' so any short-term effect on profit ultimately translates into firm entry or exit.

then there will be very little difference in price indices between the two regions, regardless of where industrial varieties are produced. Thus, shifting industrial production has only a minor impact on the relative cost of production. However, if trade is very costly, the share of varieties produced locally will have a big impact on price indices. Similar reasons show that the market-access advantage is strongest when trade costs are high.

As it turns out, the dispersion force is stronger than the agglomeration forces when trade costs are very high, but falling trade costs weaken the dispersion force more rapidly than they weaken the agglomeration forces. What this means is that, as in the CP and the FE models, at some level of trade costs, the agglomeration forces overpower the dispersion force and all industry ends up clustering in one location; a symmetric reduction in trade costs between initially symmetric regions eventually produces asymmetric regions.

8.1.2 Organization of the Chapter

The chapter has five sections after the introduction. Section 8.2 presents the CPVL model and compares it with the CP model. Sections 8.3 and 8.4 introduce the FCVL and FEVL models; the FCVL is compared to the FC and CPVL models, the FEVL model is compared to the FE and CPVL models. Section 8.5 summarizes the key features of vertical linkages models with respect to the CP model. Section 8.6 contains our concluding remarks and a brief survey of related literature.

8.2 THE CPVL MODEL

Krugman and Venables (1995) and Fujita et al. (1999, Chapter 14) modify the basic CP model to allow for input–output linkages between firms while ruling out inter-regional migration. Here, we present this model, which we call the CP model with vertical linkages, or CPVL model for short.

8.2.1 Assumptions

The basic structure of the CPVL model is shown schematically in Figure 8.1. As the diagram makes clear, the CPVL model works with the same set-up as the CP model, but incorporates three crucial modifications. In particular, as in the CP model, there are two initially symmetric regions (north and south) and two sectors (manufacture M and agriculture A). The goods of both the M and A sectors are traded, but A-sector trade is frictionless while M-sector trade is inhibited by iceberg trade costs. Specifically, it is costless to ship M goods to local consumers but, to sell one unit in the other region, an M firm must ship $\tau \geq 1$ units. In what follows, we describe the north; analogous definitions hold for southern variables and these are denoted by an asterisk.

The representative consumer in the north has the usual two-tier utility function. The upper is Cobb–Douglas and the lower tier is CES. In symbols,

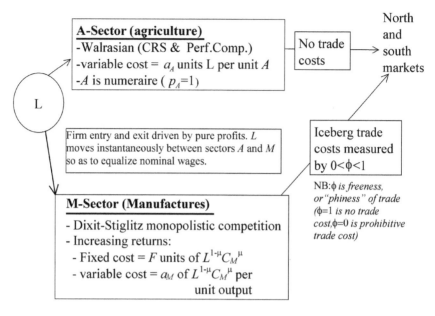

Figure 8.1 Schematic diagram of the CPVL model.

$$U = C_M^\mu C_A^{1-\mu}, \quad C_M \equiv \left(\int_{i=0}^{n+n^*} c_i^{1-1/\sigma} di \right)^{1/(1-1/\sigma)} ; \quad 0 < \mu < 1 < \sigma \quad (8.1)$$

where C_M and C_A are, respectively, consumption of the composite of all differentiated varieties in the M sector and consumption of the homogenous good A. Also, n and n^* are the mass (or number) of north and south varieties, respectively, μ is the expenditure share on M varieties, and σ is the constant elasticity of substitution between M varieties. The indirect utility function for the preferences in (8.1) is

$$V = \frac{E}{P}, \quad P \equiv p_A^{1-\mu}(\Delta n^w)^{-a}, \quad \Delta \equiv \frac{\int_{i=0}^{n^w} p_i^{1-\sigma} di}{n^w} ; \quad a \equiv \frac{\mu}{\sigma - 1} \quad (8.2)$$

where P is the perfect price index, p_A is the price of A, p_i is the consumer price of industrial variety i (the variety subscript will be dropped where clarity permits), $n^w = n + n^*$ is the world number of varieties.

The first difference between the CPVL and CP models comes in the factor endowments. While the CP model features two sector-specific factors, in the CPVL model there is only one primary factor of production, labour, which is used in both sectors. The wage of workers is denoted as w.

The second difference comes in factor mobility. While labour moves freely between sectors within the same region, it is assumed to be geographically immobile (i.e. no inter-regional migration is possible). Regional labour endowments are equal, that is, $L = L^* = L^w/2$ where L^w is worldwide labour endowment.

   The third difference between the CPVL and the CP model comes in the production technology of the M sector. The homothetic cost function of the M sector involves both labour and intermediates. Specifically, both the fixed and marginal input requirements (F and a_M, respectively) are incurred in a *composite input* consisting of labour and an aggregate of all varieties of the M good. For simplicity, we follow Fujita et al. (1999, Chapter 14) in assuming that the composite input is Cobb–Douglas in L and the usual CES aggregate of all M-sector varieties; the Cobb–Douglas expenditure share on the M-sector aggregate is μ. This way, consumers and firms devote the same shares of expenditures to manufacture and both value variety. In symbols, the cost function of a typical northern firm j is

$$C(x_j) = (F + a_M x_j)P_P, \quad P_P = w^{1-\mu}(\Delta n^w)^{-a} \tag{8.3}$$

where P_P is the producer price index and w is the wage of labour.

   The A-sector assumptions are identical to those of the CP model; producing A requires only labour; specifically, it takes a_A units of labour to make one unit of A.

   Finally, to analyse the entry decision of firms in the two regions, we assume, as usual, that agents are short-sighted. Specifically, firms enter when current profits are positive and exit when they are negative, their flow being regulated by the following simple adjustments:

$$\dot{n} = n\Pi, \quad \dot{n}^* = n^*\Pi^* \tag{8.4}$$

where Π and Π^* are pure profits. As we shall see, both Πs depend upon n and n^*.[4]

8.2.2 Short-Run Equilibrium

As usual, we distinguish between short- and long-run outcomes. In the short run, the numbers of active firms in the two regions, that is, n and n^*, are given, while in the long run these two numbers are endogenous and determined by free entry and exit that eliminate pure profit. Therefore, in the short-run equilibrium, consumers maximize utility, firms maximize profits, and all markets clear for given numbers of firms, n and n^*.

   Utility maximization yields a constant allocation of expenditures between the A and M goods. In particular, due to intermediate demand, a share μ of consumers' *and* firms' expenditures, E, falls on the M sector. Moreover, each firm faces a downward-sloping demand with constant elasticity of demand equal to σ:

$$c_j \equiv \frac{p_j^{-\sigma}\mu E}{\Delta n^w}, \quad \Delta \equiv \frac{\int_{i=0}^{n^w} p_i^{1-\sigma}di}{n^w}, \quad n^w \equiv n + n^* \tag{8.5}$$

where E is northern consumer expenditure. The southern demand curve is isomorphic.

---

[4] In contrast to the CP model, the evolution of the CPVL model is driven by two laws of motion. The reason is that it has two state variables, the mass of firms in the north, n, and the mass of firms in the south, n^*. In the CP model, the total mass (number) of manufacturing workers adds up to a constant and, thus, it is possible to reduce the number of state variables to one. As we shall see, given (8.4), a steady state (or a 'long-run equilibrium' in the jargon) is reached for $\Pi = 0$ or $n = 0$ and $\Pi^* = 0$ or $n^* = 0$.

On the supply side, marginal cost pricing in the perfectly competitive A sector implies $p_A = a_A w$ and $p_A^* = a_A w^*$. Costless trade equalizes northern and southern prices for A, so trade indirectly equalizes wage rates for labour in both regions, viz. $w = w^*$ provided that full specialization in the A sector is ruled out (given our normalizations below, this is the case if $\mu < 1/2$, which we assume throughout). In the M sector, 'mill pricing' is optimal, so the ratio of a northern variety in its local and export markets is just τ (see Chapter 2 for details). Thus,

$$p = \frac{a_M P_P}{1 - (1/\sigma)}, \qquad p^* = \frac{\tau a_M P_P}{1 - (1/\sigma)} \tag{8.6}$$

where p and p^* are the local and export consumer prices of a north-based M firm and P_P is the perfect price index from (8.3). Given mill pricing and the symmetry among firms, the closed form of Δ is

$$\Delta \equiv \frac{np^{1-\sigma} + \phi n^* \bar{p}^{*1-\sigma}}{n^w} \tag{8.7}$$

where $\bar{p}^*$ is the mill price of southern firms for southern sales. The expression for Δ^* is isomorphic.

Since there are increasing returns in the M sector, positive operating profits are needed to pay for the workers employed in the fixed component of (8.3). Under Dixit–Stiglitz competition, operating profit is simply the value of sales divided by σ (see Chapter 2 and its appendix for details). In symbols, $\pi = px/\sigma$ and an analogous expression holds for the southern operating profit, π^*. (Note that lower-case π denotes operating profit as usual while upper-case Π indicates pure profits, that is, revenue minus both fixed and variable costs). Using the demand function and mill pricing, (8.5) and (8.6), we can write these equilibrium expressions for π and π^* as

$$\pi = bB\frac{E^w}{n^w}, \qquad \pi^* = bB^*\frac{E^w}{n^w}; \qquad b \equiv \frac{\mu}{\sigma} \tag{8.8}$$

where E^w is the world aggregate expenditure (a share μ of which is spent on manufactures). Because there are trade costs, home firms sell a larger fraction of their production on the domestic market. This is captured by the Bs, which we define as

$$B \equiv P_P\left(\frac{s_E}{\Delta} + \phi\frac{1 - s_E}{\Delta^*}\right), \qquad B^* \equiv P_P^*\left(\phi\frac{s_E}{\Delta} + \frac{1 - s_E}{\Delta^*}\right) \tag{8.9}$$

where s_E is the north's share of aggregate expenditure and $\phi \equiv \tau^{1-\sigma}$ is the usual measure of trade freeness. Using (8.7) and (8.9), it is readily verified that $nB + n^*B^* = 1$ for all n and n^*, so the average operating profit in this world economy equals bE^w/n^w.

8.2.3 Choice of Numeraire and Units

We make the usual choice of numeraire and units so as to lighten equilibrium expressions. In particular, we take A as the numeraire and choose units of A such that $a_A = 1$. Hence, free trade in the agricultural good implies $p_A = p_A^* = w = w^* = 1$. This implies that the producer and consumer perfect price indices are identical, viz. $P_P = P$ and $P_P^* = P^*$. We also normalize a_M to $1 - (1/\sigma)$ and F to $1/\sigma$. Finally, we define s_n as the northern share of total active firms. To summarize,

$$p = P, \quad p^* = \tau P, \quad p_A = p_A^* = w_L = w_L^* = 1, \quad n^w \equiv n + n^* \qquad (8.10)$$

$$n = s_n n^w, \quad n^* = (1 - s_n)n^w, \quad F = \frac{1}{\sigma}, \quad a_M = 1 - \frac{1}{\sigma}, \quad L^w = 1 - \mu$$

The choice of units of L such that $L^w = 1 - \mu$ is not arbitrary; as we shall see shortly, this normalizes total expenditure E^w to unity.

8.2.4 Long-Run Location

In the long run, firms can freely enter and exit each market, so in addition to all the short-run equilibrium conditions mentioned above, the long-run equilibrium requires that no firm has any incentive to enter or exit any market; more precisely, the long run is defined as a situation where $\dot{n} = 0$ and $\dot{n}^* = 0$.

Inspection of the firm entry/exit flows given by (8.4) shows that the model has two types of long-run equilibria. An interior long-run equilibrium arises for $n > 0$ and $n^* > 0$ when $\Pi(n, n^*) = \Pi^*(n, n^*) = 0$. In such cases, there are active firms in both regions.[5] A core–periphery outcome arises whenever $\Pi(n_0, 0) = 0$ if $n_0 > 0$. As in the CP model, multiple equilibria arise and stability becomes an important issue.

The profit function associated with optimal pricing (8.6) and the cost function (8.3) is $\Pi = \pi - PF$, namely, Π is equal to operating profit π minus fixed cost PF. Thus, to find the long-run equilibria of the model, the first step is to evaluate $\Pi(n, n^*)$ and $\Pi^*(n, n^*)$ at the short-run equilibrium. Given our normalizations in (8.10), we have

$$\Pi = \frac{P}{\sigma}(x - 1), \quad \Pi^* = \frac{p^*}{\sigma}(x^* - 1) \qquad (8.11)$$

Pure profits are functions of expenditures E and E^* as well as the n's. Since markets are segmented and transportation costs are positive, the spatial distribution of E^w matters. To get an expression for E and E^*, note first that expenditures on manufactures now stem not only from consumers but also from firms. Applying Sheppard's lemma to (8.3) and Hotelling's lemma to (8.2), we find

$$\mu E = \mu[Y + s_n n^w P(a_M x + F)], \quad E = s_E E^w \qquad (8.12)$$

The second term in the square bracket in the above expression, which equals $\mu n P_P[(\sigma - 1)x + 1]/\sigma$ after simplification, is expenditure on intermediates by M firms. The term Y in this expression is consumers' income inclusive of firms' profits Π, viz.

---

[5] Under our assumption $\mu < 1/2$, both locations produce some good A in any configuration.

$$Y = s_L L^w + s_n n^w \Pi = \frac{L^w}{2} + \frac{s_n n^w P}{\sigma}(x - 1) \tag{8.13}$$

where s_L is north's share of total labour ($s_L = 1/2$ in the symmetric model under consideration) and where the second expression follows from the first due to (8.11).

Substituting (8.13) in (8.12) and using our normalization yields, after some simplification, the expression $\mu E = \mu[L^w/2 + s_n n^w P x]$. Using (8.6) along with the fact that $n^w[s_n B + (1 - s_n)B^*] = 1$ and the definition $E \equiv s_E E^w$, we find

$$E^w = \frac{L^w}{1 - \mu} \tag{8.14}$$

for all n, n^*. In other words, aggregate expenditure (and aggregate operating profits) are function of the parameters of the model only. Moreover, they are invariant in trade freeness, ϕ. By our normalization of L^w in (8.10), $E^w = 1$ and total world operating profit is equal to b. As for s_E, we get

$$s_E = \frac{1 - \mu}{2} + \mu s_n n^w B \tag{8.15}$$

Note that s_E is endogenous and a function of both s_n and n^w (and hence of the mass of firms in both north and south). From (8.9), B is itself function of Δ and s_E. Unfortunately, a complication arises in this model because Δ is not a linear function of s_n and n^w. As a result, it is impossible to characterize s_n or n^w as an explicit function of s_E. Accordingly, neither the short- nor the long-run equilibria of the model can be found analytically except in special cases such as perfect symmetry. To see this, we rewrite (8.7) with the Δs in recursive form:

$$\Delta \equiv s_n \Delta^\mu + \phi(1 - s_n)\Delta^{*\mu}, \quad \Delta \equiv \phi s_n \Delta^\mu + (1 - s_n)\Delta^{*\mu} \tag{8.16}$$

A short-run equilibrium is defined as a 5-tuple $(B, B^*, \Delta, \Delta^*, s_E)$ that satisfies the system given by (8.9), (8.15), (8.16), taking n^w and s_n as exogenous.

In a long-run equilibrium, n^w and s_n adjust so that the pure profits in (8.11) are nil for any active firms. Clearly, no closed-form solution to all endogenous variables exists. The source of this complication is twofold. First, the B's in (8.9) are non-linear functions the of Δs. Second, the definitions of the Δs in (8.16) are both simultaneous and implicit. As a result, the CPVL suffers the same fate as the CP model; most of its characteristics must be inferred from numerical simulations.[6] We shall introduce later two VL models that address either or both of these complications, making them analytically solvable.

8.2.5 Diagrammatic Solution and Forces

THE SCISSORS DIAGRAM

Analysis of the model is easily illustrated with the help of Figure 8.2. The figure plots the north's expenditure share s_E on the horizontal axis and the north's share

---

[6] It is possible to characterize the CPVL model's set of long-run equilibria in a way that shows it is isomorphic to the FEVL model. This involves even more cumbersome algebra than for the CP model, even though the strategy is similar (see Appendix 2.B).

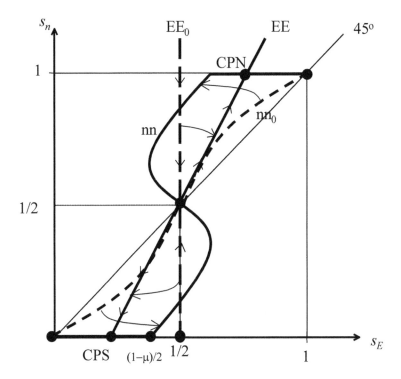

Figure 8.2 The scissor diagram for the CPVL model.

of industry s_n on the vertical axis. We keep n^w constant for this diagrammatic analysis because the most direct way the number of firms n and n^* affect s_E is via s_n. In particular, when s_n is equal to 1/2 changes in n^w have no impact on s_E.

Ideally, we would have two key expressions. The closed-form solution of (8.15) would express how relative endowments vary as the spatial allocation of firms varies. In addition, the closed-form solution to $\Pi = 0$ and $\Pi^* = 0$ would give an expression of s_n as a function of s_E such that no active firm makes pure profits. Given the complication of the model, these are not available, except in special cases.

Start with the case in which trade in M goods is impossible, viz. $\phi = 0$. Using (8.9) and (8.16), we have $B = s_E/(s_n n^w)$ (the expression for B^* is isomorphic). Plugging this in (8.15) gives the first key relationship, that is, s_E equals a constant, namely 1/2. This is plotted as the dashed line EE_0. Next, using (8.9) for $\Pi = 0$ gives the second relationship, $s_E = (s_n n^w)^c/b$, where c is a collection of parameters, $[\sigma(1 - \mu) - 1]/[(1 - \mu)(\sigma - 1)]$. This expression is plotted as nn_0. It says that a larger market supports a larger number of firms at the free-entry equilibrium, since s_E is increasing in s_n and n^w. By the no-black-hole condition (see stability analysis below), $1/c > 1$ so the slope of nn_0 is steeper than the 45-degree line.

By construction, the nn_0 line shows the combinations of s_E and s_n where pure profits are zero, keeping n^w constant. It is clear, therefore, that $\Pi > 0 > \Pi^*$ at all points to the right of the nn_0 line, because the northern market is too large for pure profits to be equal and, following the logic of the market-access effect, this corresponds to $\Pi > \Pi^*$. As a consequence, firms enter the north's market and exit the south's market (thus raising s_n) if the economy finds itself at points to the right of the nn line. For points to the left of the nn_0 line, s_n is falling.

Since EE_0 is a short-run relation (in particular it holds whether or not pure profits are zero), the combination of s_E and s_n must always lie on EE_0. As a result, out of any long-run equilibrium, the economy adjusts according to the law of motion (8.4) as shown by the arrows on the EE_0 schedule.

For more general values of ϕ, it is difficult to describe the shapes of nn and EE. However, we can characterize their shapes at three points. Start with the midpoint $(1/2, 1/2)$. This is the symmetric equilibrium at which north and south have identical numbers of firms, viz. $s_n = 1/2$. This implies $s_E = 1/2$, so EE and nn intersect at the midpoint $(1/2, 1/2)$ for any ϕ. In this case, the slope of EE can be shown to be always positive and steeper than the 45-degree line.[7] In the neighbourhood of $\phi = 0$, EE rotates clockwise around the midpoint as ϕ increases, as shown in the diagram. As for nn, this curve rotates anti-clockwise as ϕ increases for all values of ϕ. This is also indicated in the diagram. The fact that nn gets steeper as trade gets freer is an illustration of the magnification of the home-market effect.

We can also describe the endpoints of EE and nn, that is, the core–periphery outcomes $s_n = 0$ or $s_n = 1$. For any level of openness greater than $\phi = 0$, the EE curve crosses the horizontal axis at $(1 - \mu)/2$ and the upper limit at $(1 + \mu)/2$, so the endpoints of EE are unaffected by openness.[8] The endpoints of nn involve more complicated expressions, but it is enough at this stage to say that nn crosses the vertical axis for any $\phi > 0$. In summary, EE and nn cross at the midpoint $(1/2, 1/2)$, EE is steeper than the diagonal, and nn can be increasing or decreasing around the midpoint but is always above (below) the main diagonal for $s_n > 1/2$ (for $s_n < 1/2$). Note that in the case drawn, the symmetric equilibrium is unstable. Indeed, any point on EE above the midpoint is on the right of nn, hence $\Pi > 0$. By the law of motion (8.4), s_n must increase. The process stops at the point CPN at which $s_n = 1$, namely, when the equilibrium is a core–periphery outcome with the core is in the north (hence the acronym).

FORCES AT WORK

As in the CP model, there are three distinct forces governing stability in this model. Two of them—the market access and production-cost effects (also called 'demand-linked' and 'cost-linked' circular causalities, or 'backward' and 'forward' linkages)—favour agglomeration, that is, they are de-stabilizing. The third—the *market-crowding effect* (also known as the local competition effect)—favours dispersion, i.e. it is stabilizing.

---

[7] This can be assessed formally using the solutions to (8.A.1) in Appendix 8.A.
[8] This is true for any $\phi > 0$. For $\phi = 0$, there is a discontinuity, since EE is vertical in that case.

Market-Access Effect.   The expressions for the Bs in (8.9) help illustrate the first agglomeration force, namely demand-linked circular causality. Starting from symmetry, a small entry of firms in the north raises s_n. This makes the northern market bigger, for this increases s_E by (8.15).[9] In the presence of trade costs, and all else being equal, firms will prefer the big market ('market-access effect'); mathematically, B increases and B^* decreases and, as a result, Π increases and Π^* decreases, inducing firms to enter the northern market and exit the southern one. Hence, this entry-induced 'expenditure shifting' encourages 'production shifting'. As a result, we see that a small entry perturbation tends to encourage further entry in the same market via a demand-linked circular causality.

Production-Cost-Linked Agglomeration Force.   The definition of the perfect price index in (8.3) and (8.16) helps illustrate the second agglomeration force in this model, namely cost-linked circular causality, or forward linkages. Starting from symmetry, a small entry of firms in the north would increase Δ relative to Δ^*.[10] Since locally produced varieties require no trade cost, the shift in n would, other things being equal, lower the cost of production in the north relative to the production cost in the south ('cost-of-living effect', also called 'price-index effect'). This would raise the north's relative profitability and thereby induce more entry there. This is obvious from the definition of Π, viz. $\Pi \equiv \pi - PF$. Keeping π constant, P decreases relative to P^* when s_n increases. Therefore, here again some circular causality takes place: a small entry perturbation decreases the production cost in the market in which entry occurs, encouraging further entry in that market.

Market-Crowding Effect.   Both the backward and forward linkages rely on the fact that firms buy each other's output as intermediates. If they did not, then $\mu = 0$ in (8.3), (8.9), (8.15) and (8.16). By contrast, the market-crowding effect is independent of μ, hence we impose $\mu = 0$ in this discussion so as to identify this effect clearly. The relevant system of equations is now given by $\Pi = bB - F$, $s_E = 1/2$, $\Delta = [s_n + \phi(1 - s_n)]$, $B = s_E/\Delta + \phi(1 - s_E)/\Delta^*$, and the isomorphic southern variables. Clearly, B is unambiguously decreasing in Δ and Δ is larger in the market with the most firms. Hence, a higher s_n corresponds to smaller market shares for firms in the north. We call this the market-crowding disadvantage of being in the country with the larger number of firms. This is the sole dispersion force in the model.

Clearly, all these forces are decreasing in ϕ. When ϕ is large, market access is about the same for domestic and foreign firms, production costs are similar because the cost of imported varieties is only slightly larger than the cost of domestically produced varieties, and competition from foreign competitors is almost as fierce as competition from domestic producers.

---

[9] Note that s_n also enters (8.15) via B, so a priori we are not sure that $\partial s_E/\partial s_n > 0$. It can be shown, however, that $\partial(s_n B)/\partial s_n$ is always positive, hence the statement in the text is always true.

[10] In Chapter 2, we showed that Δ/Δ^* is increasing in s_n in the CP model. The proof is identical for the present model.

It can be shown that, like in the CP model, dispersion forces erode faster than agglomeration forces as ϕ increases. To prove this, we now turn to the formal stability analysis.

8.2.6 Stability Analysis

Consider first an agglomerated configuration with all active firms in one region, say $n^w = n_0$ and $s_n = 1$. This is a stable long-run equilibrium for (8.4) if and only if $\Pi(n^w, s_n) = \Pi(n_0, 1) = 0$ and $\Pi^*(n^w, s_n) = \Pi^*(n_0, 1) < 0$. Using (8.3) and (8.9)–(8.16), it is easy to find the root of $\Pi(n, 1)$. We substitute $s_n = 1$ and $n_0 = n^w$ into this system to get

$$
n_0 = \left(\frac{\mu L^w}{1 - \mu} \right)^{1/\{1 - \mu/[(\sigma - 1)(1 - \mu)]\}} = \mu^{1/c}, \quad c \equiv \frac{\sigma(1 - \mu) - 1}{(\sigma - 1)(1 - \mu)} < 1 \quad (8.17)
$$

where the second equality stems from the normalization of L^w. Note that n_0 is increasing in μ (which captures the importance of the manufacturing sector in the economy) and in $1/\sigma$ (the operating profit margin), as was to be expected. As already said, $s_n = 1$ is part of a stable equilibrium if $\Pi^*(n_0, 1) < 0$. The latter requirement is met when

$$
\frac{1 - \mu + (1 + \mu)\phi^2}{2\phi^{1 - \mu\sigma/(\sigma - 1)}} - 1 < 0 \quad (8.18)
$$

This condition is met if ϕ is larger than the sustain point ϕ^S, where ϕ^S is the smallest real root of the left-hand side of (8.18) (it is readily verified that $\phi = 1$ is also a root of this term). As it turns out, the CPVL model has the same sustain point as the CP model, which we defined implicitly in Chapter 2 as

$$
1 = (\phi^S)^{\mu/[1 - (1/\sigma)] - 1} \left[\frac{1 + \mu}{2}(\phi^S)^2 + \frac{1 - \mu}{2} \right] \quad (8.19)
$$

Turning to interior equilibria, tedious analysis reveals that the loci $\Pi(n^w, s_n) = 0$ and $\Pi^*(n^w, s_n) = 0$ always cross at least once and no more than three times. In terms of Figure 8.2, this means that EE and nn never cross more than three times. In particular, they always cross at the symmetric outcome in which $s_n = 1/2$ and $n^w = n^w_{1/2}$, where $n^w_{1/2}$ is the aggregate mass of varieties in the symmetric outcome. Using $s_n = 1/2$ in the system (8.9)–(8.16) for $\Pi = \Pi^* = 0$, we find

$$
n^w_{1/2} = n_0 \left(\frac{1 + \phi}{2} \right)^{a/(1 - \sigma a)}, \quad a \equiv \frac{\mu}{\sigma - 1} \quad (8.20)
$$

Therefore, while the number of active firms with agglomeration (n_0) is invariant to trade barriers, the number of those active in the symmetric equilibrium ($n^w_{1/2}$) is not. We will briefly come back to this point later on.

The symmetric equilibrium is stable as long as the two eigenvalues of the Jacobian associated with the laws of motion (8.4) are negative at $(n^w, s_n) =$

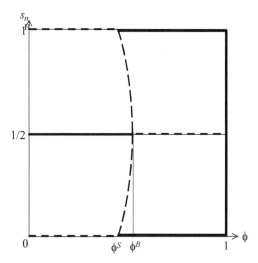

Figure 8.3   The tomahawk diagram.

$(n^w_{1/2}, 1/2)$.[11] As derived in the appendix, this is the case if ϕ is in the range $[0, \phi^B)$, where the 'break point' ϕ^B is defined as

$$\phi^B = \left(\frac{1 - \sigma a}{1 + \sigma a}\right)\left(\frac{1 - \mu}{1 + \mu}\right) \tag{8.21}$$

which is identical to the break point of the CP model of Chapter 2. Clearly, the interval $[0, \phi^B)$ is empty if $\phi^B < 0$, so we impose the 'no-black-hole' condition $1 > a\sigma$ as in the CP model. Finally, we note that the break point is decreasing in μ and increasing in σ, which means that the range of trade freeness for which the symmetric outcome is unstable expands as the expenditure share on manufacturing increases. A larger σ works in the opposite direction since it implies a lower mark-up in manufacturing and therefore weaker agglomeration forces.

The fact that the sustain and break points for the CPVL model are *identical* to the break point in the CP model is remarkable because the mechanics of agglomeration in the models are quite different.

8.2.7 The Tomahawk Diagram

Since the break and sustain points in the CP and CPVL models are identical, the nature and stability of the long-run equilibria can be conveniently summarized with the 'tomahawk' bifurcation diagram of Chapter 2 reproduced in Figure 8.3 for convenience.

The diagram plots s_n against the freeness of trade, ϕ, and shows locally stable long-run equilibria with heavy solid lines and locally unstable long-run

---

[11] See the appendix of Barro and Sala-i-Martin (1995) for an exposition on local stability analysis with two laws of motion.

equilibria with heavy dashed lines. Thus, the three horizontal lines $s_n = 1$, $s_n = 1/2$ and $s_n = 0$ are steady states for any permissible level of ϕ, but the symmetric outcome is only locally stable between $\phi = 0$ and $\phi = \phi^B$. The CP outcomes are only stable between $\phi = \phi^S$ and $\phi = 1$. The bowed line also represents steady states but all of these are unstable. Note that for most levels of ϕ, there are three long-run equilibria, while for the levels of ϕ corresponding to the bowed curve, there are five equilibria—two CP outcomes, the symmetric outcome and two interior asymmetric equilibria. Importantly, in the range of ϕ with five equilibria, there are three overlapping stable equilibria (symmetric and both CP outcomes).

8.2.8 Comparison with the CP Model

Chapter 2 pointed out seven key features of the CP model: agglomeration via the home-market effect (with magnification by freer trade), demand and cost linkages, endogenous asymmetry, catastrophic agglomeration, locational hysteresis, hump-shaped agglomeration rents, and multiple long-run equilibria in the 'overlap'.

All these features are shared also by the CPVL model since it exhibits the same equilibrium and stability properties as the CP model as summarized by the sustain and break points in (8.19) and (8.21). Accordingly, (8.19) and (8.21) also depict the crucial properties of both the CPVL and CP models.

The CPVL model also has some additional features. First, under the no-black-hole condition, (8.20) reveals that $n_{1/2}^w$ is an increasing function of ϕ. The freer trade is, the larger the number of active firms. Thus, in contrast to the CP model, trade integration fragments the market. The intuition for this result is as follows. When trade gets freer, the effective market size becomes bigger and hence profits tend to increase. By free entry, this increases $n_{1/2}^w$. All the same, when ϕ increases, the competition that arises from firms established in other regions becomes more fierce and profits tend to shrink. With free exit, this results in a lower $n_{1/2}^w$. The net effect is a priori ambiguous. Under the no-black-hole condition, it is positive.

Second, under the no-black-hole condition, (8.20) reveals that $n_{1/2}^w < n_0$, namely, the total number of firms under the symmetric equilibrium is lower than under the core–periphery equilibrium. This result is related to the previous one. Under the no-black-hole condition the market-crowding dispersion force is dominated by the agglomeration forces when ϕ is large enough. Moreover, agglomeration forces are self-reinforcing which means that, for a given ϕ, the agglomeration forces (net of dispersion forces) are larger at the core–periphery equilibrium than at the dispersed equilibrium (this is also why $\phi^S < \phi^B$). For a given number of firms, this implies that firms are more profitable in the latter configuration. By free entry, we thus have $n_0 > n_{1/2}^w$.

The CPVL model also shares the main limitation of the CP model in that the endogenous variables that are instrumental in determining the location of firms and workers (i.e. operating profits and wages) cannot be expressed as explicit functions of the spatial distribution of economic activities. This implies that the number of equilibria and their stability properties cannot be deducted but only ascertained as simulated regularities.[12]

As we shall see in subsequent parts of this book, when we analyse economic policies in the presence of vertical linkages, working with the CPVL model prevents us from identifying the role of individual parameters on the resulting outcome—and, ultimately, this blurs the exact mechanisms at work. For this reason, it is useful to develop models in which at least some result can be derived analytically. In the next sections, we propose two such models that retain the dynamic properties of the CPVL model and are nonetheless much easier to manipulate. Since both models are combinations of models we have already described at length in this chapter and others, we keep the exposition short.

8.3 The FCVL Model

The first alternative to the CPVL model is the FCVL model, due to Robert-Nicoud (2002). As its acronym suggests, the FCVL model is an extension of the FC model of Chapter 3. It combines free capital mobility and vertical linkages. As we shall see, however, it is not fully solvable even though it goes a long way towards reducing the complexity of the CPVL model. This model is used in the trade policy chapters in Part III of this book. The CPVL model is built on the empirical fact that vertical linkages are a stronger explanation of international agglomeration patterns than labour migration. However, once we move from labour to capital, the role of international mobility cannot be neglected. The FCVL model fills this gap by providing a framework in which capital mobility and vertical linkages together sustain agglomeration. This is achieved by extending the most tractable geography model—the FC model—to include intermediate inputs. The resulting model retains the same qualitative properties as the CPVL model. Moreover, its stability properties are easily determined using the method of Robert-Nicoud (2001).

The FCVL model differs from the CPVL one in three main ways. First, the cost function of the M sector is not assumed to be homothetic. Second, there are two primary factors of production. Third, one of the factors is internationally mobile. As a result, there is a single state variable. Nevertheless, most of the key equations are identical.

8.3.1 Assumptions

Tastes are described by (8.1), and on the supply side, the FCVL model works with the same set-up as the FC model (two regions, two sectors, two factors), but incorporates one crucial modification. In the standard FC model, production of a typical industrial variety entails a fixed cost of one unit of capital and a variable cost that involves only labour. Here, we suppose that the variable cost also

---

[12] However, we note that a formal proof of those regularities can be worked out along the lines of Robert-Nicoud (2001).

involves intermediate inputs, and, as in the CPVL model, we assume that this takes the form of a Cobb–Douglas aggregate of labour and C_M, where C_M is the usual CES aggregate of all industrial varieties. The expressions are simpler when the shares of firms' and consumers' spending that fall on industrial goods are the same, so we assume that μ, which is the typical consumer's expenditure share on industrial goods, is also the cost share of intermediate inputs for a typical industrial firm.[13] With these assumptions, the cost function of a typical firm j in the north, (8.3), has to be replaced by

$$C(x_j) = \pi + a_M x_j P_P, \quad P_P \equiv w^{1-\mu}(\Delta n^w)^{-a}, \quad \Delta \equiv \frac{\int_{i=0}^{n^w} p_i^{1-\sigma} di}{n^w}, \quad a \equiv \frac{\mu}{\sigma - 1} \tag{8.22}$$

where x_j is the firm's output, w and π are the rewards to labour and capital, P_P is the producer price of the Cobb–Douglas aggregate of labour and the bundle of intermediates C_M, and n^w is the worldwide mass (roughly speaking, the number) of varieties. P_P, Δ and a are defined as in the CPVL model and repeated here for convenience only.

Since the fixed cost consists only of capital, the operating profit (or Ricardian surplus) accrues to capital owners by free entry, so the operating profit π is also the capital reward.

As in the standard FC model, capital is disembodied so capital rewards are repatriated. In the long run, capital moves freely between countries/regions in search of the highest nominal reward. Labour and capital owners are immobile, so a region's labour must be fully employed locally and capital income is spent in the owner's region.

As in the CPVL model, agents are short-sighted and hence capital moves in search of the highest current nominal reward. Specifically, the flow of capital is regulated by the following law of motion:

$$\dot{s}_n = s_n(1 - s_n)(\pi - \pi^*) \tag{8.23}$$

where π and π^* are capital rewards prevailing in the north and south, respectively. Given (8.23), the system attains a steady state (long-run equilibrium) if rental rates are equalized or if firms are active in only one region. Note that, since n^w is determined by initial endowments, s_n is the only state variable and there is only one law of motion, (8.23).

A comment is in order here. In the CPVL model, we assumed that entry and exit took time and hence positive or negative pure profits could arise in the short run. By contrast, we assume here that entry and exit are instantaneous so that pure profits are eliminated and capital rewards are equal to operating profits. The implicit assumption here is that would-be entrepreneurs bid for capital and hence they forgo all rents to capital owners. So what adjusts in the long run? The assumption in (8.23) is that the spatial allocation of capital

---

[13] See Robert-Nicoud (2001) for what the expressions look like when this assumption of convenience is relaxed.

takes time and hence current operating profits might differ from the average in the short run.[14]

8.3.2 Short-Run Equilibrium

Following the distinction made in the FC model, capital is inter-regionally immobile in the short run, but perfectly mobile in the long run. Thus, in a short-run equilibrium, consumers maximize utility, firms maximize profits, and all markets clear for a given distribution of capital (and firms) between regions.

We make choices of numeraire and units similar to (8.10). In particular, we take A as the numeraire and choose units of A such that $a_A = 1$. Hence, free trade in the agricultural good implies $p_A = p_A^* = w = w^* = 1$ if no country fully specializes in M.[15] With this wage equalization, mill pricing in the M sector implies that the north's firms charge a unit price p to domestic consumers and a unit price p^* to foreign producers, where p and p^* are still defined in (8.6). Accordingly, the maximized operating profits are still governed by (8.8) and (8.9). In addition, we take the fixed cost F to be unity. This implies that the number of varieties, n^w, is equal to the world endowment of capital, K^w, by full employment. Finally, we choose units of K such that $K^w = 1$. This implies that the number and share of firms in north are the same thing, viz. $n = s_n$. These choices and some of their implications are summarized in

$$p = P, \quad p^* = \tau P, \quad p_A = p_A^* = w_L = w_L^* = 1, \quad n + n^* \equiv n^w = 1$$

$$n = s_n, \quad n^* = 1 - s_n, \quad F = 1, \quad a_M = 1 - \frac{1}{\sigma}, \quad L^w = 1 - \mu \qquad (8.24)$$

we use n instead of s_n where clarity permits.

This allows us to conclude that the producer price index, P_P, and the consumer price index, P, are both equal to Δ^{-a} (the expression for P^* is isomorphic), where $a \equiv \mu/(\sigma - 1)$, and Δ and Δ^* are defined recursively as

$$\Delta \equiv s_n \Delta^\mu + \phi(1 - s_n)\Delta^{*\mu}, \quad \Delta \equiv \phi s_n \Delta^\mu + (1 - s_n)\Delta^{*\mu} \qquad (8.25)$$

This recursion makes it impossible to fully solve the FCVL model.

8.3.3 Long-Run Location

In the long run, capital owners are free to employ their capital wherever it earns the higher return. Hence, in addition to the equations that characterize the short-run equilibrium, the long-run equilibrium requires that capital has no incentive to move, viz. $\dot{s}_n = 0$.

Given the capital allocation rule, (8.23), there are two types of long-run equilibria. An interior (or 'dispersed') equilibrium arises for $0 < n < 1$ when

---

[14] We have chosen this timing of adjustments because the algebra is easier this way. However, none of the stability results below depend on which variable we choose as the control variable.

[15] This requires μ to be low enough. In our particular case and given our normalisations, this requires $\mu(1 - 1/\sigma) < 1/2$ to hold. If $\mu < 1/2$ as in the CPVL model, then this condition holds.

$\pi = \pi^*$. In such a case, both countries have active firms. A core–periphery (or 'concentrated') outcome arises whenever $n = 0$ or $n = 1$. To find the long-run equilibria of the model, the first step is then to evaluate π and π^* at the short-run equilibrium. Given the choice of functional forms, (8.12) and (8.13) have to be replaced. Now, expenditure on manufactures is equal to

$$\mu E = \mu[Y + nPa_Mx], \quad E = s_E E^w \tag{8.26}$$

where Y is a northern individuals' income and μnPa_Mx is northern intermediate demand. Observe that the fixed cost does not enter the expression above because F consists exclusively of capital.

In the FCVL model there are no pure profits. However, there are two primary factors, L and K, so that income is now equal to

$$Y = s_L L^w + s_K K^w \bar{\pi}, \quad \bar{\pi} \equiv n\pi + (1 - n)\pi^* \tag{8.27}$$

where $\bar{\pi}$ is the average operating profit prevailing in the world economy and s_L and s_K are the north's share of world endowments of labour and capital, respectively. We work with symmetric countries, so $s_L = s_K = 1/2$. As in the FC model, the assumption behind (8.27) is that half the capital in each region belongs to northern capital owners, so capital owners earn on average $\bar{\pi}$ irrespective of their country of residence and that (8.27) holds as the result of a law of large numbers. Also, by (8.8) and $nB + n^*B^* = 1$, we obtain $\bar{\pi} = bE^w$. Using this, (8.26), (8.27) and $K^w = 1$, we find

$$E^w = \frac{L^w}{1 - \mu}, \quad s_E = \frac{1 - \mu + b}{2} + n(\mu - b)\frac{\pi}{\bar{\pi}} \tag{8.28}$$

Two comments are in order. First, $E^w = 1$ by our choice of units for labour in (8.24). Second, the north's share of expenditure increases in the number of firms active there and in their profitability. Indeed, since there are no pure profits, above-average operating profits are absorbed by the size of the firm and hence its sales and factor demands. Notice that in a long-run equilibrium, there is only one possibility for s_E to be 1/2. This arises if and only if $n = 1/2$ (in which case $\pi = \bar{\pi}$).

The short-run equilibrium is defined as the 5-tuple $(\pi, \pi^*, \Delta, \Delta^*, s_E)$ that satisfies the system of equations, (8.8), (8.9), (8.25) and (8.28), taking the spatial allocation of firms n as given. In addition, in a long-run equilibrium n adjusts so that (8.23) holds for $\dot{s}_n = 0$.

Clearly, no closed-form solution for all endogenous variables exist. The source of complication is the implicit definition of the Δs in (8.25). Nevertheless, the system of equations that characterizes both the short- and long-run equilibria is easier to manipulate than in the CPVL model for two related reasons. First, there is only one state variable, n.[16] Second, aggregate profits are constant in any equilibrium so whenever $\pi > \bar{\pi}$, it must be that $\pi^* < \bar{\pi}$. Hence, we can completely disregard what is going on in, say, the south; it is sufficient to know the values of northern variables.

---

[16] This implies that we can rely less on numeric simulations when working with extensions and, when we must use numerical simulations, we have one more degree of freedom.

8.3.4 Agglomeration and Dispersion Forces

The nature of the agglomeration and dispersion forces is as in the CPVL model. Hence, Figure 8.2 and the related analysis are also valid here. To see more clearly how they work in the present context, start from the symmetric equilibrium for simplicity, viz. $n = 1/2$ and $\pi = \pi^*$.

The first agglomeration force is the backward linkage. As usual, transportation costs imply that firms buy a disproportionately large amount of intermediates on the domestic market. Then, when more capital is allocated to the north, this production shifting results in expenditure shifting. This raises profits in the north and reduces them in the south. By the law of motion, (8.23), n rises further and the cycle repeats.

The second agglomeration force is the so-called forward linkage. Again, imagine n increases slightly. This implies that more varieties are produced in the north, which reduces the production cost P_P in the north and increases the production cost P_P^* in the south. This raises π and reduces π^*, so the cycle repeats.

Finally, the market-crowding dispersion force works against the forward and backward linkages. When more firms settle in the north, market shares decrease for existing firms in the north and hence π shrinks while π^* goes up. As a result, the initial shock is self-correcting.

As usual, agglomeration forces and dispersion forces alike are decreasing in ϕ. However, dispersion forces erode faster than agglomeration forces and hence a dispersed configuration in which there are active firms in each country prevails for low values of ϕ. Conversely, a core–periphery structure emerges for values of ϕ close to unity. To see this, however, we have to turn to stability analysis.

8.3.5 Stability Analysis

Consider first a concentrated configuration in which all firms are agglomerated in the north, viz. $s_n = n = 1$. Since π is the average profit when all capital is allocated to north, $\pi = b$ in this case. Hence, the core–periphery spatial allocation is stable if and only if $\pi^* < b$. It is readily verified that this requirement is met for any ϕ larger than the sustain point ϕ^S, where ϕ^S is implicitly defined as the smallest real root of

$$1 = (\phi^S)^{\mu-1} \left[\frac{1 + \mu - b}{2} (\phi^S)^2 + \frac{1 - (\mu - b)}{2} \right] \qquad (8.29)$$

This implies that the condition for agglomeration to be a stable long-run equilibrium in the FCVL model is qualitatively similar to the same condition in the CPVL model, namely, (8.19).

Turning to interior equilibria, tedious derivations show that the locus $\pi - \pi^*$ always crosses the horizontal axis at least once and no more than three times.[17] In

---

[17] See Robert-Nicoud (2001) for details; Appendix 2.B sketches steps for the CP model.

particular, it always crosses it at the symmetric outcome, $n = 1/2$.

The symmetric equilibrium is locally stable as long as the slope of $\pi - \pi^*$ is negative at $n = 1/2$.[18] The intuition for this stability check is as follows. If a firm moves from the south to the north, would the gap $\pi - \pi^*$ be positive (so the capital flow would be self-reinforcing), or negative (and thus self-correcting)? Formally, answering this question is equivalent to signing $d\pi/dn$ evaluated at $n = 1/2$.[19] As shown in the appendix, this changes sign at the break point ϕ^B, where ϕ^B is defined as

$$\phi^B \equiv \frac{(1 - \mu)(1 - \mu + b)}{(1 + \mu)(1 + \mu - b)} \tag{8.30}$$

which is strictly smaller than unity by inspection.

To sum up, the agglomerated configuration is sustainable for all ϕ above ϕ^S and the symmetric equilibrium is stable for all ϕ below ϕ^B. As usual, the sustain point comes before the break point ($\phi^S < \phi^B$) so the model displays hysteresis in location. In particular, the tomahawk diagram in Figure 8.3 applies to the FCVL model as well.

8.3.6 Comparison with the FC and CPVL Models

The FCVL model exhibits the same richness of features as the CPVL (and CP) model: agglomeration via the home-market mechanism (with magnification by freer trade), demand and cost linkages, endogenous asymmetry, catastrophic agglomeration, locational hysteresis, hump-shaped agglomeration rents, and multiple long-run equilibria in the 'overlap'. This is due to the presence of forward and backward linkages, which in both models stem from the input–output (or vertical) linkages among firms. In particular, in the FCVL model, free capital mobility is a necessary condition for circular causality to arise, but it is by no means sufficient. Indeed, the absence of vertical linkages means the FCVL model collapses to the FC model of Chapter 3. As a result, the FCVL model can be seen as a richer model that encompasses the simpler FC model.

The backward linkage—also known as the demand linkage—stems from the fact that firms buy each other's output as intermediates. The forward linkage—also known as the cost linkage—stems from the fact that firms benefit from the proximity of intermediate suppliers. These linkages are absent in the FC model. If there were only agglomeration forces, it would always be profitable to all firms to cluster in a single location. However, the FCVL model, like all models of Part I (including the FC model), displays the market-crowding dispersion force. Hence, generically the location equilibrium is not degenerate.

With respect to the CPVL model, the FCVL model goes some way towards

---

[18] The method developed by Baldwin (2001) ensures that this local stability test and the one that applies to core–periphery equilibria are also sufficient to assess global stability. See Appendix 2.B for details.

[19] As discussed above, by symmetry of the model, this is equivalent to signing $d(\pi - \pi^*)/dn$ at $n = 1/2$.

analytical tractability. However, we cannot express the spatial allocation of industry, namely s_n, as a closed-form function of parameters. Since the location of industry is the fulcrum of most policy analysis, this drawback makes policy analysis much more involved. Moreover, the variable that drives the spatial adjustment—operating profits—cannot be expressed as an explicit function of the spatial allocation of firms. A model that overcomes such difficulty is developed in the next section.

8.4 THE FEVL MODEL

The second alternative to the CPVL model is the FEVL model due to Ottaviano (2002). This model works with the set up of the FE model to which it adds vertical linkages. The beauty of this model is that it achieves full analytical solvability in the sense that operating profits can be written as an explicit function of the spatial allocation of firms, even though it does not yield a closed-form solution for the spatial allocation of industry. Moreover, the FEVL model retains the same qualitative properties as the CPVL model.

8.4.1 Assumptions

The FEVL model modifies the FE model in exactly the same way that the CPVL model modifies the CP model. Like the CPVL model, the FEVL model has two countries (north and south), two sectors (A and M), and one primary factor, labour.

Tastes are given by (8.1) and (8.2). As for technology, the FEVL model works with the same set-up as the CPVL model except for the fact that the production technology in the M sector is not homothetic. In particular, it assumes that fixed and marginal input requirements are satisfied by different factors: the marginal cost is incurred in terms of labour only; the fixed cost in terms of a composite input consisting of labour and the differentiated varieties of the M good. This resembles the difference between the FE and CP models, hence the acronym 'FEVL' for the present set-up.

For simplicity we assume, as in the CPVL model, that the composite fixed input is Cobb–Douglas in L and C_M with shares $1 - \mu$ and μ, respectively. This way, consumers and firms devote the same shares of expenditures to manufactures. In symbols, the cost function of the typical northern firm j is given by

$$C(x_j) = FP_P + a_M x_j w, \quad P_P \equiv w^{1-\mu}(\Delta n^w)^{-a}; \quad \Delta \equiv \frac{\int_{i=0}^{n^w} p_i^{1-\sigma} di}{n^w}, \quad a \equiv \frac{\mu}{\sigma - 1}$$

$$(8.31)$$

where P_P is the producer perfect price index.

Firms' entry decision in the two countries is governed by the same law of motion as in the CPVL model. In particular, agents are short-sighted and firms enter if pure profits are positive and exit if they are negative. Hence, (8.4) applies here as well. Observe that this system has two laws of motion for the model has two state variables, the number of firms in the north, n, and the number of firms in the south, n^*.

8.4.2 Short-Run Equilibrium

As usual, we distinguish between short- and long-run outcomes. In the short run, the numbers of active firms in the two regions are given, while there is free entry and exit in the long run. Therefore, in the short-run equilibrium, consumers maximize utility, firms maximize profits, and all markets clear for given numbers of firms, n and n^*.

We choose A as the numeraire and choose units so that A transforms one unit of labour into one unit of the numeraire as before, viz. $a_A = 1$. Hence, free trade in the agricultural good implies $p_A = p_A^* = w = w^* = 1$ if no country ever specializes in M.[20] Among other things, this implies that the producers' perfect price index is equal to the consumers' equivalent, viz. $P_P = P$.

As usual, mill pricing is optimal in the M sector, so (8.6) becomes

$$p = \frac{a_M}{1 - (1/\sigma)}, \quad p^* = \frac{\tau a_M}{1 - (1/\sigma)} \tag{8.32}$$

The fact that p and p^* depend on the parameters only comes in sharp contrast to the CPVL and FCVL models. As it turns out, this is the key to the tractability of the model. Indeed, the producer price index, P_P, and the consumer price index, P, are both equal to Δ^{-a} (the expression for P^* is isomorphic), where $a \equiv \mu/(\sigma - 1)$, and Δ and Δ^* are now explicit functions of n and n^*:

$$\Delta = s_n p^{1-\sigma} + \phi(1 - s_n)p^{*1-\sigma} \tag{8.33}$$

and the expression for Δ^* is isomorphic.

Accordingly, the maximized operating profits are still governed by (8.8) but (8.9) becomes

$$B = \frac{s_E}{\Delta} + \frac{\phi(1 - s_E)}{\Delta^*}, \quad B^* = \frac{\phi s_E}{\Delta} + \frac{1 - s_E}{\Delta^*} \tag{8.34}$$

Choosing units similar to (8.10), we get

$$p = 1, \quad p^* = \tau, \quad p_A = p_A^* = w_L = w_L^* = 1, \quad n + n^* \equiv n^w$$

$$n = s_n n^w, \quad n^* = (1 - s_n)n^w, \quad F = 1, \quad a_M = 1 - (1/\sigma), \quad L^w = 1 - b \tag{8.35}$$

again we use n instead of s_n where clarity permits. The difference with (8.10) is threefold. First, now that the variable cost is made up of labour only, the domestic and export producers prices are equal to 1 and τ, respectively. Second, the fixed cost F is assumed to be unity. Third, L^w is normalized to $1 - b$.

[20] This requires μ to be low enough. In our particular case and given our normalizations, this requires $\mu(1 - 1/\sigma) < 1/2$ to hold. As for the FCVL model, a sufficient condition for this to be the case is $\mu < 1/2$.

8.4.3 Long-Run Location

In the long run, pure profits are eliminated by entry and exit, so that $\dot{n} = 0$ and $\dot{n}^* = 0$. That is, no potential entrepreneur has any incentive to enter any market and no active firm has any incentive to exit the market in which it operates.

Inspection of the firm entry/exit flows given by (8.4) shows that the model has two types of long-run equilibria. An interior long-run equilibrium arises for $n, n^* > 0$ when $\Pi(n, n^*) = \Pi^*(n, n^*) = 0$. In such a case, there are active firms in both regions. A core–periphery outcome arises whenever $\Pi(n, 0) = 0$ and $\Pi^*(n, 0) < 0$ if $n > 0$ and $n^* = 0$ or vice versa.

The profit function associated with optimal pricing (8.32) and the cost function (8.31) is $\Pi = \pi - PF$, namely, Π is equal to operating profit π minus fixed cost PF. Thus, to find the long-run equilibria of the model, the first step is to evaluate $\Pi(n, n^*)$ and $\Pi^*(n, n^*)$ at the short-run equilibrium. By (8.8) and our normalizations in (8.35), we have

$$\Pi = \frac{x}{\sigma} - P, \quad \Pi^* = \frac{x^*}{\sigma} - P^* \tag{8.36}$$

To get an expression for s_E and E^w, note first that expenditures on manufactures now stem not only from consumers but also from firms. Sheppard's lemma applied to (8.31) and Hotelling's lemma applied to (8.2) implies

$$\mu E = \mu[Y + s_n n^w P], \quad E \equiv s_E E^w \tag{8.37}$$

The second term in the square bracket reflects the expenditure on M varieties stemming from a firm's demand for intermediates. The term Y in this expression is consumers' income inclusive of firms' profits Π, viz. $Y = L^w/2 + s_n n^w (\pi - P)$. Plugging this back into (8.37) and using (8.8), we find $E = L^w/2 + s_n n^w bBE^w$. By the same token, we find $E^* = L^w + (1 - s_n) n^w bB^* E^w$. Adding the two gives $E^w = L^w + bE^w$. Thus, the expressions for E^w and s_E simplify to

$$E^w = \frac{L^w}{1 - b}, \quad s_E = \frac{1 - b}{2} + bs_n n^w B \tag{8.38}$$

Up to now, all these expressions look very similar to the corresponding expressions of the other VL models of this chapter. What is new is that, in the present setting, we can actually get an expression for Π and Π^* as explicit functions of the variables that adjust in the long run, viz. s_n and n^w.

To start with, we use (8.34) in (8.38) to get

$$s_E = \frac{1 - b}{2} + bs_n \left[\frac{s_E}{s_n + \phi(1 - s_n)} + \frac{\phi(1 - s_E)}{\phi s_n + 1 - s_n} \right] \tag{8.39}$$

Note that (8.39) can be solved for s_E. We can then plug this closed-form solution into (8.36) together with the closed-form expression of P and P^*. Doing so, recalling (8.8) and $x = \sigma\pi$ we obtain

$$\Pi = \frac{b}{n^w} \left[1 - \frac{(1 - s_n)(s_n - 1/2)}{s_n(1 - s_n) + \dfrac{1 - Z^2}{4Z(Z - b)}} \right] - \left[\frac{1/n^w}{s_n + \phi(1 - s_n)} \right]^a \qquad (8.40)$$

$$\Pi^* = \frac{b}{n^w} \left[1 + \frac{s_n(s_n - 1/2)}{s_n(1 - s_n) + \dfrac{1 - Z^2}{4Z(Z - b)}} \right] - \left[\frac{1/n^w}{\phi s_n + 1 - s_n} \right]^a \qquad (8.41)$$

where Z is defined as $(1 - \phi)/(1 + \phi)$ and $a \equiv \mu/(\sigma - 1)$ as usual.

The expression above is very simple to analyse. Start with the first term on the right-hand side of each equation—these are operating profits, π and π^*, respectively. The expression for π confirms that there are two cases in which the prevailing operating profit in the north is equal to the world average b/n^w: when $s_n = 1$ (in which case π is the average profit by definition since no firm is active in the south) or when $s_n = 1/2$ (in which case $\pi = \pi^*$ by the symmetry of the model). The second thing to note is that $\Pi = \Pi^*$ if $s_n = 1/2$. When this is the case, the long-run solution for n^w follows from imposing $\Pi = 0$ in (8.40). By the same token, it is easy to find the long-run solution for n^w when $s_n = 1$.

More generally, the two expressions in (8.40) and (8.41) can be used to assess the stability properties of the long-run equilibria. These depend as usual on the interplay of the agglomeration and dispersion forces.

8.4.4 Agglomeration and Dispersion Forces

The nature of the agglomeration and dispersion forces is as in the CPVL model. Hence, Figure 8.2 and the related analysis are also valid here.

Agglomeration forces stem from the existence of backward and forward linkages. These linkages work exactly as in the CPVL model because the FEVL and the CPVL models differ only in their functional forms. Also the market-crowding dispersion force is identical in both models. Hence, the intuition given in Section 8.2.5 holds here too.

8.4.5 Stability Analysis

The stability analysis is very similar to that conducted for the CPVL model but is much simpler given the closed-form solutions for Π and Π^*.

Consider first the agglomerated configuration with all active firms in one region, say $(n^w, s_n) = (n_0, 1)$. This is a stable long-run equilibrium for (8.4) if and only if $\Pi(n_0, 1) = 0$ and $\Pi^*(n_0, 1) < 0$. Since closed-form solutions for Π and Π^* are available, finding the set of values satisfying these conditions is a very easy task. First, $\Pi(n_0, 1) = 0$ holds if and only if

$$n_0 = b^{1/(1-a)} \qquad (8.42)$$

where the second equality stems from the definitions of a and b. Note that given the no-black-hole condition $1 > a$, n_0 is increasing in μ (which captures the importance of the manufacturing sector in the economy) and decreasing in σ (the degree of substitutability of different varieties), as was to be expected. In particular, a larger σ is associated with a lower mark-up, so firms are more profitable if σ is low. With free entry, this translates into a larger number of firms at equilibrium.

As was already mentioned, $s_n = 1$ is part of a stable equilibrium if $\Pi^*(n_0, 1) < 0$. The latter requirement is met when

$$\frac{1 - b + (1 + b)\phi^2}{2\phi^{1-a}} - 1 < 0 \qquad (8.43)$$

This condition is met if ϕ is larger than the sustain point ϕ^S, where ϕ^S is the smallest real root of the left-hand side of (8.43) (it is readily verified that $\phi = 1$ is also a root of this term). Manipulating this expression reveals that ϕ^S solves

$$1 = (\phi^S)^a \left[\frac{1 + b}{2} \phi^S + \frac{1 - b}{2\phi^S} \right] \qquad (8.44)$$

This expression is identical to the definition of the sustain point of the FE model.

Turning to interior equilibria, the loci $\Pi(n^w, s_n) = 0$ and $\Pi^*(n^w, s_n) = 0$ always cross at least once and no more than three times (see the appendix for details). In terms of Figure 8.2, this means that EE and nn never cross more than three times. In particular, they always cross at the symmetric outcome in which $s_n = 1/2$ and $n^w = n^w_{1/2}$, where $n^w_{1/2}$ is the aggregate mass of varieties in the symmetric outcome. Using $s_n = 1/2$ in (8.40) and (8.41) for $\Pi = \Pi^* = 0$, we find

$$n^w_{1/2} = n_0 \left(\frac{1 + \phi}{2} \right)^{a/(1-a)} = b^{1/(1-a)} \left(\frac{1 + \phi}{2} \right)^{a/(1-a)} \qquad (8.45)$$

by (8.42) and the definitions of a and b. Therefore, just as in the CPVL model, the number of active firms with agglomeration (n_0) is invariant to the level of trade barriers, while the number of active firms in the symmetric equilibrium ($n^w_{1/2}$) is not (more on this below).

The symmetric equilibrium is locally stable as long as the two eigenvalues of the Jacobian associated with the laws of motion (8.4) are negative at $(n^w, s_n) = (n^w_{1/2}, 1/2)$. This is the case if ϕ is in $(0, \phi^B)$, where the 'break point' ϕ^B is defined as (see Appendix 8.A for derivations)

$$\phi^B = \frac{(1 - a)(1 - b)}{(1 + a)(1 + b)} \qquad (8.46)$$

Clearly, the interval $[0, \phi^B)$ is empty if $\phi^B < 0$; to avoid this (and thus keep the analysis meaningful), we impose the 'no-black-hole' condition $1 < a$ (as in the FE model). Observe also that, like ϕ^S, the break point above is *identical* to the break point in the FE model. This is remarkable because these models are conceptually quite different.

Note that we can rank the break-and-sustain points as usual. In particular, the break point is larger than the sustain point, viz. $\phi^B > \phi^S$.

To sum up, what we have shown in this subsection is that the tomahawk diagram in Figure 8.3 also summarizes the stability properties of the FEVL model.

8.4.6 Comparison with the FE and CPVL Models

The key features of the FEVL model can be summarized as follows. First, the FEVL model exhibits the same equilibrium and stability properties as the FE and CPVL models. In particular, the FEVL and FE models have the same break-and-sustain points. Accordingly, the FEVL model features agglomeration via the home-market mechanism (with magnification by freer trade), demand and cost linkages, endogenous asymmetry, catastrophic agglomeration, locational hysteresis, hump-shaped agglomeration rents, and multiple long-run equilibria in the 'overlap'.

Second, under the no-black-hole condition $a < 1$, (8.45) reveals that $n_{1/2}^w$ is an increasing function of ϕ. The freer trade is, the larger the number of active firms. Thus, in contrast to the FE model but like the CPVL model, trade integration fragments the market. The intuition for this result is the same as in the CPVL model.

Third, (8.45) reveals that $n_{1/2}^w < n_0$, namely, the total number of firms under the symmetric equilibrium is lower than under the core–periphery equilibrium (again assuming the no-black-hole condition). This result is related to the previous one and is also present in the CPVL model. Under the no-black hole condition, the market-crowding dispersion force dominates the agglomeration forces when ϕ is small enough. Moreover, agglomeration forces are self-reinforcing which means that, for a given ϕ, the agglomeration forces (net of dispersion forces) are larger at the core–periphery equilibrium than at the dispersed equilibrium (this is also why $\phi^S < \phi^B$). For a given number of firms, this implies that firms are more profitable in the latter configuration. By free entry, we thus have $n_0 > n_{1/2}^w$.

8.5 KEY FEATURES OF VL MODELS

Chapter 2 pointed out seven key features of the CP model: agglomeration via the home-market mechanism (with magnification by freer trade), demand and cost linkages, endogenous asymmetry, catastrophic agglomeration, locational hysteresis, hump-shaped agglomeration rents and multiple long-run equilibria in the 'overlap'. In comparing the VL models with the CP model, we discuss such features first and then we turn to new properties.

Like the FE model, the VL models display all the key features of the CP model even though the mechanism by which agglomeration is possible (input–output linkages between firms acting in an imperfectly competitive industry) is conceptually distinct from factor migration, as the FE and CP models assume.

8.5.1 Comparison with the CP Model

HOME-MARKET MAGNIFICATION

As the CP model, all the VL models feature the home-market effect. The home-market effect says that the combination of transportation costs and increasing returns imply that the larger market will host a more than proportionate share of industry. In terms of the scissor diagram of Figure 8.2, a slight increase in the northern market size leads to a shift of the EE curve to the right. Presuming that trade costs are high enough for the interior equilibrium to be stable, the shock will lead to a more than proportional increase in the north's share of industry since, in this case, the nn line is steeper than the 45-degree line. Moreover, home market magnification also occurs (i.e. the home-market effect gets stronger as trade gets freer) since freeing up trade makes the nn line steeper. Thus, the same rightward shift in the EE curve would result in a higher degree of relocation.

CIRCULAR CAUSALITY

In VL models, agglomeration is driven by and drives entry and exit of firms. Because these firms buy their inputs locally, they care about the local cost of production. This, in turn, means that entry decisions will be based on the real reward to production (operating profits deflated by production costs) so cost-linked circular causality comes into play via the production-cost effect. The fact that firms spend locally ties production shifting to expenditure shifting, so that demand-linked circular causality operates.

ENDOGENOUS ASYMMETRY

In all of the symmetric VL models, a gradual reduction of trade costs starting from a high level eventually leads to full agglomeration. Moreover, just as in the CP model, partial agglomeration is never a stable outcome—the location of industry is either symmetric or involves all industry in one region or the other. Thus, the steady lowering of trade costs results in a perfectly symmetric model becoming asymmetric.

CATASTROPHIC AGGLOMERATION

As the tomahawk diagram shows, all VL models may be subject to sudden and massive agglomerations in reaction to minor changes in trade costs. For example, when trade gets just a bit freer than ϕ^B. The same occurs in the CP model.

LOCATIONAL HYSTERESIS

Since $0 < \phi^S < 1$, whenever $\phi > \phi^S$, the VL models feature multiple stable equilibria. As in the CP model, this means that temporary shocks, including temporary policy changes, may have hysteretic effects on the location of industry.

HUMP-SHAPED AGGLOMERATION RENTS

In the VL models, as in the CP model, agglomeration rents are concave function of trade freeness. For example, this can be established in the FCVL model by considering a long-run equilibrium in which all firms are located in the north ($s_n = 1$ and $\phi^S \leq \phi \leq 1$).[21] In this case, agglomeration rents are measured as the loss that an entrepreneur would incur by relocating to the south. Formally, such rents are given by

$$\pi - \pi^*\big|_{s_{n=1}} = 1 - \phi^{\mu-1}\left[\frac{1 + \mu - b}{2}\phi^2 + \frac{1 - (\mu - b)}{2}\right] \qquad (8.47)$$

This is a function of ϕ. It equals zero at $\phi = \phi^S$ and $\phi = 1$, while it is positive in between. Moreover, in the same interval, it is concave with a maximum at $\phi = \sqrt{\phi^B}$, where ϕ^B is the break point defined in (8.30). Accordingly, as trade gets freer (i.e. ϕ rises from ϕ^S towards 1), the agglomeration rents first rise and then fall ('hump shape').

THE OVERLAP AND SELF-FULFILLING EXPECTATIONS

Since $0 < \phi^S < \phi^B < 1$, these models feature an overlap. Thus, as in the CP model, in principle, shocks to expectations may result in large spatial realloca-tions involving both symmetric and CP outcomes.

8.5.2 New Features of the FEVL and FCVL Models: Agglomeration Without Migration

The main new feature of VL models is agglomeration without inter-regional labour migration. This makes these models more appealing from an inter-national point of view since it is easier to believe that labour is mobile between sectors within a geographical region than between regions. However, the seven key features of migration models still arise, thus stres-sing their robustness.

Secondarily, the FEVL model and, to a lesser extend, the FCVL model, are analytically tractable, which makes them natural candidates for policy investiga-tion in vertical-linkage set-ups.

8.6 CONCLUDING REMARKS AND RELATED LITERATURE

8.6.1 Summary Results for Policy Modelling

While yielding valuable insights on the interactions between trade costs, imper-fect competition and agglomeration, the CP model relies on migration flows.

---

[21] Hump-shaped agglomeration rents can be derived in the CPVL and FEVL models by referring to analogous results in Chapters 2 and 4, respectively. The reason is that the CP and CPVL models as well as the FE and FEVL models are pair-wise isomorphic.

While plausible within the same country (at least in North America), such flows are seldom significant between countries. The CPVL model shows that all the insights of the CP model can be exactly recovered in a framework in which agglomeration is driven by input–output linkages between firms rather than inter-regional migration of workers. Thus, the key features of the CP model can be brought from an interregional to an international set-up.

The CPVL model, however, also shares the main limitation of the CP model—it is astoundingly difficult to work analytically, forcing numerical simulations for most results. Therefore, this chapter has presented two alternative models, FCVL and FEVL, which are easier to deal with. These models can be thought of as an extended version of the FC model and a modified version of the FE model, respectively. In particular, the FEVL model exhibits the same qualitative properties as the original CPVL model, while yielding closed-form solutions for most endogenous variables and an analytical assessment of the number of equilibria.[22] Indeed, most of the key expressions of the FEVL model are those of the CPVL model with μ divided by σ (like the break and sustain points).[23] Finally, the additional feature of the FCVL model is that it couples vertical linkages and capital mobility, which are likely to be jointly relevant in processes of international agglomeration.

8.6.2 Related Literature

The original model based on vertical linkages is due to Faini (1984). That paper proposes a model of capital accumulation in which the production of a Walrasian final good uses capital, labour and non-traded intermediate inputs. In this sense, it merges a VL model with a neoclassical growth model in the spirit of the CC model of Chapter 6.

Independently of Faini, Venables (1994, 1996a) introduced input–output linkages into the CP model. This model was refined and popularized in Krugman and Venables (1995). Its connection to the original CP model was assessed by Puga (1999). Applications to industrial development include Venables (1996b) and Puga and Venables (1996); applications to the study of trade policy and the location effects of preferential trade agreements include Puga and Venables (1996, 1997, 1999).

The FEVL model is due to Ottaviano (2002). In this model, agglomeration is supported by vertical linkages via fixed costs only, which allow for analytical solutions. The FCVL model is due to Robert-Nicoud (2002). There, capital mobility and vertical linkages through variable costs achieve the same result. Unfortunately, the FCVL model is not entirely analytically solvable. On the plus side, the FCVL model has only one state variable which makes it easier to extend to applications, as we shall see in Part III of this book.

---

[22] By the same token as in Chapter 2, the global stability of its equilibria is more easily assessed.

[23] Similarly, as argued in Chapter 4, most of the key expressions of the FE model are those of the CP model with μ divided by σ.

APPENDIX 8.A: FORMAL STABILITY TESTS IN VERTICAL-LINKAGE MODELS

8.A.1 CPVL Model: Stability of the Symmetric Equilibrium

Here, we show that in the CPVL model the symmetric equilibrium is stable if trade freeness ϕ is smaller than ϕ^B. Indeed, the symmetric equilibrium is stable as long as the two eigenvalues of the Jacobian associated with the laws of motion (8.4) are negative at $(n^w, s_n) = (n^w_{1/2}, 1/2)$. From (8.11), it is obvious that $\Pi \leq 0$ if and only if $x \leq 1$. Therefore, the symmetric equilibrium is stable if and only if x drops below 1 as a result of a shock on (n^w, s_n). Hence, to get an expression for dx we use (8.9) and find $dx/x = dB/B - dn^w/n^w + a(d\Delta/\Delta + dn^w/n^w)$, where all variables are evaluated at the symmetric long-run equilibrium. By the same token, we first differentiate the system (8.9)–(8.16) at the symmetric equilibrium, to get

$$
\begin{bmatrix} -1 & \mu - Z & 2Z \\ -\mu/2 & 0 & 1 \\ 0 & 1 - \mu Z & 0 \end{bmatrix}
\begin{bmatrix} dB/B \\ d\Delta/\Delta \\ ds_E \end{bmatrix}
=
\begin{bmatrix} 0 & -1 - \mu + Z \\ \mu & 0 \\ 2Z & \mu Z \end{bmatrix}
\begin{bmatrix} ds_n \\ dn^w/n^w \end{bmatrix}
$$

$$(8.A.1)$$

where $Z \equiv (1 - \phi)/(1 + \phi)$ is zero when $\phi = 1$ and Z is 1 when $\phi = 0$ as usual. Using Cramer's rule, we can find closed-form solutions for dB/B, $d\Delta/\Delta$, and ds_E. We then plug this back to the expression for dx/x and obtain

$$
\frac{dx}{x} = \frac{-(\sigma - 1)(\mu Z)^2 + [(\sigma - 1)(1 - \mu) + \mu^2]Z - \sigma\mu}{(1 - \mu Z)^2(\sigma - 1)} \frac{dn^w}{n^w}
$$

$$
+ 2\frac{[(\sigma - 1) + \sigma\mu^2]Z^2 + \mu(2\sigma - 1)Z}{(1 - \mu Z)^2(\sigma - 1)} ds_n \qquad (8.A.2)
$$

We then perform the symmetric exercise for dx^*/x^*. Together, the resulting expressions can be rewritten in a matrix form as

$$
\begin{bmatrix} dx/x \\ dx^*/x^* \end{bmatrix}
=
\begin{bmatrix} J_{11} & J_{12} \\ J_{21} & J_{22} \end{bmatrix}
\begin{bmatrix} dn^w/n^w \\ ds_n \end{bmatrix}
\qquad (8.A.3)
$$

where the matrix $J \equiv [J_{i,j}]$ is the Jacobian of the system under investigation.

The symmetric equilibrium is locally stable if and only if J is negative definite. Clearly, the expansion of the aggregate mass of varieties n^w has the same impact on x and x^*, hence $J_{11} = J_{21}$. By contrast, the impact of an increase in the share of varieties produced in the north s_n has opposite effects on x and x^*, so $J_{22} = -J_{12}$. Hence, the elements of the Jacobian are

$$
J_{21} = J_{11} = \frac{-(\sigma - 1)(\mu Z)^2 + [(\sigma - 1)(1 - \mu) + \mu^2]Z - \sigma\mu}{(1 - \mu Z)^2(\sigma - 1)}
$$

$$J_{22} = -J_{12} = 2\frac{[(\sigma - 1) + \sigma\mu^2]Z^2 - \mu(2\sigma - 1)Z}{(1 - \mu Z)^2(\sigma - 1)} \qquad (8.A.4)$$

J is negative definite if and only if the diagonal elements are both negative *and* $J_{11}J_{22} > \text{abs}(J_{12}J_{21})$. Given the structure of J, a sufficient condition for both of these conditions to hold simultaneously is $J_{11}, J_{22} < 0$. By inspection, $J_{22} < 0$ if and only if $Z > [(\sigma - 1) + \sigma\mu^2]/[\mu(2\sigma - 1)]$. Alternatively, expressed in terms of ϕ, J_{22} is negative if ϕ is in $[0, \phi^B)$, where the 'break point' ϕ^B is defined as

$$\phi^B = \frac{(1 - \mu)(a_M - \mu)}{(1 + \mu)(a_M + \mu)} = \frac{\sigma(1 - \mu) - 1}{\sigma(1 + \mu) - 1}\left(\frac{1 - \mu}{1 + \mu}\right) \qquad (8.A.5)$$

where the second equality stems from the definition of a_M in (8.10).

As for the sign of J_{11}, it can be shown that $J_{22} < 0$ implies $J_{11} < 0$ by the no-black hole condition ($\mu < 1 - (1/\sigma)$). As a result, ϕ^B in (8.21) is a sufficient statistics to assess the local stability of the symmetric equilibrium.

8.A.2 FCVL Model: Stability of the Symmetric Equilibrium

Here, we show that in the FCVL model, the symmetric equilibrium is stable if trade freeness ϕ is smaller than ϕ^B. The symmetric equilibrium is locally stable if the slope of $\pi - \pi^*$ is negative at $n = 1/2$. Due to the symmetry of the model, we can focus on $d\pi/dn$ evaluated at $n = 1/2$.[24] In particular, it is easy to see that $n = s_L = 1/2$ implies $s_E = 1/2$, $\pi = \pi^* = b$ and $\Delta = \Delta^* = ((1 + \phi)/2)^{1/(1-\mu)}$. Define Z as $(1 - \phi)/(1 + \phi)$; by definition, $Z > 0$. Now, first differentiating the system evaluated at the symmetric equilibrium gives

$$\begin{bmatrix} 0 & 1 - \mu Z & 0 \\ 2 & 0 & -\mu\beta \\ -2Z & Z - \mu & 1 \end{bmatrix}\begin{bmatrix} ds_E \\ d\Delta/\Delta \\ \sigma d\pi \end{bmatrix} = 2\begin{bmatrix} Z \\ \mu - b \\ 0 \end{bmatrix}dn \qquad (8.A.6)$$

Using Cramer's rule, we can solve for $d\pi/dn$. This is positive for low values of Z—or, equivalently, for high values of ϕ. The derivative $d\pi/dn$ changes sign at the break point ϕ^B, where ϕ^B is defined as

$$\phi^B \equiv \frac{(1 - \mu)(1 - \mu + b)}{(1 + \mu)(1 + \mu - b)} \qquad (8.A.7)$$

which is strictly smaller than unity by inspection.

8.A.3 FEVL Model: Stability of the Symmetric Equilibrium

Here, we show that in the FEVL model, the symmetric equilibrium is stable if trade freeness ϕ is smaller than ϕ^B. Local stability depends upon the two eigenvalues of the Jacobian associated with the laws of motion as usual. Specifically, they must be negative at $(n^w, s_n) = (n^w_{1/2}, 1/2)$. To find an expression for this

---

[24] As discussed in the main text, this is equivalent to signing $d(\pi - \pi^*)/dn$ at $n = 1/2$.

Jacobian, note first that $\Pi \leq 0$ if and only if $\ln(\pi) \leq \ln(P)$. Hence, an equivalent stability check involves signing the first derivative of $\ln(\pi) - \ln(P)$ following an infinitesimal shock of s_n and n^w. In terms of (8.40) and (8.41) this means that we are checking the sign of the first derivative of the ratio of the two terms in the right-hand side rather than their difference.

Mathematically, we write the perturbation of the system as

$$
\begin{bmatrix} d\ln(\pi) - d\ln(P) \\ d\ln(\pi^*) - d\ln(P^*) \end{bmatrix} = \begin{bmatrix} J_{11} & J_{12} \\ J_{21} & J_{22} \end{bmatrix} \begin{bmatrix} dn^w/n^w \\ ds_n \end{bmatrix} \tag{8.A.8}
$$

where the matrix $J \equiv [J_{i,j}]$ is the Jacobian of the system under investigation.

The symmetric equilibrium is locally stable if and only if J is negative definite. Clearly, the expansion of the aggregate mass of varieties n^w has the same impact on Π and Π^*, hence $J_{11} = J_{21}$. By contrast, the impact of an increase in the share of varieties produced in the north, s_n, has opposite effects on Π and Π^*, so $J_{22} = -J_{12}$. Hence, the elements of the Jacobian are

$$
J_{21} = J_{11} = -(1-a) < 0
$$

$$
J_{22} = -J_{12} = 2Z \frac{a + b - (1 + ab)Z}{1 - bZ} \tag{8.A.9}
$$

where the inequality holds under the no-black-hole condition. J is negative definite if and only if the diagonal elements are both negative *and* $J_{11}J_{22} > \mathrm{abs}(J_{12}J_{21})$. Given the structure of J, a sufficient condition for both of these conditions to hold simultaneously is $J_{11}, J_{22} < 0$. By inspection $J_{22} < 0$, if and only if $Z > (a + b)/(1 + ab)$. Alternatively, expressed in terms of ϕ, J_{22} is negative if ϕ is in $(0, \phi^B)$, where the 'break point' ϕ^B is defined as

$$
\phi^B = \frac{(1-a)(1-b)}{(1+a)(1+b)} = \frac{\sigma - 1 - \mu}{\sigma - 1 + \mu} \left(\frac{\sigma - \mu}{\sigma + \mu} \right) \tag{8.A.10}
$$

8.A.4 FEVL Model: No More than Three Interior Equilibria

A great advantage of the simplicity of the FEVL model is that we can easily show one of its central features, namely, that it does not have more than three interior long-run equilibria. As we saw, this task is extremely complicated for models like the CPVL model. Indeed, like the CP model, the CPVL model is one of the core models of Fujita et al. (1999), yet no formal proof of this central features of both the CP and CPVL models is available in that monograph.

We now provide such a proof for the FEVL model. The first step is to note that $\Pi = 0$ and $\Pi^* = 0$ if and only if $\ln(\pi) - \ln(P) = 0$ and $\ln(\pi^*) - \ln(P^*) = 0$. Hence, if we can show that the latter loci never cross more than three times then the former loci never cross more than three times either. The second step is to take the difference of these two. That is, we want to evaluate the term

$$
Q \equiv \ln\left(\frac{\pi}{\pi^*} \right) - \ln\left(\frac{P}{P^*} \right) \tag{8.A.11}
$$

Indeed, a necessary condition for $\Pi = 0$ and $\Pi^* = 0$ to hold simultaneously is that $Q = 0$ as well. Using the terms in the right-hand side of (8.40) and (8.41), it is obvious that n^w disappears from (8.A.11) which we can then refer to as $Q(s_n)$.

The third step is to take the first derivative of Q with respect to s_n. It is straightforward to show that the numerator of the resulting expression is a third-order polynomial in s_n. Therefore, Q admits at most three flat points on $[0, 1]$ and hence at most four zeroes. We claim that, actually, $Q = 0$ admits at most three solutions. To see this, note that Q is symmetric around $1/2$ given the symmetry of the system, and so is dQ/ds_n. Hence, the zeroes of this expression are symmetric as well. As a result, they come in even numbers, unless $s_n = 1/2$ is a zero as well. But if such is the case, it is easy to see that the symmetry of the model implies that this is an inflexion point, not a local extremum. This proves our claim, namely, that Q is equal to zero at most three times.

The fourth step is straightforward: if dQ/ds_n admits at most two zeros different from $s_n = 1/2$, then $Q(s_n)$ crosses the horizontal axis at most three times and hence $\Pi = \Pi^*$ at most three times, too.

Finally, it is obvious by inspection of (8.41) that, given s_n, the solution to $\Pi = 0$ for n^w is unique. Hence, the fact that $Q = 0$ for at most three distinct s_n is also a sufficient condition for $\Pi = 0$ and $\Pi^* = 0$ to cross at most three times. This is because we can disconnect the roles played by s_n and n^w. The former serves to solve the problem $\Pi = \Pi^*$; once this is done, the second is set to make pure profits nil.

As an aside, we note that this result can be used to show that the CPVL model, too, admits no more than three interior long-run equilibria.

REFERENCES

Baldwin, Richard E. 2001. The core-periphery model with forward-looking expectations. *Regional Science and Urban Economics* 31: 21–49.

Barro, R. and X. Sala-i-Martin. 1995. *Economic Growth*. New York: McGraw-Hill.

Ethier, W. 1982. National and international returns to scale in the modern theory of international trade. *American Economic Review* 72(3): 389–405.

Faini, R. 1984. Increasing returns, non-traded inputs and regional development. *Economic Journal* 94: 308–323.

Fujita, M. and J.-F. Thisse. 2002. *Economics of Agglomeration*. Cambridge: Cambridge University Press.

Fujita, M., P. Krugman and A. J. Venables. 1999. The Spatial Economy. Cities, Regions and International Trade. Cambridge, MA: MIT Press.

Krugman, Paul. 1991. Increasing returns and economic geography. *Journal of Political Economy* 99: 483–499.

Krugman, P. R. and A. J.Venables. 1995. Globalization and the inequality of nations. *Quarterly Journal of Economics* 60: 857–880.

Ottaviano, G. I. P. 2002. Models of 'new economic geography': factor mobility vs. vertical linkages. Mimeo, Graduate Institute of International Studies.

Puga, D. 1999. The rise and fall of regional inequalities. *European Economic Review* 43: 303–334.

Puga, D. and A. Venables. 1996. 'The spread of industry: spatial agglomeration in economic development. *Journal of the Japanese and International Economies* 10: 440–464.

_____. 1997. Preferential trading agreements and industrial location. *Journal of International Economics* 43: 347–368.

_____. 1999. Agglomeration and economic development: import substitution vs. trade liberalisation. *Economic Journal* 109(455): 292–311.

Robert-Nicoud, F. 2001. The structure of simple 'New Economic Geography' models. Mimeo, London School of Economics.

_____ 2002. A simple geography model with vertical linkages and capital mobility. Mimeo, London School of Economics.

Venables, A. 1994. Economic integration and industrial agglomeration. *Economic and Social Review* 26(1): 1–17.

_____. 1996a. Equilibrium location of vertically linked industries. *International Economic Review* 37: 341–359.

_____. 1996b. Trade policy, cumulative causation, and industrial development. *Journal of Economic Development* 49(1): 179–197.

General Policy and Welfare Issues

CHAPTER 9

Policy and Economic Geography: What's New?

9.1 INTRODUCTION

What makes policy analysis in a location framework interesting?

Ultimately this question must be answered by the reader after having worked thorough the policy chapters in Parts III, IV and V, but in this chapter we discuss the question at an abstract level. The basic point is that economic geography models have a number of properties that makes policy analysis very different to standard neoclassical models. Some of these properties stem from the fact that factor mobility raises a number of issues that are often ignored, but the most important of these properties arise because of the non-linearity of the models, which produce multiple equilibria, hysteresis and bifurcations.

9.1.1 Organization of the Chapter

The chapter starts with an illustration of how threshold effects, hysteresis and bifurcations matter. In Section 9.3, we go on to show that the general non-linearity of the models is crucial for policy even without the extreme forms of non-linearity in the previous section.

Section 9.4 discusses how trade freeness, and therefore trade policy, interacts with other policies. Because trade costs affect the extent to which factors are internationally mobile, trade costs are often an important 'co-factor' in determining the policy impact of, for example, liberalizing capital flows.

The location models in this book are characterized by multiple equilibria for some parameter values. As a consequence, policy may be effective in selecting which equilibria gets established, as illustrated in Section 9.5. Moreover, when agent's expectations are formed in a rational manner, the coordination of expectations decides which equilibrium gets established, as discussed in Section 9.6.

9.2 THRESHOLD EFFECTS, DISCONTINUITIES AND HYSTERESIS

When industry is already clustered spatially, agglomeration forces produce inertia that makes small policy interventions ineffective when it comes to location. That is, agglomeration produces rents which tend to hold firms and factors in place even if a policy otherwise would lead to a geographical shift. However, once the magnitude crosses some threshold—in particular when it creates a cost to firms or mobile factors that outweigh the agglomeration rents—factors will move. And as firms and factors start to locate away from the agglomeration, the size of the agglomeration rents decrease and this makes the site even less attractive. Typically, the outcome will be a massive delocation of industry.

The fact that marginal policy changes may have no impact on industrial location as long as the level of the policy instrument remains below a threshold value is the first general property that we highlight. Of course, we are not the first to identify threshold effects, but we note that they arise quite naturally and quite systematically in economic geography models. The reason, of course, is that location models almost always display multiple, locally stable equilibria.

To illustrate the general point as simply as possible, we begin by recapping the analysis of marginal trade liberalization that was presented in Part I. After that, we show the same sort of phenomenon arises when it comes to subsidies.

9.2.1 Example 1: Trade Openness and Locational Hysteresis

Figure 9.1, which shows the tomahawk diagram for a generic economic geography model, helps us to illustrate threshold effects and hysteresis when it comes to trade openness.[1] As usual, the diagram has trade openness on the horizontal axis (ϕ is a mnemonic for freeness, or 'phi-ness' of trade) and the north's share of the world's supply of the mobile factor is plotted on the vertical axis. The model features many equilibria with their number and stability properties varying with openness. The stable equilibria are shown with the bold lines—up to ϕ^S, the symmetric location outcome $s_H = 1/2$ is the only stable equilibrium, but for higher levels of openness, the model has two or three stable equilibria. For levels of openness between ϕ^S and ϕ^B, there are three stable equilibria: symmetry, full agglomeration in the north and full agglomeration in the south (i.e. $s_H = 1/2, 1$ and 0, respectively).[2] When trade is more open than ϕ^B, the only stable outcomes are full agglomeration in either the north or the south.

THRESHOLD EFFECTS

Starting from an equilibrium such as E_1 where the level of freeness is ϕ^0, a mild increase in openness to, say, ϕ', would move the equilibrium to E_2. This would involve all the customary gains from liberalization, but it would have no effect on the location of industry. The north's share of the mobile factor s_H and, thus, the north's share of industry which uses the mobile factor intensively is unchanged at 1/2. By contrast, an identical-sized increase in openness starting from ϕ' will have radically different results. Increasing freeness from ϕ' to ϕ'' would result in a sweeping shift in industry. Since the symmetric division of industry is unstable at ϕ'' (because $\phi'' > \phi^B$; see Chapter 2 or 4 for details), all industry will move north or south. To be concrete, we suppose it moves north, so E_3 is the new

---

[1] This would correspond, for example, to the CP model of Chapter 2, or the FE model of Chapter 4.
[2] There are also two unstable equilibria for each $\phi^B > \phi > \phi^S$; these are shown by the bold dashed curve.

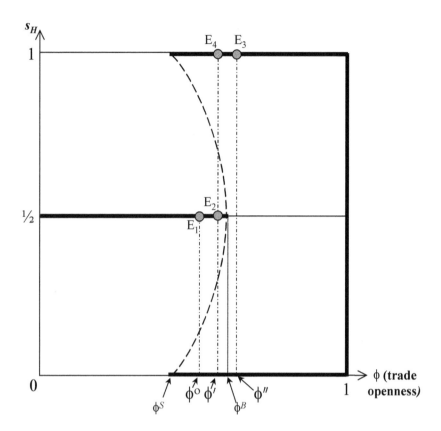

Figure 9.1   Threshold effects and hysteresis in the tomahawk diagram.

equilibrium. As before, a modest increase in trade openness would produce the customary effects, but additionally, it causes all industry to leave the south.

The main point here is that policy may have dramatically non-linear effects, contrasting sharply with the standard framework where small changes in policy lead to small responses. What does this mean in practice for policy analysis?

The main implication is one of caution—in both policy making and empirical work.. The possibility of non-linear responses to policy makes it much more difficult to forecast the effect of a given policy change. If the forecast is based on empirical work where policy variations never crossed the threshold, policy makers may conclude that location is not much affected by changes in a particular policy; they may be in for a surprise when the threshold is crossed. The new economic geography framework, thus, indicates that it can be seriously misleading to base expectations of the effects of future policies on linear approximations from the past. Secondly, empirical analysis of policy should allow for non-linear relationships. Just to take one example, trade liberalization may have very non-linear effects on industrialization and growth. Empirical studies that impose linearity on the relationship between, for example, growth and openness are likely to be mis-specified.

A separate aspect of the threshold effect arises when the model has more than one threshold. In Figure 9.1, both ϕ^B and ϕ^S are critical to policy analysis. For example, consider the impact of reversing the small policy changes that lead to the catastrophe, that is, pushing openness back down from ϕ'' to ϕ'. This makes location in the north less desirable for north-based firms, since serving the south via exports becomes more expensive. Nevertheless, this incremental policy change would not induce any relocation. Since industrial clustering in the north is a stable equilibrium at both ϕ'' and ϕ', the policy reversal will not reverse policy's impact. The equilibrium would shift from E_3 to E_4—not back to E_2. In such situations, we say the economy is subject to locational hysteresis. That is, the impact of a particular policy need not be reversed when the policy is reversed. Indeed, to get back to E_1, the economy might have to lower openness to a level below ϕ^S and then raise it back to ϕ°. This property is called hysteresis in physics. Krugman (1991), which presents several historical cases where random events lie behind the establishment of large industrial agglomerations today, calls this the 'history matters' property.

What does hysteresis mean for policy? The most direct implication is again one of caution. Bad policies, even when they are temporary, may have long-lasting bad effects. Moreover, reversing the effects may be difficult and require policy reforms that are much larger than the change that led to the initial effects. Or, as the old saying goes, it may be much easier to get the genie out of the bottle than it is to get it back in.

The example we have worked through here—symmetric changes in trade openness—is a classic in the economic geography literature, but it is rather strained as far as policy analysis is concerned. In particular the fact that it imposes symmetry on the two regions' openness and considers only coordinated shifts (i.e. ϕ is the degree of north's openness to southern exporters and south's openness to northern exporters). The next example more clearly highlights lessons for unilateral policy choices.

9.2.2 Example 2: Production Subsidies and Delocation

Many nations and sub-national regions spend substantial amounts of their taxpayers' money in attempts to attract industry. Here, we show that the impact of such subsidies is also subject to threshold effects, discontinuities and hysteresis.

Figure 9.2, which shows a 'wiggle diagram' for a generic economic geography model, facilitates the analysis. The diagram plots the north's share of the mobile factor and industry, namely s_H, against the difference in the real reward to the mobile factor in the north versus the south. As it is drawn, the northern real

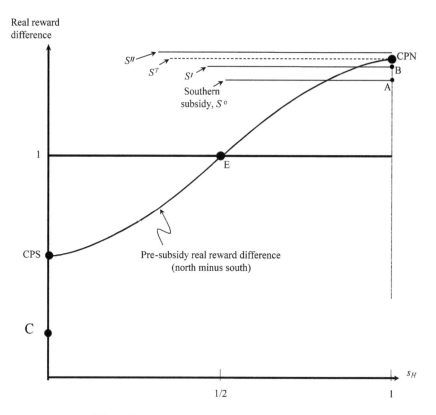

Figure 9.2   Thresholds, hysteresis and subsidies.

reward is higher than the south's when the north has more than half the mobile factor, and it is negative when the south has more than half. In such a situation— which arises when trade openness is above the break point ϕ^B—the outcome would be full agglomeration in one nation or the other. We start by assuming that the agglomeration is in the north, that is, the equilibrium is at CPN.

Now suppose the southern government provides a subsidy to the mobile factor. In practice, this might take the form of indirect ways of making the south more attractive—tax relief or subsidised infrastructure for example—but for simplicity we assume that the subsidy is just directly paid to the mobile factor. When the mobile factor is in the north, it earns the northern real reward ω. When it works in the south, it earns the southern real reward plus the subsidy, namely $\omega^* + S$, where S is the 'per head' subsidy.

If the subsidy is set at S^o, the subsidy will have no effect because the agglomeration rent—that is, the gap between the north's and south's real reward—exceeds the subsidy. Indeed, if the south increases the subsidy from S^o to S', there still would be no impact. But if the south again raises the subsidy by the same increment, $S' - S^o$ so that the subsidy becomes S'', the impact on industry will be spectacular. Indeed, since $\omega^* + S$ exceeds the maximum of ω, the new equilibrium will be at point C. Here all industry is in the south and it receives the subsidy. Plainly, the threshold subsidy in this case is S^T. Any subsidy up to S^T will be useless but beyond S^T, the reaction is extravagant. Such discontinuous behaviour is endemic to models with agglomeration forces since—unlike standard neoclassical models—factors are often not indifferent to their location in equilibrium.

Observe that this example is also subject to hysteresis. For example, if the south offers a temporary subsidy equal to S'', it will attract the industrial cluster and having done this, it could discontinue that subsidy without losing any industry since now the agglomeration rent accrues in the south.

While this stark setting is probably relevant to very few industries, the message is quite general. Temporary subsidies can have hysteretic—that is, quasi-permanent—effects when agglomeration forces are important. For example, Europe in the late 1980s and 1990s experienced signification industrial restructuring due in part to the Single Market programme. During this time, it was clear that the total number of active firms would fall, but the location and in particular the nationality of these firms was not determinant. Temporary state aids by rich member states could therefore be reasonably assumed to have long-lasting effects on Europe's economic geography. In particular, it may have ensured that Europe's industrial core stayed where it was with most of the adjustment falling on industries of member states that could not afford generous industrial subsidies.

9.3 GENERAL NON-LINEAR EFFECTS

The discontinuities and catastrophic changes discussed above may be impressive and unexpected to an economist steeped in neoclassical analysis. They are, however, merely an extreme form of non-linearity. The dynamic effects would become less crisp in a more realistic setting where dampening factors, such as heterogeneity, were introduced. As illustrated in the appendix, however, heterogeneity among agents does not per se rule out discontinuities and catastrophic events, even if it generally does dampen the tendency for extreme outcomes.[3]

We turn our attention now to the general implications of more mild forms of non-linearity that are a feature of all models in which agglomeration forces are important.

9.3.1 Tax Hikes

Non-linearity makes policy difficult. It implies, for instance, that the same intervention can have very different impacts the first and the second time it is applied.

---

[3] Another dampening effect is that firms may split up the production process geographically. This case is analysed by Ekholm and Forslid (2001), who find that the introduction of horizontal and vertical multi-national firms does decrease the tendency for extreme outcomes, but it does not rule them out.

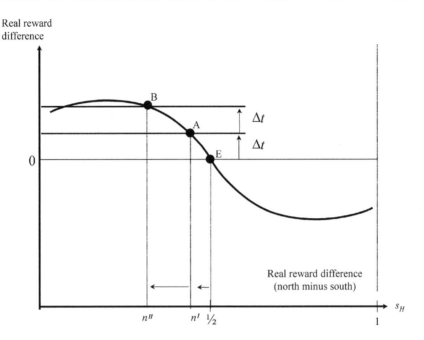

Figure 9.3   General non-linear effects of tax rises.

Assume, as an example, that the northern government wishes to raise revenues by taxation. Government revenue equals the tax rate times the tax base: $R = tB$, and the size of the tax base depends on the tax rate. Differentiating gives

$$\frac{dR}{dt} = B(1 - \varepsilon), \quad \varepsilon \equiv -\frac{t}{B}\frac{\partial B}{\partial t} \tag{9.1}$$

That is, the revenue effects of a tax hike depend on the size of the tax base B, and on the extent of erosion of the tax base (because of migration) as taxes are changed. Here, we measure the extent of the tax-base loss with the 'delocation elasticity', ε. This elasticity depends in a non-linear fashion on all parameters of the model. Moreover, it typically varies with the size of B itself.

Consider the effect of a given tax increase, say Δt, on the mobile factor in the north starting out from a stable symmetric equilibrium as shown in Figure 9.3.[4] When the north tax is raised from zero to Δt, the result will be a mild north-to-south migration of the mobile factor. Specifically, the migration goes on until the north's real reward to the mobile factor, call it ω, minus the tax just equals the south's real reward, ω^*. The result is that the equilibrium shift from E to A in the diagram and this implies the north loses some of its mobile factor; the loss amounts to exactly $1/2 - n'$. We have drawn the curves such that the drop in B is less than the rise in t so the total tax take would rise.

---

[4] This requires trade freeness to be low enough for the symmetric outcome to be stable, that is, $\phi < \phi^B$.

Suppose now that the government was happy about the revenue raising effects of the tax hike and decided to raise taxes once more by Δt. This second tax change will yield starkly different results. As illustrated in the diagram, the new equilibrium shifts to point B and this implies a much larger loss of tax base, namely $n' - n''$. As we have drawn it, the tax-base loss exceeds the tax-rate rise so the northern government would see its revenue fall.

Now, there is nothing particularly original about the possibility that tax hikes may lower tax revenue—that is the whole point of the Laffer curve—but what is important here is that in any model with agglomeration rent, Laffer-like results are inevitable. This is essentially because the industrial base remaining in the north after the first tax increase is smaller after the first tax rise and this means weaker agglomeration forces to hold industry in place. At the same time, the opposite happens in the south, which gets a larger industrial base after the first tax increase. When the second tax increase is implemented, the tax base is intrinsically more footloose, so the tax-base erosion is larger.

In a nutshell, the very nature of agglomeration forces—defined as the tendency of economic concentrations to generate tendencies that encourage further concentration—means that the delocation elasticity changes in a very non-linear fashion with the level of policies that affect the location of industry. As a consequence, the impact of policy will inevitably be very non-linear, even if we ignore situations involving jumps and hysteresis.

The implication of such non-linearity is straightforward. Past experience can be a very poor guide to the effect of a particular policy. Moreover, unless econometricians are aware of the endemic non-linearity, estimates based on historical data may provide a very misleading indication of what future policy changes will do.

9.4 INTERACTION TERMS: TRADE FREENESS ALSO MATTERS

Policy analysts tends to be a rather focused individuals, with tax experts looking at tax policies, trade experts looking at trade policy and so on. One important general message that arises from economic geography models is that such mono-minded approaches are likely to be misleading. Stated simply, the point is that the impact of a given policy will usually depend upon the economy's level of openness to trade. For instance, when we start from a situation where industry is dispersed among many locations, lowering trade costs tends to make industry more footloose, not less as might be expected. Consequently, various tax, subsidy, infrastructure, trade and/or R&D policies will typically have larger effects when trade costs are low. Conversely, when we start from full agglomeration situations, the degree of inertia, that is, the agglomeration rents, turn out to be a bell-shaped function of the level of trade freeness, so the impact of a particular policy may seem to vary in seemingly inexplicable ways in different situations.

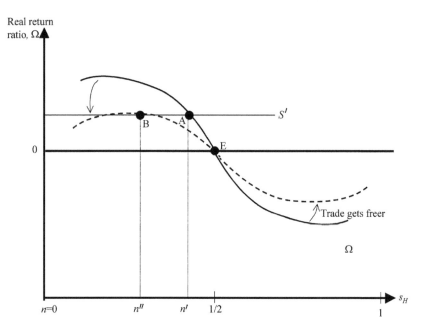

Figure 9.4   Policy making and interaction terms.

9.4.1 'De Minimus' Standards

To illustrate the importance of this point we consider the implications for 'de minimus' standards. Subsidising production in a particular location is generally frowned upon by international rules. In the World Trade Organization (WTO), for example, subsidies that distort trade patterns are explicitly forbidden, and in the European Union (EU), the European Commission spends a good deal of time fighting EU members' tendency to provide distorting 'state aids' to their industry. However, in the application of most of these rules, the authority actually charged with surveillance and enforcement typically apply 'de minimus' standards. That is, subsidies that are deemed to be small enough are ignored or even explicitly sanctioned. The EU, for instance, sets maximum subsidies that can be provided and these maximums vary according to how 'disadvantaged' the region is (this boils down it its relative income per capita).

To consider the wisdom of such rules, we consider a situation where trade costs are sufficiently high to ensure that the symmetric outcome is stable as in Figure 9.4. Suppose the de minimus subsidy is S' as shown in the diagram. If trade is not too open, the difference of real rewards to the mobile factor will be steeply downward sloping at the 1/2 point as shown with the solid bold curve. In this case, the impact of the subsidy may be minor, resulting in a shift in industry from 1/2 to n'. However, if trade integration proceeds making all regions more open to trade, the difference between the real rewards is given by a flatter curve, as shown by the dashed curve. Clearly, the same level of subsidy will now have a much larger effect. Indeed, if trade got much freer, the real-reward-gap curve would pass under the S' line implying that the subsidy, which may have been small enough to ignore when trade costs were high, now has a catastrophic impact on location.

The general point is again one of caution for policy makers and econometricians. The impact of a particular policy change may be very difficult to discern from historical data. This is especially true if empirical work ignores the fact that the policy variables should be interacted with trade openness in order to provide the full picture.

9.5 SELECTION EFFECTS

Another critical and novel property of the new economic geography models is the existence of a range of parameter values for which the models display multiple equilibria. In Figure 9.1 there are two equilibria between ϕ^B and $\phi = 1$. As we shall show, in this range, policies can have an important effect by selecting which equilibria get established.

Assume for instance that we start from a symmetric equilibrium and allow trade freeness to increase beyond the break point ϕ^B. We know that a large relocation of industry will occur. When the dust has settled, there will be complete agglomeration in one of the regions, but the model does not tell us which region will be selected. In such a situation, seemingly minor policies may have enormous effects—what we call selection effects. For instance, a direct subsidy—even if it is limited to a single firm—may ensure that one adjustment path or the other is selected. Alternatively, a policy that punishes delocation may also have large effects.

To present this argument a little bit more formally, we explicitly consider the adjustment paths that lead from the symmetric equilibrium to the core–periphery equilibria in Figure 9.5 (here assume that migrants are forward looking; see Appendix 2.B for a thorough treatment of this). The idea is that the system starts at point E where exactly half the mobile factor is in each country and the degree of openness is high enough to make this outcome unstable. The instability shows up in the fact that the real-reward-gap curve (the solid curve) is positively sloped at the midpoint. The two adjustment paths are shown as the curve with arrows showing the direction of movement. Technically speaking, we have absolutely no way of predicting which path the economy takes, but we do know that any perturbation, no matter how small, will lead us away from the symmetric situation. Selection effects of policy are essentially a form of intentional perturbation.

On the positive side, one region, say the north, might induce a single firm to migrate north using subsidies, promises of tax holidays, etc. If it succeeds, then the initial conditions are altered—specifically the system starts out to the right of the midpoint—and the only rational expectations adjustment path now leads to the core-in-the-north outcome. In other words, a potentially tiny subsidy to a single firm could swing the outcome in the north's favour. On the negative side,

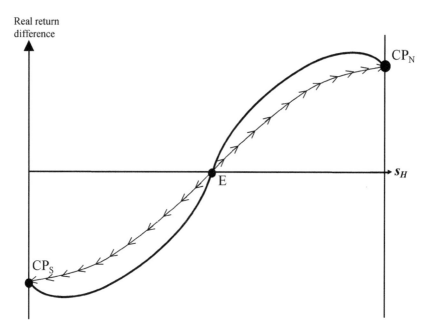

Figure 9.5   Selection effects.

one region, again say the north, might threaten departing northern firms with financial sanctions. Requiring large severance pay for fired workers, for example, or threatening to sue for environmental damage caused by abandoned production facilities. In such a situation, random perturbations that favoured the south would be negated by the threat of sanctions but random events that favoured the core-in-the-north outcome would not. Eventually, the north would win all the industry.

9.6 COORDINATION EFFECTS

As shown in Chapter 2, when migration costs are low, expectations alone can determine which equilibrium gets selected. That is, expectations rather than history matter. Agents' rational choice is to move where they believe others will move.

The situation is shown in Figure 9.6. This 'wiggle' diagram depicts the real-wage-gap curve when the level of openness is between the break and the sustain points. As Figure 9.1 showed, for such values of ϕ, there will be three locally stable equilibria (symmetry, core-in-the-north and core-in-the-south) and two unstable equilibria. In Figure 9.6, we can tell that symmetry is locally stable since the real-reward-gap is downward sloped at the midpoint. The two core–periphery outcomes are stable since the real wage gap is positive when all industry is in the north and negative when all is in the south. The unstable equilibria are

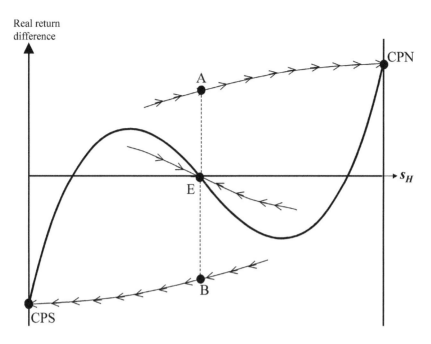

Figure 9.6 Coordination effects: self-fulfilling expectations.

where the real-reward-gap curve crosses the zero line. They are unstable since the gap is positively sloped at these crossings.

The rational expectation adjustment paths are shown with the arrows as before. As it turns out (see Chapter 2 for details), it is possible that there are three perfectly good adjustment paths at the midpoint. One path—the one touching the symmetric equilibrium—leads back to the symmetric point. Another—the one leading to CPN—takes the system away from symmetry. The third path also produces divergence but towards CPS rather than CPN.

The existence of overlapping saddle paths changes things dramatically since there is a fundamental indeterminacy. All three paths provide perfectly rational adjustment tracks. Forward-looking workers who are fully aware of how the economy works could adopt the path leading to CPN. It would, however, be equally rational for them to jump on the track that will take them to the CPS outcome.

Which track is taken cannot be decided in this model. Workers individually choose a migration strategy taking as given their beliefs about the aggregate path. Consistency requires that beliefs are rational on any equilibrium path. That is, the aggregate path that results from each worker's choice is the one that each of them believed would be the result when they made their migration decisions. Putting it more colloquially, workers choose the path that they think other workers will take. In other words, expectations matter.

Because expectations can change suddenly, even with no change in environmental parameters, the system is subject to sudden and seemingly unpredictable takeoffs and/or reversals. Moreover, the government may influence the state of the economy by coordinating the expectations of workers. For instance, regional boosterism, may work in such a setting. In fact, it may work even if the policy has no substance at all. A region that promises a subsidy can attract all activities without actually having to pay the subsidy afterwards because agglomeration externalities lock in industry.

9.7 CONCLUDING REMARKS AND RELATED LITERATURE

This chapter has discussed policy effects in a new economic geography framework from a very general perspective. The remainder of this book discusses in some detail a couple of concrete examples.

9.7.1 Related Literature

One of the earliest formal treatments of hysteresis and threshold effects is Kemp and Wan (1976). Interest in hysteretic effects was revived in 1987 by 'Hysteresis in European Unemployment' with a path-breaking paper by Blanchard and Summers (1987). After this, the hysteresis literature pursued the notion that temporary changes could lead to hysteretic effects in market structure and, thus, on prices and quantities; see the static model by Baldwin (1988), a stochastic extension in Baldwin and Krugman (1989) and the 'smooth pasting' literature by Dixit (1992).

The first exploration of selection and coordination issues is generally associated with Matsuyama (1991). The appendix 'History versus Expectations' in Krugman (1991) presents a related line of reasoning in a simpler setting. The first contributions in the specific context of economic geography models seems to be Ottaviano (2001) and Baldwin (2001).

APPENDIX 9.A. HETEROGENEOUS MOVING COSTS AMONG THE AGENTS

An important question is whether we would actually observe drastic relocations and discontinuities in a world where agents are heterogeneous. The mobile factor, especially if it is human capital, would presumably face moving costs in a more realistic setting. Moreover, if agents were heterogeneous they would face different moving costs. These costs may consist of adapting to a new region or country, learning a new language as well as purely psychological factors such as the emotional attachment to a specific region. Typically some individuals would be basically indifferent between the two locations, whereas other individuals would have a relative strong regional attachment. Here, we take as a benchmark that the moving cost is uniformly distributed over the population in each region.

9.A.1 Symmetric Case

Consider a symmetric case where industry is equally divided between two regions. Without heterogeneity, agents simply move to the north if the utility

utility difference

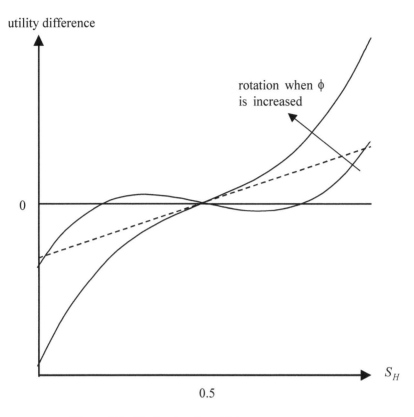

Figure 9.7   The break point with heterogeneous agents.

differential is positive. With moving costs, the mobile factor will migrate only if the utility difference is large enough to compensate for their moving costs. This implies that it is instead the dashed upward sloping line that determines migration, as illustrated in Figure 9.7.[5]

The vertical distance between the dashed curve and the zero line represents the regional bias. The positive slope represents the fact that the first ones to move away from the symmetric equilibrium are entrepreneurs that are more or less indifferent between the regions. The remaining entrepreneurs therefore get more and more reluctant to move. That is, as s_H gets larger, we dig deeper into the distribution of entrepreneurs, who's moving costs are high.

Consider now the effect of trade liberalization. This makes the utility–difference curve rotate as shown in Figure 9.7. Clearly, the basic stability properties of the model are unchanged by the introduction of heterogeneity. Once trade freeness is large enough, the symmetric equilibrium breaks down and we get catastrophic agglomeration. The only difference is that the break point occurs for a higher ϕ.

---

[5] A similar analysis can be found in Ludema and Wooton (2000).

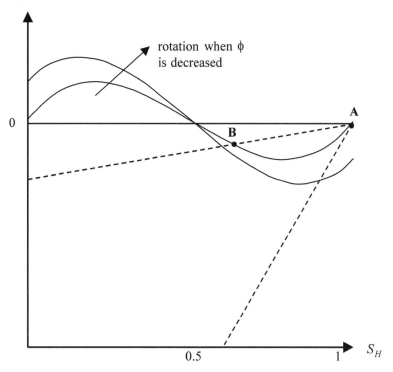

Figure 9.8   The sustain point with heterogeneous agents.

This result could, of course, be overturned by the introduction of more elaborate distributions of regional attachment. If regional attachment were not uniformly distributed over the population, the dashed curve would bend, and if it had enough curvature, we would not get a locational catastrophe. The conclusion is, thus, that heterogeneity does not per se contradict catastrophic agglomeration, but it is possible to conceive heterogeneity that does.

9.A.2 Full Agglomeration Case

Consider a case with complete agglomeration in the north ($s_H = 1$), and where the all agents in this region have varying moving costs. Again take as a base case that the regional attachment is uniformly distributed over the population. The situation is displayed in Figure 9.8. Two different distributions of migration costs are considered. The steep dashed line represents the required utility differential for migration with a wide dispersion of moving costs and the line with a less steep slope, a more narrow distribution of moving costs. The wider distribution simply implies that moving costs increase more rapidly as migration digs into the distribution of agents.

Consider now the effect of lower trade freeness. This makes the utility difference curve rotate clockwise, and the system reaches the sustain point when the tip of the curve is in point A. Two scenarios are possible as ϕ falls even more and passes the sustain point. In the first scenario, with the less sloped dashed line, moving costs are low (have a narrow distribution). In this case, the equilibrium jumps from point A to B as seen from the figure. If moving costs are high, on the contrary, there will be a gradual adjustment along the steep dashed line as ϕ is decreased.

The introduction of heterogeneity, therefore, does not rule out the possibility that locational jumps may occur when an agglomeration collapses, but it lowers the likelihood of it happening.

It may also be noted that the occurrence of a jump hinges on the non-monotonicity of the utility difference curve. This pattern is present in the CP and FE models, whereas the FC model produces a linear utility difference curve, and consequently no jump in the full agglomeration case.

9.A.3 Summary

To summarize, the introduction of heterogeneity in the mobile factor does not, in general, rule out jumps or catastrophic changes in the locational pattern. However, it certainly dampens the tendency for discontinuities, and if discontinuity exists, it decreases the size of the jump.

REFERENCES

Baldwin, Richard E. 1988. Hysteresis in import prices: the beachhead effect. *Amercian Economic Review* 78(4): 773–785.

_____. 2001. The core-periphery model with forward-looking expectations. *Regional Science and Urban Economics* 31: 21–49.

Baldwin, Richard E. and Paul Krugman. 1989. Persistent trade effects of large exchange rate shocks. *Quarterly Journal of Economics* 104(4): 635–654.

Blanchard, O.J. and L.H. Summers. 1987. Hysteresis in unemployment. *European Economic Review* 31: 288–295.

Dixit, A. 1992. Investment and hysteresis. *Journal of Economic Perspectives* 6(1): 107–132.

Ekholm, K. and R. Forslid. 2001. Trade and location with horizontal and vertical multi-region firms. *Scandinavian Journal of Economics* 103(1): 101–118.

Kemp, M.C. and H.Y. Wan. 1976. An elementary proposition concerning the formation of customs unions. *Journal of International Economics* 6(1): 95–97.

Krugman, P. 1991. *Geography and Trade.* Cambridge, MA: MIT Press.

Ludema, R. D. and I. Wooton. 2000. Economic geography and the fiscal effectsof regional integration. *Journal of International Economics* 52: 331–357.

Matsuyama, Kiminora. 1991. Increasing returns, industrialization and indeterminacy of equilibrium. *Quarterly Journal of Economics* 106: 617–650.

Ottaviano, G. I. P. 2001. Monopolistic competition, trade and endogenous spatial fluctuations. *Regional Science and Urban Economics* 31: 51–77.

CHAPTER 10

A Typology of Welfare Effects: Regional Perspective

10.1 INTRODUCTION

The nomenclature of policy effects is rich and confusing. Terms of trade effects, trade creation and diversion, dynamic effects, scale effects, growth effects are but a few of the terms applied by various authors to various channels. To provide a unified terminology for our policy analysis, this chapter presents a framework for organizing our thinking about how policy changes can affect welfare. We do not specify the connections between particular policies and the changes in the various endogenous variables; we simply identify and label the various channels through which policy changes may affect welfare. James Meade pioneered the basic approach employed here. The current application is an extension of Dixit and Norman (1980, Chapter 6) and Helpman and Krugman (1989, Chapter 2.7).

10.1.1 Organization of the Chapter

The chapter starts with a framework that allows general preferences, before specializing the organizing framework to Dixit–Stiglitz preferences in Section 10.3. Both of these sections assume factor supplies are fixed to allow us to focus on the static effects. The next two sections expand the framework to allow the accumulation of factors (typically capital). Thus, Section 10.4 allows one-off changes in capital stocks in response to policy changes, so-called medium-run growth effects, while the Section 10.5 allows for one-off changes in the rate of capital accumulation, thus encompassing the possibility of long-run growth effects.

10.2 ORGANIZING FRAMEWORK

We start by deriving an organizing framework for general preferences. We focus on the welfare of the north and work with a utilitarian social welfare function that counts the utility of all residents located within the northern region. Since we work with small changes around an equilibrium, we implicitly assume that the economy starts at a stable, interior equilibrium.

10.2.1 Assumptions

We assume two regions (north and south), two sectors (A and M), and two factors (K and L). The A sector is Walrasian while the M sector is monopolistically competitive and produces n varieties of a differentiated product. Each region's supply of L is fixed and cannot cross regional borders, but the other factor, K, may be inter-regionally mobile or not, depending upon the model (we consider both cases below). At this point, we work with general preferences given by inter-temporally separable preferences:

$$\int_{t=0}^{\infty} e^{-\rho t} V[p, n, E] dt \tag{10.1}$$

where ρ is the constant discount rate, p and n are the vectors of consumer prices and the number of varieties in each sector, and E is total consumption expenditure.

Expenditure is home income less home savings, where income is the sum of home factor income, net revenue from tariffs and other import barriers (assumed to be returned lump-sum to consumers) and pure profits, that is,

$$E = wL + rK + Tm + \Pi - S \tag{10.2}$$

where w and r, and L and K are the prices and stocks of home's labour and capital, m is the vector of sectoral trade (imports enter with a positive sign, exports with a negative sign), Π is pure profit, and S is savings. Also, $T \equiv p - p^*$, where p^* is the border price, that is, the price that the country actually pays for imports and the price it actually gets paid for exports. Thus, p^* need not equal the world price; for example, when there are frictional trade barriers, such as transport costs, the price the north pays for its imports is the price received by the exporter plus these costs.

Pure profits are related to the vector of local prices, p, the vector of sectoral outputs, Q, and the vector of average cost functions, $a[w, r, x]$, according to

$$\Pi = (p - a)Q, \quad a_i[w, r, x_i] \equiv \frac{c_i[w, r, x_i]}{x_i}, \quad Q_i \equiv n_i x_i \tag{10.3}$$

where Q_i is a typical element of the sectoral output vector, Q, a_i is a typical element in the vector of sectoral average costs, a, defined as the total cost of a typical firm (all domestic firms within a sector are assumed to be identical), $c_i[w,r,x_i]$, divided by typical firm output, x_i. As usual, total cost is a function of w, r and firm output x. Notice that pure profits are decomposed here. That is, Π is defined as if all goods in a particular sector were sold at the domestic (i.e. local) price, p. For perfect competition sectors and for sectors marked by Dixit–Stiglitz monopolistic competition, this does not matter since in both cases, firms charge the same producer price in all markets (perfectly competitive firms never price discriminate across markets, and non-discrimination, that is, mill pricing, is optimal under Dixit–Stiglitz competition). However, for oligopolistic sectors (which is a possibility with the 'linear model' of Chapter 5), producer prices can vary across markets. For such sectors, the profitability of price discrimination shows up in the term $(p - p^*)m$ in (10.2).[1]

---

[1] For example, suppose markets are segmented and there are costs to exporting, so a profit-maximizing oligopolist would typically charge a lower producer price for exports. Then, the total profit of the firm would be $p^a q^a$ plus $p^b q^b$ minus $a[w, r, q^a + q^b](q^a + q^b)$, where a indicates the producer price and quantity for local sales and b indicates the producer price and quantity for exports, but in the notation of (10.3), the profit is $p^a(q^a + q^b) - a[w, r, q^a + q^b](q^a + q^b) + (p^b - p^a)q^b$ with the last term showing up in the trade rents term.

10.2.2 Calculations

Totally differentiating V and converting utils into euros (by dividing through by the scalar V_E) yields

$$\frac{dV}{V_E} = \left(\frac{V_p}{V_E}\right)dp + \frac{V_n}{V_E}dn + dE = -Cdp + \left(\frac{V_n}{V_E}\right)dn + dE \qquad (10.4)$$

where V_p and V_n are vectors of partial derivatives; the second expression follows from the first using Roy's identity. To calculate dE, we totally differentiate the definition of E, (10.2), and use $T = p - p^*$ to get

$$dE = Ldw + Kdr + rdK + (p - p^*)dm + mdp - mdp^*$$

$$+(p - a)dQ + Q(dp - da) - dS \qquad (10.5)$$

where

$$Qda = \sum_i Q_i \frac{\partial c_i}{\partial w}\frac{dw}{x_i} + Q_i \frac{\partial c_i}{\partial r}\frac{dr}{x_i} + Q_i \frac{\partial a_i}{\partial x_i}dx_i = Ldw + Kdr + \sum_i Q_i \frac{\partial a_i}{\partial x_i}dx_i$$

$$(10.6)$$

and the summation is over all sectors i; the second expression follows from the first by Shephard's lemma.

Plugging (10.6) and (10.5) into (10.4) and using $-C \equiv -m - Q$, the expression for home welfare changes simplifies to

$$\frac{dV}{V_E} = (p - p^*)dm - mdp^*$$

$$+(p - a)dQ + Q(-a_x)dx + \left(\frac{V_n}{V_E}\right)dn$$

$$+rdK - dS \qquad (10.7)$$

where we employ the notation $\partial a/\partial x = a_x$.

This expression (10.7) is our general organizing framework.

10.2.3 Discussion

The three rows of the (10.7) categorize welfare effects into three types.

WALRASIAN EFFECTS: TRADE PRICE AND VOLUME EFFECTS

The first row shows effects that occur even when one ignores scale economies and imperfect competition. As in the public finance literature, welfare effects in a Walrasian world stem from quantity changes times initial price wedges and price changes times net trades. We refer to the first as the trade-volume effect and the second as the trade-price effect (or 'terms-of-trade' effect).

The second row shows the effects that appear when we assume the economy is marked by scale economies and imperfect competition (ICIR effects for short). The first effect is the production-rent effect. That is, if there are pure profits in a sector, increasing production in that sector tends to improve northern welfare. The second term is the scale effect. That is, since $-a_x$ is positive under scale economies—average cost falls as output increases—increased scale tends to improve northern welfare.

The third term includes two distinct effects, the well-known variety effect (i.e. an increase in the total number of varieties available tends to improve domestic welfare) and a location effect. The 'location effect' captures the welfare implications of changes in the production location of a particular variety. For example, when trade is costly, northern welfare is higher when more varieties are produced domestically instead of abroad since this allows avoidance of the trade cost. Study of this location effect is best left to the next section where concrete analysis is made possible by adoption of Dixit–Stiglitz preferences.

ACCUMULATION AND MIGRATION EFFECTS

The third row constitutes the accumulation and migration effects. In most of the Part I models, the world human or physical capital stock is fixed, so savings are zero by definition. In such cases, rdK is the impact of migration on northern expenditure. In the constructed capital, and local and global spillover models, north's capital stock depends upon savings. In such cases, the third line captures the welfare implications of induced capital formation and the induced savings that are required. In particular, induced capital formation has two counteracting welfare effects. A higher capital stock raises income and thereby expenditure. This is reflected in the first term and it is the positive aspect of induced capital formation. However, induced capital formation means consumption must be foregone. This negative influence on the current flow of utility is captured by the second, row-three term. Since the accumulation of human, physical and knowledge growth is the source of all per capita output growth, many authors refer to accumulation effects as growth effects, or dynamic effects. Interested readers can easily extend this framework to capture additional effects.

10.3 DIXIT–STIGLITZ PREFERENCES

In all but one of the Part I chapters, we assume Dixit–Stiglitz monopolistic competition and iceberg trade costs. These assumptions simplify the analysis greatly; this section exploits the resulting simplicity.

Imposing symmetry on *M* varieties made in the same nation and assuming only two nations, the Dixit–Stiglitz indirect utility function is

$$V = \frac{E}{P}, \quad P \equiv (n^w)^{\mu/(1-\sigma)} \Delta^{\mu/(1-\sigma)} p_A^{1-\mu}, \quad \Delta \equiv s_n p^{1-\sigma} + (1 - s_n) p^{*1-\sigma} \quad (10.8)$$

where p and p^* are the consumer prices of a typical domestic and imported differentiated variety (respectively), s_n is the share of world varieties produced in the north (i.e. $s_n \equiv n/n^w$ where n is the number of varieties produced in the north), E is total northern consumption expenditure, μ is the constant fraction on expenditure spent on M goods, and n^w is the total mass (number) of varieties available. As usual σ is the constant elasticity of substitution between any pair of the differentiated varieties. It is the perfect price index.

In the one-period economy, expenditure is income, that is, the sum of home factor income and pure profits, plus revenue from tariffs, taxes, etc., less any subsidy or transfer payments. Since the models allow only frictional trade barriers, tariff revenue need not be considered. Moreover, we always assume that the government runs a balanced budget so taxes, subsidies and transfers sum to zero. Thus,

$$E = wL + rK + \Pi, \quad \Pi = (p - a[w, r, x]) s_n n^w x + (p_A - wa_A) A \quad (10.9)$$

where x is the equilibrium firm size and we have used the assumption that the A sector employs only L. Recall that we choose units of K such that $n^w = 1$, so $n = s_n$, and we take A as numeraire, so $p_A = 1$.

10.3.1 Calculations

Totally differentiating (10.8) and dividing by $V_E = 1/P$ to convert utils into real euros yields

$$\frac{dV}{V_E} = dE - E \frac{dP}{P} \quad (10.10)$$

Totally differentiating the definition of E in (10.9)—using $n = s_n n^w$—yields

$$dE = \left[Ldw + Kdr - (nx)da - Aa_A dw \right] + \left[(nx)dp + Adp_A + (r - \Gamma)dK \right]$$

$$+ \left[(p - a)d(nx) + (p_A - wa_A)dA \right] \quad (10.11)$$

$$da = a_w dw + a_r dr + a_x dx$$

where Γ is a model-specific term that is discussed below.

Note that after cancelling, the terms in the first square brackets equals zero since any rise in factor payments is cancelled by a corresponding drop in Π, and firm size is invariant in the Dixit–Stiglitz approach (i.e. $dx = 0$). The terms in the third square brackets are also zero since all equilibria considered are marked by average cost pricing in both sectors. Thus, dE equals the terms in the second square brackets.

Evaluating the second term in (10.10), using the definition of the price index in (10.8), we have

$$E\frac{dP}{P} = \frac{(1-\mu)E}{p_A}dp_A + \mu E\left(s_n\frac{p^{-\sigma}}{\Delta}dp + s_n^*\frac{p^{*-\sigma}}{\Delta}dp^*\right)$$

$$+ \frac{\mu E}{1-\sigma}\left(\frac{p^{1-\sigma}-p^{*1-\sigma}}{\Delta}\right)ds_n \qquad (10.12)$$

where we have used $dn^w = 0$ to simplify, and our normalization to set $s_n^* = 1 - s_n$. Using the demand functions, the first two terms become $C_A dp_A$, and $ncdp + n^*c^*dp^*$ (c and c^* are home consumption of a typical local and a typical imported variety, respectively). The final term becomes $\mu E(s - s^*)/(1 - \sigma)$ times ds_n, where s and s^* are, respectively, the expenditure shares on a typical local M variety and a typical imported M variety; note that $(s - s^*)$ exceeds zero with positive trade costs.[2]

Plugging (10.12) and (10.11) into (10.10), the welfare effects are

$$\frac{dV}{V_E} = -mdp^B + \frac{\mu}{\sigma-1}(s-s^*)ds_n + (r-\Gamma)dK \qquad (10.13)$$

where m is the trade vector, that is, domestic consumption minus domestic production (sector by sector) and dp^B is the change in the vector of border prices, that is, dp_A, dp and dp^*). Observe that, in a symmetric equilibrium, the gap between the expenditure shares on a typical local M variety and a typical imported M variety, namely, $s - s^*$, is greater than zero in the presence of positive trade costs. This expression is our organizing framework for the restricted set of assumptions that characterize most economic geography models.

10.3.2 Discussion

Expression (10.13) shows that the CP, FE and FC models contain at most three types of welfare effects.

BORDER-PRICE EFFECT

The first term in (10.13) shows the traditional trade-price effect (or terms-of-trade effect); anything that lowers the price of imports, or raises the price of exports, will improve north's welfare. Notice that the other classic effect, the trade-volume effect, is not present since we are considering frictional barriers (i.e. the interior and border prices are identical so small changes in the volume of trade has no net welfare impact).

LOCATION EFFECT

The second term in (10.13) might be called the 'location effect', or the cost-of-living effect. What it says is that holding the number of varieties constant (so that

[2] The local demand function for a typical local variety is $p^{-\sigma}/(np^{1-\sigma} + n^*p^{*1-\sigma})$ times μE. Multiplying by p, we have that $s = pc/E$ equals $\mu p^{1-\sigma}/(np^{1-\sigma} + n^*p^{*1-\sigma})$.

the classic variety effect is absent), shifting production of one variety from the south to the north improves the north's welfare. The size of the effect increases with trade costs. Specifically, the magnitude of the effect is proportional to the difference between the share of expenditure that falls on a typical north-made variety and the share falling on a typical south-made variety.

MIGRATION EFFECT

The third term in (10.13) captures the welfare impact of migration and is, thus, model-specific. In the CP and FE models, an inflow of the mobile factor K, raises real income and so is counted as a benefit. In other words, $\Gamma = 0$ in the CP and FE model. The size of the migration effect depends upon capital's reward, r.

We note here that our strict utilitarian approach—that is, adding up the indirect utilities of all northern residents—is not the only sensible approach. Its merit is the fact that it corresponds to an observable quantity—the north's real income. However, one might, for instance, focus solely on the welfare of the initially resident. If the north had a direct democracy, or the northern government always acted in the interest of northern voters, the initial residents' welfare would be determinant. Alternatively, one might focus on average utility, but then our normalization would take on an unwanted importance. In the symmetric equilibrium, our normalizations imply that r and the wage of the immobile factor, w, are unity. Thus, migration, per se, has a neutral effect on our utility, but we could as well have chosen normalizations that implied a positive or negative effect on average utility.

In the FC model, however, capital income is repatriated so $\Gamma = r^*$, where r^* is what the north's capital earns if it migrates to the south. Note, however, that since we are starting from a stable interior equilibrium, and $r = r^*$ in the FC model in such instances, the third term in (10.13) is zero.

10.4 ALLOWING FOR VARIABLE FACTOR SUPPLIES

The models studied above, namely the CP, FC and FE models, all take the supply of K as fixed. Since capital accumulation is the essence of growth and growth is an important consideration in regional policy evaluation, we now expand our organizing framework to allow for constructed capital. We first work with the CC model, where the long-run capital stock reaches a steady-state level.

10.4.1 New Considerations

The first change is to our definition of expenditure. Since capital can be constructed, expenditure on consumption goods is income less spending on capital construction. Thus,

$$E = wL + rK + \Pi - wL_I \tag{10.14}$$

where, following the CC model, we have assumed that the capital-construction sector uses only the immobile factor, L.

The second change is to realize that maintaining K requires real resources, so the reward to K must be adjusted. In the CC model, the equilibrium reward to capital (what we called π in Chapter 6) is such that $r = (\rho + \delta)F$. Moreover, increasing K requires real resources, so dK is not 'for free'. Using the production function of the capital construction sector, that is, the I sector, we see that it takes F units of L to make a new unit of K and δF units of L to maintain one in steady state, so

$$L_I = F(\delta K + \dot{K}) \quad \Rightarrow \quad dL_I = \delta F dK + F d\dot{K} \tag{1015}$$

The third change involves the impact that dK has on income when we recognize discounting and depreciation. Presuming that future real income is discounted at the rate ρ, and using our normalization that $w = 1$, (10.15) and $r = (\rho + \delta)F$, the present value of income can be written as

$$\int_{t=0}^{\infty} e^{-\rho t}(L + \rho F K)dt - F d\dot{K} = \frac{w}{\rho}L + FK - Fd\dot{K} \tag{10.16}$$

where the term, $Fd\dot{K}$ appears outside the integral since it is a one-off cost that is incurred at time zero.

Finally, we note that we start off in a long-run equilibrium, that is, E and P are time-invariant. Thus, the present value of our indirect utility measure is

$$\int_{t=0}^{\infty} e^{-\rho t} \frac{E}{P} dt = \frac{1}{P}\left(\frac{1}{\rho}L + FK - Fd\dot{K}\right) \tag{10.17}$$

Using (10.17) instead of (10.8), we proceed through the same chain of calculation, but now we must take account of the connection between dK and the cost of its construction given by (10.15). The result is

$$\frac{dV}{V_E} = -mdp^B + \frac{\mu}{\sigma - 1}(s - s^*)ds_n + (F - F)dK \tag{10.18}$$

Plainly, the third term is zero, so induced capital formation adds nothing to utility. This result is quite intuitive. In the CC model, the capital stock rises up to the point where the value of an extra unit of K equals its cost. But then any change that induces the economy to build a marginal unit of capital will have no welfare effect, because the value of the extra unit will be exactly offset by the cost of constructing it (see Baldwin 1992 for details).

10.5 ALLOWING FOR ENDOGENOUS GROWTH

Next, we expand the framework to allow for endogenous growth. This has two implications for our calculations. First, as in the LS model, $F = 1/AK^w$, with $A = 1$ if we work with the GS model (A here is unrelated to the 'A' in the previous sections); thus, $L_I = s_K(\delta + g)/A$. Second, the discounting has to take account of the fact that the price index falls at a rate $(gs_K + g^*s_K^*)\mu/(\sigma - 1)$, where g and g^* are the rates of growth of K and K^*, respectively, and in the initial equilibrium, $g = g^*$. Finally, $r = (\delta + \rho + g)F$. With these changes, the present value of our indirect utility measure is

$$\int_{t=0}^{\infty} e^{-(\rho-ag)t} \frac{E}{P} dt = \frac{1}{P} \left(\frac{1}{\rho - a(s_K g + s_K^* g^*)} \left(L - \frac{s_K}{A} g\right) + FK - Fd\dot{K}\right)$$

(10.19)

Using this and following the usual chain of calculations, we get

$$\frac{dV}{V_E} = -mdp^B + \frac{\mu}{\sigma - 1}(s - s^*)ds_n + (F - F)dK + \frac{1}{\rho - ag}\left(\frac{aL}{\rho - ag} - \frac{1}{A}\right)dg$$

(10.20)

The new term here is the fourth one. The coefficient on dg is positive, so this could be called the growth effect.

This implies that faster growth is welfare improving. The intuition for this is straightforward. Private innovators ignore two externalities. First, being atomistic, they ignore the impact of their flow of innovations on the time path of the price index. Second, they ignore the learning externality in the innovation sector. For both of these reasons, the free market results in a growth rate that is socially sub-optimal.

REFERENCES

Baldwin, R. 1992. Measurable dynamic gains from trade. *Journal of Political Economy* 100(1): 162–174.

Dixit, A. and V. Norman. 1980. *Theory of International Trade*. London: Cambridge University Press.

Helpman, E. and P. Krugman. 1989. *Trade policy and Market Structure*. Cambridge, MA: MIT Press.

CHAPTER 11

Efficiency, Equity and Optimal Agglomeration

11.1 INTRODUCTION

The models reviewed in the previous chapters have been used to study the logic of agglomeration and regional development in the presence of monopolistic competition, increasing returns and trade costs. In this chapter, we turn to the crucial welfare questions: Is agglomeration desirable? Should policy makers foster or control it?

These and related questions can be addressed from two different points of view. From an *equity* point of view one may ask: Who are the gainers and the losers from agglomeration? Which regions are advantaged and which disadvantaged? In particular, what happens to those that are left behind in disadvantaged regions? From an *efficiency* point of view one may wonder: Can the gainers compensate the losers? Does the free working of market forces deliver the optimal degree of agglomeration? If not, is there too much or too little agglomeration for the economy as a whole? The aim of the present chapter is to answer such questions.

The distinction between equity and efficiency is crucial. If we picture the welfare of the economy as a pie, equity is about the relative size of the slices that go to different interest groups, irrespective of the overall size of the pie. Efficiency, in contrast, is about the overall size of the pie. This distinction has been under appreciated in the new economic geography, with some exceptions that include Ottaviano et al. (2002a), Ottaviano and Thisse (2002b), Ottaviano (2001) and Robert-Nicoud (2002). The reasoning in this chapter is based on Ottaviano (2001), although that paper works with the linear model while the analysis here focuses on the Dixit–Stiglitz approach adopted by, for example, the footloose capital (FC) and the footloose entrepreneur (FE) models of Chapters 3 and 4.[1]

11.1.1 Organization of the Chapter

The discussion is organized around the two models presented in Chapters 3 and 4, the FC and FE models. The former is used to point out the welfare implications of firms' location that work through the cost of living (price indices) in the two

[1] Thus, while in Ottaviano (2001) the marginal utility of the numeraire good is the same across individuals irrespective of their incomes (due to the quasi-linear demand structure), in the present context it varies, thus creating an inherent bias towards equity-driven redistribution.

regions. The latter is used to stress the welfare implications that work through factor rewards. Since the latter is richer than the former, for expositional purposes it will prove useful to start with the former. In particular, Section 11.2 studies equity and efficiency in the FC model. Section 11.3 addresses the same issues in the FE model. Section 11.4 concludes.

11.2 EQUITY AND EFFICIENCY IN THE FOOTLOOSE CAPITAL MODEL

We start with the most tractable economic geography model, the footloose capital model (FC model for short). Since the FC model is described in Chapter 3, we adopt here a streamlined presentation that focuses on what is relevant for the present discussion.

11.2.1 Three Ways to Slice Equity

In the Part I models, there are three natural ways of slicing the equity question. At the finest level, we note that each factor located in each region may have distinct and frequently conflicting welfare concerns, so in the first slice we consider four groups of individuals: the north-based and south-based owners of the immobile factor, and the north-based and south-based owners of the mobile factor. Of course, assuming that factor ownership is so highly segmented is not the only possible assumption—for instance, in the FC model we could assume that immobile workers own some or even all of the mobile capital—but analytic issues are clearest when we identify individuals with specific factors.

The second slice views all factors within a region as a group, so the question is: 'How does industrial delocation affect living standards of each region?' This is the classic approach in international trade, but the distinction is somewhat blurred by the question: 'Who is us?' that unavoidably arises when factors are mobile. To be concrete, we always consider a region's current residents as the relevant group, but we spotlight the points where this convention is important.

The third slice is to view inter-regional coalitions of factor owners as the relevant groups. Thus, northern and southern mobile-factor owners are one interest group while the northern and southern immobile-factor owners are a second group.

11.2.2 Brief Description of the FC Model

As usual, we work with two regions, north and south; when we consider asymmetric-sized regions, we adopt the convention that the south is smaller. Each region has two factors of production, physical capital, K, and unskilled workers, L. Workers are immobile across regions, so the share of the world's endowment of workers employed in the north identically equals the north's endowment of workers, and the same holds for the south. By contrast, capital is mobile albeit with an important proviso; while capital is inter-regionally mobile, capital owners are not. This assumption—which if critical to the model's tractability—forces us to adopt different symbols for the share capital *employed* in the north and share of capital *owned* by northern residents; we write the north's capital employment share as s_n (since this is also the share of firms located in the north), and north's capital endowment share as s_K.

The model assumes that there are only two sectors in each region, manufacturing, M, and agriculture, A. The A sector is Walrasian and assumed to use workers as its only input. The M sector is subject to Dixit–Stiglitz competition and increasing returns; specifically producing a variety of the manufactured good requires one unit of capital, regardless of the output level and a_M units of L per unit output made. Trade costs are crucial in the model, but for simplicity we assume that these take the 'iceberg' form and are relevant only to trade in manufactures. Trade in A is costless.

On the demand side, consumers have CES sub-utility over M varieties nested in a Cobb–Douglas upper-tier function that also includes consumption of A. The corresponding indirect utility function is

$$V = \ln\left(\frac{E}{P}\right), \quad P \equiv p_A^{1-\mu}\left(\int_{i=0}^{n^w} p_i^{1-\sigma}di\right)^{-a}, \quad a \equiv \frac{\mu}{\sigma-1}; \quad 0 < \mu < 1 < \sigma$$

(11.1)

where E is northern expenditure, P is the northern perfect price index, and n^w is the total mass (or, loosely speaking, the number) of varieties. The south's indirect utility function is given by an isomorphic expression.

NORMALIZATIONS AND THE MARKET EQUILIBRIUM

As usual, careful normalization simplifies our notation and manipulation of expressions. Since the A sector is perfectly competitive and supplies its homogeneous good under constant returns, firms charge a price equal to marginal cost, namely $p_A = a_A w_L$ where w_L is the reward to L and a_A is the unit input requirement. Since trade in A is costless, international trade equalizes international prices of A, and this, in turn, equalizes workers' wages internationally—provided only that both nations produce some of the A good. It turns out that a sufficient condition for non-specification is that $\mu < 1/2$; we adopt this parameter restriction throughout the section.[2] In the M sector, we measure M in units such that a_M equals $(1 - (1/\sigma))$ and this means that equilibrium prices in the industrial sector become $p = w_L = 1$ for domestically sold units and $p^* = \tau w_L = \tau$ for units sold abroad, where $\tau > 1$ is one plus the per-unit transport cost.

The normalization $K^w = 1$ implies that the total measure of all varieties also equals unity, viz. $n + n^* = n^w = 1$, where the n's represent, respectively, the varieties made in the north, in the south and worldwide. This allows us to write the northern and southern perfect price indices, that is, the indices that correspond to the indirect utility functions, as

$$P = \Delta^{-a}, \quad P^* = (\Delta^*)^{-a}; \quad \Delta \equiv s_n + \phi s_n^*, \quad \Delta^* \equiv \phi s_n + s_n^* \quad (11.2)$$

[2] The exact condition is $\mu < \sigma/(2\sigma - 1)$; $\mu < 1/2$ clearly meets this.

where s_n and s_n^* are the share of industrial varieties produced in the north and in the south, respectively (given our normalization, $n \equiv s_n$ and $n^* \equiv s_n^*$, so $s_n + s_n^* = 1$), $\phi \equiv \tau^{1-\sigma}$ measures the freeness of trade ($\phi = 0$ represents no trade and $\phi = 1$ represents free trade), and we have used the fact that $p_A = 1$. Observe that s_n is also the share of world capital employed in the north, since each industrial variety requires one unit of capital.

Capital flows freely across regions in search of the highest nominal reward. Thus, in equilibrium, either $\pi = \pi^*$, or all capital is concentrated in one region. In either case, the equilibrium reward to capital everywhere equals the world average, namely bE^w/K^w, where $b = \mu/\sigma$ (see Chapter 3 for details). This also means that world expenditure, which equals world income, is $E^w = L^w + bE^w = L^w/(1-b)$. Observe that in any market equilibrium, factor rewards (i.e. w_L and π) are equalized across regions. Moreover, the levels of these rewards are invariant to the location of production and the level of trade costs. Specifically workers' wage is fixed at unity and capital's reward varies inversely with the world capital-labour ratio (see Chapter 3 for details):

$$w_L = 1, \quad \pi = \beta; \quad \beta \equiv \frac{bL^w}{(1-b)K^w}, \quad b \equiv \frac{\mu}{\sigma} \qquad (11.3)$$

This, of course, is one of the reasons why the FC model is so easy to manipulate analytically.

The locational equilibrium, that is, the spatial division of capital, is found by solving the location condition, $\pi = \pi^*$, for the equilibrium spatial allocation of capital employment, s_n. When capital is not fully agglomerated in one region, the equilibrium share of world capital *employed* in the north is

$$s_n \equiv \frac{1}{2} + \frac{s_E - 1/2}{(1-\phi)/(1+\phi)}, \quad s_E - \frac{1}{2} = (1-b)\left(s_L - \frac{1}{2}\right) + b\left(s_K - \frac{1}{2}\right)$$

$$(11.4)$$

where s_n is the share of world capital employed in the north, while s_K is the north's ownership share of the world capital stock. Observe that the perfectly symmetric outcome, namely, $s_L = s_K = s_E = s_n = 1/2$, is an equilibrium, that relative market size, that is, s_E, is parametrically fixed in the FC model (since s_L and s_K reflected fixed endowments), and that $ds_n/ds_E > 1$, that is, the home-market effect is in operation here, so the bigger country hosts a more than proportionate share of industry. When s_E and ϕ are such that the s_n given by the expression in (11.4) is greater than unity, or less than zero, then we have a corner solution and s_n equals unity or zero in the obvious way.[3]

11.2.3 Pareto Welfare Analysis

We want to assess: (i) the welfare of each group of individuals at the market equilibrium; (ii) which groups of individuals can be made better off by a *fiat*

---

[3] An interior equilibrium occurs when, $s_E \in [\phi/(1+\phi), 1/(1+\phi)]$ while $s_n = 0$ for $s_E < \phi/(1+\phi)$ and $s_n = 1$ for $s_E > 1/(1+\phi)$.

relocation of M firms when no inter-group transfers are allowed for ('Pareto welfare analysis'). In the next section, we discuss whether the economy as a whole can be made better off by a *fiat* relocation of M firms when transfers are available ('global welfare analysis').

INDIVIDUAL WELFARE INDICATORS: FOUR GROUPS

At the finest level of disaggregation, there are four interest groups in this econ-omy—K owners in the north and the south, and L owners in the north and south. Their individual welfare indicators are

$$V_K = \ln\left(\frac{\beta}{\Delta^{-a}}\right), \quad V_K^* = \ln\left(\frac{\beta}{(\Delta^*)^{-a}}\right), \quad V_L = \ln\left(\frac{1}{\Delta^{-a}}\right), \quad V_L^* = \ln\left(\frac{1}{(\Delta^*)^{-a}}\right)$$

(11.5)

where we have assumed that each worker owns one unit of labour and each capital owner owns one unit of labour, and the subscript on the V's indi-cates which factor the individual owns and the asterisk, or its absence, indicates individual's region of residence (as always, the asterisk indicates the south).

Welfare analysis is particularly simple in the FC model. The 'nominal' incomes (i.e. incomes measured in terms of the numeraire) of all four groups are independent of the spatial allocation of industry, s_n, and trade costs, so all welfare effects stem from what we called the 'location effect' or the cost-of-living effect in Chapter 10, that is, changes in P and P^* due to relocation of firms. As we have seen many times, trade costs imply that the cost-of-living is lowest in the region with the most industrial firms. Consequently, any change in the location of firms that reduces P—and thus raises real incomes in the north—will increase P^*—and thus lower real incomes in the south. The opposite is also true, so there is an inherent conflict between regional interests when it comes to industrial loca-tion. Accordingly, northerners are better off than southerners whenever $s_n > 1/2$. To summarize, we write

> **Result 11.1 (regional conflict of interests).** *In the FC model, any spatial reallocation of the mobile factor and thus industry, benefits one region and penalizes the other.*

The fact that the interests of northern capital and labour owners both depend solely on P, and a similar statement holds for southern factor owners implies a further result.

> **Result 11.2 (no conflict of interest between same-region factors).** *Within the same region there is no conflict of interests between factor owners in the FC model when it comes to the spatial allocation of industry.*

This implies that for the FC model only, one of our three ways of slicing the equity question is interesting, namely the regional perspective.

Given Results 11.1 and 11.2, we can conclude the following.

Result 11.3 (no Pareto improvement is available). *The laissez-faire outcome in the FC model is Pareto efficient in the sense that no change in the spatial allocation of industry can produce a gain in the welfare of one group without harming some other group.*

To study the location effect in more detail, consider the impact of a fiat shift in s_n on two people, a northern worker and a southern worker. The sum of their welfare indicators is $\ln(1/P) + \ln(1/P^*)$, so differentiating, we get

$$-2a\frac{(1 - \phi)^2(s_n - 1/2)}{\Delta\Delta^*} \tag{11.6}$$

This shows that the inter-regional welfare conflict worsens as the spatial allocation of firms moves away from the symmetric outcome. That is, when half of industry is in each region, a small fiat reallocation of industry from the south to the north produces a gain in the north and a loss in the south, but the winners win to the same extent that the losers lose. By contrast, when s_n deviates from 1/2 to begin with, the losers lose more than the winners win. To summarize, we write the following.

Result 11.4 (concavity of the location effect). *The win-lose trade-off mentioned in Result 11.1 is concave in the sense that when the distribution of industry starts out very uneven, winners win more than the losers lose when the distribution is made less uneven.*

This result turns out to be useful in our global welfare analysis.

11.2.4 Global Welfare Analysis

No Pareto improvement over the market outcome is viable in the FC model, but we now turn to the question: 'Can a global planner with a utilitarian social welfare function improve on the decentralized equilibrium?'

In principle, there are many potential sources of inefficiency a planner may want to deal with. First, firms price above marginal cost. Second, capital owners choose where to offer their services without taking into account the impact of their decisions on consumer surpluses in the two regions. Third, they also do not take into account the impact on firms operating profits. Fourth, the effects on consumer surpluses and operating profits are also neglected in the entry decisions by firms so that the wrong number of firms may end up operating. In the present setting, however, the last source of inefficiency is irrelevant. Since the number of firms is determined only by the M-good technology (fixed costs) and the K-factor endowments ($K^w = 1$), entry is optimal. As a result, a planner will target only the other three distortions.

The global welfare indicator we adopt is the simple sum of indirect utilities across all individuals. This leads to the definition of global welfare as

$$W = K^w\left(s_K\ln\frac{\beta}{P} + s_K^*\ln\frac{\beta}{P^*}\right) + L^w\left(s_L\ln\frac{1}{P} + s_L^*\ln\frac{1}{P^*}\right) \tag{11.7}$$

since the reward to capital is β, and wage of workers is unity. Although K^w has been normalized to unity, intuition is served by leaving it explicitly in the expression.

FIRST-BEST OUTCOME

In the first-best outcome, all distortions are removed. As part of this, the planner imposes price equal to marginal cost for both local and export sales, so—given our choice of units for industrial goods—the local price of a typical variety will be $(1 - (1/\sigma))$ and the export price will be τ times this. The resulting price index is $P = (1 - (1/\sigma))^\mu \Delta^{-a}$ for the north with a similar expression for P^*. Of course, marginal cost pricing cancels operating profits, so lump-sum transfers are needed to support capital-owners' consumption. To avoid unenlightening complications, we do not model these, but rather just assume that they are set at some exogenously determined level that we call $\bar{\pi}$. Using these facts, the planner chooses s_n to maximize

$$W = \ln\bar{\pi} - \mu(K^w + L^w)\ln\left(1 - \frac{1}{\sigma}\right) + a(K + L)\ln\Delta + a(K^* + L^*)\ln\Delta^* \quad (11.8)$$

Note that the second right-hand term measures the welfare gain from marginal cost pricing and that this does not vary with the spatial allocation of firms.

Due to the concavity of the log function and constancy of the first two terms, we know W is a concave function of s_n so that the second-order condition for maximization always holds. Dividing the planner's first-order condition by the world's population, $L^w + K^w$, we can write the first order condition as

$$\frac{dW}{ds_n} = \frac{d\ln\Delta}{ds_n}s_{\text{pop}} + \frac{d\ln\Delta^*}{ds_n}(1 - s_{\text{pop}}) = 0, \quad s_{\text{pop}} \equiv \frac{L + K}{L^w + K^w} \quad (11.9)$$

where s_{pop} is the share of the world's population living in the north. This, combined with Result 11.4, shows that the optimizing planner must strike a balance between the opposing effects of changing s_n on individual well-being in the two regions, where the weights of the regions reflect their population shares. Evaluating the derivatives of Δ and Δ^*, (11.9) can be rearranged to yield

$$(1 - \phi)\left\{(1 + \phi)\left(s_{\text{pop}} - \frac{1}{2}\right) - (1 - \phi)\left(s_n - \frac{1}{2}\right)\right\} = 0 \quad (11.10)$$

This shows that when trade is perfectly free (i.e. $\phi = 1$), the planner is indifferent to firm location since this is immaterial for consumers' welfare. More interestingly, when trade is less than perfectly free (i.e. $\phi < 1$), expression (11.10) reveals that the planner chooses optimal firm location—measured here by the share of industry in the north, that is, s_n—by balancing two opposing effects. These two effects are shown as the two terms inside the curly brackets. The first is $(1 + \phi)$ times the north's share of world population, which depends on the spatial endowments of workers and capital owners. The second is $(1 - \phi)$ times the north's share of industry.

The first term reflects what we call the *trade cost-saving* effect. This means that, other things being equal, the optimal share of firms in the north should be higher, the higher is the north's share of world population. The second square-bracketed term is what we call the *individual welfare* effect. As Result 11.4 showed, the welfare trade-off between northerners and southerners worsens as the division of industry becomes more extreme. Thus, the marginal welfare cost of making the spatial distribution of industry more uneven rises as the industry distribution gets more uneven. What all this says is that the individual welfare effect is a force that favours an even distribution of industry.

Recalling the definition of trade freeness $\phi = \tau^{1-\sigma}$, (11.10) shows that the weight of trade cost saving with respect to the individual welfare loss grows as the elasticity of demand (σ) falls. In particular, the smaller is the elasticity of substitution between any two manufacturing varieties, the smaller is the relative weight of the individual loss. Such weight also falls as trade costs (τ) decrease. Thus, the lower the elasticity of demand and trade costs are, the stronger the incentive for the planner to allocate firms to the region hosting the larger number of consumers.

Solving (11.10) for s_n and labelling the result as s_n^S to emphasize the fact that this is a socially optimal allocation, we find

$$s_n^S = \frac{1}{2} + \frac{1 + \phi}{1 - \phi}\left(s_{\text{pop}} - \frac{1}{2}\right) \qquad (11.11)$$

This holds for $s_{\text{pop}} \in [\phi/(1 + \phi), 1/(1 + \phi)]$; outside this range, the planner concentrates all production in the big region. To summarize, we write the following result.

Result 11.5 (social home-market effect). *The socially optimal spatial allocation of industry requires the large region to have a more than proportional share of industry.*

This result suggests what might be called the 'social home-market effect', namely that $dn^S/ds_N > 1$. Indeed, we can write the following result.

Result 11.6 (social magnification effect). *The formula for the socially optimal spatial allocation of industry is isomorphic to that of the market outcome, with the share of population substituted for the share of world expenditure. Thus, the socially optimal spatial distribution of industry should be more uneven, not less, as trade gets freer.*

In other words, like its laissez-faire correspondent, the social home-market effect is subject to magnification.

THE SECOND-BEST OUTCOME

In the second-best outcome, we suppose that marginal cost pricing cannot be imposed, either because lump-sum transfers from consumers to firms are not available, or because the degree of surveillance necessary to enforce it is impractical. This implies that firms are free to set prices at profit maximizing levels as usual. As a result, the second-best planner maximizes an objective function that is equal to that of (11.7) with the term involving $\ln(1 - 1/\sigma)$ set equal to zero. Since s_n is not involved in the term that was zeroed, the first- and second-order conditions for the second-best planner are then the same as for the first-best planner.

Result 11.7. *The first- and second-best geographical distributions of firms coincide.*

This is due to the fact that the number of varieties is fixed by the world capital endowment, that mill pricing is optimal in Dixit–Stiglitz monopolistic competition, and that we consider only iceberg trade costs. The first implies that there is no underproduction of varieties due to above-marginal cost price, and the second implies that the ratio of imported to locally produced varieties is just τ in both the first- and second-best cases, so above-marginal-cost pricing does not distort the location decision.

11.2.5 Too Much or Too Little Agglomeration?

We are now ready to establish whether there is too much or too little spatial concentration of industry in the market equilibrium. All we have to do is to compare s_n with s_n^S. Taking the difference between (11.4) and (11.11), we obtain

$$s_n - s_n^S = \frac{1 + \phi}{1 - \phi}(s_E - s_{\text{pop}}) \tag{11.12}$$

which shows that any difference between the market and social allocation of industry depends upon the difference between the north's shares of world expenditures and its share of world population. The reason is that the utilitarian criterion, (11.7), rates individuals in the same way whatever their incomes and places of residence. To put it differently, the market criterion cares about expenditures, which implies that richer individuals count more. This leads to the two differential terms in the last expression on the right-hand side.

Result 11.8. *The market outcome has too many firms in the big region, if and only if the big region has a higher per capita income.*

The big region's per capita income depends on two things. The region's relative factor endowment and the relative reward of the two factors. To take a natural case, suppose the income of capital owners is higher than that of workers. In this case, the big region is richer and there is too much agglomeration, when the north is relatively well endowed with capital. Mirror conditions apply for the south.

There are two special cases when the market outcome is optimal, when the two regions are scaled versions of each other ($s_L = s_K$), or when remunerations are equalized across factors, i.e. $\beta = 1$.[4] We can summarize this in the following result.

---

[4] This requires the world capital/labour ratio, K^w/L^w, to just equal $b/(1 - b)$.

Result 11.9 (inefficient agglomeration). *Except in the knife-edge cases where regions have exactly the same relative factor endowment, or the rewards to K and L are identical, the spatial distribution in the market outcome is socially sub-optimal.*

The location inefficiency is larger, the larger is the factor price and the relative factor endowment differentials—the more so the lower is the trade costs ϕ. However, in terms of welfare levels, substituting s_n from (11.4) and s_n^S from (11.11) into (11.7) shows that the absolute welfare loss of the market with respect to the first-best outcomes is independent of the level of openness. To see this, note that

$$W^S = \ln\bar{\pi} + \mu(K^w + L^w)\ln\left(1 - \frac{1}{\sigma}\right)$$

$$+ a(K^w + L^w)\left[\ln(1 + \phi) + s_{\text{pop}}\ln s_{\text{pop}} + (1 - s_{\text{pop}})\ln(1 - s_{\text{pop}})\right] \quad (11.13)$$

$$W^M = \ln\beta + a(K^w + L^w)\left[\ln(1 + \phi) + s_{\text{pop}}\ln s_E + (1 - s_{\text{pop}})\ln(1 - s_E)\right]$$

where W^S and W^M are welfare criteria evaluated at, respectively, the social optimum and the market outcome. The result that $W^S - W^M$ is independent of trade freeness stems from the fact that the terms involving $\ln(1 + \phi)$ cancel. The independence of $W^S - W^M$ from ϕ together with the fact that W^M is increasing in trade freeness implies that the welfare loss, as a fraction of world market welfare, is greater when trade is more restricted.

Result 11.10. *As trade barriers fall, the geographical distribution of firms at the market outcome is increasingly different from the optimal one. Nonetheless, the relative welfare loss diminishes.*

11.2.6 Over- or Under-Agglomeration: Analysis by Factor Groups

This overall result hides a potential conflict between factor-owner groups. While there are no conflicts between different factor owners within a region (Result 11.2), the preferred spatial allocation of industry for the inter-regional coalition of workers will differ from the preferred allocation of the inter-regional coalition of capital owners. Defining W_L as the sum of workers' utilities worldwide and W_K as the analogous sum for capital owners worldwide, it is easy to show that the optimal divisions for the two groups are

$$s_n^L = \frac{1}{2} + \frac{1 + \phi}{1 - \phi}\left(s_L - \frac{1}{2}\right), \quad s_n^K = \frac{1}{2} + \frac{1 + \phi}{1 - \phi}\left(s_K - \frac{1}{2}\right) \quad (11.14)$$

where the superscripts on the left-hand side variables indicates the group-wise optimal allocation. Comparing the first expression in (11.14) with (11.4) and (11.11), we have the following result.

Result 11.11. *From the point of view of L owners, both the market and the planner allocate too many firms to a capital abundant region (i.e. the* *region which has a larger share of world capital than it does of world labour).*

This result is clearly more relevant in a situation where north and south are two regions within a nation, since it is easier to think of ways in which inter-regional interest groups can be effective when both regions are within the same political system. From the perspective of the inter-regional coalition of K owners, the mirror result holds.

11.3 SYMMETRIC FOOTLOOSE ENTREPRENEUR MODEL

The FC model is the simplest and most analytically tractable of the Part I models and its welfare was, correspondingly, quite simple. In this section, we consider the FE model, which is less tractable than the FC model but displays a much wider range of features. Indeed, as Chapter 4 showed, the features of the FE model are virtually identical to those of the original CP model.

The key source of intractability in the FE model is the fact that the price index involves a non-integer power. Since the mobile factor does consider price indices when deciding where to locate, and the location decision itself affects the price indices, one is not able to analytically solve for the equilibrium spatial distribution of industry in the FE model. However, when regions are intrinsically equal in size—that is, both are endowed with half the world's immobile factor—one can say quite a few things about the symmetric outcome. For this reason, we focus on the symmetric FE model in this section. Formally, this means that we maintain the assumption that $s_L = 1/2$ throughout the section.

11.3.1 The FE Model

The basic set-up of the FE model is almost identical to that of the FC model. There are two regions, two factors, and two sectors. One sector is Walrasian and this faces costless trade and uses only the immobile factor in production. The other sector is Dixit–Stiglitz, using only the mobile factor as the fixed-cost factor and only the immobile factor as its variable-cost input; inter-regional trade in its output is subject to iceberg trade costs.

The naming conventions are the same as before with the exception of the mobile factor. In recognition of the fact that the mobile factor consists of people in the FE model, we call it H (mnemonic for human capital) and its reward will be called w instead of K and π as in the FC model. Specifically, we think of the mobile factor as 'entrepreneurs' and assume that they locate in the region that provides them with the highest real reward.

11.3.2 Normalizations and the Market Equilibrium

We continue with all the normalizations imposed on the FC model above. In the symmetric case of $s_L = 1/2$, the equilibrium reward of north-based entrepreneurs is

$$w = \left(\frac{bL^w/2}{1-b}\right)\frac{1 - Z[b + 2(Z-b)(s_n - 1/2)]}{1 - Z[b + 4(Z-b)(s_n - 1/2)^2]}, \quad b \equiv \frac{\mu}{\sigma}, \quad Z \equiv \frac{1-\phi}{1+\phi}$$

$$(11.15)$$

where Z is a measure of closed-ness, which is handy in simplifying expressions when $s_L = 1/2$. Note that $Z = 1$ when $\phi = 0$, that is, trade costs are infinite, and $Z = 0$ when trade is perfectly free, that is, $\phi = 1$. The equilibrium expression for southern entrepreneurs is analogous, but it proves more revealing to write the ratio of entrepreneurs' rewards in the north and in the south:

$$\frac{w}{w^*} = \frac{1 - Z[b + 2(Z-b)(s_n - 1/2)]}{1 - Z[b - 2(Z-b)(s_n - 1/2)]}$$

$$(11.16)$$

This clearly shows that the location of industry, namely s_n, affects the nominal reward to the mobile factor.

Entrepreneurs move to the region that affords them the highest real income. At interior equilibria, the division of entrepreneurs (which is identical to the division of industry since one entrepreneur per variety is required) is such that real rewards are equalized. Given the model's symmetry, $s_n = 1/2$ is always an equilibrium, but it is not always stable. At the core–periphery, that is, full agglomeration, outcomes, the region with the agglomeration has the higher real wage. As Chapter 4 explains in detail, $s_n = 1/2$ is a stable equilibrium only for sufficiently low levels of trade freeness ($\phi < \phi^B$, the 'break' point), while core–periphery outcomes are stable only for sufficiently high levels of trade freeness ($\phi > \phi^S$, the 'sustain' point). The two threshold levels for trade freeness are defined by

$$\phi^B = \frac{(1-a)(1-b)}{(1+a)(1+b)}, \quad 2(\phi^S)^{1-a} - (1+b)(\phi^S)^2 - (1-b) = 0 \quad (11.17)$$

where ϕ^B is the break point and ϕ^S is the sustain point. It is always the case that $\phi^B < \phi^S$ with $\phi^B > 0$ when the 'no-black-hole' condition, namely $a < 1$, holds. If this condition is violated, then the symmetric outcome $s_n = 1/2$ is never stable and long-run outcomes are always associated with full agglomeration of industry. As usual, we assume that the no-black-hole condition holds.

11.3.3 Pareto Welfare Analysis

As usual, the finest disaggregation identifies four groups of individuals, namely workers and entrepreneurs in the two regions. The welfare of northern and southern workers in the FE model varies with the spatial allocation of industry and with trade freeness exactly as it does in the FC model.

In particular, because the reward to workers in both regions is fixed at unity, their utility levels vary only with the price indices. As we saw in Result 11.1, this implies a conflict of interest between northern workers and southern workers. For example, increasing the share of industry in the north helps northern workers and hurts southern workers. Thus, even without considering entrepreneurs, we have the following result.

Result 11.12 (no Pareto improvement possible). *As in the FC model, no Pareto-improving reallocation of firms is available in the FE model. A corollary is that, when multiple stable equilibria exist, they cannot be Pareto-ranked.*

Can multiple stable equilibria be Pareto-ranked from the point of view of H owners? As Chapter 4 showed, the FE model can have up to three stable equilibria corresponding to a single level of openness, namely $s_n = 0$, $s_n = 1$ and $s_n = 1/2$. By inspection of (11.15) and (11.16), the actual reward paid to H owners is $bL^w/(1 - b)$ in all three of these outcomes since w is irrelevant when $s_n = 0$ and w^* is irrelevant when $s_n = 1$. This implies that, in the comparison of equilibria, all that matters is the cost of living. Because we know that the price index is lower in the region where all firms are clustered, we have the following result.

Result 11.13. *The agglomerated outcomes $n = 0$ and $n = 1$ Pareto-dominate the dispersed outcome $n = 1/2$ from the point of view of H owners.*

Accordingly, for H owners, whatever the initial conditions, the market outcome is Pareto-efficient only if $\phi > \phi^B$, that is, when full agglomeration is the only equilibrium. When trade $\phi < \phi^B$, individually rational decisions by H owners can keep them at the Pareto-inferior dispersed equilibrium.

11.3.4 Global Welfare Analysis

Moving from equity to efficiency, we ask whether a planner can improve on the decentralized equilibrium. The sources of efficiency that the planner has to tackle are the same as in the FC model with the additional feature that production relocation also leads to expenditure relocation in the FE model. Our global welfare indicator is again the simple sum of individual utility.

FIRST-BEST OUTCOME

In the first-best case, all distortions are removed at once and this requires, inter alia, that the planner imposes marginal cost pricing which drives the market reward to the mobile factor to zero. To maintain a positive level of consumption of H owners, a lump sum transfer from workers is necessary. As before, we do not model this, but rather merely assume that it is constant. After having imposed marginal cost pricing, the planner's objective is

$$W = \ln\bar{w} - \mu(H^w + L^w)\ln\left(1 - \frac{1}{\sigma}\right) + a(s_n\ln\Delta + (1 - s_n)\ln\Delta^*) + \frac{aL^w}{2}\ln(\Delta\Delta^*)$$

$$(11.18)$$

where the Δs are defined as in (11.2). Note that the first two terms represent the invariant per capita transfer to H owners and the gain from marginal cost pricing, respectively. The third term show the impact of the price indices on H owners' utility (recall that $P = \Delta^{-a}$ and that the geographic division of industry, s_n, exactly equals the geographic division of H owners). The last term shows the welfare of the immobile L owners because their wage is unity and half of them are located in each region.

The fact that the mobile factor's wage is fixed by fiat at $\bar{w}$ greatly simplifies the analysis. In particular, H owners always prefer more agglomeration to less. Under full agglomeration ($s_n = 0$ or 1), all H owners—and thus all industry—is clustered in one region, so every H owner faces the minimum value of the price index, namely $P = 1$ when the core is in the north and $P^* = 1$ when it is in the south. For any division of industry/entrepreneurs that is strictly between zero and unity, all H owners face price indices that are greater than unity. In short, the welfare of H owners is strictly convex in s_n, attaining its maximum at the core–periphery outcomes.

The welfare of immobile workers is quite different. Since workers cannot move and half are located in each region, the sum of their utilities is maximized by a perfectly even division of industry (this is a direct implication of the reasoning behind Result 11.4). Of course, the sum hides the fact that northern workers like agglomeration in the north, but dislike agglomeration in the south (southern workers have the reverse preferences). To summarize these points we write the following result.

Result 11.14 (regional and factor conflicts of interest). *Workers in the two regions have opposite preferences for agglomeration, with northern workers preferring agglomeration in the north and southern workers preferring it in the south. Since the inter-regional utility trade-off in this conflict is concave, an even division of industry maximizes the sum of workers' utility over the two regions. All owners of the mobile factor, by contrast, always prefer full agglomeration, but they are indifferent as to which region gets the core.*

This result helps us interpret the planner's first-order condition for welfare maximization:

$$\frac{dW}{ds_n} = \ln\left(1 + \frac{2(1 - \phi)}{\Delta^*}\left(s_n - \frac{1}{2}\right)\right) + a(1 - \phi)\frac{2\phi - L^w(1 - \phi)}{\Delta\Delta^*}\left(s_n - \frac{1}{2}\right)$$

$$\geq 0, \quad s_n \leq 1 \tag{11.19}$$

where at least one of the equalities must hold strictly (to reduce notation we only consider the core-in-the-north possibility). To understand this condition intuitively, we note that the first right-hand term captures the effect of reallocating H owners on their own welfare, holding price indices constant. This term is positive for $s_n > 1/2$ and negative for $s_n < 1/2$ for all levels of openness, ϕ. The second right-hand term reflects the impact of a marginal reallocation of industry on the price indices from the point of view of H owners (this is the part involving 2ϕ) and from the point of view of L owners (this is the part involving $-(1 - \phi)L^w$). The sign of the second term depends upon both s_n and the freeness of trade.

Specifically, when ϕ exceeds $L^w/(2 + L^w)$, the term is positive when $s_n > 1/2$ and negative when $s_n < 1/2$.

What all this goes to say is that a sufficient condition for the planner to find full agglomeration optimal is $\phi > L^w/(2 + L^w)$. When trade is freer than this value, the government's objective function is everywhere rising in s_n, so setting s_n to the corner solution value ($s_n = 1$) is optimal. Given Result 11.14, this result is quite intuitive. $L^w/(2 + L^w)$ is the ratio between the number of people who lose from a departure from symmetry ($L^w/2$), and the number of people who gain from it ($1 + L^w/2$). Thus, $s_n = 1/2$ is a minimum of the planner's problem when the share of L owners left behind in the deserted region ($L^w/2$) is small and/or trade is very free. This provides a very intuitive condition. A departure from symmetry is good from a Benthamite perspective when relatively few immobile L owners are affected by the rise in living costs in the de-industrializing region and/or when trade is quite free so that differences in regional costs of living are minor.

The Social Break Point. To more tightly characterize the range where full agglomeration is socially optimal, we note that $s_n = 1/2$ is always a solution to (11.19), but we cannot be sure that symmetry represents a maximum rather than a minimum. To check, we see that the second-order condition is

$$\left.\frac{d^2 W}{ds_n^2}\right|_{s_n=1/2} = \frac{4a(1 - \phi)}{(1 + \phi)^2}((3 + L^w)\phi + 1 - L^w) \tag{11.20}$$

and this is negative when ϕ is less than

$$\phi_{FB}^B \equiv \frac{L^w - 1}{L^w + 3} \tag{11.21}$$

where the subscript *FB* stands for first best. As the above intuition suggests, $n = 1/2$ is a local minimum when trade is sufficiently free and the immobile part of the population is small with respect to the mobile part (recall that we normalized $H^w = 1$). In such a case, symmetric dispersion would minimize global welfare. Thus, we write the following result.

Result 11.15. *When there are fewer L owners than H owners, $n = 1/2$ is a local minimum whatever the level of trade barriers.*

Thus, $L^w > H^w = 1$ is the 'no-black-hole' condition for the first-best planner.

The Social Sustain Point. We turn now to completing the global picture. Standard analysis reveals that (11.18) is symmetric around $s_n = 1/2$ and changes concavity at most twice, which implies that it has at most three zeroes. In other words, the planner's first-order condition has at most five solutions: three interior and two corner ones. This mirrors the market outcome. Specifically, there exist only three possible cases. These are shown in Figure 11.1, which portrays global welfare, (11.18), on the vertical axis as a function of a firms' distribution n on the horizontal axis. The three curves capture the three possible scenarios. Specifically, the bottom curve has a unique maximum at $s_n = 1/2$. The planner chooses

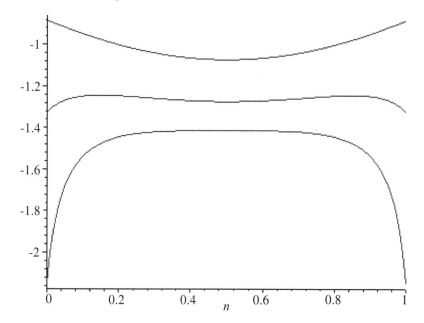

Figure 11.1   The first-best welfare objective ($\sigma = 4$, $\mu = 0.3$, $L^w = 1.1$, $\phi = 0.02, 0.09$, 0.2).

symmetry. The middle curve achieves a local minimum at $s_n = 1/2$ and two interior global maxima are symmetric around the minimum: the planner chooses partial agglomeration. The top curve still has a local minimum at $s_n = 1/2$ and two global maxima, but these are at corners $s_n = 0$ and $s_n = 1$; the planner chooses full agglomeration.

We have already determined that $s_n = 1/2$ is a local maximum when ϕ is less than the social break point, so it must be a local minimum when ϕ exceeds this critical value. Thus, we know that we are *not* in the bottom case when ϕ is greater than ϕ_{FB}^B. All that is left to do is to discriminate between the top and middle cases. In other words, to establish the conditions under which agglomeration is a local maximum (top curve) or a local minimum (middle case).

The middle case can be distinguished by the requirement for dW/ds_n to be negative at $s_n = 1$. The top case requires that dW/ds_n is positive at $s_n = 1$. The key then is to find the critical value of ϕ where dW/ds_n changes sign at $s_n = 1$. The critical value is ϕ, which solves

$$L^w + 2\phi_{FB}^S \frac{\ln \phi_{FB}^S - (1 - \phi_{FB}^S)}{(1 - \phi_{FB}^S)^2} = 0 \qquad (11.22)$$

Because full agglomeration is socially optimal only when $\phi > \phi_{FB}^S$, the threshold ϕ_{FB}^S can be interpreted as the first-best 'sustain point'. However, differently from the free market equilibrium, numerical investigations show that the first-best sustain point is above the break point: $\phi_{FB}^S > \phi_{FB}^B$.

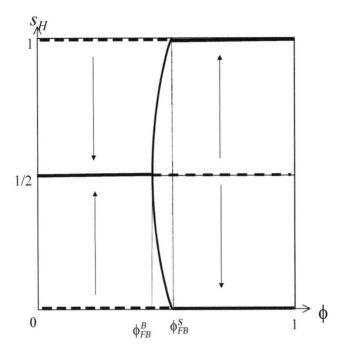

Figure 11.2   First-best location.

To sum up, if $\phi < \phi_{FB}^B$, the bottom curve applies—the planner implements symmetric dispersion. If $\phi_{FB}^B < \phi < \phi_{FB}^S$, the middle curve applies and the planner implement partial agglomeration. Finally, if $\phi > \phi_{FB}^S$ the top curve applies and the planner implements full agglomeration. This is represented in Figure 11.2, which depicts the optimal distribution of firms as trade freeness varies. Solid lines represent the globally maximizing locations.

THE SECOND-BEST OUTCOME

In the second-best outcome, lump sum transfers to H owners are not available to the planner, who must therefore refrain from imposing marginal cost pricing. This implies that prices are set at profit maximizing levels and the second-best planner's objective is

$$W = \ln w^{s_n} w^{*1-s_n} + a \ln \Delta^{s_n} \Delta^{*1-s_n} + a\left(\frac{L^w}{2}\right)\ln \Delta \Delta^* \qquad (11.23)$$

where w and w^* are given by (11.15) and (11.16), respectively. The first right-hand term shows the crucial difference with respect to the first-best objective. It measures the social welfare value of H factor rewards, which depends on the rewards in the two regions and the distribution of H across regions. At $s_n = 1/2$, that term is a concave function of s_n, which shows that H owners would like to be

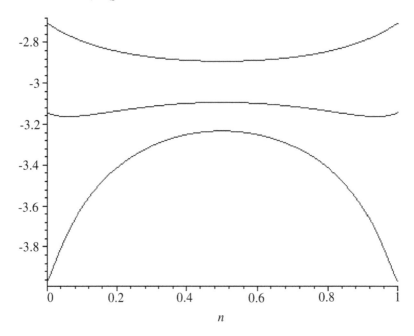

Figure 11.3   The second-best welfare objective function.

dispersed were nominal income all that mattered. On the contrary, as already discussed, they would rather be agglomerated were the cost of living all that mattered. Thus, with respect to the first-best problem, income considerations introduce an additional dispersion force.

Again applying standard analysis, we find that (11.23) has at most three interior maxima or minima, so the planner's first-order condition has at most five solutions as in the free market and first-best outcomes. As before, this means there are three possible cases to consider; these are shown in Figure 11.3, which portrays global welfare (11.23) on the vertical axis as a function of firms' spatial distribution on the horizontal axis. The three curves capture the three possible scenarios. Specifically, the bottom curve has a unique maximum at $s_n = 1/2$. The middle curve achieves a local maximum at $s_n = 1/2$ and two interior global minima are symmetric around the maximum. The top curve has a local minimum at $s_n = 1/2$ and two global maxima at corners $s_n = 0$ and $s_n = 1$.

The passage between the middle curve and the top one happens for ϕ such that $d^2 W/dn^2 = 0$ at $s_n = 1/2$. The passage between the bottom curve and the middle one happens for the value of ϕ, call it ϕ_{SB}, such that (11.23) takes the same value at $s_n = 0$, $s_n = 1/2$ and $s_n = 1$:

$$(\phi_{SB})^{L^w/2} - \left(\frac{1 + \phi_{SB}}{2}\right)^{1+L^w} = 0 \qquad (11.24)$$

This is the crucial threshold. For ϕ below it, the global maximum is at $s_n = 1/2$ so that the planner implements symmetric dispersion. Above ϕ_{SB}, global maximization requires corner allocations $s_n = 0$ or $s_n = 1$ so that the planner implements agglomeration.

TOO MUCH OR TOO LITTLE AGGLOMERATION?

To establish whether the market outcome is globally efficient, we have to compare the five thresholds ϕ^B, ϕ^S, ϕ_{FB}^B, ϕ_{FB}^S and ϕ_{SB}. In so doing, we restrict our attention to the focal case where all five thresholds are defined in the relevant range of values $\phi \in [0, 1]$.

Three facts are crucial. First, under a free market, as trade freeness rises from zero to one, agglomeration becomes sustainable before symmetry breaks:

$$\phi^S < \phi^B \tag{11.25}$$

Second, numerical investigation shows that the second-best threshold falls within the two first-best ones:

$$\phi_{FB}^B < \phi_{SB} < \phi_{FB}^S \tag{11.26}$$

Third, since both ϕ^B and ϕ^S are independent of L^w while optimal ϕ_{FB}^B, ϕ_{FB}^S, and ϕ_{SB} are not, the ranking of thresholds changes as L^w varies while all other parameters are kept constant. In particular, we have $d\phi_{FB}^B/dL^w > 0$ as well as $d\phi_{FB}^S/dL^w > 0$ and $d\phi_{SB}/dL^w > 0$ provided $\phi < L^w/(2 + L^w)$, which needs to be the case for ϕ_{FB}^S to fall in the relevant range.

Thus, the following ranking holds when L^w is low enough:

$$\phi_{FB}^B < \phi_{SB} < \phi_{FB}^S < \phi^S < \phi^B \tag{11.27}$$

whereas, if L^w is large, the following holds:

$$\phi^S < \phi^B < \phi_{FB}^B < \phi_{SB} < \phi_{FB}^S \tag{11.28}$$

The former case is depicted in Figure 11.4, which represents equilibrium and first-best locations as functions of trade freeness. The figure reveals the presence of an intermediate interval of trade freeness that supports agglomeration under free market and dispersion under the planner. Figure 11.5 represents the latter case, in which intermediate freeness leads to opposite results.

We can be more precise by assessing the analytical conditions under which the second scenario applies. By (11.17) and (11.21), ϕ_{FB}^B is larger than ϕ^B whenever

$$L^w - 1 > 2\frac{(1 - a)(1 - b)}{a + b} \tag{11.29}$$

where both sides are positive when both the first-best and the market no-black-hole conditions hold.

Moreover, under those conditions, the right-hand side of (11.29) is an increasing function of σ and a decreasing function of μ. The intuition behind this result is the following. When σ is small and μ is large, operating profits are large,

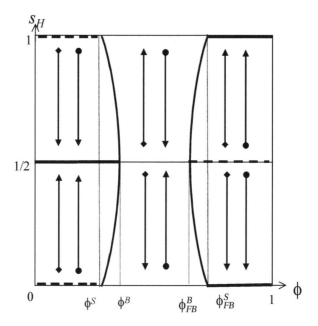

Figure 11.4   Inefficient agglomeration.

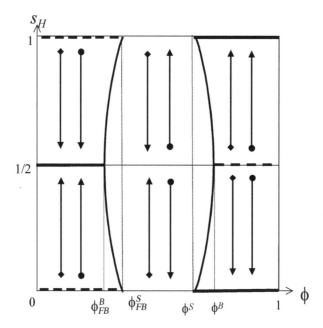

Figure 11.5   Inefficient dispersion.

which implies large H-factor rewards. In this case, the market assigns a large weight to H-owners desires. If L^w is large with respect to $H^w = 1$, such weight is likely to be too large from the point of view of the planner, who cares about heads and not about their incomes. Since H owners prefer agglomeration, small σ, large μ, and large L^w deliver agglomeration at the market outcome while the planner would rather have dispersion ($\phi^B < \phi^B_{FB}$).

To sum up, conditions (11.27), (11.28) and (11.29) imply the following result.

Result 11.16. *When agglomeration forces are strong (i.e. $1/\sigma$ and μ are large), and L^w is large relative to H^w, there exists an intermediate range of openness where the market delivers agglomeration while the planner implements dispersion. The opposite is true for weak agglomeration forces and a low L^w/H^w ratio.*

11.3.5 Over or Under Agglomeration: Analysis by Factor Groups

As in the FC model, it is interesting to analyse the conflict between the owners of different factors when considered as two separate interest groups. Starting with the L owners, their aggregate welfare as a group is still given by (we continue to assume $s_L = 1/2$)

$$W_L = a\left(\frac{L^w}{2}\right)\ln(\Delta\Delta^*) \tag{11.30}$$

which is concave in s_n with a maximum at perfect symmetry, $s_n = 1/2$, and two minima at $s_n = 0$ and $s_n = 1$.

As to H owners, we have already pointed out that complete agglomeration Pareto-dominates symmetric dispersion. This result can be complemented by studying their aggregate welfare:

$$W_H = \ln w^{s_n} w^{*1-s_n} - \ln P^{s_n} P^{*1-s_n} \tag{11.31}$$

which is convex in s_n with a minimum at $s_n = 1/2$ and two maxima at $s_n = 0$ and $s_n = 1$.

Therefore, we have the following result.

Result 11.17. *In the FE model, L factor owners as a group favour dispersion while H factor owners favour agglomeration.*

11.4 CONCLUSION

Market outcomes are driven by the geographic allocation of expenditure. Given a simple utilitarian social welfare functional, the socially optimal outcome is driven by the geographic dispersion of population. When the spatial dispersion of expenditure does not match the spatial dispersion of population, the market will lead to a geographical distribution of firms that is socially inefficient.

REFERENCES

Ottaviano, G. I. P. 2001. Home market effects and the (in)efficiency of international specialization. Mimeo, Graduate Institute of International Studies.

Ottaviano, G. I. P. and J.-F. Thisse. 2002a. Integration, agglomeration and the political economics of factor mobility. *Journal of Public Economics* 83: 429–456.

Ottaviano, G. I. P., T. Tabuchi and J.-F. Thisse. 2002b. Agglomeration and trade revisited. *International Economic Review* 43: 409–435.

Robert-Nicoud, F. 2002. A simple geography model with vertical linkages and capital mobility. Mimeo. London School of Economics.

PART III

Trade Policy

CHAPTER 12

Unilateral Trade Policy

12.1 INTRODUCTION

The economic geography literature is a bit like Hamlet without the Prince. Trade policy should play *the*, or at least *a*, leading role in the literature—or that is what one might expect since trade barriers are at the very heart of the models and the literature's founding fathers are famous for their theoretical trade policy analysis. Alas, the literature is surprisingly short on trade policy analysis. For example, in Peter Neary's excellent overview (Neary 2001), not a single article on trade policy is referenced.

The reason for this lacuna is uncomplicated. The policy implications implicit in the standard models do not seem to provide useful insights. As Neary (2001) remarks:

> The key problem is that the policy implications of the basic core–periphery model are just too stark to be true. The model turns Sartre's 'Hell is other people' on its head: agglomeration is unambiguously good for you. Because the cost of living is lower in the core, it is always better to live there than in the periphery, with the level of utility in a diversified economy lying in between. Faced with multiple equilibria that have a clear welfare ranking, it is tempting to suggest a role for government in 'picking equilibria'. This in turn may encourage a new sub-field of 'strategic location policy', perhaps drawing on fifteen years' work on strategic trade policy, which, as Brander (1995) and Neary and Leahy (2000) argue, has produced much interesting theory but no simple robust rules to guide policy making."

Neary concludes with, "No harm then that FKV are mostly neutral on the applicability of the models to policy."

12.1.1 Organization of the Chapter

This chapter begins by taking up the challenge that is implicit in Neary's analysis of the CP model's appropriateness for policy analysis. It does this by first using our more tractable models (see Part I) to study precisely how 'strategic location policy' works when agglomeration forces are present—that is, how unilateral protection can lower prices in the protecting nations (what we call the price-lowering-protection effect). We then introduce a series of enrichments that makes economic geography models 'ambiguous enough to be true', to paraphrase Neary.

Refuting the price-lowering-protection (PLP) effect, however, is not really sufficient for showing that economic geography models are suitable tools for trade policy analysis. Even with the our enrichments, unilateral protection always fosters industrialization in the sense that a nation can always increase its share of world industry by imposing a unilateral import barrier. Since unilateral protection is not generally viewed as a sure-fire route to industrialization in the real world, the next section explores variants of simple economic geography models in which trade *liberalization* can foster industrialization. This involves consideration of imported intermediate goods.

We turn next to the question of why small countries have trouble attracting industries in which agglomeration forces are important. Of course, the economic geography models are perfectly suited to answer this question. We focus on the interplay between domestic and foreign protection, domestic and foreign market size and comparative advantage.

The last substantive section considers an old chestnut in trade policy analysis—the non-equivalence of tariffs and quotas. As it turns out, these two policies can have very different effects on the spatial allocation of industry. The final section provides our concluding remarks and a discussion of related literature.

12.2 PRICE-LOWERING PROTECTION (PLP)

The prime example of the protectionist implications of economic geography models is the price-lowering effect of protection. In a typical new trade theory model an increase in unilateral protection lowers the domestic price level. Venables (1987) first showed this surprising and counter-intuitive effect in a model without agglomeration forces; Baldwin (1999) shows that the presence of agglomeration forces serves to strengthen the effect.

This result flies in the face of empirical evidence and common sense, but it does have clear-cut protectionist implications. In the CP model, for instance, a nation that erects import barriers (even barriers that generate no tariff revenue or quota rents) experiences a Pareto welfare improvement in the sense that each factor-owner gains, the mobile factor gaining both from agglomeration-induced higher nominal wage and lower prices, while the immobile factor gains only from the latter. While unilateral protection can be both pricing-lower and welfare-improving in other models, the PLP effect is novel; see Box 12.1 for details.

To fix ideas, this section first presents a decomposition of PLP that highlights its source and points to theoretical factors that could reverse it. We then present a simple model in which the effect can be simply and analytically demonstrated.

12.2.1 Decomposition of Price-Lowering Protection (PLP)

Most economic geography models, including the standard CP model, feature monopolistic competition where all differentiated varieties enter the representative consumer's preferences in a symmetric fashion, and all varieties produced in a given nation are symmetrically priced. The perfect price index for such preferences can be expressed as

---

BOX 12.1 PRICE LOWERING EFFECTS IN NEOCLASSICAL TRADE MODELS

In a neoclassical trade model (e.g. Ricardian or Heckscher–Ohlin), a sufficiently small tariff can induce a welfare-improving price reduction in any nation that is not atomistic. This so-called optimal tariff reduces the home nation's demand for imports and this in turn lowers the international price for its imports. This differs greatly from the PLP effect discussed in this chapter. The classical 'optimal tariff' works by pushing down the border price and indeed it requires the domestic price of imports to rise. For this reason, the optimal tariff argument does not apply to 'frictional' trade barriers such as unilateral changes in iceberg trade costs. To put it differently, the optimal-tariff gain stems from the fact that part of the tariff's incidence falls on foreigners, it therefore only works for trade barriers that generate domestic revenue; the 'optimal tariff' is just a tricky way of taxing foreigners.

$$P = P[nv[p], n^* v[p^*]], \quad P_1, P_2, v' < 0 \tag{12.1}$$

where n and n^*, are the mass (number) of locally produced and imported varieties; the asterisk indicates foreign variables, as usual. Also, p and p^* are the consumer prices of local and imported goods. The partials of the implicit function $P[\ ,\ ]$ are negative (this reflects the love of variety aspect of the assumed preferences, and the derivative of $v[\ ]$ is negative, so at any price rise P is raised. The impact of unilateral protection on such a price index is

$$\frac{dP}{d\tau} = P_1\left(nv'\frac{dp}{d\tau} + v\frac{dn}{d\tau}\right) + P_2\left(n^* v'\frac{dp^*}{d\tau} + p^* v\frac{dn^*}{d\tau}\right) \tag{12.2}$$

where τ measures the level of home protection, and P_1 and P_2 are the partials of $P[\ ,\ ]$ with respect to the first and second arguments, respectively. Since protection can alter factor prices and market structure, the derivatives in this expression are, in general, quite complex. Intuition, however, is served by a few of the simplifying assumptions commonly made in the economic geography literature.

If varieties are symmetric across nations as well as within nations, we have that $P_1 = P_2$ and for brevity, we write $P_1 = P_2$ as P'. Economic geography models often work with frameworks where mill pricing is optimal since this assumption eliminates pro-competitive effects; the result is that p is proportional to w and p^* is proportional to $w^* \tau$, where w and w^* are the home and foreign wage rates. In some economic geography models, a change in τ will affect w and w^*, however, if we start at the symmetric point with symmetric nations, all effects will be equal and opposite; for example, $dw/d\tau = -dw^*/d\tau$ starting from a point where $w = w^*$ and $\tau = \tau^*$. Finally, it proves convenient to write n and n^* in terms of shares and the global number of varieties, viz. $n = s_n n^w$ and $n^* = (1 - s_n)n^w$. Using these assumptions and evaluating (12.2) at the symmetric point yields

$$\frac{dP}{d\tau} = -n^w(-P')(v[p] - v[p^*])\frac{ds_n}{d\tau} + \frac{n^w}{2}(-P')\left(-v'[p]\frac{dp}{d\tau} - v'[p^*]\frac{dp^*}{d\tau}\right)$$

$$-\left(\frac{-P'}{2}\right)(v[p^*] + v[p^*])\frac{dn^w}{d\tau} \tag{12.3}$$

DISCUSSION

Equation (12.3) decomposes the price-index impact into three parts. The first right-hand term reflects what we called the 'location effect' in Chapter 10. The idea here is that $p^* > p$ with mill pricing (the price of imported varieties includes trade costs), so $v[p^*] < v[p^*]$ and this means that if protection yields inward delocation—that is, $ds_n/d\tau > 0$—then protection tends to lower the price index. More heuristically, the location effect simply reflects the fact that the index tends to falls when a large fraction of varieties are produced locally since this allows home consumers to avoid the trade costs on a wider range of goods.

The second effect—which corresponds to the 'trade price effect' in Chapter 10—shows how a protection-induced change in p and p^* affects the price index. Note that since the $(-P')$ and $(-v')$ terms are positive, increases in either p or p^* tend to raise P. We normally expect the direct effect to raise P for two reasons. First, an increase in trade costs τ will raise p^* automatically given mill pricing, and second, general equilibrium factor price effects are likely to result in a rise in p (since the protection boosts demand for domestic output and thus factors), or at least no change.

The final effect—captured by the third right-hand term—is the famous variety effect. Given that $v > 0$ and $P' < 0$, an increase in n^w lowers the price index. We note that most economic geography models (including the CP model) make assumptions that render the total number of varieties, that is, n^w, invariant to trade barriers. For such models, the third term drops out leaving us with two effects, the direct effect, which tends to raise P, and the delocation effect, which tends to lower it. In short, PLP only works in mainstream economic geography models, when the 'delocation elasticity' is sufficiently high. Specifically, when

$$\frac{ds_n}{d\tau} > \frac{1}{2}\frac{v'[p]\frac{dp}{d\tau} + v'[p^*]\frac{dp^*}{d\tau}}{v[p] - v[p^*]} \tag{12.4}$$

To summarize this analysis, we write the following result.

Result 12.1. *Unilateral protection can lower prices in standard economic geography models since the direct price-raising impact of protection may be more than offset by the delocation of firms into the home market. PLP only works when the 'delocation elasticity' is sufficiently high.*

12.2.2 Stark Results in Simple Models: PLP in the FC and CC Models

In the model with which Venables (1987) first showed the PLP effect, the elasticity of delocation is very high. This section shows that this is also true of simple economic geography models by reproducing and analysing the PLP using simple models. In the models we employ—the FC model of Chapter 3 and the CC model of Chapter 6—the global number of varieties is invariant to trade policy, just as it is in the CP model and in Venables (1987). We start with the FC models where unilateral protection leads to gradual delocation, postponing issues of catastrophic agglomeration to the subsequent section.

PLP IN THE FC MODEL

The FC model that we employ is described at length in Chapter 3, so here we just remind readers of the key assumptions and reproduce the equilibrium conditions. The basic set-up consists of two nations, home and foreign (in the trade chapters we use home and foreign instead of north and south, with home taking north's notation), two factors (labour, L, and physical capital, K) and two sectors (M and A). Physical capital can move freely between nations, but capital owners cannot, so all K reward is repatriated to the country of origin. Industrial and agricultural goods are traded. Trade in A is costless. Industrial trade is impeded by frictional (iceberg) import barriers such that $1 + t \geq 1$ units of a good must be shipped in order to sell one unit abroad (t is the tariff equivalent of the trade costs). Countries have identical preferences and technology. To keep things simple, we assume that nations have identical endowments, but to allow for unilateral protection, we suppose that they have potentially different iceberg trade costs for industrial imports. Preferences of the representative consumer comprise the usual Cobb–Douglas nest of a CES aggregate of industrial varieties and consumption of the A good. The representative consumer owns the entire nation's L and K and his/her income (and expenditure) equals $wL + \pi K$ (there is no tariff revenue with iceberg barriers).

Combing free trade and perfect competition in A, with our standard normalizations, we get $p_A = p_A^* = w = w^* = 1.$[1] Also, with 'mill pricing' in the M sector, home M firms charge $p = 1$ for local sales and $p = \tau$ for export sales. Using this, the operating profit of a typical northern industrial firm reduces to

$$\pi = Bb\frac{E^w}{K^w}, \quad B \equiv \frac{s_E}{\Delta} + \frac{\phi^* s_E^*}{\Delta^*}; \quad \Delta \equiv s_n + \phi s_n^*, \quad \Delta^* \equiv \phi^* s_n + s_n^*, \quad b \equiv \frac{\mu}{\sigma} \tag{12.5}$$

where $\phi \equiv \tau^{1-\sigma}$ and $\phi^* \equiv \tau^{*1-\sigma}$ are measures of north's and south's openness (i.e. $\tau - 1$ is the tariff equivalent of the frictional barriers faced by southern firms selling to the north, and $\tau^* - 1$ is the corresponding value for northern exports to the south). The rest of the notation is standard (E^w and $K^w = n^w$ are world

---

[1] We assume that the no-specialization condition holds; $\mu < 1/2$ is sufficient (see Chapter 3 for details).

expenditure and world capital stock, K^w is normalized to unity, s_E is the north's share of E^w, and s_n is the share of n^w made in the north, and finally s_n^* equals $1 - s_n$). As usual, B measures the extent to which a northern variety's sales exceed the world average per variety sales (which is $\mu E^w/K^w$), and thus the extent to which π exceeds the world average operating profit (which is $bL^w/K^w(1 - b)$ as Chapter 3 shows in detail). Similar foreign expressions hold with foreign variables denoted with an asterisk.

Capital movements are assumed to be costless, so capital moves and thus $n = s_n$ and $n^* = 1 - s_n$ adjust until $\pi = \pi^*$.[2] This has several important implications. First, it means that each unit of capital earns the global average reward $bL^w/K^w(1 - b)$ and, importantly, this does not vary with the level of protection or the spatial allocation of industry. For simplicity, we work with two nations that have identical endowments, and since π's are equalized in equilibrium and remitted, home's share of world expenditure, s_E, never varies and by symmetry it equals 1/2.

With $s_E = 1/2$, the location condition $\pi = \pi^*$ can be solved for s_n to yield a closed-form solution for the equilibrium spatial distribution of industry and its dependence on openness, that is,

$$s_n = \frac{1}{2} + \frac{1}{2} \frac{\phi^* - \phi}{(1 - \phi)(1 - \phi^*)} \tag{12.6}$$

This is the model's key equilibrium condition. Plainly, with symmetric protection, industry would be evenly divided between the two regions regardless of the level of trade freeness. Observe that raising home protection unambiguously raises home's share of industry and raising foreign protection unambiguously lowers it. Specifically, from (12.6), the delocation derivatives, $ds_n/d\tau$ and $ds_n/d\phi$, in this model evaluated at symmetric trade freeness are

$$\frac{ds_n}{d\tau} = \frac{(\sigma - 1)\tau^{-\sigma}}{2(1 - \tau^{1-\sigma})^2} > 0, \quad \frac{ds_n}{d\phi} = \frac{-1}{2(1 - \phi)^2} \tag{12.7}$$

This gets arbitrarily large as the level of freeness increases. This is summarized in the following result.

Result 12.2. *Unilateral protection raises a nation's share of global industry in the FC model. The size of this 'delocation derivative' rises with the initial level of openness.*

The increasing sensitivity of industrial location to asymmetric protection should be thought of as a corollary to the 'home-market magnification effect' discussed in Part I.

UNILATERAL PROTECTION IN THE SYMMETRIC FC MODEL

Here, we focus on home unilateral protection and its impact on the home price index, namely

---

[2] We focus on interior equilibria here; see Chapter 3 for an analysis of core–periphery outcomes.

$$P = (n^w \Delta)^{-a}, \quad a \equiv \frac{\mu}{\sigma - 1} > 0 \tag{12.8}$$

since $p_A = 1$ and both home and foreign varieties are priced at unity for local sales (see Chapter 3 for a detailed derivation of this 'perfect' price index). Plugging (12.6) into the definition of Δ and differentiating, we get

$$\frac{dP/d\phi}{P} = -\frac{a}{\Delta}\left(1 - s_n + (1 - \phi)\frac{ds_n}{d\phi}\right) = a\left(\frac{\phi^*}{1 - \phi\phi^*}\right) > 0 \tag{12.9}$$

The first term in the large parentheses in (12.9) is the direct effect of liberalization on the price index. The second term is the location effect. The second expression follows from the first after evaluating $ds_n/d\phi$ with (12.7) and the equilibrium value of s_n with (12.6). As inspection reveals, $dP/d\phi$ is always positive (as indicate by the inequality), so unilateral liberalization always *raises* the liberalizer's price index. The reason, of course, is that the delocation derivative $ds_n/d\phi$ is so large. This is summarized in the following result.

Result 12.3. *Unilateral protection lowers the protecting nation's price index in the symmetric FC model.*

Discussion. Three observations can be made concerning this result. First, PLP stems entirely from protection-induced relocation of industrial firms. To see this observe from (12.9) that the magnitude of the effect rises with manufactures' expenditure share, μ, and falls as the M varieties become better substitutes since $a \equiv \mu/(\sigma - 1)$. In the limit, when varieties are perfectly substitutable, that is, $\sigma = \infty$, or home consumers spend nothing on M, that is, $\mu = 0$, policy-induced delocation has no price implications. The same point can be seen by noting that if $ds_n/d\phi$ were zero, liberalization would lower prices.

Second, the gain from unilateral protection rises as the initial overall level of protection falls. For instance, suppose the two nations start with $\phi = \phi^*$ and home is considering a marginal decrease in its trade freeness. By inspection of (12.9), the size of the welfare gain from such protection gets very large as the initial level of symmetric freeness approaches costless trade. The reason, of course, is that when trade costs are almost zero, firms are almost indifferent to their location so any small locational advantage has an outsized impact on location of industry. Thus, in some sense, the temptation for a nation to 'cheat' on a reciprocal trade liberalization increases as the depth of integration rises. This so-called magnification effect of globalization (Baldwin 2000) may help explain why deep integration schemes—such as the EU and the EEA—seems to require much stronger trans-national mechanisms for surveillance, enforcement and adjudication than free trade areas, such as NAFTA and EFTA. To spotlight this, we write the following result.

Result 12.4. *The welfare gains from a slight, unilateral increase in protection are larger when starting from a position of initially liberal trade. Thus, a nation's incentive to 'cheat' is higher, not lower as intuition might suggest, when trade is quite free to begin with.*

Third, if we had worked with an economic geography model with more powerful agglomeration forces, the amount of industry that would delocate in response to unilateral protection would be even greater. (Recall from Part I that the FC model is the economic geography model with the weakest agglomeration forces.)

RETALIATION

Delocation in this model is a zero sum game and since a reduction in the share of varieties that are produced locally always harms a nation, home's unilateral protection harms foreigners. To see this more carefully, note that protection has no impact on E or E^* so differentiating the foreign indirect utility function, $V^* = E^*/P^*$, yields $(dV^*/d\phi)/V^* = a(d\Delta^*/d\phi)/\Delta^*$, where

$$\frac{d\Delta^*/d\phi}{\Delta^*} = \frac{(1 - \phi^*)}{(1 - \phi)(1 - \phi\phi^*)} \tag{12.10}$$

Thus, foreigners lose when home unilaterally raises its level of protection (i.e. when $d\phi < 0$). Again, the size of the welfare loss rises as the initial level of symmetric trade freeness rises.

Given this win–lose aspect of unilateral protection, foreigners are unlikely to view home protection benignly. Indeed, if the two nations play a Nash protection game, the only equilibrium is prohibitive barriers. The point is easily made. Taking the indirect utility function (i.e. $V = E/P$) as the objective of the home government, the home government's first order condition can be written as

$$\frac{dV/d\phi}{V} = \frac{-a\phi^*}{1 - \phi\phi^*} \leq 0, \quad \phi \geq 0, \quad \text{w.c.s.} \tag{12.11}$$

where w.c.s. stands for 'with complementary slackness'. By symmetry, we can solve for the Nash equilibrium level of freeness by imposing symmetry. Employing $\phi^{ne} = \phi = \phi^*$ in (12.10), we get $\phi^{ne} = 0$ is the only solution. Thus, we have he following result.

Result 12.5. *If nations play Nash in their level of openness, the only equilibrium entails prohibitive trade barriers.*

This extreme result is intuitively obvious. Any delocation of firms to home is welfare improving. The optimal home policy is thus to set home trade freeness, ϕ, low enough to ensure that all M firms are in the home. From (12.6), this holds for any ϕ that is more protectionist than $(2\phi^* - 1)/\phi^*$, subject to $0 \leq \phi$. Of course, a symmetric full relocation condition holds for foreigners, so both governments would be driven to setting the protection at prohibitive levels.

What all this goes to say is that PLP acts very much like an extreme form of the terms-of-trade-shifting argument for tariff protection in Walrasian trade models. Thus, just as in the old literature, unilateral protection engages governments in a prisoners' dilemma; reciprocal free trade may be the best realistic option even if unilateral free trade is not.

CATASTROPHIC PLP EFFECT: THE CC MODEL

The PLP effect illustrated above works in a smooth way, but how does it work in a model where catastrophic agglomeration is a possibility? As Chapter 6 showed, it is simple to add demand-linked circular causality to the FC model. The result, the CC model, yields a closed-form solution for the spatial division of industry in a model where agglomeration can collapse catastrophically.

The two key expressions for the CC model (see Chapter 6 for derivations and motivation) are

$$s_n = \frac{(1 - \phi^*\phi)s_E}{(1 - \phi)(1 - \phi^*)} - \frac{\phi}{1 - \phi}, \quad s_E = (1 - \beta)s_L + \beta s_n \quad (12.12)$$

where $\beta \equiv b\rho/(\rho + \delta)$ and $b \equiv \mu/\sigma$. The first expression, which is identical to the corresponding condition for the FC model, shows that expenditure shifting leads to production shifting in the CC model. The second expression shows that, unlike the FC model, production shifting also leads to expenditure shifting in the CC model (in the FC model, s_E is fixed parametrically).

The interior equilibrium becomes catastrophically unstable when the slope of the first expression with respect to s_E exceeds the inverse of the slope of the second expression with respect to s_n. The reason is that for such levels of openness, a shock to firm location sparks a self-reinforcing cycle of expenditure shifting and production shifting that results in all industry being located in one nation.

The easiest way to characterize the collapse is to find the closed-form solution for the north's share of industry (we do this by plugging the second expression in (12.12) into the first), and check when a slight increase in northern protection would induce *all* industry to decamp to the north. The result of the closed-form solution for s_n with asymmetric protection, but symmetric endowments is

$$s_n = \frac{1}{2} \frac{1 + \phi\phi^* - 2\phi - (1 - \phi\phi^*)\beta}{(1 - \phi)(1 - \phi^*) - (1 - \phi\phi^*)\beta} \quad (12.13)$$

To complete the analysis, we start out with identical levels of protection, so $\phi = \phi^*$, and parameterize the north's unilateral protection by introducing the parameter $\varepsilon \equiv \phi/\phi^* \leq 1$. Then, we differentiate the resulting expression for s_n with respect to ε and evaluate the derivative as $\varepsilon = 1$. The result is

$$\frac{ds_n}{d\varepsilon} = \frac{-\phi/2}{(1 - \phi)^2 - (1 - \phi^2)\beta} \quad (12.14)$$

By inspection, this 'delocation derivative' is infinite when $\phi = (1 - \beta)/(1 + \beta)$. This critical value is none other than the break point of the symmetric CC model. This is summarized in the following result.

Result 12.6. *In the CC model, which allows for self-reinforcing agglomeration, that is, circular causality, a slight unilateral increase in protection by one nation, can cause a catastrophic agglomeration of industry into the protecting nation when the level of openness is near the break point. This massive delocation will lower prices and raise welfare in the protecting nation, and do the opposite in the other nation.*

12.2.3 What's Wrong with this Picture?

In the model described above, import substitution is always a winning policy in the sense that unilateral protection is a sure-fire route to promoting industrialization and the national interest. Putting the conclusion in this way brings at least three qualifications to mind.

First, relocation of industrial activity is expensive. While the notion of costly relocation is perfectly reasonable, parsimony has led standard economic geography models to ignore this important facet of the real world. As it turns out, including it has important implications.

Second, import substitution is an attempt to boost an industry (which amounts to forcing relocation in this economic geography model) by creating a sheltered market for firms. If the protected nation is very small, such policies may be ultimately fruitless; even near-prohibitive import barriers may result in no relocation.

The third qualification is that comparative advantage matters. The standard economic geography models ignore comparative advantage for simplicity. However, by making firms a priori indifferent to location on the supply side, the standard model stacks the odds in favour of PLP by making dramatic delocation easier. While such a simplification is reasonable for many purposes, it is clearly inappropriate for trade policy analysis. For instance, when thinking about why import substitution failed in Latin America, it is impossible not to point to the fact that these nations had massive comparative disadvantages in many of the industries they were trying to foster.

We turn now to extending the model to capture the first of these qualifications. We do so by introducing the concept of relocation barriers, that is, barriers to capital movement.

12.2.4 Ambiguity with Relocation Barriers

It is costly to relocate production abroad. This section shows that allowing for this natural factor can reverse the stark PLP result. For simplicity, we consider a 'per unit' relocation cost, that is, a relocation cost that is the same for all firms and is unaffected by the amount of relocation that has occurred. A key insight in this section is that the stark protectionist implications of PLP are not intrinsic to economic geography models. Rather, they stem in a large part from the simplifying assumption that moving firms is costless, but moving goods is costly.

FLAT RELOCATION COSTS: DISCONTINUOUS PLP

Some relocation costs are natural, but some are man-made. Natural costs include linguist, cultural and climatic differences between a firm's host and home nations, coordination costs over distance, etc. The list of man-made barriers is much longer. Nations, especially developing nations, have many policies that implicitly make it difficult for foreign firms to produce locally. For instance, foreign firms may require a large and uncertain number of permits in order to do business. Or they may be made to strictly adhere to local tax, labour, heath and environmental laws, while local firms may be allowed to skirt them. Foreign firms may also be systematically subject to greater pressures to directly or indirectly pay off local officials. Finally, foreign firms may have much higher costs of acquiring information about local production conditions, legal systems and local consumers. Clearly, the most satisfactory route would be to provide micro-foundations for each of the factors separately. Doing so, however, would take us too far afield.

To illustrate the importance of relocation costs as clearly as possible, we continue to work with the symmetric FC model, but we now allow for a relocation cost. Specifically, we assume that a firm relocating from one nation to another pays a *proportional* cost of $1 - \kappa$, where $0 \leq \kappa \leq 1$ is a measure of the freeness of capital's mobility. That is, $\kappa = 1$ indicates costless capital mobility and $\kappa = 0$ indicates zero (infinitely costly) capital mobility. (Note that both trade freeness and capital freeness are parameterized such that 1 is perfectly free and 0 is perfectly closed.) Importantly, we assume that this is a one-time cost and focus on situations where it has already been incurred so that the relocation cost has no impact on current earnings.[3]

The No-Delocation Band. Begin by considering what would happen to π and π^* if same-size nations had different trade barriers, but relocation was forbidden.[4] As usual, higher home protection makes home more attractive in the sense that $\pi > \pi^*$ when s_n is held at 1/2. Now given this difference, would firms relocate from foreign to home if they faced relocation costs? Plainly, relocation would only occur if relocation were sufficiently cheap, that is, if the relocation costs $1 - \kappa$ were sufficiently small. Specifically, firms would move only if $\pi\kappa > \pi^*$ (evaluated at $s_n = 1/2$). This is captured by the following inequalities that hold with complementary slackness[5]

$$\phi < \phi^* \quad \Rightarrow \quad \pi\kappa \leq \pi^*, \quad s_n \geq \frac{1}{2}, \quad \text{w.c.s.}$$

$$\phi > \phi^* \quad \Rightarrow \quad \pi^*\kappa \leq \pi, \quad s_n \leq \frac{1}{2}, \quad \text{w.c.s.} \tag{12.15}$$

The first of these applies when home protection (i.e. $\phi < \phi^*$) creates an incipient inflow of firms/capital. If any foreign firms do relocate to home—which, given the initial symmetry, is tantamount to $s_n > 1/2$—they will do so up to the point where $\kappa\pi = \pi^*$ with $\kappa \leq 1$. The second equation covers the mirror-image case where foreign is more protectionist.

---

[3] We have worked out an alternative model—the melting capital model—where κ represents a flow cost. The results are broadly similar, but the analysis is more complex since regional expenditure levels depend upon capital flows.

[4] This is identical to the short-run analysis in Chapter 3.

[5] Here, we assume, as usual in the economic geography literature, that firms are myopic. If they were forward looking, the condition would compare the present value of the π difference to the one-off cost. We could repeat all the analysis using $\rho\kappa$ to reflect this; nothing important would change.

To characterize the range of ϕ where delocation is not worthwhile (so s_n remains at 1/2), we solve $\kappa\pi = \pi^*$ and $\pi = \kappa\pi^*$ for the critical levels of ϕ using (12.5). We refer to this as the 'no-delocation band', or 'hysteresis band'. The task, however, is complicated by the fact that even though s_n remains unchanged in the band, s_E changes since π does not equal π^* with $\phi \neq \phi^*$. For example, starting at full symmetry, home protection raises π and lower π^*, even if s_E stayed at 1/2. This increase in home earning power, however, also raises s_E and this in turn leads to a further increase in π and a decrease in π^*. In other words, the model with relocation costs displays a form of demand-linkage that was not present above.

To deal with this demand link, we solve $s_E = E/E^w$ for s_E (with s_n fixed since we are in the band) to get

$$s_E = \left(\frac{1}{2}\right) \frac{(1 + \phi)[(1 + \phi^*)b - (1 + \phi^*)]}{(1 - \phi\phi^*)b - (1 + \phi^*)(1 + \phi)} \qquad (12.16)$$

A demand linkage of sorts can be seen since s_E rises as home protection increases. For example, $ds_E/d\phi$ equals $-b/[2(1 + \phi)(1 - b + \phi(1 + b)] < 0$ when evaluated at the symmetry point. As long as protection levels stay within the band, the change in relative market sizes has no impact on location of industry, so inside the band this is just half of the demand-linked circular causality that exists in operation (see Chapters 3 and 4 for details).

Using (12.16) in (12.5) and its foreign analogue, we can implicitly define the limits of the band with symmetric-sized nations with the equations $\kappa\pi = \pi^*$ and $\pi = \kappa\pi^*$. Solving these, we find the range of ϕ for which $s_n = 1/2$ given ϕ^* and κ. This is the no-delocation band, namely

$$\phi^{\text{lower}} = \frac{2\kappa\phi^* - (1 - b)(1 - \kappa)}{2 + (1 + b)(1 - \kappa)\phi^*}, \quad \phi^{\text{upper}} = \frac{2\phi^* + (1 - b)(1 - \kappa)}{2\kappa - (1 + b)(1 - \kappa)\phi^*} \quad (12.17)$$

For values of ϕ within this range, the delocation elasticity is zero. Note that the band widens as ϕ^* increases since the gain from asymmetric protection diminishes as the overall level of barriers falls. Figure 12.1 shows that the band partitions protection space into three regions. Inside the band, no delocation occurs, but on either side, home protection will increase s_n. The figure also illustrates the point that the band narrows as delocation costs fall; that is, the degree of capital mobility, κ, rises.

The Price Implications.   In the no-delocation band, unilateral protection has the usual price-rising impact on the price index (since $ds_n/d\phi = 0$ inside the band, only the 'direct effect' operates). For example, if ϕ^* remains constant and home lowers ϕ starting from $\phi = \phi^*$, the home price index rises as ϕ approaches ϕ^{lower}. The reason is that lowering ϕ raises the home price index by increasing the price of imported varieties without affecting the price of local varieties or the number of varieties produced locally.

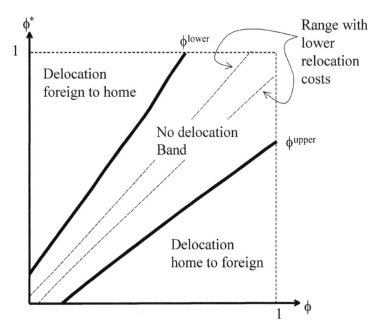

Figure 12.1   The no-delocation band.

Result 12.7. *Unilateral changes in openness have the classical effect on prices as long as the openness levels are within the no-delocation band defined by (12.17), that is, a unilateral opening by home lowers the home price index.*

When the level of home freeness drops below this critical value, that is, $\phi < \phi^{\text{lower}}$, foreign firms begin to delocate to home according to the modified location condition, $\pi\kappa = \pi^*$. The s_n that solves this is

$$s_n = \frac{1}{2} \frac{(1 - \phi\phi^*)(1 - \kappa)b + 2[\kappa - \phi(1 - \kappa\phi^*)]}{(1 + \kappa)(1 + \phi\phi^*) - 2(\phi + \kappa\phi^*)} \tag{12.18}$$

where this is only valid for $\phi < \phi^{\text{lower}}$. It is clear that s_n rises as ϕ continues to fall below the band, specifically,

$$\frac{ds_n}{d\phi} = -(1 - \kappa\phi^*)\{[2 - b(1 - \kappa)](1 - \phi^*) + 2\phi^*(1 - \kappa)\} \tag{12.19}$$

where D is the denominator from (12.18). This is negative since κ and ϕ^* are less than unity. In fact, the price-lowering effect of the delocation outweighs the price-rising effect on varieties that continue to be imported, so the price index falls.[6] In other words, PLP outside of the band. This persists until all M varieties are produced locally, or ϕ reaches zero.

---

[6] We have an analytic expression for $dP/d\phi$ below the band, but it is too awkward to be revealing; see UniTradPo.mws.

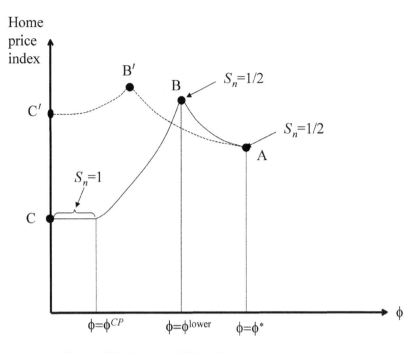

Figure 12.2 Truncated PLP effects with costly relocation.

The solid lines in Figure 12.2 show an example of the price implications of decreasing home's trade freeness from $\phi = \phi^*$ to $\phi = 0$. The point labelled A is the initial, symmetric protection position, where half world industry is in home. Initially, a decrease in home freeness raises prices as shown, up to ϕ^{lower} because the price of imports rises and there is no delocation of varieties. Further reductions in home trade freeness produce delocation-induced price-index reductions, as (12.19) shows. In the solid-line example in Figure 12.2, all firms have delocated to home when ϕ reaches ϕ^{CP}, so the price index is flat (and equal to unity) for lower levels of ϕ. In this case, it is simple to show that PLP is in operation. At point C—where $\phi = 0$ and $s_n = 1$—no varieties are subject to trade costs so $P = 1$. At point B—where $s_n = 1/2$—we know that some varieties are imported and subject to positive trade costs, so P at B must be greater than unity.

The solid-line example, however, is not the only possibility. When foreign trade has a sufficiently high level of protection, then even fully closing off imports, that is, setting $\phi = 0$, will not be enough to induce full agglomeration in the home country.[7] In this case, illustrated in the diagram with point C′, it turns out that P at B′ is below P at this point but establishing this is more involved (for details, see analysis in the Maple worksheet UniTradPo.mws available on http:// heiwww.unige.ch/~baldwin/). To summarize this, we write the following result.

―――――――――

[7] Note that $\phi^{CP} = (2\phi^*\kappa - 1)/\phi^*$ is only positive when ϕ^* or κ are sufficiently small; when this condition is not met, $\phi = 0$ does not entail full agglomeration.

Result 12.8. *Unilateral reductions in openness lead to lower prices in the protecting nation when the protecting nation's level of openness is below the no-delocation band defined by (12.17).*

Truncated and Overall PLP. The fact that the home price index falls when it raises its level of protection beyond the no-delocation band can be thought of as a 'truncated' PLP effect. A natural question, however, is whether home prices rise or fall when home moves its level of openness from the symmetric position, where $\phi = \phi^*$, to the extreme position where $\phi = 0$. In other words, would home see its prices fall if it were to shut off all imports of manufactured varieties? If the answer is no, home will clearly be better off staying with symmetric protection. As we shall see, the answer depends upon κ, ϕ^* and b.

To study this, we define a test for what we call the 'overall PLP' effect, that is, a test for whether a shift from symmetric protection to prohibitive protection lowers home's price index. Maintaining our assumption of symmetric sized nations, the test is[8]

$$\frac{b + \kappa(2 - b)}{2[\kappa(1 - \phi^*) + 1 - \kappa\phi^*]} > \frac{1 + \phi^*}{2} \qquad (12.20)$$

where the left-hand side is $\Delta = s_n + \phi(1 - s_n)$ where s_n is from (12.18) evaluated at $\phi = 0$, and the right-hand side is $\Delta = s_n + \phi(1 - s_n)$ evaluated at $s_n = 1/2$ and symmetric openness levels.

To characterize the constellation of parameters where the overall PLP effect holds, we first point out that if capital movement is perfectly free, that is, $\kappa = 1$, then the PLP test is positive (??please check) since we are in the standard FC model where PLP holds (see Result 12.3). If capital movements are perfectly restricted, that is, $\kappa = 0$, then the PLP effect does not hold; this is an implication of Result 12.7 and the fact that the entire openness space is inside the no-delocation band when capital movement is prohibitively expensive. To make a more precise statement about how free capital movements must be to yield the PLP result, we impose an equality sign on (12.20) and solve for κ. This tells us that when capital movements are freer than κ', where $\kappa' = (1 - \phi - b)/(1 - \phi - b + 2\phi^2)$, the PLP result holds. This is summarized in the following result.

Result 12.9. *If capital movements are sufficiently costly, unilateral protection raises the domestic price index in the protecting nation. The critical level of capital movement cost is lower when the other nation has very low trade barriers and agglomeration forces (as measured by $b = \mu/\sigma$) are strong.*

This result is quite intuitive. When foreign is very open to trade, firms find it cheap to supply foreign consumers from the home country and thus they are easily induced into moving to the home nation. The impact of agglomeration

---

[8] The ratio of price indices equals the ratio in the expression raised to the power of $\mu/(1 - \sigma)$, but since this is compared to unity, we can dispense with the power.

forces is similarly straightforward. When agglomeration forces are strong, delocation of firms from foreign to home are self-reinforcing and so are more easily induced.

12.2.5 Political Economy of Protection with Entry Barriers

In the real world, import substitution policies typically end up sustaining a few, poorly run and economically inefficient firms that are—not coincidentally— controlled by politically powerful groups. This section considers political economy forces that help make sense of this common outcome. In short, we suggest that import protection creates conditions in which entry barriers become very attractive to domestic industry. The reasoning is based on Baldwin and Robert-Nicoud (2002).

We continue to work with the previous section's model, namely the FC model with costly capital relocation. To illustrate the reasoning, consider two extreme policy combinations—capital market barriers without unilateral protection, and unilateral trade protection without capital market barriers. Under the first combination ($\phi = \phi^*$ and $\kappa < 1$), relocation costs have absolutely no impact; starting at equilibrium, specifically at $\pi = \pi^*$, no relocation would occur in any case so the costs are irrelevant. The important point is that home capital owners would have no incentive to lobby for entry restrictions if there were no protection.

Under the second combination ($\phi < \phi^*$ and $\kappa = 1$), the unilateral reduction in home trade freeness would tend to attract foreign firms and since firms can move costlessly, the location condition implies that new firms enter until the condition $\pi = \pi^*$ is restored. We have seen that the equalized reward to capital $\pi = \pi^*$ is invariant to trade freeness and the spatial allocation of firms.[9] The key point here is that because the reward to capital is completely unaffected by protection, lobbying for protection has no effects on capital owners' incomes and thus industry would have no incentive to lobby.[10]

To summarize these results we write the following result.

> **Result 12.10.** *If capital movements are costless, industry has no incentive to lobby for protection since foreign entry continues until the reward to capital is force back down to the pre-protection level. Moreover, if the home market is not more protected than the foreign market (i.e. home and foreign have the same levels of openness), there is no gain from lobbying for capital flow restrictions since no capital will flow in any case.*

However, as we saw above, the *combination* of unilateral protection and entry barriers does raise the earnings of local capital owners. Thus, protection creates an incentive for local capitalist/industrialists to lobby for relocation barriers, and vice versa. This suggests the following sequence of events. A government deci-

---

[9] The typical operating profit is invariant to trade policy and in fact it equals $bL^w/(1 - b)n^w$, where $b = \mu/\sigma$ and both $n^w = K^w$ and L^w are fixed by endowments.

[10] This line of reasoning is pursued in greater depth in Baldwin and Robert-Nicoud (2002).

des to impose unilateral protection, justified perhaps under the rubric of import substitution. Once the trade barriers are in place, restrictions on capital inflows become a source of gain for local capital owners. We can go somewhat further and argue that the utility levels, as well as the incomes, of capital owners be raised by a package of protection and entry barriers under certain circumstances. The reason is that for a fairly wide range of parameter values, protection-cum-relocation costs can raise the *real* income of K owners. This is obviously true if the package lowers the local price index (since $\kappa < 1$ raises their nominal earnings), but it can also hold in some cases where the package raises local prices.

To look at this more closely, we take the real reward to local K owners as the objective function of the K owners' lobby group (thus ignoring coordination problems within the lobby). The policy package considered is a combination of $\phi < \phi^*$ and $\kappa < 1$, such that the nation stays inside the no-delocation band; this guarantees that the package raises the local price index. For simplicity, we focus on a perturbation of the symmetric situation so the economy stays in the no-delocation band even if κ is very close to unity (i.e. relocation costs were small). Formally, consider the impact on π/P when $\kappa < 1$ and ϕ is lowered slightly, starting from $\phi = \phi^*$. Using (12.5) and (12.16), the derivative at symmetry is

$$\frac{d(\pi/P)}{d\phi} = \frac{b(1+Z)^{1-a}}{4(1-bZ)}[2a - 1 - (1 + 2ab)Z], \quad Z \equiv \frac{1-\phi}{1+\phi} \quad (12.21)$$

The first multiplicative term is always positive, so the sign of the term in square brackets determines whether the policy package raises or lowers K owners' real incomes. Since the level of 'closedness' Z is between zero and unity, inspection shows that the term in square brackets is always negative when $a < 1/2$, and even when this condition fails, it is negative when the initial level of protection is high enough. This is summarized in the following result.

> **Result 12.11.** *A small increase in unilateral protection (which tends to attract foreign capital), packaged together with an increase in the cost of capital that is sufficient to prevent any inflow, will always raise the real incomes of capital owners. Thus, if local capital owners have the political power to set protection levels and to impose regulations, taxes, etc. that discourage capital inflows, political pressure may ensure that import substitution policies never work.*

To phrase this result differently, import substitution policies may fail on purpose since local capital owners can raise their real incomes by ensuring that the import substitution policies do not expand domestic industrial output. While it would be too bold to assert that this is the main explanation of why import substitution policies have typically failed, the logic is at least consistent with the common observation that nations who pursued import substitution policies also typically imposed many other barriers that made it hard to do business. This fact that firms protected by import substitution policies are often controlled by politically powerful individuals or groups makes it easier to believe that the logic is in operation.

12.2.6 Ambiguity with Size Asymmetry

Even enthusiastic supporters of import substitution policies admit that home-market size matters. For example, if scale economies are important and a nation is sufficiently small, unilateral protection will encourage very little home production and thus make it likely that import substitution fails. This point also comes through clearly in the model laid out above.

Given the analysis above, we have a simple way to see the impact of size. Specifically, we consider the test for the overall PLP effect as described in (12.20) but allowing for size asymmetry, we get[11]

$$\frac{\phi^* s_K [\kappa + (1 - \kappa)(1 - s_K)] - (1 - s_K)[\phi^*(1 - \kappa\phi^*) + (1 - b)(1 - \kappa)s_K]}{(1 - \kappa)(1 - s_K) + \kappa(1 - \phi^*)} > 0$$

(12.22)

Here, s_K measures home's relative size since we have assumed that the two nations have identical factor endowment ratios, that is, that $s_K = s_L$. Plainly, if s_K is sufficiently small, the condition fails which means that home has higher prices with prohibitive barriers than it does with symmetric trade barriers.

12.2.7 Ambiguity with Comparative Advantage

The result that unilateral protection can lower the domestic price index is surprising and counter-intuitive. In a large measure, the result stems from the assumption that firms are—apart from issues of import protection—entirely indifferent to producing in the two locations. However, when considering the impact of a real-world trade policy—say, protection-led development strategy—the first order of business would be to investigate the nation's natural comparative advantage. Hereto, we have been working with models that did not permit this. Assuming identical factor endowment ratios eliminated Heckscher–Ohlin comparative advantage and positing identical technology across nations ruled-out Ricardian comparative advantage.

This section introduces Ricardian comparative advantage within the manufacturing sector and shows that the price-lowering impact of import protection depends critically on the protecting nation's comparative advantage. In particular, a nation that has a comparative disadvantage in manufactures unambiguously loses from raising its import barriers if the comparative disadvantage is strong enough.

RICARDIAN COMPARATIVE ADVANTAGE IN THE FOOTLOOSE CAPITAL MODEL

Here, we introduce a single modification to the model described above. The modified model is similar to that of Forslid and Wooton (2001).

We continue to assume that nations are identical in all respects, except in terms of manufacturing technology. Specifically, manufactured variety is produced subject to a fixed cost and constant marginal cost, as before, but now fixed costs are assumed

---

[11] When considering size asymmetries, we impose $s_L = s_K$, since, with this assumption, the two nations differ only in terms of size.

to differ both within and across national manufacturing sectors. These differences in fixed cost generate comparative advantage in the sense that the number of varieties produced is determined endogenously. Recall that, in the model above, the number of varieties was determined solely by capital endowments.

With this change, the cost of producing x_i in home is

$$rF_i + wa_m x_i; \quad F_i = \beta i^\chi, \quad \chi \geq 0, \ \beta > 0 \tag{12.23}$$

where F_i, the variety-specific amount of K associated with the fixed cost, r, is K's reward, and β and χ are parameters. The functional form of F_i requires us to order home varieties from lowest fixed cost to highest fixed cost in each nation. The cost function for foreign is isomorphic but, we assume that the order of fixed costs by variety in home is exactly the reverse of foreign's. These assumptions mean that the variety that is most cheaply produced in home would be the most expensive to produce in foreign.

Observe that if χ (a mnemonic for comparative advantage) is zero and β is unity, then this model is identical to the footloose capital model described above (i.e. there is one unit of K required per variety for all varieties). As χ rises above zero, the ratio of home and foreign production costs for a given variety diverges from unity; in other words technology-driven comparative advantage emerges. In this sense, χ allows us to parameterize the importance of comparative advantage. Note that the marginal production cost continues to be identical across all varieties worldwide as in the standard FC model.

Although this modelling choice—putting comparative advantage in via fixed costs instead of in the variable costs—is somewhat unconventional, it permits us to illustrate, simply and analytically, the main link between comparative advantage and the PLP effect.

Altering the fixed cost assumptions does not affect the operating profit earned per variety. Here, as in the standard footloose capital model, the symmetry of marginal costs, mark-up pricing and factor price equalization (due itself to free trade in A and perfect capital mobility) implies that all home and foreign goods are priced at unity in their local markets. The price in their exports markets is just $1 + t$ for goods imported into home and $1 + t^*$ for goods imported into foreign (t and t^* are the tariff equivalents of home and foreign iceberg import barriers). What this means is that the formula for operating profit in (12.6) and its foreign analogue are still applicable.

The variable fixed cost input leads to two important changes in the model. The first is the international arbitrage equation. Since the fixed costs, which continue to consist solely of capital, vary across varieties and nations, the arbitrage condition must take account of how many units of K are necessary to produce a given variety. Thus, the arbitrage equation becomes

$$\frac{\pi[s_n, n^w]}{F[s_n n^w]} = \frac{\pi^*[s_n, n^w]}{F^*[s_n n^w]} \tag{12.24}$$

where we express the number of home and foreign firms as $n = s_n n^w$ and $n^* = (1 - s_n)n^w$.

The other important change concerns the global number of varieties that can be affected by trade policy. In the standard model, K's full employment condition was simply $n^w = K^w$ and was thus independent of trade costs. Given (12.23), however, K's full employment condition becomes

$$K^w = \beta \frac{s_n^{\chi+1} + (1 - s_n)^{\chi+1}}{1 + \chi}(n^w)^{\chi+1} \tag{12.25}$$

Finally, since size asymmetry plays no role in the insight to be illustrated, we assume symmetric sized nations, that is, $s_E = 1/2$. To make this airtight, we assume that capital owners hold a perfectly diversified global portfolio, so that they earn half the operating profit generated worldwide regardless of the location equilibrium.

ANALYTIC SOLUTIONS FOR SPECIAL CASES

Since (12.25) involves a potentially non-integer power, we cannot solve the model analytically for general values of χ. Nevertheless, the model can be solved for particular χ values, the easiest being $\chi = 0$ and $\chi = 1$.

When $\chi = 0$, all varieties have the same fixed cost, so the model reduces to the standard FC model. Consequently, (12.9) is valid and the PLP effect is always in operation.

When $\chi = 1$, we can solve the capital mobility condition, (12.24), for the equilibrium, s_n. There are two solutions, with the economically relevant one being

$$s_n = \frac{1 + \phi\phi^* + \phi - \phi^* - \sqrt{(1 + \phi^2)(1 + \phi^{*2})}}{2(\phi - \phi^*)} \tag{12.26}$$

The full employment of the capital condition in this case takes a particularly simple and intuitive form:

$$n^w = \sqrt{\frac{K^w}{\beta(s_n^2 + (1 - s_n)^2)/2}} \tag{12.27}$$

Note that the denominator on the right-hand side includes the sum of squared national shares of industry, that is, something akin to the Herfindahl index of concentration. As usual this sum of squared shares attains its minimum at $s_n = 1/2$ and its maximum at $s_n = 1$ and 0. Since any deviation from symmetric protection moves s_n away from $s_n = 1/2$, (12.27) tells us that any unilateral protection will reduce the total number of varieties available for consumption. In essence, asymmetric trade barriers will distort the allocation of resources in a way that reduces n^w. What all this means is that unilateral protection has an additional impact on the price index, namely the 'negative variety effect of protection'.

Using (12.26) in the full employment of capital condition, yields the equilibrium number of varieties. Again there are two roots. The relevant one is

$$n^w = \sqrt{\frac{2K^w}{\beta}\left(1 + \frac{1 + \phi\phi^*}{\sqrt{(1 + \phi^2)(1 + \phi^{*2})}}\right)} \tag{12.28}$$

The negative variety effect of protection is seen by noting that the quotient in the radical attains its maximum at $\phi = \phi^*$.

To check for the PLP effect in the $\chi = 1$ case, we use (12.26) and (12.28) in the definition of the price index, differentiate with respect to home trade freeness and evaluate the derivative at $\phi = \phi^*$. This gives

$$\frac{d\ln(P)}{d\phi} = -a\frac{1 + \phi + 2\phi^2}{2(1 + \phi)(1 + \phi^2)} < 0 \qquad (12.29)$$

This shows that unilateral liberalization lowers the price index since the expression is manifestly negative for all relevant parameter values. In short, the PLP effect fails when comparative advantage is sufficiently strong.

As noted above, home liberalization has three effects on the price index. The direct effect of lowering the price of imported goods, the delocation effect that depends upon $ds_n/d\phi$, and the negative variety effect. Since the negative variety effect is tightly linked to our specification of comparative advantage, it is worth noting that even holding n^w constant, liberalization lowers P. Specifically, $d\Delta/d\phi$ evaluated at symmetric protection equals the term in square brackets in (12.29), which is itself unambiguously positive. The point, of course, is that sufficiently strong comparative advantage reduces the delocation elasticity to the point where the direct price-lowering impact of liberalization is not offset by the loss of location manufacturing production.

NUMERICAL SOLUTIONS FOR NON-INTEGER CASES

What we have shown is that when comparative advantage forces are sufficiently weak ($\chi = 0$), the PLP effect appears, but when they are sufficiently strong ($\chi = 1$), it does not. To investigate intermediate values of χ, we turn to numerical simulations. Figure 12.3 shows the results. The diagram has χ on the horizontal axis and the value of the derivative on the vertical axis. The simulation is done assuming that the initial level of ϕ is 0.5, and that $\mu = 4/10$ and $\sigma = 4$. The results confirm that the PLP effect holds only when comparative advantage is weak. Numerically, the crossing point is between $\chi = 1/20$ and $\chi = 1/100$. When we perform similar simulations for higher and lower values of the initial level of trade freeness, we find qualitatively similar results. This line of exploration, however, does reveal that for any level of χ, the PLP effect is more likely to hold when the initial level of trade freeness is high. This is expected since the elasticity of delocation in this model increases dramatically with ϕ.

12.3 Liberalization and Industrialization

The notion that unilateral protection always lowers the domestic price level by enticing industry to relocate is certainly one of the most outlandish policy implications of simple economic geography models. The preceding section showed that this was in fact an artefact of several simplifying assumptions rather than a

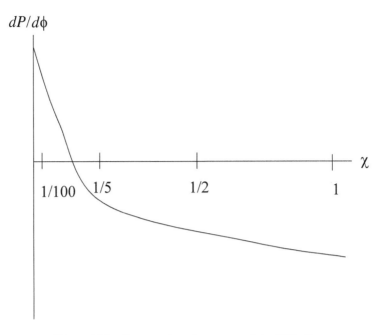

Figure 12.3   Comparative advantage and the PLP effect.

deep result. Refuting the PLP effect, however, is not really sufficient for showing that economic geography models are suitable tools for trade policy analysis. Even with the extensions discussed above, unilateral protection always fosters industrialization in the sense that a nation can always increase its share of world industry by imposing a unilateral import barrier. Unilateral protection, of course, is not generally viewed as a sure fire route to industrialization. The many and varied experiments with import substitution failed throughout the developing world.

This section explores variants of the simple economic geography model in which trade *liberalization* can foster industrialization. The possibility that liberalization might be pro-industry in an economic geography model was first addressed by Puga and Venables (1997, 1999) in a series of numerical examples using the vertical linkages version of the core–periphery model (see Chapter 8 for a presentation of this 'CPVL' model). For instance, their 1999 paper uses a two-country, two-sector model where consumers have non-homothetic preferences (the spending shares on industrial goods rises with the level of income). The small nation has only 1/3 the endowment of the big country and 'natural' trade costs have a tariff equivalent of 15%. The big country imposes no other import barriers, but the small country potentially imposes additional import barriers. For the particular parameters they choose, Puga and Venables show that if the small country imposes an additional import tariff of between approximately 30% and 60%, then there will be no industry in the small country. Raising the small-nation tariff beyond 60%, or lowering it below 30% both result in industrialization. The acute intractability of the core–periphery model prevents them from pinning down a precise relationship between their result and their particular assumptions (on the size asymmetry, the level of natural trade costs, the extent of the non-homotheticity, the strength of agglomeration forces, etc.). Their discussion, however, provides intuition that suggests their findings are more general than the specific examples. This section uses a variant of the vertical linkages variant of the footloose capital model to analytically illustrate the Puga–Venables intuition.

12.3.1 Footloose Capital Model with Vertical Linkages

Studying the possibility of pro-industry liberalization, requires us to extend our simple economic geography models to include intermediate goods, that is, 'vertical linkages'. The point is quite simple.

Without intermediates the only role of unilateral protection is to shift expenditure from foreign varieties to domestic varieties, so unilateral liberalization can only reduce the attractiveness of the liberalizing nation to industry. If, however, we make the natural and realistic assumption that industrial firms use imported intermediates, liberalization takes on a new role. To the extent that liberalization lowers the cost of imported intermediates, liberalization can lower the local cost of production and thus—other things being equal—increase the attractiveness of setting up an industrial firm in the liberalizing nation.

To make this point, we work with the 'vertical linkages' version of the footloose capital model (or FCVL model for short). The model, due to Robert-Nicoud (2002), is described at length in Chapter 8, so we just briefly review its main features here. The basic set-up is identical to that of the FC model, namely two sectors (M and A), two nations (home and foreign), and two factors (L which is immobile and K which is perfectly mobile internationally). The supply assumptions for the Walrasian A sector are identical to those of the FC model, but quite different for the M sector. Manufacturing firms use only capital as a fixed cost as in the FC model while the variable costs compromise a Cobb–Douglas composite of labour and intermediates. In particular, the intermediates are aggregated in the standard CES composite, so the cost function for a typical variety is given by $\pi + a_M w^{1-\mu} P_m^{\mu}$, where P_m is the standard CES price index.

Since capital moves freely in search of the highest reward, the location condition for an interior equilibrium is $\pi = \pi^*$. The local price indices are unimportant since all capital earning is spent in the capital owner's nation, regardless of where the capital is employed. The condition for a core–periphery outcome is $\pi > \pi^*$, for the core-in-the north outcome and the opposite for the core-in-the-south outcome. Importantly, in any of these equilibria, the reward to capital is always the same regardless of the degree of openness and the spatial pattern of capital employment.

The FCVL model displays both demand linkages (production shifting leads to expenditure shifting since firms buy industrial goods as intermediates) and cost linkages (since the CES price index falls as the local share of industry rises). As such, it is not fully tractable in the sense that we cannot get a closed-form solution for the spatial allocation of firms, s_n. Nevertheless, the model is significantly more tractable than the vertical linkages version of the core–periphery model because we can derive a function that gives the mobile factor's reward in terms of the spatial allocation of industry. See Chapter 8 for more on this comparison.

The location equilibrium can be described by three equilibrium expressions. The expression for north and south rewards to capital is (with our normalizations $E^w = 1$, $n^w = K^w = 1$)

$$\pi = b\left(\frac{s_E}{\Delta} + \frac{\phi^* s_E^*}{\Delta^*}\right)\Delta^\mu, \quad \pi^* = b\left(\frac{\phi s_E}{\Delta} + \frac{s_E^*}{\Delta^*}\right)(\Delta^*)^\mu \qquad (12.30)$$

where ϕ and ϕ^* are the north's and south's degree of trade freeness as usual and the denominators of the demand functions, that is, the Δs, are implicitly defined by

$$\Delta = n^w(s_n\Delta^\mu + \phi(1 - s_n)(\Delta^*)^\mu), \quad \Delta^* = n^w(\phi^* s_n\Delta^\mu + (1 - s_n)(\Delta^*)^\mu)\,(12.31)$$

and the north's relative market size is given by

$$s_E \equiv \frac{E_m}{E_m^w} = (1 - \mu)s_L + bs_K + \frac{\mu - b}{b}\pi s_n \qquad (12.32)$$

where E_m stands for total expenditure on manufactures (this encompasses final and intermediate demands). Before proceeding with the analysis, it is worth noting several aspects of these expressions. First, the expression for π is very similar to the one in the FC model, but it includes the extra term Δ^μ, which reflects the impact of the price of intermediates on a typical northern firm's sales. That is, if the CES price index, $P_m \equiv \Delta^{-\mu/(\sigma-1)}$, is particularly high in the north, then northern sales and, thus, π will be low. Second, the expressions for the Δs cannot be solved analytically (except for special cases), so unlike the standard FC model, the FCVL model is not fully tractable. Third, in the special case of symmetric endowments (i.e. $s_L = s_K = 1/2$), an even division of industry ($s_n = 1/2$) is always a solution, but it may not be stable. Moreover, as argued in the Appendix 2.B, the break point comes before the sustain point, so the model is subject to catastrophic agglomeration and locational hysteresis.

To explore the impact of liberalization, we first separate the role of protection into its two components.

FINAL AND INTERMEDIATE GOODS: EFFECTIVE RATE OF PROTECTION

Protection affects industry through two distinct channels in a model with imported intermediates—one channel functions via the local costs of imported intermediates, the other by protecting local producers from import competition. Intuition is served by separating these and to this end we suppose that the southern government can, somehow, impose distinct import barriers on: (1) imports that are sold to southern consumers; and (2) imports sold to firms as intermediate inputs. For simplicity's sake, we work with nations that are symmetric in terms of endowments. Moreover, to focus on industrialization, we assume that the common level of openness is just at the sustain point and all industry is agglom-erated in the north. That is, writing the π's as implicit function of the north's share of industry, n, and the level of trade freeness, ϕ, we have that $\pi[\phi^S, n] = \pi^*[\phi^S, 1 - n]$, where $n = 1$. The axis of investigation is to determine whether the southern government can, using an uneven liberalization, raise π^*; if it can, some industry will be attracted to the south since we start from the sustain point. In other words, liberalization will foster industrialization.

The core–periphery outcome is one of the special cases where we can find the Δs. With $n = 1$, (12.31) implies that $\Delta = 1$ and $\Delta^* = \phi$. Using these, and noting that with $n = 1$, northern demand depends on final and intermediate demand while southern demand stems only from consumers, the expression for π^* becomes

$$\pi^* = \frac{1}{\sigma}\left(\frac{\phi E_m}{1} + \frac{E_m^*}{\phi^*}\right)(\phi^* \gamma)^\mu, \quad \phi^* = \phi = \phi^S \tag{12.33}$$

where ϕ^S is the sustain point level of openness and $\gamma > 1$ reflects the extent to which southern protection is higher on final goods than on imported intermediates. Using Max Corden's concept of the effective rate of protection, $\gamma > 1$ implies that the effective rate of protection on final goods is higher than ϕ^S.

Simple inspection of (12.33) reveals that increasing γ—that is, liberalizing imports of industrial goods for intermediate use—raises π^*. Since π^* was just equal to π with $n = 1$ in this example, we know that such a liberalization would attract some industry to the south.

This type of trade liberalization can foster industrialization and indeed, most developing nations do maintain higher levels of protection on final goods than they do on intermediates. These practices lead to the creation of the notion of the 'effective rate of protection'. That is, when intermediates and final goods are protected at different rates, the true level of protection—the effective level—is not well captured by the tariff rate on the final good.

EVEN PROTECTION

Is it possible that across-the-board liberalization could also foster industrializa-tion? To check, we set $\gamma = 1$ and differentiate (12.33) with respect to ϕ^* to get

$$\frac{d\pi^*}{d\phi^*} = \frac{1}{\sigma}\left(\mu\frac{\phi E_m}{1} - (1 - \mu)\frac{E_m^*}{\phi^*}\right)(\phi^*)^{\mu-1} \tag{12.34}$$

If this is positive, we know that unilateral liberalization can be beneficial to industry. To characterize the sign of this expression, we solve for the ϕ^* that makes it just zero. For any level of ϕ^* above this critical value, liberalization will be pro-industry. The critical value is $(1 - \mu)E^*/(\mu\phi E)$. Since ϕ^* cannot exceed unity, we see that liberalization can be pro-industrialization when the northern market is relatively large and relatively open, and when the share of expenditure on industrial goods is not too large. Intuition for these findings is simple. A small size of the home market means that the part of the liberalization that affects import competition is small since home firms are mainly interested in the foreign market to begin with. The openness of the foreign market plays the same role. When the foreign market is very open, firms initially sell a large share of their output to the foreign market, so the change in home openness has a dampened impact on profits.

To summarize these results we write the following result.

Result 12.12 (pro-industrialization liberalization). *Liberalization that reduces the cost of imported intermediates without increasing import competition in the market for final industrial goods tends to make the liberalizing nation more attractive to industry. Moreover, even an across-the-board liberalization can stimulate industry when the liberalizing nation is relatively small and the foreign market is relatively open.*

12.4 INDUSTRIAL DEVELOPMENT, MARKET SIZE AND COMPARATIVE ADVANTAGE

The previous section studied liberalization in a model where the cost of imported intermediates affects the competitiveness of a nation's industrial firms, showing that, under some circumstances, unilateral opening could promote industrial development. This section continues to focus on industrial development but focuses on market size, comparative advantage and foreign trade barriers.

12.4.1 The Underdevelopment Puzzle

While rich country labour unions frequently bemoan the loss of 'good' manufacturing jobs to poor countries, most poor countries have the opposite complaint. Given their low wages, why isn't industry more interested in poor nations, that is, why are poor countries so 'underdeveloped' in terms of industry?

The principal focus of economic geography models is industrial location, so they provide a natural vehicle for studying the lack of industry in poor countries. Before turning to the models, however, we address and then put aside the most obvious answer.

Surely it is possible that poor countries have a comparative disadvantage in manufacturing. Poor country wages are low because their workers are not very productive. If this lack of productivity is either evenly spread across all sectors or especially concentrated in manufacturing, then the unit cost of producing industrial goods in developing nations will be higher than the unit cost in rich countries. The lower wages fail to offset the lower productivity, or—to use David Ricardo's terminology—poor nations have a comparative disadvantage in manufacturing. No wonder, then, that they have little industry. Even in a perfectly flat world (no trade costs, no imperfect competition, no increasing returns), firms would prefer manufacturing in rich countries.

While this classical explanation seems to account for the fact when it comes to many poor nations, the rapid industrialization of several formerly poor nations makes one wonder whether the full answer is not a bit more complex.

12.4.2 The 'Peripherality Point' in the FC and CC Models

The location of industry in a geography model depends upon relative market size as well as the degree of domestic and foreign openness. Here, we add a third concern, namely comparative advantage.

A convenient way to study the interaction of all these forces is to calculate what we call the 'peripherality point', that is, the smallest market size that permits the small/poor nation to attract at least some industry. Following the principle of progressive complexity, we start with the easiest model, the FC model of Chapter 3.

To be concrete, we consider the north to be the small (poor) nation that is struggling to promote industrial development when all industry is initially located in the large (rich) south. To add an important real-world element to the equation, we modify the standard FC model to allow for technology differences.

Ricardian comparative advantage can be easily introduced into the FC model by assuming that the ratio of labour input coefficients differs in the two nations. In particular, we assume that the north's ratio a_M/a_A differs from the south's a_M^*/a_A^*, where the a_i's are sectoral unit labour requirements using our standard notation. To introduce this enrichment with the least complication, we assume that, as in the basic FC model, $a_A = a_A^* = 1$, so free trade in A goods continues to equalize nominal wages in both nations (i.e. we assume that the no-full-specialization condition holds; see Chapter 3 for details). With this modification, the rewards to capital are

$$\pi = b\left(\frac{s_E}{\Delta} + \frac{\phi^*(1 - s_E)}{\Delta^*}\right)\chi, \quad \pi^* = b\left(\frac{\phi s_E}{\Delta} + \frac{1 - s_E}{\Delta^*}\right), \quad \chi \equiv \left(\frac{a_M}{a_M^*}\right)^{1-\sigma}$$

(12.35)

where

$$\Delta = \chi s_n + \phi(1 - s_n), \quad \Delta^* = \phi^*\chi s_n + 1 - s_n$$

and χ (a mnemonic for comparative advantage) measures comparative advantage with $\chi > 1$ indicating a comparative advantage for the north in industry; note that the χ here is entirely unrelated to the χ in (12.25). Recall that in the FC model, the north's relative market size, as measured by s_E, is exogenous.

Solving the location condition $\pi = \pi^*$ for the spatial division of industry, s_n, allowing for differences in size, openness and comparative advantage, we have

$$s_n = \frac{[(1 - s_E)\phi\phi^* + s_E]\chi - \phi}{(\chi - \phi)(1 - \chi\phi^*)}$$

(12.36)

where, as usual, this is only valid for economically relevant shares; if the right-hand side exceeds unity or is less than zero, then s_n is one or zero as appropriate.

As usual, real incomes depend upon industrial location and openness. If both countries are equally open, then, as usual, the small country will have less industry and, thus, a higher price index. In other words, the small country will also be the poor country.

Although our expressions are general, we are particularly interested in the case where $\chi > 1$, that is, where the small/poor/un-industrialized nation actually has a fundamental comparative advantage in industry. The interest lies in the fact that, in a neoclassical model, the small north would always have some industry regardless of trade costs. In an economic geography model, by contrast, market-access considerations can allow a pattern of specialization that contradicts comparative advantage. Furthermore, since wages are equalized, yet the north has a lower labour input coefficient in industry, the unit cost of industrial production is lower in the north.

To find the peripherality point, we find the s_E where s_n is just equal to zero, that is, where the core-in-the-south is just barely sustained. Solving $s_n = 0$, where s_n is (12.36), for s_E, we get the critical market size of the rich/northern market to be

$$s_E^P = \frac{\phi}{1 - \phi\phi^*}\left(\frac{1}{\chi} - \phi^*\right) \tag{12.37}$$

where s_E^P is the peripherality point, that is, the size of the small northern market that implies it has no industry. Since (12.36) is increasing in s_E, we know that the north will be without industry (i.e. will be the periphery) for any market size that is less than s_E^P.

A particularly salient feature of (12.37) is that, even if the north has a native comparative advantage in industry ($\chi > 1$) so that the unit labour cost of producing in the north is below that of the big south, industry can still be fully concentrated in the south. In other words, this is an example of agglomeration producing a trade pattern that contradicts the pattern predicted by comparative advantage.

DISCUSSION

Expression (12.37) conveniently organizes the various forces that foster industrial underdevelopment. By inspection, s_E^P is decreasing in χ and in ϕ^*, and increasing in ϕ. This means that the greater is the north's comparative advantage in manufacturing, the smaller its market must be to sustain peripherality. Moreover, protection of the big market (the south in this case) makes location in the small north less advantageous, so higher big-market protection ($d\phi^* < 0$) allows northern peripherality at a higher northern market size. The impact of small-nation protection on the small country was thoroughly explored in the previous section so there is no need to repeat it here. To summarize, we write the following results.

Result 12.13 (size matters). *If agglomeration forces are important and trade is not completely costless, small nations will tend to be without industry. The minimum market size that is necessary to attract some industry depends upon openness and comparative advantage (these are the subject of subsequent results).*

Result 12.14 (GSP logic). *The higher are industrialized nations' barriers against the industrial exports of the poor countries, the more likely it is that small nations will be without industry and thus poor.*

This may be thought of as providing some intuition for why the WTO's General-ised System of Preferences (GSP) was thought to be pro-development.[12]

The final result concerns the small nation's trade barriers. The more open the small nation is to big-nation industrial exports, the larger must be the small nation's market to attract at least some industry. Of course, we have seen in the two previous sections that this import-substitution logic can be reversed when one allows for other real-world elements such as capital relocation costs and intermediates.

12.4.3 Allowing for Self-Reinforcing Agglomeration

While the FC model is supremely amenable to analysis, it achieves this by assuming away many interesting aspects of more general economic geography models. We can restore one major element—circular causality, that is, self-rein-forcing agglomeration—by re-doing the analysis in the CC model of Chapter 6. That model allows for demand-linked circular causality by assuming that capital is constructed (rather than endowed) and that it must be employed in its region of origin. Forces that encourage industry in a particular nation result in an incentive to raise that nation's capital stock. Because national expenditure also rises with the capital stock, we have that forces that tend to 'shift' production to a nation also tend to 'shift' expenditure to that same nation. Since this cycle of production and expenditure strengthens agglomeration forces, it also exaggerates the spatial implications of any given policy change.

The main difference that appears when we shift from the FC model to the CC model is that the spatial division of expenditure, that is, the relative market sizes—as measured by s_E—becomes endogenous. In particular, the expressions (12.35) and (12.36) are equally valid for the CC model, but additionally we have

$$s_E = (1 - \beta)s_L + \beta s_n, \quad 0 < \beta \equiv \frac{b\rho}{\rho + \delta} < 1 \qquad (12.38)$$

where $b \equiv \mu/\sigma$ as usual, ρ is the discount rate and $\delta > 0$ is the rate of deprecia-tion (see Chapter 6 for details). Solving the location condition, $\pi = \pi^*$, using (12.35) and (12.38), we get a formula for s_n and solving this for the s_L where $s_n = 0$, we find the CC-model's peripherality point to be

$$s_L^P = \frac{\phi}{1 - \phi\phi^*} \left(\frac{1}{\chi} - \phi^* \right) \frac{1}{1 - \beta} \qquad (12.39)$$

To compare this to the equivalent expression for the FC model, suppose that north and south have identical relative endowments (i.e. $s_L = s_K$), so that $s_E = s_L$. In this case, we can directly compare (12.39) and (12.37). Because $0 < \beta < 1$, the point of peripherality is higher in the CC model. This is quite intuitive. It says that the small nations need a bigger market to attract at least some industry when agglomeration forces are stronger. Indeed, β is a measure of the strength of

---

[12] GSP is a GATT waiver of the non-discrimination principle. It allows rich nations to provide preferential market access to the industrial exports of poor nations.

agglomeration forces in the CC model (e.g. the break point is $(1 - \beta)/(1 + \beta)$ with symmetric nations), so we get the very believable result that the stronger are agglomeration forces, the larger a nation must be before it can support some industry. To summarize, we write the following result.

Result 12.15 (agglomeration forces and the peripherality point). *The peripherality point calculated for the FC model is higher than that for the CC model since agglomeration forces are stronger in the CC model. Moreover, the stronger are agglomeration forces in the CC model, the larger a nation must be before it can support some industry.*

12.5 LOCATION AND POLICY NON-EQUIVALENCES

When firms operate in a competitive environment, tariffs and quotas are 'equivalent' under a broad range of assumptions. That is, a tariff and a quota that restrict imports to the same extent, have the same impact on prices—be they consumer prices, producer prices or import prices. The distribution of trade rents (i.e. imports times the gap between domestic and border prices) between foreign and domestic residents may differ depending upon how the quota is administered, but if the government auctions the quota licences, then tariffs and quotas are equivalent in this aspect as well.

This section explores the implications of economic geography for the classical tariff–quota equivalence. Before turning to the geography models, we illustrate the basic equivalence insight with a partial equilibrium to fix ideas and introduce notation. Consider first a specific tariff equal to the difference between the domestic and border prices shown as p^b and p^d in Figure 12.4. This drives a wedge between the import demand curve (MD) and the import supply curve (MS), so compared to the free trade outcome, the tariff reduces imports from M to M'. The gain in trade rents (i.e. tariff revenue), which equals $A + B$, tends to offset the loss in private surplus, namely $-A - C$. Indeed, the tariff enables home to tax foreigners (B is the incidence of the tax on foreigners) and if the incidence on foreigners exceeds the part of the deadweight loss that falls on domestic residents, that is, C, the tariff raises domestic welfare as measured by the unweighted sum of private and public surpluses.

A quota that restricted imports to M' would have identical effects on prices and quantities. If quota rights are allocated to home residents, the trade rents continue to count towards the home surplus and the total welfare impact is identical to that of the tariff. If the quota rights are allocated to foreigners, the trade rents no longer count in the sum of domestic surpluses and the result is a sure loss for home of $-A - C$. It is worth noting that since p^d is the price home pays for its imports when foreigners have the quota rights, the impact on home welfare is identical to the terms of trade loss that would result from a rise in the border price from the free-trade price to p^d.

This reasoning suggests that it is useful to categorize trade barriers according to their trade rent allocation implications. Trade barriers, such as tariffs and

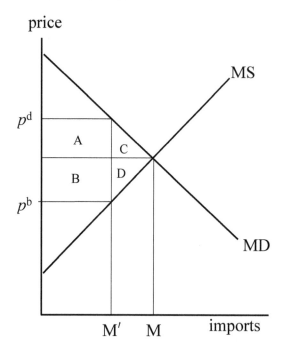

Figure 12.4 Equivalence of tariffs and quotas under perfect competition.

quotas exercised by domestic residents, are here called 'domestically captured rent' barriers, or DCR barriers for short. Barriers that grant the trade rent to foreigners—voluntary export restraints (VERs) and price undertakings are the classic examples—are called 'foreign captured rent' barriers, or FCR barriers for short. Barriers that create a wedge without generating trade rents are called frictional barriers (technical barriers to trade are classic examples of this).

12.5.1 Non-Equivalence of Location Effects

Neoclassical trade models make so many simplifying assumptions that firms can be ignored entirely without further loss of generality. While this is useful for a first exploration of the subject, one naturally wonders whether the simple and stark results obtained in neoclassical models would go through once important, real-world considerations such as imperfect competition and increasing returns are allowed for. Fortunately, much of this wondering was done in the 1970s and 1980s by a number of economists working in what was known as the 'new trade theory'.[13] This work, which is nicely synthesized in Helpman and Krugman (1989), shows that the tariff–quota equivalence was an artifice of simplifying assumption rather than a deep fundamental result. In general, a tariff and a quota that restrict imports by the same extent have different effects on prices.

[13] A number of important points were made before this (see Bhagwati 1965), but since these were made without the benefit of game theory, they were inevitably idiosyncratic.

The basic reasons why tariffs and quotas are not equivalent under imperfect competition and increasing returns are well understood. However, the differential impact that such policies have on the spatial allocation of industry has not been explored. This section is a first attempt to highlight the main issues and provide insight on the non-equivalent location effects of tariffs and quotas. Following the principle of progressive complication, we start with a very simple example to provide intuition, before moving on to a more standard framework (Dixit–Stiglitz monopolistic competition).

12.5.2 Tariff vs. Quota: The Case of the 'Lonely' Monopolist

We start with a simple example, namely, the case of a monopolist and this is most easily embedded in the linear FC model of Chapter 5. The model is developed at length there, but we present the basic elements here for the reader's convenience. The supply side of the economy is identical to that of the FC model employed above, so again there are two sectors, two nations and two factors. Costless trade in the Walrasian sector and costless capital mobility equalize factor prices internationally. Each variety of industrial good entails a fixed cost of one unit of capital, so the spatial distribution of capital and industry are identical. The main difference comes on the demand side. Preferences are assumed to be quasi-linear with the Walrasian good acting as the 'outside' good and tastes for industrial varieties given by a quadratic sub-function. The preferences yield linear demand curves for each industrial variety; spending on the Walrasian good is a residual.

To deal with monopoly power as simply as possible in this section, we assume away substitutability among different industrial varieties in consumer tastes, so that each producer can be thought of as a 'lonely' monopolist. Finally, we assume that the monopolist we focus on is currently located in the south and transportation costs are low enough so that he/she serves both markets.

Demands by northern and southern consumers are $L(a - bp)$ and $L^*(a - bp^*)$, respectively, where p and p^* are consumer prices, L and L^* are market sizes, and a and b are positive parameters (the a and b in this section are completely unrelated to the a and b used above). For simplicity, we normalize marginal production costs to zero. Inter-regional transportation costs are τ, and trade is further restricted by a specific tariff equal to λ (recall that transportation costs involve the numeraire good in the linear model so they are not iceberg costs). Tariffs are collected in the numeraire good and returned lump sum to domestic residents, so tariff revenue has no effect on demand. Finally, we assume that markets are segmented in the sense that firms can price discriminate between the two markets without worrying about arbitrage.

With these assumptions, the monopolist chooses prices to maximize operating profits, which are

$$\pi^* = L(a - bp)(p - \tau - \lambda) + L^*(a - bp^*)p^* \qquad (12.40)$$

since the monopolist is in the south. As usual, optimal pricing with linear demand implies $p^* = a/2b$ and $p = p^* + (\lambda + \tau)/2$. Since the monopolist must hand over

λ units to the northern government for every unit sold in the north, equilibrium profits are

$$\pi^* = b(L + L^*)(p^*)^2 - bL(\lambda + \tau)p^* + bL\left(\frac{\lambda + \tau}{2}\right)^2, \quad p^* = \frac{a}{2b} \quad (12.41)$$

Clearly, profits decrease with both the transportation cost, τ, and the trade barrier, λ, over the parameter space for which we get interior solutions for prices and quantities (so that some trade occurs at equilibrium).

WHO GETS THE TRADE RENTS?

We have started by supposing that λ is a tariff, so the northern government collects tariff revenues (i.e. trade rents) worth

$$R = \lambda Lb\left(p^* - \frac{\tau + \lambda}{2}\right) \quad (12.42)$$

If the trade barrier takes the form of a quota, the monopolist, who can perfectly price discriminate across markets, will charge a price to northern consumers that is just high enough to ensure that they only want to consume (i.e. import) an amount equal to the quota. Supposing that the quota is set to restrict imports to exactly the same level that would have been observed under a tariff equal to λ, the monopolists will continue charging the same consumer prices that he/she did under the tariff, and this means that the trade rents, (12.42), accrue to the southern monopolist rather than the northern government.

The formal argument behind this result can be found in Helpman and Krugman (1989), but the intuition is easy. If the monopolist charges a northern consumer price below $p^* + (\lambda + \tau)/2$, demand will exceed the quota, so some other agent will have to absorb the rents created by the quantity rationing. This plainly is not profit-maximizing behaviour for the monopolists. If the monopolist found it optimal to charge a price above $p^* + (\lambda + \tau)/2$, northern demand will be less than the quota and the quota is not binding. But if the quota is not binding, the monopolist would ascribe a shadow price of zero to the restriction and thus his/her optimal price in the northern market would be $p^* + \tau/2$ and this would result in a level of imports that exceeded the quota. What this shows is that the hypothesis that the monopolist might find it optimal to charge a price above $p^* + (\lambda + \tau)/2$ leads to a logical contradiction and so must itself be false. Finally, we note that both tariff and quota reduce profits vis-à-vis free trade (i.e. $\lambda = 0$) since they impose constraints on the monopolist's otherwise unconstrained problem. In summary, we have the following result.

Result 12.16. *A tariff and a quota that result in the same level of imports both reduce the profit earned by a foreign monopolist, but the quota is less harmful to profits since the home government gets the trade rents with the tariff, while monopolist gets them with a quota. The two policy instruments have the same impact on consumer prices.*

IMPLICATIONS FOR LOCATION

With this simple framework in mind, we now make two simple points related to the non-equivalence of the location effects of tariffs and quotas.

First, we note that even in this framework, protection may lower domestic prices. Starting with symmetric nations and free trade, any northern tariff or quota—however small—will induce the monopolist to relocate to the protected market. To see this in the case of a tariff, write π as the profit of the producer when located in the north. Since the expression for the equilibrium, π, is isomorphic to (12.41) with $\lambda = 0$, the gain from relocating to the north is

$$\pi - \pi^* = \frac{\lambda L}{2}\left(a - b\frac{\lambda + 2\tau}{2}\right) \tag{12.43}$$

which is positive by virtue of the usual parameter restriction. In addition, because $p > p^*$, this relocation would lower the price faced by northern consumers (they would no longer pay the share of transportation costs that was previously passed onto them). The result is that any positive trade barrier, λ, would produce the PLP effect.

Second, the *nature* of the trade barrier matters for the location equilibrium and, in turn, for the cost-of-living (the consumer price index). To see this, assume now that the two regions are of different sizes. In particular, we take north to be the small market ($L < L^*$). Now, starting from a situation where the monopolist is in the south, suppose the north imposes a tariff. A relocation to the north would yield a net gain of

$$\pi - \pi^* = \frac{\lambda L}{2}\left(a - b\frac{\lambda + 2\tau}{2}\right) - \frac{\tau(L^* - L)}{2}\left(a - b\frac{\tau}{2}\right) \tag{12.44}$$

which reduces to (12.43) when $L = L^*$. The terms in both large parentheses above are positive. The first term on the right-hand side represents, as before, the profits saved on tariffs by relocating to the protectionist country. The second term represents the loss of profits involved by relocating away from the large country; obviously, this loss is nil when transportation costs, τ, are zero. Since the two terms pull profits in opposite directions, the net impact of λ on the relocation decision is ambiguous. To illustrate the non-equivalence of tariffs and quota on location, assume that λ and L/L^* combine such that the profit change in (12.44) is just positive, namely

$$\frac{\lambda}{\tau}\left(a - b\frac{\lambda + 2\tau}{4}\right) = \frac{L^* - L}{L}\left(a - b\frac{\tau}{2}\right) + \varepsilon \tag{12.45}$$

where ε is an arbitrarily small positive number, so the monopolist would delocate to the north.

We now ask: What happens if home is forced to replace its tariff with an equivalent quota? Since a quota is less harmful to a south-based monopolist than a tariff, the gain from delocating to the north would be lower. Since the monopolist was almost indifferent to relocation with the tariff, he/she would be against relocation if the protection took the form of a quota. Specifically, using (12.42), the prospective gain (12.44) is now replaced by

$$\pi - \pi^* = L\left(\frac{\varepsilon\tau}{2} - \lambda\frac{a - b(\lambda + \tau)}{2}\right) \quad (12.46)$$

which is negative for ε and τ small enough. Hence, when regions are of different sizes, the small region might fail to attract the foreign producer.

The key implication of this is that a tariff would result in lower domestic prices, while a quota would result in higher domestic prices. Moreover, although the tariff and the quota would have the same impact on imports without delocation, the tariff ends up reducing imports to zero, while the quota restricts imports less drastically. This is summarized in the following result.

Result 12.17. *A tariff and a quota calculated to result in the same level of imports based on initial production patterns can have radically different effects once relocation possibilities are allowed for. In particular, if the tariff is just large enough to induce the foreign monopolist to delocate to the north, the 'equivalent' quota will fail to induce delocation. As a consequence, the tariff would result in a drop in domestic prices and a cessation of imports, while the quota would raise domestic prices and only partially restrict imports. This suggests that policies that favour tariffs over quotas have an impact on location in themselves.*

The point that relative market size matters for the PLP effect was made in the previous section. The additional insight here is that the nature of the protection also matters.

Having made these simple points in a simplistic model, we turn to verifying the main insights in a richer economic environment. In particular, our example was also extreme in the sense that the monopolist had no interaction with any other producer. We turn to showing that these points generally hold in the other extreme case, namely, in the FC model.

12.5.3 Tariff vs. Quota in the FC Model

In the FC model, each producer has a monopoly in the product for his/her specific variety, competing with other firms only indirectly. Having shown above that a monopolist earns higher operating profit in a market that is protected with a quota than in a market that is protected with a tariff, we know that quotas will typically affect the reward to capital. Because operating profit is part of expenditure, this sort of effect will alter the two region's relative expenditures and thus remove a great deal of the FC model's tractability. Since this sort of connection between market size and the nature of protectionist barriers is surely of second-order importance in the real world, we neutralize the connection by working with quasi-linear preferences (see Appendix 2.A for details). The main implication is that the demand functions for industrial goods no longer depend upon region incomes. In particular, the demand functions are

$$c^* = \frac{(\mu/2)p^{*-\sigma}}{np^{1-\sigma} + n^*p^{*1-\sigma}}, \quad c = \frac{(\mu/2)p^{-\sigma}}{np^{1-\sigma} + n^*p^{*1-\sigma}} \quad (12.47)$$

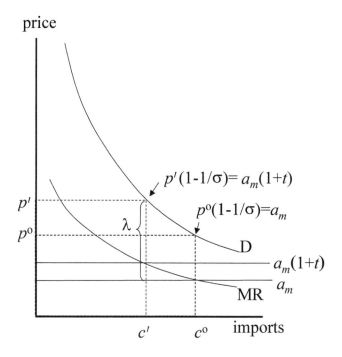

Figure 12.5   Pricing with tariffs and quotas in the FC model.

where μ stands for world spending on all differentiated varieties, which, by symmetry, is split evenly between the two regions. The demand and supply of the homogenous good, A, is a residual that we can ignore as long as both countries produce something in each sector.

To study the full general equilibrium effects of a tariff and a quota, we note that under Dixit–Stiglitz competition, each atomistic firm ignores the denominators of its demand functions and so acts as if it faces an iso-elastic demand function. The pricing decision in this case for a tariff and a quota are illustrated in Figure 12.5. The demand and marginal revenue curves corresponding to the iso-elasticity case are shown as the D and MR curves (as usual the MR curve is flatter than the D curve in the iso-elastic case). With no protection, the exporting firm faces a marginal cost of selling equal to a_M (a_M is the unit labour input coefficient in the M sector and, as usual in the FC model, international trade in A and our normalizations imply north and south wages are equal to unity) and so sets the consumer price and p^o. The corresponding sales are c^o. If a tariff rate equal to t is imposed (this is collected in terms of the product itself, just like an iceberg transport cost), then the marginal selling cost rises to $a_M(1 + t)$ and the firm responds by raising price to p' and reducing sales to c'.

If the same degree of protection is to be achieved with a quota, the government can impose a quota of c'. As we argued above, as long as the quota licence holders are atomistic, the exporting firm will manage to attract all the rent by setting a price equal to p'. In other words, the Lagrangian multiplier on the quota constraint must be equal to the λ shown in the diagram. Plainly, the operating profit margin is higher with a quota than with the 'equivalent' tariff and, as a result, southern operating profit earned on northern sales is higher under a quota. Specifically, it is higher by the rectangle $(1 + t)c'$.

THE SPATIAL EQUILIBRIUM

We now turn to a more formal treatment of the problem. As a matter of convention, we take the north as the protecting economy and consider the effects of the trade policies on south-based producers of industrial varieties.

As usual, the fulcrum for our investigation is operating profits of south-based and north-based firms. As before, τ represents either the iceberg transportation cost or an ad valorem tariff, and λ reflects the shadow price of any quota. Here, however, it proves insightful to allow for both natural transport costs, what we call 'T' and a tariff, denoted as 't'. Thus, $\tau \equiv 1 + T + t$, where T is an exogenously given parameter while t is chosen by the northern government. The problem of a typical south-based firm is

$$\max_{p,p^*}(p_{SS} - a_M)x_{SS} + (p_{SN} - a_M\tau)x_{SN} \quad \text{s.t.} \quad x_{SN} \leq Q \qquad (12.48)$$

Here, we adopt a more explicit notation where, for example, p_{ij} is the price charged by a firm located in market i for sales in market j; the x's indicate sales using the same notation.

The solution to this maximization problem provides optimal prices and a shadow value on the quota. Employing our usual normalization of $\beta = 1 - (1/\sigma)$, these are

$$p_{SN} = \tau + \lambda/a_M, \quad p_{SS} = 1 \qquad (12.49)$$

Using these in (12.48), and using the standard FC model solution for northern operating profits (only the north imposes barriers in our example), we have

$$\pi = b(\frac{1}{\Delta} + \frac{\phi^*}{\Delta^*}), \quad \pi^* = b\left(\frac{\phi\zeta}{\Delta} + \frac{1}{\Delta^*}\right)$$

$$\phi \equiv \left(\tau + \frac{\lambda}{a_M}\right)^{1-\sigma}, \quad \zeta \equiv \left(\frac{\tau + \lambda\sigma/a_M}{\tau + \lambda/a_M}\right) \geq 1 \qquad (12.50)$$

where the northern trade freeness, ϕ, allows for tariff or quota protection, and the Δs are defined as in (12.5).[14] The ζ term, which exceeds unity when the quota is binding, reflects the fact that south-based firms earn an extra high operating profit margin on sales to a market protected with a quota.

[14] Having assumed a segmented market, we can explain the term with ζ by dealing only with the sub-problem of a typical southern firm's sales to the north: $\max_p(p - \beta\tau)x$, s.t. $Q \geq x$. The first-order condition is $p(1 - (1/\sigma)) = \beta\tau + \lambda$, where λ is the Lagrangian multiplier on the quota. Rearranging this, we have $(p - \beta\tau)x = px/\sigma + \lambda x$. As long as the quota is binding, $\lambda > 0$ and the operating profit earned on sales to the north exceeds the usual amount, that is, px/σ. Using $\zeta \equiv 1 + \sigma\lambda/p$ and the first-order condition, with $\beta \equiv (1 - (1/\sigma))$, yields the result.

Capital searches for the location with the highest reward so the interior equilibrium is where $\pi = \pi^*$. Solving this location condition for the spatial equilibrium, s_n, gives

$$s_n = \frac{1}{2} + \frac{\phi^* - \phi + \phi^*(1 + \phi) - (1 + \phi^*)\phi\zeta}{2(1 - \phi^*)[2 - (1 + \zeta)\phi]} \qquad (12.51)$$

so when the north imposes no protection ($\lambda = t = 0$, so $\phi = \phi^* = (1 + T)^{1-\sigma}$), this says that industry is evenly split, that is, $s_n = 1/2$.

EQUALLY PROTECTIONIST TARIFFS AND QUOTA

tariff and a quotaThe difference between tariff and quota protection can be illustrated with the following experiment. Suppose in the first case that the north unilaterally protects its market with a tariff only ($t > \lambda = 0$), and the south does not respond. The northern market will be less open than the southern market and, to be specific, we define the difference as $\delta \equiv \phi^*/\phi \geq 1$. In the second case, the north imposes the same degree of protection—in the sense that $\delta \equiv \phi^*/\phi$—but now it uses only a quota ($\lambda > t = 0$). Both instruments will alter the locational equilibrium; specifically,

$$s_n = \frac{\phi^2\delta + 1 - (1 + \zeta)\phi}{(1 - \delta\phi)(2 - (1 + \zeta)\phi)} \qquad (12.52)$$

When the protectionist instrument is a tariff, $\zeta = 1$, and when it is a quota, $\zeta > 1$. By inspection, we can see that the delocation effect of the tariff is greater than that of the quota. The intuition for this is straightforward. The fact that the quota tends to boost the profitability of southern exports to the north means that the quota tends to keep more of the southern firms in place.

Given this, we can use the reasoning of the previous section to say that a tariff will have a more negative impact on north's price than will a quota.

There is another more important difference between the tariff and quota protection. In the case of a tariff, the delocation flow continues until the reward to north-based capital returns to the level it was at before the protection. Specifically, it equals b before and after the tariff protection. With a quota, however, both the northern and southern rewards to capital are higher with the quota than without. Intuitively, the reason is that the quota raises the operating profit margin on one trade flow (southern exports to the north) and this raises the total level of operating profit worldwide. While relocation ensures equalization of π, the equalization takes place at a higher level. It has often been remarked that firms typically prefer quota protection to tariff protection. Our analysis suggests one possible explanation. If the north-based firms manage to overcome the free-rider problem and organize to lobby for a tariff, the potential rise in their earnings that a tariff tends to create will be entirely eroded by foreign entry. By contrast, lobbying for a quota will allow them to raise their reward and so may justify the lobbying expense. Note also, that the foreign producers will similarly prefer a quota to a tariff.

More formally, using (12.52) in (12.50), the sum of world operating profit, namely $n^w[s_n\pi + (1 - s_n)\pi]$, is

$$b\left(\frac{1 - \delta\phi^2\zeta}{(1 - \delta\phi^2)}\right)\left(\frac{1 - \phi(1 + \zeta)/2}{1 - \zeta\phi}\right) \tag{12.53}$$

where we have used the standard normalization of $n^w = 1$. Since each term in the large parentheses is greater than unity when $\zeta > 1$, we see that world profits are higher under a tariff than under a quota. This is summarized in the following result.

Result 12.18. *A quota and tariff that produce the same level of imports have different effects on the geographical dispersion of industry, on domestic prices and on the reward to capital. In particular, since a quota is better for foreign exporters than a tariff, the quota produces less delocation into the protected economy (i.e. the tariff-jumping delocation will be greater than the quota-jumping delocation). The reduced delocation also means a quota has a dampened PLP effect. Furthermore, the quota will raise the equilibrium reward to capital in both regions, while the tariff's profit boosting effect is entirely offset by delocation.*

Of course, if the level of protection is high enough to induce total delocation to the protected economy, then a trivial equivalence is restored.

POLITICAL ECONOMY CONSIDERATION AND FURTHER CONSIDERATIONS

We have examined tariffs and quotas in a setting where the PLP effect always works; above we saw that this was really just an artefact of the model's simplifying assumptions. In richer frameworks, the price-index-lowering effect of protection-induced delocation may or may not offset the direct price-index-raising effect of protection. It is clear that we could easily build an example in which a tariff would reduce domestic prices whilst a quota would increase them.

We have left aside an important, potentially interesting, issue here. In both our examples, market conduct is either trivial (the lonely monopolist) or simplistic (monopolistic competition). In either case, each producer does not interact directly with others. It would be interesting to know how the market *conduct* could be affected by the nature of the policy instrument. For instance, can we imagine a situation where a quota so strongly boosts the profits of foreign exporters that the quota leads to delocation out of the protected economy? More generally, how do the location effects of VERs and quotas differ in settings of imperfect competition? Our preliminary explorations suggest that these issues are harder to answer than one might think; we leave them for future research.

12.6 CONCLUDING REMARKS

This chapter just scratches the surface of what seems to be a field rich in interesting results. For instance, we have looked only superficially at the underdeveloped puzzle. The numerical examples in Puga and Venables (1998) suggest that many more interesting results could be demonstrated in the more tractable models in Part I. Another example of 'low hanging fruit' concerns path dependencies. The chapter does not follow up on one of the most usual aspect of geography models, namely locational hysteresis. It would be of some interest, for instance, to consider how temporary unilateral protection could permanently alter trade patterns, perhaps creating 'un-natural' comparative advantages.

REFERENCES

Baldwin, Richard E. and F. Robert-Nicoud. 2002. Asymmetric lobbying: why governments pick losers. Working Paper No. 8756, National Bureau of Economic Research.

Bhagwati, J. 1965. On the equivalence of tariffs and quotas. In *Trade, Growth and the Balance of Payments*, ed. R. E. Caves, H. G. Johnson and P. B. Kenen. Amsterdam: North-Holland.

Forslid, R. and I. Wooton. 2001. Comparative advantage and the location of production. *Review of International Economics* in press.

Helpman, Elhanan and P. Krugman. 1989. *Trade Policy and Market Structure*. Cambridge, MA: MIT Press.

Puga, Diego and A. Venables. 1997. Preferential trading arrangements and industrial location. *Journal of International Economics* 43(3–4): 347–368.

_____. 1999. Agglomeration and economic development: import substitution vs trade liberalisation. *Economic Journal* 109(455): 292–311.

Robert-Nicoud, F. 2002. A simple model of agglomeration with vertical linkages and capital mobility. Mimeo, London School of Economics.

CHAPTER 13

Reciprocal Trade Agreements

13.1 INTRODUCTION

In virtually any model that displays agglomeration forces, two-way trade liberalization between a big and a small nation has a tendency to boost the large nation's share of world industry at the expense of the small nation. This is just a straightforward application of an effect that was explored at length in Part I—the home-market magnification effect (the tendency for large nations to attract disproportionate shares of industry is magnified by trade openness). These results might be taken as explaining or justifying the fact that small nations often fear that trade liberalization with larger, richer nations will erode their industrial bases. In practice, these concerns are recognized in free trade agreements and multilateral trade liberalizations since small nations are explicitly or implicitly allowed to maintain higher trade barriers. For example, the EU allowed Central European nations to phase out their tariffs on EU exports more slowly than the EU did on Central European exports. Likewise, the WTO/GATT has traditionally allowed developing nations to benefit from tariff reductions by industrialized nations without requiring them to lower their tariffs. By contrast, standard WTO negotiating rules (reciprocity) state that rich nations get freer access to other rich nation markets, only if they themselves cut tariffs.

In this chapter, we study this small-to-big delocation effect and evaluate schemes that permit liberalization without such delocation. The main reasoning is based on Baldwin and Robert-Nicoud (2000) and Robert-Nicoud (1996).

13.1.1 Organization of the Chapter

The workhorse model in this chapter is the footloose capital (FC) model of Chapter 3, so we first review its equilibrium expressions in Section 13.2 and characterize the forces that yield delocation when trade liberalization is symmetric and incomplete in Section 13.3. We then turn to exploring a no-delocation liberalization scheme and evaluate its welfare implications in Section 13.4. Section 13.5 studies international transfers as an anti-delocation tool and Section 13.6 contains our concluding remarks.

13.2 THE MODEL

To treat delocation issues formally, we adopt the FC model. While Chapter 3 explores the model at length, we repeat the assumptions briefly for the reader's convenience. Readers who have worked through Chapter 3 will find it easier to follow the reasoning.

We assume two regions (north and south), two sectors (agriculture, A, and manufactures, M), and two factors (capital, K, and workers, L). The A sector is Walrasian and uses only L to produce its homogenous good. Inter-regional and intra-regional trade in A is costless. The monopolistically competitive M sector uses only K in its fixed cost (one unit of K per variety) and only L in the variable cost. Intra-regional sales are costless, but inter-regional trade in M goods is subject to iceberg trade costs. Each region's supply of L is fixed and cannot cross national borders. Capital is perfectly mobile across nations, but labourers own all capital so capital income is fully repatriated to its country of origin. Preferences over the two sectors consist of CES preferences for M varieties nested in an upper-tier Cobb–Douglas function that ensures a constant fraction of expenditure, namely μ, is spent on M goods.

As Chapter 3 shows in detail, the equilibrium price in both the northern and southern A sectors is unity and this equalizes wages internationally as long as neither country specializes completely in one sector (a sufficient condition for this is $\mu < 1/2$ and we assume this henceforth). With equal wages, we know that marginal costs and thus producer prices in the M sectors are also equalized, and we choose units such that these equalized producer prices are unity.

Using the usual expressions for operating profits in north and south, namely π and π^*, we solve the location condition, that is, $\pi = \pi^*$, for the share of world industry in the north (see Chapter 3 for details). Allowing for asymmetric degrees of openness, the answer is

$$s_n = \frac{s_E(1 - \phi\phi^*) - \phi(1 - \phi^*)}{(1 - \phi^*)(1 - \phi)}, \quad 0 \le \phi \equiv \tau^{1-\sigma} \le 1 \qquad (13.1)$$

where s_E is the north's share of global expenditure, and an isomorphic definition holds for the south's degree of trade freeness, ϕ^* (recall that ϕ is a mnemonic for the 'freeness', or phi-ness of trade, so ϕ ranges from zero, with infinite barriers, to unity, with zero barriers). Expression (13.1) holds for interior solutions of s_n, namely when parameters are such that $0 < s_n < 1$. Outside this parameter space, s_n equals zero or unity in an obvious manner. The south's share of firms, which we sometimes denote as s_n^*, equals $1 - s_n$.

In this chapter, we allow for different relative endowments, that is, different capital/labour ratios, so s_E is given by

$$s_E = (1 - b)s_L + bs_K, \quad b \equiv \frac{\mu}{\sigma} \qquad (13.2)$$

where s_L and s_K are the north's share of the global labour and capital stock. It is useful to note that s_E is related to the north's share of world capital and its capital abundance by the simple expression $s_E = s_K - \psi$, where ψ is defined as $(s_K - s_L)(1 - b)$.

13.3 SYMMETRIC LIBERALIZATION AND DELOCATION

This section opens our analysis of delocation and trade liberalization by showing that the symmetric liberalization between asymmetric-sized regions does lead to de-location from the small nation to the big nation. To keep things simple, the south and north differ only in their economic size and relative factor endowments (i.e. $\phi = \phi^*$ in this section) and we shall—to be concrete—take the north to be the big nation.

When the nations have the same degree of openness, (13.1) simplifies to

$$s_n = \frac{1}{2} + \frac{1 + \phi}{1 - \phi}\left(s_E - \frac{1}{2}\right) \tag{13.3}$$

This says that when trade barriers are prohibitive, that is, $\phi = 0$, the division of industry matches national income/expenditure share. Liberalization from this point implies a progressive shift of industry from the small nation to the large nation, as long as $s_E \neq 1/2$, and indeed, all industry will be clustered in the big nation at some level of openness that ϕ is close to, but short of, free trade. The critical value ϕ, that is, the sustain point, is just $(1 - s_E)/s_E$. This is summarized in the following result.

Result 13.1. *A symmetric, reciprocal freeing of trade between asymmetric-sized nations will produce a relocation of industry from the small nation to the big nation.*

The intuition for this result is straightforward. In all economic geography models, imperfect competition and trade costs tend to foster location of industry in the larger nation. This pro-agglomeration 'market-access' effect is countered by a pro-dispersion 'local competition' effect. The strength of both effects erodes with liberalization, but the pro-dispersion force's strength erodes faster than that of the pro-agglomeration force. Consequently, a progressive and symmetric liberalization between asymmetric-sized nations produces a monotonic de-industrialization of the small nation.

13.3.1 Allowing for Factor Endowment Asymmetries

The path to de-industrialization, however, can be more complex when the big nation is also relatively capital abundant. To trace out the full path, we introduce a 'delocation metric', namely $s_n - s_K$. This metric ranges from zero with no delocation (i.e. when nations are autarkic both in terms of trade and capital flows) to $1 - s_K$ when complete delocation has occurred, that is, when $s_n = 1$ (recall that s_K is a parameter representing capital endowments while s_n is an endogenous variable representing the equilibrium spatial allocation of industry). From (13.1), with trade in manufactures restricted by a common ϕ, we find the delocation metric varies with size and factor endowment differences. Specifically,[1]

---

[1] This holds for interior solutions of s_n, in other words when $\phi^G < (1/s_E) - 1$. For ϕ^G below this, $s_n = 1$.

$$s_n - s_K = \frac{2\phi}{1-\phi}\left(s_E - \frac{1}{2}\right) - \psi, \quad \psi \equiv (s_K - s_L)(1-b) \quad (13.4)$$

where ψ is a measure of the north's relative capital abundance. As before, this expression holds for interior solutions of s_n; outside this parameter space, the metric equals zero or $-\psi$ in an obvious manner.

Expression (13.4) illustrates the two fundamental forces driving delocation in this model—the market-crowding effect and the market-size effect that are described at length in Chapters 2 and 3. For example, if trade barriers are prohibitive (i.e. $\phi = 0$), the first term is zero and the delocation metric would be determined entirely by endowment differences as measured by ψ. This can be thought of as the market-crowding effect since with $\phi = 0$, firms locate in a way that equalizes the amount of local expenditure per firm (recall that capital's reward is proportional to sales). If, on the other hand, countries have identical endowments (i.e. $\psi = 0$), the second term is zero, so our delocation metric is determined by openness and relative size.

We turn now to the welfare effects of this delocation for the case of general size and factor-endowment asymmetries.

13.3.2 Welfare Analysis: Gains Despite Delocation

The welfare yardsticks we employ are the indirect utility functions of north and south labour. These are (see Chapter 3 for details):

$$V = s_E\big(s_E(1 + \phi)\big)^a, \quad V^* = (1 - s_E)\big((1 - s_E)(1 + \phi)\big)^a; \quad a \equiv \frac{\mu}{\sigma - 1} \quad (13.5)$$

The north's function has two elements. The first term, s_E, is invariant as usual in the FC model. The second term, which depends on s_E and ϕ, captures the net impact of what we called the 'location effect' in Chapter 10 (i.e. delocation's impact on the price index) and the direct gain from unilaterally liberalizing imports. Plainly, (13.5) shows that both nations gain from any degree of reciprocal liberalization, despite any ensuing delocation. The result is easy to understand for the north since the two forces on its price index—the location effect and the direct effect—pull in the same direction. The positive gain for the south, however, is less intuitive. The southern price index can be written as $(\phi s_n + 1 - s_n)^a$. The direct effect, $d\phi > 0$, lowers the price index. By contrast, the location effect, which stems from the fact that s_n is non-decreasing in ϕ, tends to raise the price index as southern consumers are forced to pay for trade barriers on a larger fraction of their purchases. However, when both nations liberalize, the rate of delocation is insufficient to induce an overall loss to the small nation (the south). As we shall see below, this simple analysis is more complicated when the trade barriers take the form of tariffs. To summarize, we write the following result.

Result 13.2. *A symmetric, reciprocal reduction of frictional trade barriers between asymmetric-sized nations is welfare improving for both nations despite the small-to-large delocation induced by the liberalization.*

13.4 TRADE LIBERALIZATION WITHOUT DELOCATION

Having seen that symmetric market opening is good for both large and small nations despite any liberalization-induced delocation, small-country fears of liberalization may seem misplaced. Nevertheless, it is a simple fact that many policy makers view de-industrialization per se as unfavourable. This may reflect sophisticated concerns, such as technological externalities and national security issues, which are excluded from our simple model. It may also reflect political economy factors that lead policy makers to judge outcomes by a measure other than national welfare. Be that as it may, this section takes the desire to avoid de-industrialization as a primitive and investigates the nature of trade-barrier asymmetries that would be necessary to allow liberalization without delocation.

To make the argument as cleanly as possible, we work with an exaggerated form of policy makers' concern about delocation. That is, we assume that nations coordinate their tariff cutting in a manner that allows both to reach free trade *without any delocation*. Of course, real-world policy makers operate with many goals and constraints that we ignore here, but the extreme policy objective highlights the novel aspects of asymmetric liberalization that are aimed at reducing liberalization-induced delocation.

Specifically, we shall assume that both levels of trade freeness, ϕ and ϕ^*, will be brought from zero to unity, but that asymmetric ϕ's are allowed during the transition. Our task is to characterize the trade barrier asymmetry that is necessary to ensure *no* delocation occurs, that is, to ensure that each region keeps the number of firms it has in autarky.[2] Formally, we characterize the levels of ϕ and ϕ^*, necessary to keep

$$s_n = s_K \tag{13.6}$$

during the whole trade liberalization process (since shares sum to unity, this also implies that the south holds on to all its industry).

As will become clear in a moment, what counts is the relative importance of the ϕ's, not their levels. Hence, we treat the north's liberalization path (namely the level of ϕ at any point in time) as exogenous and focus on the corresponding level of ϕ^* that is necessary to prevent delocation. Finally, we note that we continue in the long-standing tradition of ignoring time in economic geography models. While this prevents us from looking at many interesting issues, for example, adjustment costs, it allows us to parsimoniously highlight the key links between asymmetric barriers and delocation.

13.4.1 The General Rule

Substituting (13.6) into (13.1) and using (13.2) yields the no-delocation level of ϕ^* that corresponds to any given ϕ. We write this in implicit form as

[2] The autarky level is a convenient benchmark that simplifies calculations. Working with some arbitrary, initial distribution of industry would complicate the analysis without introducing any important considerations.

$$1 - \phi^* = \frac{s_E}{s_K(1 - \phi) + (1 - s_E)\phi} (1 - \phi) \qquad (13.7)$$

Note that all right-hand side variables are independent of ϕ^* and that s_E and s_K depend only on endowments and parameters. Thus, the no-delocation path for ϕ^* is dictated by the north's path of liberalization, which, as mentioned above, is taken to be exogenous.

Three general results are immediately available. First, the left-hand side can be taken as a measure of the remaining distance to free trade ($\phi^* = 1$ under free trade). Second, the right-hand side of the expression is everywhere decreasing in ϕ, so the no-delocation rule implies that the two levels of openness must move in the same direction. In other words, the no-delocation rule never requires the south to respond to northern liberalization with a *rise* in southern barriers. Third, if the two trading areas were identical ($s_K = s_L = s_E = 1/2$), the no-delocation rule would require symmetric liberalization.

Considering special cases provides further insight. We first consider size asymmetries in isolation by supposing that nations have equal relative endowments ($\psi = 0$) but the north is larger ($s_E > 1/2$). Under these provisos, (13.7) simplifies to

$$1 - \phi^* = \frac{s_E}{s_E(1 - \phi) + (1 - s_E)\phi} (1 - \phi) \qquad (13.8)$$

By inspection of this expression, $\phi^* = \phi$ in only two cases, when barriers are prohibitive (both ϕ's are zero) and when trade is perfectly free (both ϕ's are unity). Between these two extreme cases, the convexity of the right-hand side of (13.8) implies that in the size-difference-only case, the larger nation should always be more open than the small nation (the south) all along the path to perfectly free trade. The convexity also implies that the protection asymmetry must be greatest at intermediate values of ϕ. To summarize we write the following result.

Result 13.3 (big nation opens faster). *If nations differ only in size, the no-delocation liberalization path requires the large nation to maintain lower import barriers along the entire path. The protection asymmetry must be greatest at intermediate levels of protection.*

To understand this result intuitively, note that delocation when trade barriers are very high is less advantageous since the migrating southern firms face very large barriers when re-exporting to the small southern market. Delocation at very low barriers brings few advantages since, with low barriers, the degree of competition is almost as high in the south as it is in the north. Consequently, the incentives to delocate are strongest for intermediate levels of trade cost. This, of course, is very similar to the hump-shaped-agglomeration-rents property that we highlighted in Part I, but here it appears for an interior equilibrium. Given that agglomeration forces are strongest at intermediate trade costs, the offsetting asymmetry in trade barriers must be greatest for intermediate trade barriers.

The second special case highlights factor-endowment asymmetries by considering countries of equal size but allowing the north to be relatively capital abundant ($\psi > 0$). In this case, the implied protection asymmetry is reversed.

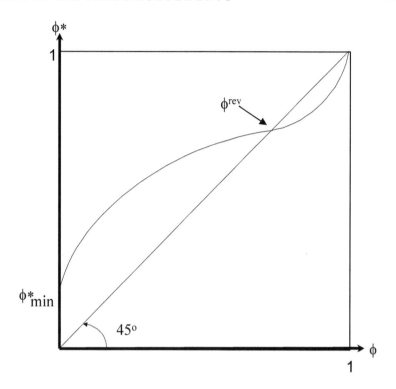

Figure 13.1 The no-delocation liberalization path.

When $s_E = 1/2$ but $\psi > 0$, the ratio of closed-ness, namely $(1 - \phi^*)/(1 - \phi)$, must be equal to $[1 + 2\psi(1 - \phi)]^{-1}$. Since the latter is always less than unity, the no-delocation rule requires the south to be *more open* than the north. Intuitively, the lack of size differences means that the only force operating is the decentralizing market-crowding effect. That is, with no market-size advantage to attract firms to the northern market, northern capital tends to shift to the south in order to reduce its exposure to competition. Offsetting this tendency requires northern barriers to exceed those of the south.[3]

Finally, consider what might be called the 'European case' of $s_E > 1/2$ and $\psi > 0$, that is, where the north is larger and relatively capital abundant. Here, the competition and size effects work in opposite directions yet the relative strengths of the two effects vary with ϕ.[4] Consequently, the prevention of delocation requires the south to maintain *lower* barriers than the north in the first phase of liberalization (i.e. when northern barriers are high) but to maintain higher barriers in the final phase (i.e. when northern barriers are sufficiently low). This relationship is summarized graphically in Figure 13.1.

[3] A similar result can be found in the three-nation endogenous growth model of Martin and Ottaviano (1996).

[4] Specifically, Section 13.3 showed that the market-crowding effect does not depend upon ϕ, but size-effect's strength grows with ϕ.

To characterize the rule more precisely, we focus on two specific levels of ϕ^*. First, note that southern trade barriers never need to be infinitely high, even when northern barriers are. Specifically, when $\phi = 0$, the no-delocation southern openness equals $(1 - b)\psi/s_K$, given (13.2) and (13.8). This minimum level of southern openness provides a handy landmark, so we denote it as ϕ^*_{min}.

Second, from (13.7) there is some intermediate value of ϕ, call it ϕ^{rev} (mnemonic for 'reversal') where the market-crowding effect just offsets the size effect. At this point, the south's import barriers on industrial goods must exactly equal those of the north's in order to prevent delocation. When trade is freer than this, the small south's barriers must be *above* those of the big north in order to prevent southern firms from moving northward. Intuition for this is straightforward. As we showed at length in Part I, both the dispersion and agglomeration forces get weaker as trade costs drop to zero. However, the 'natural tendency' of capital to migrate from the capital-rich region (the capital abundant north) to the capital-poor region is a force that remains intact right up to the point where location is irrelevant ($\phi = \phi^* = 1$). What this means is that if trade is sufficiently restricted, the natural tendency becomes the dominant force. To counterbalance this force, the north must be more closed than the south.

To find ϕ^{rev} formally, we look for the fixed point in (13.7), namely

$$\phi^{rev} = \frac{\psi}{2(s_E - 1/2) + \psi} \qquad (13.9)$$

Several aspects of (13.9) are worth pointing out. First, ϕ^{rev} is never smaller than ϕ^*_{min} and they coincide at zero when $\psi = 0$. Thus, when nations have identical relative endowments, the no-delocation combination of ϕ and ϕ^* lies strictly below the 45° line for ϕ in $(0, 1)$. In words, this says that relative endowment differences are a necessary and sufficient condition to get reverse asymmetry (i.e. the situation where south must be more open than the north). Second, if the only difference between the two countries is that the north is relatively capital abundant, then there always exists an incentive for some north firms to delocate to the south. This incentive is stronger, the larger are the trade barriers. Finally, note that both ϕ^{rev} and ϕ^*_{min} are increasing with ψ and decreasing with s_E. This means that delocation in the large, capital-abundant country is more likely when capital/labour ratios are close to each other and/or when its market size is larger.

13.4.2 Welfare Analysis

We now evaluate this asymmetric no-delocation liberalization scheme against two possible benchmarks. The first of these is the 'no liberalization' case. This may be somewhat extreme, but, for many years, developing nations refused trade liberalization in part because they feared that symmetric liberalization would eliminate the uncompetitive industries that had been created by import-substitution policies. The second benchmark, the 'symmetric trade liberalization' studied in Section 13.3, is perhaps a more natural point of reference. To avoid a proliferation of special cases, we focus on the 'European' case where north is larger and relatively capital abundant.

The first benchmark is simple to use. The only effect distinguishing asymmetric trade liberalization from autarky is the direct gains from unilateral trade liberalization because there is no delocation under either scheme. We can therefore directly assert that even partial asymmetric liberalization of the no-delocation type is welfare improving for both nations with respect to isolation. To summarize this, we write the following result.

Result 13.4. *The no-delocation liberalization scheme is welfare superior to no liberalization for both nations.*

The second benchmark is more involved. To fully compare asymmetric versus symmetric trade liberalization, one would have to account for the speed of liberalization. For instance, at one extreme, a 'big-bang' autarky-to-free-trade liberalization makes the issue of delocation irrelevant (location is indeterminate when all trade is costless). Including these issues, however, complicates the analysis without providing much compensating insight. We choose, therefore, to take as our metric the difference in southern utility levels under the no-delocation scheme and the symmetric liberalization scheme at any given level of northern openness.

For the north, the individual indirect utility function depends directly on ϕ, and indirectly on ϕ and ϕ^* via s_n (see (13.1) for the exact relationship). V can, therefore, be expressed implicitly as $V[s_n(\phi, \phi^*), \phi]$. Under the symmetric-liberalization benchmark, which we denote as V_S, the level of utility is given by $V_S[s_n(\phi^G, \phi^G), \phi^G]$, where ϕ^G is our notation for the common level of trade freeness ('G' is a mnemonic for global). Under the no-delocation rule, northern utility, which we denote as V_A (A is a mnemonic for asymmetric) is given by $V_A[s_K, \phi]$ since in this case s_n always equals s_K. Analogous functions, $V_A^*[\ ]$ and $V_S^*[\ ]$ can be defined for southern utility levels. To streamline the expressions, we take the ratios of the utility levels by nation, namely V_A/V_S and V_A^*/V_S^*. The asymmetric no-delocation policy is preferred only when these ratios exceed unity. Dropping the G superscript and using (13.7), (13.9) and (13.5), we get

$$\frac{V_A}{V_S} = \left(\frac{s_E(1 + \phi) - \psi(\phi - \phi^{\mathrm{rev}})/\phi^{\mathrm{rev}}}{s_E(1 + \phi)} \right)^a \tag{13.10}$$

Since $a > 0$, we see that $V_A > V_S$, that is, the large nation prefers the no-delocation scheme to symmetric liberalization—if and only if $\psi(\phi - \phi^{\mathrm{rev}})/\phi^{\mathrm{rev}}$ is negative. From (13.9), ϕ^{rev} lies between zero and unity in the 'European' case, so $\psi(\phi - \phi^{\mathrm{rev}})/\phi^{\mathrm{rev}}$ definitely changes sign over the $[0, 1]$ range for ϕ, and this means that the large, rich country prefers symmetric liberalization at high levels of openness, but prefers asymmetric liberalization at low levels of openness. The switchover in ranking occurs exactly at $\phi = \phi^{\mathrm{rev}}$.

The intuition for this finding is straightforward. Under symmetric liberalization, north firms migrate southwards when barriers are very high (in order to avoid competition), but southern firms shift to the north when barriers are sufficiently low. According to the location effect, the southward delocation harms northern welfare while the northward delocation benefits the north. Since the no-delocation scheme shuts off the location effect, north prefers the no-delocation scheme when trade barriers are high (ϕ is low), but prefers symmetric liberalization when barriers are low. Note that as factor-endowment differences between nations disappear (i.e. ψ limits to 0), the reference point ϕ^{rev} approaches zero and $\psi(\phi - \phi^{\text{rev}})/\phi^{\text{rev}}$ limits to $2\phi(s_E - 1/2)$. In this case, where size is the only asymmetry, the large country always fairs better under the symmetric liberalization scheme.

Plainly, the overall welfare comparison of the two schemes would, in the general case, require more detailed information on the time path of ϕ. For instance, suppose, as is often the case, that the process lowers barriers rapidly in the beginning but slowly at the end. In this case, the north could lose in welfare terms from the no-delocation scheme.

The ratio for the south can be written as

$$\frac{V_A^*}{V_S^*} = \left(\frac{(1 - s_E)(1 + \phi) + \psi(\phi - \phi^{\text{rev}})/\phi^{\text{rev}} - \Gamma}{(1 - s_E)(1 + \phi)} \right)^a \tag{13.11}$$

where

$$\Gamma = \frac{s_K(1 - \phi)\psi(\phi - \phi^{\text{rev}})/\phi^{\text{rev}}}{s_E - \psi(\phi - \phi^{\text{rev}})/\phi^{\text{rev}}}$$

This expression is quite similar to the north's expression apart from the Γ term, which captures the direct southern welfare impact of having a higher or lower tariff under the no-delocation scheme.

If we could ignore the Γ term, we could immediately say that the small country's welfare ranking is exactly opposite to that of the large country's. That is, the small country would prefer the symmetric scheme whenever the large country preferred the asymmetric one and vice versa. As it turns out, this statement is true even allowing for Γ, but its demonstration is somewhat involved. We turn first to signing Γ. The denominator of Γ can be re-written as $(s_E + \psi)(1 - \phi) + \phi(1 - s_E)$ with the help of (13.11). This is clearly positive, so the sign of Γ depends only on the sign of its numerator. Thus, by inspection, Γ is positive for $\phi > \phi^{\text{rev}}$ but negative for $\phi < \phi^{\text{rev}}$. Given this, the Γ term tends to dampen the small countries preferences for symmetric liberalization in the high-barrier region and tends to dampen its preference for asymmetric liberalization in the low-barrier region. We can, however, go beyond this.

Solving $V_A^*/V_S^* = 1$ for ϕ, we find that the only two roots are zero and ϕ^{rev}. Thus, the small country's ranking changes only once over the [0, 1] range of ϕ (because $0 < \phi^{\text{rev}} < 1$ when the north is larger and more capital abundant). Moreover, since Γ approaches zero as ϕ approaches its free trade level of unity, we know that in the neighbourhood of free trade, $V_A^* > V_S^*$. Due to the single-crossing feature, we can therefore say that $V_A^* < V_S^*$ for $\phi < \phi^{\text{rev}}$ but $V_A^* > V_S^*$ for $\phi > \phi^{\text{rev}}$. In words, the south prefers the symmetry rule when trade is very restricted but prefers the no-delocation rule when barriers are low. Again, the dividing line is ϕ^{rev}.

As with V_A/V_S, much of the complexity of V_A^*/V_S^* stems from factor-endowment differences. As ψ limits to zero—so $\psi(\phi - \phi^{\text{rev}})/\phi^{\text{rev}}$ limits to $2\phi(s_E - 1/2)$—we find that V_A^*/V_S^* is always greater than unity and V_A/V_S is always less than unity. In words, when there is only a size asymmetry between them, the rankings of large and small countries do not change with ϕ. In terms of welfare, the large country prefers the symmetric liberalization scheme while the small country prefers the asymmetric scheme. Of course, as discussed above, the large nation may still prefer the no-delocation scheme on grounds that are not reflected in our simple aggregate welfare calculation.

13.4.3 Global Welfare Analysis

Another natural question concerns total world welfare. Let us define the world welfare measure as the simple sum of south and north utility levels, that is, $V^W[\phi,\phi^E] = V[\ ] + V^*[\ ]$. As before, we compare the liberalization schemes by taking the ratio of V^W evaluated under the asymmetric and symmetric liberalization rules. The world ratio is

$$\frac{V_A^W}{V_S^W} = \lambda\frac{V_A}{V_S} + (1-\lambda)\frac{V_A^*}{V_S^*}; \quad \lambda \equiv \frac{s_E^{1/(1-b)}}{s_E^{1/(1-b)} + (1-s_E)^{1/(1-b)}}, \quad b \equiv \frac{\mu}{\sigma}$$

$$(13.12)$$

where the ratios of V's are given by (13.10) and (13.11).

A few aspects of (13.12) are noteworthy. First, when $\phi = \phi^{\text{rev}}$, V_a^W/V_s^W equals unity since both V_a/V_s and V_a^*/V_s^* do (as we showed above). Moreover, numerical simulations show that V_a^W/V_s^W exceeds unity for $\phi < \phi^{\text{rev}}$. In words, for this range of trade freeness, we find that an asymmetric liberalization can be a good idea from a global utilitarian point of view. This means that there are particular circumstances when the no-delocation rule, teamed with international income transfers, could be Pareto improving. However, in this range the asymmetry prevents delocation of firms from the large nation to the small (since the market-crowding effect outweighs the market-size effect when $\phi < \phi^{\text{rev}}$). In the range of ϕ where $\phi > \phi^{\text{rev}}$ (i.e. where the no-delocation asymmetry is blocking incipient small-to-large delocation), we find that symmetric liberalization is superior from a global perspective, although asymmetry may be adopted for political reasons.

We turn next to evaluating an alternative policy—namely international income transfers—that could yield the same no-delocation effect as asymmetric protection.

13.5 Avoiding Delocation via International Transfers

In Europe, but also elsewhere, economic disparities are viewed as a danger to social and political cohesion. Reflecting this, the European Union (EU) spends about 30% of its budget on so-called structural programmes that are aimed at encouraging economic activity in Europe's peripheral and disadvantaged regions. It seems natural, therefore, to investigate the magnitude of transfers that would be necessary to offset delocation. As we shall see, the size of the required transfers would appear to make this solution infeasible.

Let us define international transfers, T, in units of A that the north gives to the south. Transfers alter aggregate expenditure patterns and since the equilibrium price of A is unity, we have

$$E_{\text{net}} = L + \pi K - T, \quad E^*_{\text{net}} = L^* + \pi K^* + T \quad\quad (13.13)$$

Our task is to characterize the level of T that is necessary to allow liberalization without delocation, in the sense of (13.6). To focus on key issues, we consider only symmetric, reciprocal liberalization as in Section 13.3, so $\phi = \phi^*$. Using (13.13) to define the north's post-transfer relative market size (i.e. $[E - T]/E^W$), plugging the result into (13.1) and imposing the no-delocation condition (13.6), endogenizes T as a function of the common level of openness ϕ.

It proves convenient to express this endogenous transfer as a share of world income E^w:

$$\frac{T}{E^w} = \frac{\psi(\phi - \phi^{\text{rev}})}{\phi^{\text{rev}}(1 + \phi)} \quad\quad (13.14)$$

Observe that the necessary transfer is negative for low levels of trade freeness—specifically for $\phi < \phi^{\text{rev}}$—but positive for high levels of openness. This is intuitively obvious, given the results above; the market-crowding effect dominates with high barriers (so firms would tend to move southward) but the market-size effect dominates with low trade barriers (so firms would tend to move northward). As before, the expression is simplified in the size-asymmetry-only case (i.e. when ψ and thereby ϕ^{rev} are zero). Namely, (13.14) becomes $T/E^w = 2(s_E - 1/2)\phi/(1 + \phi)$. Here, we see that the size of the required transfer is increasing with trade freeness for all ϕ.

13.5.1 Feasibility

To get some idea of the massive-ness of the implied transfers, consider (13.14) in the neighbourhood of free trade when the nations differ only in terms of size. In this case, the required T/E^w approximately equals $(s_E - 1/2)$, so the implied T as a fraction of northern income is $(s_E - 1/2)/s_E$. If the north's pre-transfer income were three-fourths of world income, then the north would have to transfer one-third of its income to the south in order to stymie northward delocation. Since this is roughly equal to the existing tax burden in advanced industrialized nations, the transfer scheme would require a radical re-orientation of spending policies, or a hefty tax rise. The least we can say is that it is difficult to imagine that the population of rich countries would agree to pay such a cost for allowing trade integration to proceed without delocation.

13.6 CONCLUDING COMMENTS

This chapter has illustrated two main insights that economic geography models can add to the standard literature on two-way trade liberalization. First, in almost any model in which agglomeration forces are important, reciprocal liberalization between a large and small nation will, all else being equal, lead to an erosion of the small nation's industrial base. Although we have examined the issue only in the context of the simplest model with agglomeration forces (the FC model), we conjecture that it would go through in other new economic geography models. The point is that our finding is nothing more than a corollary of the home-market magnification effect that we found to characterize all the models we considered in Part I. Thus, while the predictions of our simple model should not be taken literally (there are many dispersion forces in the real world that are not captured in our simple models), the analysis in this chapter has illustrated how the logic of agglomeration and trade liberalization affect the spatial allocation of industry.

The second insight concerns the role of asymmetric liberalization in preventing, or reducing liberalization-induced delocation. To wit, countries that differ in size can achieve fully open trade without any delocation occurring, if the large country maintains lower barriers during the transition to free trade. This finding may not be only of theoretical interest. Small and poor nations often fear that free trade agreements with larger, richer nations will erode their industrial base. Although the reverse concern also can be heard, large, rich nations often implicitly recognize the concerns of their smaller partners by allowing the small nation to maintain higher trade barriers during the transition to free trade. In Europe, this principle is explicitly incorporated in the Europe Agreements (the EU phased out its tariffs more rapidly than the Central and southern European countries, although both go to zero). In other cases, the asymmetry occurs automatically. Under the US–Mexico FTA, for example, progressive tariff cuts were specified as percentages of the remaining tariff levels. Although these percentage cuts are symmetric, Mexican tariffs on US exports were initially four times higher (on average) than US barriers against Mexican exports. As a result, Mexico's tariff levels were higher than those of the United States during the entire transition phase to zero duties.

REFERENCES

Baldwin, R. E. and F. Robert-Nicoud. 2000. Free trade agreements without delocation. *Canadian Journal of Economics* 33(3): 766–786.

Martin, P. and G. Ottaviano. 1996. The geography of multi-speed Europe. *Economie Internationale* 67: 45–65 (in English: Discussion paper No. 1292, Centre for Economic and Policy Research).

Robert-Nicoud, F. 1996. Reciprocal but asymmetric trade liberalisation in a hub and spoke system. Masters thesis No. 543. Graduate Institute of International Studies, Geneva.

CHAPTER 14

Preferential Trade Agreements

14.1 INTRODUCTION

Preferential trade liberalization is a pervasive aspect of the world trading system. More than a hundred such arrangements have been announced to the WTO. Although only a handful of them function well, that handful accounts for a massive share of world trade. For instance the sum of intra-EU and intra-NAFTA trade accounts for about 40% of all world trade. It is, therefore, important to investigate the insights that economic geography models can add to the study of preferential liberalization. In this chapter, we address two main questions: 'What effect does the formation of a free trade agreement (FTA) have on the location of industry?' and 'What are the welfare effects of the changing geography for both the participating countries and the countries left out?'

There are, as it turns out, a number of important insights that come from the consideration of agglomeration forces. The first, and most robust, insight—the so-called production-shifting effect—can be thought of as a corollary of the home-market effect. If two or more nations remove all trade barriers among them, they create a large 'home' market, and in an economic geography model this tends to favour industry in the newly enlarged market. In short, new economic geography models suggest that in industries where agglomeration forces are important, formation of a trade bloc will lead to 'investment creation' and 'investment diversion'. While the idea is not new—this was part of the intellectual justification for Latin American regionalism in the 1960s, for example—its internal logic has not been thoroughly explored theoretically. For instance, we conjecture that this effect is subject to the caveats that we explored in Chapter 12; if industrial relocation is expensive and/or the integrating nations have a comparative disadvantage in the sector, preferential liberalization may not produce a large inflow of industry.

The second insight concerns the impact of preferential liberalization on the spatial distribution of industry inside a trade bloc. This effect is best thought of as a two-tier home-market effect. That is, as a group of nations begin lowering their barriers preferentially, the first home-market effect—the one we just discussed above—tends to favour industry in all members of the trade bloc. However, as the integration deepens, a second home-market effect—what might be called the internal home-market effect—kicks in. This tends to favour the largest bloc members as an industrial location. Indeed, we show that even before all internal barriers are removed, all of the trade bloc's industry will be clustered in the member with the largest market.

A third insight concerns the incentives for nations to join a trade bloc. This is most easily thought of as the political economy implication of the investment diversion and production shifting discussed above. The share of world industry that is attracted to a given trade bloc depends upon the bloc's size. Moreover, having a large share of world industry produced locally boosts real incomes, so both the benefits of joining a bloc, and the costs of not joining, rise as the bloc gets bigger. This suggests a dynamic whereby formation of a trade bloc creates a gravitational force—a force for inclusion—that is self-reinforcing; the bigger the bloc, the stronger is the incentive for new members to join, thus making it more likely that the bloc enlarges. In short, an idiosyncratic impulse that led to the creation of a trade bloc may trigger a domino effect that results in a progressive spreading of preferential liberalization.

The fourth insight concerns a particular, but common, form of preferential liberalization called a 'hub-and-spoke' arrangement. This involves one nation, the hub, at the centre of a number of bilateral free trade agreements (FTAs) with its trading partners (the spokes), but no FTAs among the spokes. Here, the main insight is the so-called 'hub effect' whereby superior market access favours the hub as a location for industry.

To illustrate these points as simply as possible, we employ the footloose capital (FC) model of Chapter 3 and several variants. With the exception of the last substantive section, we ignore the sort of demand-linked and supply-linked 'circular causality' that leads to spectacular shifts in the core–periphery model. This is not because we think they are unimportant; it is because the basic insights come through without them—basically circular causality just amplifies the direction of the changes we get in the FC model—and including them typically renders the models much more difficult to work with.

Puga and Venables (1997) seems to be the first article to explore the location effects of preferential liberalization. They work with the CP model, so as usual, they must rely on numerical simulation to provide a gallery of examples that are suggestive of general conclusions.

14.1.1 Organization of the Chapter

Section 14.2 presents a multi-nation version of the FC model. Sections 14.3–14.6 use this model to study the basic insights that economic geography models provide for the study of preferential liberalization schemes. Section 14.6 studies preferential trade agreements using the vertical-linkages version of the FC model (the FCVL model from Chapter 8) that allows for catastrophic agglomeration. Section 14.7 contains our concluding remarks and literature review.

14.2 THE MULTI-NATION FOOTLOOSE CAPITAL MODEL

To illustrate the main insights, we employ the simplest economic geography model, the FC model of Chapter 3. This allows us to derive a closed-form solution for the spatial distribution of industry, but it rules out catastrophic agglomeration. Such catastrophes do play an interesting role in the analysis of preferential liberalization, but they also introduce analytic complications that would cloud the basic forces, so we delay their consideration to the next section.

The footloose capital (FC) model is presented in detailed in Chapter 3, but here we merely recall the main outlines of the model for the reader's convenience. The model assumes:

- —Two sectors (A and M) and two factors (K and L).
- —The A sector is Walrasian and uses only L to produce its homogenous good. Inter-regional and intra-regional trade, A, is costless.
- —The monopolistically competitive industrial sector (M sector) uses only K in its fixed cost (one unit of K per variety) and only L in the variable cost. Intra-regional sales are costless, but inter-regional trade in M goods is subject to iceberg trade costs.
- —Each region's supply of L is fixed and cannot cross regional borders. Labourers own all capital.
- —Preferences over the two goods consist of CES preferences for M varieties nested in an upper-tier Cobb–Douglas function that ensures a constant fraction of expenditure, namely μ, is spent on industrial goods.

14.2.1 Formal Presentation of the Model

Discussion of preferential trade agreements requires at least three regions, so we extend the FC model to allow for $R > 2$ regions. Before turning to the policy analysis, we briefly review the positive aspects of the multi-national FC model.

To start simply, we abstract from asymmetries in openness and endowments, supposing that trade costs between any two regions are identical and that each nation is endowed with the same capital/labour ratio. We do consider size asymmetries, however, so we index regions with the superscript j, so s_E^j is region j's share of world expenditure and s_n^j denotes the share of industry located in region j. Using this notation, the equal relative endowment assumption is $s_K^j = s_L^j$ and $s_E^j = s_L^j$, for all j.

As in the two-nation FC model, some regions will be without industry when trade gets sufficiently free—at least as long as regions are not perfectly symmetric in size. We shall explore this possibility below, but for the moment we assume that trade is restricted enough to ensure that there are some firms operating in every nation. In this case, the operating profit of a firm located in nation j is

$$\pi_E^j = \left(\frac{s_E^j}{\Delta^j} + \phi \sum_{i \neq j} \frac{s_E^i}{\Delta^i} \right) b \frac{E^w}{K^w}, \quad \Delta^j \equiv s_n^j + (1 - s_n^j)\phi \qquad (14.1)$$

Capital mobility equalizes the equilibrium rewards to capital. As argued in Chapter 3, this means that every unit of capital earns the average capital reward, that is, b. Solving this location condition, we get

$$s_n^j - \frac{1}{R} = \left(1 + \frac{\phi R}{1 - \phi}\right)\left(s_E^j - \frac{1}{R}\right) \qquad (14.2)$$

where R is the number of regions. This expression tells us that if a region j is larger than the average region, then region j will host a share of world industry that is larger than its share of world expenditure. The converse is also true, so regions that are relatively small have industry shares that are less than proportionate to their size. Since a nation is a net exporter of industrial goods when $s_n^j - s_E^j > 0$, re-arrangement of (14.2) shows that every nation that is larger than average, that is, $s_E^j > 1/R$, is a net exporter and all other nations are net importers. Note also that an increase in a nation's size (s_E^j) produces a more than proportional increase in its share of industry. Moreover, the factor of proportionality increases as trade gets freer (the factor also rises with the number of regions), so we have the following result.

Result 14.1 (multi-nation home-market effect). *The multi-nation FC model displays the home-market effect (HME) since countries that are larger than average are net exporters of goods marked by imperfectly competition; moreover, the 'home-market magnification' effect also holds since the size of the HME is magnified by openness.*

We note that the very simple form of (14.2) is not robust. For example, if trade costs are unequal, as they surely are in reality, the home-market size alone, that is, s_E^j, is not sufficient to predict s_n^j. Rather, the expression involves a term that resembles a market-potential index involving trade costs and the full distribution of market sizes.

An alternative way of seeing a consequence of the HME is to use (14.2) and compute the variance of s_n as a function of the variance of s_E:

$$\sum_{j=1}^{R} \left(s_n^j - \frac{1}{R}\right)^2 = \left[\frac{1 + (R-1)\phi}{1 - \phi}\right]^2 \sum_{j=1}^{R} \left(s_E^j - \frac{1}{R}\right)^2$$

Clearly, the term in the square brackets in the expression above is larger than unity, which justifies the claim that, in a multi-region extension of the FC model, the spread of industrial activity is more uneven that the spread of income or expenditure.

MFN LIBERALIZATION AND PERIPHERALITY POINTS

It is also clear from (14.2) that global liberalization increases the share of industry in large nations and decreases the share of industry of small nations. A nation of size $s_E^j < 1/R$, will have no industry for any level of trade freeness greater than ϕ^{pj} (here, the superscript p is a mnemonic for periphery) where ϕ^{pj} is implicitly defined by

$$\frac{1}{1/R - s_E^j} = R\left(1 + \frac{\phi^{pj} R}{1 - \phi^{pj}}\right) \qquad (14.3)$$

This, together with (14.2), tells us that as ϕ increases, small regions become specialized in the Walrasian good one after another, starting from the smallest. By the time trade is perfectly free, all industry will be agglomerated in the largest region—except, of course, in the knife-edge case where regions are exactly equal in size. To summarize, we write the following result.

> **Result 14.2 (core–periphery pattern).** *In this simple model, global liberalization favours industrial location in larger than average nations and disfavours it in relatively small nations (due to the home-market magnification effect). During a process of multilateral liberalization, the smallest nation is the first to lose all industry and, as liberalization proceeds, other nations become 'peripheral' (i.e. have no industry) in order of their smallness (the level at which a small region first has no industry is defined by (14.3). Before trade is fully free, all industry will be agglomerated in the nation with the largest market.*

Caveats. This result is driven by exactly the same forces that produce the PLP effect in the two-nation FC model, so all the provisos raised in Chapter 12 apply. Specifically, if we allowed for any number of realistic dispersion forces—for example, capital relocation costs, or comparative advantage differences among nations—this stark result will be modified. Nevertheless, it does illustrate a quite general implication of models that display agglomeration forces. We also repeat our warning that the definition of size is far more complicated when trade costs are not perfectly symmetric.

14.3 Production Shifting and Investment Diversion

The most basic new insight that comes from models with agglomeration forces concerns the way in which a preferential trade arrangement tends to favour industry inside the trade bloc. This effect—what Baldwin and Venables (1995) call 'production shifting'—features frequently in policy-makers reasoning. For instance, it was often asserted that the competitiveness of European industry suffered compared to US and Japanese industry from the 'Euro disease' of too-many-too-small markets. A major argument in favour of the European Union's Single Market programme was to remedy this by creating a home market that was as big or bigger than the one enjoyed by American and Japanese firms.

It is best to think of the production-shifting effect as a corollary of the home-market effect (HME). Preferentially lowering trade barriers among members of a preferential trade arrangement (PTA) essentially expands the 'home' market of all members and this, in turn, makes location inside the bloc more attractive to industrial firms for the standard HME reasons. The easiest way to illustrate this formally is to consider the effects of forming a 'perfect' free trade area (FTA) between two of the R nations in the world when all regions are of equal size. By symmetry, we know that the two prospective members of the FTA account for a share of world industry equal to $2/R$. After they form their FTA, they become a large region in the sense that the FTA's home market is twice that of every other region. Having demonstrated that the HME works in the multi-nation FC model, it is obvious that the FTA's share of world industry will now exceed their share of world expenditure. Since the FTA members' shares equalled their shares of expenditure before the preferential liberalization, this tells us that FTA formation will shift some industry into the FTA.

The production-shifting effect also obtains when we consider less than perfect free trade areas, that is, marginal preferential liberalizations. For example, suppose the members of the PTA impose a two-way freeness of ϕ' while all other trade flows are governed by ϕ. Working with $R = 3$ for simplicity's sake (the expressions for equilibrium, s_n, become unwieldy when we have uneven trade freeness parameters and/or more than three nations), and solving the location conditions $\pi^1 = \pi^2$, and $\pi^2 = \pi^3$ (this assumes that trade costs are high enough to maintain some industry in all nations) for the share of industry in nation 1, we get, for example

$$s_n^1 = \frac{(1 + \phi' - 2\phi^2)[s_E^1 + (s_E^1 - s_E^2)(\phi' - \phi)/(1 - \phi')]}{(1 - \phi)(1 - \phi + \phi' - \phi)} - \frac{\phi}{1 - \phi + \phi' - \phi} \tag{14.4}$$

The expression for the s_n^2 is isomorphic, while the expression for s_n^3 is just $1 - s_n^1 - s_n^2$. Plainly this is increasing in nation 1's size (s_E^1), in its relative size within the PTA, as measured by $s_E^1 - s_E^2$ and in both the freeness of intra-PTA trade ϕ', and overall trade freeness, ϕ.

Denoting the pre-PTA national industry shares as s_n^1 and s_n^2, (14.2), and comparing this sum of their shares post-PTA, we find (using (14.1) and the corresponding expression for nation 2's share) that

$$s_n^{PTA} - (s_n^1 + s_n^2) = \frac{2\phi(\phi' - \phi)[1 - (s_E^1 + s_E^2)]}{(1 - \phi)(1 - \phi + \phi' - \phi)} > 0 \tag{14.5}$$

where s_n^{PTA} is the sum of nation 1's and nation 2's shares post-PTA. There are three salient points here. First, what we might call the marginal production-shifting effect is increasing in the freeness of trade inside the PTA, viz. ϕ'. Also, if we hold the margin of preference $\phi' - \phi$ constant, the degree of production shifting also increases with the general freeness of trade, namely ϕ.[1] This latter result could be thought of a corollary of the 'home-market magnification' effect that we saw in the simple two-nation case. That is, since industry becomes more footloose as trade gets freer, the production-shifting effect of preferential liberalization gets stronger as global trade gets freer. Finally, the absolute size of the production-shifting effect increases as the economic size of the PTA, that is, $s_E^1 + s_E^2$, decreases. The reason for this result is quite simple. If the PTA encompassed the whole world, there would be no industry to shift into the PTA, so it is natural that the amount of shifting depends upon that amount of industry that can be shifted.

---

[1] More formally, $d(\text{LHS})/d\phi' = 2\phi s_E^3/(1 - \phi' - 2\phi)^2 > 0$ and $d(\ln[\text{LHS}])/d\phi = (1 - \phi^2 + \delta)/(\phi(1 - \phi)(1 - \phi + \delta)) > 0$, where δ is the constant margin of preference, and LHS is the left-hand side of (14.5).

We also note that in the FC model, industrial delocation is synonymous with international capital flows, so the industrial delocation induced by the formation of a PTA would induce what Baldwin et al. (1996) call the investment diversion effect. To summarize these results, we have the following results.

Result 14.3 (production-shifting effect and investment diversion). *Preferential liberalization induces industry to delocate from outside the PTA to inside it. This induces capital flows from excluded nations into the PTA, so the production-shifting effect also implies 'investment diversion'.*

Result 14.4 (size of production-shifting effect). *The magnitude of production shifting increases with the freeness of trade within the PTA. Also, if one holds constant the margin of preference that PTA membership implies, then the production-shifting effect increases with the degree of overall trade freeness. Finally, the degree of production shifting increases as the economic size of the PTA decreases.*

In closing this section, we note that there is an interesting effect implicit in (14.4). If the preferential liberalization is incomplete ($\phi' < 1$) and the integrating nations are not equal in size, then preferential liberalization may reduce industry in the small partner. More on this after we consider the welfare effects.

14.3.1 Welfare Implications

In the FC model, the indirect utility function for a representative consumer in a typical regions is

$$V = \frac{E}{P}; \quad P \equiv p_A^{1-\mu} \Delta^{-a}, \quad \Delta \equiv \left(\int_{i=0}^{n^w} p_i^{1-\sigma} di \right), \quad a \equiv \frac{\mu}{\sigma - 1} \quad (14.6)$$

Since $p_A = 1$, and nominal incomes are constant in any equilibrium, the price index Δ^{-a} is a sufficient statistic to assess the welfare effect of any change in policy. In particular, since $a > 0$, welfare increases whenever Δ increases. The expressions for the welfare changes are unambiguous, so we can, without loss of generality, concentrate the discussion on the formation of free trade areas that involve a marginal (upward) shift in ϕ' starting from $\phi = \phi'$.

In the three-nation case that we study, Δ for nation 1 is $\Delta_1 \equiv s_n^1 + \phi' s_n^2 + \phi s_n^3$. The analogous expression for the non-FTA member, nation 3, is $\Delta_3 \equiv \phi s_n^1 + \phi s_n^2 + s_n^3$. This permits us to decompose the welfare effect into the direct effect and the result of production shifting (an indirect effect):

$$\frac{\partial \Delta_1}{\partial \phi'} = s_n^2 + (1 - \phi) \frac{\partial s_n^1}{\partial \phi'} + (\phi' - \phi) \frac{\partial s_n^2}{\partial \phi'}, \quad \frac{\partial \Delta_3}{\partial \phi'} = (1 - \phi) \frac{\partial s_n^3}{\partial \phi'} \quad (14.7)$$

The welfare impact on typical PTA members (nations 1 and 2 by convention) is shown by the first expression, while the second expression captures the welfare effect on the excluded nation, nation 3.

Focusing on the first expression, we note that the direct effect consists of the fall in consumer prices for those goods that are imported from the partner region (this is the first right-hand term in the first expression, namely s_n^2). The second and third terms shows that the production-shifting effect has two components. To the extent that PTA formation raises s_n^1, the indirect effect improves nation 1 welfare since nation 1 consumers no longer pay the trade costs on the goods that are now produced within their nation; the weight on this shift is $1 - \phi$. The preferential liberalization will also typically increase production in the partner nation, nation 2. This is captured by the third term. Since trade with the partner country is more open than it is from the rest of the world (country 3), the weight on this shift is $\phi' - \phi$ is positive, so an increase in s_n^2 at the expense of s_n^3 tends to be welfare improving. Of course, if s_n^1 falls sufficiently, the overall impact of the indirect effect could be negative (more on this below). Note that the logic behind this welfare is distinctly related to the price-lowering protection effect analysed in Chapter 12. As such, all the provisos raised in that chapter apply here. The total impact on the FTA, summing across real incomes in both PTA member nations, is also unambiguously positive since $s_n^1 + s_n^2$ rises. To summarise, we write the following result.

Result 14.5 (PTA normative effects on members). *Formation of a prefer-ential trade arrangement unambiguously raises the total real income of PTA residents.*

Note that nominal incomes (i.e. incomes measured in the numeraire good) are invariant to trade policy in the FC model, so there is no intra-national distribution issue. Regardless of the factor ownership, all residents of a given nation either gain, or all lose from the PTA formation. This, of course, is an artifice of the model's simplifying assumption rather than a fundamental result; more generally, any type of liberalization will alter factor prices.

The impact of the PTA on the rest-of-the-world nation (nation 3) is given by the second expression in (14.7). Since we showed that PTA formation lowers s_n^3, this shows that the rest of world is harmed by the preferential liberalization between nations 1 and 2.

Result 14.6 (normative effects on the rest of world). *Formation of a PTA always harms the excluded nations.*

This result, which arises in a much broader class of models, but not always so unambiguously, helps us explain why the GATT placed restrictions on prefer-ential liberalization (e.g. GATT Article 24).

14.3.2 Two-Tier Home-Market Effect: Spatial Inequality and PTAs

We now focus more sharply on the important question of how preferential liberal-ization affects the allocation of industry *within* a trading bloc.

As noted in the introduction, one of the basic effects is what we call the two-tier home-market effect. As we saw, preferential liberalization favours industry inside the bloc because the bloc as a whole becomes a bigger home market. However, as

Number of firms

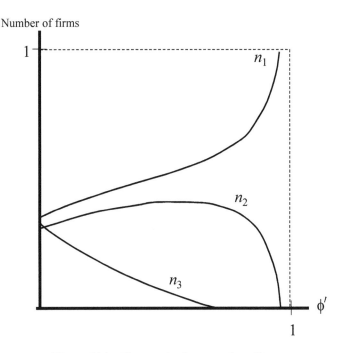

Figure 14.1   The two-tier home-market effect.

long as trade inside the bloc is not perfectly free, a second-tier HME operates. That is, as internal trade gets freer, industry will tend to move towards the larger markets inside the bloc. Thus, the largest market in a PTA will unambiguously gain industry, but the impact on the smaller market can go either way.

We shall examine this two-tier HME in some detail in this section, but it may be useful to illustrate the main issues by plotting the equilibrium values for n_1, n_2 and n_3 implied by (14.4) and its correspondent for region 2. The result, shown in Figure 14.1, illustrates how preferential liberalization clearly shifts industry away from the excluded nation, and clearly favours industry in the largest PTA member. The small PTA member, however, first gains firms (in this example, n_2 rises until all industry has left the excluded nation) from the PTA versus rest-of-world HME, but then loses industry due to the within-PTA HME that directs industry to the largest member. (The parameter values used here set the external trade freeness, ϕ, equal to 0.55, $s_E^1 = 1/3 + \delta$, $s_E^3 = 1/3 - \delta$ and $s_E^2 = 1/3$, where $\delta = 1/200$.)

To study the within-PTA spatial inequality more precisely, we use (14.4) and the corresponding expression for nation 2's share of industry to express within-union inequality as

$$s_n^{1'} - s_n^{2'} = \frac{(1 - \phi^2 + \phi' - \phi'^2)(s_E^1 - s_E^2)}{(1 - \phi)(1 - \phi')} \tag{14.8}$$

where this is only valid for parameters that yield interior values of both s_n's. This is plainly positive as long as nation 1 is larger than nation 2 and some preferential liberalization has taken place, that is, $\phi' \geq \phi$. Four remarks are useful in making this expression 'talk'.

First, inspection reveals that the larger is the size asymmetry, that is, $s_E^1 - s_E^2$, the larger is the inequality in the spatial allocation of industry within the trade bloc. Second, by inspection we see that as trade within the bloc gets freer, that is, ϕ' rises, the degree of spatial inequality rises.

The third point is that the impact of external openness on internal inequality is ambiguous.[2] If the rest of the world is very closed, additional rest-of-world openness increases internal inequality since the two partners are close to the classic two-region FC model when ϕ is near zero (and hence the classic HME dominates). The sign, however, is reversed when ϕ is high and the margin of preference is small.

Importantly, we should note that as long as the regions are not perfectly symmetric in terms of size, progressive internal liberalization will eventually result in a core–periphery pattern within the trade bloc. To make this concrete, we consider the following thought experiment. Suppose that the two PTA members jointly account for two-thirds of world expenditure, and the size asymmetry between them is parameterized by ε, where $s_E^1 = (1 + \varepsilon)/3$ and $s_E^2 = (1 - \varepsilon)/3$. The critical value of internal freeness beyond which the core–periphery outcome occurs is defined as

$$\frac{-2\varepsilon(1 - \phi - \phi^2) + \phi(3 - \phi) + (1 - \phi)\sqrt{(2 - \phi)^2 + (2\phi\varepsilon - 2)^2 - 4(\varepsilon\phi^2 + 2\varepsilon\phi + 1)]}}{2(1 + \varepsilon)}$$

$$(14.9)$$

This says that the critical value of internal freeness is lower for high levels of size asymmetry (high ε) for any given level of external openness (ϕ), and the critical value is higher for any level of external openness, for any given ε. To summarize, we have the following results.

Result 14.7 (two-tier HME). *Gradual preferential liberalization raises the amount of industry inside the bloc since PTA formation expands the group's home market and this triggers the usual HME. However, bloc formation also shifts industry within the bloc. Specifically, what might be called the internal HME magnification mechanism implies that industry delocates to the largest member nation, thus raising that degree of spatial inequality of industrial production inside the bloc.*

Result 14.8 (PTA's 'sustain point'). *If intra-bloc liberalization is progressive, all industry inside the trade bloc will be agglomerated in the large market at some point that is short of perfectly free internal trade. The critical value for internal trade freeness beyond the core–periphery pattern emerges as given by (14.9). This shows that the sustain point comes sooner (i.e. lower ϕ') when the intra-bloc size asymmetry is large and when trade with the rest of the world is highly restricted.*

---

[2] Specifically, the derivative with respect to ϕ is $(s_E^1 - s_E^2)[(1 - 2\phi)(1 - \phi) + \phi' - \phi]/(1 - \phi)^2(1 - \phi')$.

This latter result suggests that it is easier to maintain a spatially dispersed equilibrium when internal liberalization is teamed with external liberalization. To emphasis this policy implication, we write the following result.

Result 14.9 (preferential liberalization teamed with multilateral liberalization). *The appearance of an intra-bloc core–periphery pattern is hindered if internal liberalization is accompanied by external, multilateral liberalization. This also suggest that, in terms of industry, small members of a trade bloc may be more interested in multi-lateral liberalization.*

In closing this line of analysis, we note that this sort of internal dislocation of industry can be avoided in two ways.

Result 14.10 (avoiding spatial inequality). *A big-bang liberalization that quickly removes all internal trade barriers would result in no delocation. If industrial delocation creates political resistance (as might be expected), then a very gradual preferential liberalization might be politically unsustainable while a 'shock therapy' policy change might be feasible. Additionally, an asymmetric liberalization scheme where the large member lowers its barriers faster could also allow the members to achieve full integration without increase the internal spatial inequality (see Chapter 13).*

14.3.3 Welfare Implications

The welfare implications on intra-bloc spatial inequality are fully described by expression (14.7). The above analysis, however, has shown that unless the two PTA members are exactly equal in size, then the delocation derivative (i.e. $ds_n^i/d\phi'$) for the small nation will be negative over some range of ϕ'. This suggests that the welfare effects on the small PTA member country may be ambiguous for some ranges of internal trade freeness. To check this, we again parameterize the size asymmetry with ε, so $s_E^1 = (1 + \varepsilon)/3$ and $s_E^2 = (1 - \varepsilon)/3$, and use the explicit solutions for s_n^1 and s_n^2 in the Δ's. Recalling that $V = E/P$ and $P = \Delta^{-a}$, it is clear that changes in Δ are a sufficient statistic for welfare changes (recall that E is unaffected by liberalization in the FC model). Using (14.4) and its analogue for s_n^2, we find that

$$\Delta_1 = \frac{1 + \varepsilon}{3} \frac{1 + \phi' - 2\phi^2}{1 - \phi}, \quad \Delta_2 = \frac{1 - \varepsilon}{3} \frac{1 + \phi' - 2\phi^2}{1 - \phi} \qquad (14.10)$$

Interestingly, this shows that although the large PTA member gains more than the small member, the small PTA member always gains (since $\varepsilon < 1$ and $1 + \phi' - 2\phi^2$ is positive when $1 > \phi' > \phi$). To summarize, we write the following result.

Result 14.11 (no PTA losers). *In the FC model, the degree of internal delocation is small enough to ensure that the all PTA members gain from any level of preferential liberalization.*

By way of caution, we note that Puga and Venables (1997) find a counterexample to this result in a different model. They present a numerical example where gradual preferential liberalization harms one member of a PTA in the CP model with vertical linkages (i.e. the CPVL model of Chapter 8) over a certain range of trade costs. While it seems impossible to verify the generality of their result given the intractability of the CPVL model, we conjecture that it is due to the fact that the CPVL model has much stronger agglomeration forces so that the internal HME may act much more rapidly, thus favouring a negative outcome for the small partner.

14.4 DOMINO EFFECTS AND ENDOGENOUS BLOC SIZE

The results discussed above imply that the welfare gain from joining a trade bloc rises as the size of the trade bloc increases. The point is simply an application of the home-market effect, as the bloc size rises, the share of world industry inside the bloc rises more than proportionally, so the cost of living in the bloc falls with bloc size. Likewise, the cost of *not* joining a trade bloc also rise as the bloc expands because the cost of living in excluded nations is driven up by the bloc-induced delocation of industry. This sort of logic suggests that the formation of trade blocs may be influenced by a 'domino effect' (Baldwin 1993, 1997).

Heuristically, the domino effect stems from the fact that forming a preferential trade area, or deepening an existing one, produces trade and investment diversion. This diversion generates new political economy forces in non-participating nations. The pressure for inclusion increases with the size of the trade bloc, yet bloc size depends upon how many nations join. Clearly, then, a single incidence of regionalism may trigger several rounds of membership requests from nations that were previously happy as non-members. Of course, the idea underlying the domino effect is quite old. A presentation can be discerned in Jacob Viner's account of how dozens of German principalities and city states were cajoled and coerced into joining Prussia's Zollverien between 1819 and 1867 (see Viner 1950, Chapter V.3).

14.4.1 Illustrating the Effect

The easiest way to illustrate this more precisely is to look at a very stylized world consisting of many identically sized nations, all of whom initially impose the same MFN trade barrier. We then exogenously form a perfect free trade area between two of the nations and exogenously add nations to the FTA until eventually the world is one great big free trade area. The main axis of investigation is the impact of this bloc expansion on the geographical distribution of industry. With this distribution in hand, we compare the welfare of a representative consumer inside the trade bloc to that of a representative consumer living in an excluded nation.

The first step is to specify the operating profit of firms based in a member nation and firms based in an excluded nation. These are (with the usual normalizations $K^w = 1$, $E^w = 1$)

$$\pi = b\left(\frac{M/R}{\Delta} + \phi\frac{(R-M)/R}{\Delta^*}\right), \quad \pi^* = b\left(\frac{\phi M/R}{\Delta} + \frac{\phi(R-M-1)/R}{\Delta^*} + \frac{1/R}{\Delta^*}\right)$$

$$\Delta \equiv s_n + \phi(1 - s_n), \quad \Delta^* \equiv \phi\left(1 - \frac{1 - s_n}{R - M}\right) + \frac{1 - s_n}{R - M} \qquad (14.11)$$

where R is the number of nations, M is the number of them that have joined the FTA, s_n is the share of industry located in the FTA (summing over all FTA members), Δ and Δ^* are the denominators of the demand functions in a typical FTA nation and in a typical non-member nation, respectively; ϕ is the level of trade barriers that all nations apply to all trade flows, except those within the FTA (for these trade is completely unhindered). Observe that in this notation, the share of industry in one of the $R - M$ nations that are not in the FTA is $(1 - s_n)/(R - M)$.

Solving the location condition $\pi = \pi^*$, we get that the share of industry inside the FTA is related to the share of nations inside the FTA and ϕ by

$$s_n^{\mathrm{FTA}} = \frac{m(1 + (1 - m)R\phi) - \phi}{1 - \phi}, \quad m \equiv \frac{M}{R} \qquad (14.12)$$

where this is valid for s_n^{FTA} between zero and unity. If the expression implies an s_n^{FTA} that is outside this band, then either $s_n^{\mathrm{FTA}} = 0$, or $s_n^{\mathrm{FTA}} = 1$ in the obvious manner. Observe that, as expected, the share of industry in the FTA is increasing in m over the whole range of m where s_n^{FTA} is between zero and unity (due to the HME). Also, it is important to note that, if there are many nations (R is large), then all industry agglomerates inside the FTA when the number of FTA members is higher than a fairly low number. In particular, solve (14.12) for $s_n^{\mathrm{FTA}} = 1$, we find that the 'sustain point' membership is

$$m^S = \frac{1}{\phi R} \qquad (14.13)$$

so, for example, if there are ten identical nations and the MFN level of trade freeness is 0.7 (with an elasticity of substitution equal to 3 this corresponds to a tariff equivalent of 16.3%), then the FTA will have attracted all the world's industry when it consists of just 1/7th of the world's nations. The reason for this rather extreme finding is that our simple set-up leads to a very rapid increase in size asymmetry since each non-member has a home market that is just 1/Rth of world expenditure, but the FTA has a home market that is M/Rth of world expenditure.

The welfare implications of bloc expansion are simple to track. As usual, indirect utility indicators are proportional to real income and these in turn depend upon the Δ's raise to a positive power $a = \mu/(\sigma - 1)$.[3] Thus, to gauge the welfare gain that a nation would get from shifting from non-member to member status,

---

[3] That is, utility is inversely related to the price index, but the price index is Δ^{-a}, $a > 0$.

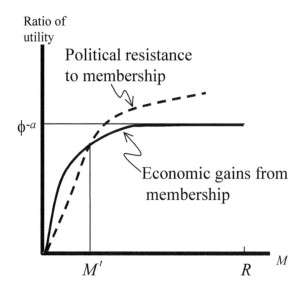

Figure 14.2   Domino theory of regionalism.

we use (14.12) in the definitions of the Δ's in (14.11), to find the ratio of indirect utility of an agent based inside the bloc, that is, E/P, to that of one based outside the bloc, that is, E^*/P^*. Remarkably, this ratio simplifies to

$$\frac{E/P}{E/P^*} \equiv \left(\frac{\Delta}{\Delta^*}\right)^a = M^a \tag{14.14}$$

Obviously then, the gain from joining the bloc rises with the bloc size. The ratio, however, goes on rising until all industry is inside the bloc (i.e. until $M = m^S R$, where (14.13) defines m^S), after which the ratio is constant at ϕ^{-a}.

14.4.2 Dominos

Telling the dominos story precisely would require a dynamic political economy model, but the basic intuition can be illustrated with the help of Figure 14.2. The solid curve shows the ratio of utility for a representative agent inside the bloc to that of one outside the bloc. This gives us a measure of the economic gains from joining the bloc. Joining a free trade area, however, typically involves some loss of sovereignty and this engenders political resistance in most nations. This resistance, typically, varies according to various cultural and historical factors. In the diagram, we have arranged nations in order of increasing resistance, so the most resistant nation is nation R. The level of political resistance is thus given by the dashed curve.

   As we have drawn it, the political resistance is below the economic benefit up to the bloc size M'. Again, we have not specified a fully dynamic framework, but it is easy to think of an idiosyncratic shock starting a process by which nations enter the bloc one-by-one in order of their political resistance.

A simple extension of this, which we leave to the reader, would be to allow some trade barriers inside the FTA. This would lower the 'economics gains' curve without altering the 'political resistance' curve, so the result bloc size would be smaller. In this case, a renewed effort of bloc members to deepen intra-FTA integration, for example, to complete their internal market, would trigger another round of membership applications.

14.5 Hubs and Spokes: The Hub Effect

A very common form of preferential trade liberalization in the real world is the so-called 'hub and spoke' arrangement in which one country—typically a large region like the United States or the European Union—finds itself at the centre of many bilateral free trade agreements with smaller nations.[4] Such arrangements are not typically orchestrated; they emerge in an ad hoc manner, driven by standard political economy logic.[5]

Whatever the cause, such arrangements produce what Krugman (1993) called the 'hub effect'.That is, just as an all-roads-lead-to-Paris transportation system favours industrial location in Paris, a hub-and-spoke arrangement favours industry in the hub nation at the expense of industry in the spoke nations.

14.5.1 Imperfect Bilateral FTAs with the Hub

To illustrate the hub effect and its welfare consequences as simply as possible, we suppose that there are three nations in the world and that nations 2 and 3 (the spokes) have signed bilateral FTAs with nation 1 (the hub). The level of trade freeness between the two spokes is given by ϕ, while the degree of hub–spoke trade openness is ϕ'; since we are considering preferential liberalization hub–spoke trade is more open, that is, $\phi' > \phi$. To keep things simple, we assume each nation accounts for a third of world expenditure. With these assumptions, we have

$$\pi = b\left(\frac{1/3}{\Delta} + \phi'\frac{2/3}{\Delta^*}\right), \quad \pi^* = b\left(\phi'\frac{1/3}{\Delta} + \frac{1/3 + \phi/3}{\Delta^*}\right)$$

$$\Delta \equiv s_n + \phi'(1 - s_n), \quad \Delta^* \equiv \phi's_n + (1 + \phi)\left(\frac{1 - s_n}{2}\right) \tag{14.15}$$

where π and π^* are the operating profit earnings by typical hub and spoke firms (respectively), and s_n is the share of world industry located in the hub, that is, nation 1 (this means that $(1 - s_n)/2$ is the share in each spoke).

---

[4] See Kowalcyz and Wonnacott (1992) for a discussion of such agreements in the Western Hemisphere and Baldwin (1994) for an analysis of such agreements in Europe.

[5] The idea is that exporters in small nations are willing to fight harder for FTAs with the main trade partner than with minor trade partners. Thus, pro-trade exporters often win the political battle to get FTAs with the main partner (the hub), but anti-trade import competitors win the battle when it comes to FTAs with minor partners (other spokes); see Baldwin (1994, Chapter 5.2) for details.

Solving the location condition, $\pi = \pi^*$, as usual yields

$$s_n^H = \frac{1}{3} + \frac{2\phi'(\phi' - \phi)}{3(1 - \phi')(1 + \phi - 2\phi')}, \quad s_n^S = \frac{1}{3} - \frac{\phi'(\phi' - \phi)}{3(1 - \phi')(1 + \phi - 2\phi')} \tag{14.16}$$

where the superscripts H and S indicate the industry shares of the hub and a typical spoke economy, respectively. As usual, when parameters are such that the s_n's implied by these formulas are outside their natural limits, then they equal zero or one in an obvious manner.

It is important to note that the 'hub effect' (the tendency of a hub-and-spoke arrangement to favour location in the hub) does not always work. Formally, the difference between s_n^H and s_n^S provides a measure of the hub effect since without any preference, that is, $\phi = \phi'$, both shares are a third. Subtracting the two expressions in (14.16) yields $\phi(\phi' - \phi)/[(1 - \phi')(1 + \phi - 2\phi')]$. The numerator of this is always positive when the FTAs provide at least some preferential access, but the denominator is negative when the margin of preference is large enough. Specifically, if ϕ' is greater than $(1 + \phi)/2$ (i.e. if the FTA freeness is more than half way between the MFN degree of openness and free trade), then the denominator is negative. Moreover, when the degree of preference is this high, the expression for s_n^H is out of bounds in the sense that it would imply a very negative value. In such cases, we know that the boundary is binding, so $s_n^H = 0$.

Intuitively, the source of the hub effect's ambiguity is the fact that the market-access effect and the local competition effect pull in opposite directions. Clearly, location in the hub implies better market access, however, it also implies stiffer competition. As it turns out, when the spokes maintain very high levels of protection but the FTA make hub–spoke trade quite free, then the local competition effect dominates and we see that there will be less than a third of world industry in the hub. However, if the margin of preference, that is, $\phi' - \phi$, is small, then the second right-hand terms of both expressions in (14.16) are positive, so there will be more industry in the hub than in either spoke. In this case, we say that the hub effect dominates.

14.5.2 Welfare

A sufficient statistic for evaluating the welfare effect of any change in policy is the policy's impact on Δ, as usual, with welfare increasing whenever Δ increases. Differentiating the definition from (14.15), we have

$$\frac{\partial \Delta}{\partial \phi'} = (1 - s_n) + (1 - \phi')\frac{\partial s_n}{\partial \phi'} \geq 0, \quad \frac{\partial \Delta^*}{\partial \phi'} = s_n - \left(\frac{1 - \phi}{2}\right)\frac{\partial s_n}{\partial \phi'} < 0 \tag{14.17}$$

For each expression above, the first term on the right-hand is the direct effect; the second term is the production-shifting effect. Starting from $\phi' = \phi$, it is clear that the creation of a hub-and-spoke system increases welfare in the hub.

Both the direct and the indirect effect work in the same direction, so as shown, the hub never loses from the arrangement and gains strictly for interior solutions for s_n.

The impact of MFN liberalization (i.e. liberalization between the spokes in our simple three-nation example), on the other hand, is negative for the hub since for a given ϕ' it entails a reduction in the hub effect. Indeed, using (14.16) and the analogue to (14.17), we find

$$\frac{\partial \Delta}{\partial \phi} = \frac{-2(1 - \phi')\phi'}{3(1 + \phi - 2\phi')^2} \tag{14.18}$$

This expression holds for interior solutions of s_n only. Otherwise, $\partial \Delta / \partial \phi$ is equal to 0 or 1 when $s_n^H = 1$ or 0, respectively.

What about the welfare of the residents of the spokes? Clearly, the direct effect of reducing the trade cost incurred on those goods imported from the hub is positive. All the same, the production-shifting effect hurts them. The net effect is thus ambiguous; algebraic steps similar to those conducted for Δ reveal

$$\frac{\partial \Delta^*}{\partial \phi'} = \frac{2(1 - \phi')^2 - (1 - \phi)}{3(1 - \phi')^2} \tag{14.19}$$

This expression holds for interior solutions of s_n only; for $s_n^H = 1$ or 0, $\partial \Delta^* / \partial \phi'$ is equal to -1 or 1, respectively. For an incremental liberalization, namely, starting at $\phi' = \phi$, we find

$$\lim_{\phi' \to \phi} \frac{\partial \Delta^*}{\partial \phi'} = -\frac{1 - 2\phi}{3(1 - \phi)} \tag{14.20}$$

This is negative when trade barriers are low, implying that production shifting dominates in such cases. On the other hand, the direct effect dominates when trade barriers are important, so that the creation of a hub-and-spoke system is favourable to the spokes as well. Finally, it becomes less costly to be in a spoke when trade becomes freer, so $\partial \Delta^* / \partial \phi \geq 0$.

Thus far, we have looked at incremental changes. One of the merits of the FC model's simplicity is that it allows closed-form solutions and this enables us to establish the welfare effects of discrete changes in policy.

WELFARE EFFECTS OF DISCRETE POLICY CHANGES

As long as $\phi' - \phi < 1 - \phi$, any form of hub-and-spoke implementation—marginal or discrete—is welfare improving for the hub. To see this, we start from a situation where everything is perfectly symmetric, in particular $\phi' = \phi$, and consider an increase of ϕ' beyond ϕ. The welfare effects of such a change in policy are (still for values of s_n strictly in the unit interval)

$$\frac{2(1 - \phi' + \phi)(\phi' - \phi)}{3(1 + \phi - 2\phi')}, \quad \frac{(1 - 2\phi')(\phi' - \phi)}{3(1 - \phi')} \tag{14.21}$$

where the first expression is for the hub and the second for the spokes. The sign of the spoke's welfare effect is the same as the sign of the expression in (14.20), so the interpretation there remains valid for a discrete change.

14.6 FREE TRADE AREAS AND INTERNAL CATASTROPHES

Our analysis of free trade areas in the presence of agglomeration forces showed two important and quite fundamental effects. Preferential liberalization tends to: (1) shift industry from the bloc at the expense of excluded nations (the production-shifting effect); and (2) increase the spatial inequality inside the bloc (the two-tier home-market effect). Puga and Venables (1997) show that in the vertical-linkages variant of the core–periphery model (what we call the CPVL model), preferential liberalization can lead to a very spectacular form of spatial inequality, namely an internal catastrophic agglomeration where all industry inside the bloc shifts to a single member nation. These authors' use of the CPVL model forces them to rely on numerical examples. This section illustrates the internal catastrophe point using a more tractable model, namely the vertical-linkages version of the FC model (FCVL model for short) due to Robert-Nicoud (2002), which was described at length in Chapter 8.

We start with the positive analysis.

14.6.1 The Multi-Region FCVL Model

Vertical linkages create some complementarities in the firms' location decisions and this gives rise to multiple equilibria for some parameter values and the possibility of 'catastrophic agglomeration'. Before turning to policy analysis we recall the key expressions of the FCVL model (see Chapter 8 for details and derivations), extended to allow for multiple regions.

In addition to consumers, a typical industrial firm sells part of its production to other firms; these firms use this output as intermediates. For simplicity, the intermediates are built into the same CES aggregate as that of the consumers. In other words, the elasticity of substitution σ is the same in final demand as well as in intermediate demand. Moreover, we assume that firms spend the same fraction of their costs on industrial goods as intermediates, as do consumers on industrial goods as final goods.[6] The basic expressions for the FC model are modified by vertical linkages in the following way:

$$\pi^j = (\Delta^j)^\mu \left(\frac{s_E^j}{\Delta^j} + \phi \sum_{J \neq j} \frac{s_E^J}{\Delta^J} \right) b, \quad \Delta^j \equiv s_n^j (\Delta^j)^\mu + \phi \sum_{J \neq j} s_n^J (\Delta^J)^\mu \quad (14.22)$$

where R is the number of nations worldwide. Note that the definition of the Δ is now implicit in the sense that the Δ's are the solution to R equations similar to the second one in (14.22).

[6] See Robert-Nicoud (2002) for a more general treatment that does not impose this restriction.

The second important change is that with vertical linkages, national market sizes, that is, the s_E^j, are endogenous. This is so because local expenditure comprises both consumer expenditure (which is fixed by our assumptions that people do not migrate and because capital rewards are repatriated) and expenditure on intermediates arising from other firms; the latter is mobile as firms are mobile. More precisely, we write

$$s_E^j = s_L^j + (\mu - b)(s_n^j - s_L^j) + (\mu - b)\frac{\pi^j - \bar{\pi}}{\bar{\pi}} s_n^j, \quad \bar{\pi} \equiv \frac{bL^w}{(1 - \mu)K^w} \quad (14.23)$$

where $\bar{\pi}$ is the equilibrium return on capital. It is obvious from the expression above that s_E^j increases in the mass of people (s_L^j) and firms (s_n^j) located in region j as well as on the rate of profits of the latter (π^j). This is so because profits are proportional to output and output is proportional to the composite input, which includes intermediates. Clearly, expenditure is proportional to population size (i.e. $s_E^j = s_L^j$) if the proportion of the firm matches capital ownership ($s_n^j = s_K^j = s_L^j$) and if local firms make non positive pure profits ($\pi^j = \bar{\pi}$).

Finally, we close the model by imposing the location condition, which can be written as $\pi^j = \bar{\pi}$, for all j. It is obvious from (14.22) and (14.23) that we can no longer obtain closed-form solutions for the key locational variables s_n^j.

THE BREAK AND SUSTAIN POINTS IN THE MULTI-CASE

Here, we provide the expression for the 'break' and 'sustain' points for the R-country FCVL model when all countries are symmetric, that is, when all countries have identical endowments, viz. $s_L^j = 1/R$, for all $j = 1, ..., R$ and all countries apply the most-favoured-nation (MFN) clause universally, viz. ϕ characterizes the trade/transportation barriers of any pair of countries.

In such a case, it is easy to show that there exists an equilibrium in which all endogenous variables are the same for any ϕ. This equilibrium is said to be unstable, however, if a perturbation to the system of the form of an exogenous decrease in the share of firms located in, say, country 1, is not self-correcting. In our context, such a perturbation is self-correcting if the operating profit of the firms that relocate away from 1 decrease, so that they (or others since all firms are identical) will have an incentive to relocate back to country 1 (more on this below). This is so if the dispersion forces are stronger than the agglomeration forces, which is the case whenever $\phi \in [\phi_{MFN}^{break}, 1)$, where

$$\phi_{MFN}^{break} = \frac{(1 - \mu)(1 - \mu + b)}{(R - 1 + \mu)(1 + \mu - b) - (1 - \mu)(R - 2)} \quad (14.24)$$

the denominator of which is strictly larger than the numerator, all $R > 1$.

Conversely, a pattern in which the whole industry clusters in a single location j is sustainable if no firm that considers a unilateral de-location away from the cluster—in country J, say—would find it profitable to do so. Formally, this is the case if $\max_{J \neq j} \pi^J \leq \pi^j$, where π^j is evaluated at $s_n^j = 1$. It can be shown that this will be the case for any $\phi > \phi_{MFN}^{sust}$, where ϕ_{MFN}^{sust} is implicitly defined as the smallest root of the following polynomial:

$$f(\phi) = \phi^2[1 + (\mu - b)(R - 1)] + (1 - \mu + b)[1 + (R - 2)\phi] - R\phi^{1-\mu}$$

(14.25)

This expression is the simple generalization of the break point in the two-nation version of the model. It can be shown that $\phi_{MFN}^{sust} < \phi_{MFN}^{break}$ for all admissible parameter values.

14.6.2 Positive Analysis of FTA's with Catastrophic Agglomeration

As usual, a dispersed equilibrium configuration becomes unstable when trade becomes sufficiently free. What is the implication for countries forming a free-trade area? As we showed above, preferential liberalization triggers a two-tier home-market effect. The integrated market looks bigger thanks to the reduction in internal trade costs and this brings in new firms at the expense of the countries that are left out of the agreement; vertical linkages reinforced this effect. Second, and more important, circular causation stemming from vertical linkages may produce a collapse of industry to a single nation *within* the FTA. This section develops the argument.

Take three ex-ante identical countries, that is, each of them is endowed with one-third of total factor endowments. Using the FTA openness levels, we rewrite (14.22) and (14.23) as

$$\frac{\pi^1}{\bar{\pi}} = (\Delta^1)^\mu \left(\frac{s_E^1}{\Delta^1} + \phi \frac{s_E^2}{\Delta^2} + \phi^* \frac{(1 - s_E^1 - s_E^2)}{\Delta^*} \right)$$

$$\Delta^1 = s_n^1(\Delta^1)^\mu + \phi s_n^2(\Delta^2)^\mu + \phi^*(1 - s_n^1 - s_n^2)(\Delta^3)^\mu \qquad (14.26)$$

$$s_E^1 = \frac{1}{3} + (\mu - b)\left(s_n^1 - \frac{1}{3}\right) + (\mu - b)\frac{\pi^1 - \bar{\pi}}{\bar{\pi}} s_n^1$$

where ϕ now stands for the intra-FTA trade freeness, ϕ^* stands for the level of openness governing all other trade flows and $\bar{\pi}$ is the average earnings of capital. Expressions for country-2 variables are isomorphic. The expressions for country 3 (the excluded nation) are

$$\frac{\pi^3}{\bar{\pi}} = (\Delta^3)^\mu \left(\phi^* \frac{s_E^1}{\Delta^1} + \phi^* \frac{s_E^2}{\Delta^2} + \frac{(1 - s_E^1 - s_E^2)}{\Delta^*} \right)$$

$$\Delta^3 = \phi^* s_n^1(\Delta^1)^\mu + \phi^* s_n^2(\Delta^2)^\mu + (1 - s_n^1 - s_n^2)(\Delta^3)^\mu \qquad (14.27)$$

$$s_E^3 = \frac{1}{3} + (\mu - b)\left(s_n^3 - \frac{1}{3}\right) + (\mu - b)\frac{\pi^3 - \bar{\pi}}{\bar{\pi}} s_n^3$$

The expressions for s_E^j in (14.26) and (14.27) show when s_E^j is larger than 1/3, namely when the country is a net importer of capital or when firms located there make pure profits, viz. $\pi^j > \bar{\pi}$. As usual, this feeds back into the price index and the profit functions (the second and first expression in (14.26), respectively).

Using the usual terminology, (14.26) defines an instantaneous equilibrium of the model. By contrast, a 'long-run' equilibrium is defined as a 9-tuple $\{s_E^j, s_n^j, \pi^j\}_{j=1}^3$ that solves (14.26) such that $\pi^j \leq \bar{\pi}$, $s_n^j \geq 0$ and $s_n^j(\pi^j - \bar{\pi}) = 0$. In plain English, in a long-run equilibrium, all active firms must make non-positive pure profits. As usual, we assume that the s_n^j's evolve according to the ad hoc law of motion,

$$\dot{s}_n^j = s_n^j(1 - s_n^j)(\pi^j - \bar{\pi}) \tag{14.28}$$

By symmetry between regions 1 and 2, we know that $s_n^1 = s_n^2$, together with $s_E^1 = s_E^2$, $\Delta^1 = \Delta^2$ and $\pi^1 = \pi^2$ is always a solution to (14.26). We call this long-run equilibrium the 'FTA-symmetric equilibrium'. Moreover, we conjecture that there exists a long-run equilibrium such that $s_n^3 < 1/3$ because $\phi^* < \phi$. To verify this, we use the following argument. First, $\phi = \phi^*$ implies that the fully symmetric equilibrium is a solution to (14.26)–(14.28) with $s_n^j = 1/3$. Second, it is straightforward to check that $\partial s_n^3/\partial\phi$ evaluated at the symmetric equilibrium and $\phi = \phi^*$ is negative. By a continuity argument, it must be that an equilibrium for which more than two-thirds of firms locate in the FTA exists for all $\phi^* < \phi$.

Now we want to describe the circumstances where firms located in the FTA are evenly spread between member countries, namely countries 1 and 2. To answer this question, we look at the circumstances under which the FTA-symmetric equilibrium is stable. Formally, this involves signing $\partial\pi^1/\partial s_n^1$ evaluated at the FTA-symmetric equilibrium. The value of ϕ such that this term is zero gives us the 'FTA break point'.

Formally, we are interested in the combination of parameters at which the FTA-symmetric equilibrium is on the verge of being broken—which is the case if (14.26), (14.27) and (14.28) hold with $s_n^1 = s_n^2$ *and* if $\partial\pi^1/\partial s_n^1 = 0$ holds. (Remember that $\partial\pi^1/\partial s_n^1$ equals $-\partial\pi^2/\partial s_n^1$ at the FTA-symmetric equilibrium.) A priori, two cases can occur: either the country that is not part of the agreement is already specialized in the production of good A when the FTA-symmetric equilibrium is broken. In this case, $s_n^3 = 0$ (and $s_n^1 + s_n^2 = 1$), or there are still some active firms in country 3 when this phenomenon occurs, in which case we have $s_n^3 > 0$.

CASE I

Here, we are interested in a configuration in which industry is evenly spread between both countries part of the FTA but absent from country 3, and ask under which circumstances this long-run equilibrium is unstable. We show that this can never be part of a stable long-run equilibrium. Therefore, only cases like Case II occur. The reader not interested in the algebraic details can skip the remainder of this section and go directly to Case II without loss of continuity.

We impose $s_n^1 + s_n^2 = 1/2$. Since countries 1 and 2 are perfectly symmetric, we omit the country superscripts from now on. Conversely, we superscript variables pertaining to country 3 with an asterisk. When country 3 is entirely specialized in A, viz. $s_n^* = 0$, (14.26) and (14.27) reduce to

$$\frac{\pi}{\bar{\pi}} = \Delta^\mu \left((1 + \phi) \frac{s_E}{\Delta} + \phi^* \frac{1 - 2s_E}{\Delta^*} \right) = 1,$$

$$\frac{\pi^*}{\bar{\pi}} = (\Delta^*)^\mu \left(2\phi^* \frac{s_E}{\Delta} + \frac{1 - 2s_E}{\Delta^*} \right) \le 1 \qquad (14.29)$$

and

$$\Delta^{1-\mu} = \left(\frac{1 + \phi}{2} \right), \quad \Delta^* = \phi^* \Delta^\mu, \quad s_E = \frac{1}{3} + \frac{\mu - b}{6}, \quad s_E^* = \frac{1}{3} - \frac{\mu - b}{3} \qquad (14.30)$$

The inequality in (14.29) holds because $s_n^* = 0$ implies that shadow pure profits in country 3 are non-positive.

We now ask two related questions. First, under what circumstances is it true that $\pi^* < \bar{\pi}$? And, second, when is it the case that the FTA-symmetric equilibrium in which $s_n^1 + s_n^2 = 1/2$ holds is stable? Only when these two conditions are simultaneously satisfied is the configuration that we are considering in this section part of a stable long-run equilibrium. We start with the first question. A sufficient and necessary condition for $\pi^* < \bar{\pi}$ to hold is

$$P^*(\phi, \phi^*) \equiv \left(\frac{2\phi^*}{1 + \phi} \right)^2 (2s_E) + \frac{2}{1 + \phi} s_E^* - \left(\frac{2\phi^*}{1 + \phi} \right)^{1-\mu} \le 0 \qquad (14.31)$$

The P stands for 'periphery': when this condition is satisfied, country 3 is a periphery in that no firms settle there. Observe that the expression above is strictly decreasing in ϕ, so that a necessary condition for this condition to be satisfied is

$$P_N^*(\phi^*) \equiv (\phi^*)^2 2s_E + s_E^* - (\phi^*)^{1-\mu} \le 0 \qquad (14.32)$$

because $\phi < 1$; the subscript N stands for 'necessary'. Any ϕ^* larger than the smaller root of the polynomial above would do. Conversely, making use of the fact that $\phi > \phi^*$, a sufficient condition for (14.31) to hold is

$$P_S^*(\phi^*) \equiv \left(\frac{2\phi^*}{1 + \phi^*} \right)^\mu \left(\frac{2\phi^*}{1 + \phi^*} (2s_E) + \frac{s_E^*}{\phi^*} \right) - 1 \le 0 \qquad (14.33)$$

It can be shown that the lowest ϕ^* at which (14.32) and (14.33) are satisfied is decreasing in μ and increasing in σ (decreasing in b). Unsurprisingly, this implies that these conditions are more likely to hold when agglomeration forces are strong (see any chapter of Part I of this book). The shape of the curves P_N^* and P_S^* can be shown to be as depicted in Figure 14.3. Obviously, $P_S^*(\phi^*) > P^*(\phi, \phi^*) > P_N^*(\phi^*)$ for all ϕ^* and for all ϕ such that $\phi > \phi^*$. Clearly, all these conditions are satisfied when ϕ^* is large enough.

We observe that (14.32) and (14.33) are violated at the limit $\phi^* = 0$. The interpretation for this result is, once more, well known to the reader familiar

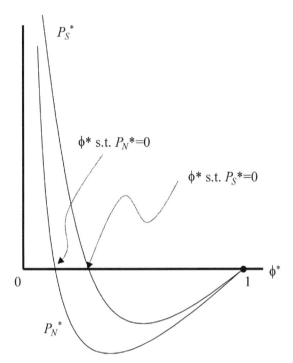

Figure 14.3 Necessary and sufficient conditions for the FTA-symmetric equilibrium.

with the material in Part I. When $\phi^* = 0$, the manufacturing market of country 3 is perfectly isolated, and hence the only way to serve in this market is to locate production there. But has any firm the incentive to do so in the first place? The answer is 'yes', simply because the functional forms we have chosen to describe tastes and production, namely a CES embedded in a Cobb–Douglas upper-tier aggregate, fulfil the Inada conditions.

To answer our second question, we need to sign $\partial\pi^1/\partial s_n^1 = -\partial\pi^2/\partial s_n^1$ when the operating profits are evaluated at the FTA-symmetric equilibrium; for this equilibrium to be stable, the sign of this must be negative. Indeed, we can see from (14.28) that a perturbation of the initial equilibrium in the form of an exogenous increase of s_n^1 would be self-correcting only if π^1 falls after such a shock. Formally, we first differentiate (14.26) at the FTA-symmetric equilibrium and obtain[7]

$$\left.\frac{\partial\pi}{\partial s_n}\right|_{s_n=1/2} \geq 0 \quad \Leftrightarrow \quad \phi \geq \frac{(2-3\mu)(1-\mu+b)}{3(1+\mu)(1+\mu-b)-(1-\mu+b)} \equiv \phi_{\mathrm{FTA}}^{\mathrm{break}}$$

$$(14.34)$$

This expression says that, whenever it exists, the FTA-symmetric equilibrium is unstable if trade-cum-transportation costs between the two integrating countries are substantially reduced, that is, provided that ϕ is large enough. Two remarks are in order. First, if $\mu > 2/3$, this equilibrium is always unstable. Second, ϕ^* does not

[7] See any chapter of Part I for the methodology needed to derive that kind of result.

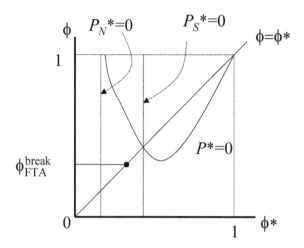

Figure 14.4 FTA.

enter the expression for the 'FTA-break point' in (14.34) because the degree of trade integration with the non-participating country 3 is irrelevant to the firms located within the FTA as far as their location choice *within* the area is concerned.

Turn to Figure 14.4. The axes represent the ϕ's, and hence we are interested in the area above the diagonal because $\phi > \phi^*$ in an FTA. All the loci described in (14.31)–(14.34) are drawn on this graph. Start with the locus $P_N^*(\phi^*) = 0$. From Figure 14.3, it is clear that the necessary condition for the FTA-symmetric equilibrium to be compatible with $\pi^* \leq \bar{\pi}$, which is given by (14.32), is satisfied at the right of this line. A similar reasoning shows that $P_S^*(\phi^*) < 0$ at the right of the $P_S^*(\phi^*) = 0$ vertical line. Turn now to the locus described in (14.31). By definition of $P_N^* = 0$, we know that this is a vertical asymptote of $P^*(\phi, \phi^*) = 0$. By definition of $P_S^* = 0$, we know that $P^*(\phi, \phi^*) = P_S^*(\phi^*)$ if and only if $\phi = \phi^*$. Graphically, these two loci must cross on the 45-degree line. Finally, it is easy to see that $P^*(1, 1) = 0$, so the $P^*(\phi, \phi^*) = 0$ curve has the shape as drawn in the figure. It is also straightforward to show that the condition in (14.31) is satisfied for any pair (ϕ, ϕ^*) above the curve.

Next, simulations show that $P_S^*(\phi_{FTA}^{break}) > 0$ for *any* admissible parameter values, hence the sufficient condition (14.33) is violated at the FTA break point.[8] As a consequence of this, the graph reveals that $P^*(\phi, \phi^*) > 0$ for all $\phi > \phi^*$; this is so because, first, P_S^* is decreasing in the range for which it takes positive values (see Figure 14.3) and, second, $\phi^* < \phi$. In such a situation, there does not exist any ϕ such that $s_n^1 + s_n^2 = 1/2$ is part of a sustainable equilibrium in the first place, so the FTA break point is somewhat irrelevant.

A final remark is in order here: we just showed that whenever (14.31) is satisfied, (14.34) is violated; but it might very well be that a condition akin to (14.34) for some $s_n < 1/2$ becomes violated before we actually reach the $P^* = 0$

[8] This claim can certainly be proved formally in the same way that we show $\phi^{break} > \phi^{sust}$ in the two-region models of Part I.

locus. This would mean that, provided it is a long-run equilibrium, a configuration in which $s_n < 1/2$ and $s_n^* > 0$ would be unstable. When this occurs, we have a 'bang-bang' solution and all firms within the FTA cluster are in a single location, say 1, and hence $s_n^1 > 0$ and $s_n^2 = 0$. This brings us to Case II.

CASE II

In this section, we are interested in a configuration in which a cluster forms within the FTA while some firms are still active in country 3, and ask under what circumstances this long-run equilibrium is unstable.

To answer that question, let us start with two observations: first, countries 1 and 2 are perfectly symmetric, including in their position vis-à-vis country 3. This implies that the variables in country 3 are irrelevant to a firm considering relocating from country 2 to country 1. (A simple way of seeing this is to use (14.26) and note that $\pi^1 - \pi^2 = 0$ at the FTA-symmetric equilibrium.)

Second, the fact that $s_n^3 > 0$ implies $\pi^3 = \bar{\pi}$. This implies that (14.31) is violated and that (14.30) must be replaced by

$$\Delta = (1 + \phi)s_n\Delta^\mu + \phi^*(1 - 2s_n)(\Delta^*)^\mu, \quad \Delta^* = 2\phi^*s_n\Delta^\mu + (1 - 2s_n)(\Delta^*)^\mu$$

$$s_E = \frac{1}{3} + (\mu - b)\left(s_n - \frac{1}{3}\right), \quad s_E^* = \frac{1}{3} - (\mu - b)\left(2s_n - \frac{2}{3}\right) \quad (14.35)$$

where we have used the same notation as before, namely, variables free of superscripts denote variables pertaining to countries 1 and 2 and variables with the asterisk denote variables pertaining to country 3. $s_n^* > 0$ now implies that shadow pure profits in country 3 are non-negative; by free entry, this implies that both expressions in (14.29) hold with equality.

Ideally, we would now proceed as in the previous case to get the equivalent of (14.34). That is, we would ask, for given values of b, μ and ϕ^*, what is the threshold value for ϕ above which the FTA equilibrium is unstable, that is, which is the smallest ϕ such that $\partial \pi / s_n = 0$? This was an easy task in the previous case because we had imposed $s_n = 1/2$, $s_n^* = 0$ (and hence $\pi^* \leq \bar{\pi}$). In the present case, we impose $\pi^* = \bar{\pi}$ which implies $s_n \leq 1/2$, $s_n^* \geq 0$. The difficulty stems from the fact that the latter variables are now endogenous. Unfortunately, the system given by (14.29), $\pi^* = \bar{\pi}$ and (14.35) cannot be solved for s_n explicitly. Consequently, no closed-form solution for the FTA break point exists in this generic case. We denote the FTA break point in the general case considered in this subsection as $\phi_F^{\text{break}}(\phi^*)$ so as to make the dependence of ϕ_F^{break} upon ϕ^* explicit.

However, we can still do some pencil-and-paper work. Indeed, we already know three things. First, when $\phi = \phi^*$ (i.e. when all three countries apply the 'most-favoured-nation' rule to each other), then $s_n = s_n^* = 1/3$. Hence, for ϕ arbitrarily close to ϕ^*, the fully symmetric equilibrium is unstable if ϕ^* is larger than $\phi_{\text{MFN}}^{\text{break}}$ as defined in (14.24). Put differently, $\phi_F^{\text{break}}(\phi^*) = \phi_{\text{MFN}}^{\text{break}}$ when $\phi^* = \phi$. But is the core–periphery pattern sustainable when the fully symmetric equilibrium is unstable? By this we mean, if all firms cluster in 1 (viz. $s_n^1 = 1$), is it true that shadow operating profits in countries 2 and 3 are below the normal rate of return on capital $\bar{\pi}$? Using (14.26) and (14.27), we find

$$\frac{\pi^2}{\bar{\pi}} \leq 1 \quad \Leftrightarrow \quad \phi^2 s_E + s_E^*(1 + \phi) - \phi^{1-\mu} \leq 0$$

$$\frac{\pi^3}{\bar{\pi}} \leq 1 \quad \Leftrightarrow \quad (\phi^*)^2 s_E + s_E^*\left(1 + \frac{(\phi^*)^2}{\phi}\right) - (\phi^*)^{1-\mu} \leq 0 \qquad (14.36)$$

where $s_E = [1 + 2(\mu - b)]/3$ and $s_E^* = [1 - \mu + b]/3$ in the present case. Since $\phi > \phi^*$, a sufficient condition for both conditions in (14.36) to hold is that the first of the two holds. Observe that this is equivalent to the definition of the sustain point in (14.25) by definition (with $R = 3$). The sustain point proper $\phi_{\text{MFN}}^{\text{sust}}$ is defined as the smallest root of this polynomial and any ϕ, ϕ^* larger than this satisfy the conditions in (14.36). Remember that $\phi_{\text{MFN}}^{\text{sust}} < \phi_{\text{MFN}}^{\text{break}}$, so whenever the fully symmetric equilibrium is unstable, a core–periphery pattern is sustainable. Simulations consistently show that no other stable long-run equilibria exist, hence it must be that whenever the equilibrium $s_n^j = 1/3$ (for all j) is unstable, only outcomes with $s_n^j = 1$ (either j) are stable.

Second, if ϕ is above ϕ^*, this has two effects. On the one hand, $\phi > \phi^*$ makes each market in the FTA look bigger, hence $s_n > 1/3$ at the FTA-symmetric equilibrium. On the other hand, the overall degree of trade freeness has increased in our world economy, and hence agglomeration forces increase relative to dispersion forces; thus, the FTA break point ϕ_F^{break} is smaller than $\phi_{\text{MFN}}^{\text{break}}$.

Finally, if ϕ is low enough, then $s_n = 1/2$, $s_n^* = 0$ by continuity of the previous argument. In such a case, the FTA break point is defined by (14.34), viz. $\phi_F^{\text{break}}(\phi^*) = \phi_{\text{FTA}}^{\text{break}}$ when ϕ^* satisfies (14.31). Simple algebra confirms that $\phi_{\text{FTA}}^{\text{break}} < \phi_{\text{MFN}}^{\text{break}}$. This must be true, as agglomeration forces are self-reinforcing; remember that $\phi_{\text{FTA}}^{\text{break}}$ is evaluated at $s_n = 1/2$ while $\phi_{\text{MFN}}^{\text{break}}$ is evaluated at $s_n = 1/3$. Numerical simulations confirm that for FTA-symmetric equilibria for which the value of s_n lies in the interval $(1/3, 1/2)$, the FTA break point $\phi_F^{\text{break}}(\phi^*)$ belongs to the interval $(\phi_{\text{FTA}}^{\text{break}}, \phi_{\text{MFN}}^{\text{break}})$ and is increasing in ϕ^*.

DISCUSSION

All these findings suggest a picture like Figure 14.5. This figure plots ϕ against ϕ^*, and, again, the part of the graph under scrutiny is the one above the 45-degree line. We have drawn or redrawn three loci on this graph. First, we have repeated the locus $P^* = 0$ for convenience. We have also drawn the sustain point: any pair of ϕ and ϕ^* on the right of $\phi_{\text{MFN}}^{\text{sust}}$ (and above the main diagonal) implies that any core–periphery configuration is a stable long-run equilibrium. Lastly, the BB$'$B locus represents the FTA break point ϕ_F^{break} as a function of ϕ^*, that is, BB$'$B plots the combinations of ϕ and ϕ^* at which the FTA-symmetric equilibrium is on the verge of instability, viz. $\partial \pi/s_n = 0$; above this locus, $\partial \pi/s_n > 0$.

As Figure 14.5 shows, BB$'$B is made of two segments (BB$'$ and B$'$B). Start with $\phi^* = 0$. First is the horizontal segment BB$'$: we know from the analysis

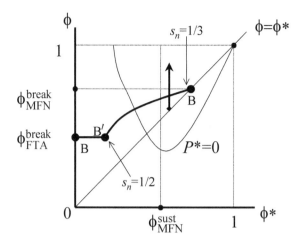

Figure 14.5 Catastrophic agglomeration within a FTA.

above that the FTA break point ϕ_F^{break} cannot be lower than $\phi_{\text{FTA}}^{\text{break}}$; moreover, the FTA break point is non-decreasing in ϕ^*; clearly, BB$'$ must be horizontal over some non-trivial range of ϕ^*. But we know from Case I that this segment is irrelevant because condition (14.31) is violated on this segment. Graphically, this reads as BB$'$ being strictly below the locus $P^* = 0$.

Next, as ϕ^* keeps increasing, BB$'$B becomes upward-sloping to the right of point B$'$ and s_n decreases as we move towards the north-east along B$'$B. Eventually, the FTA-symmetric equilibrium is on the verge of instability when $s_n = 1/3$; this occurs when $\phi = \phi^* = \phi_{\text{MFN}}^{\text{break}}$. For any ϕ, ϕ^* above this threshold, no FTA-symmetric equilibrium is ever stable, and hence the BB$'$B locus stops precisely at the point $(\phi_{\text{MFN}}^{\text{break}}, \phi_{\text{MFN}}^{\text{break}})$, as drawn.

Next, let us raise an important issue. We know that whenever the fully symmetric equilibrium is unstable, a core–periphery pattern is sustainable. By contrast, the main result exposed in Case I is that an FTA-symmetric equilibrium in which no firm settles in country 3 is never part of a long-run equilibrium. By a continuity argument, we infer from these results that, in the neighbourhood of point B$'$, no FTA symmetric equilibrium exists (and hence the BB$'$B locus is irrelevant on this parameter range). Conversely, still invoking a continuity argu- ment, we expect any FTA-symmetric equilibrium to exist on B$'$B for pairs of (ϕ, ϕ^*) close enough to the end point B. Hence, there must exist a point on B$'$B such that for any pair (ϕ, ϕ^*) on the right of this point the FTA-symmetric equilibrium exists on the B$'$B curve. For a given ϕ^*, we write the corresponding ϕ as $\phi_{\text{FTA}}^{\text{bust}}$, where 'bust' is a mnemonic for 'break' and 'sust' because the FTA- symmetric equilibrium is not sustainable for ϕ's lower than this threshold.

This discussion allows us to tell the following tale with the help of Figure 14.6. This figure is the (in)famous 'tomahawk' diagram in its version for the three-country FTA case. It plots industry shares as a function of trade freeness, ϕ. Fix ϕ^* low enough and ask how the s_n's evolve as ϕ increases above ϕ^*. Initially, the only fully

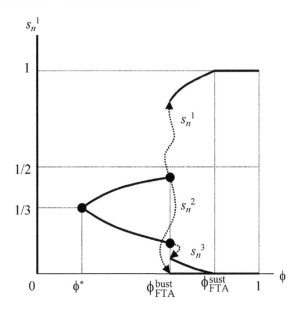

Figure 14.6 The tomahawk diagram for a FTA.

symmetric equilibrium is stable. Then, as ϕ increases, relocation from the left-out country into the FTA occurs smoothly; within the FTA, industry is evenly spread because only the FTA-symmetric equilibrium is stable for ϕ low enough. But, eventually, the FTA-symmetric equilibrium goes bust and catastrophic agglomeration occurs within the FTA. We shall assume country 1 gains firms.

In the graph, this can be seen by the sudden rise of s_n^1 and the discrete decline of s_n^2; s_n^2 may or may not go even all the way down to zero, as pictured, depending on whether $\phi_{\text{FTA}}^{\text{bust}}$ is larger or smaller than $\phi_{\text{FTA}}^{\text{sust}}$. Whether this is the case or not, this catastrophic agglomeration within the FTA has an ambiguous effect on s_n^3 (in the figure, we draw it as a downward blip). Intuitively, this is because the balance between agglomeration and dispersion is altered by this phenomenon. Indeed, when s_n^1 increases and s_n^3 stays constant, both s_E^1 and Δ^1 increase relative to s_E^2 and Δ^2. This affects the profitability of firms currently in country 3 in an ambiguous way, as can be seen from the expression for π^3 in (14.27).

Finally, as ϕ keeps increasing above $\phi_{\text{FTA}}^{\text{bust}}$, agglomeration forces are reinforced relative to dispersion forces and s_n^1 keeps increasing until no firm is left in country 3. As an aside, note that the graph shows that $\phi_{\text{FTA}}^{\text{sust}} > \phi_{\text{FTA}}^{\text{bust}}$ but this need not be the case; the tale as we tell it would remain the same, however.

This concludes our discussion of the positive effects of the FTA. We turn next to the welfare effects of such a preferential trade agreement.

14.6.3 FTA and Agglomeration: Normative Analysis

Nominal incomes remain unchanged in the FCVL model (see Chapter 8), so sufficient statistics for welfare effects are the Δ's. We note that the Δ's change due to changes in trade costs, holding the spatial allocation of industry as given, and due to changes in this spatial allocation. To be concrete, take any Δ^j and totally differentiate to get

$$d\Delta^j = \frac{\partial \Delta^j}{\partial \phi} d\phi + \frac{\partial \Delta^j}{\partial \phi^*} d\phi^* + \sum_{j=1}^{3} \frac{\partial \Delta^j}{\partial s_n^j} ds_n^j \qquad (14.37)$$

The first two terms on the right-hand side of the (14.37) are the direct effect of any trade liberalization on welfare; keeping location constant, a reduction of trade barriers of any kind is always welfare enhancing as it decreases consumer prices. The third term in this expression represents the indirect, or relocation, effect. Clearly, Δ^j increases in s_n^j, as indicated in (14.37). As we have argued at length in Section 14.6.1, changing the ϕ's has an impact, often a big impact at that, on the location equilibrium. This implies that the indirect effect of the ϕ's on the Δ's is potentially important. Indeed, the higher the share of varieties produced at home, the less consumers have to pay for transportation costs.

The previous section has told us a lot about the indirect effect; we now add the direct effect to this. The analysis for levels of openness that imply stable interior outcomes is the same as in the analysis we saw without vertical linkages, so we do not repeat it. We only remind the reader that, keeping ϕ^* constant, relocation out of country 3 as ϕ increases hurts country 3 and is beneficial to countries 1 and 2; this can be seen in (14.26), (14.27) and (14.37). For country 3, the direct effect is absent (ϕ^* does not change by assumption) whilst the indirect effect hurts it, viz. s_n^3 decreases. For countries 1 and 2, both the direct and the indirect effects are favourable.

However, when catastrophic agglomeration occurs, something really interesting happens. Turn to Figure 14.7, which is the welfare counterpart of Figure 14.6. When ϕ increases beyond the break point ϕ_{FTA}^{burst} marginally, there is a discrete jump in s_n^2 and hence it must be that 2 loses from further discriminatory trade liberalization with 1 in the neighbourhood of this point. In other words, even though they are ex-ante symmetric, the countries parts of the FTA *diverge* both in terms of their production structure and in per capita incomes. Interestingly, country 2 might be worse off than country 3 in the upper neighbourhood of the break point, as we draw it in Figure 14.7. However, as ϕ increases further towards unity, welfare increases in 2 (the direct effect of trade integration), welfare in 1 increases (by the home-market effect ever more firms accrue to the FTA) and welfare in 3 shrinks (for symmetric reasons).[9] Eventually, real incomes converge again within the FTA.

14.6.4 Hub-and-Spoke Agreements and Catastrophic Agglomeration

When self-enforcing agglomeration forces are absent, the location equilibrium is unique and is a smooth function of ϕ. This is no longer the case when these forces

---

[9] If s_n^2 did not shrink down to zero discretely in the first place, it will do so over time as ϕ increases. However, the positive, direct effect will eventually come to dominate.

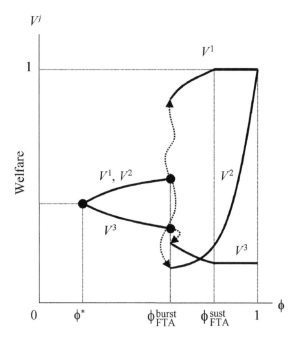

Figure 14.7 Welfare effects for the FTA.

are present. The effects of adding such forces to the setting of the previous section should be intuitive. We have seen that, analytically, the FTA and the HS are somewhat symmetric. Also, we know that the equilibrium location in the case without circular causality is a lower bound for the location equilibrium in the current, richer setting. Hence, we shall keep the analysis of this section at an informal level.

Again, we assume that $\phi - \phi' < 1 - \phi$ holds. As ϕ steadily increases above ϕ^*, that is, as bilateral liberalization (between country 1 on the one hand and countries 2 and 3 on the other) proceeds, production starts shifting into the hub, the more so the more important the vertical linkages (as captured by μ) among firms. Eventually, however, a configuration in which some industry remains in the hubs becomes unstable and some catastrophic agglomeration occurs; industry clusters in country 1. Depending on parameter values, however, it is reasonable to imagine a situation in which some industry remains in the spokes. In such a case, the HS-symmetric equilibrium in which both countries 2 and 3 have the same share of industry becomes unstable as well, and one of the spokes becomes entirely specialized in the production of the numeraire.

The welfare effects, again, are unambiguous for country 1. This country benefits directly from lower prices for its imports from the spokes; it benefits even beyond this direct effect, since some production shifting takes place and ever more firms relocate into the hub. By contrast, the effect on welfare in the spokes is ambiguous. These countries do benefit from lower consumer prices for the goods they import from 1, but their industrial base shrinks and hence they import more and more manufacturing goods. When some catastrophic agglomeration occurs in the form of a discrete increase in the number of firms in the hub, the consumers in the spokes are clearly worse off. Since we have assumed that ϕ^* is unchanged, countries 2 and 3 will not converge to the real incomes of country 1's citizens.

14.7 Concluding Remarks and Related Literature

The chapter has highlighted four key insights that consideration of agglomeration forces adds to the study of preferential trade arrangements: the production-shifting effect, the internal inequality effect, the domino effect and the hub effect. With the exception of the internal inequality effect, we have not explored the impact of including mechanisms that would result in self-reinforcing agglomeration. This is certainly a topic for future research. We conjecture that looking at preferential liberalization in models that allow for such circular causality linkages would not alter the qualitative nature of our results, but this is nothing more than a conjecture.

14.7.1 Related Literature

There has been relatively little written on preferential liberalization in the presence of agglomeration forces. A section of Baldwin and Venables (1995) is devoted to the topic and Baldwin et al. (1996) explore investment creation and diversion in a computable general equilibrium model, but Puga and Venables (1997) seems to be the only article fully devoted to the subject. Forslid et al. (2002) use a computable general equilibrium model to investigate several aspects in the European context. See also Martin and Ottaviano (1996). The literature on the domino effect started with Baldwin (1993) and more recently includes Albertin (2001), Krishna (1998) and Levy (1997).

References

Albertin, G. 2001. Will regional blocs expand? Mimeo, London School of Economics.
Baldwin, Richard E. 1993. A domino theory of regionalism. Working Paper No. 4465, National Bureau of Economic Research.
———. 1994. Towards an Integrated Europe. London: Centre for Economic and Policy Research.
———. 1997. The causes of regionalism. *The World Economy* 20(7): 865–888.
Baldwin, Richard E. and A. J. Venables. 1995. Regional economic integration. In *Handbook of International Economics*, Volume III, ed. G. Grossman and K. Rogoff. Amsterdam: North-Holland.
Baldwin, Richard E., Rikard Forslid and Jan Haaland. 1996. Investment creation and diversion in Europe. *The World Economy* 19(6): 635–659.
Forslid, R., J. Håland, K. Midlefart Knarvik. 2002. A U-shaped Europe? A simulation study of industrial location. *Journal of International Economics* 57(2): 273–297.

Kowalcyz, C. and R. Wonnacott. 1992. Hubs and Spokes, and Free Trade in the Americas. Working Paper No. 4198, National Bureau of Economic Research.

Krishna, P. 1998. Regionalism and multilateralism: a political economy approach. *Quarterly Journal of Economics* 113(1): 227–251.

Krugman, Paul. 1993. The hub effect: or threeness in interregional trade. In *Theory, Policy and Dynamics in International Trade*, ed. W. Ethier, E. Helpman and J. Neary. Cambridge: Cambridge University Press.

Levy, P. 1997. A political-economic analysis of free-trade agreements. *American Economic Review* 87(4): 506–519.

Martin, P. and G. Ottaviano. 1996. The geography of multi-speed Europe. *Economie Internationale* 67: 45–65 (in English: Discussion paper No. 1292, Centre for Economic and Policy Research).

Puga, Diego and A. Venables. 1997. Preferential trading arrangements and industrial location. *Journal of International Economics* 43: 347–368.

Robert-Nicoud, F. 2002. A simple model of agglomeration with vertical linkages and capital mobility. Mimeo, London School of Economics.

Viner, Jacob. 1950. *The Customs Union Issue*. New York: Carnegie Endowment for International Peace.

PART IV

Tax Policy

Agglomeration with Taxation and Public Goods

15.1 INTRODUCTION

One of the most exciting applications of new economic geography models to policy questions lies in the area of taxation and tax competition. Almost without exception, the public finance literature on tax competition and the effects of international taxation has relied on 'smooth' models. That is to say, models in which small changes lead to small effects. Economic geography models are 'lumpy' by their very nature and this, as we shall see, casts new light on a number of old issues.

This chapter, which is the first of two devoted to tax policy, shows as simply as possible what agglomeration forces mean for tax policy and the provision of public goods. The chapter also looks at the reverse implications, namely how consideration of taxes and public goods affects agglomeration. Many insights can only be studied in the context of explicit strategic tax-setting games, but these introduce an element of complexity that often obscures the underlying insight. For this reason, we postpone such issues to the next chapter.

15.1.1 Organization of the Chapter

We open the chapter with a review of the main results from the standard international tax competition literature, that is, the literature that ignores trade costs and agglomeration forces. This provides a basis for comparison against which we contrast the insights that arise when one allows for agglomeration forces. Section 15.3 introduces the general notion that trade costs—as well as capital mobility—can have important effects on tax competition when agglomeration forces are present. We continue to pursue this idea in Section 15.4 by focusing on the case where all capital is agglomerated in one region.

As it happens, the locational effects of taxes are distinctly different when industry is already agglomerated (core–periphery case) as opposed to being dispersed geographically, so Section 15.5 considers the case where capital is evenly dispersed between two mirror-image regions.

The subsequent sections enrich the standard geography model by introducing public goods. The provision of tax-financed public goods turns out to be a destabilizing force and this is illustrated in Section 15.6. Following this line of thinking, Section 15.7 suggests that competition between regions in the provision of public goods could in some situations lead to a result that is reminiscent of the famous Tiebout conjecture (closer integration improves governmental efficiency), but it also shows that closer integration could achieve the opposite.

Up to this point, the chapter has worked with the assumption that the immobile factor was either not taxed, or it was taxed at the same rate as the mobile factor. In Section 15.8, we consider the implications of allowing differential taxation on the two factors. Surprisingly, we find that shifting taxation from the mobile factor to the immobile factor tends to promote stability of the dispersed outcome.

Section 15.9 contains our concluding remarks and comments on related literature.

15.2 THE STANDARD TAX COMPETITION LITERATURE

Theorists have long studied the links between taxation and international economic integration. The early literature, for example Tiebout (1956), viewed inter-jurisdictional tax competition as a form of competition that forces efficiency on governments and thus tends to view tax competition as welfare enhancing. By contrast, the dominant theme in the modern literature is the 'race to the bottom,' which asserts that competition for a mobile tax base produces sub-optimally low taxes, with the mobile factor bearing too little of the tax burden. The seminal papers here are Gordon (1983), Zodrow and Mierzkowski (1986), Wilson (1986), and Wildasin (1988), with subsequent important contributions from de Crombrugghe and Tulkens (1990), Bucovetsky (1991), Wilson (1991), Wildasin (1991), Kanbur and Keen (1993), and Edwards and Keen (1996).

A major proviso to the sub-optimal-taxation result is the so-called Leviathan government hypothesis, which asserts that self-interested policy makers tend to set taxes too high; the race-to-the-bottom thus may actually yield a second best improvement.

Remarkably, almost the entire tax competition literature focuses on capital mobility as the sole dimension of economic integration. For instance, most models assume costless trade and work with a single good model. One exception is Janeba (1998) who adds tax competition into a strategic trade model.

15.2.1 The Basic Tax Competition Model

The literature on tax competition has focused on a very simple, very special model. Here, we present a version of the 'basic tax competition model' (Zodrow and Mierzkowski 1986). This section draws heavily on the excellent survey by Wilson (1999); the structure of the synthesis was inspired by Krogstrup (2002).

BASIC SET UP

Our version of the 'basic tax competition model' (BTCM for short) involves two nations, which we call north and south, and two factors of production, which we call capital, K, and labour, L.[1] Each Walrasian (perfect competition and constant

---

[1] Some versions of the BTCM assume infinitely many small nations, but we can mimic this by assuming that the north acts as if it was small in the sense that its tax policy has no impact on the post-tax reward to capital.

returns) economy produces the same, homogenous private good using K and L. The output is traded costlessly, so international prices are equalized; factor prices are not equalized since there are more factors than goods. Capital is viewed as physical capital in that it can move internationally without its owner, and indeed, labourers are assumed to be perfectly immobile.

The sole role of government in the model is to set the tax rate, and collect tax revenue that it turns costlessly into a public good. Capital and labour are taxed in the nation in which they are employed (this is the 'origin principle' in tax lexicon). For simplicity, the tax rate on labour and capital are constrained to be identical.

Since the model assumes away so many complicating factors (imperfect competition, scale economies, trade costs, etc.), we can work with implicit functional forms. Technology for north and south is given by the standard neoclassical production function

$$Y = F[K,L]; \quad F_L, F_K, F_{KL} > 0 > F_{KK}, F_{LL}, \quad Y = LF_L + KF_K \qquad (15.1)$$

where subscripts indicate partials, as usual. The restrictions on the partial derivatives impose constant returns and diminishing marginal products.[2] For convenience, the good's price is normalized to unity.

The representative consumer is a labourer, who owns all the economy's L and K, and has preferences and post-tax income given by

$$U = U[G,C] \qquad (15.2)$$

where G is a public good (this is provided only by government) and C is consumption. Southern consumers have identical tastes.

CAPITAL MOBILITY AND TAXATION

The main focus of the BTCM literature is the impact of capital mobility on equilibrium tax rates, but for simplicity, mobility is not modelled as a continuous variable—capital is assumed to be either perfectly mobile, or perfectly immobile. Normally, considering only extreme policies would hide a rich array of non-linear or even non-monotonic effects, but because the underlying economy is so convex, the loss of generality from focusing on extremes is minor.

Notation.   As usual, we use n and n^* to indicate the amount of the mobile factor (capital in this case) that is *employed* in the north and south, respectively, while K and K^* indicate the amount of capital that each region *owns*. We also continue with our practice of choosing units such that the world's fixed capital stock K^w is normalized to unity, that is, $n + n^* = K^w = 1$; this normalization is without loss of generality.

The spatial allocation of capital is determined by the equalization of post-tax rates of return, when capital is perfectly mobile. When capital is assumed to be

---

[2] To ensure interior equilibria (all regions have some capital), we could assume that the marginal product of capital becomes infinite as the capital/labour ratio goes to zero.

perfectly immobile, the spatial allocation is fixed by endowments. Since factors are paid their marginal products, we can write the location conditions as

$$F_K[n, L](1 - t) = F_K[1 - n, L^*](1 - t^*), \quad \text{with } K \text{ mobile}$$

$$n = K, \quad 1 - n = K^*, \qquad\qquad\qquad \text{with } K \text{ immobile}$$

(15.3)

where t and L are home's tax rate and labour force, while t^* and L^* are the corresponding variables for the south; given our normalization, $1 - n$ is the amount of capital employed in the south.

Government's Problem and the Social FOC.   The two governments play Nash in tax rates, so taking the southern tax rate as given, the northern government's problem is to choose the tax rate, t, to maximize welfare of the representative consumer subject to (15.3) and a balanced budget requirement. In symbols the problem is

$$\max_t U[G, C]; \quad G = tY, \quad C = (1 - t)I \tag{15.4}$$

where Y is GDP, that is, the northern tax base, and I is northern GNP, that is, northern income (GDP and GNP may diverge since capital is internationally mobile and this matters since taxation is based on location rather than ownership). More specifically,

$$Y = F[n, L], \quad I = \{F[n, L] - F_K[n, L]n\} + F_K[n, L]K$$

where subscripts indicate partial derivatives as usual (recall that n indicates the amount of K employed in the north, so $F_K[n, L]$ is the partial of $F[K, L]$ with respect to K evaluated at $n = K$). The term in curly brackets represents northern labour income (i.e. labour gets paid all the output that is not paid to capital) and, due to constant returns, this equals $F_L[n, L]L$.[3] The remaining term in the expression for I is northern capital's pre-tax income.[4] Also, G is a public good (this is provided only by government), and we have assumed that the cost of G is unity, so home's provision of the public good just equals home's tax revenue.[5]

The government's first-order condition is

$$\frac{U_G}{U_C} = \frac{-dC/dt}{dG/dt} \tag{15.5}$$

where the left-hand side of the first expression is the marginal rate of substitution between private and public goods, that is, the social benefit of higher tax revenue.

---

[3] It proves convenient to express labour's income in this way since it allows us to avoid consideration of the cross partial F_{LK}.

[4] Since some northern capital may be working in the south, it might seem like we should have separate terms for K working in the north and south. However, the location condition (top expression in (15.3)) ensures that $(1 - t)F_K = (1 - t^*)F_K^*$, so we can write $(1 - t)I$ *as if* all northern capital earned F_K and paid t.

[5] Taxes are collected in the numeraire good, X, and thus the assumed production function for G is $G = X$, or alternatively, $G = F[K,L]$ where K and L are hired by the government using the collected X.

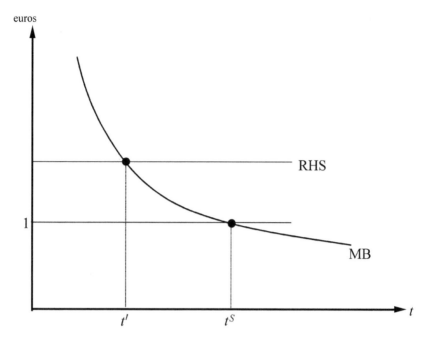

Figure 15.1 Standard tax competition model results.

Also[6]

$$\frac{-dC/dt}{dG/dt} = \frac{I}{Y\left(1 + \dfrac{dn/n}{dt}t\eta\right)}; \quad \eta \equiv \frac{n}{Y}F_K[n, L]$$

where $\eta > 0$ is the capital-output elasticity and dn/dt is the spatial responsiveness of capital to northern taxes, taking the southern tax rate as given. Totally differentiating the location condition (15.3) when capital is mobile, we find

$$\frac{dn/n}{dt} = \frac{F_K/n}{(1 - t)F_{KK} + (1 - t^*)F^*_{KK}} < 0 \qquad (15.6)$$

where the F_{KK} terms, which show how fast capital's marginal product declines, are negative; as usual, these derivatives are evaluated at the equilibrium point.

To solve the tax game we would specify the southern government's first-order condition and then use the two conditions to solve for the two tax rates, but we can illustrate the main results without doing so.

---

[6] Note that $dC/dt = -I + (dI/dn)(dn/dt)$, but by the envelope theorem, $dI/dn = 0$; intuitively, since there is no distortion between K and L employment, a tax change that induces a small increase in capital employment raises output (GDP) by F_K, but since the extra capital must be paid (F_K), there is no change in domestic income (GNP). Note that in many formulations of the BTCM, only capital is taxed; since the K/L choice is distorted in this case, a tax change that induces extra capital employment does affect national income.

15.2.2 Major Results from the BTCM Literature

The various results from the standard tax competition model literature can be illustrated with the help of Figure 15.1. The MB curve represents that left-hand side of the first expression in (15.5); the second-order condition of the government's problem ensures that it is downward sloped at the optimum.

BTCM Result 1. *Capital mobility results in a capital tax rate that is too low from the social perspective.*

This is seen directly from the diagram. If the capital were entirely unresponsive to the tax rate ($dn/dt = 0$), as it would be without capital mobility, the right-hand side (RHS) of (15.5) would equal unity so that $U_G = U_C$ (note that $I = Y$ when $n = K$). Thus, without capital mobility the social first best is achieved and the equilibrium tax rate is t^S. Perfect capital mobility results in a positive delocation effect, that is, $dn/dt < 0$, so the RHS exceeds unity and this results in a tax rate, t', which is below the socially optimal rate. The positive corollary of this is as follows.

BTCM Result 2. *There is a negative correlation between capital mobility and the tax rate on capital.*

The policy corollary of this is also straightforward.

BTCM Result 3. *A slight, uniform rise in capital tax rates is Pareto improving when capital is mobile.*

ASYMMETRIC COUNTRY SIZE

A second set of results corresponds to the implications of asymmetric country size as measured by the supply of the fixed factor, L. To be concrete we assume that north is larger than south, that is, $L > L^*$ but that nations all have the same relative factor endowment, that is, $K/L = K^*/L^*$.

To argue that the large country has higher taxes in equilibrium, we suppose instead that tax rates are equal and show that this leads to a contradiction whose resolution requires the large nation to have a higher rate. Given diminishing returns, it is clear that if taxes were equal, perfect capital mobility would equalize the capital/labour ratios internationally (marginal products in a neoclassical production function like F depend only on capital/labour ratios, so equalizing F_K equalizes K/L). This means there would be no capital movement since the nations are endowed with identical capital/labour ratios. With this fact in mind, inspection of (15.6) shows that if taxes were equal, the country with the largest employment of capital, would have a lower $(dn/n)/dt$ since $n = K > n^* = K^*$ under the hypothesis we are considering. In words, this says that the tax base is less sensitive to changes in t in the larger country. From (15.5) and the corresponding diagram, this implies different tax rates, so our hypothesis that they have equal tax rates must be incorrect.

Using the standard smoothness properties of a neoclassical economy and the objective functions, this line of thought demonstrates that the large country government will find it optimal to allow some of its capital to move abroad in exchange for setting its tax rate closer to the social optimum. Thus, in equilibrium $t > t^*$ and $n < K$. Since with equal taxes the model predicts $K/L = K^*/L^*$, the equilibrium capital/labour ratio is lower in the big country, that is, $n/L < n^*/L^*$. This is summarized in the following result.

BTCM Result 4. *Large countries should have higher tax rates than small countries, where size is defined in terms of supplies of the immobile factor.*

BTCM Result 5. *Large countries should have lower capital/labour ratio, that is, we should observe a negative correlation between tax rates and capital/labour ratios. Other things being equal, this means that small nations should have higher per capita incomes.*

BTCM Result 6. *Large countries should be exporters of capital and small countries importers of capital, that is, capital should flow from poor countries to rich countries when richness is defined in terms of per capita income.*

The foundation of these results is that a country with more of the immobile factor can more easily hold on to its industry (due to diminishing returns). Thus, we can also state the following result.

BTCM Result 7. *The responsiveness of tax base to tax rate should be lower in nations with large shares of the world supply of immobile factors.*

CAPITAL VS. LABOUR TAXATION

If we expand the model to allow for different taxes on labour and capital, it is obvious that all governments will set zero tax rates on capital but positive rates on labour, in the presence of capital mobility. The reason is quite simple. Since labourers own all capital in the representative consumer setting, income–distribution considerations are absent, so the government chooses the most efficient tax structure. Capital taxation is distortionary with capital mobility, but labour taxation is not.

When capital is immobile, the tax structure is not uniquely determined. That is, the level of taxation will rise until its marginal benefit equals unity, but the division of this tax burden between K and L is indeterminate because both are supplied inelastically. Stepping slightly outside the model, however, and allowing for an unequal distribution of capital among labourers, income distribution considerations would resolve the indeterminacy of the tax structure. The exact taxation on capital would depend upon details, but the capital tax rate would not be zero as it is with capital mobility.

BTCM Result 8. *There should be a negative correlation between capital mobility and capital's share of the tax burden.*

As we shall see, the analysis of capital taxation in a new economic geography framework affords a host of new insights since it enriches the underlying economy.

15.3 LUMPY WORLD TAXES: IMMOBILITY OF PERFECTLY MOBILE CAPITAL

Perhaps the most important insight that the economic geography models provide for the tax competition literature concerns the way in which agglomeration makes the world 'lumpy', as shown by Kind et al. (2000), and Ludema and Wooton (2000). That is, agglomeration forces can turn mobile factors into quasi-fixed factors. Agglomeration forces mean that spatial concentration of economic activity—including the activity of the mobile factor—creates forces that favour further spatial concentration. This is in sharp contrast to the standard neoclassical situation where concentrating the mobile factor spatially tends to reduce its reward and so creates forces that tend to reverse the concentration. Lumpiness has several important implications for tax competition.

The basic point is quite general and can be shown in any model with agglomeration forces. To keep the analysis as general as possible, we illustrate the point with a 'wiggle diagram' for a generic economic geography model (see Chapter 2 for a detailed presentation of the wiggle diagram). As usual, the vertical axis of Figure 15.2 plots the ratio of the mobile factor's real reward in the north versus the south. The horizontal axis shows the north's share of the mobile factor,

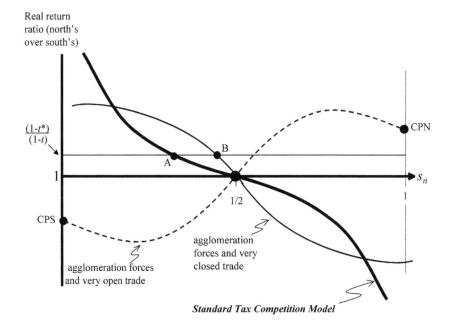

Figure 15.2   Lumpiness vs. neoclassical diminishing returns.

denoted as s_n (a mnemonic for share of world capital employed in the north). Presuming that the mobile factor is attracted by a higher reward, we know that the north's share of mobile factors is increasing whenever it has a higher reward, and the converse is true when it has a lower real reward.

Consider first what the wiggle diagram looks like for a neoclassical model. Assuming the two nations are ex ante identical, forcibly moving industry from the south to the north always lowers the north's relative reward. Moreover, the north's rate will be above the south's whenever the north has less than half the world capital, but below the south's when it has more than half. This is depicted by the heavy solid line; diminishing returns mean it is everywhere downward sloped and it is unity (i.e. real rewards are equalized) at the symmetric point $s_n = 1/2$.

Asymmetric taxation in the neoclassical case will result in a moderate reallocation of capital. For example, if the northern tax rate is above the south's, that is, $(1 - t^*)/(1 - t)$ exceeds one, capital would migrate from the north to the south until the post-tax rewards were re-equalized. In the diagram, this is shown as point A; here the real reward ratio is high enough in the north to exactly compensate capital for the higher taxation. As it turns out, the same sort of behaviour can be observed when agglomeration forces are present, but only when trade is sufficiently restricted.

As Part I showed, every model with agglomeration had a stable symmetric equilibrium when trade was sufficiently closed (the exact condition is that the freeness of trade was less than the 'break point'). An example of such a case is shown with the narrow solid line that is downward sloped at the midpoint. A positive tax gap in this case also produces a moderate reallocation of capital; point B shows the post-tax equilibrium.

However, when agglomeration forces are present *and* trade is free enough, the impact of asymmetric taxes is quite different. When trade gets free enough, the relationship between the reward ratio and the dispersion of capital is reversed. This situation is shown with the dashed line that is upward sloped at $s_n = 1/2$. The positive slope indicates that at this level of openness, agglomeration forces outweigh dispersion forces so the benefit of agglomerating in one region tends to increase as the extent of the agglomeration increases. Importantly, the real reward in the north is higher when all capital is in the north—this corresponds to point CPN—and the real reward in the south is higher when all capital is in the south, that is, at CPS.

Asymmetric taxation in this case may have *no* effect on location. For instance, if the economy were at CPN, the asymmetric tax shown would not lead any capital to leave the high tax region. The point is that the ratio of real rewards at CPN is higher than the tax gap, so capital is still strictly better off in the high-tax north.

To summarize, industry tends to clump together even in the absence of differential tax incentives when agglomeration forces are present. This has a series of implications for tax policy. The first concerns the general importance of trade costs.

Result 15.1 (trade costs matter). *When trade is sufficiently free, agglom-eration forces induce mobile factors to cluster geographically. In this case, mobile factors respond to tax differentials in a manner that is quite different to the one predicted by the BTCM. When trade is quite closed, however, economic geography models display diminishing-returns-like behaviour similar to that of the BTCM.*

This result implies that many of the standard tax competition model's predictions will go through only when trade costs are sufficiently high, or when agglomeration forces are very weak.

15.4 Agglomeration and the Tax Gap: the CP Thought Experiment

Many of the standard tax competition results depend upon the 'smoothness' of the underlying economies. As illustrated above, things can be quite different when agglomeration forces are in operation. One pervasive feature of agglomeration forces is that it matters a great deal if we start out from symmetry or from an agglomerated equilibrium. Here, we explore the extreme case where all industry and capital are in the north, that is, we start at the core-in-the-north (CPN) outcome.

To set the stage, we consider the real rewards to capital in the CPN outcome and how they vary with trade costs. In essence this is the analytic equivalent to looking at the height of point CPN in Figure 15.2.

It is important to note that we assume perfect capital mobility throughout the section and focus on changes in economic integration due to changes in trade costs.

15.4.1 The Sustain Point Tax Gap

As we illustrated extensively in Part I, all the new economic geography models we work with feature hump-shaped agglomeration rents. That is, when the entire supply of the mobile factor is in the one region, increasing the degree of trade openness first increases and then decreases the ratio of real rewards. We refer to the ratio of real rewards in the core-in-the-north outcome as Ω^{CP} and plot this for a typical new economic geography model in Figure 15.3 (see Box 15.1 for intuition on the bell shape).

The question now is: For any given southern tax rate on capital, what is the highest tax that north can charge on its capital without any of its capital relocating to the south? To characterize the highest tax gap that the north can sustain without losing industry—what we call the 'sustain-point tax gap'—we note that none of the mobile factor will move as long as the real-reward ratio is large enough to offset the tax gap. Defining the tax gap as $T = (1 - t)/(1 - t^*)$, the formal condition for no relocation is

$$T < T^S, \quad T^S \Omega^{CP} = 1 \tag{15.7}$$

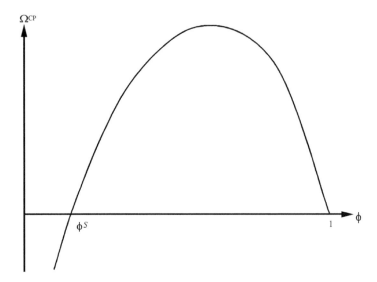

Figure 15.3   Hump-shaped agglomeration rents.

where T^S is the 'sustain-point tax gap'. As this expression shows, agglomeration forces create a rent that can be taxed. This is summarized in the following result.

Result 15.2 (agglomeration creates taxable rents). *Agglomeration forces can be thought of as creating location-specific rents. These rents can be taxed up to some point without affecting the location of capital.*

The intuition for this result is straightforward. The agglomeration forces imply that capital earns a higher reward when it is located near a large agglomeration of capital. Since capital's only alternative is to move to a region without a concentration of capital, the core region may extract some of the agglomeration rent without losing any of its capital.

It also follows immediately from (15.7) that the region with the most capital can have *higher* tax rates. Specifically, when trade is sufficiently free and trade costs are below the sustain point, that is, $\phi > \phi^S$, the agglomeration rent exceeds one, so the core's tax rate may exceed the periphery's. However, for levels of openness that are inferior to ϕ^S, $\Omega^{CP} < 1$ and the north must have lower tax rates, if it wants to hold on to all industry. This is summarized in the following result.

Result 15.3 (conditioning the negative correlation). *The BTCM predicts a negative correlation between concentrations of mobile factor and relative tax rates, that is, the region with the highest capital/labour ratio should, ceteris paribus, have the lowest tax rate. When agglomeration forces are present, this correlation only holds when trade is very restricted. When trade is free enough (i.e. $\phi > \phi^S$), it is entirely possible for the region with the highest capital/labour ratio to have the highest tax rate.*

BOX 15.1 INTUITION FOR THE HUMP

In words, the fact that the agglomeration rent is hump-shaped can be seen by first considering the two end points. When trade is highly restricted, it is very unprofitable for firms in the core to service the periphery market, and at the same time any firm operating in the periphery is heavily protected from competition, so the reward to being in the core is inferior to that of being in the periphery, that is, the real reward ratio is less than one. At perfectly free trade, the ratio is exactly one since location has no impact on profitability. In between these two extremes, agglomeration is both possible and profitable.

To be more precise, we use the FE model of Chapter 4. Separating the components of the real reward ratio provides more intuition. Using the standard expressions for capital's reward (which we call π here but is called w in Chapter 4) and the price indices definitions, we have

$$\frac{P^*}{P} = \phi^{-a}, \quad \frac{\pi}{\pi^*} = \frac{2\phi}{2 - (1 + b)(1 - \phi^2)} \tag{15.8}$$

Turning to the first term, note that because all firms are located in the north, the northern price index is lower than the south's. This is the supply link, which tends to lock firms into the core northern region. Observe that it gets stronger as trade gets more closed, and as agglomeration forces get stronger (i.e. as a and b rise). The impact of trade costs is obvious (higher trade costs make living more expensive in the south since all manufactured goods must be imported), the impact of a and b works in a similar way.

The ratio of operating profits—the second expression in (15.8)—illustrates the combined effect of the dispersion force and the demand link. This displays the usual non-monotone relationship. For high trade costs the dispersion force dominates, and this makes the π^* in the periphery south higher. For low trade costs, by contrast, $\pi > \pi^*$ so all entrepreneurs will stay in the core if there is no tax gap. The effect of ϕ, finally, is non-monotone, being strongest at intermediate trade costs. The intuition for this is straightforward. At very high trade costs, agglomeration is not really possible, since servicing distant markets is prohibitively expensive. At very low trade costs, agglomeration is not really necessary since trade is so cheap. At intermediate trade costs, however, agglomeration is both possible and necessary.

It is also clear from (15.7) and Figure 15.3 that the sustain-point tax gap, T^S, varies with the level of trade freeness and agglomeration forces. In particular, the more strongly industry is tied down to the large region by agglomeration forces, the larger is the scope for differential taxation. To summarise, we write the following result.

Result 15.4 (hump-shaped tax gap). *The sustain-point tax gap, T^S, depends upon the level of trade freeness in a hump-shaped fashion, since agglomeration rents are a hump-shaped function of trade freeness. In* *particular, agglomeration is most important to firms—and thus can be most highly taxed—when trade costs are at an intermediate level (this is when geographic clustering is both necessary and possible). When trade costs are sufficiently high, the core region's tax rate must be below that of the periphery if it is to hold on to the core.*

This also suggests that agglomeration forces increase the degree of tax independence of regions that already have an agglomeration of industry.

The non-monotone relationship between agglomeration rents and trade costs implies that, in practice, one may expect tax competition between an industrial core and a periphery to be dampened at early stages of integration and attenuated only at later stages. To summarise, we write the following result.

Result 15.5 (race to top and bottom). *Starting from a high level of trade barriers, trade integration may lead to a 'race to the top' where the high tax region raises its rate more rapidly than the low tax region. At later stages of trade integration, we may see something that looks like a race to the bottom where the high-tax country cuts its rate faster than the low tax country.*

The result is written in terms of conditionals ('may' rather than 'will') since determining what taxes regions choose requires consideration of strategic tax-setting issues; formal analysis of this is postponed to the next chapter.

The results described above hold for any of the models with agglomeration forces discussed in Part I since the results depend only on the hump-shaped feature of agglomeration rents illustrated in Figure 15.3. However, to be more precise about the size of the tax gap, we work through the expressions using the FE model in Box 15.2.

We note that if we slightly extended our models to allow for many manufacturing sectors (i.e. Dixit–Stiglitz sectors) and many countries, we could find a situation where several countries have an agglomeration of different sectors as shown in Fujitia et al. (1999, Chapter 16). In such a model, Result 15.4 would suggest that agglomeration forces might increase the ability of nations to set different tax rates in different sectors.

15.5 TAXES WITH SYMMETRIC COUNTRIES

Tax competition between two symmetric regions is, as we shall see, very different in nature from the core–periphery case. While strong agglomeration forces give a core region more independence in choosing taxes, the opposite is true for symmetric regions; strong agglomeration forces threaten to destabilize a symmetric equilibrium, and therefore leave very little scope for unilateral tax increases on the mobile factor.

In this section, we work with a situation where industry is dispersed, that is, the economy starts at the symmetric equilibrium and trade is sufficiently restricted for this outcome to be stable (i.e. $\phi < \phi^B$). In what follows, we consider the

BOX 15.2 EXPLICIT EXPRESSIONS FOR THE FE MODEL

As shown in Chapter 4, the real-reward ratio in the full agglomeration outcome (core in the north) is

$$\Omega^{CP} \equiv \left.\frac{\pi/P}{\pi^*/P^*}\right|_{s_H=1} = \frac{2\phi^{1-a}}{2 - (1+b)(1-\phi^2)}; \quad a \equiv \frac{\mu}{\sigma-1}, \quad b \equiv \frac{\mu}{\sigma} \quad (15.9)$$

where we have imposed equal shares of the immobile factor in each region.

Several aspects of this are noteworthy. First, the ratio is unity when trade is perfectly free ($\phi = 1$), and it gets very negative as trade freeness drops towards zero. Also, as the analysis in Chapter 4 showed, this is positive when trade is sufficiently free, that is, ϕ exceeds the sustain point ϕ^S. The fourth point is that the ratio is increasing with trade openness when trade is relatively closed yet decreasing in openness when trade is relatively free. To see this, we log differentiate the ratio to get

$$\frac{d\Omega^{CP}/\Omega^{CP}}{d\phi/\phi} = (1-a) - \frac{2\phi^2(1+b)}{2 - (1+b)(1-\phi^2)} \quad (15.10)$$

Since the first right-hand term must be positive by the no-black-hole condition (see Chapter 4 for details) and the second term is increasing in ϕ, the derivative is clearly positive up to some critical value of ϕ and after this the derivative is negative. The level of trade freeness that maximizes Ω^{CP} is

$$\phi^{max} = \sqrt{\left(\frac{1-a}{1+a}\right)\left(\frac{1-b}{1+b}\right)} \quad (15.11)$$

Note that ϕ^{max} is the square root of the break point.

The fifth point is that the maximum level of Ω^{CP} increases in the agglomeration forces (as measured by a and b; see Chapter 4 for details). The final point concerning (15.9) is rather obvious, but greatly eases the analysis when we model tax competition explicitly in the next chapter; the real-return ratio, Ω, depends only on trade costs and parameters.

impact of trade openness on the 'foot looseness' of capital, and then the impact of agglomeration forces on the same. We conclude the section with some discussion on how tax competition is altered by the possibility of catastrophic agglomeration.

Our point of departure is the location condition for capital in the presence of taxes. The location condition (15.7) was written for the CP outcome. Its correspondent for the symmetric outcome is

$$\Omega T = 1, \quad T \equiv \frac{1-t}{1-t^*} \quad (15.12)$$

that is, geographically mobile entrepreneurs will be indifferent between the two regions if the ratio of real returns, Ω, is exactly compensated by the tax gap.

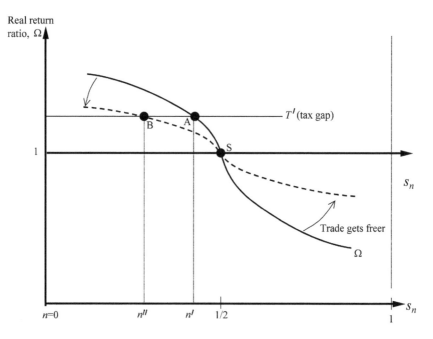

Figure 15.4 Taxation and delocation with dispersed industry.

15.5.1 Tax-Base Responsiveness and Openness

Recalling that Ω is downward sloped when the symmetric equilibrium is stable (see Figure 15.2), it is clear that a higher tax rate, ceteris paribus, makes a region less attractive. But how sensitive is the mobile factor to the tax gap?

This question is analysed in Figure 15.4, which plots Ω and T against the north's share of capital, s_n. As before, we wish to keep the analysis as general as possible at this point so the diagram reflects only the common properties of the new economic geography models explored in Part I. In particular, we showed that in every model, a gradual opening of trade flows between initially symmetric regions will produce catastrophic movement of the mobile factor to one region or another, once a threshold level of trade freeness is exceeded.[7] In terms of wiggle diagrams such as Figure 15.4, this means that the line depicting the real-reward ratio is negatively sloped as it crosses the midpoint when trade is highly constrained, but the slope at the midpoint tends towards zero as trade freeness approaches the break point. With this result in hand, we turn to the link between openness and the responsiveness of the tax base to the tax rate.

We start with a perfectly symmetric situation where half the world's industry and capital is in the north, and tax rates are equal so $T \equiv (1 - t)/(1 - t^*) = 1$. We disturb this state of affairs with an exogenous increase in the tax gap—say north raises its rate but the south does not. This will clearly induce some entrepreneurs

[7] In the FC model of Chapter 3, this occurs only when trade is perfectly free.

to head south. In the diagram, the new tax gap is shown as T'. As the T line shifts up to T', S is no longer a stable point since at S, the real rewards are equal but northern taxes are higher. As entrepreneurs move south, the real-reward ratio rises and this movement continues until $\Omega = 1/T'$, that is, at point A. The effects of an exogenous tax change are, thus, quite neoclassical in the sense that a marginal tax change gives a marginal relocation of the mobile factor. In the no-capital mobility case, the tax change has no effect on location, so we find— as in the BTCM—that capital mobility makes the tax base more responsive to the tax rate.

Notice, however, that the degree of relocation depends largely upon the level of trade costs—not just the degree of capital mobility as in the BTCM. When trade is freer, the relevant Ω curve is flatter. This is shown as the dashed Ω curve. Now the same tax gap brings the system to point B, not point A. It is immediately clear that the same tax increase has stronger effects on the location of the mobile factor. In short, the balance between dispersion and agglomeration forces narrows as trade gets freer and this means that initial equilibrium becomes more fragile. To summarize, we write the following result.

Result 15.6 (trade costs affect tax competition). *The extent to which a given tax rise reduces a region's tax base via capital delocation depends upon trade openness. In particular, since industry gets more footloose as trade gets freer, a given tax gap results in a greater tax-base loss when trade is very open.*

This results rests on what we called the 'home-market magnification' effect in Part I; as trade gets freer industry gets more footloose, not less.

Using an analogy with the government's tax problem in the BTCM, this result suggests that lower trade costs would exacerbate the race to the bottom when regions are similar. While this proposition turns out to be true, formal evaluation of it would require a game-theoretic setting and is therefore postponed to the next chapter.

15.5.2 Tax-Base Responsiveness and Agglomeration Forces

It is straightforward to show that tax-base responsiveness also increases with the strength of agglomeration forces. The argument has two steps. Part I showed that the break point of each model comes at a lower level of openness when agglomeration forces are stronger. Graphically, the break point is the level of openness where the slope of the Ω curve at the midpoint becomes zero, so we know that for any given level of openness (where $\phi < \phi^B$), the Ω curve becomes flatter as agglomeration forces become stronger. In other words, the Ω curve rotates counter clockwise around point S in Figure 15.4 as agglomeration forces become strong, so it is clear that stronger agglomeration forces heighten tax-base responsiveness.

In short, agglomeration forces tend to reduce the degree of independence in tax setting. To summarize, we write the following result.

BOX 15.3 DELOCATION RESPONSIVENESS IN DETAIL

The tractability of the FE model allows us to be more precise. If we totally differentiate the condition that characterizes the locational equilibrium, namely $T\Omega = 1$, with respect to the tax gap, T, and the spatial distribution of industry, $n = s_H = s_n$, and evaluate at the initially symmetric point, we get

$$\left.\frac{dn}{dT}\right|_{s_n=1/2,\ t=t^*} = \frac{-1}{\partial\Omega/\partial n} = \frac{(1 - bZ)/4Z}{(1 + ab)Z - a - b}, \quad Z \equiv \frac{1 - \phi}{1 + \phi} \qquad (15.13)$$

where this derivative, what we call the 'tax-base responsiveness', is only defined for $\phi < \phi^B$, and Z is a measure of the closed-ness of trade ($Z = 0$ at free trade, and 1 with no trade). Specifically, it is the share of expenditure on locally made industrial goods minus the share on imported varieties. To see that the delocation elasticity gets bigger as trade gets freer, all we have to do is note that the derivative of Ω with respect to s_n falls as Z rises (i.e. as trade gets more closed). And indeed, since the breakpoint is defined as the ϕ where $d\Omega/dn = 0$, we see that the delocation elasticity approaches negative infinity as ϕ approaches ϕ^B.

Result 15.7. *Starting from a situation where industry is not already fully grouped in one region, stronger agglomeration forces increase the cost—in terms of lost tax base—of raising the tax rate relative to that of other regions. In a sense, this implies that agglomeration forces tend to reduce the scope for independent tax setting when regions are similar to begin with.*

The contrast between this and Result 15.4 is peculiar enough to warrant writing it as a result.

Result 15.8. *Agglomeration forces tend to increase tax-setting independence when the mobile factor is initially agglomerated, but they tend to reduce independence when the mobile factor is spatially dispersed.*

As before, these results hold for all the Part I models. To be complete and specific, we illustrate the exact points with the FE model in Box 15.3.

15.5.3 Catastrophes and Taxes: the CP Tax Gap

A tax change may produce dramatic effects when ϕ is large enough, as Figure 15.5 shows. Consider the case where trade is quite free so the real reward ratio is given by the dashed Ω curve. Starting from symmetry, that is, point S, even a fairly large tax gap, say T', only results in moderate loss of industry, namely from $n = 1/2$ to n''. However, even a small increase in the tax gap beyond this, say from T' to T'', will result in a catastrophic delocation of industry. That is, with T'', the only stable location equilibrium is point C, where industry is fully agglomerated in the south.

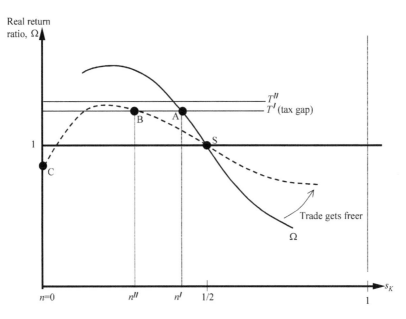

Figure 15.5 Catastrophes and taxes.

The catastrophic possibility requires the Ω curve in the diagram to have the right curvature. In particular, it must be hump-shaped to the left of the symmetric point as is the case in Figure 15.5. As it turns out, not all of the Part I models display this feature. In fact, there is an exact correspondence between the existence of what we called the overlap (i.e. a range of ϕ's where both CP outcomes and symmetry are locally stable) and existence of this curvature. Consequently, such a possibility does not arise in all models. As Chapter 4 showed, the FE model does display this feature, so we work with the FE model in the rest of the section.

Given the FE model's tractability, we can characterize this possibility more fully by calculating the tax gap beyond which the symmetric equilibrium would break down and the core–periphery outcome would become stable—we call this the break-point tax gap. Clearly, when the symmetric point is not stable—that is, $\phi > \phi^B$—then even the slightest tax gap would break symmetry, so we limit our attention to $\phi < \phi^B$.

Two cases are of interest. When trade is quite restricted, the Ω curve has a negative slope over the entire range of industry distribution. In this case, the only way to make the CP outcome stable is to have the tax gap so large that $T\Omega^{CPS} > 1$, where Ω^{CPS} is the value of Ω when all industry is in the south, that is, $n = 0$. When trade is freer, but still restricted enough to make the symmetric equilibrium stable (i.e. $\phi < \phi^B$), the Ω curve may have an interior maximum in the range $n = (0, 1/2)$. In this case, the CP tax gap is defined by the height of the Ω curve at its interior maximum.

To characterize the partition between these two cases, we focus on the slope of Ω at $n = 0$. The first case, where the maximum Ω occurs at $n = 0$, the slope of Ω with respect to n at $n = 0$ will be negative. When the maximum occurs at an interior n, then the slope of Ω at $n = 0$ will be positive (see Chapter 4 on Ω's concavity properties). The dividing line is where the slope is just zero. Log differentiating (15.9), setting the result to zero and solving for Z, we find the threshold Z. We call this Z^c, since it defines the boundary of the region in which small tax changes may lead to catastrophic location effect. It equals

$$Z^c = \frac{\psi - \sqrt{\psi^2 - 4(a + b)^2}}{2(a + b)}, \quad \psi \equiv 1 + b(b + 2a) > 0 \qquad (15.14)$$

Recall that Z is a measure of closed-ness, that is, $Z \equiv (1 - \phi)/(1 + \phi)$, so this says that when trade is closed enough, namely $Z > Z^c$, the sustain-point tax gap is just Ω evaluated at $n = 0$—what we called Ω^{CPS}.

For $Z < Z^c$, the ratio of real rewards is hump-shaped in n. To find the interior maximum of this hump, we differentiate Ω with respect to n and set the result equal to zero. The n that solves this, what we call n^{max}, is

$$n^{max} = \frac{1}{2} - \frac{\sqrt{(1 - bZ)A[a(bZ - 1) + Z - b]}}{2AZ} \qquad (15.15)$$

$$A \equiv \psi Z - (a + b)Z^2 - b(1 + ab)$$

We are not principally interested in n^{max} but rather in the value of real-reward ratio at this level of n. To find this, we substitute n^{max} into (15.9). While this does yield a closed form solution, it is too unwieldy to be revealing so we do not reproduce it here; we merely note that the result is labelled Ω^{max}.

With all this in hand, we can write the sustain-point tax gap as

$$T^S = \begin{cases} 1/\Omega^{CPS}, & Z \geq Z^c \\ 1/\Omega^{max}, & Z < Z^c \end{cases} \qquad (15.16)$$

where T^S is the sustain-point tax gap, and Ω^{max} is the Ω evaluated at n^{max} from (15.15).

This is again an example of the strong non-linearity of the model. It implies that it can be a serious mistake to gauge the effects of a tax change on a linear interpolation from the past. This is summarized in the following result.

Result 15.9 (endemic non-linearity of tax competition and economic integration). *The responsiveness of a region's tax base to the tax gap is highly non-linear. Moreover, the impact of a given tax gap will vary with the level of trade openness, and this in a very non-linear manner. Consequently, attempts to empirically determine the impact of taxes on industry location using standard functional forms and assuming separability of effects may produce thoroughly misleading results.*

15.6 TAX-FINANCED PUBLIC GOODS AS A DESTABILIZING FORCE

The previous sections have highlighted results where the consideration of agglomeration forces extends the standard results in tax competition models. Here, we show that the tax literature has something to teach the economic geography literature.

The mobile factor, entrepreneurs or H for short, naturally seek to locate in the region that can afford them the highest level of utility. In the basic FE model, this boils down to looking for the region with the highest real reward. However, once we allow for public goods, entrepreneurs will typically take into account the level of public goods available in each region when making their location decision. As we will see, this introduces an extra agglomeration force into the model, as shown by Andersson and Forslid (2003).

15.6.1 Additional Assumptions

We follow Andersson and Forslid (2003) and assume that tax revenue is used to produce a public good that is appreciated by L and H alike. Specifically, preferences are

$$U = C_M^\mu C_A^{1-\mu} G^\gamma \tag{15.17}$$

where G is the supply of the public good, and $\gamma > 0$ determines the importance of public goods in utility. The indirect utility function of the mobile factor is $V = \xi \pi G^\gamma / P$ where ξ represents a group of parameters, namely $\xi \equiv \mu^\mu (1 - \mu)^{1-\mu}$. This formulation implies that at least a rudimentary public sector is necessary if agents are to enjoy non-zero utility.

For simplicity, we assume that the public good is produced by the means of the average consumption basket, that is, a fraction of the tax revenue equal to $1 - \mu$ is spent on agricultural goods, and a fraction μ on manufactures. Since this implies that the composition of demand is independent of the level of taxation, we can avoid having to re-work all the FE model's equilibrium expressions taking account of the possibility that government spends its 'income' in a pattern that differs from that of the average consumer. In other words, with this assumption, wages and prices are unaffected by the level of taxes; the goods market impact of government and private spending are identical since they buy exactly the same basket of goods. We also assume that the government's budget is always balanced.

Finally, for convenience, we assume that only the mobile factor is taxed, so the balanced budget assumption implies

$$PG = tn\pi, \quad G = C_m^\mu C_A^{1-\mu} \tag{15.18}$$

and an isomorphic condition for the south.

15.6.2 Stability of the Symmetric Equilibrium

The extra agglomeration force is most easily illustrated at the symmetric equilibrium. With symmetric tax rates, the relative utility of the mobile factor is

$$\frac{V}{V^*} \equiv \frac{\pi(1-t)P^*(t\pi n)^\gamma(P^*)^\gamma}{\pi^*(1-t^*)P(t^*\pi^*n^*)^\gamma(P)^\gamma} = T\Omega^{1+\gamma}\left(\frac{tn}{t^*n^*}\right)^\gamma \qquad (15.19)$$

where we use the standard FE model normalization, $n = s_H = s_n$, to lighten the notation (see Chapter 4 for details) and note that the tax gap, T, is defined as in (15.12). To investigate the stability properties of the symmetric equilibrium, we differentiate (15.19) with respect to n and evaluate this derivative at the symmetric equilibrium ($n = 1/2$ and $t = t^*$). Recalling that $n^* = 1 - n$, this gives

$$(1+\gamma)\frac{\partial\Omega}{\partial n}\bigg|_{1/2} + 4\gamma \qquad (15.20)$$

where

$$\frac{\partial\Omega}{\partial n}\bigg|_{1/2} = 4Z\frac{Z(1+ab)-a-b}{bZ-1}$$

The first term in (15.20) is proportional to the standard partial that we get without public goods. As Chapter 4 showed in detail, this partial can be decomposed into a three effects. A stabilizing market-crowding effect and two destabilizing cycles of circular causality, demand linkages and cost linkages. The new element here is the second term, 4γ. Since it is positive, it tends to make the symmetric equilibrium unstable and, thus, we classify it as an agglomeration force and call it the 'amenities linkage'.

AMENITIES LINKAGES

Intuitively, this agglomeration force arises from something that is akin to the cost-of-living effect. Production shifting leads to 'tax-base shifting' and this in turn results in a change in the level of public goods provided in the two regions. In particular, migration implies that the receiving region can afford better public goods while the sending region can offer only a poorer set of public goods. Since migrants care about the relative availability of public goods, the migration creates forces that tend to induce further migration. The stronger are preferences for the public good (as measured by γ), the stronger is this force. Essentially this is an instance of scale economies in the production of public goods that makes a larger region more attractive. Notice that it does not involve trade costs. Moreover, the force exists also when taxes are symmetric.

Result 15.10 (bright lights, big city effect). *The spending of tax revenue on public goods creates a destabilizing agglomeration force.*

Importantly, the magnitude of this destabilizing force is *not* related to trade costs. It depends only on preferences for public goods.

15.7 DUELLING PUBLIC AMENITIES: A MODIFIED TIEBOUT HYPOTHESIS

Governments do spend money on public goods, but also on other goods and services that do not directly make their region more attractive to mobile factors.

Moreover, governments may differ in the efficiency with which they transform tax revenues into public amenities. What we investigate here is the implications for location when nations have identical tax rates, but produce different levels of public goods with their revenue.

To keep the discussion concrete, we introduce a parameter, Γ (a mnemonic for government efficiency), that measures that relationship between tax revenue and the public goods. That is,

$$PG = \Gamma tn\pi, \quad P^*G^* = \Gamma^* t^* n^* \pi^* \tag{15.21}$$

where $\Gamma = 1$ implies full efficiency, and $\Gamma = 0$ implies zero efficiency. All other assumptions are maintained.

Repeating the same calculations we used above with this new 'production function' for public goods, and with symmetric taxes we find

$$\frac{V}{V^*} = \Omega^{1+\gamma} \left(\frac{n}{1-n} \right)^{\gamma} \Lambda^{\gamma}, \quad \Lambda \equiv \frac{\Gamma}{\Gamma^*} \tag{15.22}$$

where we refer to Λ as the 'amenities gap', or 'government efficiency gap'.

The axis of investigation now turns to the connection between the amenities gap and industrial location. Comparing (15.19) with (15.22), it is clear that there is an almost perfect symmetry between the tax gap with symmetric efficiency, and the amenities gap with symmetric tax rates. Consequently, there is no need to repeat the calculations; we just re-interpret the results from above.

Using the analogy with the tax gap, we can use Result 15.2 to note that when industry is already clustered, the government in the core region can sustain a higher level of inefficiency without losing industry. Result 15.3 says that we may observe a negative correlation between industrial location and government efficiency. Moreover, Result 15.4 implies that the maximum government-efficiency gap is hump-shaped with respect to openness. This suggests a modification to the Tiebout hypothesis that competition for the mobile factor improves governmental efficiency:

Result 15.11 (Tiebout modified). *Competition among jurisdictions for mobile factors tends to improve efficiency, but only when trade is sufficiently restricted. When trade is free enough, economic agglomerations appear and the core-region's government can be less efficient than the periphery's without losing capital due to the hump-shaped nature of agglomeration rents. In particular, increased goods market integration will first weaken pressure on the core-government and then strengthen it.*

This result suggests that the governments of agglomerated regions—large cities for example—could get away with a higher level of wastefulness, corruption and frivolous spending than can smaller communities.

In the case where industry is even distributed, Results 15.7 and 15.8 imply that freer trade and/or stronger agglomeration forces tend to have the opposite effect on government's independence; in terms of lost industry, the greater the cost of a given government-efficiency gap, the freer is trade and the stronger are agglomeration forces. Once again, we see that the presence of agglomeration forces has very different effects when industry is clustered and when it is dispersed.

In summary, trade integration may decrease or increase pressures on governments to provide public amenities more efficiently. The key determinants are the level of trade costs and the initial spatial allocation of industry.

15.8 REDISTRIBUTIVE TAXES: OPENNESS AND TAXATION OF MOBILE FACTORS[8]

Consider two symmetric countries where public goods are financed by potentially different tax rates on mobile and immobile factors. The tax rate on the entrepreneurs' income is denoted t_H and the tax on the immobile factor's income is t_A. To isolate effects, we will assume that taxes are completely harmonized between the north and the south: $t_H = t_H^*$ and $t_A = t_A^*$. The government's budget is assumed to balance, which gives $PG = t_H n\pi + t_A L$ for the north and an isomorphic expression for the south. The relative indirect utility in the two countries is now

$$\frac{V}{V^*} = \Omega^{1+\gamma}\left[\frac{L/\pi + n(t_H/t_A)}{L/\pi^* + (1-n)(t_H/t_A)}\right]^\gamma \tag{15.23}$$

The effect of redistributive taxes can be gauged from the following differential:

$$\left.\frac{\partial^2(V/V^*)}{\partial(t_H/t_A)\partial n}\right|_{1/2} = \frac{4\gamma b(1-b)(1-Z^2)}{(1-bZ)[1-b+b(t_H/t_A)]^2} > 0 \tag{15.24}$$

Since higher t_H/t_A has a positive effect on the 'wiggle curve' at symmetry, it is clear that a higher tax on the mobile factor strengthens agglomeration forces. Also it can be seen that a higher γ amplifies this agglomeration force. The higher is t_H/t_A, the more important it is to be located in a country with a large stock of the mobile factor, since the stock of mobile factors becomes more important in financing the public good. This last fact suggests a very interesting interpretation of trends in the taxation of mobile factors.

Increasing trade openness tends to foster agglomeration, that is, to make it more difficult for governments to hold on to their industry. One element of the destabilization stems from amenities linkages and these in turn depend upon the extent to which the tax base is linked to the location of the mobile factor. If all governments shift the tax burden from the mobile factor to the immobile factor, it becomes easier for all governments to hold on to their own mobile factors.

Result 15.12. *Shifting the burden of taxation from the mobile to the immobile factor tends to stabilize the dispersed-industry outcome and this in turn tends to counter the destabilizing effects of freer trade.*

[8] This section is based on Andersson and Forslid (2003).

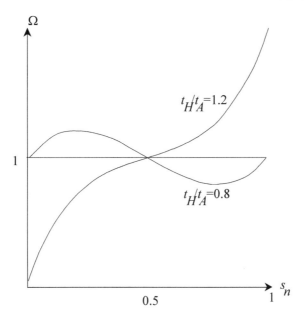

Figure 15.6 Stability and taxation of mobile factors.

Figure 15.6 displays the 'wiggle diagram' of relative indirect utility as $n = s_H = s_n$ varies for from zero to unity.[9] The downward sloping curve, which is drawn for $t_H/t_A = 0.8$, implies that the symmetric equilibrium is stable. When $t_H/t_A = 1.2$, the symmetric equilibrium is unstable. Thus, a higher t_H/t_A has exactly the same effect as a higher ϕ on the stability of the symmetric equilibrium.

An interesting implication of this analysis is that tax harmonization may not suffice to maintain a stable symmetric allocation of industry. It may also be necessary to shift the tax burden on to the immobile factor to dampen the tendencies for agglomeration.

15.9 CONCLUDING REMARKS

This chapter shows that studying taxation and public goods in a new economic geography framework yields several important insights. First, taxation when agglomeration has already occurred is radically different from tax competition between two symmetric regions (more precisely two regions at a stable interior equilibrium). Anything that strengthens agglomeration forces will have a tendency to lock industry into the core, and therefore give the core region an increased freedom to tax the mobile factor. There is, thus, in essence a 'large

---

[9] The parameter values used are $\sigma = 3$, $\mu = 0.4$, $L^w = 1$, $g = 0.4$, $\phi = 0.4$ and $t_H/t_A = 0.8$ and 1.2, respectively.

country advantage'. In a symmetric case, stronger agglomeration forces have just the opposite effect. They make the symmetric equilibrium more fragile, and therefore decrease the scope for taxation. One key parameter that affects agglomeration forces is the openness of trade. Since agglomeration forces are hump-shaped in openness, the scope for taxation is maximal for intermediate trade costs for a core region and minimal in a symmetric equilibrium. Second, the presence of public goods introduces an extra agglomeration force, since a large region implies a large tax base to finance the public good. Moreover, this effect is larger the more taxes are levied on the migrating factor. One implication of this is that tax harmonization may not suffice to maintain a stable symmetric equilibrium as trade is liberalized.

The review of related literature on taxes and agglomeration is postponed until the end of the next chapter.

REFERENCES

Andersson, F. and R. Forslid. 2003. Tax competition and economic geography. *Journal of Public Economic Theory* 5: in press.

Bucovetsky, S. 1991. Asymmetric tax competition. *Journal of Urban Economics* 30: 67–181.

de Crombrugghe, A. and H. Tulkens. 1990. On Pareto improving commodity tax changes under fiscal competition. *Journal of Public Economics* 41: 335–350.

Edwards, J. and M. Keen. 1996. Tax competition and leviathan. *European Economic Review* 40: 113–134.

Fujita, M., P. Krugman and A. Venables. 1999. The Spatial Economy: Cities, Regions, and International Trade. Cambridge, MA: MIT Press.

Gordon, R. 1983. An optimal tax approach to fiscal federalism. *Quarterly Journal of Economics* 98: 567–586.

Janeba, E. 1998. Tax competition in imperfectly competitive markets. *Journal of International Economics* 44: 135–153.

Kanbur, R. and M. Keen. 1993. Tax competition when countries differ in size. *American Economic Review* 83: 877–892.

Kind, H., K. H. Midelfart Knarvik and G. Schjelderup. 2000. Competing for capital in a "lumpy" world. *Journal of Public Economics* 78: 253–724.

Krogstrup, Signe. 2002. What do theories of tax competition predict for capital taxes in EU countries? A review of the tax competition literature. HEI manuscript, Geneva.

Ludema, R. and I. Wooton. 2000. Economic geography and the fiscal effects of regional integration. *Journal of International Economics* 52: 331–357.

Tiebout, C. 1956. A pure theory of local public expenditures. *Journal of Political Economy* 64: 416-424.

Wildasin, D. 1988. Nash equilibria in models of fiscal competition. *Journal of Public Economics* 35: 229–240.

_____. 1991. Some rudimentary duopoly theory. *Regional Science and Urban Economics* 21: 393–421.

Wilson, J. 1986. A theory of interregional tax competition. *Journal of Urban Economics* 19: 296–315.

_____. 1991. Tax Competition with interregional differences in factor endowments. *Regional Science and Urban Economics* 21: 423–452.

_____. 1999. Theories of tax competition. *National Tax Journal* LII(2): 269–304.

Zodrow, G. and P. Mieszkowski. 1986. Pigou, Tiebout, property taxation and the under-provision of local public goods. *Journal of Urban Economics* 19: 356–370.

Tax Competition and Agglomeration

16.1 Introduction

The previous chapter provided a series of insights that would seem to be important for our thinking on international tax competition. That chapter, however, stopped short of actually modelling the full set of interactions. In particular, tax rates were taken as given in the economic geography models, so issues concerning the interaction among governments could not be addressed. The aim of this chapter is to remedy the omission.

16.1.1 Organization of the Chapter

This chapter first considers a formal tax game between similar countries. This allows us to more formally show that free trade and stronger agglomeration forces tend to magnify international tax competition, leading, for instance, to lower Nash tax rates. Section 16.3 follows up on the issue of an 'amenities competition'. Specifically, we demonstrate that the socially first-best tax rate is chosen even though capital is perfectly mobile. The deep fundamentals of this result, which is reminiscent of the famous Tiebout hypothesis, are that when capital and labour owners share common preferences and the government cares about the representative consumer, the government's first-order condition mimics the location condition. Consequently, the tax rate that is most attractive to the mobile factor is also the social first-best rate.

Section 16.4 considers international tax competition in the absence of capital mobility. One of the Part I models—the constructed capital, or CC model—does display agglomeration forces without capital mobility. Indeed, as we showed in Chapter 5, agglomeration forces are stronger without capital mobility. This, as we shall see, implies that contrary to the received wisdom in the public finance literature, capital mobility in the presence of agglomeration forces may lessen tax competition.

Section 16.5 looks at tax competition between similar countries when catastrophic agglomeration is possible. Section 16.6 studies tax competition when capital is already agglomerated in one nation. This shows that most of the main results of the 'basic tax competition model' can be overturned in the presence of agglomeration forces and trade costs. We close the chapter with a summary section that includes a review of the most relevant literature.

16.2 Tax Competition between Similar Countries: Simplest Case

We start with a set-up that is as close as possible to the 'basic tax competition model' (BTCM) presented in the last chapter. Specifically, we work with two nations that play Nash in tax rates. For simplicity, we continue to assume that the mobile and immobile factors are taxed at the same rate, and that the nations are symmetric in all aspects. The key new ingredient is an agglomeration force. Specifically, the economic framework adopted is a variant of the 'footloose capital' (FC) model of Chapter 3.

16.2.1 The Economic Framework: A Quasi-Linear FC Model

The model we employ, the quasi-linear FC model, is best thought of as the FC model with a simpler utility function. The FC model is detailed in Chapter 3 but we recall its main features here for the convenience of the reader before pointing out how the quasi-linear FC model differs from the standard FC model.

The model works with two sectors, two factors, and two regions (north and south). As usual, one sector is Walrasian and the other is Dixit–Stiglitz with only the latter being subject to iceberg trade costs. One factor is the immobile factor and we call this 'labour', while the other factor—capital—is perfectly internationally mobile. The world capital supply, K^w, is fixed and so without loss of generality we normalize the total to one. With this, the sum of capital employed in the north, n, and in the south, n^*, is unity. The n's therefore are both the level of capital *and* the share of world capital working in their respective regions (this allows us to substitute n for the more explicit but more cumbersome share notation, e.g. s_n). Moreover, since the model assumes that each Dixit–Stiglitz variety requires the same amount of capital (one unit to be concrete), n is also the share of industrial varieties made in the north. For simplicity, we work with the symmetric-region version of the model, so regions have identical endowments, tastes, technology and trade costs.

Labourers own all the capital, and since they are immobile, they repatriate all capital earnings. This means that capital's post-tax income gets spent in its home market, and, importantly, that capital's location decision is based on a comparison of post-tax nominal rewards (i.e. rewards measured in the numeraire good rather than in terms of basket of goods). Also recall that standard, FC model normalizations take A as numeraire, and chooses units of A such that $w = 1$. We assume costless trade in A so L's reward is equalized internationally, that is, $w = w^* = 1$ (see Chapter 3 for derivations).

16.2.2 Additional Assumptions

The FC model without taxes does not display demand linkages since capital's income is repatriated. With taxation, however, the standard FC model does have demand linkages. The mechanism is simple. Taxation means that the home government retains part of foreign capital's income and spends this locally. While this is surely a second-order consideration as far as the profitability of locations is concerned, taking account of this greatly complicates the analysis. Indeed, although we can easily derive the Nash equilibrium tax rate in such a set-up, the expression is too cumbersome to be revealing. To avoid relying on numerical simulation, we instead modify preferences and the public good technology in a way that eliminates the demand linkage.

Specifically, we assume quasi-linear preferences with consumption of Walrasian good, A, entering linearly, and the consumption of Dixit–Stiglitz varieties entering as a CES composite.[1] As usual, quasi-linear preferences eliminate all income effects on demand and thereby eliminate demand-linkages. Thus, instead of the usual Cobb–Douglas CES nest, the preferences assumed here are

$$U = C + \ln(G), \quad C \equiv C_A + \mu \ln C_m, \quad C_M \equiv \left(\int_{i=0}^{n+n^*} c_i^{1-(1/\sigma)} di \right)^{1/(1-1/\sigma)} ; \tag{16.1}$$

$$\sigma > 1 > \mu > 0$$

where μ measures the strength of preferences for differentiated goods and G is the amount of public good provided. This specification implies that, as normal, marginal utility from G is positive but diminishing. The fact that C_A enters linearly means that total expenditure on M varieties is unaffected by the level of income.

Adding the public good permits us to introduce rudimentary micro-foundations for the government's objective function but to avoid interactions between the level of government spending and demand for differentiated varieties, G, is assumed to be produced directly from the A good (i.e. G's production function is just $G = A_G$ where A_G is the amount of A employed by the government to make the public good).

16.2.3 Key Equilibrium Expressions

We normalize each economy's total labour endowment to unity, so optimal aggregate demand for a typical industrial variety, and the aggregate demand for A are (see Appendix 2.A for the derivation)

$$c_j = \frac{\mu p_j^{-\sigma}}{\int_{i=0}^{1} p_j^{1-\sigma} di}, \quad C_A = (1 - t)(L + \pi K) - \int_{i=0}^{1} c_j p_j di \tag{16.2}$$

where p_i is the consumer price of a typical M sector variety, t is the northern tax rate, $(1 - t)I$ is northern, after-tax factor income consisting of labour income L (the wage is unity since L is numeraire) and capital income πK, where π is capital's reward and K is north's fixed supply of capital.[2] These expressions imply that private spending on A is a residual, that is, equal to post-tax income that is not spent on industrial goods. (Total demand for A will also reflect government purchases used to make G; here, C_A represents only private demand.)

---

[1] This model can equally be thought of as a modified version of the linear model in Chapter 5.

[2] It may seem odd that northern disposable income depends only on the north's tax rate since some northern capital may work in the south. A unit of northern capital working in the south would remit $(1 - t^*)\pi^*$, but due to the location condition below, this exactly equals $(1 - t)\pi$.

As usual, the producer price for a typical industrial firm is related to marginal costs according to $p_j(1 - 1/\sigma) = a_m$. By choice of units (viz. $a_M = 1 - 1/\sigma$), we can—without loss of generality—set the producer price to unity for all differentiated varieties. Recalling that costless trade in A equalizes northern and southern rewards to labour, the southern producer price is also unity. Consequently, the nominal reward to entrepreneurs working in the north—namely π—is related to the location of industry (n), and trade openness (ϕ) by

$$\pi = bB, \quad B \equiv \frac{1}{\Delta} + \frac{\phi}{\Delta^*}; \quad \Delta \equiv n + \phi n^*, \quad \Delta^* \equiv \phi n + n^*, \quad b \equiv \frac{\mu}{\sigma}$$

$$(16.3)$$

where b represents a group of parameters that frequently arises; it is a handy measure of the strength of agglomeration forces since it rises with the share of spending on M goods and with the size of the profit margin, $1/\sigma$. The expression for the reward to capital employed in the south, what we call π^*, is isomorphic. Notice that unlike the standard FC model, π here does not depend upon expenditure shares.

The spatial allocation of the mobile factor is defined by the location condition and since we focus on the stable, symmetric outcome in this section, this is

$$\left(\frac{1-t}{1-t^*}\right)\frac{\pi}{\pi^*} = 1 \tag{16.4}$$

Notice that mobile capital does not care about price levels or public-good provision in choosing its location since capital's post-tax income is always spent in its home market. Using (16.3) and its southern equivalent, the equilibrium location of capital (as characterized by n) and the responsiveness of capital to north's tax (taking t^* as given) are, respectively,

$$n = \frac{1}{2}\left(1 - \frac{t - t^*}{2 - t - t^*}\left(\frac{1+\phi}{1-\phi}\right)^2\right), \quad \left.\frac{\partial n}{\partial t}\right|_{n=1/2} = -\frac{1}{4(1-t)}\left(\frac{1+\phi}{1-\phi}\right)^2$$

$$(16.5)$$

where the derivative is evaluated at symmetry. This clearly illustrates that with symmetric taxes, we get an even division of capital. Also we note that capital's responsiveness to tax changes depends upon the degree of trade openness, with the response approaching infinity as trade becomes entirely free. As we shall see, this fact implies that trade openness will play an important role in tax competition.

16.2.4 Government Objective Function

The government's preferences for G and private consumption, C, are

$$W = W[G, C]; \quad G \equiv tY, \quad C \equiv C_A + \mu \ln C_M \tag{16.6}$$

Using (16.2), and the fact that locally made varieties are priced at unity while imports are priced at ϕ, we get

$$C = I(1 - t) - \mu + \mu \ln \mu + a \ln \Delta, \quad a \equiv \frac{\mu}{\sigma - 1} \qquad (16.7)$$

where Δ is defined in (16.3), Y is the total of locally generated income, namely $Y = L + \pi n$ (in other words, Y is GDP), I is GNP, a is a group of parameters that frequently appears in expressions, and we have used the solution to the consumer problem to express C_A and C_M in terms of prices and post-tax income. The south has analogous variables and functions.

The class of models that corresponds to (16.6) includes models where the government cares only about a representative consumer (so the W function is identical to the U function), models where the government cares only about G for its own purposes (Leviathan governments), and convex combinations of the two. To parallel our presentation of the BTCM in the previous chapter, this section assumes that the government maximizes utility of the representative consumer, so its objective is

$$W = I(1 - t) - \mu + \mu \ln \mu + a \ln \Delta + \ln(tY) \qquad (16.8)$$

16.2.5 Nash Equilibrium Taxes: Openness and Agglomeration Matter

The governments choose taxes to maximize (16.8) taking as given the other nation's tax rate; the equilibrium concept is Nash in tax rates. Differentiating the objective function with respect to t, holding t^* constant, yields the northern government's first-order condition

$$\frac{U_G}{U_C} = \frac{-\partial C / \partial t}{\partial G / \partial t} \qquad (16.9)$$

By the symmetry of the nations, this single condition and the imposition of symmetry, $t = t^*$, can be used to characterize the Nash equilibrium.

FIRST-BEST AND RACE-TO-BOTTOM

Before we turn to the Nash equilibrium, we calculate the first-best tax rate, that is, the tax rate when capital is perfectly immobile. When capital is immobile, I and Δ are parameters in the government's problem so the first-order condition is

$$\frac{U_G}{U_C} = 1 \quad \Rightarrow \quad t^{FB} = \frac{1}{1 + b} \qquad (16.10)$$

The expression for the first-best tax rate comes from the fact that the left-hand side equals $1/G$, and income in equilibrium is $(1 + b)$. We also note that the left-hand side of (16.10) is declining in t. Thus, the first-best tax corresponds to point FB in Figure 16.1; the left-hand side of (16.10) is plotted as MB (a mnemonic for marginal benefit).

When capital is mobile, I, Y and Δ all depend upon n and, thus, upon t via the location condition. Combining our definitions of I, Y, Δ and π with the expressions for n and $\partial n / \partial t$, it can be shown that the right-hand side of the government's first-order condition, (16.9), equals

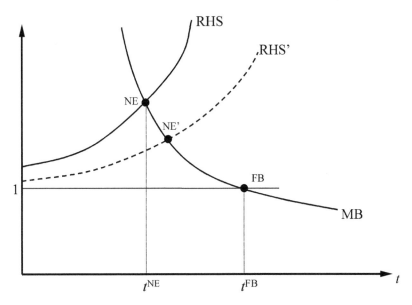

Figure 16.1 Social inefficiency of the Nash tax equilibrium.

$$\frac{-dC/dt}{dG/dt} = \frac{(1-t)[b + (2+b)Z^2] + Za}{(1-t)[b + (2+b)Z^2] - b(1-Z^2)}, \quad Z \equiv \frac{1-\phi}{1+\phi} \quad (16.11)$$

where the symmetry taxes in equilibrium has used been to simplify expressions.

Using (16.11) to solve the first-order condition, (16.9), we find that the Nash equilibrium tax rate $t^{NE} =$

$$\frac{Y(4Z^2 + aZ + b) + b^2Z^2 + b - \sqrt{(b^4 - 8bY)Z^4 + DZ^3 + EZ^2 + ab(4+2b)YZ + b^4 + 4b^2Y}}{2Y[(2+b)Z^2 + b]}$$

$$(16.12)$$

$$D \equiv [8a + ab(2b^2 + 16 + 10b], \quad E \equiv [2b^3(2+b) + (a^2 + 8)bY + a^2Y],$$

$$Y = 1 + b$$

It is possible to show directly that $t^{FB} > t^{NE}$, but indirect reasoning is simpler and more intuitive. As we saw in the previous chapter's review of the BTCM, whenever the right-hand side of (16.9) exceeds unity, taxes are set at a level that is too low from the social point of view. It is seen from (16.11) that the right-hand side is indeed greater than one since $a > b > 0$ and Z is less than unity. Figure 16.1 shows this graphically. In the diagram, the RHS curve is shown as lying everywhere above unity, as we just showed, and by inspection of (16.11), the RHS is positively sloped and convex, so we know that the two curves intersect to the left of the first-best rate. The curve RHS' shows the right-hand side when trade is more restricted, in which case the Nash tax rate is closer to the first-best rate in this case. This can be summarized in the following result.

Result 16.1 (race to the bottom). *International tax competition for a mobile factor leads social welfare maximizing governments to choose a tax rate that is too low. As in the standard tax competition model, removing capital mobility removes the inefficiency.*

Having established the fact that our model yields a BTCM-like result (see Chapter 15), we turn now to consider how changes in trade freeness and changes in agglomeration forces affect the Nash equilibrium tax rates.

AGGLOMERATION FORCES, TRADE OPENNESS AND NASH TAX RATES

Expression (16.5) showed that as trade gets freer, capital becomes more footloose. Since the crux of tax competition is the attempt to attract more tax base by lowering rates, it seems intuitively obvious that openness will have much to do with the harmfulness of tax competition. Indeed, by inspection of (16.11), we see that as Z falls (i.e. trade becomes less closed), the Nash tax rate falls.

Since both a and b rise with agglomeration forces (i.e. as μ or $1/\sigma$ rise), the analytics of the impact on the Nash tax rate is highly complex. Graphical methods using the closed-form solution, (16.12), however, easily show the intuitive result that tax competition gets harder—in the sense that Nash rates fall—when agglomeration forces increase. To summarise this, we write the following result.

Result 16.2 (mobility of goods and agglomeration forces also matter). *Capital mobility is not the only factor affecting the impact of tax competition on tax rates. In particular, the level of trade openness and the extent of agglomeration forces have important effects on equilibrium tax rates when similar countries engage in Nash tax competition.*

The exact direction of the effect is summarized as the following result.

Result 16.3. *Tax competition becomes harder, and Nash tax rates fall, as trade gets freer and/or agglomeration forces becomes stronger. As trade becomes perfectly free, the Nash tax rates fall towards zero.*

This result suggests that the impact of given tax rate differentials might be quite different across industries, so empirical work that pools across very different sectors may produce misleading results.

A direct policy corollary of these results concerns the gain from tax harmonization between similar nations.

Result 16.4. *The gain from cooperative tax harmonization between similar nations increases, as trade gets freer.*

The next section shows that the nature of capital matters enormously for these results. In particular, if capital owners move with their capital, then their location decision will involve the local provision of public goods as well as the tax rate. We shall see that this may change everything.

16.3 Harmless Tax Competition: Tiebout and Agglomeration[3]

At one level, the result that tax competition leads to an under-provision of public goods is somewhat curious. If a nation wants to attract foreign capital, providing the optimal level of public amenities (and, thus, charging the optimal tax rate) would seem to be a good place to start. In the previous section and in the BTCM literature in general, this conjecture is wrong since foreign capital does not benefit from the host nation's amenities; capital is assumed to spend its income in its home nation. This may seem reasonable and relevant when speaking about physical capital—it is quite easy for physical capital owners to be physically separated from their capital. However, for many other forms of capital, especially human capital, it is not easy to employ the factor without its owner being present physically. The same can be said for many forms of knowledge capital which are 'embedded' in trained workers.

The importance of this point lies, in the first instance, in the fact that many economic geography models work in a framework where productive factors can only move with their owner. Labour migration, for instance, is the key agglomerative mechanism in the CP model and the same can be said about FE and linear FE models. Since the ability to spatially separate capital and its owner was crucial to the race-to-the-bottom result, and many economic geography models assume this is not possible, it is important to check the implications of tax competition in other models. That is the task of this section.

In the second instance, the important issue is that assuming capital owners move together with their capital turns out to produce a stark result.

When factors move with their owners, international tax competition can lead to the socially optimal tax rate. In other words, tax competition may be harmless in this case. This is certainly not a new result to public economics—it is basically a corollary of the famous Tiebout hypothesis—but it does highlight the sort of assumptions that are necessary to generate harmful tax competition.

16.3.1 The Economic Framework: Standard FE Model

In this section we work with the standard FE model. This was detailed in Chapter 4, so we merely recall the model's main features here.

The model's basic set-up is identical to the one in the previous section: two nations, two sectors and two factors. One sector is Walrasian while the other is Dixit–Stiglitz. The mobile factor is used only as the fixed-cost input in producing the Dixit–Stiglitz varieties. The immobile factor, labour, provides the variable inputs into the Dixit–Stiglitz sector as well as being the sole factor of production employed by the Walrasian sector. As usual, costless trade in Walrasian goods equalizes labourers' wage rates internationally, and, thus, it also equalizes marginal costs in the Dixit–Stiglitz sector in the two nations. The main difference is that the mobile factor, which we call 'entrepreneurs', cannot be moved without

---

[3] The section is based on Baldwin and Forslid (2002a).

its owner; thus, entrepreneurs can also be thought of as human capital. Entrepreneurs search for the nation that provides the highest level of utility, taking into account taxes, prices and public amenities.

Also in contrast to the previous section, we revert to the standard preferences over private goods, that is, a Cobb-Douglas nest of consumption of the homogenous Walrasian good and a CES composite of the differentiated varieties.

Public goods are at the heart of our story. To introduce them as simply as possible, we follow Andersson and Forslid (2003) in assuming that the public good is produced using the same composite of A and M as in the consumers utility function.[4] Thus, the cost function of producing G units of the public good, G, is just P times G in the north, where P is the usual consumer price index corresponding to the standard two-tier utility function of the representative consumer. Consumers' preferences are

$$U = G^\gamma C^{1-\gamma}, \quad C \equiv C_M^\mu C_A^{1-\mu}, \quad C_M \equiv \left(\int_{i=0}^{n+n^*} c_i^{1-(1/\sigma)} di \right)^{1/[1-(1/\sigma)]} \quad (16.13)$$

where $0 < \gamma < 1$ measures the intensity of taste for the public good.

GOVERNMENT OBJECTIVE FUNCTION

Following the last section, we continue to assume that both factors are taxed at the same rate and that the government chooses the tax rate, and thus indirectly the level of public goods, to maximize the utility of residents. The governments play Nash in tax rates and the northern government's payoff function is

$$W = U[G, C], \quad G = \frac{tY}{P}, \quad C = \frac{(1-t)Y}{P}, \quad P = \Delta^{-a} \quad (16.14)$$

where Δ and a are as defined in (16.3) and (16.7), and we have used the solution of the consumer's problem to write utility in its indirect form. The south's payoff function is isomorphic. It is important to note that in contrast to the case of disembodied capital, both consumption and public-goods provision are based on GDP, that is, Y.

Since there is no difference between GDP and GNP in this model (i.e. there are no factors repatriating earnings), we can use a handy simplification of the government's objective function. Since the utility function in (16.13) is homogenous of degree one in Y/P, we can write

$$W = U[t, 1-t]\left(\frac{Y}{P}\right) \quad (16.15)$$

The southern government has an isomorphic objective function.

LOCATION CONDITION

Since the mobile factor spends its income locally, its location decision takes account of taxes, the price level and the provision of public goods. Specially,

[4] This implies that the level of taxation does not change the demand pattern. See also Trionfetti (2001).

assuming that trade is sufficiently restricted to allow the symmetric outcome to be stable, and the relative utility curve to be everywhere downward sloping (i.e. the level of openness is sufficiently below the 'break point'; see Chapter 4 for details),[5] the location condition is

$$\frac{G^{\gamma}((1-t)\pi/P)^{1-\gamma}}{(G^*)^{\gamma}((1-t^*)\pi^*/P^*)^{1-\gamma}} = 1 \tag{16.16}$$

where the π's in here are *not* given by (16.3), but rather by

$$\pi = bB\frac{E^w}{n^w}, \quad \pi^* = bB^*\frac{E^w}{n^w}; \quad B \equiv \frac{s_E}{\Delta} + \frac{\phi s_E^*}{\Delta^*}, \quad B^* \equiv \frac{\phi s_E}{\Delta} + \frac{s_E^*}{\Delta^*}, \quad b \equiv \frac{\mu}{\sigma} \tag{16.17}$$

where s_E and s_E^* are north's and south's share of world expenditure, respectively (so $s_E + s_E^* = 1$), and the Δ's are defined in (16.3). Finally, recall that the standard normalizations that ensure that world expenditure, E^w, equals unity and $n + n^* \equiv n^w = 1$ (see Chapter 4 for details).

16.3.2 Nash Competition for Entrepreneurs

The most direct method of establishing the Tiebout hypothesis in this model is to assert that the first-best tax rate is an equilibrium, and then to show that no nation would deviate from this equilibrium. Given our functional forms, the first-best tax rate is trivial to calculate. If all factors are perfectly immobile, Y/P is a parameter, so $W = t^{\gamma}(1 - t)^{1-\gamma}$, the maximum of which obtains at $t = \gamma$.

Now allowing capital mobility, we wish to establish that $t = t^* = \gamma$ is a Nash equilibrium of the tax game. To do this, we ask whether north could improve its payoff by varying its tax rate slightly when the amount of capital in the north, that is, n, can vary in response to tax differentials. Starting off at $t = t^* = \gamma$, any deviation will, by definition of the optimal tax rate, decrease utility in the region and therefore lead to delocation of entrepreneurs until utility is equalized in the two regions. The resulting asymmetric equilibrium implies lower welfare because the relative utility curve is downward sloping. Put differently, any deviation from the optimal tax rate (which is positive due to the welfare effects of the public good) means a static welfare loss as well as a loss due to delocation of entrepreneurs, which erodes the tax base. Consequently, north would not want to deviate from $t = t^* = \gamma$ and south would come to the same conclusion, so this is a Nash equilibrium.

The Nash equilibrium can also be established by mechanically differentiating the payoff function, W, and evaluating the derivative at the Nash tax rate. This exercise is facilitated by noting that W can be broken into two sub-functions, one involving only t and the other involving only n. That is, $W = f[t]g[n]$, where $f[t] \equiv t^{\gamma}(1 - t)^{1-\gamma}$ and $g[n] \equiv Y/P$. Using this, we find

---

[5] Assuming an everywhere-downward-sloping, relative utility curve rules out catastrophic agglomeration.

$$\frac{dW}{dt} = \frac{d(t^{\gamma}(1-t)^{1-\gamma})}{dt}\Bigg|_{t=\gamma} \frac{Y}{P} + \left((\gamma^{\gamma}(1-\gamma)^{1-\gamma})\frac{d(Y/P)}{dt}\right)\Bigg|_{n=1/2} \qquad (16.18)$$

we already know that the first right-hand term is zero, so the sign of dW/dt depends only on the sign of the second term. Using $Y = L + \pi n$, and our definition for P, (16.14), we find

$$\frac{d(Y/P)}{dt}\Bigg|_{n=1/2} = \left(\frac{\pi}{P}\left(1 + \frac{n}{\pi}\frac{d\pi}{dn}\right)\frac{dn}{dt} - \frac{Y}{P}\left(\frac{dP/dn}{P}\right)\frac{dn}{dt}\right)\Bigg|_{n=1/2},$$

$$\pi\left(1 + \frac{n}{\pi}\frac{d\pi}{dn}\right) = \frac{b}{1-b}\left(\frac{1-Z^2}{1-bZ}\right), \qquad \frac{dP/dn}{P} = -2aZ \qquad (16.19)$$

where derivatives are evaluated at the symmetric outcome, $L = 1/2$ by normalization, and Z is a measure of trade 'closed-ness' which varies from zero (free trade) to unity (no trade). By inspection, all terms in this expression are positive with the possible exception of dn/dt. Indeed, inspection of (16.19) reveals that the sign of $d(Y/P)/dt$ depends only on the sign of dn/dt (and, thus, the sign of dW/dt depends only on the sign of dn/dt). This intermediate result is quite intuitive; a deviation from the proposed equilibrium will improve northern welfare only if doing so raises northern real income by attracting more capital.

To investigate dn/dt, we totally differentiate the location condition, (16.16), with respect to n and t (taking t^* as given) and evaluate the result at the proposed equilibrium, that is, where $t = \gamma$ and $n = 1/2$. Noting that again we can separate the left-hand side of the location condition into two sub-functions, $f[t] \equiv t^{\gamma}(1 - t)^{1-\gamma}$ and the other involving only n—call it $g[n]$—the result of this calculation is

$$g\left[\frac{1}{2}\right]\frac{d(t^{\gamma}(1-t)^{1-\gamma})}{dt}\Bigg|_{t=\gamma} dt + f(t)\frac{d}{dn}\frac{Y^{\gamma}\pi^{1-\gamma}/P}{(t^*Y^*)^{\gamma}[(1-t^*)\pi^*]^{1-\gamma}/P^*}\Bigg|_{n=1/2} dn = 0 \qquad (16.20)$$

While it is simple to calculate the second term explicitly, this is not necessary. Noting that the first term must be zero (since $t = \gamma$ optimizes this sub-function), we know that dn must also be zero, that is, $dn/dt = 0$ at the proposed equilibrium. This implies that $dW/dt = 0$, so we know that north would not gain from deviating from the proposed equilibrium. By symmetry, south would also not wish to deviate, so the proposed equilibrium is a Nash equilibrium. To summarize this, we write the following result.

Result 16.5 (Tiebout corollary). *When factor owners move with their factor, and these owners have the same tastes as the owners of immobile factors, and governments have Benthamite objectives, Nash tax competition over the mobile factor will result in the first-best tax rate being set. In this sense, tax competition is harmless.*

The intuition behind this result is straightforward. Since taxes are used to provide public goods and the mobile factors care about local provision of public goods, the mobile factor acts as if they like taxes—at least up to a point. Since mobile and immobile factors have identical preferences, the tax rate that is most attractive to the mobile factor is also the tax rate most preferred by the immobile factor, so the government's attempt to attract the mobile factor ends up maximizing social welfare.

COMMENTS ON THE RESULT

This result is certainly not a proof that tax competition is harmless. What it tells us is that if tax competition is to be harmful in the standard economic geography models—that is, models where factors and their owners cross borders—then it is necessary to get away from one of the key assumptions. In particular, we either need that capital and its owners can be spatially separated, as in the FC model, or we need the government's objective function to be different from that of the mobile factor. Since we do wish to continue exploring harmful tax competition in the context of models where factor owners cross borders with their factors, the way forward is to revise the government's objective function.

Fortunately, the public finance literature has already provided many examples of non-Benthamite government objective functions. As we explain in detail below, the way that we favour rests on political economy explanations—the median voter model in particular.

16.4 Tax Competition and Capital Mobility

One of the primary tenants of the BTCM literature is that international capital mobility is the most important source of inefficient tax competition. The previous section showed that this focus misses a number of important points—mobility of goods also matters.

This section goes further and shows that even without capital mobility, international mobility of goods is enough to imply that tax competition among similar nations can be harmful. Moreover, in our example, capital mobility actually makes tax competition less harmful. We demonstrate this in the context of the 'constructed capital' (CC) model of Chapter 6.

16.4.1 The CC Model

For the reader's convenience, we quickly repeat the main assumptions and key expression of the 'constructed capital' model here; for details and motivations, see Chapter 6.

In its basic set-up, the constructed capital (CC) model closely resembles the FC model described above. There are two regions, two sectors, two factors, and all the naming conventions are the same. In particular, we think of capital as physical capital. On the demand side, the CC model works with the standard two-tier preferences (consumption of the Walrasian good and the CES composite of differentiated varieties are nested in a Cobb–Douglas function). The difference comes in the factor-supply and factor-mobility assumptions.

The CC model assumes that neither labourers nor capital are internationally mobile. Industry can only 'move' via an indirect mechanism. That is, industrial production can increase in one nation and decrease in the other via the construction and destruction of capital (as before, each unit of capital is associated with a specific differentiated variety). In this way, pressures that induced capital to physically cross borders in the FC model, lead to the creation of capital in the favoured nation and the destruction of capital in the disfavoured nation. In particular, the northern and southern capital stocks rise or fall until post-tax the reward to capital (measured in units of numeraire) equals the normal long-run return to capital, that is,

$$(1 - t)\pi = F(\rho + \delta), \quad (1 - t^*)\pi^* = F(\rho + \delta) \qquad (16.21)$$

where F is the marginal cost (in terms of the numeraire) of constructing a unit of capital, $F(\rho + \delta)$ is the equilibrium rate of return to capital and δ is the depreciation rate. In this section, we assume trade is sufficiently restricted so as to ensure that the symmetric interior equilibrium is stable (i.e. the level of openness is less than the 'break point'; see Chapter 6 for details). Importantly, depreciation takes a special form. Capital remains in perfect working order, until it 'dies', at which time it is perfectly useless and the variety/firm it was associated with disappears. Each unit of capital faces a constant probability, namely δ, of 'dying' at every instant; by the law of large numbers, exactly δ times the capital stock of each nation disappears each instant. Observe that capital's immobility means that GDP always equals GNP and north's share of world capital always equals its share of industry, that is, $s_K = s_n$. The π's in (16.21) for this model are given by (16.17) with $s_n \equiv n$.

Solving (16.21) for n, we get the so-called nn curve,

$$s_n - \frac{1}{2} = \left(\frac{1}{2Z}\right)\frac{2Z(s_E - 1/2) - (1 - T)/(1 + T)}{Z - 2(s_E - 1/2)(1 - T)/(1 + T)}, \quad T = \frac{1 - t}{1 - t^*} \qquad (16.22)$$

where $0 < Z < 1$ is our usual measure for trade 'closed-ness'. This expression says that when the tax rates and market sizes are equal, industry is evenly split between the two nations, that is, $n = 1/2$, and, thus, the national capital stocks are also equal. Moreover, it shows that the equilibrium n is decreasing in t and increasing in s_E, that is, the north's share of industry declines as it raises its tax rate (holding the southern rate constant), and an increase in the northern market size also tends to increase its share of industry (as expected from the home-market effect).

As far as the mechanics of the model are concerned, the equilibrium number of firms in each nation is maintained by the continual replacement of depreciated capital. More importantly, since capital's income is spent locally, a shift in the equilibrium number of firms affects relative market size, that is, s_E. As explained at length in Chapter 6, this introduces circular causality into the model and, thus, opens the door to catastrophic agglomeration and locational hysteresis. Specifi-

cally, using the definition of world expenditure, and the north's capital construction condition, $\pi(1 - t) = F(\rho + \delta)$, we can solve for E^w and n^w. Using these in
the definition of the north's share of world expenditure, we find the 'EE curve',

$$s_E - \frac{1}{2} = \left(\frac{b}{2}\right)\frac{2(1 - \delta[(1 - t)/(\rho + \delta)])(s_n - 1/2) - (1 - T)/(1 + T)}{1 - 2(s_n - 1/2)(1 - T)/(1 + T)}\,(16.23)$$

Again notice that with symmetry, that is, $s_K = 1/2$, and $t = t^*$, the north has half
the world's expenditure.

The CC model is tractable enough to allow the division of industry/capital to
be expressed as a simple function of parameters and the tax rates. Solving (16.22)
and (16.23), we get

$$s_n - \frac{1}{2} = \left(\frac{1}{2Z}\right)\frac{(1 - bZ)(1 - T)/(1 + T)}{b - Z - 2(1 - t)\beta}, \quad \beta \equiv \frac{b\delta}{\delta + b}\qquad (16.24)$$

With this, (16.21) and the definition of world expenditure, we can find the amount
of capital in the north and how it varies with tax rates. The solution is

$$n = \frac{b(1 - \beta)(1 - t)\big((1 + Z^2)(1 + T) - 2(1 + ZZ^B)\big)}{R[(4 - [(1 + Z)(1 + T) + 2ZZ^B](1 - Z))(1 + T) - 4(1 - b^2Z)}\qquad (16.25)$$

where n is the level of capital in the north, T is the tax gap, that is, $(1 - t)/(1 - t^*)$,
as usual and Z^B is the break point Z; throughout this section we limit ourselves to
levels of Z that are more closed than Z^B. Setting $T = 1$, we can readily see that the
amount of capital in the north varies with the tax rate, trade closed-ness and
agglomeration forces even when taxes are symmetric.

GOVERNMENT'S OBJECTIVE FUNCTION: MEDIAN VOTERS AND BIASED PUBLIC GOODS

In order to provide rudimentary micro-foundations for the government's objective function in the tax game, we continue to assume the existence of a public
good as a means of explaining why the government wants to boost its tax base.
How does the public good enter the government's objective function? The most
straightforward set of assumptions—that labour and capital owners have identical
preferences and the government is Benthamite—is unfortunately not fruitful. As
the previous section demonstrated, tax competition is harmless in such situations.
Since we do believe harmful international tax competition is an important facet of
reality, we need to follow a different path. The path we choose is that of the
median voter model.

The median voter model implies that the majoritarian group uses electoral
competition to force the government to adopt its preferences. Here, we make
assumptions that ensure that workers have a majority, so the government's objective function will be the preferences of workers. In this economy, the normalization that yields $E^w = 1$ requires that the labour supply in each economy is
measured in units such that $L = 1 - b$. Moreover, we measure units of capital
such that the capital stock in each nation is 1/2. The number of labourers and

capital owners, however, are not constrained by these assumptions since we have not specified the number of units of labour and capital owned, respectively, by labourers and capitalists. If each capitalist owns one unit of capital and each labourer own less than $2(1 - b)$ units of labour each, we know that the political voice of workers will always dominate the governmental choices.[6]

Our final political economy assumption concerns the nature of public goods. We assume that the nature of the public good provided is biased towards the interest of workers and against those of capitalists. The simplest form of such 'biased public goods'—the form assumed here—takes the extreme form that the public good provides utility to workers but not to capitalists.

For the sake of parsimony, we continue to assume that all consumers' tastes for private goods are identical, and that the tax rate on the two groups is identical. In particular, the preference of the two groups, are

$$U^L = G^\gamma C_L^{1-\gamma}, \quad U^K = C_K; \quad G = t\frac{Y}{P}, \quad C_L = (1-t)\frac{L}{P}, \quad C_k = (1-t)\frac{n\pi}{P}$$
(16.26)

where $Y = L + n\pi$, and we have used the solution for the consumers' problem to write demand for the private consumption composite in terms of incomes and the perfect price index.

16.4.2 Nash Tax Competition between Similar Nations

Governments play Nash in tax rates, so the northern government's first-order condition is

$$\frac{U_G^L}{U_C^L} = \frac{-\partial C_L/\partial t}{\partial G/\partial t}, \quad \frac{-\partial C_L/\partial t}{\partial G/\partial t} = \frac{1 - (1-t)(-P_n/P)(\partial n/\partial t)}{[1 + t(Y_n/Y - P_n/P)(\partial n/\partial t)]Y}$$
(16.27)

where $Y = L + \pi n$ as before. The expression for the right-hand side is found using (16.26) and the definitions of the price index and Y. We note that an increase in capital, that is, n, raises Y and P, so the size of the right-hand side is governed by the responsiveness of capital to the tax northern tax rate. Recalling that the left-hand side of the government's first-order condition is diminishing in t, we know that anything that increases the right-hand side diminishes the Nash equilibrium tax rate.[7] This line of reasoning directs us to investigate dn/dt more closely.

Differentiating (16.25) with respect to the north's tax rate and evaluating the result as the symmetric point, we find

$$\frac{\partial n}{\partial t} = \left(\frac{-b(1-\beta)}{4RZ}\right)\frac{1 + Z^2 - (1+Z)Z^B}{(1-bZ)^2(Z-Z^B)}$$
(16.28)

which is negative since $Z > Z^B$ and $Z^B < 1$. Using the above reasoning, this

---

[6] While this may seem like legerdemain, it merely says, for example, that we can decide how many identical labour owners there are independently of how much labour there is in the economy.

[7] As in the previous section, this single first-order condition plus symmetry, viz. $t = t^*$, allows us to find the Nash equilibrium tax rate.

means that the RHS of the government's first-order condition is less than unity, so the tax rate is below the social optimal. This result is not unusual except for the fact that capital is internationally immobile in this model.

Result 16.6. *In a model where capital is constructed rather than endowed, international tax competition leads to tax rates that are too low from the social perspective—even when capital is perfectly immobile. This contrasts sharply with the BTCM where capital mobility was the key cause of inefficient tax competition and removing capital mobility produced first-best taxation.*

Moreover, since Z is proportionally more important in the denominator than in the numerator in (16.28), we know that $d(dn/dt)/dZ$ is positive, that is, as trade gets less closed, capital becomes more responsive to tax changes (i.e. dn/dt gets more negative).[8] What this means is that the Nash equilibrium tax rate will fall as trade gets more open. Indeed, as Z approaches the break point, dn/dt become unboundedly large, so the Nash tax rate would drop to zero.

Result 16.7. *Since the industry becomes more 'footloose' as trade becomes freer, the Nash equilibrium tax rates are negatively correlated with trade openness—even when capital mobility is absent. Of course, here industry does not literally cross borders, but construction and destruction of capital leads to the same outcome.*

16.4.3 Tax Competition with Perfect Capital Mobility

As Chapter 6 showed, it is simple to re-solve the CC model for the case of perfect capital mobility and here we show that doing so is fruitful. We continue to assume that capital owners are immobile.

As Chapter 6 showed in detail, capital mobility is stabilizing when capital owners do not move with their capital. What this means is that the location of industry is *less* responsive to tax rates when capital is mobile. Following the reasoning from above, this tells us that dn/dt is lower when capital is mobile, so the degree of tax competition is less, in the sense that the Nash equilibrium tax rate would be higher with mobility than without it. This is summarized in the following result.

Result 16.8. *In a model where capital is constructed rather than endowed, we find a positive correlation between capital mobility and Nash equilibrium tax rates. This, of course, is just the opposite of the correlation generated by the BTCM.*

The policy corollary of this is stated in the following result.

Result 16.9. *International tax competition is less harmful when capital is mobile than when it is immobile. Thus, the incentive for similar nations to engage in tax harmonization is lower when capital is mobile. This reverses the correlation predicted by the BTCM.*

[8] More precisely, $d^2n/dtdZ = b(1 - \beta)(2Z - Z^B)/[(Z - Z^B)^2(1 - Z^B)RZ^2]$.

CONCLUDING REMARKS

Perhaps the main message of this section is that, in the long run, capital is always 'mobile' since capital can be constructed when conditions are favourable and it can depreciate when they are not. An important side effect of forcing capital to adjust to international differences via construction and destruction, rather than physical mobility, is that the former leads to knock-on effects on market size and these in turn can exaggerate initial differences. Thus, the finding that capital mobility may actually reduce tax competition may not be quite as other-worldly as it sounds.

16.5 TAX COMPETITION AND CATASTROPHIC AGGLOMERATION

In the previous chapter, we showed that when the relative real reward is sufficiently concave, a sufficiently large tax gap might result in a sudden displacement of industry to the low-tax region. In Figure 16.2, for instance, if the tax gap, that is, $(1 - t)/(1 - t^*)$, exceeded the maximum of the ratio of rewards to capital, that is, $\Omega^{\max}$, all industry would decamp to the south. This section considers how this possibility affects Nash tax competition.

To investigate this possibility, we need a model in which it can arise, and this requires us to switch to a model with stronger agglomeration forces. The FC and CC models we used in the previous sections have the merit of being entirely

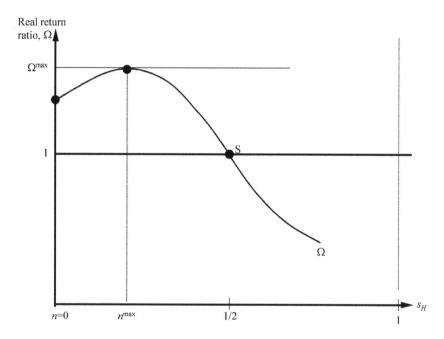

Figure 16.2 Taxation and catastrophes.

amenable to analytical reasoning, but the very linearity that makes them tractable rules out the possibility in which we are interested. For this reason, we turn to the FE model.

16.5.1 The FE Model, Tax Structure and Strategic Assumptions

The underlying economies assumed in the FE model were described briefly above and at length in Chapter 4. The basic tax structure we assume here is that of the previous section. Namely, political economy considerations lead the government to adopt labourer's utility as its objective and to spending tax revenue on a public good that favours labourers over capital owners ('entrepreneurs' in this model). Thus, the objective function is given by $W = U_L$, where U_L is defined in (16.26).

Given the discontinuous nature of the competition—a feature that is endemic to the lumpy-economy models of the economic geography literature—it is handy to realize that the government's problem cannot be fully captured by simple maximization techniques. In particular, two cases are of interest. If the Nash equilibrium exists, it will be symmetric and, given the underlying symmetry of nations, this means that half of the mobile factor will be in each nation. If a deviation from the Nash equilibrium occurs, it will involve all industry concentrated in, say, the south. The government's objectives in the two cases are

$$W^{sym} = \left(\frac{Y^s}{P^s}t\right)^{\gamma}\left((1-t)\frac{L}{P^s}\right)^{1-\gamma}, \quad W^p = \left(\frac{Y^p}{P^p}t\right)^{\gamma}\left(\frac{L}{P^p}(1-t)\right)^{1-\gamma};$$

$$Y^s = \frac{L^w + \pi}{2}, \quad Y^p = \frac{L^w}{2}$$

(16.29)

where the superscripts, s and p, refer to the symmetric outcome and the core–periphery outcome with the periphery in the north. Recall that with our normalizations, $L^w \equiv 1 - b$, $Y^s = 1/2$ and $Y^p = (1 - b)/2 < 1/2$. The two objective functions are depicted in Figure 16.3, with the higher bell-shaped curve representing W^{CPS}.

16.5.2 Nash Taxation

To build intuition, we first consider why the standard procedure for finding a Nash equilibrium does not work here. If we maximize W^s with respect to t, taking t^* as given, and then solve for t imposing symmetry, we will find a value of t, call it t'. As usual, tax competition implies that t' is to the left of the first-best outcome, marked as FB in Figure 16.3. The problem with solving for t' using the Nash first-order conditions is that this presumes that the local maximum, that is, t', is also the global maximum. Yet because the economy is lumpy, there may well be a non-marginal deviation that makes the north better off if the south stays at $t^* = t'$. To see this requires a bit of background.

In the previous chapter, we identified two cases. When trade is quite restricted, Ω is negatively sloped over the entire range of industry distribution, n. In this

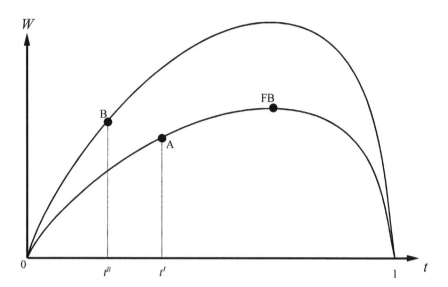

Figure 16.3 Nash taxation and non-marginal deviations.

case, the Nash tax game is globally stable in the sense that a small increase in the tax gap, what we call $T = (1 - t)/(1 - t^*)$, results in a small delocation of industry. In this case, the marginal analysis above is valid and t' is indeed the Nash equilibrium. However, when trade is freer, but still restricted enough to make the symmetric equilibrium stable (i.e. $\phi < \phi^B$), the Ω curve will have an interior maximum in the range $n = (0, 1/2)$, as shown in Figure 16.2. In this case, a tax gap that is just a little bit above the height of the Ω curve at its interior maximum, will lead all industry to move to the south.

The latter case—where there is a possibility of catastrophic agglomeration from a small tax change—is the case of interest to us in this section. In the previous chapter, we worked out the range of trade closed-ness, that is, the level of Z, where this possibility exists. We repeat it for convenience, that is, catastrophic tax competition is possible when

$$Z^P > Z > Z^B; \quad Z^P = \frac{\zeta - \sqrt{\zeta^2 - 4(a + b)^2}}{2(a + b)}, \quad Z^B = \frac{a + b}{1 + ab}, \quad (16.30)$$

$$\zeta \equiv 1 + b(b + 2a) > 0$$

where Z^B is just the break point level of trade closed-ness, and, as usual, $a = \mu/(\sigma - 1)$ and $b = \mu/\sigma$. Of course, when trade is freer than Z^B, the symmetric outcome is unstable, so any slight tax deviation would lead to emergence of the core–periphery outcome.

Limiting ourselves to Z's that respects (16.30), Ω has an interior maximum. This level is of great interest to us. As explained in the previous chapter, it occurs at the level of n equal to $n^{\max}$ where

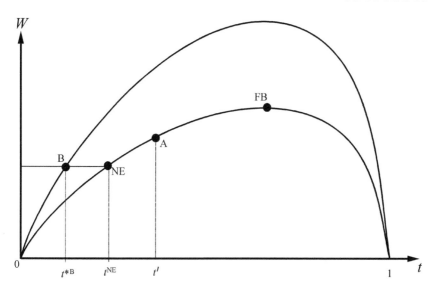

Figure 16.4   Nash solution with catastrophes.

$$n^{\max} = \frac{1}{2} - \frac{\sqrt{(1-bZ)A[a(bZ-1)+Z-b]}}{2AZ};$$

$$A \equiv \psi Z - (a+b)Z^2 - b(1+ab), \tag{16.31}$$

$$\lambda \equiv (1-Z^2)[(b-a)(1+Z^2) + (1-(b-2a)b)Z]$$

Using this, we can define the 'break point tax gap', T^B, as the minimum level of T where the sudden jump to the CP outcome occurs:

$$T^B = (\Omega^{\max})^{-1} \tag{16.32}$$

where $\Omega^{\max}$ is the Ω evaluated at $n^{\max}$ from (16.31).

By way of explanation, we note that the reasoning is conducted as if the south is the deviating region, so T^B implicitly defines the extent to which the south would have to undercut the north's tax in order to get the core. Given the definition of T, this break point southern tax is just $t^{*B} = 1 - (1-t)\Omega^{\max}$.

Returning to Figure 16.4, if t^{*B} is greater than zero (we limit the analysis to non-negative taxes), then the south may find that its welfare rises when it deviates from $t^* = t'$ by setting $t^* = t^{*B}$. One such case is illustrated in Figure 16.3; at t^{*B} the south's welfare with the core is given by point B. Because point B is higher than point A, the non-marginal deviation, from t' to t^{*B}, is welfare improving. In short, the south would have an incentive to deviate from the $t = t^* = t'$ outcome, so this is not a Nash equilibrium. But what is the equilibrium in this case?

The key to finding the Nash tax equilibrium is to define what must be true about the symmetric Nash rate, call this t^{NE}, so that deviation is not interesting to the south. If this condition holds, symmetry tells us that deviation is also not interesting to the north, so t^{NE} is Nash. The 'no deviation' condition is

$$W^p(t^B) \le W^s(t^{NE}), \quad 0 < t^B = 1 - (1 - t^{NE})\Omega^{max} \quad (16.33)$$

This is illustrated in Figure 16.4. The crucial point is that the Nash tax *level* must be so low that the degree of tax undercutting that is necessary to 'steal' the core is unattractive. Specifically, the degree to which the deviation rate, t^B, is below the Nash rate (i.e. the horizontal distance between points NE and B in the diagram) is related to the Nash rate itself by

$$t^{NE} - t^B = (1 - t^{NE})(\Omega^{max} - 1) \quad (16.34)$$

Thus, the Nash rate gets pushed down until deviation is unattractive.

In Figure 16.4, the 'naive' Nash equilibrium, t', that is, the one that only considers local deviations, is above the global Nash equilibrium, t^{NE}. Investigating this ordering analytically would involve comparing the level of Ω at a given point, Ω^{max}, with the derivative of Ω at the symmetric point. While the derivative is simple, Ω^{max} is too complex to work with. To get around this difficulty, we numerically solve for the naive and true Nash equilibria for a variety of trade costs and a range of agglomeration forces. What we find is that for weak and moderate agglomeration forces, the naive rate is always higher than the global rate, so the global rate is binding. For strong agglomeration forces, the global rate is only binding for sufficiently low levels of trade closed-ness.[9]

16.6 UNEVEN TAX COMPETITION AND ASYMMETRIC NATIONS: RACE TO THE TOP AND BOTTOM

Not surprisingly, some of the most unexpected insights from adding agglomeration forces to a model with tax competition are found when agglomeration is most important, namely, when all industry is already agglomerated in a single region. This leads us to study the impact of agglomeration forces on tax competition between uneven regions. As we shall see, tax competition in this situation can reverse most of the results from the 'basic tax competition model'. This section is based on Baldwin and Krugman (2000).

16.6.1 FE Model, Additional Assumptions and the Tax Game

We model the underlying economy with the FE model, but we need to make a few additional assumptions.

We start with the case where all industry is agglomerated in one region, the north to be specific, so implicitly we are limiting ourselves to a level of openness where full agglomeration is stable, that is, where the level of trade freeness, ϕ, exceeds the sustain point, ϕ^S (see Chapter 4 for details).

It might seem that the most straightforward tax game set-up would be a simultaneous-move Nash, as was employed above. However, this is not possible in the

[9] The numerical calculations are in the Maple worksheet 'cat_tax_comp.mws' freely available on http://heiwww.unige.ch/~baldwin/

current setting. By the usual logic of economic geography models, when trade is free enough to sustain the core–periphery outcome, the movement of capital becomes very discontinuous. If the north's tax rate is high enough to induce one entrepreneur to delocate to the south, then all will (see Chapter 4 for details). This discontinuity implies that the government's reaction functions are discontinuous, and this, in turn, implies that the Nash tax game has no pure strategy equilibrium (more on this below).

Instead, we follow Baldwin and Krugman (2000) in assuming a 'limit taxing' game. Specifically, north (the nation that initially has the core) sets its tax rate, t, in the first stage, south sets its rate, t^*, in the second stage, and then migration and production occur in the third stage. Clearly this structure maximizes the ability of the south to engage in fiscal competition. We continue to assume that each nation applies the same tax rate to both factors of production, and, as before, we assume the government cares only about the median voters and supplies only a biased public good.

The second significant extension concerns the impact of national wealth on preferences for public amenities. The tendency of rich voters to desire more government spending is well documented so this could be viewed as a natural assumption. But more to the point, it is crucial to one of the main results in this section. One of the stylized facts we would like to account for is that rich, capital abundant nations often have higher tax rates, and indeed poor, capital-scarce regions often see their capital moving to high-tax regions. As it turns out in our tax game, this requires the core region to have a stronger preference for taxation in the sense that in the absence of tax competition, the core would choose a higher rate than the periphery. Median voters in the core nation are richer than they are in the periphery regions (since the price index is lower in the core; see Chapter 4 for details), so all we need to assume is that preferences for public goods are stronger when consumers are richer. Figure 16.5

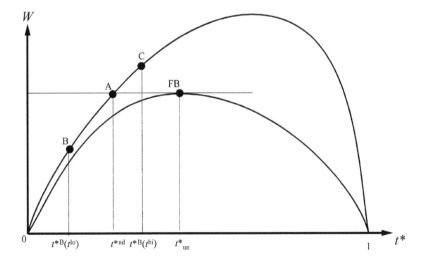

Figure 16.5 Second stage choice by the south.

shows an example of such preferences. In the diagram, the top curve shows the utility as a function of the tax rate for a rich region (i.e. the region with the core) and the bottom curve is for a poor region. The key point is that the utility maximum occurs at a higher tax rate for the rich region.

16.6.2 Intermediate Results and Equilibrium Expressions

The tax game is solved last stage first, but the last stage yields an economic outcome that is described by the equilibrium conditions laid out in the previous chapter. For completeness and convenience, we repeat the key expressions; for details see the previous chapter.

AGGLOMERATION AND THE TAX GAP

We assume that entrepreneurs migrate to the nation that offers the highest post-tax real reward, so it is useful to have an expression for what the ratio of real rewards would be without taxes. Using the equilibrium expressions for the reward to capital in the north and south as well as the definition of price indices, the ratio of the real rewards with all capital in the north (i.e. $s_n = s_H = n = 1$) is

$$\Omega^{CP} \equiv \left.\frac{\pi/P}{\pi^*/P^*}\right|_{n=1} = \frac{\phi}{1 - (1 - \phi^2)[s_L(1 - b) + b]} \qquad (16.35)$$

where π and π^* are the rewards to capital in the north and the south, respectively, P and P^* are the northern and southern price indices and s_L is the north's share of the world's supply of the immobile factor (this measures the intrinsic size difference between the two nations). Parsimony leads us to work with intrinsically symmetric nations, so $s_L = 1/2$ throughout this section.

Two aspects of (16.35) are particularly important for what follows. First, the before tax real return ratio in the CP outcome, Ω^{CP}, does not depend upon taxes as long as the CP outcome is stable. In this 'lumpy' world, marginal tax changes never induce marginal changes in Ω^{CP}; either all capital is in the north and the real reward ratio (pre-tax) is Ω^{CP}, or all capital is in the south and the ratio is just the inverse of Ω^{CP}. Second, as we saw in the previous chapter, the agglomeration rent, Ω^{CP}, is hump-shaped in the freeness of trade.

THE SUSTAIN POINT TAX GAP

The question now is: How much can north tax its entrepreneurs without provoking a tax exodus? One way to answer this is to find the highest tax gap that the north can sustain without losing industry. As in the previous chapter, we call this the 'sustain point tax gap' and denote it as T^B. More precisely, none of the mobile factor will move as long as the tax gap satisfies the 'break point condition'

$$T\Omega^{CP} > 1 \quad \Leftrightarrow \quad T < T^B \equiv \frac{2 - (1 + b)(1 - \phi^2)}{2\phi} \qquad (16.36)$$

16.6.3 Equilibrium Taxes

In solving the second stage, it is important to observe that the southern objective function is discontinuous. If the south chooses a sufficiently high tax rate, no industry/entrepreneurs will move from north to south; southern tax revenue is then just t^* times its supply of the immobile factor, L^*. If, however, the south chooses a tax rate low enough to attract all industry, that is, to capture the core, it has a higher tax base and, thus, higher revenue for any given tax rate. We refer to the threshold south tax rate as t^{*B}, and note from (16.36) that $t^{*B} = 1 - \Omega^{CP}(1 - t)$.

Figure 16.5 illustrates the discontinuous problem facing southern tax setters in the second stage. The vertical axis shows the metric for the government's objective function and the horizontal axis plots the southern tax rate, t^*. The top bell-shaped curve is the southern objective function when the core has delocated to the south. The lower bell-shaped curve is the southern objective function when the core remains in the north.

To find the optimal southern tax rate for a given t, we compare the optimal t^* from the two cases. In the core-stays-in-north case, the southern government is unconstrained by its desired to have the core. Indeed, the delocation elasticity is zero, so the south's unconstrained choice will be the first-best, marked FB in the diagram. The southern government's alternative is choose a tax rate low enough to get the core. Here, the southern government's objective function is the upper bell-shaped curve, but in this case, t^* must be no higher than t^{*B}, or else the core would not migrate southward. (Since the core-in-the-south objective function is necessarily increasing at t^{*B}, the south would actually choose t^{*B}, if it decides to go for the core). It is important to note that the level of t^{*B} depends upon the level of t set by the northern government in the first stage. Figure 16.5 shows two possibilities. When the north chooses a high t, t^{*B} is also high, for example, at the level marked as $t^{*B}(t^{hi})$. When north chooses a low t, t^{*B} is also low, for example at $t^{*B}(t^{lo})$. As drawn, the southern government would lower t^* to t^{*B}—and, thus, steal the core—if the northern government had chosen t^{hi}, but not if the north chose t^{lo}. If the northern government chose t^{lo}, the south would find it optimal to allow the core to remain in the north, choosing t^*_{un} instead of $t^{*B}(t^{lo})$. In short, moving to the higher schedule would be worth paying the price of a constrained tax rate when t is at t^{hi}, but not when it is at t^{lo}.

NORTH'S CHOICE IN STAGE ONE

Of course, the north is aware of its influence over the south's decision. The lower is the t chosen, the lower will be t^{*B} and, thus, the less attractive will be the core-stealing option to the south's government. In the first stage, the north will presumably want to set its rate such that the south will *not* find it worthwhile to 'snatch' the core. What the north has to do, then, is to push its tax rate low enough so that the south is indifferent between its unconstrained optimum without the core and its constrained optimum with it—a situation illustrated in Figure 16.6. The top

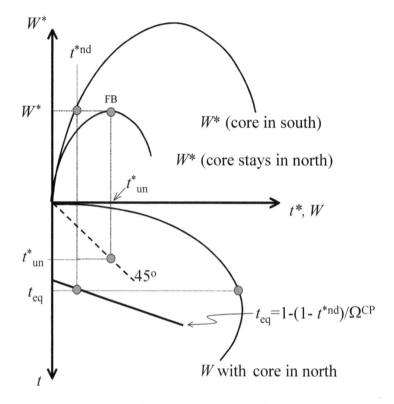

Figure 16.6 North's stage one choice.

panel of the diagram reproduces the stage-two sub-game for the south. Mechanically, the equilibrium north rate—call this t_{eq}—is calculated by first finding t_{un}^* and its corresponding objective function level, marked FB in Figure 16.6. Using this level, we find the corresponding t^{*B} which would make the south just indifferent to taking the core. This is labelled t^{*nd} since it is defined by a 'no deviation' condition

$$W^{*core}(t^{*nd}) \leq W^*(t_{un}^*) \tag{16.37}$$

in the diagram. Finally we find the implied northern tax rate, what we call t_{eq}, we use the 'no break point condition' (16.36) for the case when $t^{*B} = t^{*nd}$.

Plainly this 'limit tax' game is akin to the equilibrium of a Stackleberg oligopoly game where the leader 'limit prices' a potential entrant.

We must also check that the north actually prefers the tax rate it needs to keep the core to the tax rate it would have if it surrendered the core, but at least when $s_L = 1/2$, this is easy. In this case, the 'with-core' and 'without-core' W's for the north are the same as those for the south. Since t_{eq} is greater than t^{*nd} and the north has the core, we see that the north is better off charging t_{eq} and keeping the core than it would be letting the core go and charging t_{un}.

To summarize, the analytical expression for the north tax rate is

$$t_{eq} = 1 - \frac{1 - t^{*nd}}{\Omega^{CP}} \tag{16.38}$$

Three facts are noteworthy. First, t_{eq} rises and falls with the level of agglomeration rents, Ω^{CP}. Second, the tax competition only constrains the high-tax country on the margin, and third, the north's rate is linked to a 'shadow' southern rate—that southern rate that would make the south just indifferent to having the core—rather than to the actual rate t^*_{un}.

WHICH NATION CHARGES A HIGHER RATE?

Because t_{eq}, is linked to the southern no-deviation rate rather than the south's applied rate, t^*_{un}, we cannot be sure that t_{eq} is above the rate that the south actually applies. To investigate the issue, we apply a log-linear approximation to (16.38) so we can write $t_{eq} - t^{*nd}$ as approximately equals $\Omega^{CP} - 1$. To find the difference between t^*_{un} and t^{*nd}, we note that the southern government's payoff function can be written as a function of the tax rate and the amount of capital/industry in the south, that is, $W[t^*, n^*]$. Approximating around the t^{*nd} point, $W[t^*_{un}, 0] \approx W[t^{*nd}, 1] + W_t[t^{*nd}, 1](t^*_{un} - t^{*nd}) + W_n[t^{*nd}, 1](0 - 1)$, where subscripts on W indicate partials as usual. Since $W[t^*_{un}, 0] = W[t^{*nd}, 1]$ by definition of t^{*nd}, the gap $t^*_{un} - t^{*nd}$ is approximately equal to $W_n[t^{*nd}, 1]/W_t[t^{*nd}, 1]$. Combining these two approximations, we have

$$t_{eq} - t^*_{un} \approx \Omega^{CP} - 1 - \left(\frac{\partial W / \partial n}{\partial W / \partial t} \right) \tag{16.39}$$

Plainly, depending upon the size of agglomeration rents and the precise shape of the southern government's objective function, the applied-rate gap may be positive or negative. In Figure 16.6, we have drawn it for the case where the applied-rate gap is positive. This is the point where it is crucial that we assume that richer nations want higher tax rates. If preferences instead were as in Figure 16.4, the core would never *want* to charge a higher rate than the south.

NON-EXISTENCE OF PURE NASH EQUILIBRIUM

It should be clear now why we cannot rely on a simultaneous-move Nash tax game. If the south took the north's rate as given, it would not want to deviate; however, if the north took the south's rate as given, it would wish to raise its rate. But if it raised its rates, the south would find it optimal to 'steal' the core, and then the north's rate would no longer be optimal. In short, the discontinuities in the reaction functions—and these are inevitable in a lumpy economy—rule out the existence of a Nash equilibrium in pure strategies.

16.6.4 First Results

The situation just described differs quite markedly from that of the standard tax competition model (BTCM). The countries are symmetric in size, according to the BTCM definition (equal amounts of the fixed factor), but they have different tax rates. In particular, the nation with the larger market, higher capital/labour ratio and higher per capita income may have the higher tax rate. Moreover, if the situation started from a stable symmetry outcome that become unstable as trade became freer, during the emergence of the core, we would observe capital moving from the poor, low-tax region to the rich, high-tax region with the process continuing until all of the mobile factor had left the poor south.

As we showed in Chapter 4, the CP outcome is more likely (happens at a lower level of openness) when the nations are asymmetric in size. Thus, if the north were intrinsically bigger, the core would be more likely to be in the north. Furthermore, size asymmetries strengthen agglomeration forces in the core as we can see from (16.35).

To summarize the new results with asymmetric countries, that is, the results that could not be derived in the BTCM, we write the following results.

Result 16.10. *Tax competition with perfectly mobile capital implies that countries that are intrinsically of equal size (size defined in terms of supplies of the immobile factor) end up with different tax rates when trade becomes sufficiently free.*

Result 16.11. *Tax competition bears on the two nations in a very asymmetric manner. The large, rich country is constrained to charge a rate that is lower than what its government would wish, but the small poor country feels no constraint from international tax competition. Consequently, from the governmental perspective, only the big country's tax rate is too low.*

Result 16.12. *The predicted negative correlation between high taxes and capital/labour ratios predicted by the BCTM may be reversed.*

Result 16.13. *Large, rich countries may be importers of capital despite the fact that they have higher tax rates.*

16.6.5 Tax Competition and Trade Liberalization: Race to the Top?

Next, we look at how international economic integration in the form of trade opening would affect international tax competition and equilibrium tax rates.

The first point rests on the fact that the agglomeration rent, Ω^{CP}, is a hump-shaped function of trade freeness. The previous chapter demonstrated this in detail, but roughly speaking, agglomeration forces are strongest at intermediate levels of trade costs since that is when agglomeration is both feasible (trade costs are low enough so that the periphery market can be readily serviced via exports) and necessary (trade costs are high enough to make it important to be in the big market).

Given this, inspection of (16.39) together with our knowledge of the hump-shape of Ω^{CP} shows that the tax gap tends to be bell-shaped. In particular, if W_n/W_t does not change too much with trade costs, the north rate first raises and then lowers the tax gap in response to trade integration. What this says is that during an initial phase of economic integration, making trade freer tends to relax the extent to which tax competition constrains the north, but after trade gets free enough, the correlation is reversed in the sense that tighter integration of goods markets corresponds to a narrower dispersion of tax rates on the mobile factor. Note that this result does not rely on the assumption that public goods are luxury goods. The tax gap is driven by the hump-shaped agglomeration rent even if $t_{eq}^* < t_{un}^*$ at all levels of openness.

The second point rests on the fact that trade liberalization will make the southern median voters progressively richer. As usual, reduced trade costs make imported varieties cheaper and this raises the real wage of southern workers. Given our assumption that public amenities are a luxury good, we know that the south's applied tax rate, that is, t_{un}^*, will rise with trade integration. Again, assuming that W_n/W_t does not change too much with trade costs, the rising t_{un}^* will result in a rising t^{*nd}. Using this result in (16.38) and recalling the bell-shaped nature of Ω, we could get something that resembled a 'race to the top'. In other words, trade liberalization raises real per capita incomes in both north and south for the usual static reasons, so the south—whose government is unconstrained by tax competition in equilibrium—will raise its rate, t_{un}, as trade liberalization proceeds. Since the north's rate is essentially the south's rate plus the agglomeration rent, the north's rate will also tend to rise. Initially—when trade freeness was fairly low (i.e. on the upward slope of the bell)—the northern rate would rise faster than the southern rate, although both would be rising. Later when agglomeration rents begin their descent down the downward slope of the bell, the northern rate would fall relative to the south's rate. We cannot say a priori whether it would fall in absolute terms or merely in relative terms. Graphically, this would look like a tilted bell in Figure 16.7. To summarize, we write the following results.

> **Result 16.14.** *The correlation between international tax gaps and openness should be positive over some range of trade openness, but negative over another. Specifically, the correlation should be positive when trade is relatively restricted and negative when it is relatively free.*

> **Result 16.15.** *If the preference for public goods rise with per capita income, international tax competition together with trade liberalization may produce a 'race to the top'—in the sense that low-tax poor nations and high-tax rich nations both raise their tax rates with liberalization, but the rich nation should raise it more quickly—for some range of trade openness.*

16.6.6 Tax Harmonization

As it turns out, this set-up suggests that tax harmonization has somewhat unexpected results. In the basic tax competition model, tax harmonization is basically

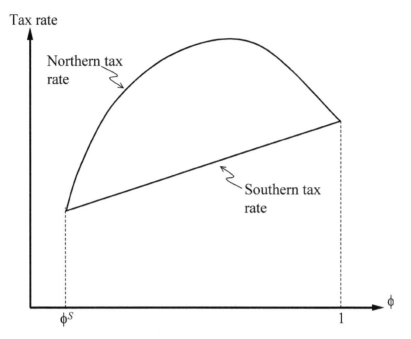

Figure 16.7 Tilted bell tax competition: race to top and bottom.

a shift from a non-cooperative tax game to a cooperative tax game. As a result, harmonization leads to a Pareto improvement from the government's perspective almost by definition.

Consider first the most straightforward tax harmonization scheme, that is, adoption of a common rate that lies between the two initial rates, t_{eq} and t_{un}^*. As it turns out, this split-the-difference harmonization makes both north and south worse off as Figure 16.8 shows. First, note that this single rate, t_A in the diagram, would not lead to a shift in the core from north to south since with equal taxes, firms prefer to stay agglomerated in the large region. Given that the south remains without industry, the south's loss follows directly from the fact that its pre-harmonization rate was an unconstrained maximum. The loss for the north is similarly clear. Compared to the initial equilibrium, the harmonization forces the north to lower its tax rate, when in fact the north would have preferred to raise it.

A second possible candidate for the single-rate harmonization would entail a rise in both nations' rates to something like t_C in the diagram. Here, the north would gain (since its tax-competition constraint would be relaxed) but the south would lose for the reasons just mentioned; any change in the equilibrium southern rate lowers the south's welfare as measured by its government's objective function. Lowering of both rates to something like t_B would also make both governments worse off.

Intuition for this result is simple. When the underlying economic geography is lumpy, tax competition is a rather one-sided affair. The capital-rich, high-tax

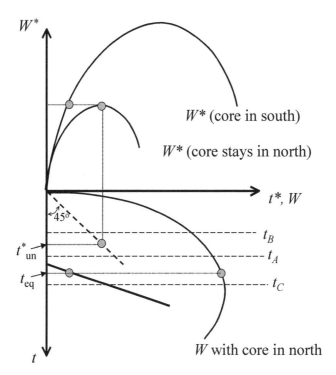

Figure 16.8   Welfare worsening tax harmonization.

region continuously worries that the poor south will steal its industry, and this threat constrains it to charge a rate that it considers too low. The capital-poor region, on the other hand, understands that the capital-rich region will never allow it to win the competition for industry clusters, so its rate is set without regard to tax competition. Given this asymmetry, there is no mutual gain to harmonization. To summarize, we write the following result.

> **Result 16.16.** *Simple tax harmonization, that is, adoption of a common rate, cannot be Pareto improving, and depending upon the rate chosen, such harmonization may make both nations worse off.*

As a corollary, we write the following result.

> **Result 16.17.** *Tax harmonization should be very difficult politically since tax competition in the presence of agglomeration forces implies that big rich nations will want it only if it raises their tax rates, but tax setting in poor small nations is not particularly constrained by tax competition, so they will be unwilling to change their rate without being compensated by substantial transfers.*

While the most straightforward tax harmonization scheme would never be agreed to, there is a simple proposal that would be weakly Pareto improving from the government's perspectives, namely a simple tax floor set just below the equilibrium tax rate of the low-tax nation. The reasoning is uncomplicated. In order to dissuade the south from 'stealing' the core in the limit tax game, the north must ensure that even if the south did get the core, it would be no better off than if it did not have the core. This, in turn, requires the north to base its rate on the off-equilibrium southern tax t^{*nd}—and this despite the fact that the south ends up charging the higher rate t^*_{un} in equilibrium. By setting the minimum just below the south's equilibrium rate, the minimum tax scheme rules out the off-equilibrium t^{*nd} by fiat. Given this, the north can now base its rate on the higher equilibrium southern rate, t^*_{un}. This effectively relaxes a binding constraint on the north's choice, so the tax-floor scheme raises the level of the north's objective function. The scheme has, by construction, no impact on the south's situation.

> **Result 16.18.** *Since tax competition in the presence of agglomeration is one-sided, with the big, rich country feeling the brunt of the pressure, a tax floor set at the level of the small country's tax rate can lessen the tax pressure in the big country without altering the situation for the small country. This would be a weak Pareto improvement.*

16.7 Concluding Remarks and Related Literature

This chapter has demonstrated that, allowing for the sort of considerations that are at the heart of the new economic geography, new light can be shed on issues of international tax competition. Some of the insights may have direct relevance to the world of policy. For instance, it offers an explanation for why it is so hard to agree on tax harmonization and it suggests one scheme that might be more politically acceptable. Other insights may help us to understand the stylized facts of taxation—for example, that despite increased capital mobility almost all European nations *raised* their tax rates on mobile factors during the 1970s and indeed the rich nations raised them faster than did the poor nations. Many other insights, however, are cautionary. For example, we have repeatedly seen that the level of trade integration affects tax competition so empirical studies that focus solely on the degree of capital mobility are missing an important element. Moreover, the relationships are rife with non-linearity, non-monotonicity and catastrophes that empiricists may have to account for in their regression.

16.7.1 Related Literature

Relatively few papers to date address issues of taxes and tax competition in an economic geography framework. The first paper was probably Ludema and Wooton (2000), who focus on the effects of integration on the intensity of tax competition in a framework with homogeneous-good oligopoly and moving costs (as opposed to the differentiated-product approach). They conclude that integration interpreted as decreasing trade costs, contrary to popular notions, attenuates tax competition because of the inertia resulting from concentration of the mobile factor in one region.

The first paper illustrating the lumpiness due to the hump-shaped agglomeration rents in a standard trade and location model was Kind et al. (2000). They show that a country hosting an agglomeration may find it optimal to levy a source-based tax on capital income, whereas it is optimal to subsidize if countries are symmetric. Andersson and Forslid (1999) introduce public goods and redistributing taxes. Trionfetti (2001) analyses a model with a home market bias in the procurement of public goods. Because of this, the introduction of public goods constitutes a dispersion force. Norman (2000) analyses tax competition and public goods in a regional setting.

Baldwin and Krugman (2000) analyse a limit-tax game between a large leader country and a small follower. Ottaviano and Van Ypersele (2002) obtain similar results in a simultaneous-move game based on the linear FC model of Chapter 5. In particular, in the case of asymmetrically sized countries, they show that tax competition can be beneficial from a global welfare viewpoint for high trade barriers, and detrimental otherwise. Finally, Forslid and Midelfart Knarvik (2001) analyse optimal taxation of an industrial cluster of upstream and downstream goods, using the FEVL model of Chapter 8.

REFERENCES

Andersson, F. and R. Forslid. 2003. Tax competition and economic geography. *Journal of Public Economic Theory* 5: 279–304.

Baldwin, R. E. and R. Forslid. 2002a. Tiebout efficiency, agglomeration and trade costs. HEI manuscript, Geneva.

———. 2002b. Tax competition and the nature of capital. HEI manuscript, Geneva.

Baldwin, R. E. and P. Krugman. 2000. Agglomeration, integration and tax harmonisation. Discussion Paper No. 2630, Centre for Economic Policy Research.

Forslid, R. and K. H. Midelfart Knarvik. 2002. Internationalisation, industrial policy and clusters. Discussion Paper No. 3129, Centre for Economic Policy Research..

Kind, H., K. H. Midelfart Knarvik and G. Schjelderup. 2000. Competing for capital in a "lumpy" world. *Journal of Public Economics* 78: 253–274.

Ludema, R. and I. Wooton. 2000. Economic geography and the fiscal effects of regional integration. *Journal of International Economics* 52: 331–357.

Norman, E. B. 2000. Agglomeration, tax competition and local public goods supply. Working Paper No. 49, Samfunns-og Næringslivsforskning AS.

Ottaviano, G. I. P. and T. Van Ypersele. 2002. Market access and tax competition. Mimeo, Graduate Institute of International Studies and Facultés Universitaires Notre-Dame de la Paix de Namur (FUNDP).

Trionfetti, F. 2001. Public procurement, marekt integration, and income inequalities. *Review of International Economics* 9(1): 29–41.

P A R T   V

Regional Policy

Infrastructure Policies and Economic Geography

17.1 INTRODUCTION

This chapter proposes a very simple way to analyse some of the effects of regional policies on industrial geography, regional income disparities and growth. For this, we use the 'localized spillovers' model of Chapter 7 in which both the location and the endogenous growth rate of industry are simultaneously determined. The model is extended to allow explicit consideration of different public policies such as infrastructure policies, transfers and subsidies to technology transfers. An important message of this section, which is based on Martin (1998, 1999), is that the presence of localized technology spillovers implies that a trade-off exists between spatial efficiency and equity when infrastructure policies reduce transport costs either between or inside regions. Public policies that facilitate the inter-regional diffusion of technology spillovers have very different implications and do not face this trade-off. European policy makers believe that regional policies are not only necessary to improve equity but also efficiency. To give a chance to this argument, we analyse regional policies in the presence of congestion effects. Multiple equilibria may appear even with capital mobility: a 'good' equilibrium with high growth and low spatial concentration and a 'bad' equilibrium with low growth and high spatial concentration. In the presence of congestion costs, policies that improve infrastructure in the poor region can improve growth and reduce inequality. Again, however, policies that facilitate the inter-regional diffusion of technology spillovers are better.

17.1.1 Organization of the Chapter

Section 17.2 introduces inter-regional and intra-regional trade costs in the 'localized spillovers' model and analyses different policy experiments: transfers to the poor regions, better transport infrastructures inside regions, better transport infrastructures between regions and policies towards technology spillovers. It then extends the analysis to a three-region geography. Congestion effects are introduced in Section 17.3. Finally, non-linear effects of public policies are discussed in Section 17.4 in a model with agglomeration.

17.2 PUBLIC POLICIES: GROWTH AND GEOGRAPHY EFFECTS

17.2.1 The Extended LS Model

The workhorse model in this chapter is an extended version of the local spillovers (LS) model that was presented at length in Chapter 7. For the reader's convenience, we repeat the main features of the LS model before introducing the extensions.

The model's basic set-up has two regions (north and south), two factors (workers and capital) and two final good sectors (manufactures, M, and a homogenous good, A). The manufactured goods sector is marked by Dixit–Stiglitz monopolistic competition and its output is subject to iceberg trade costs. The A sector is Walrasian and its output is traded costlessly both within and between regions. Capital is used only in the manufacturing sector and then in a very specific way. Each variety of the manufactured good requires one unit of capital as its fixed cost, but all variable costs are accounted for by labour inputs. The A good is produced according to constant returns using labour as the only input. Neither labour nor capital owners are mobile between regions, but since capital is a 'disembodied' factor (think of physical capital or patents), it can be employed in the other region. To keep things simple, suppose that capital is perfectly mobile in the sense that it can move between regions without cost. All capital earning is repatriated to the region where its owner is located. To allow for growth, the model has an innovation sector (the I sector) that produces new units of capital. This sector employs only labour and, to allow for ceaseless growth, the sector is assumed to be subject to a learning curve in the sense that the amount of labour needed to produce a new unit of capital falls as the cumulative number of units produced rises. The idea is that experience on past production improves the productivity of current production. Importantly, the model assumes that this sort of learning spillover is partially localized. That is, northern I sector workers learn more from northern innovations than they do from southern innovations (see Chapter 7 for details and motivation).

The extension involves the addition of another transport cost and, thus, another dimension for policy intervention. Specifically, we introduce transaction costs inside regions (as usual, these costs compromise all costs of selling at a distance), so trade costs exist both *between* regions (*inter*-regional trade costs) and *inside* regions (*intra*-regional trade costs). We presume that public infrastructure can affect both kinds of costs independently.

As public policies alter trade costs, they influence economic geography, and, because of localized learning spillovers, this in turn affects the growth rate. The model displays, from a theoretical point of view, a policy trade-off between aggregate growth and regional equity.[1] This implies that regional policies that improve regional equity, improving, for instance, infrastructures in the poor region in order to attract firms, may not generate the geography most favourable to growth.[2] This type of trade-off should be quite ubiquitous in many geography

---

[1] Quah (1996) and Martin (1998) provide some empirical evidence for such trade-off for European regions. Quah finds that European countries which did not experience rising regional inequalities had lower growth.

[2] Martin and Ottaviano (1999) analyze this trade-off from a welfare point of view to show that the optimal geography may entail more or less spatial concentration than the market equilibrium depending on the level of transaction costs. Matsuyama and Takahashi (1998) present a model where economic geography can be characterized by excessive or insufficient agglomeration due to the absence of certain markets and the lack of coordination of agents.

models. Agglomeration does create benefits either because of increasing returns at the level of the firms or because of spillovers, which generate benefits of agglomeration as an external effect. In this section, we, on purpose, give no chance to agglomeration to have negative efficiency effects because no congestion effect is introduced. This is done in the next section.

For analytical convenience, we simplify the geography within each region such that the cost of selling every locally produced industry variety to every local resident involves the intra-regional iceberg trade cost denoted by τ_D, while the inter-regional trade cost is denoted as τ_I (D and I are mnemonics for domestic and international). As in Martin and Rogers (1995), we interpret these costs as directly related to the quality of infrastructures. We will regard a reduction of τ_D as an improvement of intra-regional infrastructure and a drop in τ_I as an improvement in inter-regional infrastructure. For example, the construction of a highway between Milan and Naples will be an improvement in inter-regional infrastructure while a road between Milan and Florence is an improvement of the intra-regional infrastructure of northern Italy. Differences in intra-regional trade costs can also be interpreted as differences in the physical geography of regions.

To study policy choices, we want to be able to distinguish between policies that improve northern and southern infrastructure separately, so we allow the southern intra-regional trade cost, namely τ_D^*, to differ from the north's. However, we will assume that the infrastructure that facilitates transactions between the two regions is shared so that the inter-regional trade costs are the same in either direction. Finally, we assume that $\tau_I > \tau_D \geq \tau_D^*$, that is, that it is more costly to trade with an agent from the other region than with an agent in the same region and that the cost of intra-regional transactions in the north is at least as low as in the south.

Capital moves in search of the highest nominal reward (i.e. the reward defined in terms of the numeraire rather than in terms of the price index), and so interior equilibria can be characterized by the location condition $\pi = \pi^*$, where

$$\pi = bB\frac{E^w}{K^w}, \quad \pi^* = bB^*\frac{E^w}{K^w}; \quad b \equiv \frac{\mu}{\sigma} \tag{17.1}$$

where E^w and K^w are world expenditure and capital stock (recall that with one unit of capital per variety, K^w is also the number of varieties made globally, i.e. $K^w = n^w \equiv n + n^*$), and where

$$B \equiv \frac{s_E\phi_D}{\Delta} + \frac{\phi_I s_E^*}{\Delta^*}, \quad B^* \equiv \frac{\phi_I s_E}{\Delta} + \frac{\phi_D^* s_E^*}{\Delta^*}$$

$$\Delta \equiv \phi_D s_n + \phi_I(1 - s_n), \quad \Delta^* \equiv \phi_I s_n + \phi_D^*(1 - s_n)$$

Here, s_E and s_E^* are the north's and the south's share of world expenditure (so $s_E +$

$s_E^* = 1$), and where, using an obvious extension of the standard notation, $\phi_D \equiv \tau_D^{1-\sigma}$ and $\phi_D^* \equiv (\tau_D^*)^{1-\sigma}$ represent the freeness of trade within the northern and southern regions, and $\phi_I \equiv \tau_I^{1-\sigma}$ reflects the freeness of inter-regional trade.

Solving the location condition $\pi = \pi^*$ shows how the spatial allocation of industry (as characterized by the north's share of industry, s_n) depends on the relative market sizes (as characterized by the north's share of world expenditure, s_E) and the various trade costs (and, thus, on different types of infrastructure policies). Specifically,

$$s_n = \frac{1}{2} + 2\frac{(\phi_D\phi_D^* - \phi_I^2)(s_E - 1/2) + \phi_I(\phi_D - \phi_D^*)}{2(\phi_D - \phi_I)(\phi_D^* - \phi_I)} \tag{17.2}$$

Note that our restrictions on the τ's ensure that the denominator is positive. Also, location still depends on the difference in the shares of expenditures between the two regions, however, a second effect is introduced. Everything else being equal, the region with the best domestic infrastructures (i.e. free intra-regional trade) will attract more firms. The reason is that high intra-regional transaction costs diminish the effective size of the local market for local producers and, as usual, a smaller market attracts fewer firms. It can also be checked that the location of firms becomes very sensitive to intra-regional infrastructure quality when inter-regional infrastructure quality is itself high. However, these are not general equilibrium results as this equation takes the northern share of expenditure, s_E, as given.

With equal-sized regions ($s_L = 1/2$), the north's share of world expenditure depends upon its endowment share of the world capital stock and upon the equilibrium growth rate, viz. (see Chapter 7 for details)[3]

$$s_E = \frac{1}{2} + \frac{b\rho}{g + \rho + \delta}\left[s_K - \frac{1}{2}\right] \tag{17.3}$$

where s_K is the north's endowment share of world capital, g is the endogenous growth rate of the world's capital stock, ρ is the subjective discount rate, and δ is the depreciation rate. Note that since capital is mobile, but capital owners are not, the share of capital working in the north, that is, s_n, may differ from s_K. Since s_E is the north's share of world consumption, we may interpret ($s_E - 1/2$) as a measure of regional income inequality, so this expression says that income inequality increases with inequality in capital endowments and decreases with growth.

Finally, we turn to the equilibrium growth rate. Because learning spillovers are partially localized, the average productivity of the north's innovation sector (only the north innovates in equilibrium) depends on the spatial allocation of industry. Specifically, the growth rate of the world's capital stock is (see Chapter 7 for details)[4]

$$g = 2bL[s_n + \lambda(1 - s_n)] - \rho(1 - b) - \delta, \quad 1/2 < s_n \le 1 \tag{17.4}$$

where λ parameterizes the degree of learning localization (at the two extremes, $\lambda = 0$ implies spillovers are only within a region, and $\lambda = 1$ implies that they are

---

[3] To find (17.3), use the definition of $E = L + \rho vK$, (7.9) and $\pi = E^w/K^w$.
[4] To find (17.4), use (7.20) where s_K is replaced by s_n, and the usual condition $q = v/F = 1$.

fully global). This expression says that the spatial concentration of firms (a higher s_n) implies a lower cost of innovation and therefore a higher growth rate.

The equilibrium is fully characterized by the s_n, g and s_E that solve the three equilibrium expressions (17.2), (17.3) and (17.4).

NOMINAL AND REAL INCOME INEQUALITIES

One of our primary concerns is the impact of the different public policies on the industrial geography, s_n, on the geography of incomes and expenditures, s_E, and on the growth rate of the world capital stock, g. The location of firms matters for immobile agents in our set-up because a region that has more firms also benefits from a lower price index. This is due to the fact that, for locally produced goods, trade costs (intra-regional) are less than for goods imported from the other region. The perfect price index that corresponds to our nested CES utility function is

$$P \equiv \Delta^{-a}, \quad P^* \equiv (\Delta^*)^{-a}; \quad a \equiv \frac{\mu}{\sigma - 1} > 0 \qquad (17.5)$$

so, as usual, an increase in the share of firms in the north benefits consumers in the north and hurts consumers in the south.

The disparity in real income across the regions depends on the disparity in nominal incomes, s_E, given by (17.3), and on the disparity in the price indices defined above which itself depends on s_n. If changes in s_E and s_n go in the same direction, then the impact on real income disparity is unambiguous. For example, an increase in s_E and s_n implies that real income disparities increase between the north and the south as nominal income disparities increase at the same time as the price index decreases in the north and increases in the south. On the contrary, if nominal income disparity increases but industrial agglomeration decreases, the effect on real income inequality is ambiguous. In general, the impact of industrial agglomeration on the price index will be less important the better the public infrastructures. In particular, if inter-regional transaction costs are not very high, then the location of production will have little effect on the price indices and, therefore, on the real income disparities. In this case, the real income disparities will follow the nominal income disparities.

17.2.2 A Continuous Income Transfer to the South

We first look at a direct monetary transfer[5] to the south that persists forever. A convenient way of modelling this is to view it as a transfer of some of the north's capital endowment to the south, that is, a decrease in s_K. This and other policies can be simply analysed using the four-quadrant diagram of the type shown in Figure 17.1. The three equilibrium expressions, (17.2), (17.3) and (17.4), are

[5] These are very important in the European context of large social transfers even outside the realm of European regional policies. Davezies (2001) insists on the fact that regional economies get most of their income from mechanisms that are not directly linked to production. In France, for example, Ile de France and Alsace are the only two regions for which the sum of private sector income is larger than social transfers.

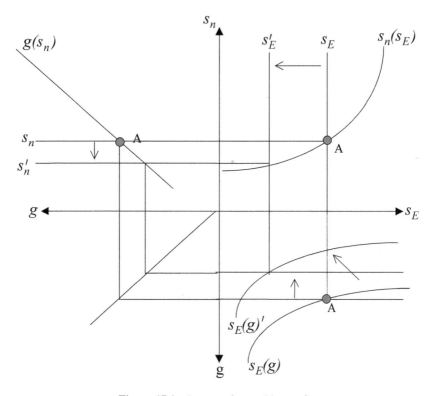

Figure 17.1 Impact of a wealth transfer.

plotted in the northeast (NE), southeast (SE) and northwest (NW) quadrants of the diagram, respectively. The points A indicate the initial equilibrium.

The initial impact of the transfer is to lower s_E for any given growth rate as per (17.3). This shift is shown in the SE quadrant of Figure 17.1. In turn, the transfer in purchasing power (s_E decreases) increases the market size of the south, attracting firms there (s_n decreases as shown in the NE quadrant). Because of local spillovers, the geography becomes less conducive to innovation so that the growth rate decreases (see the NW quadrant). The economic geography in terms both of industrial location and nominal incomes becomes less unequal, so that real income inequality decreases but at the expense of the growth rate. To summarize this , we write the following result.

Result 17.1 (income transfer). *An income transfer to the poor region lowers income inequality and spatial concentration but lowers the growth rate of the whole economy.*

17.2.3 A Decrease of Intra-Regional Trade Costs in the South

Consider next a policy that improves local infrastructures in the south and thus raises the freeness of south–south trade, that is, ϕ_D^* increases. The effect of such a

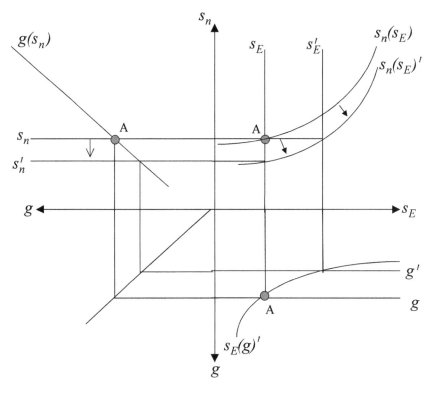

Figure 17.2   Improved local infrastructure in the south.

policy is shown with the help of Figure 17.2. In this case, s_n decreases for any given level of s_E (see the NE quadrant in the diagram). The intuition is that, as public infrastructure improves, transaction costs on goods produced and consumed in the south decrease, increasing the effective demand. Given increasing returns to scale, firms in the differentiated goods sector relocate to the south and s_n decreases. Relocation from the north, where the innovation sector is located, to the south brings about an increase in the cost of innovation reducing the growth rate of innovation. In this sense, the improvement in infrastructure of the south generates a less growth conducive geography and, through a reduction in the growth rate of innovation, it lessens competition, increasing monopoly profits to the benefit of capital owners in both regions. As capital owners are more numerous in the north, the inter-regional inequality in expenditures, measured by s_E, rises (see the SE quadrant). The net effect on real income inequality is, however, ambiguous. Nominal income inequality has increased but the price index has decreased in the south compared to the north. This is due to the fact that more firms produce in the south and that the cost of transporting locally produced goods to consumers in the south has decreased.

Note also that economic geography has not only an impact on inter-regional income inequality but also on a particular form of intra-regional inequality between workers and capital owners. When monopolistic profits increase due to a less concentrated geography (lower s_n) and a lower growth rate, this increases the relative income gap between capital owners and wage earners because the value of capital increases in both regions. The mirror image of this is that the marginal cost of capital increases with a less concentrated geography. This is true in both regions. This is an important point. In policy discussions, it is often assumed that reducing regional inequalities through regional policies that induce firms to relocate in the poor regions reduces inequalities in a larger sense. However, it is important to identify those inequalities that are targeted. Here, reducing regional inequalities leads to an increase in another type of inequality, this time, among economic agents. Hence, not only do regional policies face a trade-off between equity and efficiency, they also face a trade-off between reducing spatial inequalities and reducing inter-individual inequalities. To summarize this, we write the following result.

> **Result 17.2 (local infrastructure).** *Infrastructure that facilitates intra-regional trade in the south lowers spatial concentration, decreases growth in the whole economy and increases nominal income inequality between north and south and between workers and capital owners.*

17.2.4 A Decrease in Inter-Regional Trade Costs

The effect of improving inter-regional infrastructure in a way that makes trade between the regions freer can also be seen using Figure 17.2. In this case, as long as the north has a larger market size than the south, or that its domestic infra-structures are better than those in the south (i.e. $s_E > 1/2$ or $\phi_D > \phi_D^*$), this improvement in inter-regional infrastructure will increase the attractiveness of the north, since, from (17.2) we know that $\partial s_n / \partial \phi_I > 0$ under these conditions. Hence, the curve labelled $s_n(s_E)$ shifts as shown in the NE quadrant and the effect of such a policy is qualitatively the exact opposite to the effect of a decrease of intra-regional trade costs in the south. An improvement in inter-regional infra-structure has the opposite effect of an improvement in intra-regional infrastructure in the south. As s_n increases, the growth rate of innovation, g, increases, and s_E decreases as monopolistic profits of each capital owner decrease. The result that improved transport infrastructure between regions of different size increases regional agglomeration in the sense that it increases the attractiveness of the largest or richest regions would hold in many 'new economic geography' models, with or without growth.

The impact on real income disparities is ambiguous. The nominal income disparity (as measured by s_E) decreases but the impact on the price index in the two regions is more complex. In the south, the increased freeness of inter-regional trade lowers the cost of importing goods from the north. However, as some firms relocate to the north (s_n increases), more of the goods have to be imported bearing a higher transaction cost (the inter-regional one) than the one faced if the good was produced locally. It can be shown that the first effect is larger than the second so that, following a decrease in the inter-regional transaction cost, the price index in the south decreases. In the north, both effects go in the same direction. The cost of importing goods from the south decreases and more firms decide to produce in the north. It can be shown that the price index decreases more in the south than in the north. The net effect on real income inequality is therefore ambiguous. As shown in Martin and Ottaviano (1999), if transaction costs between the two regions are already sufficiently low, the impact on price indices will not be very important. So, an improvement in infrastructures that helps to decrease the inter-regional transaction costs further will lower real income inequality between the regions.

A decrease in the intra-regional transaction costs in the north would have the same qualitative effect as those described here for the improvement of inter-regional infrastructures. To summarize this, we write the following result.

Result 17.3 (inter-regional infrastructure). *Infrastructure that facilitates inter-regional trade between north and south increases spatial concentration, increases growth in the whole economy and decreases nominal income inequality between north and south and between workers and capital owners.*

17.2.5 A Policy Towards Technology Spillovers

In the case of the policies described above, all regional in nature, a trade-off exists because they all have an undesirable side effect. They either lead to lower growth, to higher nominal income inequality or to more industrial agglomeration. A public policy that makes technological spillovers less localized does not face this trade-off since, as was shown in Chapter 6, making knowledge spillovers more global is both pro-growth and pro-dispersion. For example, a policy that improves telecommunication infrastructures, which improves internet access or which focuses on human capital may be interpreted as a policy that increases the parameter λ as it helps the diffusion of new technologies from one region to another. One can think of this type of policy as one that facilitates trade in ideas rather that trade in goods. It could be argued that transport infrastructures that help facilitate human capital movements will have such effect because it facilitates the 'transport' of ideas which often requires face to face communication.

In this case, the $g(s_n)$ line shifts to the left and the equilibrium growth rate increases as the cost of innovation decreases (see the NW quadrant in Figure 17.3). More firms enter the market reducing the monopolistic power of existing firms and, therefore, the income of capital owners. This reduces the income differential between north and south, between workers and capital owners inside each region, and leads to relocation of firms to the south.

It can be shown that the exogenous decrease in the cost of innovation more than compensates the endogenous decrease in spatial concentration so that the net effect is an increase in the growth rate. It should be noted that any policy that reduces the cost of innovation could attain both the objectives of higher growth

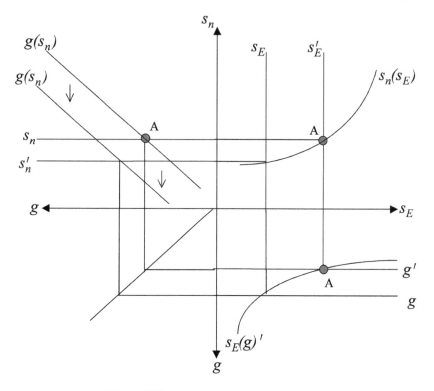

Figure 17.3   Improved knowledge spillovers.

and more equity. If subsidies to R&D, increased competition on goods markets and labour markets, improved education infrastructure, etc., can decrease the cost of innovation for firms, then, this kind of policy may yield more desirable outcomes than traditional transfers or regional policies. Note that such a policy, leading to the relocation of economic activities to the south, helps the creation of new economic activities and firms without any of the local bias that regional policies usually have.

Our analysis draws a sharp distinction between policies that decrease the transaction costs on goods and those that decrease the transaction costs on ideas and technologies. This is useful because, in the case of the European Union, until recently the emphasis has been put on the first type of policy. It should be clear that our framework gives a strong rationale to favour the latter type of policy which does not face either the trade-off between equity and efficiency or the trade-off between spatial equity and inter-individual equity. However, this result comes from the sharp analytical distinction that we can make in our model between transaction costs on goods and on ideas. Obviously, the reality is more complex: facilitating trade in goods also facilitates trade in ideas simply because trade in goods often implies that agents familiarize themselves with new technologies. To summarize this, we write the following result.

Result 17.4 (technology spillovers). *A public policy that facilitates inter-regional technology spillovers increases growth in the whole economy, decreases nominal income inequality between north and south and between workers and capital owners, and decreases spatial concentration.*

17.2.6 Transport Infrastructures in a Three-Region Framework

A caveat in the framework developed in the previous sections is that it is a two-region model and that these regions are basically points. This is important in particular for the result that says that a poor region always loses industries when transaction costs are lowered with a rich region. This may not be true in a three-region model if the poor region is at the crossroad of rich regions. In this case, lowering transaction costs between the poor region and the rich regions may actually induce firms to relocate in the poor region. Hence, the effect of public infrastructures depends crucially on physical geography. While, the building of highways between the north and the south of Italy has not helped the south and may even have increased industrial delocation to the north, the same policy applied to a poor region such as Nord-Pas de Calais in the north of France seems to have been much more conducive to industrial relocation in that region. Nord-Pas de Calais is a region in industrial decline (formerly specialized in textiles and metallurgy), which has benefited from important transport infrastructure projects (highways, the fast train TGV to Paris, London and Brussels). In this case, the lowering of transaction costs with the rich regions—such as Ile de France, the London area and the Brussels area—seems to have generated industrial relocation to Nord-Pas de Calais. The fact that this region, even though poor in terms of income per capita, is located at the crossroad of some rich and large regions has been the key to explaining the effect of the infrastructure policy. This effect is similar to the hub effect analysed in Krugman (1993).

To see this point, we can extend our analysis to a simple three-region model: the three regions are called A, B and C and we will assume that B is located between A and C. In particular, firms in A which export to A transport goods through B, and vice versa so that the structure of transport costs is the following:

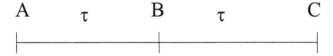

Hence, the transport cost between A and C is τ^2 and τ between A and C as well as between B and C. To facilitate the analysis, we assume that A and C are perfectly symmetric (in particular, in terms of capital endowments) and that there are no intra-regional transaction costs. We note that s_{nB} is the share of firms located in region B, and s_{EB} is the share of total expenditures in B. We assume that $s_{EB} < 1/3$ so that indeed region B is a relatively poor region because its share in capital endowment is itself less than one-third. In this case, it is easy to derive the equilibrium relation between regional income inequality and industrial location:

$$s_{nB} = 1/3 + \frac{(3s_{EB} - 1)(1 + \phi)}{3(1 - \phi)^2} + \frac{2}{3}\left(\frac{\phi}{1 - \phi}\right)^2 \qquad (17.6)$$

There are two effects driving the location of firms. The first, represented by the second term on the right-hand side in (17.6), is the usual home-market effect. If, as we assume, region B is poor, that is, $s_{EB} < 1/3$, then this second term is negative and any policy that reduces transaction costs (an increase in ϕ) will induce a decrease in the share of firms in the poor regions. This is the usual effect that we have already analysed. However, a second effect comes with the particular geographical structure that we have assumed which makes region B a 'central region' even though it is a poor region. This second effect is given by the third term on the right-hand side of (13.5). It is positive because, being 'central' is an attracting feature to firms. Being located in B, even though B is not itself a large market, helps secure an easy access to the large markets A and C. Here, we see that a policy that reduces transaction costs between regions (an increase in ϕ) reinforces this effect and therefore induces firms to relocate in the poor 'central' region. The two effects, the 'home-market' effect and the 'central place' effect go in opposite direction so that an infrastructure policy that leads to a decrease in transaction costs between regions has an ambiguous effect on relocation towards the poor region. There will be relocation towards the poor region, that is, $\partial s_n / \partial \phi > 0$ if

$$s_{EB} > \frac{1 - \phi}{3 + \phi} \qquad (17.7)$$

Hence, an infrastructure policy that reduces transaction costs between a 'central ' poor region and two rich regions will be successful in attracting firms to the poor regions only if the market size of the 'poor' region is not too small and/or if existing transaction costs between the poor and the rich regions are not too small. Another way to say this is that an 'empty' place, even if it is at the crossroads of rich regions, cannot become an industrial base; a large enough local market is necessary. Also, to be attractive as a location that saves on transaction costs, those costs must be high enough. This example shows that the impact of a transport infrastructure policy depends crucially on physical geography, the existing market sizes and on existing infrastructures. To summarize this, we write the following result.

> **Result 17.5 (three-region).** *A policy that facilitates trade between a centrally located poor region and two rich regions leads to relocation to the poor region if its share of expenditure is sufficiently high.*

17.3 AGGLOMERATION, CONGESTION AND GROWTH

Up to now we have focused on the positive effects of agglomeration on growth, even though we also made clear that agglomeration will have unwelcome effects on regional inequalities. This, of course, follows the large empirical literature that has insisted on the importance of localized technological spillovers. We now want to present a simple framework in which, despite the presence of internal increasing returns, the agglomeration process, if pushed too far, can also be detrimental to growth. The interesting point of this analysis is not the way we model congestion, which will be admittedly quite ad hoc, but the fact that the possibility of congestion can lead to a stable equilibrium with low growth, high regional inequality and high inequality between regions as well as between workers and capital owners. We are not the first to look at this; see for example Tabuchi (1998) and Monfort and Nicolini (2000).

To do this, we use the model of the preceding sections in the case of perfect capital mobility. The only modification with this section is that the cost of innovation in the north will be given by

$$F = a_I, \quad a_I \equiv \frac{1}{K^W A}, \quad A \equiv s_n + \lambda(1 - s_n) - \gamma\left(s_n - \frac{1}{2}\right)^2 \quad (17.8)$$

λ still measures the degree of localization of technology spillovers. We have now introduced a further effect to take into account the possibility that at high levels of agglomeration (high s_n), the effect of an increase in the proportion of firms in the north may increase the cost of innovation. This congestion effect is measured by the parameter γ. Note that in the symmetric case ($s_n = 1/2$), the congestion effect is zero with our specific form.

It is easy to check that in this case, the growth rate of the economy is now given by

$$g = 2bL[s_n + \lambda(1 - s_n) - \gamma s_n^2] - \rho(1 - b) - \delta, \quad \frac{1}{2} < s_n < 1 \quad (17.9)$$

Growth increases with spatial economic concentration at low levels of concentration but then decreases at high levels of concentration if $\gamma > (1 - \lambda)/2$ which we will assume to make the story interesting. The other two equilibrium relations are still valid: (17.2) gives the relation between s_n, the equilibrium location of firms, and the growth rate, and (17.3) gives the relation between s_E, the income inequality and the location of firms. Put together, we get a second relation between growth and the equilibrium location firms

$$s_n = \frac{1}{2} + \frac{(\phi_D \phi_D^* - \phi_I^2)\dfrac{\rho b}{g + \rho}\left(s_K - \dfrac{1}{2}\right) + \phi_I(\phi_D - \phi_D^*)}{2(\phi_D - \phi_I)(\phi_D^* - \phi_I)} \quad (17.10)$$

The relation is negative. An increase in growth decreases monopolistic profits (market crowding or 'competition' effect) and the income of capital owners who are more numerous in the north ($s_K > 1/2$). Hence, due to the home-market effect, an increase in the growth rate in turn induces a lower level of spatial concentration.

The first relation always holds in equilibrium as long as the equilibrium growth rate is positive. The second relation implies that, for this combination of spatial concentration and growth rate, profits are equalized in the two regions. If however, in the core–periphery (CP) equilibrium ($s_n = 1$), profits are higher in

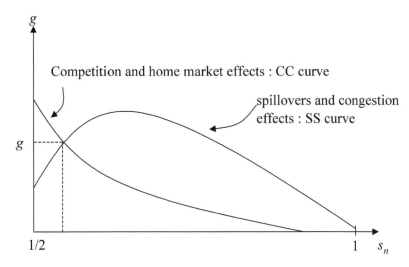

Figure 17.4   Growth and concentration: high inter-regional trade costs.

the north than in the south, this relation does not need to hold for the CP to be an equilibrium.

Depending on the parameters, four typical situations will emerge. We will focus on different levels of inter-regional trade costs to compare those situations. At high levels of trade costs, a unique stable equilibrium will exist as described by Figure 17.4 that relates the growth rate and the spatial concentration as given by (17.9) and (17.10) which are given by the SS and the CC curves, respectively, in Figure 17.4.

This situation is quite similar to the one we saw in the previous section. Because of high trade costs, income inequality between the two regions does not translate in strong spatial concentration. From the point of view of growth, spatial concentration in the north is too low because we are still in the situation where positive localized spillovers dominate the congestion effects.

What happens if we lower inter-regional transaction costs to medium values? The SS curve, which shows how growth is affected by spatial concentration, is not affected. However, the CC curve, the competition and home-market effect, shifts to the right. Lower trade costs imply that with the same growth rate, and therefore the same income inequality, profits will be equalized between the two regions at a higher level of spatial concentration. Hence, a second equilibrium emerges as shown by the top panel of Figure 17.5. Note that the same movement of the CC curve will occur if the policy consists of infrastructures that mainly lower transaction costs in the rich region.

The 'low concentration equilibrium' still exists, even though at a higher level of concentration, and is still characterized by too little concentration from the point of view of growth. However, a second equilibrium appears with high concentration and low growth. This second equilibrium, for which profits are equalized in the two regions, is not stable though. It is easy to check this from the

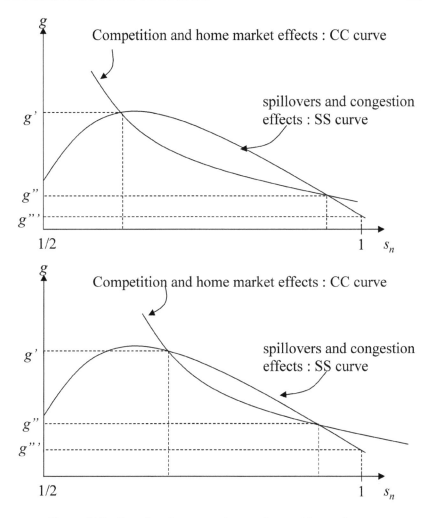

Figure 17.5 Growth and concentration: medium and low trade costs.

level of s_n that corresponds to g; a small increase in spatial concentration will increase profits in the north and decrease profits in the south so that firms will relocate to the north. Symmetrically, a small decrease in spatial concentration will decrease profits in the north and increase profits in the south so that firms will relocate from the north to the south. Hence, two stable equilibria exist, the 'low concentration' equilibrium and the CP equilibrium. The latter is stable because it can be checked that profits are higher in the north than in the south in this situation.[6] The intuition is that low growth increases the value of existing mono-polistic firms owned mainly by the north so that income inequality between the two regions is high, which, through the home-market effect, implies that profits

[6] For the R&D sector to remain in the north in the extreme equilibrium, we also need $\lambda < 1 - \gamma$, which we assume for simplicity.

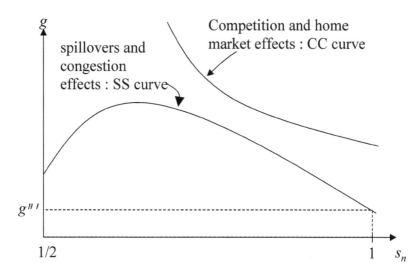

Figure 17.6   Growth and concentration: very low inter-regional trade costs.

are higher in the north than in the south. In turn, the extreme concentration of industries in the north generates congestion effects that are detrimental to growth. Such a situation obviously legitimizes some sort of public intervention that would lift the country out of the low growth–high concentration trap.

With lower inter-regional trade costs (or lower trade costs inside the rich region), the CC curve keeps shifting to the right as shown in the bottom panel of the diagram. Two stable equilibria exist: the CP equilibrium with low growth and a partial concentration equilibrium with higher growth. The difference is that even the interior equilibrium displays too much concentration relative to the growth maximizing equilibrium.

A further decrease in inter-regional trade costs (or a decrease in trade costs in the rich region) implies that the interior equilibrium disappears so that the only stable equilibrium is the CP with low growth. This is described in Figure 17.6.

Hence, the general conclusion is that for low and very low trade costs, the degree of agglomeration generated by market forces will always be too strong if some congestion effect exists. This, of course, will especially be the case when the market equilibrium leads to full agglomeration in one region. The fact that lowering inter-regional trade costs in the presence of congestion effects leads, even in the presence of increasing returns sectors, to sub-optimal spatial concentration is interesting. It can be interpreted as making legitimate the claims of the European Commission and of some European governments, that progress in the European integration process must be accompanied by public policies such as the Structural Policies that aim to help poor regions to attract economic activities and more generally lead to a decrease of the spatial concentration of economic activities in a few core regions.

However, public policies that lower transport costs between poor and rich regions will not help, on the contrary. In the presence of congestion effects, this may shift the economy from a high growth, low industrial concentration and low-income inequality into an equilibrium with low growth, high industrial concentration and high-income inequality. It suggests again that it is important to identify the market failures (here localized technological spillovers and congestion costs) and to act directly at the source of those market failures rather than further lowering transport costs on goods, which can magnify the effects of these market failures. This implies again that public policies that foster the diffusion of technology spillovers and diminish congestion costs are first-best. In our graphical framework, these policies would be represented by an upward shift of the SS curve. Policies that give incentives to firms that relocate in poor regions will also help. In our framework, in the case of high congestion costs, the financing of infrastructures that lower transactions inside the poor regions will both decrease regional inequalities and increase growth. To summarize this, we write the following result.

Result 17.6 (congestion). *In the presence of congestion costs, better infrastructure that lowers trade costs between regions may put the economy in an equilibrium with low growth, high spatial concentration and high regional income inequality.*

17.4 NON-LINEAR EFFECTS OF PUBLIC POLICIES

One central message of the 'new economic' geography is that decreases in trade costs may have no effect on economic geography but when those costs fall below a certain threshold, the effect of a small decrease may have very dramatic implications on economic geography. The implications of this message for public policies should by now be quite clear (see also Puga 2002, on this theme). In the presence of agglomeration processes, infrastructure policies, whether they imply a decrease of inter-regional transaction costs or intra-regional transaction costs may have very non-linear effects. To see this, we will use the model developed in Chapter 7 in the case of no capital mobility. The analysis of the previous section, showed that capital mobility coupled with congestion effects can give rise to multiple equilibria with very different properties in terms of growth and regional inequalities, so that even with capital mobility, a small change in public policies can have non-linear effects. If it succeeds in changing the equilibrium, the policy has an enormous impact on geography and growth. However, a small change may also have a small impact if it does not move the economy from one equilibrium to another.

We will simplify the analysis, compared to the previous sections, by eliminating localized technology spillovers and congestion effects so that we will focus on the non-linear effects of infrastructure policies on economic geography and forget their effects (which in this context may also be very non-linear) on growth. Growth is therefore given by (17.4) with $\lambda = 1$, and

$$s_E = \frac{1}{2} + \frac{\rho(2s_K - 1)}{2(2L + \rho)} \qquad (17.11)$$

defines how the share of expenditures in the north is related to the share of capital in the north. However, the share of capital, when we take into account the presence of intra-regional trade costs is now

$$s_K = \frac{1}{2} + 2\frac{(\phi_D\phi_D^* - \phi_I^2)(s_E - 1/2) + \phi_I(\phi_D - \phi_D^*)}{2(\phi_D - \phi_I)(\phi_D^* - \phi_I)} \qquad (17.12)$$

Note that, of course, this is the same as (17.2) except that it defines both location and the share of capital, as capital is now immobile. The interior equilibrium where both regions accumulate capital still exists but is not the symmetric equilibrium as long as intra-regional trade costs are different in the poor and in the rich region. If we assume, as before, that $\tau_I > \tau_D \geq \tau_D^*$, that is, the rich region is better endowed in transport infrastructures, then even with an equilibrium in which both regions accumulate capital at the same pace, it is easy to check that this equilibrium will be such that $s_E > 1/2$ and $s_K > 1/2$. Hence, with different levels of public infrastructures, the two regions may accumulate capital at the same pace in the steady-state equilibrium but, at any point in time, the north will have a higher stock of capital and therefore a higher level of income. In this case, public infrastructure policies will have quite different effects. Lowering inter-regional transaction costs, as long as the north has better infrastructure than the south, will increase the steady-state share of capital and income in the north. The reason is that by doing so, it increases demand and profits in the best-endowed region so that it increases the incentive to accumulate capital there. An improvement in infrastructures in the poor region will have the opposite effect as it increases the effective size of the market and therefore profits in that region. As long as the interior equilibrium is stable, a small change in public infrastructures will have a small impact on capital accumulation and steady state incomes.

However, changes in public infrastructures may also have dramatic effects if they contribute to make the interior equilibrium where both regions accumulate unstable. Again, to look at the question of stability, we can use different tools which all give the same answer. For example, we can ask: When does the interior equilibrium become unstable; that is, for what level of inter-regional transaction cost, which we call ϕ_{ICP}, will an increase in the share of capital in the north increase profits and Tobin's q in the north? Or for what level of ϕ_I do we get $\partial q/\partial s_K = 0$? It can be shown that this transaction cost is such that

$$\phi_I > \phi_{\mathrm{ICP}} = \frac{(2L + \rho)(\phi_D + \phi_D^*) - \sqrt{(2L + \rho)^2(\phi_D - \phi_D^*)^2 + 4\rho^2\phi_D\phi_D^*}}{4(L + \rho)}$$

$$(17.13)$$

This is also the level of inter-regional transaction cost such that the CP equilibrium becomes stable, that is, no agent in the south has any incentive to accumulate capital when all the capital is owned by the north. Note, of course, that when $\phi_D = \phi_D^* = 1$, we get $\phi_{ICP} = \phi_{CP} = L/(L + \rho)$.

The implications for infrastructure policies are quite important. If public investment lowers inter-regional trade costs so that ϕ_I goes above the threshold level defined in (17.13), then the effect on inter-regional divergence will be quite dramatic. An improvement in public infrastructures inside the poor region, a decrease in intra-regional trade costs, will have also very non-linear effects. It may have a small positive effect for that region if we are in the interior equilibrium (see above). It may prevent a process of 'catastrophic agglomeration' in the north, if inter-regional trade costs are around the threshold defined in (17.13). Indeed, it can be checked that an increase in that ϕ_D^* increases ϕ_{ICP}. Also, if we start from the core–periphery equilibrium, a small improvement in infrastructures in the poor region will have no effect if the difference in public infrastructures between the north and the south is large enough or if the inter-regional trade costs between the two regions are low enough. The reason is that such policy will not make investment profitable in the south so that the core–periphery equilibrium stays stable. However, in the opposite case, a small improvement in infrastructures in the south may have a dramatic impact as it may be sufficient to make investment profitable in the south (i.e. to make ϕ_I go below ϕ_{ICP}). This in turn will make the south enter a virtuous circle. As capital accumulation starts in the south, income and expenditures increase so that this reinforces the incentive to accumulate through an increase in profits in the south. The south, however, will not converge fully to the north even with such a 'miracle' as long as public infrastructures in the north are better than in the south.

We saw in Section 17.1 that public policies that facilitate the inter-regional diffusion of technological knowledge could increase growth and decrease regional inequalities. What is their role in the presence of agglomeration effects? In the simple example just presented, there are no localized spillovers so it is difficult to discuss the effects of such policy. However, we can use the results of Chapter 7 for that purpose, more precisely those in the section with localized spillovers and no capital mobility. We showed that starting from the CP equilibrium, an increase in inter-regional learning spillovers (an increase in λ) would first have no effect on the geography of accumulation (the south would still have no incentive to accumulate) but then at a threshold level, a 'miracle' would take place in the south as it would start innovating (the cost of innovation is sufficiently low). This would in turn boost its income and expenditures, and therefore local profits, so that the incentive to innovate would increase. Again, this example confirms that public policies may have, if agglomeration forces are at work, very non-linear effects. To summarize this, we write the following result.

Result 17.7 (non-linear effects). *In the presence of agglomeration effects, infrastructure projects have non-linear effects. An improvement of infrastructures inside the poor region may have no effect until a threshold is reached where convergence occurs between the poor and the rich region.*

*An improvement of infrastructures that facilitate trade between regions
may have no effect until a threshold is reached where divergence occurs
between the two regions.*

17.5 CONCLUDING REMARKS AND RELATED LITERATURE

17.5.1 Summary Results

This chapter has shown that economic geography models can be used to analyse
some concrete regional policy questions such as the impact of public infrastructures on spatial agglomeration, regional income inequality and growth. When
positive localized spillovers exist, spatial concentration of economic activities
has a beneficial effect on innovation and growth. This implies that public infrastructure policies have to deal with a fundamental trade-off between regional
equity and efficiency. Hence, a policy that invests in public infrastructure in
the poor regions (e.g. that facilitates intra-regional trade in the poor region)
will attract firms towards that region. However, this makes the geography less
inefficient and less conducive to growth. By increasing the return to capital, this
policy also increases the income differential between the poor and the rich region.
An infrastructure policy that facilitates trade between regions of different size
will aggravate regional inequalities, a result that comes directly from the home-
market effect. In this case, because geography would become more conducive to
spillovers, growth would be increased.

To escape the trade-off between spatial equity and spatial inefficiency, this
chapter has shown that the public policy should attack the market failure which is
at the source of the possible inefficiency. In the context of the model presented,
the market failure is the imperfection or the localization of the technology spillovers. Infrastructure policies that facilitate the 'trade' in ideas between regions,
and therefore make the spillovers less localized, decrease the cost of innovation
and increase the growth rate. By spurring the entry of new firms, such a policy
increases competition and the return to capital declines which favours the poor
region. Hence, regional income inequality is reduced which leads to less spatial
concentration. Examples of such a 'win-win' policy are infrastructure policies in
telecommunication, internet, human capital formation and passenger transport.

If agglomeration has at some point some congestion effect, then infrastructure
policies that facilitate trade between regions may lead to a 'bad' equilibrium with
agglomeration, congestion, low growth, low competition, low growth and high
income inequalities. In this case, again public policies should identify the relevant market failure which in this context is congestion and not the lack of transport infrastructure between regions.

In models with possible catastrophic agglomeration, public policies have non-
linear effects: a large infrastructure project may not have any impact on the
location of economic activities if it does not alter the stability of the equilibrium.
On the contrary a small improvement in infrastructure can have a very large effect
if it succeeds in putting into motion a circular causality mechanism.

17.5.2 Related Literature

Puga (2002) provides a very useful review on how regional policies can be analysed in the light of the new economic geography literature. Caminal (2000) also studies a related set of issues.

Other interesting aspects of public policies have not been analysed in this chapter. In particular, public procurement policies are potentially important because of the effect they can have on regional demand and therefore industry location in models with scale effects. This issue has been studied by Trionfetti (2000, 2001) and Brulhart and Trionfetti (2000) who show that, from a theoretical and empirical point of view, public procurement policies can counteract agglomeration forces. The financing of public infrastructures, at the local, national or European level is also an important issue. The issue is touched on by Martin and Rogers (1995) and is analysed in more depth by Justman et al. (2001) who show that it can lead to a process of fiscal agglomeration when regions compete on infrastructure quality to attract firms. Public infrastructures, such as public amenities, can have an effect on transport and on firms but they can also have a direct impact on the utility of agents. In models with labour mobility, where location choice by mobile agents is driven by utility differentials, this could be an important determinant of location.

If infrastructure policies can attract policies, then such policies can become strategic tools in the hands of regional governments as argued by Maurer and Walz (2000). They show that the strategic interaction can lead to sub-optimal provision of local infrastructure. Combes and Linnemer (2000) analyse the impact of different transport infrastructure on location choice and equilibrium geography. A step towards the endogenization of the transport sector in economic geography models is taken by Mori and Nishikimi (2002) who show that economies of transport density (a higher demand for inter-regional transport leads to a decrease in the transport cost) can trigger industrial agglomeration. The impact of infrastructures as a determinant of industrial location in developing countries is analysed by Bjorvatn (2001).

From an empirical point of view, many papers have shown the importance of infrastructure as a determinant of the location of economic activities. Combes and Lafourcade (2001) show that the decline in transport costs in France has led to more spatial concentration and specialization at the regional level, a result consistent with the theoretical framework presented here. Limao and Venables (2001) show that infrastructure quality is an important determinant of transport costs and as such has a strong effect on trade flows. A positive impact of transportation infrastructure on the location of new foreign-owned plants is found by Coughlin and Segev (2000).

A related and very large literature has analysed the impact of public infrastructure on productivity (see Morrison and Schartz 1996 for a regional analysis). An analysis that explicitly takes into account the geographical dimension of the question can be found in Haughwout (2002).

REFERENCES

Bjorvatn, K. 2001. Infrastructure and industrial location: a dual technology approach. Working Paper, The Norwegian School of Economics and Business Administration.

Brulhart, M. and F. Trionfetti. 2000. Public expenditure and international specialisation. Working Paper No. 00.23, University of Lausanne.

Caminal, R. 2000. Personal redistribution and the regional allocation of public investment. Discussion Paper No. 2627, Centre for Economic Policy Research.

Combes, P.-P. and M. Lafourcade. 2001. Transport cost decline and regional inequalities: evidence from France. Discussion Paper No. 2894, Centre for Economic Policy Research.

Combes, P.-P. and L. Linnemer. 2000. Intermodal competition and regional inequalities. *Regional Science and Urban Economics* 30(2): 131–184.

Coughlin, C. and E. Segev. 2000. Location determinants of new foreign-owned manufacturing plants. *Journal of Regional Science* 40(2): 323–351.

Davezies, L. 2001. Revenu et territoires. *Aménagement du Territoire*. Conseil d'Analyse Economique, 173–193.

Haughwout, A. 2002. Public infrastructure investments, productivity and welfare in fixed geographic areas. *Journal of Public Economics* in press.

Justman, M., J.-F. Thisse and T. van Ypersele. 2001. Taking the bite out of fiscal competition. Discussion Paper No. 3109, Centre for Economic Policy Research.

Krugman, P. 1993, The hub effect: or threeness in international trade. In *Trade Policy and Dynamics of International Trade*, ed. W. J. Ethier, E. Helpman and J. P. Neary. Cambridge: Cambridge University Press, 29–37.

Limao, N. and A. J. Venables. 2001. Infrastructure, geographical disadvantage, transport costs and trade. *World Bank Economic Review* 15(3): 451–479.

Martin, P. 1998. Can regional policies affect growth and geography in Europe? *World Economy* 21(6): 757–774.

———. 1999. Public policies, regional inequalities and growth. *Journal of Public Economics* (73)1: 85–105.

Martin, P. and G. I. P. Ottaviano. 1999. Growing locations: industry location in a model of endogenous growth. *European Economic Review* 43(2): 281–302.

Martin, P. and C. A. Rogers. 1995. Industrial location and public infrastructure. *Journal of International Economics* 39: 335–351.

Matsuyama, K. and T. Takahashi. 1998. Self-defeating regional concentration. *Review of Economic Studies* 65(2): 211–234.

Maurer, B. and U. Walz. 2000. Regional competition for mobile oligopolistic firms: does public provision of local inputs lead to agglomeration? *Journal of Regional Science* 40(2): 353–375.

Monfort, P. and R. Nicolini. 2000. Regional convergence and international integration. *Journal of Urban Economics* 48: 286–306.

Morrisson, C. and A. Schwartz. 1996. State infrastructure and productive performance. *American Economic Review* 86(5): 1095–1111.

Puga, Diego. 2002. European Regional Policies in the light of recent location theories. *Journal of Economic Geography* in press.

Quah, D. 1996. Regional cohesion from local isolated actions: 1. Historical outcomes. Mimeo, London Sschool of Economics.

Tabuchi, T. 1998. Agglomeration and dispersion: a synthesis of Alonso and Krugman. *Journal of Urban Economics* 44: 333–351.

Trionfetti, F. 2000. Discriminatory public procurement and international trade. *World Economy* 23: 57–76.

_____. 2001. Government procurement, economic integration, and income inequality. *Review of International Economics* 9(1): 29–41.

CHAPTER 18

The Political Economics of Regional Subsidies

18.1 INTRODUCTION

A striking features of OECD economies is the regularity with which governments favour rural regions to an extent that seems far out of proportion with their population shares. The classic example is the subsidization and protection of agriculture, but rural regions also often receive direct economic aid. In Western Europe, for example, governments routinely subsidize industry in rural/poor regions. Some of this is direct, taking the form of tax breaks and/or production subsidies, and some of it is indirect, taking the form of regional infrastructure such as roads, airports and industrial parks.

This chapter takes a first look at the political economy of regional subsidies. While there are undoubtedly many, many explanations to be explored, we focus primarily on the story—put forth by Robert-Nicoud and Sbergami (2002)—that emphasizes political homogeneity of rural regions. In a nutshell, this line of reasoning asserts that rural populations are more homogenous politically, perhaps as a result of decades of self-selection in the face of massive rural-to-urban migration. Given this, politicians find that a given subsidy level will buy more votes when the subsidies are paid to rural-based firms. Or, using the terminology of Persson and Tabellini (2000), there are more swing voters in rural regions. The chapter also briefly considers two other explanations: legislative over representation, and legislative bargaining.

In addition to asking how geography affects politics, the chapter also explores how politics affects economic geography. In particular, we revisit the impact of falling trade costs on the location industry in a model where regional subsidies are politically determined.

18.1.1 Organization of the Chapter

We begin the analysis by presenting the footloose capital (FC) model of Chapter 3 augmented to include subsidies and a political economy module that endogenizes the size and direction of such subsidies. Section 18.3 uses this model to address questions such as: When voters are heterogeneous, which population subsets are most attractive to politicians? How does this translate in the implemented regional policy? What are the effects on the spatial equilibrium?

Section 18.4 considers a different channel that may account for the disproportionate subsidies received by rural regions in many nations. The legislature in many nations, the United States being a prime example, is based on geographic as well as demographic principles. As a consequence, the number of legislative votes per citizen can vary enormously; both Montana and California have two US senators even though California's population is many times that of Montana. Section 18.4 also considers how the design of constituencies shapes the spatial allocation of firms in the political equilibrium.

Section 18.5 focuses on a third channel linking regions, political outcomes and industrial location. If the sole conflict of interest in a legislative body is the spatial allocation of industry, then small constituencies prove very attractive as coalition partners and are thus typically part of any winning coalition. Finally, this section also asks how elections of representatives interact with the coalition formation that arises once the legislative body is elected. Section 18.6 presents our concluding remarks.

AN IMPORTANT NOTE ON NOTATION

For the remainder of this chapter, we will use interchangeably the terms 'poor', 'small', and 'south' in referring to the less industrialized region. The other region is referred to as the 'rich', 'large', or northern region.

18.2 THE AUGMENTED FC MODEL

The FC model on which this chapter builds is described at length in Chapter 3, so here we merely recall the main assumptions and focus instead on the additional assumptions we require. As usual, the basic set-up consists of two regions (north and south) that belong to the same nation; two factors (labour, L, and physical capital, K) and two sectors, manufacturing, M, and agriculture, A. Individuals have identical preferences, endowments, and technology. Regions differ in their size only, so that the north is just the scaled-up version of the south. In particular, the north's endowment of both capital and labour is $\Lambda > 1$ times the south's endowment of capital and labour. For this reason, we will sometimes refer to Λ as the relative economic strength of north (or, equivalently, as the relative economic weakness of south).

Turning to technology, both labour and capital are used to produce the differentiated good M under increasing return to scale and monopolistic competition. Production of each manufacturing variety involves a one-time fixed cost consisting of one unit of K and a per-unit-of-output cost consisting of a_M units of L. Sector A produces a homogenous good under constant return to scale and perfect competition using one unit of labour per unit of output (labour is the only input). This good is also chosen as the numeraire. As usual, we choose units of A such that the wage equals unity in both regions (this assumes no full specialization; see Chapter 3 for details). Labour is perfectly mobile across sectors, but immobile across regions.

Physical capital can move freely between regions, but capital owners cannot, so all K reward is repatriated to the country of origin. Industrial and agricultural goods are traded. Trade in A is costless. Industrial trade is impeded by frictional (i.e. 'iceberg') import and barriers and transportation costs such that $\tau \geq 1$ units of a good must be shipped in order to sell one unit abroad. In this chapter τ is mostly interpreted as technical trade barriers (τ generated no tariff revenue). Accordingly, we refer to regional integration as a gradual fall in τ.

Preferences of the representative consumer comprise the usual Cobb–Douglas nest of a CES aggregate of industrial varieties and consumption of the A good. More precisely, in this chapter we take a logarithmic functional form, $U = \mu \ln(M) + (1 - \mu) \ln A$, where M is the CES composite of all manufacturing varieties (see Chapter 3 for a precise definition) and A is the amount of good A consumed.

As always, the key to the spatial equilibrium is the region-specific reward to the mobile factor (capital in this case). Capital's reward in the FC model is the operating profit of a typical industrial variety (see Chapter 3) and these are

$$\pi = bB\frac{E^w}{K^w}, \quad \pi^* = bB^*\frac{E^w}{K^w}; \quad b \equiv \frac{\mu}{\sigma} \tag{18.1}$$

where the notation is standard; π is the operating profit, E^w and K^w are economy-wide levels of expenditure and capital, respectively. Also the B's are

$$B \equiv \frac{s_E}{\Delta} + \phi\frac{1 - s_E}{\Delta^*}, \quad B^* \equiv \phi\frac{s_E}{\Delta} + \frac{1 - s_E}{\Delta^*} \tag{18.2}$$

where s_E defines the north's share of total expenditure, $E^w \equiv E + E^*$, where the E's are region-specific expenditure (an asterisk indicates southern variables as usual) and the Δ's are

$$\Delta \equiv s_n + \phi(1 - s_n), \quad \Delta^* \equiv \phi s_n + 1 - s_n \tag{18.3}$$

where s_n is the share of industrial firms operating in the north.

18.2.1 The Nature of Subsidies

To keep things simple, we assume that subsidies are paid on a per firm basis, that is, independent of output. Given that the one-time fixed cost consists of one unit of K, such subsidies actually represent a subsidy to capital.

THE θ NOTATION

As it turns out, the equilibrium expressions are neater and more easily manipulated when subsides are defined in a rather unconventional way. To explain the notation, we first specify the equilibrium conditions using standard notation. When subsidies are provided to firms that are located in the south, the spatial allocation of firms (s_n) adjusts to the point where the pre-subsidy reward to employing capital in the north, that is, π, just equals the post-subsidy reward in the south, that is, $\pi^*(1 + z^*)$, where z^* is the per firm payment and π^* is the pre-subsidy reward to south-based capital. When north-based firms are subsidized, the division of firms (s_n) adjusts until $\pi(1 + z)$ equals π^*, where z is the per firm payment. These conditions, expressed in ratios, become $\pi/\pi^* = 1/(1 + z)$ when northern production is favoured and $\pi/\pi^* = (1 + z^*)$ when the south is favoured.

Alternatively, we can define the size and direction of the subsidy implicitly with the *equilibrium* ratio of *pre-subsidy* operating profits,

$$\theta \equiv \frac{\pi}{\pi^*} \tag{18.4}$$

With this notation, we know that if $\theta > 1$ *in equilibrium*, then it must be that southern production is subsidized; the size of the subsidy is $\theta - 1$. When $\theta < 1$, we know that northern production is favoured and the per firm subsidy rate is $1/\theta - 1$. Clearly $\theta = 1$ means that capital is not subsidized anywhere (viz. $z = z^* = 0$) and the lower is the absolute value of $\theta - 1$, the smaller is the subsidy.[1]

To put this differently, when production takes place in both regions, perfect capital mobility equalizes the post-subsidy rewards to capital across regions, that is, $\rho = \rho^*$ in equilibrium. Due to subsidies, however, the π's (i.e. the rewards before taxes or subsidies are paid) can differ. In particular, when a firm setting up in the south is subsidized (viz. $\theta > 1$), the prevailing equilibrium private return on capital, ρ, is equal to $\pi = \theta\pi^*$. When $\theta < 1$, namely when firms in the north are subsidized, $\rho = \pi/\theta = \pi^*$.

In what follows, the location subsidy is determined implicitly as the result of a political game between the two regions. We assume that at most one region at a time is subsidized, viz. $\min\{z, z^*\} = 0$. This is without loss of generality because, in the model we are using, only relative size matter. Moreover, $\min\{z, z^*\} = 0$ is always an equilibrium of the game we depict below even in the more general case in which both regions can be subsidized.[2]

18.2.2 The Nature of Taxation

The subsidies in our model are paid for by lump-sum taxation. We identify each unit of labour with an individual, so the per person tax can be expressed as a per unit of L tax (the labour supply is perfectly inelastic on a region-by-region basis). Moreover, we assume that the government budget is always in balance, so the level of taxation is tied to the level of subsidies. For example, if firms in the south are subsidized ($\theta > 1$), the government budget is balanced if and only if

$$TL^W = (\theta - 1)(1 - s_n)K^W\pi^*, \quad L^W \equiv L + L^* \tag{18.5}$$

where T is the per capita lump-sum tax. The left-hand side is the government revenue and the right-hand side represents the subsidy paid to the $n^* = (1 - s_n)K^W$ firms that operate in the south.

---

[1] To be precise, we could imagine a situation in which firms in both regions are subsidized. Hence, $\theta = (1 + z^*)/(1 + z)$ and θ is equal to 1 whenever $z = z^*$. Moreover, z and z^* have no influence on the spatial equilibrium or on welfare beyond the ratio θ (the latter follows from our assumption that capital ownership is uniformly distributed in this economy). Hence, it is only a minor abuse of language to say that $\theta > 1$ ($\theta < 1$) represents a subsidy to firms in the south (north).

[2] We can also use perturbations to the game so that this would be the unique equilibrium.

In keeping with our interpretation of the two regions as areas within a nation, the tax per capita is the same for residents of both north and south.

18.2.3 Equilibrium Market Size

Each region's representative consumers own the entire region's L and K and their income (and expenditure) equals $wL + \rho K$, where ρ is the subsidy-inclusive return on capital. The typical northern consumer pays lump-sum tax, T, so his/ her disposable income is $w + \rho K/L - T$. There are no savings in this static model, so private expenditure equals disposable income. Therefore, with wages equal to unity, we can write

$$E = L + \rho K - LT, \quad E^* = L^* + \rho K^* - L^*T \tag{18.6}$$

Here, we assume that north and south have the same capital/labour ratio, so $LT/E = L^*T/E^*$, namely, taxes paid by northern and southern residents as a share of their expenditure are the same.

To find the E's in terms of primitives, we rely on the standard normalizations, the standard result that $\pi = px/\sigma$ and $\pi^* = px/\sigma$, where p is producer price and x is typical output, and the standard result that $\mu(E + E^*) = npx + n^*p^*x^*$ (see Chapter 3). These facts and using (18.5) and (18.6), we have $\rho[s_n + (1 - s_n)/\theta](1 - b) = bL^w/K^w$, where $b \equiv \mu/\sigma$ as usual. Employing this implicit expression for ρ in (18.5) and (18.6), we get

$$\Lambda = \frac{E}{E^*}; \quad E = \frac{L}{1 - b}, \quad E^* = \frac{L^*}{1 - b}; \quad b \equiv \frac{\mu}{\sigma} \tag{18.7}$$

where Λ is our notation for relative market size. Observe that the expressions for the E's are identical to those we find without subsidies. To summarize this, we write the following result.

> **Result 18.1.** *Relative expenditure—namely E/E^*—is a function only of relative labour endowments.*

To understand this result, note that since taxes are collected in a lump-sum fashion, taxation has no efficiency loss associated with it. Moreover, each individual is both a taxpayer and an owner of capital and labour, so the government's budget balance condition means that on net, capital owners' incomes are unaffected by the tax-cum-subsidy. The final point to note is that free capital mobility means that capital owners who receive the subsidy earn no more than those who receive no subsidy, so netting out the tax-cum-subsidy, capital owners' incomes are unaffected by taxation. Labourers, of course, always earn their marginal product and this is unaffected by the subsidies. Of course, if capital ownership were not uniform, the tax-cum-subsidy policy would have redistributive effects.

We now have everything at hand to solve for the spatial equilibrium of industry.

18.2.4 Equilibrium Location

To close the model, we invoke the location condition that states that north-based and south-based capital earn the same post-subsidy rate of return. The distribution of industry that solves this is

$$s_n = \frac{s_E(1 - \phi^2) - \phi(\theta - \phi)}{(1 - \phi)[(\theta - \phi) - s_E(\theta - 1)(1 + \phi)]} \tag{18.8}$$

This expression holds for admissible values of s_n, namely when parameters are such that $0 < s_n < 1$. Outside this parameter space, s_n equals zero or 1 in an obvious manner. This expression is more informative than what might be inferred at first sight. By inspection, s_n is increasing in s_E (and hence in the north's relative size Λ) and is decreasing in the north's relative cost of capital θ. Denoting as $s_n/(1 - s_n)$, the number of northern firms relative to the south's, it can be shown, using (18.8), that η is larger than Λ if $\Lambda > 1 > \theta$. These inequalities illustrate effects that will be recurrent in what follows.

Expression (18.8) is the fulcrum of our analysis, so it is worth studying it in the absence of subsidies, that is, when $\theta = 1$ (in this case we are back to the case studied in Chapter 3). The equilibrium η in this case is

$$\eta|_{\theta=1} = \frac{\Lambda - \phi}{1 - \Lambda\phi}; \quad \Lambda \equiv \frac{s_E}{1 - s_E}, \quad \eta \equiv \frac{s_n}{1 - s_n} \tag{18.9}$$

When 1 is larger than $\Lambda\phi$, making trade freer ($d\phi > 0$), this results in a delocation of firms to the big region. More specifically, the home-market effect (HME) manifests itself as

$$\frac{\partial \eta}{\partial \Lambda}\bigg|_{\theta=1} = \frac{1 - \phi^2}{(1 - \Lambda\phi)^2} > 1; \quad \lim_{\phi \to 1/\Lambda} \eta = +\infty \tag{18.10}$$

The first expression says that a larger region will get a more than proportional share of industry. It holds whenever $\phi < 1/\Lambda$. On the other hand, when $\phi \geq 1/\Lambda$, the second expression in (18.10) says that all firms cluster in 1, viz. $\eta = +\infty$ or $n = 1$. In words, all firms cluster in the larger region when trade costs are low enough (ϕ sufficiently close to unity), yet strictly positive (ϕ strictly lower than unity). Note also the magnification effect of trade liberalization of the first term, viz. $\partial^2 \eta/\partial \Lambda \partial \phi > 0$. These results are described more fully in Chapter 3.

In order to isolate the effect of a subsidy on the firm allocation share, we now take the opposite simplifying case and calculate the equilibrium, η, for $\Lambda = 1$ and take the derivative of this with respect to $1/\theta$. Using (18.8), it is easy to show that $\partial \eta/\partial(1/\theta)$ is larger than one when $\Lambda = 1$. This says that one additional unit of subsidy given to the north leads to a more than proportional change in the share of firms in the north. We call this property the home-subsidy effect by analogy with the HME. Trade liberalization magnifies this effect as well, viz. $\partial^2 \eta/\partial(1/\theta)\partial \phi > 0$. We can summarize this in the following result.

Result 18.2. *Ceteris paribus, the region that has the larger income or the region that is subsidized has an equilibrium share of industrial firms that is larger than its share of income or than its relative subsidy. These biases are magnified by high levels of openness.*

Both the home-market and the home-subsidy effects will be used in the following sections to help boost intuition.

The equilibrium conditions for the A sector are the standard ones from the FC model, and, since they play no role in our analysis, we omit them here (see Chapter 3).

18.3 THE VOTE MARKET EFFECT

Our ultimate goal is to determine the equilibrium size and direction of subsidies, but before adding political economy elements to our analysis, it proves instructive to see how exogenous changes in subsidies affect welfare and the spatial allocation of firms.

We start with the following definitions:

$$\underline{\theta} \equiv \max\{\theta : s_n = 1\}, \quad \bar{\theta} \equiv \min\{\theta : s_n = 0\}, \quad \Theta \equiv [\underline{\theta}, \bar{\theta}] \tag{18.11}$$

where s_n is given by (18.8). The latter shows the minimum level of subsidization necessary to attract all firms in the small region (south). The former shows the minimum level of subsidy (possibly negative) to firms located in the north that is necessary to concentrate industry there. Substituting $s_n = 0$ and $s_n = 1$ in (18.8), these two parameters and the interval they form are defined respectively as

$$\bar{\theta} \equiv \frac{\Lambda + \phi^2}{(1 + \Lambda)\phi}, \quad \underline{\theta}^{-1} \equiv \frac{1 + \Lambda\phi^2}{(1 + \Lambda)\phi}, \quad \Theta \equiv [\underline{\theta}, \bar{\theta}] \tag{18.12}$$

Θ is the vertical interval between the two curves.

Figure 18.1 plots $\bar{\theta}$ and $\underline{\theta}$ as a function of trade freeness, ϕ, for a given value of Λ. As is possible to see from the top curve, the freer is trade, the smaller is the subsidy required to attract all the firms to south because liberalization amplifies the effect of a subsidy. This is just a straightforward application of the home-market magnification effect we explored at length in Part I. That is, since industry becomes *more* footloose as trade becomes free, the impact of a given subsidy is magnified when trade becomes freer. Note that, since $\bar{\theta} > 1$ holds for all ϕ, the minimum level of subsidy to industries in the south that makes this small region the core is always positive. In other words, an active regional policy is necessary to offset the tendency of the small region to lose firms as ϕ rises. (See Chapter 13 for an analysis of liberalization-linked delocation with asymmetric regions and no subsidy.)

The converse is not necessarily true, as a look at $\underline{\theta}$ (the bottom curve) shows: the relationship between the minimum level of subsidies to firms located in the north necessary to keep all the firms in the same region and the level of trade integration is bell-shaped. The reason is that the HME works in favour of the

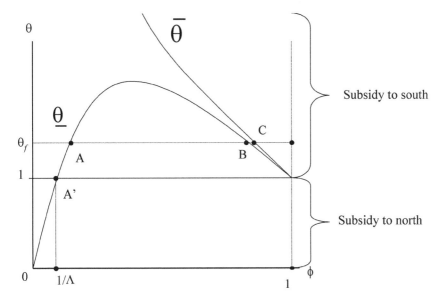

Figure 18.1   Subsidies and equilibrium location.

large region, so that a small tax on firms there (or, equivalently, a small subsidy on potential firms in south) is ineffective in making any firm move to the smaller region for any $\phi > 1/\Lambda$. The fact that taxing capital in the core does not necessarily lead it to relocate comes in sharp contrast to the classical results on tax competition (see Chapter 16).

It is also instructive to consider the effectiveness of a given level of subsidy to the firms in the south along the integration path. In particular, consider what the location effects are when ϕ varies but θ is fixed at some arbitrary level (shown as θ_f in the diagram). When ϕ is relatively close to zero, there is some economic activity in both regions since $\theta \in \Theta$. As the two regions become more integrated, the HME starts dominating the subsidy effect. From point A onwards, the relative strength of the HME is so reinforced by an ongoing integration process that this level of subsidy to industrial activity in the south is completely ineffective and this small region becomes the periphery region ($s_n = 1$) in spite of the subsidy on offer. As ϕ continues to increase, the relative strength of the HME decreases and eventually, when point B is reached, some of the firms start leaving the north (which is hence no longer a core). Things get even worse for the larger region as transportation costs fall further: to the right of point C, the core is in the south. Again, if we take the model literally, this shows how effective regional policy is when ϕ is close to unity. Without any subsidy ($\theta = 1$), the core would be (and remain) in the north from point A$'$ onwards.

Lastly, note that an increase in $\Lambda \equiv E/E^*$ strengthens the home-market effect. As it is possible to see from (18.12), a higher value of Λ makes both $\underline{\theta}$ and $\bar{\theta}$ shift upward. As a result, the minimum subsidy to south's firms needed to keep the core there has to be higher. Likewise, the upward shift of $\underline{\theta}$ implies that the minimum subsidy level needed to ensure that the core is in the north is now lower. Conversely, the range of trade freeness, for which a small subsidy offered to locations in the south, still compatible with the core remaining in the north, is wider.

18.3.1 The 'Subsidy Effect' on Welfare

Since equilibrium nominal incomes are function of the parameters only, in particular they are invariant to η and θ, the welfare of the representative individual is a function of the price index prevailing in the region where he/she lives. Mathematically, the assumed functional forms give us the following expressions for the indirect utility functions:

$$V(\theta; \phi) = \ln\left(\frac{\mu}{\sigma - \mu}\right) + \frac{\mu}{\sigma - 1}\ln[\phi + (1 - \phi)s_n(\theta)] \qquad (18.13)$$

for the north's representative consumer and

$$V^*(\theta; \phi) = \ln\left(\frac{\mu}{\sigma - \mu}\right) + \frac{\mu}{\sigma - 1}\ln[1 - (1 - \phi)s_n(\theta)] \qquad (18.14)$$

for the south's representative consumer, with η taken from (18.8). The first term on the right-hand side of each expression above is the (log of) per capita income and the second term is the true price index for each representative consumer. As can be easily inferred from these expressions, welfare is monotonically increasing in the ratio of firms that locate in the agent's region as this person would then save on transportation costs.

This implies that $\partial V/\partial s_n > 0$ and $\partial V^*/\partial s_n < 0$. Since s_n itself is decreasing in θ, we have the obvious relationship between indirect utilities and the subsidy given to the south: $\partial V/\partial \theta < 0$ and $\partial V^*/\partial \theta > 0$. Of course, (18.13) and (18.14) hold for values of s_n in $(0, 1)$ or, which is the same thing by (18.12), for values of θ in Θ. Hence, we have the following result.

Result 18.3. $\underline{\theta}$ *and* $\bar{\theta}$ *are the bliss points of any individual in the north and south, respectively.*

With this analysis at hand, we now turn to the political process that will determine θ and s_n.

18.3.2 The Voting Model

The political environment is as follows. Both regions belong to the same constituency. All voters, whether living in the north (as L of them do) or in the south (as L^* of them do), choose a candidate from the same set of candidates. This set is exogenously given for simplicity.

The political game belongs to the Hotelling–Ledyard class of models and makes the following assumptions (see Osborne 1995 and Ledyard 1984):

1. The policy space Θ as defined in (18.12) is one-dimensional.
2. The set of candidates $\{A, B\}$ is fixed and finite.

3. Each candidate is 'Downsian' in that he/she cares only about winning office and is assumed to maximize his/her expected number of votes.

4. The number of citizens, whose preferences are monotonic on Θ, is finite and equal to L^w.

5. Candidates simultaneously choose a position on Θ (their 'platform').

6. Having observed the candidates' platform, voters decide whether to vote or not and, if so, for which candidate. Voting is costless.

Additionally, our formulation of the voting model follows Lindbeck and Weibull (1987). Candidates differ not only on the policy issue (i.e. in their platform), but also on a second dimension, orthogonal to the policy space—call it ideology or party membership. The ideology of a candidate is not part of his/her platform because he/she cannot credibly change it, by assumption.[3]

Voters derive utility both from consumption and how much their own ideology matches the winning candidate's; ideology is assumed to be unrelated to consumption for simplicity. Hence, their utility function has two components. The materialistic component—V and V^* as in (18.13) and (18.14)—is directly affected by the subsidy policy and is known to both candidates. The other component of people's utility is derived from other policies proposed by the competing parties or by attributes specific to the candidates. Importantly, the candidates know only the *distribution* of the voters along this dimension. Hence, in effect, voters face a discrete choice between two candidates that they perceive as different, even if the latter choose the same platform θ. This parallels the discrete choice theory of product differentiation, in which firms cannot observe all the variables affecting consumer choices (see Anderson et al. 1992 for a concise treatment of this theory). In other words, even if each consumer or voter chooses a single option (to vote for one candidate or the other), outside observers (the candidates) see utility as a random variable reflecting unobservable preferences. We adopt this interpretation of the model, although other interpretations are also possible.

At the time they simultaneously announce their platform, candidates know only the distribution of voters along the ideological dimension. If candidates A and B share the same platform, a given voter prefers the first of the two if candidate A's ideology is closer to his/hers. If, on the other hand, candidate B proposes a platform on the policy issue that suits this voter better than A's, the voter trades off his/her ideological preference against his/her policy one. The extent to which he/she is willing to do so depends upon the strength of his/her ideology, a variable that is unknown to anybody but him/her. This assumption will ensure that each candidate's best response correspondence will be a smooth, continuous function.[4]

---

[3] This dimension is assumed to merge all the issues that voters might care about—that is, all but regional policy. For example, it may include the parties' manifesto on moral issues (e.g. death penalty) as well as on long-standing economic positions like commitment to free trade. The key assumption here is that, on all these issues, the candidates are already pre-committed, whilst they are (credibly) campaigning on the regional policy issue only.

[4] Anticipating the results, the assumptions just listed will ensure the convergence of the candidates' platform to a unique equilibrium policy. This outcome is a Condorcet winner, that is, a policy that beats in probability any other feasible policy in a pair-wise vote.

As far as the voting rule is concerned, we abstract from entry issues and assume that two candidates, belonging to two distinct parties, compete for office. Each candidate $i \in \{A, B\}$ proposes a value θ_i in Θ, that is, suggests to what extent he/she wishes to subsidize the south. Voters cast a ballot for one of the candidates, according to their idiosyncratic preference and to the candidates' platforms. The elected candidate sticks to his/her policy platform once in office; his/her promise is credible in game theoretical terms, since candidates do not care about the policy outcome.

To illustrate voters' payoffs, consider a particular northern voter, voter j. If candidate B is elected, then voter j's utility (both materialistic and derived from his/her ideology) is assumed to be equal to $V(\theta_B) + \varepsilon_j/2$, where $V(\ )$ is the materialistic utility and measures the voter's economic welfare derived from the implementation of candidate B's economic platform, whereas ε_j is voter j's idiosyncratic ideological bias towards party B and measures the utility he/she derives from B's political leadership. This latter term is negative if voter j is ideologically closer to candidate A, and equal to zero if he/she is ideologically neutral and cares only about economic policy. Conversely, if candidate A is elected, voter j enjoys utility $V(\theta_A) - \varepsilon_j/2$. Voter j is indifferent between candidates A and B for the platforms θ_A and θ_B if and only if

$$V(\theta_A) - V(\theta_B) = \varepsilon_j \qquad (18.15)$$

When (18.15) holds, j votes for candidate A with probability 1/2, but would vote for the same candidate with probability one or with probability zero if this expression held with strict inequality. Given θ_A and θ_B, this voter is ideologically neutral. We call such a voter a 'swing voter'. Hereafter, we refer to the value of his/her idiosyncratic parameter as ε_S (subscript S stands for 'swing'). Similar expressions hold in the south, therefore

$$\varepsilon_S = V(\theta_A) - V(\theta_B), \quad \varepsilon_S^* = V^*(\theta_A) - V^*(\theta_B) \qquad (18.16)$$

18.3.3 Timing of the Game

The timing of the elections is as follows. First, both candidate A and candidate B announce their platforms simultaneously and non-cooperatively, knowing the preferences of voters over θ and the probability density function of ε_j and ε_j^*. Second, uncertainty is resolved and voting takes place. Finally, the elected candidate implements the platform he/she announced in the first stage.

We now introduce an important assumption. In each region, all ε's are drawn from a continuously differentiable, symmetric cumulative distribution function (cdf) that has mean zero. We denote the two cdfs as $F(\varepsilon)$ in the north and $F^*(\varepsilon)$ in the south. These cdf's are known to all so there is no aggregate uncertainty. We assume that $F(\varepsilon)$ and $F_2(\varepsilon)$ belong to the same family.

Our working assumption is that social and economic activities are more variegated and heterogeneous in the big, urban region. Indeed, it is a stylized fact that larger cities tend to be more diversified (Duranton and Puga 2000). Mathematically, we assume that this translates into a higher dispersion of the cumulative distribution around the mean in the big region. Hence, if ψ^2 is the variance of $F(\varepsilon)$ and ψ^{*2} the variance of $F^*(\varepsilon)$, we assume $\psi > \psi^*$.[5] There is a technical issue here. To be rigorous, double-sided uncertainty is needed for the equilibrium to exist. That is, some of the attributes of the candidates are unknown to the voters at the time candidates choose their platforms. As a consequence, the mean of both $F(\varepsilon)$ and $F^*(\varepsilon)$ is itself a random variable. We take it to be symmetrically distributed around 0. The algebra below is unaffected by other parameters of the distribution of the common mean (like its variance that we assume to be finite) so we leave this issue in the background from now on.

It can be shown that $F(\varepsilon)$ and $F^*(\varepsilon)$ together with $V(\theta)$ and $V^*(\theta)$ fulfil the sufficient conditions for a Nash equilibrium in the platform-setting game to exist because they are quasi-concave in θ. To see this, note that the V's are concave with respect to s_n and that s_n is a monotonic function of θ; together, these facts ensure the result.[6] In particular, it is sufficient for the V's to be concave in n— which they are—given our assumptions on the F's. Details can be found in Robert-Nicoud and Sbergami (2001, 2002).

Given these assumptions, and making use of the definition of Λ (viz. $\Lambda \equiv L/L^*$), candidate A's expected vote share is

$$s_A = \frac{\Lambda}{\Lambda + 1} F(\varepsilon_S) + \frac{1}{\Lambda + 1} F^*(\varepsilon_S^*) = \frac{1}{2} + \frac{\Omega(\theta_A, \theta_B)}{2} \tag{18.17}$$

where s_A is candidate A's share of votes, and

$$\Omega(\theta_A, \theta_B) \equiv \frac{\Lambda}{\Lambda + 1} F[V(\theta_A) - V(\theta_B)] + \frac{1}{\Lambda + 1} F^*[V^*(\theta_A) - V^*(\theta_B)] \tag{18.18}$$

Candidate A's probability of winning the election is increasing in $\Omega(\theta_A, \theta_B)$. Candidate B's expected vote share is equal to $1 - s_A$.

If the ε's were uniformly distributed, Ω would look like a weighted social welfare function, with the weights to V and V^* being proportional to the 'economic' sizes $s_E = \Lambda/(\Lambda + 1)$ and $1 - s_E = 1/(\Lambda + 1)$, respectively, and inversely proportional to the standard deviations of the idiosyncratic ideological preferences (ψ and ψ^*). In other words, a north vote is worth Λ/ψ and a south vote is worth $1/\psi^*$ to the politicians. This is due to the underlying uncertainty in the ε's. The same intuition carries over for more general distributions, F.

To understand the incentives the candidates face when setting their plat-form, suppose for a while that candidate A is considering a shift in his/her

---

[5] Another way of interpreting this assumption is as follows. Assume that $F_1(\varepsilon)$ and $F_2(\varepsilon)$ are identical with variance 1, but that the spatial distribution of industry is a more salient issue to those voters left behind in the periphery than to those living in the core, as it presumably is. That is, assume now that the welfare of individual j in 1 or 2 is $(1 - \psi')V_1(\theta) + \psi'\varepsilon_j$ or $(1 - \gamma)V_2(\theta) + \gamma\varepsilon_j$, respec-tively. The assumption that regional policy is more salient in 2 is equivalent to assuming $\psi' > \gamma$. In aggregate terms, the two interpretations are equivalent. (Indeed, with $\psi' = \psi/(1 - \psi)$ and $\gamma = \psi^*/(1 + \psi^*)$ all the analytical results below are strictly identical.) In what follows, we use the termi-nology of the interpretation developed in the text.

[6] See, for example, Theorem 2 in Lindberg and Weibull (1987) for details.

platform from θ_A to θ'_A. A higher θ will boost the equilibrium number of firms in the south at the expense of the north, causing an increase in southern voters' materialistic utility and a reduction in northern voters' materialistic utility. This shifts the identity of the swing voters in both regions, as can be seen from expression (18.16). As a result of his/her unilateral deviation, candidate A gains some votes in the south and loses others in the north. Candidate A has no longer any incentive to deviate when the number of votes lost in the latter is equal to the number of votes gained in the former. This brings us to the solution of the candidates' problem.

18.3.4 The Nash Equilibrium of the Platform Setting Game

Candidate A maximizes his/her expected number of votes given by (18.17) and (18.18), announcing a certain policy θ_A taking θ_B as given. Candidate B instead will seek to minimizes the votes A receives by choosing θ_B for a given θ_A. Hence, $\theta_A^{NE} = \mathrm{argmax}\{\Omega(\theta_A, \theta_B^{NE}) : \theta_A \in \Theta\}$ and $\theta_B^{NE} = \mathrm{argmin}\{\Omega(\theta_A^{NE}, \theta_B) : \theta_B \in \Theta\}$, where the function Ω is defined in (18.18) and NE stands for 'Nash equilibrium'. In words, the objectives of candidates A and B are perfectly symmetric and so they face the same optimization problem. In equilibrium, they both find it optimal to announce the same level of subsidies, which we call θ_{NE}.

Using (18.8), (18.13), (18.14), (18.17), and (18.18), the equilibrium policy announcement θ_{NE} is the solution to the following first-order condition of this problem for both candidates, which reduces to

$$\left[\Lambda f(0) \frac{\partial V}{\partial n}(\theta_{NE}) + f^*(0) \frac{\partial V^*}{\partial n}(\theta_{NE}) \right] \frac{\partial n}{\partial \theta}(\theta_{NE}) = 0 \qquad (18.19)$$

where f and f^* are the pdfs of F and F^*, respectively. The second-order condition is satisfied by the quasi-concavity of the V's with respect to θ. Notice that, due to standard statistical properties of probability distribution functions belonging to the same family, we have $f^*(0)/f(0) = \psi/\psi^*$. Define m as the ratio of the two standard deviations, viz.

$$m \equiv \frac{\psi}{\psi^*} = \frac{f^*(0)}{f(0)} > 1 \qquad (18.20)$$

We can interpret m as the relative 'political strength' of the south.

In (18.19), $\Lambda f(0)$ and $f^*(0)$ represent the mass of swing voters in the north and south, respectively (up to a factor $1 + \Lambda$)—namely, the mass of those voters that are marginally indifferent between the two candidates at equilibrium. This mass is increasing with the size of the region electorate (L or L^*) and inversely related to the spread of the population along the political dimension (ψ or ψ^*). Finally, solving for θ_{NE} gives

$$\theta_{NE} = 1 + \frac{(m-1)(1-\phi)}{1+\phi m} \qquad (18.21)$$

if $\theta_{NE} \in \Theta$, or θ_{NE} is equal to either boundary of Θ in an obvious manner otherwise.[7] Since $\phi < 1$, this is larger than unity under the assumption that $\psi > \psi^*$.[8] To get the political equilibrium location, plug (18.21) into (18.8) to get

$$\eta_{NE} = \frac{\Lambda - m\phi}{m - \Lambda\phi} \tag{18.22}$$

Simple derivations give the expected signs for the following partial derivatives: $\partial\eta_{NE}/\partial\Lambda > 0$ and $\partial\eta_{NE}/\partial m < 0$, namely, the share of firms in the north increases with its size and decreases in the south's political strength. To sum up, we have shown the following result.

Result 18.4. *At the political equilibrium, each region's share of industry is increasing in its size and in its ideological homogeneity. The equilibrium subsidy is increasing in a region's ideological homogeneity.*

18.3.5 The Vote-Market and the Net-Market Effects

Many interesting results stem from (18.21) and (18.22). Since the ultimate concern of voters is to attract economic activities in the region where they live, let us focus first on η_{NE}. As it is clear from (18.22), once we introduce the political dimension as a determinant of the policy decision, the equilibrium industry share does not depend solely on the economic forces. Indeed, the equilibrium share of industry of, say, the north is increasing with its (relative) expenditure size Λ—essentially an economic parameter—and decreasing in its ideological heterogeneity—a socio-economic parameter that reflects the relative salience of the regional policy issue for those living in the south.

The first of these two effects is well known and is an alternative formulation of the standard home-market effect. The second one is what Robert-Nicoud and Sbergami (2001, 2002) call the 'vote-market effect' (VME) by analogy. Recall that in the standard model (viz. $m = 1$), the HME is defined as $\partial\eta/\partial\Lambda > 1$ whenever $\Lambda > 1$. Likewise, when the two regions have the same size ($\Lambda = 1$), the VME is defined as $\partial\eta/\partial(1/m) > 1$ if and only if $1/m > 1$.

In order to determine which dominates, we define a third effect shortly, namely the *net-market effect* (NME). To this aim, we need to introduce a new variable,

$$\Lambda_{\text{swing}} \equiv \frac{\Lambda}{m} \equiv \frac{L/L^*}{\psi/\psi^*} \tag{18.23}$$

representing the overall relative force of the two regions. Particularly, Λ_{swing} is the ratio of the mass of swing voters in the north to the mass of swing voters in the south. Note that Λ_{swing} can be below or above unity. Using this definition in (18.22), it is easy to check that

---

[7] Note that the utilitarian optimum is the laissez-faire outcome. Indeed, the utilitarian planner puts equal weights on anybody's welfare as does the candidate facing the population with identical ideological spreads (see Chapter 9).

[8] The attentive reader might have noticed that apparently regional size does not matter in determining the equilibrium subsidy; we get back to this in Section 18.3.6.

$$\frac{\partial \eta_{NE}}{\partial \Lambda_{swing}} = \frac{1 - \phi^2}{(1 - \phi \Lambda_{swing})^2} > 1 \quad \Leftrightarrow \quad \Lambda_{swing} > 1 \qquad (18.24)$$

In other words, we have the following result.

Result 18.5 (net-market effect). *At equilibrium, the region that has more swing voters will get a more than proportionally larger share of industries.*

To put it differently, in equilibrium, the big region (north) will have a more-than-proportional share of industry only if its economic strength (measured by its relative expenditure Λ) more than compensates its political weakness due to the higher dispersion of its population over the political dimension $(1 < m)$. Conversely the economically small region (south) can attract a more-than-proportional share of industry if it has enough political power, that is, if it has a sufficiently large mass of swing voters. Thus, when the VME is added to the basic model, predictions may differ from those induced by the standard economic HME and the political game may qualitatively reverse the laissez-faire outcome.

A final point deserves attention here. When trade barriers are sufficiently low, but still positive, our model features a core–periphery outcome (unless $\Lambda_{swing} = 1$). In particular, all the economic activities concentrate in the large region ($\eta_{NE} = +\infty$) whenever $\phi > 1/\Lambda_{swing}$, while the south becomes the core ($\eta_{NE} = 0$) whenever $\phi > \Lambda_{swing}$. Note that the two are mutually exclusive because $\phi \in [0, 1)$.

The novelty of this analysis is that when political factors are included, we find that the standard prediction (the big region becomes the core) does not necessarily hold. In other words, the political environment does matter in shaping the equilibrium geography.

Having analysed the equilibrium location of economic activities, we can now turn to the analysis of the equilibrium subsidy level which delivers η_{NE}.

18.3.6 The Equilibrium Subsidy Level: Does Size Matter?

As expected, interior solutions for θ_{NE} are increasing in m—see (18.25). Candidates want to attract swing voters and the less dispersed group has a larger mass of such voters, ceteris paribus. Hence, the wider is the difference in the homogeneity degree of the two regions, the higher is the subsidy level that the relatively more homogeneous region receives. Besides, θ_{NE} is larger than unity and, hence, the south is subsidized because $m > 1$. This departure from a majoritarian result, which is due to the fact that regional policy is more salient to a minority of citizens, is one of the sources of non-majoritarian outcomes discussed in Besley and Coate (2000).

The attentive reader might have noticed that apparently regional size does not matter in determining the equilibrium subsidy θ_{NE}. Indeed, the economic weight Λ does not appear in (18.21) and the region that gets the subsidy is the more homogeneous one, independently from its size. As we shall see, this is clearly a knife-edge result that depends on the logarithmic transformation of the aggregate consumption index in the utility function, U. More generally, the relative size of the two populations matter, and the effect of an increase of Λ on θ_{NE} is ambiguous.

This is best understood from the dual nature of Λ. On one hand, this represents the ratio of electorates and hence, since candidates try to get as many votes as possible, a larger Λ implies a lower θ, ceteris paribus. But on the other hand, Λ also represents the ratio of expenditures and, given (18.8), a larger Λ implies a larger η. Hence, for a constant political equilibrium η_{NE} in (18.22), a larger Λ must be compensated by a larger θ so that the solution to the economic relationship (18.8) is unchanged. In other words, if the result of the political process decides for some location equilibrium, η_{NE}, a larger subsidy θ will be needed do accomplish this if Λ is larger.

This point is easily made mathematically. Let us untangle the two natures of Λ and write Λ_V when we talk about electorate sizes (the subscript V for voters) and Λ_C when we talk about economic sizes (the subscript C for consumers). Hence, since (18.8) is an economic equilibrium relationship, we write, using the η notation,

$$\eta = \frac{(1 - \theta\phi)\Lambda_C - \phi(\theta - \phi)}{-(1 - \theta\phi)\Lambda_C\phi + (\theta - \phi)} \tag{18.25}$$

Conversely, the Λ's in Section 18.3.2 clearly represent electorate sizes. Hence, we rewrite (18.22) as

$$\eta_{NE} = \frac{\Lambda_V - m\phi}{m - \Lambda_V\phi} \tag{18.26}$$

Obviously, the two η's must be consistent, so θ_{NE} solves $\eta = \eta_{NE}$. Using (18.8), the solution to this problem is

$$\theta_{NE} = 1 + (1 - \phi)\frac{(m - 1)\Lambda_C + m(\Lambda_C - \Lambda_V)}{(1 + \phi m)\Lambda_C - (\Lambda_C - \Lambda_V)} \tag{18.27}$$

Obviously, the solution to (18.27) is identical to the solution to (18.21) if and only if there are as many electors as consumers (or, more generally, when the participation rates are the same in the two regions).

For reasons explained earlier, (18.27) reveals the following result.

Result 18.6. *The equilibrium subsidy to the south is increasing in the north's relative market size, Λ_C, and decreasing in the north's electorate size, Λ_V.*

When Λ_C and Λ_V are equal, they cancel out *because of our choice of functional forms.*

Interestingly (18.26) tells us that only political variables matter in the determination of the η_{NE}. Indeed, η_{NE} is entirely determined by tastes, participation rates and ideological heterogeneities. Conversely, (18.27) suggest that economic variables matter only for the determination of the level of the instrument needed to accomplish the equilibrium policy.

A final remark is in order here. Different participation rates have the same qualitative effects on the equilibrium location and subsidies as different ideological heterogeneities. To fix ideas, take $m = 1$ but imagine instead that in the larger region the participation rate is m' times lower than in the small region—possibly because there are larger foreign populations in big cities and foreigners are forbidden to vote by law. This assumption implies $\Lambda_V = \Lambda_C/m'$.

Then, it is readily seen from both (18.26) and (18.27) that the solutions in (18.21) and (18.22) are identical, with Λ replaced by Λ_C and m replaced by m'. In short, we can either assume that large regions are socially more heterogeneous or that participation rates are lower there than in small regions. Both of these are reasonable assumptions that yield the same result: at the political equilibrium, small regions get a larger share of industry than in the laissez-faire equilibrium and, when trade costs are low enough, it is possible that the industrial cluster ends up in the economically disadvantaged region.

To summarize, the political equilibrium of this section game has removed the original definite prediction made in the original models like Krugman (1980) regarding the identity of the core. Taken at its face value, the analysis conducted in this chapter has shown that it is no longer obvious that the large, rich region or trading partner will eventually attract all the industrial activity.

18.4 THE ROLE OF THE ELECTORAL SYSTEM IN A DECENTRALIZED STATE

We have seen how consideration of political heterogeneity enriches the set of outcomes in a simple economic geography model. In this section, we analyse how the electoral system itself has an impact on the spatial equilibrium. To do this, we abstract from the considerations we have dealt with thus far. Rather, we take a much less centralized electoral system where C regions, as defined economically, would exactly match C electoral constituencies (hence the 'C'). We first extend the FC model to allow for $C \geq 2$ regions.

18.4.1 The Footloose Capital Model with Many Regions

It is a well-known result that the HME makes the equilibrium distribution of n more uneven than the underlying distribution of s_E, as we recall in the sequel (see Chapter 14 for details).

Assume that ϕ is low enough so that there are firms operating in every region $c = 1, \ldots, C$. Generalizing the FC model, the operating profit π^i of any firm located in some region $i \in \{1, \ldots, C\}$ is easily shown to obey

$$\pi^i = bB^i \frac{E^w}{K^w}; \quad B^i = \frac{s_E^i}{s_n^i + (1 - s_n^i)\phi} + \phi \sum_{c \neq i} \frac{s_E^c}{s_n^c + (1 - s_n^c)\phi} \quad (18.28)$$

Under laissez-faire and free capital mobility, the equilibrium rewards, π, must be equal in all i, as they are proportional to the operating profit at equilibrium. Therefore, using expression (18.28), we have

$$\frac{(1-\phi)s_E^i}{s_n^i + (1-s_n^i)\phi} + \sum_{c\neq i,j}\frac{\phi s_E^c}{s_n^c + (1-s_n^c)\phi} = \frac{(1-\phi)s_E^j}{s_n^j + (1-s_n^j)\phi} + \sum_{c\neq i,j}\frac{\phi s_E^c}{s_n^c + (1-s_n^c)\phi}$$

(18.29)

for any pair $i,j \in \{1,...,C\}$. Rearranging and summing over all j's, we get

$$s_n^i - s_E^i = \frac{\phi C}{1-\phi}\left(s_E^i - \frac{1}{C}\right)$$

(18.30)

Clearly, a region i will be a net importer of capital if and only if its total expenditure is larger than the average $1/C$. Note also that the multiplicative term in front of the large bracket in (18.30) is larger than zero and increasing in ϕ (this is the usual magnification effect of trade freeness) since C is a positive integer. Using this expression, it is easy (although cumbersome) to show that the HME, as usually defined, still holds.

The final step is to use (18.30) to calculate the variance of n as a function of the variance of e:

$$\sum_{i=1}^{C}\left(s_n^i - \frac{1}{C}\right)^2 = \left[\frac{1 + (C-1)\phi}{1-\phi}\right]^2\sum_{i=1}^{C}\left(s_E^i - \frac{1}{C}\right)^2$$

(18.31)

Clearly, the term in the square brackets is larger than unity, which proves the following claim.

Result 18.7. *In the multi-region FC model, the spread of industrial activity is more uneven that the spread of income or expenditure.*[9] *Moreover, the HME holds as in the simple two-region FC model.*

It is also clear from (18.30) that s_n^i is increasing with openness ϕ if and only if $s_E^i > 1/C$. As ϕ increases, each region loses industries one after the other, starting from the smallest. (In (18.30), C should actually be replaced by the number of regions j for which $s_n^j > 0$ and s_E^i calculated as j's share of income among the same pool of regions.) When ϕ is close to unity, only the largest one still has some industry.

18.4.2 A Simple Federation

In a C-region country, the regional policy instrument, θ, is a C-dimensional vector, viz. $\theta \equiv [\theta^1,...,\theta^C]'$. (For reasons discussed in Section 18.2, we can normalize one of the entries of θ to unity.)

We start by treating the legislature as a black box and assume that all members of parliament are equally powerful in shaping regional policy. In such a setting, it is clear that if constituencies are of different population sizes, a person in the small region would be over-represented. Call this system a federal one.

More formally, the game is defined as follows.

---

[9] More generally, the pdf of s_n is similar to the pdf of s_E, up to the factor $[1 + (C-1)\phi]/[1-\phi]$.

There are $C \geq 2$ constituencies, each represented by one member of parliament (MP). To abstract from electoral concerns, we assume here that the MPs are perfect delegates of their own constituency, c. A random coalition of size $S \leq C$ is drawn and chooses θ by bargaining. We use the solution concept of Cooperative Game Theory, the Shapley value.[10] Any MP is chosen with equal probability S/C to be part of the coalition of agenda setters. If the coalition disagrees, it is dissolved and a new, random coalition is put in charge. To make the point more forcefully, we also make the extreme assumption that no outsider has any amendment power. Clearly, each member of the coalition would now agree on a platform that gives $1/S$ firms to all member constituencies.[11] Since each constituency has the same probability S/C to be part of a ruling coalition by assumption, the expected share of industry for all c is $s_n^c = 1/C$, because $s_n^c = 1$ or $s_n^c = 0$ with probability S/C and $1 - S/C$, respectively.

Therefore, we have the following result.

Result 18.8. *In the simple federation, each region or constituency has the same political clout. Hence, the small regions get a larger share of industry in expected terms by comparison to the laissez-faire solution.*

Of course, this model is embarrassingly simplistic. For instance, there is no time dimension, and it suggests that the location equilibrium vector would change every time a new house is elected. Nevertheless, it points to the fact that we should expect the political process to interfere with economic forces to shape the spatial economic configuration of a country in a way that may favour the small regions.

18.5 LEGISLATIVE BARGAINING AND STRATEGIC DELEGATION

In Section 18.3, we concentrated on the voting stage; in the subsection above, we have discussed some issues that focus on the legislative stage. This was very much simplified. A third source of over-representation of the special interests of the small regions is related to the *non-cooperative* 'legislative bargaining' game (Baron and Ferejohn 1989) and to the 'strategic delegation' of representatives.[12] This game assumes that one of the elected candidates is chosen to form a coalition; who then needs to 'buy' the votes of a qualified majority of the legislature. The cheapest votes to buy are those for which the default payoff is lowest. If the deputy of each constituency cares only about the fate of his/her region, then the MPs having the lowest default payoffs are those representing the smallest regions. In such a framework, one would expect the smallest constituencies to

---

[10] See, for example, Mas-Colell et al. (1995, Chapter 18).

[11] This would, for instance, require a (shadow) tax to be put on firms locating in constituencies not part of the coalition and to subsidize the smallest regions part of the coalition.

[12] Except for the fact that it is applied to location policy, nothing is really new in what follows, so we keep the discussion at an informal level. The interested reader can refer to Persson and Tabellini (2000, Chapter 7) for a self-contained treatment of this issue, as well as for further references.

be part of any coalition.[13] Later on, we will add to this game a stage in which voters of different constituencies elect a representative.

More formally, the two-stage game looks like this. In stage one, each constituency/region elects a representative. One of them, the agenda setter, is picked at random in stage two and asked to submit a C-dimensional policy proposal, θ. To become law, this proposal has to be accepted by a qualified majority $M \leq C$ of the House of Representatives. If the House rejects the proposal, we assume that the default policy implemented is the laissez-faire solution $\theta = 1$. As usual, we solve the game by backward induction, so we start with the legislative bargaining.

18.5.1 Legislative Bargaining

At stage two, a given representative will accept any policy proposal under which his/her constituency is no worse off than under the default policy. Otherwise he/she opposes it. The agenda setter, a, chooses θ so as to maximize the welfare of his/her own constituency, given that at least $M - 1$ of the remaining representatives are no worse off than under the default policy. As anyone's welfare is increasing with the number of firms located in one's constituency and the total number of firms is fixed, the agenda setter chooses θ such that s_n^a is maximized given that the s_n^j are equal to their laissez-faire level for all j in $M \backslash \{a\}$. Obviously, $s_n^c = 0$ for all $c \notin M$. Clearly, the cheapest votes to buy are those for whom the default policy brings the lowest economic well-being—in the present model, the smallest regions by the HME.

To sum-up, we write the following result.

Result 18.9. *In a legislature, the agenda setter builds the coalition which is cheapest to buy in terms of votes. In our spatial setting, this coalition is made up of the smallest regions. As a result, the coalition chooses θ such that the largest regions have no industry.*

In short, if the sole policy issue the legislature has to raise is the spatial allocation of industry (through regionally based set-up subsidies), then the parliamentary coalition will be made of the representatives of the smallest (or 'southernmost') constituencies. This simple point is illustrated by the current debates about institutional reforms and the enlargement of the European Union: there is a coalition of the countries (e.g. France) that might lose most if the CAP is scrapped together with those that currently benefit from the Structural Funds(with Spain as the most vociferous of them) but most regions of which would no longer qualify as Objective 1 regions when Central and Eastern European Countries join.

If, on the other hand, we allow for the representatives to be of different types, some strategic delegation at an earlier voting stage might occur. By 'strategic delegation' we mean that a voter of some type might elect a representative of a different type. This principle has been famously highlighted by Rogoff (1985, p.

---

[13] Obviously, this assumes that the policy issue is one-dimensional and that this dimension is the spatial distribution of economic activity.

1169) in the case of monetary policy: "Society can sometimes make itself better off by appointing a central banker who does not share the social objective function." Here, voters might elect somebody with a different type not to solve a time-inconsistency problem, but to make him/her more attractive in the second stage. We now turn to this issue.

18.5.2 Strategic Delegation

At stage one, voters in every region elect one of their fellow citizens as the representative of their constituency. These 'citizen candidates' are self-interested and, unlike Downsian candidates, care only about the policy actually implemented.[14] Let us generalize further the model depicted in this section to allow for heterogeneous factor ownership. We now assume that the capital ownership K^ι of every individual ι is symmetrically distributed around the aggregate average $k \equiv K^w/L^w$. Assume also that the lower and upper bounds for K^ι are the same in any region c. Define these bounds as K^L and K^H, respectively. Who is going to be elected?

As usual we solve the game backwards. Remember from the analysis above that the constituencies left out of the running coalition lose all industrial activity (i.e. their s_n is zero). The voters in $c = 1, \ldots, C$ will then try to make their representative as attractive as possible.[15]

In the original model as described in Section 18.2, individual incomes remain unchanged because what you pay as a taxpayer you get back as a capital owner. This is no longer the case if you own a number of units of capital different than k. As a result, we can no longer normalize one of the elements of θ to unity. For instance, take two vectors, θ and θ', such that the resulting spatial equilibrium is the same and such that all elements of θ are larger than the elements of θ'. Hence, somebody relatively well endowed with capital would prefer a the policy vector θ to be implemented rather than the policy vector θ', and conversely. By contrast, somebody endowed with the average k is perfectly indifferent between the two options.

In other words, a wealthy capital owner prefers high subsidies to set-up costs than a poor person, ceteris paribus. Hence, if elected, his/her vote is easier to buy as he/she is now willing to trade off a lower s_n for his/her constituency against a larger aggregate level of subsidies. This is bad news for the people who elected him/her, but they would nevertheless strategically elect a representative whose capital ownership corresponds to the upper bound, K^H.

They would do so because their constituency is engaged in a Bertrand-type competition with the other regions. The argument goes as follows. Imagine that every constituency but constituency 1 elects a mean-type capital owner ι, $K^\iota = k$, and that the agenda setter is constituency 2's MP. Then, everything else being equal, if voters in region 1 elect a person with an epsilon-higher capital ownership instead, the latter is more likely to be part of the coalition because he/she would

---

[14] That is, their utility function is as anybody's. See Besley and Coate (1997) for details.

[15] We assume that C is large enough so that the expected utility of electing the actual agenda setter does not affect the result.

accept a slightly more generous subsidy to the constituency, while still bargaining for a subsidy to his/her own region, namely, region 1. Assuming that all other elements of the vector θ are unaffected, a more generous subsidy to firms in region 2 has north's MP rewarded with a higher (gross) rental on capital. (Taxes have increased as well, but as a wealthy person, the net effect on his/her income is positive.)

Obviously the voters in each region reason in that way, and they all elect a high-type person. This is a case of strategic delegation because the elected person's first-best policy vector θ is different to most of his/her electorate's. The outcome will entail an even more uneven distribution of s_n than in the simple federation because even the members of the coalition will now agree on a smaller industrial base in their constituency as they are rewarded by a larger after-tax income. To sum-up, we write the following result.

Result 18.10. *At stage 2, as in the case of a simple federation, regions whose MPs are not part of the coalition have no industry in the political equilibrium and these regions are the largest ones. At the voting stage (stage 1), voters engage in strategic delegation that makes their MPs more attractive to the agenda setter when building a coalition. This arises if the candidates to parliamentary elections are not indifferent between policies that have the same spatial outcome but distinct distributive effects. As a result, all regions whose MP is part of the coalition get a smaller share of industry than under the simple federation.*

18.6 CONCLUDING COMMENTS

Using the simple FC model enriched to allow for endogenously determined regional policy, we have analysed the impact of regional interventions on the spatial distribution of the industrial sector. Two regions of the same country/constituency are considered: north, the largest one, and south, whose population is assumed to be 'socially' more homogenous. Voters vote on national elections for candidates belonging to national parties.

More importantly, interesting results emerge in spite of the simplicity of the framework. First, the two candidates converge towards the same policy announcement, which is not far from what actually happens in many industrialized countries. Ideological homogeneity does play a role in the location-policy decision-making process. Particularly, it is the more homogenous group (and not necessarily the larger one) that gets regional aid, no matter how small it is compared to the population as a whole. This is consistent with a well known stylized fact, that is, that farmers, although not a numerous group, are so effective in focusing attention on their needs and getting policy-created rents.

Second, the size of the group has an ambiguous effect on the equilibrium magnitude of the subsidy. However, the effectiveness of this aid in slowing down the agglomeration process that comes as a by-product of regional integration does depend upon the relative size of the two populations: for a given amount of regional aid, the location policy will be less effective in attracting industrial activity in the small region if the size of the large region increases (this is a consequence of the well-known home-market effect'). Thus, the political factor determines the amount of aid and the economic factor decides its effectiveness.

Finally, the very fact that regional policy is a political issue (we have made the extreme assumption here that it is, in a sense, the sole relevant one) may even reverse the regional specialization pattern predicted by economic theory, giving rise to what we dubbed the vote-market effect. If the small region is much more homogenous compared to the large one, then regional policy might do even more than just slowing down the agglomeration-in-north process that goes along with the deepening of trade integration. Eventually, the effects of the regional intervention can dominate the economic home-market effect and make the core end up in the small region.

At the political economy equilibrium, integration fosters agglomeration in the big region if its relative economic strength overcomes its eventual relative political weakness. Thus, the political effect may lead to less clear-cut (and qualitatively somewhat different) predictions than those suggested by the standard economic home-market effect.

We have also hinted at how the political system itself might favour the small regions. For instance, small regions would be over-represented in a representative democracy that attributes the same number of MPs to each region irrespective of the size of their electorates (provided that the policy outcome is like an average of the preferences of the MPs). In a better-specified extension, we have seen that the agenda setter has strong incentives to form a coalition with the MPs representing the small regions. Their default option—if they are left in the parliamentary opposition—is lower than for those elected in the richer regions, so they are easier to please. Extending this even further showed how strategic delegation might occur and yield an even more uneven distribution of industrial activity.

Along the same lines, Persson and Tabellini (2000, Chapters 7 and 8) have shown that majoritarian elections concentrate electoral competition in some key districts and entail more targeted spending. If for some reason these key districts happen to coincide with the smallest ones, then again we have a source of explanation for the stylized fact we have sought to describe in this chapter.

Another mechanism by which 'losers pick government policy' is described in Baldwin and Robert-Nicoud (2002)—although in a different setting. In a New Economic Geography framework, this could be translated as follows. Imagine that some kind of regional policy creates local rents, and immigration occurs until these rents are eroded, via some congestion costs. Assume also that migration costs are sunk, at least in parts. Then, if a negative idiosyncratic shock affects a given region, lowering the shadow value of immigration to this region below the value of the sunk cost, it is clear that people stuck in the depressed area can effectively lobby for regional aid without fearing these quasi-rents to be eroded by immigration if these rents are not too large.

To sum up, poor regions have a natural set of reasons to be politically powerful, despite—and sometimes because of—their relatively small size.

REFERENCES

Anderson, S., A. De Palma and J. Thisse. 1992. *Discrete Choice Theory of Product Differentiation*. Cambridge, MA: MIT Press.

Baldwin, R. and F. Robert-Nicoud. 2002. Entry and asymmetric lobbying: why governments pick losers. Working Paper No. 8756, National Bureau of Economic Research.

Baron, D. and J. Ferejohn. 1989. Bargaining in legislature. *American Political Science Review* 83: 1181–1206.

Besley, T. and S. Coate. 2000. Issue unbundling via citizens' initiatives. Mimeo, London School of Economics and Cornell University.

Duranton, G. and D. Puga. 2000. Diversity and specialization in cities: why, where and when does it matter? *Urban Studies* 37(3): 533–555.

Krugman, P. 1980. Scale economies, product differentiation, and patterns of trade. *American Economic Review* 70: 950–959.

Ledyard, J. 1984. The pure theory of large two-candidate elections. *Public Choice* 44: 7–41.

Lindbeck, A. and J. Weibull. 1987. Balanced-budget redistribution as the outcome of political competition. *Public Choice* 52: 273–297.

Mas-Colell, A., D. Whinston and J. Green. 1995. Microeconomic Theory. Oxford: Oxford University Press.

Osborne, M.. 1995. Spatial models of political competition under plurality rule: a survey of some explanations of the number of candidates and the positions they take. *Canadian Journal of Economics* 27: 261–301.

Persson, T. and G. Tabellini. 2000. *Political Economics: Explaining Economic Policy*. Cambridge, MA: MIT Press.

Robert-Nicoud, F. and F. Sbergami. 2001. Endogenous regional policy in a model of agglomeration. Working Paper No. 02-2001, HEI.

Robert-Nicoud, F. and F. Sbergami. 2002. The vote-market effect: location equilibrium in a probabilistic voting model. *European Economic Review* in press.

Rogoff, K. 1985. The optimal degree of commitment to an intermediate monetary target. *Quarterly Journal of Economics* 100: 1169–1189.

CHAPTER 19

Concluding Remarks and Directions for Future Research

IN THIS CLOSING CHAPTER, we limit ourselves to two tasks: we summarize the insights that have been illustrated in the various chapters; and we list our conjectures concerning future research.

19.1 SUMMARY OF INSIGHTS

To be systematic, we go through each chapter, grouping them by parts.

19.1.1 Part II: General Welfare and Policy Issues

Part II considers general welfare and policy issues. The first chapter in Part II, Chapter 9, considers what sort of new insights can arise in models that allow for agglomeration forces. Perhaps the most important and general point is that many policies have very non-linear or even non-monotonic effects on prices, trade flows, industrial location, and the like. Moreover, the impacts of policies often interact with trade openness, sometimes in unexpected ways. The key ramification of this is for empirical researchers. When dealing with sectors that are marked by agglomeration forces, it is possible that standard specifications and the typical assumption of separability will lead to very incorrect inferences. For instance, results from an empirical study of tax harmonization among countries that are open to trade and have fairly similar industrial structures may be entirely misleading when applied to nations that are very dissimilar and/or very closed to trade.

The next two chapters look at general welfare issues. Specifically, Chapter 10 explores the various ways in which policy can affect welfare by presenting an organizing framework for welfare effects that arise for marginal changes in the neighbourhood of a stable interior equilibrium.

Chapter 11 looks at equity and efficiency issues in the context of the two main models used in this book, the FC model and the FE model. The key questions are: Who wins and loses from agglomeration? Does the market produce too much or too little agglomeration? As it turns out, there are no easy answers, but this is probably a merit since ambiguity seems an important aspect of the real world.

19.1.2 Part III: Trade Policy

It is surprising that the economic geography literature has almost entirely avoided trade policy. Neary (2001) suggests an explanation: "The key problem is that the policy implications of the basic core-periphery model are just too stark to be true.'' In particular, unilateral protection always *lowers* domestic prices. While this price-lowering-protection (PLP) effect flies in the face of real-world experience, it is endemic to existing economic geography models.

The first chapter in Part III, Chapter 12, begins by taking up the challenge that is implicit in Neary's analysis of the CP model's appropriateness for policy analysis. It does this by introducing a series of enrichments that make economic geography models 'ambiguous enough to be true', to paraphrase Neary. With these enrichments, we show that the PLP is an artifice of several simplifying assumptions rather than a fundamental property of models with agglomeration forces.

Refuting the PLP effect, however, is not really sufficient for showing that economic geography models are suitable tools for trade policy analysis. Even with the enrichments introduced, protection always fosters industrialization in the sense that unilateral protection always increases a nation's share of world industry. Since unilateral protection is not generally viewed as a sure-fire route to industrialization in the real world, the next section explores variants of the simple economic geography model in which trade *liberalization* can foster industrialization. This involves consideration of imported intermediates.

The following section continues to focus on industrial development but it turns the focus to market size, comparative advantage and foreign trade barriers. It considers why small countries have trouble attracting industries where agglomeration forces are important—a question to which economic geography models are perfectly suited. This section focuses on the interplay between domestic and foreign protection, domestic and foreign market size, and comparative advantage.

The last section in Chapter 12 considers an old chestnut in trade policy analysis—the non-equivalence of tariffs and quotas. As it turns out, these two policies can have very different effects on the spatial allocation of industry. What we find is that quotas tend to have less effect on industrial location than do tariffs.

Chapter 13 focuses on reciprocal trade liberalization. The main axis of investigation is to characterize reciprocal trade liberalization schemes that can remove all trade barriers while simultaneously avoiding all industrial delocation.

Preferential trade policy is the subject of Chapter 14. As it turns out, economic geography models provide at least four insights for the analysis of preferential trade arrangements. The first, and most robust, insight—the so-called production shifting effect—can be thought of as a corollary of Paul Krugman's famous home-market effect (Krugman 1980). If two or more nations remove all trade barriers among them, they create a large 'home' market, and this, as usual, induces some, or even all, industry to move from its initial location to the newly enlarged market. In short, new economic geography models suggest that, in industries where agglomeration forces are important, formation of a trade bloc will lead to 'investment diversion'. This effect is subject to the usual caveats that we explored in Chapter 12; if industrial relocation is expensive and/or the integrating nations have a comparative disadvantage in the sector, preferential liberalization may not produce a large inflow of industry.

The second insight concerns the impact of preferential liberalization on the spatial distribution of industry *inside* a trade bloc. This effect is best thought of as a two-tier home-market effect. That is, as a group of nations beginning lowering their barriers preferentially, the first home-market effect—the production shifting effect discussed above—tends to favour industry in all members of the trade bloc at the expense of excluded nations. However, as the internal integration deepens, a second home-market effect—what might be called the internal home-market effect—kicks in. This tends to favour the largest bloc member as an industrial location.

A third insight concerns the incentives for nations to join a trade bloc. This is most easily thought of as the political economy implication of the investment diversion and production shifting discussed above. The share of world industry that is attracted to a given trade bloc depends upon the bloc's size. Moreover, having a large share of world industry boosts real incomes inside the bloc and lowers it outside the bloc, so both the benefits of joining a bloc, and the costs of not joining, rise as the bloc gets bigger. This suggests a dynamic whereby formation of a trade bloc creates a gravitational force—a domino effect—that is self-reinforcing. The bigger the bloc, the stronger is the incentive for new members to join and thus enlarge the bloc.

The fourth insight concerns a particular, but common, form of preferential liberalization called a 'hub and spoke' arrangement. This involves one nation, the hub, at the centre of a number of bilateral free trade agreements (FTAs) with its trading partners (the spokes), but no FTAs among the spokes. Here, the main insight is the so-called 'hub effect' whereby superior market access favours the hub as a location for industry.

19.1.3 Part IV: Tax Policy

Perhaps the most exciting applications of new economic geography models to policy questions lies in the area of taxation and tax competition. Almost without exception, the public finance literature on tax competition and the effects of international taxation has relied on 'smooth' models. That is, models in which small changes lead to small effects. Economic geography models are 'lumpy' by their very nature and this, as it turns out, casts new light on a number of old issues.

Chapter 15, which is the first of two chapters devoted to tax policy, shows as simply as possible what agglomeration forces mean for tax and public goods policy as well as for their effects. Many insights can only be studied in the context of explicit strategic tax-setting games, but these introduce an element of complexity that can obscure the underlying insight. For this reason, such issues are postponed to Chapter 16.

Chapter 15 opens with a review of the main results from the standard international tax competition literature. This provides a basis for comparison against which we contrast the insights that arise when one allows for agglomeration forces. The following section introduces the general notion that trade costs—as well as capital mobility—can have important effects on tax competition when agglomeration forces are present. We continue to pursue this idea in the two subsequent sections by first focusing on the case where all capital is agglomerated in one region and then by focusing on the case where industry is dispersed. The main insight here is that agglomeration forces tend to relax the constraints of tax competition when industry is already agglomerated, but they tend to exacerbate harmful tax competition when industry is dispersed. Moreover, we find that a number of the main findings of the traditional literature only hold when trade costs are sufficiently high.

The subsequent sections enrich the standard geography model by introducing public goods. As it turns out, the provision of tax-financed public goods creates a new agglomeration force, what we call the 'amenities linkage' (production shifting leads to tax-base shifting which in turn allows the 'winning' government to provide a more attractive package of public amenities, which, in turn tends to attract more production). Following this line of thinking, the next section suggests that competition between similar regions in the provision of public goods could in some situation lead to 'harmless tax competition'. That is, it can result in the first-best level of taxation. We also show that this Tiebout hypothesis-like result is reversed if the closer integration occurs between very dissimilar regions.

Up to this point, the chapter has worked with the assumptions that the immobile factor was either not taxed, or it was taxed at the same rate as the mobile factor. The last substantive section shows that shifting taxation from the mobile factor to the immobile factor tends to promote stability of the dispersed outcome.

Chapter 15 provides insights for international tax competition but stops short of actually modelling the outcome when governments set taxes in an explicit game theoretic set-up. Chapter 16 redresses this omission.

Chapter 16 first considers tax competition between similar countries where we more formally show that free trade and stronger agglomeration forces tend to magnify international tax competition, leading, for instance, to lower Nash tax rates. The subsequent section follows up on the issue of an 'amenities competition', demonstrating that the socially first-best tax rate is chosen even though capital is perfectly mobile. The deep fundamentals of this result, which is reminiscent of the famous Tiebout hypothesis, is that when capital and labour owners share common preferences and the government cares about the representative consumer, the government's first-order condition mimics the location condition. Consequently, the tax rate that is most attractive to the mobile factor is also the social first-best.

The next section considers international tax competition in the absence of capital mobility. One of the Part I models—the constructed capital model— does display agglomeration forces without capital mobility. Indeed, as we showed in Chapter 6 and 7, agglomeration forces can be stronger without capital mobility. This, as it turns out, implies that in a model where demand-link circular causality is present, capital mobility lessens tax competition since it de-links expenditure shifting from production shifting. This, of course, is diametrically opposed to the main result of the traditional tax competition literature, that capital mobility produces a race-to-the-bottom. Here capital mobility prevents a race-to-the-bottom.

Not surprisingly, some of the most unexpected insights from adding agglomeration forces to a model with tax competition are found when agglomeration forces are most important, namely, when all industry is already agglomerated in a single region. This leads us to study the impact of agglomeration forces on tax competition between uneven regions. As it turns out, most of the main results of the 'basic tax competition model' can be overturned in this case. For example, the region with the most capital may also have the highest tax rate; trade integration may lead to something that looks like a race-to-the-top over some ranges of trade costs, but a race-to-the-bottom over others. Finally, we show that tax harmonization will—contrary to the traditional literature's predication—harm at least one nation.

19.1.4 Part V: Regional Policy

Up to this point in the book, the analysis views nations as having an extremely simple geography—they were points in space—so all physical geography features are captured with bilateral trade costs, including man-made trade barriers. While convenient when focusing on national trade policies, this abstraction is clearly wanting when it comes to providing insights for regional policies, such as the EU's Structural Funds.

Part IV therefore begins by introducing internal geography into each nation. The best way to approach this is to view geography as a seamless two-dimensional space, as is common in the old geography literature (Lösch 1940) and less common in the new (e.g. Krugman and Venables 1997). Such models, however, are not analytically tractable except in very special cases. The alternative, pursued in the first chapter of Part V, is to assume that the internal geography of nations can be represented as points within a nation. This permits us to model infrastructure policies as changing inter-regional (i.e. within nations) trade costs independently from inter-regional trade costs. Since the stated goal of regional policy in most nations is to disperse economic activity and promote income growth in 'backward regions', the chapter works with the Chapter 7 model where economic geography affects economic growth and vice versa. The reason is that when learning externalities are localized, the dispersion of economic activity may affect a nation's long-run growth rate. An important message that emerges is that the presence of localized positive technology spillovers implies that a trade-off exists between spatial efficiency and equity. The main policy implications are: (1) infrastructure policies that facilitate transport between regions will increase regional inequality and national growth; (2) infrastructure policies that facilitate transport within poor regions will decrease regional inequality and national growth; and (3) public policies that facilitate the inter-regional diffusion of technology spillovers decrease regional inequality and increase national growth. The chapter then allows for congestion effects at high levels of spatial concentration and this creates the possibility of multiple equilibria—some of which are 'good' and some of which are 'bad' equilibrium from the growth perspective. This is important since, in the presence of congestion costs, policies that improve infrastructure in the poor region can improve growth and reduce inequality.

Chapter 18 turns to the political economy of regional policy asking: 'What is the mechanism that actually determines the magnitude the regional subsidies?' This chapter seeks to provide an answer in an economic geography model that is extended to include a fully specified political economy process of policy selection.

19.2 FUTURE RESEARCH

Writing the policy chapters in Parts III, IV and V was exciting and frustrating. Exciting since we kept stumbling across insights. Frustrating since we did not have time to nail them all down. This was particularly true in the trade chapters, where we did not follow up on a whole series of issues involving the connections between openness, urbanization, industrialization and growth. Likewise, it seems that many other aspects of international tax competition could have usefully been explored from the perspective of economic geography models. One line of reasoning we did not illustrate is the point first put forth by Trionfetti (1997). He considers the interaction between debt sustainability and goods market integration. The story is that a given level of debt services corresponds to a given level of taxation. As Chapter 15 showed, however, the location impact of different tax rates changes with the degree of goods market integration. Thus, one can imagine a situation where a nation's debt switches from sustainable to unsustainable due to goods market integration (raising taxes high enough to service the debt becomes impossible since this would produce a massive erosion of the tax base due to industrial delocation that would occur with the lower trade costs). Our coverage of regional policy issues also just scraped the surface. We did not, for instance, address issues of educational policy. The leaders of many peripheral regions believe that it is essential to have a university in their district. It would be interesting and fruitful to explore this assertion in a model where agglomeration forces were present and location mattered. As we have shown repeatedly in this book, analyses based on the assumption that the economy is 'smooth' often miss important insights.

Given the large, rich and insightful literature that has explored the political economy of trade policy, it strikes us, as usual, that so little has been done on the political economy of regional policy. After all, distortionary and seemingly inefficient regional policies are a hallmark of virtually every advanced industrialized nation—and this, despite the great diversity of political architectures. For example, one line of reasoning that we did not pursue in the book concerns the correlation between winners, losers and movers. During a transition between locational equilibria, the mobile factor is typically either indifferent to location, or happy that he/she has moved. The immobile factors, however, especially in the region that is de-industrializing, are not indifferent. Systematically, the voters left behind in the emptying region are unhappy about the change. We conjecture that in the right political framework, the fact that voters left behind actively oppose agglomeration, while voters who move are indifferent on the margin would systematically favour anti-agglomeration policies. While the idea did resonate with us, we did not have time to examine its internal logic in a formal model.

One line of policy research that we actually started, but had to abandon to get the book done, concerns the impact of subsidies in an economic geography model (for the analysis, see Dupont and Martin 2003). The draft chapter started to analyse the effects of subsidies in a very simple model with agglomeration forces. We concentrated on the different effects of different forms of subsidies (to production, per firm, to particular inputs, to exports, etc.) as well as the impact of different financing schemes (nationwide versus region-specific taxation, for example). We came across three insights. First, while regional subsidies do attract firms in almost any model, our first insight concerned the interaction between regional subsidies and degree of goods–market integration. This is nothing more than a corollary of the home-market magnification effect we stressed in Part I, but it may be unexpected. For example, if the EU continues to lower intra-EU trade barriers without changing the level of permissible subsidies to firms in remote regions, the subsidies will lead to an increasing distortion of the spatial allocation for industry. The second insight is that when firms are mobile, regional subsidies to firms in one region lead to higher operating profits in *all* regions. Thus, even firms that do not directly benefit from regional subsidies gain indirectly through the distortion on regional competition. This has the interesting implication that a subsidy given to firms that locate in the poor region can actually worsen nominal inequality. If profits increase due to the subsidy and most capital owners are in the rich region then these capital owners will disproportionately benefit from the subsidy intended for the poor region. The third insight concerns the effect of the way subsidies are financed. Regional subsidies that are financed at the trans-regional level have the largest effect on relocation. An interesting result is that even when financed locally, regional subsidies lead to relocation in the region that gives the subsidy. Another way to put it is that the negative effect of taxing regional expenditure is more than compensated by the subsidies to regional production. A related line of thought, which we did not have time to synthesize, has been explored by Federico Trionfetti and co-authors (e.g. Trionfetti 1997, 2001). This concerns the locational effects of the nature and financing of public procurement. The insight here is that it matters greatly *where* the government buys its goods. In essence, government procurements change market size by fiat, and this, by the usual logic, affects the location of industry.

Competition policy is another area that deserved a chapter or two, but had to be set aside in the interest of time. Imperfect competition is the heart-and-soul of the home-market effect. It therefore stands to reason that anti-trust and unfair competition policies will affect the location of production. One key insight that is likely to emerge from such analysis is that lax competition policy in both regions tends to favour industrial location in the large region since high mark-ups correspond to very strong home-market effects. In a strategic setting, this suggest a race-to-the-bottom in regional competition policies when regions are not too similar. Moreover, following the insights from the tax chapter, it is likely to be the case that competition policy would have very different effects in the symmetric case and the core–periphery case. All of these conjectures need to be verified and refined, but it seems to us that there is a lot to be learned here. The standard analysis of competition policy has, to a large extent, ignored issues of agglomeration, catastrophic delocation and hysteresis.

Another set of 'low hanging fruit' that we did not have time to 'pick' concerns the analysis of factor market integration policies—for example, immigration policy, and openness to foreign direct investment (FDI)—in the light of economic geography models. In Chapter 7, we briefly studied the locational effects of changing to a degree to which knowledge spillovers were localized. Since FDI and high-skill migration are likely to foster knowledge spillovers, we conjecture that there are a number of insights in these policy areas that should be illuminated by economic geography models.

Development economics would also seem to be a natural place to apply economic geography models. Indeed, the early development thinkers—people like Chenery, Myrdal and Rostow—who were not hindered by the need to mathematically model the points they made, often stressed backward and forward linkages and other agglomeration-related channels.

We hope that this final chapter illustrates how much more work still needs to be done on the theory side of economic geography. We close by repeating the old adage: 'nothing is ever done, it's just due.'

REFERENCES

Dupont, V. and P. Martin. 2003. Regional policies and inequalities: are subsidies good for you? Mimeo, CERAS, Paris.

Krugman, P. 1980. Scale economies, product differentiation, and the pattern of trade. *American Economic Review* 70: 950–959.

Krugman, P. and A. J. Venables. 1997. Integration, specialization and adjustment. *European Economic Review* 40: 959–968

Lösch, A. 1940. *The Economics of Location*, translation published in 1954 by Yale University Press, New Haven, CT.

Neary, J. P. 2001. Of hype and hyperbolas: introducing the new economic geography. *Journal of Economic Literature* 49: 536–561.

Trionfetti, F. 1997. Public expenditure and economic geography. *Annales d'Economie et de Statistique* 47: 101–125.

_____. 2001. Public procurement, market integration, and income inequalities. *Review of International Economics* 9(1): 29–41.

www.ingramcontent.com/pod-product-compliance
Ingram Content Group UK Ltd.
Pitfield, Milton Keynes, MK11 3LW, UK
UKHW041938130225
455056UK00003B/88